Life History and Ecology of the Slider Turtle

J. WHITFIELD GIBBONS

WITH CONTRIBUTIONS BY

Harold W. Avery
Justin D. Congdon
Arthur E. Dunham
Carl H. Ernst
Gerald W. Esch
Robert E. Foley
Nat B. Frazer
William R. Garstka

J. Whitfield Gibbons
Timothy M. Goater
Judith L. Greene
Thomas G. Hinton
Dale R. Jackson
Kym C. Jacobson
John M. Legler
Jeffrey E. Lovich

David J. Marcogliese
Clarence J. McCoy
Joseph C. Mitchell
Don Moll
Edward O. Moll
Christopher A. Pague
William S. Parker
Robert R. Parmenter

Joseph P. Schubauer
David E. Scott
Kim T. Scribner
Michael E. Seidel
Michael H. Smith
James R. Spotila
Edward A. Standora
Richard C. Vogt

Smithsonian Institution Press
Washington, D.C.
London

Library of Congress Cataloging-in-Publication Data

Gibbons, J. Whitfield, 1939–
  Life history and ecology of the slider turtle.

  Bibliography: p.
  Includes index.
  1. Pseudemys scripta. I. Title.
QL666.C547G53 1989   597.92   88-600294
ISBN 0-87474-468-7

British Library Cataloguing-in-Publication Data is available.

⊚ The paper used in this publication meets the minimum requirements of the
American National Standard for Permanence of Paper for Printed Library Materials
Z39.48-1984.

Printed in the United States of America
10 9 8 7 6 5 4 3 2 1
98 97 96 95 94 93 92 91 90

For permission to reproduce individual illustrations appearing in this book, please
correspond directly with the owners of the images, as stated in the picture captions. The
Smithsonian Institution Press does not retain reproduction rights for these illustrations
individually or maintain a file of addresses for photo sources.

Contents

Foreword

Truth is stranger than fiction. No cliché is more appropriate for the ecological research programs on the Savannah River Plant (SRP) in the Upper Coastal Plain of South Carolina. The initial sponsoring agency, the Atomic Energy Commission; its successor, the Department of Energy (DOE); and Du Pont, the SRP's management company, are commonly thought of in association with environmental degradation, not with habitat and wildlife conservation. Yet at the SRP these organizations manage one of the largest nature reserves in the Southeast and sponsor a major program for long-term studies of plant and animal ecology.

In establishing the Savannah River Ecology Laboratory (SREL) as an adjunct research organization to a nuclear facility, the intent was obviously to foster a research program to examine and understand the ecological impact such a facility has on natural environments. Such research has remained a major thrust of SREL; however, the ecologists have had the freedom and foresight to expand their studies into life history and population biology of the local animals and plants, thereby placing the thermally disturbed or other environmentally altered populations and communities in proper perspective. Turtles have been major research animals at SREL for the past two decades. There are any number of reasons why they are particularly appropriate species for monitoring the effects of thermal effluents in natural systems, but certainly a primary reason is Whit Gibbons. Whit is a naturalist with wide-ranging interest; nevertheless, turtles and turtle ecology are a constant to which his attention is frequently focused. The presence of turtles in the thermally polluted lakes and streams certainly in no way hindered his enthusiasm or DOE's interest in the study of SRP turtles. Thus, turtle ecology has become a mainstay of SREL's program, and Whit and his colleagues have contributed greatly to our knowledge of turtle life history and population ecology as well as to the biology of other amphibians and reptiles.

Many species of turtles have been studied on the SRP, none more extensively than *Trachemys scripta*. The data extend across 21 years and encompass three major and many minor populations of sliders. These data provide the core for this book, both for retrospection and for planning future research paths. Few animal populations have been studied for such a long time, and the data for even fewer are summarized and integrated into a single publication. This feature alone makes this book a landmark study in animal biology; however, the contents of the book encompass the entire spectrum of slider biology, from fossil history and slider systematics to population genetics and parasitology. The breadth of this book is evident from a quick glance at its table of contents. What is not evident, though, is the intellectual thread that ties together many of the research objectives and researchers in this book.

The intellectual link is Fred Cagle. Turtles fascinated him as well, and his earliest publications centered on turtle natural history. As it so happens, *Trachemys scripta* was one of the more abundant turtles in Cagle's research area. The eventual result was the publication of his *Life History of the Slider Turtle, Pseudemys scripta troostii* (Holbrook), which may be considered a scholarly precursor of this multiauthored book (that link, however, is coincidental). The intellectual link was forged by Cagle's commitment to detailed studies of life history and population ecology. Turtles remained a lifelong research interest, but he became increasingly convinced of the necessity for a thorough inventory of life history and population characteristics of any animal studied. Not surprisingly, Cagle was only one of several mid-twentieth-century ecologists who advocated a more rigorous and holistic approach to animal ecology. He promulgated this commitment to the herpetological community in 1953 with the publication of "An Outline for the Study of Reptile Life History." More important, he instilled this holistic approach to reptilian ecology in his students, and in one, Don Tinkle, it took particularly deep root. Reptilian ecology, indeed ecology and evolutionary biology, was profoundly influenced by Tinkle's research and ideas. The range of ecological and evolutionary concepts in this book is due in no small measure to the way Don Tinkle thought about reptile ecology and life history. Although it was not intended to be, this book can be viewed as a memorial to Cagle and Tinkle for their pioneering research in life history and population biology studies of reptiles.

GEORGE R. ZUG
Department of Vertebrate Zoology
(Amphibians and Reptiles)
National Museum of Natural
History
Washington, D.C.

Preface

In one sense this book had its beginning about 20 years ago on July 21, 1967, when I captured my first slider turtle on the Savannah River Plant (SRP) in South Carolina. I would have had a hard time beginning the writing at that time, or even choosing the title, because actually I did not know what species I had caught. Although I had captured 1,001 painted turtles during the previous three years in Sherriff's Marsh in Michigan and was familiar with red-eared sliders by benefit of an Alabama childhood, I had never seen the eastern subspecies of the common pond slider. During the remainder of that summer, however, with the capture of other regional species of turtles for comparison, and with the aid of Roger Conant's *A Field Guide to Reptiles and Amphibians of the United States and Canada East of the 100th Meridian* and Archie Carr's *Handbook of Turtles,* I became confident that I was dealing with what was then called *Chrysemys scripta* by some herpetologists and *Pseudemys scripta* by others.

A rationale for initially selecting turtles as study organisms is that they have certain life history characteristics that make them demographically distinct when compared with lizards, the most thoroughly studied group of reptiles. The main life history qualities that all turtles possess, in contrast to most lizards or other animals, are extended longevity and delayed maturity. These two factors alone qualify the group for attention by ecologists and demographers. Turtles also have a variety of other traits that make them ideal for life history and demographic studies, such as being relatively easy to capture, handle, and mark for permanent identification. Among the most useful determinations that can be made on individuals of many freshwater species, including slider turtles, without harm to the animal, are quantifications of body size, age, sex and state of maturity of both sexes, and reproductive condition of females.

The SRP in South Carolina, where the majority of the populations mentioned in this book are located, has been an ideal site for establishing long-term field research efforts because of the protection from public disturbance that results from the tight security of a defense site. This book will reveal some of the research advantages and insights that can accrue from long-term field studies of specific natural populations in such a situation.

As a herpetologist interested in turtles, I could not have fallen upon better times with a better species. The U.S. Atomic Energy Commission (AEC), the source of most of my research support, wanted to know how thermal effluent from nuclear reactors affected environments and their natural inhabitants. Anyone could have convinced the commission, as we did, that slider turtles were a species worth looking into because the evidence was soon clear that turtles in this group not only survived but actually thrived in polluted waters, including waters heated to temperatures unsuitable for most native flora and fauna. Fortunately for us, and I hope for other researchers, the AEC recognized that in order to conduct studies that demonstrated effects on organisms from industrial operations, the scientist must also examine populations of the same species under natural conditions. One must observe natural phenomena when and where there are no effects before industrial, domestic, or agricultural impacts can be ascertained. Thus, we were allowed, even encouraged, to pursue ecological research on slider turtles in thermally unaffected habitats on the SRP and in other geographic regions, in addition to those receiving heated water from reactors.

Although I am not an expert in theoretical biology, mathematical modeling, or statistics, I have been able to deal with these areas through the help of numerous associates and collaborators. And with the help of willing students, technicians, and others, I have been able to catch turtles. During the two decades following the capture of my first slider turtle, we have collected an average of more than 3 turtles per day (3.4 per day as of December 1987). Of these 24,754 turtles representing more than a dozen species, 46% (11,297) have been slider turtles. Some were new individuals, but more and more were turtles that had been caught before. Naturally, the length of time between the first and last capture of some individuals increased, so almost every year we broke the previous year's record for time between captures. It became apparent that not only were we documenting that individuals lived for several years, but we were also gradually compiling records in several populations with large proportions of individuals whose ages we knew precisely. Many of these were older individuals and represented a situation unusual for most studies of long-lived animals. That is, a fairly good representation of the age structure was available for some populations, including individuals in the older age classes.

As a matter of course, we collected data applicable to understanding the life history and ecology of turtles, most of it without experimental or theoretical design. We just took measurements that seemed like they might provide some level of enlightenment to the knowledge and information about turtles. I am afraid that today's highly experimentally minded, theoretically based scientific approach discourages this type of behavior among young scientists. A challenge to this attitude is that if all scientists had waited for the right hypothesis or question before making their observations, our core of information and fundamental knowledge in biology would be a structure too weak for most theory to stand on. I take the stand that the simple collection of data for its own sake, even though a specific hypothesis of theory is not addressed, can sometimes be valuable. Charles Darwin demonstrated this, and I feel certain that an impressive array of other scientific advancements could be brought forth as examples of how observational data can advance and set a crucial foundation for much of biology.

One distinction between most long-term research projects and short-term studies is that the latter often have a single hypothesis that is being tested or a specific question that is being asked. Long-term projects are different in that the investigator probably did not begin the research with the intent of extending it beyond a few years at most. Therefore, a study that has lasted for many years may provide the empirical evidence needed to address certain biological issues, although the study was not designed initially with such issues in mind.

After about 13 or 14 years of capturing, marking, and recapturing turtles, we began to recapture individuals that we knew were more than 20 years old by virtue of their having been at least 6 or 7 when they were first captured.

Somehow the approach of the 20-year mark clicked as a milestone, and I decided that I should compile the information we had on sliders and other turtles into a form that would be useful to other interested ecologists. Although we published several papers in which older, known-age individuals were capitalized upon, it seemed that a book on the subject might be in order.

The importance of long-term ecological studies of animal populations has been recognized, as in Don Tinkle's *BioScience* article in 1979, yet fewer than 15% of the life history studies of natural populations are based on research of more than three years (according to a survey of studies of natural populations of animals published in *Ecology* and *Ecological Monographs* from 1980 to 1984). Short-term studies often result in interpretations and conclusions about a particular species without the benefit of comparative data in different years or under different environmental conditions, so the extent of natural variability may not be recognized. Local environmental conditions in an area have been shown to have dramatic effects on important life history features for a variety of organisms. However, given the limited time span of most population studies, it is difficult to identify the level of variability that can occur within the same population at different times and under different environmental conditions. An awareness of this variability would appear to be critical in the formulation of life history theory.

An initial objective of this book was to examine the variability in selected life history attributes in natural populations of a long-lived animal species that has been studied for a relatively long period of time. The findings reported were to be based primarily on 20 years of continual surveillance of several populations of a freshwater turtle. The primary study species was the yellow-bellied slider turtle (*Trachemys scripta*). However, life history data were also gathered on other turtles that resided with the slider turtle in the Upper Coastal Plain of South Carolina. These included the chicken turtle (*Deirochelys reticularia*), cooter (*Pseudemys floridana*), eastern mud turtle (*Kinosternon subrubrum*), snapping turtle (*Chelydra serpentina*), and stinkpot (*Sternotherus odoratus*). Comparable information was also gathered on the painted turtle (*Chrysemys picta*) from population studies conducted in southern Michigan between 1964 and 1987. Data from these studies are used when appropriate for comparison with findings about slider turtles.

As I began to consolidate my own data and consider what I might contribute about slider turtles in particular and the ecology of turtles in general, I came to realize that although I had more data of this sort than most other investigators who did long-term mark-recapture studies on long-lived species, there were many gaps in what my associates and I could say. Therefore, I elected to invite other ecologists who had worked with slider turtles to contribute chapters to augment my own work. I was pleased that of the 17 individuals who were invited to submit chapters, only one declined outright because of other commitments. If this book is indeed a contribution to the knowledge and understanding of sliders and other turtles, it will be in great part because of the efforts of these individuals.

A major value of the analysis, synthesis, and interpretation of the data taken in these studies should be the addition to our base of information on the ecology and life history of turtles as a significant group of modern-day reptiles. Also, I hope that the empirical evidence from these studies will provide the basic ingredients to successfully support or refute many of the theoretically derived impressions that population ecologists have about natural populations of animals. Collectively, the studies on the SRP and those from other areas by other investigators should provide a definitive foundation for ecological studies of freshwater turtles in particular, with general applicability to marine or terrestrial species. A final product of these presentations should be the identification of the most critical questions that should now be asked in the study of turtles.

J. Whitfield Gibbons

Acknowledgments

A major acknowledgment should be given to a group of people who are part of an organization that has had three different names since I first became associated with it. The parent organization was known as the U.S. Atomic Energy Commission. In 1974 the name was changed to the Energy, Research and Development Administration. The final product is what we know as the U.S. Department of Energy. This trinomial organization has done more to support basic ecological work than almost any other government agency. The data on freshwater turtles presented in this book could not have been collected for the most part without its help and the encouragement of certain individuals. I would particularly single out Bill Osborne, who operated as a scientist within their ranks and, as far as I can tell, was supportive of the turtle research from the very beginning. Many others (the names have changed more often than the agency's) have also provided the background support necessary to conduct these studies, and it is only proper that we should occasionally bring them from behind the scenes to indicate our appreciation. Notable among them have been Heyward Hamilton and Helen McCammon. Special thanks also go to the people at the Department of Energy's Savannah River Operations Office for their assistance with logistical and administrative tasks over the years. These include Karl Herde, Liz Goodson, Don Day, Bill Wisenbaker, Dick Jansen, and Steve Wright as well as many others.

I would also like to thank the National Science Foundation for Grant DEB79-04758, which was awarded to me for the study of the basic ecology of turtles in the 1970s. Information on the turtles was also gathered under grants and contracts from the American Philosophical Society, the South Carolina Wildlife and Marine Resources Division, the Environmental Protection Agency, the National Science Foundation Education Programs, Oak Ridge Associated Universities, the University of Georgia Institute of Ecology, Sigma Xi Research Awards, and the Kiawah Island Company. All of these organizations in some way enhanced our collection of data on turtles. I also thank George R. Zug and the Smithsonian Institution for permitting me to spend a sabbatical year at the National Museum of Natural History during the initiation of plans and preparations for this book.

I will have a lasting gratitude to the many associates at the University of Georgia's Savannah River Ecology Laboratory, including the SREL faculty, technicians, students (high school, undergraduate, graduate, and postdoctoral), visiting faculty, secretaries, clerical staff, and maintenance personnel for their endless contributions, both direct and indirect, to the collection, analysis, and presentation of data on slider turtles for the past 20 years. The most notable of these has been Judith L. Greene, who was responsible for the successful collection of many years of field and laboratory data and who was the primary force involved in compiling, editing, and analyzing the data set. Others who have contributed through direct involvement in bringing SREL turtle research to fruition through publication include John M. Aho, Harold W. Avery, David H. Bennett, Joseph Bourque, I. Lehr Brisbin, William C. Cale, Jr., E. Jennifer Christy, David B. Clark, John W. Coker, Justin D. Congdon, Michael E. Douglas, Gerald W. Esch, Herman E. Eure, Joseph Evans, James O. Farlow, David L. Forney, Kim Fowler, J. Christian Franson, Laurie Goldner, Julian R. Harrison III, Michael F. Hirshfield, James T. Hook, Glennis Kaufman, Garfield Keaton, Trip Lamb, Jeffrey E. Lovich, Joseph R. McAuliffe, Richard W. Miller, Tony Mills, Don Moll, Gary B. Moran, Stephen J. Morreale, Thomas M. Murphy, Jr., David H. Nelson, Susan Novak, Sarah Watson Oliver, Tim Owens, E. Davis Parker, Robert R. Parmenter, Karen K. Patterson, Joseph P. Schubauer, Cindy Scott, Kim T. Scribner, Richard A. Seigel, Raymond D. Semlitsch, Rebecca R. Sharitz, Gary C. Smith, Michael H. Smith, Edward A. Standora, Donald W. Tinkle, Laurie J. Vitt, and Larry Wright. I also appreciate the support and encouragement of Rebecca R. Sharitz (acting director) and Michael H. Smith (director) of SREL during the completion of this seemingly endless project of preparing a book.

Credit for the preparation of the book itself must be extended to several individuals at SREL, including Judith L. Greene, who performed most of the analyses for the SRP research, and Jeffrey E. Lovich, who read all of the chapters and offered many valuable comments on the manuscripts of others, especially those from people at SREL. Their efforts are greatly appreciated. Sarah Collie and L. Marie Fulmer were invaluable for their coordination of graphics and text. Chuck Segal's contribution in the transfer of material between computer files and in the typesetting of tables was vital to the completion of the book. I also thank Linda Orebaugh, Jean Coleman, Rebecca Schneider, and Mary Jackson for the preparation of figures and maps. Jean Coleman was particularly helpful in the revision of figures for final publication. Jim Knight conducted literature searches that were useful in several of the chapters. I am extremely indebted to the SREL Word Processing Center; its supervisor, Miriam Stapleton; and the typing staff, including Pat Davis, Jan Hinton, Malinda Doherty, Marianne Reneau, Susan Kinlaw, Teresa Taylor, and Shirley Mabe. Rosemary Sheffield is to be credited for having done the most thorough job of manuscript editing that most of the authors and I had ever experienced. We are deeply grateful for her attention to detail and organization.

Finally, I give everlasting credit to my wife, Carol, and to Laura, Jennifer, Susan Lane, and Michael for the type of family support that any field biologist needs if he is going to have a wife and children.

Introduction

J. WHITFIELD GIBBONS
Savannah River Ecology Laboratory
Drawer E
Aiken, South Carolina 29802

1

The Slider Turtle

Abstract

A general overview is given of the systematic status and natural history of the slider turtle, *Trachemys scripta*.

Introduction

In Charleston, South Carolina, the year 1855 was a notable one, although the significance of particular events depended—as it does today—on where your interests lay. For politicians, a significant issue was the recent passage of the Kansas-Nebraska Act, which opened settlement of the two territories to both slave owners and non–slave owners. For those interested in the military defense of the city, a key concern was the condition of Fort Sumter, a small facility in Charleston Harbor. But for people who were interested in natural history, the capture of a particular turtle near the city would mark an altogether different beginning. The ultimate significance was that the specimen that Louis Agassiz had captured would later be cataloged under the name of *Emys serrata* as the first reptile entered into the vertebrate collections of the newly formed U.S. National Museum in Washington, D.C. Its nomenclature would change over the years from *Emys serrata* to *Trachemys scripta* to *Pseudemys scripta* to *Chrysemys scripta*, depending upon the year and the turtle biologist who was using the name. The specimen, which now resides in a jar of alcohol in the support center of the Smithsonian Institution, is a slider turtle, the subject of this book.

A basic question in the study of an animal or plant species is, Why does the species function in the manner in which it does, rather than in some other way? This question can be formulated at all levels, from the precise physiological, morphological, or genetic questions to the more complex questions of why it has a certain behavior pattern or community association. However the question is posed, some of the first answers required are how the organism performs biologically, how it is structured, and where it lives.

In the thinking of some scientists the idyllic study in ecology is a project undertaken to address a theoretical question that is recognized as being of current interest and that has been posed in order to satisfy or refute a model. The study organisms are used simply to test the model and provide generalities that can then be broadly applied, thus eliminating the need for detailed observation of each species. However, no matter how esoteric a model or how theoretical a question is, the final answers must come from empirical evidence emanating from the examination of particular species—their habits, morphology, physiology, genetics, behavior, and community relationships.

Another approach is to begin investigation of the ecology of a species with the objective of unraveling and understanding as much of its natural history as possible. A common approach with studies of this nature is to use the findings later to test a theoretical question or model. This is frowned upon as the ideal, but its widespread use bespeaks its practicality. Yet another approach in scientific writing for those interested in theoretical questions is to use earlier presentations of basic ecological information on a species that are appropriate for testing the model or addressing the theoretical question.

The information presented in this book is a mixture of approaches, including the last, in that it should provide information that may later be used by others. I do not pass judgment on which is the best approach to science, but I do maintain that our fundamental question is to understand how animal and plant species function; that is, Why are they the way they are? Any information that can contribute toward this understanding is, in my opinion, useful and should not be belittled.

The objective of this work is to use the ecological observations on the turtles of a selected geographic region in order to understand the natural history of the species as thoroughly as possible. The life history features of common freshwater turtles in selected populations have been examined by ecologists on the Savannah River Plant (SRP) in South Carolina since 1967 (Appendix 1.1). By far the most ubiquitous and abundant of these turtles is the slider, *Trachemys scripta*. These studies on the SRP have been augmented by the research of others on slider turtles in the same or other regions. I hope that collectively the research presentations will be revealing of the life history, ecology, and evolution of the slider turtle as well as of turtles as a group. These findings, or any hypotheses generated from this information, should allow us to address some of the basic questions posed by ecologists about how the world's environments and attendant organisms function.

Turtle Populations

In the study of turtles, countless questions may be asked about individuals, populations, or species and why they function in the way they do. The individual is accepted as the primary unit of selection, and although no one has difficulty defining what an individual turtle is, the individual's characteristics that are subject to natural selection may be difficult to ascertain. At the next level, the population, where the overall expression of selection is observed, a definition of the unit of study itself can present problems. How are the populations of a species of turtle in a region defined and demarcated? Which individuals are included in the population?

Among the variously stated definitions of a population is the classic one that a population is a group of individuals that intermix genetically with other members of the group more so than they do with similar neighboring groups. In my early studies of turtle populations, I often declared that some species of freshwater turtles were ideal for population studies because they occurred in circumscribed bodies of water (e.g., lakes), so that the population was an identifiable unit. Several thousand marked turtles later, I concluded that this is a fallacy. Exchange among individuals from neighboring habitats is commonplace, and such well-defined genetic populations seldom exist, or at least have not been identified empirically.

The population concept as applied to turtles, and most other animals, must be viewed as a continuum ranging from groups of individuals that fit the true population model (having practically 100% genetic mixing with no outside interlopers or interloping) to the other extreme, in which gene flow is panmictic over a large region. Defining the boundaries of a population may be confounded by discovery of areas where turtles congregate for winter dormancy or for summer feeding and that include individuals from a variety of different genetic units. I do not have evidence of this phenomenon, but it is certainly conceivable, considering the complexity of behavior and population structure that is being revealed in turtle populations.

But to do population studies, one must define the population, and with freshwater turtles this is not easy. After coming full circle, I would once again define a freshwater turtle study population in terms of the body (and nearby bodies) of water that a group of individuals inhabit. So the term "population" becomes the word of convenience when referring to groups of animals that live in an area (defined as the study area) and intermix genetically. It must be understood in the use of this term that some populations are more tightly structured genetically than others. That is, gene flow has at least some probability of occurrence even in the most remote populations as long as there are other populations of the species in existence. The critical factor becomes the establishment and definition of the study area, as that will be what the investigator must use in defining the population.

My studies with turtles have led me to the belief that populations, however defined, and our expressions of them (such as population structure, life tables, and survivorship curves) are consequences of a variety of temporal and spatial stochastic events. Although a particular population of turtles may be quantified in terms of population parameters, the specific quantification will be applicable only to the group of individuals at the particular time and place but not necessarily to groups of individuals in other places or to those in that place at another time. Thus, the defining of population characteristics must be viewed with caution in terms of their applicability to the species. A comparison of population parameters of different populations of the slider turtle will make this point in various chapters of the book. In essence, each individual is operating only to increase its own fitness, and its mode of operation will vary to fit the local demographic and environmental conditions to which it is subjected.

Our general conclusions about population dynamics of turtles may be far more limited than we presently believe. In short, populations are merely assemblages of individuals of a species as we perceive them, and they have few inherent properties that are consistent across different populations. Furthermore, I believe that if this concept of population is critically examined for most species of animals or plants, the same will be able to be said. That is, populations of a species cannot be depended upon for consistency but are based only on the stochastic history of the individuals that constitute them.

The Study Species

The pond slider (*Trachemys scripta*) has one of the more extensive geographic ranges of the vertebrate species in the Western Hemisphere and has numerous subspecies, some of which are contested to be true species. The subspecies-species controversy notwithstanding, the yellow-bellied slider turtle is generally accepted as a subspecies of *Trachemys scripta* that inhabits the eastern United States. The populations on the SRP in South Carolina belong to the subspecies *T. s. scripta*.

The questionable phylogenetic relationships of the slider turtle and related species have led to taxonomic confusion about the genus or genera to which these species belong. This confusion is evident in the fact that this species has been referred to in the refereed scientific literature by three different generic names (*Pseudemys*, *Chrysemys*, *Trachemys*) in a single decade (Table 1.1). For purposes of the present writing, it should be understood that a single species, or even subspecies if one wishes to drop to that level, occurs within the geographic range of the samples from South Carolina. I believe everyone would agree

Table 1.1. Brief chronological summary of selected classification schemes proposed for the *Chrysemys/Pseudemys/Trachemys* complex

Reference	Chrysemys (picta)	Pseudemys	Trachemys (scripta)
Agassiz (1857)	C	P	T
Cope (1875)	C	P	P
Boulenger (1889)	C	C	C
Carr (1952)	C	P	P
Conant (1958)	C	P	P
McDowell (1964)	C[a]	C[a]	C[a]
Zug (1966)	C	P	T
Weaver and Rose (1967)	C	C	C
Parsons (1968)	C[a]	C[a]	C[a]
Ernst and Barbour (1972)	C	C	C
Conant (1975)	C	C	C
Ernst and Ernst (1980)	C	P	P
Vogt and McCoy (1980)	C	P	P
Seidel and Inchaustegui Miranda (1984)	C	P	T
Ward (1984)	C	P	T
Obst (1985)	C	C	C
Iverson (1986)	C	P	T
Seidel and Smith (1986)	C	P	T

Note: Taxonomic designations are those of Seidel and Smith (1986), in which *Chrysemys* contains only *C. picta*, *Trachemys* contains *T. scripta* and the West Indian species of slider turtles (Iverson, 1986), and *Pseudemys* contains all other members of the complex. The generic recognition of each taxon by an author is indicated by its first letter.
[a]The taxonomic designations of Seidel and Smith (1986) for the species are allocated to subgeneric status under the genus *Chrysemys*.

about that. What people do not agree about is the phylogenetic status of this species relative to closely related species. All authorities, to my knowledge, also agree that the genus that includes slider turtles, no matter which species are included, is restricted to the Western Hemisphere, except for modern introductions elsewhere.

A difficult decision for me in considering the preparation of this book was whether to allow authors to use the genus name of their choice or to recommend strongly that they use a particular one in order to standardize the presentation. The dilemma was of course whether to confront turtle researchers whose foundation in systematics far excelled my own. In the end, the choice was not a difficult one for me. I elected to use *Trachemys* and make my choice known to the other contributors whose manuscripts arrived using the names *Trachemys*, *Pseudemys*, and even *Chrysemys*. Contributors then used the name that they preferred without the requirement that justification be given.

From the viewpoint of an ecologist, the role of a name is to identify what you are talking about. This is the important feature in the study of a species as a functional unit in an ecosystem. The significance of the name of an organism from the standpoint of the systematist can be based on either of two issues. The first is the assessment and interpretation of the phylogenetic relationship of the species to other members of the genus or to closely related genera. This issue is often shrouded in opinion, and because inter-

Table 1.2. Nomenclatural origins of names of the slider turtle

emys--Gr. *emys*, genit. *emydos*, a freshwater tortoise
pseud--Gr. *pseudēs*, false, deceptive
script--L. *scriptus*, written, p.p. of *scrībo*, to write
chrys--Gr. *chrysos*, gold
trachy--Gr. *trachys*, rough

Source: Jaeger, 1944.

pretive science is not a democratic process, we have no jury processes for indictment and conviction. The second issue is etymological and often comes down to the rather basic process of which letters of the alphabet are used. Biologists have built careers and fed their families through addressing these two issues, especially the former, with their chosen organisms. In fact, the slider turtle may have fed more people, in this indirect manner, than any other North American turtle. An accounting of what the slider turtle has been called generically during the last 130 years is presented in Table 1.1. Figure 1.1 indicates the geographic ranges of the various North American species that are or have been included in the same genus as *T. scripta*, under the names *Pseudemys* or *Chrysemys*.

Taxonomic Pronunciation

As best as I can tell, the slider turtle is indeed among the front-runners in the number of accepted generic epithets that have been used in the last decade. Of equal interest are the numerous pronunciations that have been used for each of the generic names. The word *emys* is Greek and means turtle. All of the genus names thus have been of Greek origin (Table 1.2), whereas *scripta* is from Latin.

I have heard *Pseudemys* pronounced as 'süd ə mēz, süd 'em ēz, süd 'em es, and even süd 'ē mis (diacritical marks are those used in *Webster's Ninth New Collegiate Dictionary*). *Chrysemys* has been pronounced by reputable turtle biologists I have known as 'kri sə mēz, 'kris ə mēz, kri 'sem es, kris 'em ēz, and even kris 'sēm es. *Trachemys* is a new one for most of us, and so far I have heard it called only 'trāk ə mēz, 'trak ə mēz, and trak 'em es. I am sure we need only a little more time with this one.

Ernst and Barbour (1972) offer cry'-sĕ-mēz ('kri sə mēz) as the proper pronunciation of *Chrysemys* and do not give pronunciations for *Pseudemys* or *Trachemys*. So far, I think everyone agrees that *scripta* is pronounced skrĭpt'-a, as in Ernst and Barbour (1972).

Natural History of the Slider Turtle

Several excellent accounts have been given of the life history, ecology, and behavior of the slider turtle in general works (Carr, 1952; Ernst and Barbour, 1972) and monographs on the species (Cagle, 1950; Moll and Legler,

1971). Perhaps the greatest number of turtle ecology studies have been on the closely related painted turtle *Chrysemys picta* (Cagle, 1954; Sexton, 1959b; Gibbons, 1967b, 1968c,d; Ernst, 1971c,d; Wilbur, 1975a; and others), and they augment our understanding, although most were conducted in colder temperate areas outside the range of *T. scripta*.

Trachemys scripta is a semiaquatic species in which individuals remain in aquatic areas, generally where submerged and floating vegetation is heavy, except for terrestrial excursions, which have several readily identifiable purposes that include travel of hatchlings overland from a terrestrial nest to water, travel by the female to a nesting site, movement to and from hibernation sites or alternate feeding areas, departure from an unsuitable habitat (Cagle, 1944b; Gibbons et al., 1983; Parker, 1984), and travel by males in search of females (Morreale et al., 1984). The basking habit is well noted in all species of the group, and a significant portion of time is spent in absorbing sunlight on the bank or protruding objects or in basking aquatically (see Chapter 22).

The basic life cycle of the species in temperate regions is one in which eggs are laid in early spring in an underground nest dug by the female, with the young hatching in about three months. The hatchlings usually remain in the nest cavity for the duration of fall and winter (Gibbons and Nelson, 1978). Upon emergence in early to late spring, the hatchlings enter the aquatic habitat and begin feeding, approximately one year after being deposited as eggs. The juveniles are preferential carnivores (Clark and Gibbons, 1969), as are the adults when a high-protein diet is available (Parmenter, 1980). Individuals can subsist on a vegetative diet, although growth rates may be significantly slower than in populations in which individuals have carnivorous diets.

Growth rates are influential in the attainment of maturity in that males in a region tend to reach maturity at a set size range whereas females reach maturity more as a function of age (Gibbons et al., 1981). Therefore, males in a population of fast-growing turtles tend to reach maturity at a younger age, and females at a larger size, than those in a population of slow-growing individuals. However, it should be stated that the age-size relationships to maturity in the sexes are highly complex and await further detailed studies to refine our understanding of them.

Sexual dimorphism is apparent in foreclaw length and tail length (both significantly longer in adult males than in females) and in the much smaller size of males than females within a geographic region. Geographic variation is evident in that both sexes of this species from Panama (Moll and Legler, 1971) are dramatically larger than those in the United States (Conant, 1975). However, variation in size can be significant among populations within a geographic region, as is evidenced by the much larger size of slider turtles in the Par Pond Reservoir (which

FIGURE 1.1.   Geographic ranges of North American species of turtles that have been included in the same genus (*Pseudemys*, *Chrysemys*, or *Trachemys*) as the slider turtle during the last 10 years. Genus and species epithets are those currently accepted by Seidel and Smith (1986). Geographic ranges are based on those given by Conant (1975).

receives thermal effluent from a nuclear reactor) than of the natural population at Ellenton Bay less than 20 km away (Gibbons, 1970d). Also, individuals in some tropical populations are not larger than those in typical temperate populations. Geographical variation in body size is another issue that is in no way resolved.

Mating occurs in the spring, although courtship behavior by males has been observed in both fall and winter and may occur to some degree year-round. Observations of slider turtles in the tropics suggests that they are reproductively active from early fall to spring (Moll and Legler, 1971). Females presumably retain viable sperm for many months, as is reported for other turtles (for a review, see Ehrhart, 1982), so the timing of copulation relative to ovulation would not be critical. Slider turtles display the typical reptilian activity pattern in response to seasons and temperatures. The periods of greatest overland and aquatic movement are in the spring and fall. During the winter, individuals become dormant, but in areas where winter observations have been made, some individuals are active on sunny days, even when water temperatures are below 4° C. Summer appears to be a period of reduced activity, relative to spring and fall. Some individuals estivate under banks or beneath terrestrial surface litter during periods of high temperature.

Although most slider turtles in the world die before they leave the nest, because of predation or other factors, those that reach the water and ultimately achieve adulthood have higher survival rates than most other animals. Sliders, as well as other species of turtles, live for more than a quarter of a century (Gibbons and Semlitsch, 1982; Gibbons, 1987). Senility does not seem to be a characteristic of slider turtles.

Habitats and Relative Abundance of the Slider Turtle

A consideration of a species' population characteristics under different habitat conditions can establish whether the species is a habitat specialist or generalist and can provide insight into its ecology and evolutionary history. The slider turtle is unmistakably a habitat generalist, compared with other species of turtles. A survey of the habitats where slider turtles have been sampled by investigators conducting life history studies reveals the spectrum of habitats where sliders not only survive but also flourish. Slider turtles are noted for the ubiquity of their habitat throughout their range. Carr (1952) reported slider turtles from a wide variety of habitats, including intermittent streams, sloughs, sinkholes, and oxbow lakes. Cagle (1950), who conducted the most extensive natural history studies on the species in the United States, found populations living in lakes, ponds, swamps, slow-moving streams, and roadside ditches with little or no vegetation. Moll and Legler (1971) found tropical popula-

tions that inhabited large permanent rivers with abundant vegetation and contiguous backwaters. Legler (1960c) found Big Bend slider turtles (*T. s. gaigeae*) inhabiting large rivers in desert regions of northern Mexico.

Not surprisingly, then, slider turtles have been found in almost every conceivable aquatic habitat in, on, and around the SRP. These include Carolina bays that fluctuate from having water 2 m deep in some years to being dried-up fields in others; seepage basins with radioactive waste materials and a variety of chemical pollutants; farm ponds; natural stream systems; and the Savannah River. One population near the SRP is in a runoff habitat from a hog farm that is estimated to have more than 2,000 slider turtles occupying a body of water with an area of less than 2 ha. No other vertebrates live in the habitat, no aquatic invertebrates are apparent, and a sample of 6 turtles dissected by G. W. Esch at Wake Forest University had no helminth parasites. Thus, turtles are the only apparent, or at least one of the few, multicellular animals that can live in the habitat. Slider turtles can thrive even in waters receiving thermal effluent, as observed in an Illinois reservoir (Thornhill, 1982) and in the thermally elevated reservoirs, streams, and swamps of the SRP.

Primary limitations to the geographic range of slider turtles in the United States might at first appear to be cold weather along the northern edge of the range and arid conditions along the western edge, although the subspecies *T. s. nebulosa* apparently lives in situations in Baja California where drought is a constant specter (Carr, 1952), and the species clearly does well in Illinois, where winters can be harsh (Cagle, 1950). No ready explanation is available for why slider turtles occur in Florida's panhandle but not in the lower part of the state. Competition with *Pseudemys nelsoni* is suspected as an explanation, but no documentation is available to support this contention.

Turtles are an apparent and significant component of the vertebrate fauna of many freshwater, terrestrial, and marine systems, and numerous studies have focused on population features of various species. However, relatively little research with turtles has been directed toward interspecific interactions or other community and ecosystem considerations, although understanding the role of species components is considered to be of critical importance in such studies. This lack of research may be, in part, a consequence of turtles' usually being represented by only one or a few species in most habitats where they occur and of their constituting only a small proportion of the faunal biomass, individual numbers, and productivity. Nonetheless, their potential role in community function has been noted (Congdon and Gibbons, 1989a).

An important initial step toward understanding aquatic or terrestrial communities is to have accurate estimates of standing crop biomass and annual productivity of the species components. Initial steps have been taken toward understanding the role of turtles in aquatic ecosystems

(Congdon et al., 1986), but data on standing crop biomass are few and have usually been limited to single species (Iverson, 1982) rather than the whole turtle community. Estimates of biomass production in turtle species populations or communities are even rarer (Congdon and Gibbons, 1989a).

Many studies have reported estimates of population size and density for freshwater and terrestrial species; however, most density calculations have been based on rough estimates of population sizes and on arbitrary delineations of habitat boundaries. Few studies have considered species interaction among turtles (Berry, 1975), although studies on species composition and relative abundance, and their importance to competition and predation, have been presented for lizards (e.g., Dunham, 1980; Pianka, 1986).

We have compared standing crop and annual biomass productivity for several turtle populations in southern and northern freshwater wetlands (Congdon et al., 1986; Congdon and Gibbons, 1989a). Biomass production rates of turtles were estimated for a six-species community in a Carolina bay (Ellenton Bay) in South Carolina and for a three-species community in a marsh (East Marsh) in southeastern Michigan. *Trachemys scripta* was the numerically dominant species and had the highest standing crop biomass in most southern populations examined.

Of the six common species within the Ellenton Bay community, total biomass production (eggs plus soma) rates ranged from a low of 0.2 kg/ha/yr for *Sternotherus odoratus* to 5.2 kg/ha/yr for *T. scripta*. Total biomass production for the entire six-species community was 9.7 kg/ha/yr. In East Marsh, biomass production ranged from 1.8 kg/ha/yr for *Emydoidea blandingii* to 4.0 kg/ha/yr for *Chelydra serpentina*. Biomass production in the numerically dominant species, *Chrysemys picta*, was 2.4 kg/ha/yr. Total biomass production for the three-species community was 7.3 kg/ha/yr. This should not be taken as a definitive statement that southern turtle communities have a higher standing crop and biomass production rate than North Temperate ones, although this finding may serve as the basis for future comparisons.

Biomass production rates of turtles averaged less than 0.05% of the estimated total primary productivity of similar wetland habitats. Although the standing crop biomass and biomass productivity of turtles are dramatically lower than those of plants in aquatic systems, turtles have a potentially high impact on such systems, particularly in transient wetlands, and may have a previously unsuspected influence on natural wetland habitats that is disproportionate to their comparative standing crop biomass.

The few biomass estimates of single-species populations of turtles presented in the literature do not usually include all species in the habitat. However, enough information has been gathered that certain general hypotheses

can be advanced. Iverson (1982) gave a thorough review of the subject, concluding that (1) populations of herbivorous turtles tend to have higher biomasses than do either carnivorous or omnivorous species; (2) populations of semiaquatic species tend to have lower biomasses than do species that are primarily aquatic; and (3) islands, ponds, and springs, compared with all other habitats studied, have populations with the highest biomasses. In contrast, we (Congdon et al., 1986) have suggested that species-specific densities and biomass are more closely related to habitat suitability, body size of the species, and population age structure than to trophic position. Clearly, the topic is one deserving of further consideration.

The purpose of studying ecological patterns in the slider or any other turtle species is to be able to understand why turtles make decisions to do one thing rather than another. In the simplest measure and most basic terms, the goal of science is to have as firm a grasp as possible on natural phenomena, including the organisms with which we live. Knowing what the potential gains and expenses are to an individual turtle when it moves, eats, or breeds can give us not only a predictability about the behavior and activity patterns of turtles but also insight into the evolutionary background that has led to turtles' behaving the way they do. Knowing what turtles do may lead to ideas about other animals that may have faced similar decisions during their own evolution. The following sections consider fundamental steps in the life of slider turtles based on what is known today and may be instructive in posing questions for future studies.

Life Movement Patterns of the Slider Turtle: An Overview

A premise in the discussion of movement patterns is that alternative choices relating to movement by individual turtles are ultimately under genetic control. It is not necessary to assume that a single allele is involved in any particular movement pattern, and in fact it is more likely that a variety of physiological and ecological considerations must be weighed in terms of their risks and benefits in a manner that natural selection can operate on. The changing probabilities of whether one movement pattern is more likely to be successful than another are an explanation for the inherent variability in movement patterns among individuals. However, consistent patterns of activity and movement in a population are identifiable in a generalized manner, which speaks to the shaping of movement strategies by natural selection through an inheritable genetic medium.

Based on the information available at this time, a scenario can be constructed using a risk-benefit analysis for why slider turtles move from one place to another during their lifetime. The initial travel by all species of freshwater turtles is from the nest to the water, and the decision by a slider turtle about when to make the trip involves potential risks and benefits. Exposure to predators, desiccation, and thermal extremes, and the acquisition and apportionment of energy, are factors that can influence success or failure of the individual and are affected by the individual's choice of activity pattern.

Slider turtles from all reported areas characteristically delay emergence from the nest after hatching. In South Carolina even the clutches of eggs laid latest in the season complete incubation before the onset of cold temperatures. Therefore, the hatchlings are at a developmental state that would permit their departure from the nest cavity and entry into the aquatic environment in late summer or fall.

The benefits that could accrue to an individual from immediate departure from the nest upon hatching would be the initiation of growth at an earlier age and a subsequent size advantage. However, the risk of entering a habitat at an inopportune time can be high if resources are not available, because exposure to predators would be increased and growth would not be enhanced. In addition, it would be necessary in South Carolina to locate a sanctuary for the upcoming period of cold weather. The benefit of remaining in the nest is that the individual is already occupying a safe site prior to a several-month period that is likely to yield minimal returns energetically. A springtime emergence has the benefit of the highest assurance of available resources for a longer period of time.

One prediction regarding hatchling emergence is that in climatic regions where the end of the incubation period coincides with what will be a predictably long period suitable for growth, slider turtles should not delay emergence from the nest but enter the aquatic environment immediately. A corollary prediction is that in areas where the risk is increased for hatchlings that remain in the nest for an extended period, such as certain floodplain systems in which winter flooding is a common occurrence, natural selection should operate on any genetic component associated with the timing of emergence, and immediate emergence from the nest should be the rule. Because it is unknown how labile the timing of emergence might be genetically, it is uncertain whether immediate or delayed departure from the nest might be habitat-specific, with some populations of sliders or other species exhibiting one approach and other populations in that same region exhibiting another. This is an interesting problem that bears investigation.

Once a slider turtle has entered the aquatic environment, movement as a juvenile should be limited to the location of effective areas for eating, basking, and inactivity at night and during cold weather. In situations where habitat conditions remain stable, I see no reason why juvenile slider turtles should travel other than intrapopulationally, and even then only to the extent of taking advantage of microhabitat distributions of resources. Small turtles characteristically limit their activity to areas of heavy floating vegetation and would incur the risk of exposure to predators by making any excursions outside such areas, especially trips across open water.

Preliminary evidence indicates that juvenile turtles become active later in the spring and retire earlier in the fall than adults, presumably because the benefit of limited food acquisition does not outweigh the increased exposure to predators. One possible explanation for extensive intrapopulational or even extrapopulational movement by juvenile turtles is exploratory behavior that might benefit the individual by giving it a more complete awareness of the resource potential of the local habitat and surrounding areas. A prediction is that wanderlust in juvenile turtles inhabiting an area of adequate resources increases as a function of body size, which would reduce the risk of susceptibility to predators.

In slider turtle habitats with adequate resources, extrapopulational movement associated with reproduction should not commence until an individual reaches maturity. The potential benefits to a male slider turtle for moving from one body of water to another are an increase in encounters with females and the subsequent increase in fitness if mating can be achieved. The potential risks are not only exposure to a new suite of predators but also the possibility of being in the terrestrial environment during unexpected environmental extremes, such as a cold front or a prolonged period of high temperatures. Any of these risks would presumably diminish with an increase in size of the animal. Indeed, long-distance travel is proportionately higher in larger individuals than smaller ones. One aspect of overland travel between bodies of water that deserves mention is the question of how slider turtles initially make such a move. Although documentation has not been presented at this time, I hypothesize that slider turtles, and perhaps other species that are frequent interhabitat transients, are able to detect the presence of other bodies of water visually by some mechanism involving the properties of reflected light. Sun-compass orientation has been demonstrated in the closely related *Chrysemys picta* (DeRosa and Taylor, 1982), but this would be of little value unless the individual has visited another site on a previous occasion. Although long-distance movements should be abruptly correlated with the attainment of maturity and the clear benefits to be derived from overland travel, intrapopulational movements should increase throughout the population with an increase in body size that would result in more effective utilization of microhabitat resources with increased impunity from predation.

The primary terrestrial movements of female freshwater turtles are associated with nesting activities. A size-related aspect of nesting excursions might be that larger females would be at less risk during terrestrial excursions than would smaller females. A benefit could definitely be derived from extensive searching by the female until she locates a site she considers highly suitable for nesting. I am unaware of any study that has considered the relationship between body size of females and the amount of distance covered and times spent on land in search of nesting sites, although nesting studies conducted on the George Reserve in Michigan could address this question (Congdon, pers. com.). If large females are more likely than small females to make long nesting forays, large females would be more likely to approach the vicinity of aquatic habitats other than the one in which they normally reside. Thus, larger females would be expected to relocate at greater distances from their original aquatic habitat.

The final area of concern regarding movement patterns is that of travel that is not a predictable seasonal or age-related response but is a response to conditions that are unsuitable for the individual. In this situation the potential benefits of overland or aquatic travel have a greater than even probability of outweighing the risks of such travel. Travel that finds its basis in conditions that are unsuitable for an entire population is of course more likely to be observed, because individuals of all or many size and age classes respond. Even as juveniles, individuals are confronted with situations in which resources may be less than desirable, so a decision must be made as to whether travel is warranted in terms of the risks that might be encountered in the search for more suitable habitat.

A testable hypothesis that seems reasonable is that individuals would respond differently to a particular resource situation and would evaluate the risk-benefit ratio differently, which would of course explain the variability observed among individuals in their propensity to engage in overland travel. Resources for juveniles would presumably be restricted to those involving opportunities for growth and survival, whereas those for adults would have the added component of reproductive success. Larger body size would presumably confer an advantage in reducing predator and environmental risks to turtles; therefore, the documentation of a correlation between movement, particularly overland travel, and body size would be expected for other species as well. Even small turtles are observed in transit between bodies of water, possibly because the potential benefits of available resources have diminished to a level that the risk of movement is judged to be less than the potential benefits to be derived elsewhere.

Lifetime Energetics Decisions of the Slider Turtle

As with movement, the initial decision point in the life cycle of a turtle regarding energy apportionment and acquisition comes while the turtle is in the nest. Energy will be expended whether the turtle remains in the nest or attempts to enter the aquatic environment, but only the latter approach offers any opportunity to acquire addi-

tional energy through feeding. It is possible, however, for the turtle to enter the aquatic environment at an inopportune time for foraging such that lipid stores of the embryo may be used during a futile effort to find food. This then becomes an additional factor associated with the decision not to leave the nest at what may seem to be a propitious time in the fall.

The energy required by a juvenile can be partitioned primarily into that required for maintenance and that required for growth. Presumably, a juvenile turtle will eat and grow at the maximum rate that is possible under the circumstances. The variability observed among individuals within a population presumably reflects the variability in opportunities each has had in foraging in different microhabitats. I can see no reason why juvenile turtles, prior to the advent of any secondary sexual traits or other changes associated with incipient maturity, should differ in their growth rates and patterns of growth on the basis of sex. Achieving a large size as rapidly as possible should be of equal benefit to either sex and thus be equally favored by natural selection. I know of no evidence to the contrary in turtles, and our evidence from slider turtles in South Carolina is that males and females grow at equal rates when they are immature. However, because male slider turtles begin to reach maturity at a smaller size than females, their growth rate slows considerably relative to that of immature females that are the same size. It is at this point in a slider turtle's life history that males begin to partition energy resources into reproduction in lieu of growth.

The mortality risks and energetics costs associated with reproductive activity in male turtles are probably less well appreciated than are those for female turtles, in which egg production and nesting are so obvious. However, a male's reproductive fitness can be equated with the number of successful mating encounters. The probability of successful mating would presumably increase in relation to the probability of finding receptive females (Fig. 1.2). A male turtle in search of females, especially when the search entails long-distance excursions, experiences major metabolic costs for its activity and spends less time foraging and acquiring energy resources. Although it has not been documented, my assumption is that males divert all available energy into such reproductive activity until all possibilities of locating receptive females have been exhausted.

The apportioning of energy by female slider turtles is possibly easier to measure because of the relative ease by which egg production can be expressed quantitatively in terms of energy. However, measurements have not been made of the energetics expenditures for various forms of reproductive activity, such as searching for proper nesting sites, so-called prenesting exploratory behavior, and the documented overland and aquatic movement of immature females that are large but not reproductively active. Nor is the cycle of energy transfer from lipid stores into

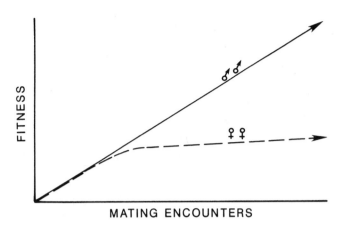

FIGURE 1.2.   Relationship between potential reproductive fitness and number of mating encounters of both sexes of the slider turtle, a species whose females are capable of sperm storage.

ovarian follicles fully understood (Tinkle et al., 1981).

In the final years of life, both mature males and mature females would presumably partition their energy resources in a manner that emphasizes reproduction at the cost of growth. However, the observation of continued growth in large individuals in both sexes suggests that in certain years there may be circumstances in which the reproductive effort is expended for the year, and the acquisition of resources can be converted into an increase in body size. I imagine that careful measurements of the seasonal timing of growth in adult turtles would reveal that the major portion of incremental growth occurs after any potential for reproductive activity between the sexes has ceased. Also, because available lipid reserves would presumably have been shunted into reproduction, and the initial energy harvested would be used for replenishing those reserves, a lag time between the end of reproductive activity and the initiation of any growth in body size of adults would be expected.

Clearly, these are matters for future investigations and will be resolved through the gathering of careful empirical evidence both in natural situations and experimentally. The life history questions associated with bioenergetics are some of the most intriguing ones turtle biologists will face during the next few years.

Literature Survey

One problem that certainly will become more prevalent with the increase in scientific knowledge is the unintentional omission of pertinent references through oversight or ignorance. I assume that the intentional omission of references because someone does not like someone else will stay at about the same level as always. Not citing a publication because of personal animosities or insecurities is of course petty and unprofessional, as I am sure all who are professional and not petty would agree.

I have no delusions of any sort that every reference of turtle biology that would be appropriate in this book has been cited. I speak not only for myself but also for any of the other authors when I apologize for the omission of studies that should have been included somewhere but were not. Furthermore, I request that the author of the chapter be notified of such errors so that the appropriate citation can be given if subsequent editions of the book are printed. Scientists are often reluctant to make a case that their own work should have been cited in a particular presentation. In many instances, however, an uncited author would be providing a service by making another author aware of such omissions.

One source of literature that can sometimes be overlooked because of its unavailability is doctoral dissertations and master's theses. A list of the doctoral dissertations from the United States that have been written about turtles and of which I am aware are listed in Appendix 1.2. I have not attempted to list the numerous master's theses that have focused on the biology of turtles, although many outstanding ones are shelved away in biology departments around the country. Turtle biologists will recognize many of the dissertations because of the open-literature publications that resulted from them. However, a great deal of useful information about turtles is still harbored in dissertations and theses that will never be published.

Acknowledgments

Research and manuscript preparation were made possible by contract DE-AC09-76SROO-819 between the University of Georgia and the U.S. Department of Energy and by National Science Foundation grant DEB-79-04758. I appreciate the assistance of Judy Greene and Jeff Lovich.

APPENDIX 1.1.   Savannah River Ecology
Laboratory publications on turtles

Avery, H. W., and L. J. Vitt
  1984.   How to get blood from a turtle. *Copeia* 1984:209–210.
Bennett, D. H.
  1972.   Notes on the terrestrial wintering of mud turtles (*Kinosternon subrubrum*). *Herpetologica* 28:245–247.
Bennett, D. H., J. W. Gibbons, and J. C. Franson
  1970.   Terrestrial activity in aquatic turtles. *Ecology* 51:738–740.
Bourque, J. E., and G. W. Esch
  1974.   Population ecology of parasites in turtles from thermally altered and natural aquatic communities. In *Thermal ecology*, U.S. Atomic Energy Commission Symposium Series (CONF-730505), edited by J. W. Gibbons and R. R. Sharitz, 551–561. National Technical Information Service, Springfield, Va.

Breitenbach, G. L., J. D. Congdon, and R. C. van Loben Sels
1984. Winter temperatures of *Chrysemys picta* nests in Michigan: Effects on hatchling survival. *Herpetologica* 40:76–81.

Christy, E. J., J. O. Farlow, J. E. Bourque, and J. W. Gibbons
1974. Enhanced growth and increased body size of turtles living in thermal and post-thermal aquatic systems. In *Thermal ecology*, U.S. Atomic Energy Commission Symposium Series (CONF-730505), edited by J. W. Gibbons and R. R. Sharitz, 277–284. National Technical Information Service, Springfield, Va.

Clark, D. B., and J. W. Gibbons
1969. Dietary shift in the turtle *Pseudemys scripta* (Schoepff) from youth to maturity. *Copeia* 1969:704–706.

Congdon, J. D., and J. W. Gibbons
1983. Relationships of reproductive characteristics to body size in *Pseudemys scripta*. *Herpetologica* 39:147–151.
1985. Egg components and reproductive characteristics of turtles: Relationships to body size. *Herpetologica* 41:194–205.
1987. Morphological constraint on egg size: A challenge to optimal egg size theory? *Proceedings of the National Academy of Sciences of the United States of America* 84:4145–4147.

Congdon, J. D., J. W. Gibbons, and J. L. Greene
1983. Parental investment in the chicken turtle (*Deirochelys reticularia*). *Ecology* 64:419–425.

Congdon, J. D., J. L. Greene, and J. W. Gibbons
1986. Biomass of freshwater turtles: A geographic comparison. *American Midland Naturalist* 115:165–173.

Esch, G. W., J. W. Gibbons, and J. E. Bourque
1979. The distribution and abundance of enteric helminths in *Chrysemys s. scripta* from various habitats on the Savannah River Plant in South Carolina. *Journal of Parasitology* 65:624–632.
1979. Species diversity of helminth parasites in *Chrysemys s. scripta* from a variety of habitats in South Carolina. *Journal of Parasitology* 65:633–638.

Gibbons, J. W.
1967. Variation in growth rates in three populations of the painted turtle, *Chrysemys picta*. *Herpetologica* 23:296–303.
1968. Population structure and survivorship in the painted turtle, *Chrysemys picta*. *Copeia* 1968:260–268.
1968. Reproductive potential, activity, and cycles in the painted turtle, *Chrysemys picta*. *Ecology* 49:399–409.
1969. Ecology and population dynamics of the chicken turtle, *Deirochelys reticularia*. *Copeia* 1969:669–676.
1970. Reproductive characteristics of a Florida population of musk turtles (*Sternothaerus odoratus*). *Herpetologica* 26:268–270.
1970. Reproductive dynamics of a turtle (*Pseudemys scripta*) population in a reservoir receiving heated effluent from a nuclear reactor. *Canadian Journal of Zoology* 48:881–885.
1970. Sex ratios in turtles. *Researches on Population Ecology* (Kyoto) 12:252–254.
1970. Terrestrial activity and the population dynamics of aquatic turtles. *American Midland Naturalist* 83:404–414.
1982. Reproductive patterns in freshwater turtles. *Herpetologica* 38:222–227.

1983. Reproductive characteristics and ecology of the mud turtle *Kinosternon subrubrum* (Lacepede). *Herpetologica* 39:254–271.
1986. Movement patterns among turtle populations: Applicability to management of the desert tortoise. *Herpetologica* 42:104–113.
1987. Why do turtles live so long? *Bioscience* 7:262–269.

Gibbons, J. W., and J. W. Coker
1977. Ecological and life history aspects of the cooter, *Chrysemys floridana* (Le Conte). *Herpetologica* 33:29–33.
1978. Herpetofaunal colonization patterns of Atlantic Coast barrier islands. *American Midland Naturalist* 99:219–233.

Gibbons, J. W., and J. L. Greene
1978. Selected aspects of the ecology of the chicken turtle, *Deirochelys reticularia* (Latreille) (Reptilia, Testudines, Emydidae). *Journal of Herpetology* 12:237–241.
1979. X-ray photography: A technique to determine reproductive patterns of freshwater turtles. *Herpetologica* 35:86–89.

Gibbons, J. W., and J. R. Harrison III
1981. Reptiles and amphibians of Kiawah and Capers Islands, South Carolina. *Brimleyana* 1981(5):145–162.

Gibbons, J. W., and D. H. Nelson
1978. The evolutionary significance of delayed emergence from the nest by hatchling turtles. *Evolution* 32:297–303.

Gibbons, J. W., and R. D. Semlitsch
1981. Terrestrial drift fences with pitfall traps: An effective technique for quantitative sampling of animal populations. *Brimleyana* 1981(7):1–16.
1982. Survivorship and longevity of a long-lived vertebrate species: How long do turtles live? *Journal of Animal Ecology* 51:523–527.

Gibbons, J. W., and R. R. Sharitz
1974. Thermal alteration of aquatic ecosystems. *American Scientist* 62:660–670.
1981. Thermal ecology: Environmental teachings of a nuclear reactor site. *Bioscience* 31:293–298.

Gibbons, J. W., D. H. Nelson, K. K. Patterson, and J. L. Greene
1976. The reptiles and amphibians of the Savannah River Plant in west-central South Carolina. In *Proceedings of the First South Carolina Endangered Species Symposium*, edited by D. N. Forsythe and W. B. Ezell, Jr., 133–143. South Carolina Wildlife and Marine Resources Department and the Citadel, Charleston, S.C.

Gibbons, J. W., J. L. Greene, and J. P. Schubauer
1978. Variability in clutch size in aquatic chelonians. *British Journal of Herpetology* 6:13–14.

Gibbons, J. W., G. H. Keaton, J. P. Schubauer, J. L. Greene, D. H. Bennett, J. R. McAuliffe, and R. R. Sharitz
1979. Unusual population size structure in freshwater turtles on barrier islands. *Georgia Journal of Science* 37:155–159.

Gibbons, J. W., R. R. Sharitz, and I. L. Brisbin, Jr.
1980. Thermal ecology research at the Savannah River Plant: A review. *Nuclear Safety* 21:367–379.

Gibbons, J. W., R. D. Semlitsch, J. L. Greene, and J. P. Schubauer
1981. Variation in age and size at maturity of the slider turtle (*Pseudemys scripta*). *American Naturalist* 117:841–845.

Gibbons, J. W., J. L. Greene, and K. K. Patterson
 1982.   Variation in reproductive characteristics of aquatic turtles. *Copeia* 1982:776–784.
Gibbons, J. W., J. L. Greene, and J. D. Congdon
 1983.   Drought-related responses of aquatic turtle populations. *Journal of Herpetology* 17:242–246.
Knight, J. L., and R. K. Loraine
 1986.   Notes on turtle egg predation by *Lampropeltis getulus* (Linnaeus) (Reptilia: Colubridae) on the Savannah River Plant, South Carolina. *Brimleyana* 1986(12):1–4.
Lamb, T.
 1983.   On the problematic identification of *Kinosternon* (Testudines: Kinosternidae) in Georgia, with new state localities for *Kinosternon bauri. Georgia Journal of Science* 41:115–120.
 1983.   The striped mud turtle (*Kinosternon bauri*) in South Carolina, a confirmation through multivariate character analysis. *Herpetologica* 39:383–390.
Lamb, T., and J. D. Congdon
 1985.   Ash content: Relationships to flexible and rigid eggshell types of turtles. *Journal of Herpetology* 19:527–530.
Morreale, S. J., and J. W. Gibbons
 1986.   *Habitat suitability index models: Slider turtle.* United States Fish and Wildlife Service Biological Report no. 82(10.125).
Morreale, S. J., J. W. Gibbons, and J. D. Congdon
 1984.   Significance of activity and movement in the yellow-bellied slider turtle (*Pseudemys scripta*). *Canadian Journal of Zoology* 62:1038–1042.
Parker, E. D., M. F. Hirshfield, and J. W. Gibbons
 1973.   Ecological comparisons of thermally affected aquatic environments. *Journal of Water Pollution Control Federation* 45:726–733.
Parmenter, R. R.
 1980.   Effects of food availability and water temperature on the feeding ecology of pond sliders (*Chrysemys s. scripta*). *Copeia* 1980:503–514.
Schmidt, G. D., G. W. Esch, and J. W. Gibbons
 1970.   *Neoechinorhynchus chelonos,* a new species of acanthocephalan parasite of turtles. *Proceedings of the Helminthological Society of Washington* 37:172–174.
Schubauer, J. P.
 1981.   A reliable radio-telemetry tracking system suitable for studies of chelonians. *Journal of Herpetology* 15:117–120.
Schubauer, J. P., and R. R. Parmenter
 1981.   Winter feeding by aquatic turtles in a southeastern reservoir. *Journal of Herpetology* 15:444–447.
Scott, D. E., F. W. Whicker, and J. W. Gibbons
 1986.   Effect of season on the retention of ^{137}Cs and ^{90}Sr by the yellow-bellied slider turtle (*Pseudemys scripta*). *Canadian Journal of Zoology* 64:2850–2853.
Scribner, K. T., M. H. Smith, and J. W. Gibbons
 1984.   Genetic differentiation among local populations of the yellow-bellied slider turtle (*Pseudemys scripta*). *Herpetologica* 40:382–387.
Scribner, K. T., J. E. Evans, S. J. Morreale, M. H. Smith, and J. W. Gibbons
 1986.   Genetic divergence among populations of the yellow-bellied slider turtle (*Pseudemys scripta*) separated by aquatic and terrestrial habitats. *Copeia* 1986:691–700.

Spotila, J. R., R. E. Foley, J. P. Schubauer, R. D. Semlitsch, K. M. Crawford, E. A. Standora, and J. W. Gibbons
 1984.   Opportunistic behavioral thermoregulation of turtles, *Pseudemys scripta,* in response to microclimatology of a nuclear reactor cooling reservoir. *Herpetologica* 40:299–308.

APPENDIX 1.2.   Doctoral dissertations pertinent to studies on the life history, ecology, or evolution of turtles

Ackerman, R. A.
 1975.   Diffusion and the gas exchange of sea turtle eggs. University of Florida.
Andrews, R. D.
 1966.   Leptospiral flora of aquatic turtles in Illinois. University of Illinois.
Barone, M. C.
 1968.   Effect of induced cold torpor and time of year on blood coagulation, serum proteins, and other blood properties of the turtles *Pseudemys scripta* and *Chrysemys picta.* St. Bonaventure University.
Barzilay, S. S.
 1980.   Orientation and homing of the wood turtle (*Clemmys insculpta*). Rutgers.
Baumann, T. W.
 1966.   A study of brain and cervical spinal cord in *Chrysemys picta.* St. Louis University.
Beall, R. J.
 1970.   An investigation on the effect of cold exposure on the cardiac metabolism of the turtle, *Chrysemys picta.* State University of New York at Buffalo.
Belkin, D. A.
 1961.   Anaerobic mechanisms in the diving of the loggerhead musk turtle, *Sternothaerus minor.* University of Florida.
Bourque, J. E.
 1974.   Studies on the population dynamics of helminth parasites in the yellow-bellied turtle, *Pseudemys scripta scripta.* Wake Forest University.
Boyer, D. R.
 1958.   Biological implications of the basking habit in turtles. Tulane University.
Brown, L. M.
 1971.   Comparative blood studies of turtles as related to environment and tolerance of submersion. University of Southern Mississippi.
Bull, J. J.
 1977.   Evolution in karyotypes: I. Sex determination, and II. Chromosomes of side-necked turtles. University of Utah.
Bury, R. B.
 1972.   Habits and home range of the pacific pond turtle, *Clemmys marmorata,* in a stream community. University of California, Berkeley.
Bush, W. G.
 1973.   A qualitative and quantitative electron-microscopic study of the retina of the turtle, *Pseudemys scripta elegans.* University of Delaware.

Cagle, F. R.
1943.   The growth of the slider turtle, *Pseudemys scripta elegans*. University of Michigan.

Carras, P. L.
1983.   Passive electrical properties of horizontal cells in the retina of the turtle, *Pseudemys scripta elegans*. University of Illinois.

Cipolle, M. D.
1983.   The renin-angiotensin system in the freshwater turtle *Pseudemys scripta*. University of Illinois.

Clark, V.
1971.   Studies on anaerobic metabolism in the freshwater turtle (*Pseudemys* species). University of North Carolina at Chapel Hill.

Cowan, F. B. M.
1970.   Comparative studies on the cranial glands of turtles with special reference to salt secretion. University of Toronto.

Crenshaw, J. W., Jr.
1955.   The ecological geography of the *Pseudemys floridana* complex in the southeastern United States. University of Florida.

Crouse, D. T.
1985.   The biology and conservation of sea turtles in North Carolina (marine, population, *Caretta caretta*, demography, Georgia). University of Wisconsin—Madison.

Cunningham, B.
1920.   Some phases in the development of *Chrysemys cinerea*. University of Wisconsin—Madison.

Dalrymple, G. H.
1975.   Variation in the cranial feeding mechanism of turtles of the genus *Trionyx geoffroy*. University of Toronto.

Dantzler, W. H.
1964.   The role of the kidneys and bladder in the handling of water and solutes in the freshwater turtle, *Pseudemys scripta,* and the desert tortoise, *Gopherus agassizii*. Duke University.

Davis, M.
1981.   Aspects of the social and spatial experience of eastern box turtles, *Terrapene carolina carolina*. University of Tennessee at Knoxville.

DeRosa, C. T.
1977.   A comparison of orientation mechanisms in aquatic, semi-aquatic, and terrestrial turtles (*Trionyx spinifer, Chrysemys picta,* and *Terrapene c. carolina*). Miami University.

Desan, P. H.
1984.   The organization of the cerebral cortex of the pond turtle, *Pseudemys scripta elegans*. Harvard University.

Dobie, J. L.
1966.   Reproduction and growth in the alligator snapping turtle, *Macroclemys temmincki* (Troost). Tulane University.

Dorando, S. L. S.
1978.   The energy and nitrogen budgets of the common snapping turtle, *Chelydra serpentina serpentina* (Linne). Rutgers.

Dubois, W.
1982.   Testis structure and function in the freshwater turtle *Chrysemys picta*. Boston University.

Dunson, W. A.
1965.   Sodium regulation in freshwater turtles. University of Michigan.

Ehrenfeld, D. W.
1966.   The sea-finding orientation of the green turtle (*Chelonia mydas*). University of Florida.

Ernst, C. H.
1969.   Natural history and ecology of the painted turtle, *Chrysemys picta* (Schneider). University of Kentucky.

Feuer, R. C.
1966.   Variation in snapping turtles, *Chelydra serpentina* Linnaeus: A study in quantitative systematics. University of Utah.

Fisher, J. E.
1968.   The life histories of *Spirorchis scripta* Stunkard 1923, and *Spirorchis neurophilus*, species nova (Trematoda), from *Chrysemys picta picta*. Virginia Polytechnic Institute and State University.

Fox, M. A. M.
1961.   Transport of some sugars by intestinal segments of *Chrysemys picta*. St. Louis University.

Frair, W. F.
1962.   Comparative serology of turtles with systematic implications. Rutgers.

Frazer, N. B.
1983.   Demography and life history evolution of the Atlantic loggerhead sea turtle, *Caretta caretta* (Georgia). University of Georgia.

Froese, A. D.
1974.   Aspects of space use in the common snapping turtle, *Chelydra s. serpentina*. University of Tennessee at Knoxville.

Fulbrook, J. E.
1982.   Motion sensitivity of optic nerve axons in turtle, *Pseudemys scripta elegans*. University of Delaware.

Gaffney, E. S.
1969.   The North American baenoid turtles and the cryptodire-pleurodire dichotomy. Columbia University.

Gatten, R. E., Jr.
1973.   Aerobic and anaerobic metabolism during activity in the turtles *Pseudemys scripta* and *Terrapene ornata*. University of Michigan.

Gibbons, J. W"
1967.   Population dynamics and ecology of the painted turtle, *Chrysemys picta*. Michigan State University.

Glidewell, J. R.
1984.   Life history energetics of the red-eared turtle, *Pseudemys scripta*, in north central Texas (reptiles). North Texas State University.

Graf, V. A.
1967.   A spectral sensitivity curve and wavelength discrimination for the turtle, *Chrysemys picta picta*. Bryn Mawr College.

Graham, T. E.
1972.   Temperature-photoperiod effects on diel locomotor activity and thermal selection in the turtles *Chrysemys picta* (Schneider), *Clemmys guttata* (Schneider), and *Sternotherus odoratus* (Latreille). University of Rhode Island.

Grassman, M. A.
1984.   The chemosensory behavior of juvenile sea turtles: Im-

plications for chemical imprinting (*Chelonia mydas, Lepidochelys kempi*). Texas A&M University.

Gutzke, W. H. N.
1984.   The influence of environmental factors on eggs and hatchlings of painted turtles (*Chrysemys picta*). Colorado State University.

Hammer, D. A.
1973.   Ecological relations of waterfowl and snapping turtle populations. Utah State University.

Hart, D. R.
1979.   Resource partitioning among Louisiana turtles of the genus *Chrysemys*. Tulane University.

Hartweg, N. E.
1934.   A study of genetic variation in the genus *Chrysemys*. University of Michigan.

Hartwell, E. M.
1881.   Notes on some points in the anatomy and physiology of the slider terrapin (*Pseudemys rugosa*). Johns Hopkins University.

Herbert, C. V.
1983.   The physiological responses of the turtle, *Chrysemys picta bellii*, to apnea, as a function of temperature. Brown University.

Hirschfeld, W. J.
1964.   The effect of bleeding and starvation on erythropoiesis in the turtle, *Pseudemys scripta elegans*. New York University.

Hudson, D. M.
1984.   Studies on the immunoparasitology of eastern painted turtles (*Chrysemys picta picta*) and snapping turtles (*Chelydra serpentina*) exposed to spirorchid blood flukes (*Spirorchis scripta*). University of Rhode Island.

Hutton, K. E.
1955.   Variations in the blood-chemistry of turtles under active and hibernating conditions. Purdue University.

Jackson, C. G., Jr.
1964.   A biometrical study of form and growth in *Pseudemys concinna suwanniensis* Carr (order: Testudinata). University of Florida.

Jackson, D. R.
1977.   The fossil freshwater emydid turtles of Florida. University of Florida.

Killebrew, F. C.
1976.   Comparative osteology of *Graptemys flavimaculata* Cagle and *Graptemys nigrinoda* Cagle (Testudines, Emydidae). University of Arkansas.

Lagler, K. F.
1940.   Ecological studies of turtles in Michigan with special reference to fish management. University of Michigan.

Legler, J. M.
1959.   The life history and ecology of the ornate box turtle, *Terrapene ornata ornata* Agassiz. University of Kansas.

Lieb, J. R.
1953.   Biophysical and biochemical studies of the blood of the central painted turtle: *Chrysemys picta marginata*. St. Louis University.

Lucey, E. C.
1975.   Cardiovascular and respiratory responses to temperature, diving, carotid occlusion and hemorrhage in the turtle *Pseudemys scripta elegans*. Idaho State University.

Madden, R. C.
1975.   Home range, movements, and orientation in the eastern box turtle, *Terrapene carolina carolina*. City University of New York.

Magliola, L.
1983.   Effects of estrogen on skeletal calcium metabolism and plasma parameters of vitellogenesis in the male, three-toed box turtle (*Terrapene carolina triunguis*). University of Missouri.

Mahmoud, I. Y.
1960.   The comparative ecology of the kinosternid turtles of Oklahoma. University of Oklahoma.

Manton, M. L.
1972.   Chemoreception in the migratory sea turtle, *Chelonia mydas*. Columbia University.

Masat, R. J.
1964.   Environmentally induced changes in blood serum proteins in *Chrysemys picta*. St. Louis University.

McKnight, T. J.
1959.   A taxonomic study of the helminth parasites of the turtles of Lake Texoma. University of Oklahoma.

McKown, R. R.
1972.   Phylogenetic relationships within the turtle genera *Graptemys* and *Malaclemys*. University of Texas at Austin.

Mehaffey, L., III
1971.   The spectral sensitivity of the turtle *Pseudemys scripta elegans*. Ohio State University.

Meylan, A. B.
1984.   Feeding ecology of the hawksbill turtle (*Eretmochelys imbricata*): Spongivory as a feeding niche in the coral reef community. University of Florida.

Mitchell, J. C.
1982.   Population ecology and demography of the freshwater turtles *Chrysemys picta* and *Sternotherus odoratus*. University of Tennessee at Knoxville.

Moll, D. L.
1977.   Ecological investigations of turtles in a polluted ecosystem: The central Illinois River and adjacent flood plain lakes. Illinois State University.

Moll, E. O.
1969.   The life history of a neotropical slider turtle, *Pseudemys scripta* (Schoepff), in Panama. University of Utah.

Mortimer, J. A.
1981.   Reproductive ecology of the green turtle, *Chelonia mydas*, at Ascension Island. University of Florida.

Mosimann, J. E.
1956.   A morphometric analysis of allometry in shells of the turtles: *Graptemys geographica, Chrysemys picta*, and *Sternotherus odoratus*. University of Michigan.

Murphy, G. G.
1970.   Orientation of adult and hatchling red-eared turtles, *Pseudemys scripta elegans*. Mississippi State University.

Northcutt, R. G.
1968.   The telencephalon of the western painted turtle (*Chrysemys picta belli*). University of Illinois.

Obbard, M. E.
1984.   Population ecology of the common snapping turtle, *Chelydra serpentina*, in north-central Ontario. University of Guelph, Ontario.

Owens, D. W.
1976. Endocrine control of reproduction and growth in the green sea turtle *Chelonia mydas*. University of Arizona.
Patterson, W. C.
1965. Hearing in the turtle. University of Delaware.
Perry, S. F.
1972. The lungs of the red eared turtle, *Chrysemys (Pseudemys) scripta elegans*, as a gas exchange organ: A histological and quantitative morphological study. Boston University.
Pert, A.
1973. Instrumental behavior in the turtle (*Chrysemys picta picta*) as a function of amount of award. Bryn Mawr College.
Pindzola, R. R.
1984. Olfactory pathways in the soft-shell turtle (*Trionyx spiniferus*). University of Delaware.
Plummer, M. V.
1976. Population ecology of the softshell turtle, *Trionyx muticus*. University of Kansas.
Pluto, T. G.
1983. Habitat utilization and movements of the map turtle, *Graptemys geographica* (Pennsylvania). Pennsylvania State University.
Rainey, W. E.
1984. Albumin evolution in turtles. University of California, Berkeley.
Rapatz, G. L.
1955. Metabolic studies of the turtle, *Chrysemys picta*, during a state of cold torpor and during a state of fast. St. Louis University.
Reagan, D. P.
1972. Microenvironmental aspects of habitat selection in the three-toed box turtle, *Terrapene carolina triunguis*. University of Arkansas.
Ream, C. H.
1967. Some aspects of the ecology of painted turtles, Lake Mendota, Wisconsin. Ph.D. thesis. University of Wisconsin—Madison.
Richardson, J. I.
1982. A population model for adult female loggerhead sea turtles (*Caretta caretta*) nesting in Georgia. University of Georgia.
Robbins, D. O.
1970. Wavelength and intensity effects on the responses of single optic tectal units in the turtle, *Pseudemys scripta elegans* (Wied). University of Delaware.
Russo, P. M.
1972. Behavioral thermoregulation and energy budget of the eastern box turtle, *Terrapene carolina carolina* (Linne). Rutgers.
Salhanick, A. R.
1979. Binding proteins for estradiol-17-beta in the plasma and oviduct of the turtle, *Chrysemys picta*. Boston University.
Scanlon, T. C.
1982. Anatomy of the neck of the western painted turtle (*Chrysemys picta belli* Gray; Reptilia, Testudinata) from the perspective of possible movements in the region. University of Michigan.

Scott, A. F.
1976. Aquatic and terrestrial movements of farm pond populations of the eastern mud turtle (*Kinosternon subrubrum subrubrum*) in east-central Alabama. Auburn University.
Seidel, M. E.
1973. Osmoregulatory adaptations of the spiny softshell turtle, *Trionyx spiniferus*, from brackish and fresh waters. University of New Mexico.
Sexton, O. J.
1957. The spatial and seasonal distribution of a population of the painted turtle, *Chrysemys picta marginata* Agassiz. University of Michigan.
Shaner, R. F.
1920. The anatomy of a 9.5 mm. turtle, *Chrysemys picta:* A study in comparative embryology. Harvard University.
Sharber, J. F.
1973. A telemetric study of activity of the common snapping turtle *Chelydra serpentina*. Middle Tennessee State University.
Shealy, R. M.
1973. The natural history of the Alabama map turtle, *Graptemys pulchra* Baur, in Alabama. Auburn University.
Skoloda, T. E.
1973. Ipsilateral visual evoked potentials in the turtle, *Pseudemys scripta elegans*. University of Delaware.
Smith, C. G.
1967. Variations in the blood proteins of the musk turtle, *Sternotherus odoratus* (Latreille). Southern Illinois University at Carbondale.
Snow, J. E.
1984. Feeding ecology of juvenile turtles (*Chrysemys*) under experimental conditions. University of Oklahoma.
Standora, E. A.
1982. A telemetric study of the thermoregulatory behavior and climate-space of free-ranging yellow-bellied turtles, *Pseudemys scripta*. University of Georgia.
Stephens, G. A.
1976. Blood pressure regulation in the pond turtles *Pseudemys scripta elegans* and *Chrysemys picta:* Absence of an arterial baroreceptor reflex. University of Kansas.
Stickel, E. L. F.
1949. Populations and home range relationships of the box turtle, *Terrapene carolina* (Linnaeus). University of Michigan.
Stuart, M. D.
1985. Helminth parasites of the eastern box turtle, *Terrapene c. carolina,* from North Carolina. North Carolina State University at Raleigh.
Sturbaum, B. A.
1972. Thermoregulation in the ornate box turtle, *Terrapene ornata*. University of New Mexico.
Sullivan, J. B., III
1966. Structure, function, and evolution of turtle hemoglobins. University of Texas at Austin.
Thiruvathukal, K. V.
1960. The histology of the digestive tract of the freshwater turtle, *Chrysemys picta*. St. Louis University.

Timken, R. L.
  1968. The distribution and ecology of turtles in South Dakota. University of South Dakota.
Tinkle, D. W.
  1957. Systematics and ecology of the *Sternothaerus carinatus* complex (Testudinata). Tulane University.
Vogt, R. C.
  1978. Systematics and ecology of the false map turtle complex *Graptemys pseudogeographica*. University of Wisconsin— Madison.
Walker, W. F.
  1946. The development and adult morphology of the shoulder region of the turtle *Chrysemys picta marginata*, with special reference to the musculature. Harvard University.
Ward, F. P.
  1979. Disparities in turtle populations on Carroll Island, Maryland, as a measure of past environmental impacts. Johns Hopkins University.

Ware, S. K.
  1980. Cardiovascular responses to diving in the turtle, *Pseudemys scripta*. Iowa State University.
Webb, R. G.
  1960. Recent softshell turtles of North America (family, Trionychidae). University of Kansas.
Winokur, R. M.
  1973. Cranial integumentary specializations of turtles. University of Utah.
Wood, J. R., Jr.
  1974. The amino acid requirements of the hatchling green sea turtle, *Chelonia mydas*. University of Arizona.
Zug, G. R.
  1969. Locomotion and the morphology of the pelvic girdle and hindlimbs of cryptodiran turtles. University of Michigan.
Zwick, H.
  1968. Behaviorally determined dark-adaptation functions in the turtle (*Pseudemys scripta elegans*). University of Delaware.

J. WHITFIELD GIBBONS
Savannah River Ecology Laboratory
Drawer E
Aiken, South Carolina 29802

2

Turtle Studies at SREL: A Research Perspective

Abstract

Descriptions are given of the aquatic habitats and climate of the Savannah River Plant in South Carolina. The techniques used and data collected by investigators at the Savannah River Ecology Laboratory during 20 years of research on freshwater turtles are also described. Historically significant events in the study of turtles, such as the discoveries that mud turtles hibernate on land, that clutch size can be determined by x-ray photography, and that radioactive turtles occur on the Savannah River Plant are discussed.

Introduction

The purpose of this chapter is to discuss the research program on freshwater turtles, particularly the slider turtle (*Trachemys scripta*), initiated at the University of Georgia's Savannah River Ecology Lab (SREL) in July 1967. Details of habitats and techniques that are referred to in other chapters of the book are provided, as well as a general chronology of research findings, anecdotes, and my personal assessment of the situations that arose. Much of the material is based on my 20 years' worth of scattered field notes and data sheets, and a hazy memory.

One objective of this book is to reveal some of the research advantages and insights that accrue from long-term field studies of specific natural populations. Such long-term studies can best be carried out as a consequence of two important factors: protected field sites and long-term funding. The U.S. Department of Energy's (DOE) Savannah River Plant (SRP) has been an ideal site for establishing long-term field research efforts because of the protection from public disturbance that results from the tight security of a defense site. The other critical consideration that has made these studies possible is that funding of SREL by DOE [i.e., AEC (Atomic Energy Commission), 1952–74, and ERDA (Energy Research and Development Administration), 1974–77] has been continuous throughout the study period. A reliable source of funding is essential to planning and carrying out intensive long-term field studies. This fundamental support of SREL was a major factor in the completion of the turtle studies.

The Study Site

SREL is located on the SRP, whose northern boundary is about 12 miles south of Aiken, South Carolina (Fig. 2.1). The security measures taken by DOE for a national defense facility result in the largest area (almost 300 square miles) of restricted-access land not only in South Carolina but also in the entire eastern United States. One product is the protection of natural habitats and wildlife.

The protection from poaching results in an undesignated wildlife preserve for most of the native plant and animal species of the South Carolina Coastal Plain. Furthermore, the SRP operational plan results in the ironic situation that the nuclear reactor site has suffered less environmental impact on a broad scale than typical agricultural and urban areas of South Carolina. To be sure, some of the SRP industrial releases, such as cadmium, mercury, and low levels of radioisotopes, are potentially

hazardous, but they are mostly confined to prescribed areas that are a small portion of the SRP. Thus, the environmental impact of reactor operations has been relatively consistent over the years, unlike some of the major environmental abuses and disruptions that have been perpetrated on the many other parts of the South Carolina Coastal Plain and other regions.

Most of the natural ecosystems in the South Atlantic Upper Coastal Plain are represented on the SRP. Bottomland hardwood forests, swamp forests, and the shorelines of ponds and reservoirs constitute a wealth of wetland habitats. The floodplain of the Savannah River on the SRP includes beautiful swamps of majestic bald cypress and water tupelo. Although few turtles are to be found in the heavily canopied area, the swamps are habitat for a diverse array of reptiles, birds, and other wildlife. The swamp margins are breeding and feeding habitats for many species, including large populations of frogs and salamanders that rely on these areas for breeding. Some of the same habitats serve as feeding grounds for the northernmost nesting colony of wood storks. A natural stream, Upper Three Runs Creek, that is virtually unpolluted by domestic, agricultural, or industrial sources flows through 20 miles of bottomland hardwood forests of oak, holly, and maple. This blackwater stream (a term used for streams rich in dissolved humus) has a higher reported diversity of invertebrates than any other stream in the Southeast. Although unpolluted blackwater streams are a fast-vanishing habitat, Upper Three Runs is home for untold numbers of water snakes, wood ducks, and other native species.

On the SRP is the 2,800-acre reservoir known as Par Pond, where the only boats are those of ecologists, and slider turtles are among the most prevalent animals. Dozens of Carolina bays are found on the site. These natural lentic wetlands attract all species of wading birds native to the region and serve as the primary habitat for thousands of semiaquatic turtles, snakes, frogs, and salamanders (Table 2.1) as well as aquatic invertebrates. Despite the seasonal drying of many of these habitats, slider turtles venture into most of them when water levels are high, and all of the habitats seem to have resident populations of eastern mud turtles. Sundews, pitcher plants, and native orchids grow on the periphery of these Carolina bay wetlands.

Paradoxically, the natural environments of the SRP have been saved by the characteristic mode of operation of a U.S. defense facility. The SRP has become an outdoor laboratory that permits comparison of natural communities with those influenced by human hands. For example, many of the wetland habitats where turtles live have been protected for a third of century from major environmental impacts typically caused by today's society. Yet some streams and areas of the cypress-tupelo swamp affected by thermal pollution support impressive populations of

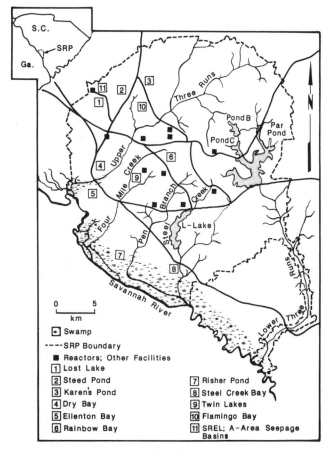

FIGURE 2.1.   The Savannah River Plant and some of the sites important in the study of freshwater turtles.

⊡ Swamp
- - - - SRP Boundary
■ Reactors; Other Facilities
1 Lost Lake
2 Steed Pond
3 Karen's Pond
4 Dry Bay
5 Ellenton Bay
6 Rainbow Bay
7 Risher Pond
8 Steel Creek Bay
9 Twin Lakes
10 Flamingo Bay
11 SREL; A-Area Seepage Basins

Table 2.1. Checklist of the amphibians and reptiles of the SRP

Table 2.1 -- *Continued*

Class Amphibia
  Order Caudata (salamanders)
    Proteidae

Necturus punctatus	Dwarf waterdog

    Amphiumidae

Amphiuma means	Two-toed amphiuma

    Sirenidae

Siren intermedia	Lesser siren
Siren lacertina	Greater siren

    Ambystomatidae

Ambystoma maculatum	Spotted salamander
Ambystoma opacum	Marbled salamander
Ambystoma talpoideum	Mole salamander
Ambystoma tigrinum	Tiger salamander

    Salamandridae

Notophthalmus viridescens	Red-spotted newt

    Plethodontidae

Desmognathus auriculatus	Southern dusky salamander
Eurycea bislineata	Two-lined salamander
Eurycea longicauda	Three-lined salamander
Eurycea quadridigitata	Dwarf salamander
Plethodon glutinosus	Slimy salamander
Pseudotriton montanus	Mud salamander
Pseudotriton ruber	Red salamander

  Order Anura (frogs and toads)
    Pelobatidae

Scaphiopus holbrooki	Eastern spadefoot toad

    Bufonidae

Bufo quercicus	Oak toad
Bufo terrestris	Southern toad

    Hylidae

Acris crepitans	Northern cricket frog
Acris gryllus	Southern cricket frog
Hyla avivoca	Bird-voiced treefrog
Hyla chrysoscelis	Cope's gray treefrog
Hyla cinerea	Green treefrog
Hyla crucifer	Spring peeper
Hyla femoralis	Pinewoods treefrog
Hyla gratiosa	Barking treefrog
Hyla squirella	Squirrel treefrog
Hyla versicolor	Gray treefrog
Limnaoedus ocularis	Little grass frog
Pseudacris nigrita	Southern chorus frog
Pseudacris ornata	Ornate chorus frog
Pseudacris triseriata	Striped chorus frog

    Microhylidae

Gastrophryne carolinensis	Eastern narrow-mouthed toad

    Ranidae

Rana areolata	Carolina gopher frog
Rana catesbeiana	Bullfrog
Rana clamitans	Green frog (bronze frog)
Rana grylio	Pig frog
Rana palustris	Pickerel frog
Rana utricularia	Southern leopard frog
Rana virgatipes	Carpenter frog

Class Reptilia
  Order Crocodilia (crocodilians)
    Alligatoridae

Alligator mississippiensis	American alligator

  Order Chelonia (turtles)
    Chelydridae

Chelydra serpentina	Common snapping turtle

    Kinosternidae

Kinosternon baurii	Striped mud turtle
Kinosternon subrubrum	Eastern mud turtle
Sternotherus odoratus	Stinkpot

    Emydidae

Chrysemys picta	Painted turtle

Class Reptilia

Clemmys guttata	Spotted turtle
Deirochelys reticularia	Chicken turtle
Pseudemys concinna	River cooter
Pseudemys floridana	Florida cooter
Terrapene carolina	Eastern box turtle
Trachemys scripta	Slider turtle

    Trionychidae

Trionyx spiniferus	Spiny softshell turtle

  Order Squamata (snakes and lizards)
    Suborder Lacertilia (lizards)
     Iguanidae

Anolis carolinensis	Green anole (chameleon)
Sceloporus undulatus	Eastern fence lizard

     Teiidae

Cnemidophorus sexlineatus	Six-lined racerunner

     Scincidae

Eumeces fasciatus	Five-lined skink
Eumeces inexpectatus	Southeastern five-lined skink
Eumeces laticeps	Broadhead skink
Scincella lateralis	Ground skink

     Anguidae

Ophisaurus attenuatus	Slender glass lizard
Ophisaurus ventralis	Eastern glass lizard

    Suborder Serpentes (snakes)
     Colubridae

Carphophis amoenus	Worm snake
Cemophora coccinea	Scarlet snake
Coluber constrictor	Racer (black racer)
Diadophis punctatus	Ringneck snake
Elaphe guttata	Corn snake
Elaphe obsoleta	Rat snake
Farancia abacura	Mud snake
Farancia erytrogramma	Rainbow snake
Heterodon platyrhinos	Eastern hognose snake
Heterodon simus	Southern hognose snake
Lampropeltis getulus	Common kingsnake
Lampropeltis triangulum	Milk snake (scarlet kingsnake)
Masticophis flagellum	Coachwhip snake
Nerodia cyclopion	Green water snake
Nerodia erythrogaster	Red-bellied water snake
Nerodia fasciata	Banded water snake
Nerodia sipedon	Northern water snake
Nerodia taxispilota	Brown water snake
Opheodrys aestivus	Rough green snake
Pituophis melanoleucus	Pine snake
Regina rigida	Glossy crayfish snake
Regina septemvittata	Queen snake
Rhadinaea flavilata	Yellow-lipped snake
Seminatrix pygaea	Black swamp snake
Storeria dekayi	Brown snake
Storeria occipitomaculata	Red-bellied snake
Tantilla coronata	Southeastern crowned snake
Thamnophis sauritus	Eastern ribbon snake
Thamnophis sirtalis	Common garter snake
Virginia striatula	Rough earth snake
Virginia valeriae	Smooth earth snake

     Elapidae

Micrurus fulvius	Coral snake

     Viperidae (= Crotalidae)

Agkistrodon contortrix	Copperhead
Agkistrodon piscivorus	Cottonmouth
Crotalus horridus	Timber rattlesnake (canebrake rattlesnake)
Sistrurus miliarius	Pygmy rattlesnake

Source: Gibbons and Semlitsch, 1989.

slider turtles that thrive by benefit of the slightly elevated temperatures and higher primary productivity. Some of the largest alligators reported from South Carolina have been found on the SRP, presumably because of their unintentional but effective protection from poachers before the Endangered Species Act. The restriction on public hunting has resulted in Par Pond's having large overwintering flocks of waterfowl and population sizes of many native wildlife species that are unparalleled in the region.

The SRP scheme of controlled industrial facilities nested within an array of natural habitats has created unusual opportunities for ecological study. Environmental questions applicable not only to local problems but also to some national and international problems have been able to be addressed. Thus, the major portion of the SRP is a paradise for environmental protection and, consequently, for ecological research with freshwater turtles.

Climate

The general temperature and rainfall patterns on the SRP where most populations are located consist of hot, humid summers and mild winters, with an average precipitation of about 100 cm (39 inches) per year (Fig. 2.2). January temperatures for the SRP region are normally lows approaching freezing and highs around 13° C

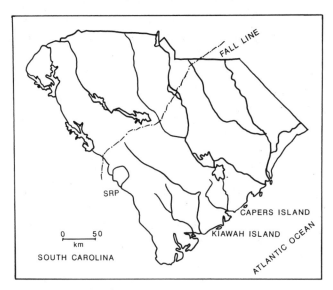

FIGURE 2.3. Major river systems and reservoirs of South Carolina. The Fall Line, which separates the Piedmont and Coastal plains, is indicated by the dotted line running northeast to southwest across the state. Note the location of the Savannah River Plant (SRP) and Kiawah and Capers islands.

(56° F). July low temperatures average around 21° C (70° F), and average highs are around 32° C (90° F). Snow or freezing rain is an occasional occurrence, but most of the precipitation is from rains during the winter and spring and from summer storms, with unpredictable amounts of rainfall deposited in a sketchy pattern over the region. Because of the localized nature of the numerous thunderstorms in the region, the water levels of fluctuating habitats, such as the Carolina bays, can vary significantly from one another, even though they may be located within a few kilometers of each other.

Populations of *T. scripta* were also examined on Kiawah Island and Capers Island, barrier islands near Charleston, South Carolina (Fig. 2.3). The coastal temperature and precipitation regimes of the islands are similar to one another but differ from those of the mainland. Rainfall occurs primarily in the spring and summer (snow is a rare event), and temperatures average about 1.6° C (2.9° F) higher throughout the year than on the SRP.

Regional and Local Characteristics

The SRP is located in west central South Carolina (Fig. 2.3) and encompasses portions of Aiken, Barnwell, and Allendale counties. The site's southwest boundary is the Savannah River, a typical large southern river with extensive floodplains and oxbow lakes. The northern boundary is approximately 32 to 48 km (20 to 30 miles) south of the Fall Line, which represents the transitional zone between montane or piedmont and coastal plain environments throughout a major portion of the Southeast (Fig. 2.3).

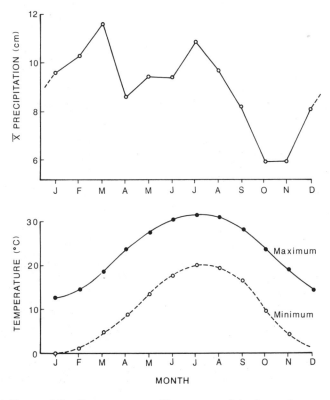

FIGURE 2.2.   Long-term monthly mean precipitation and temperatures of the Savannah River Plant, based on 1955-86 records from Augusta, Georgia.

The Fall Line is also considered to form the northern boundary for numerous species and subspecies found on the SRP and is a zone of intergradation for many others. The entire SRP site lies within the Atlantic Coastal Plain physiographic province. The SRP acreage consists of several major soil types, primarily sand overlying sandy clay-loam.

The area of the SRP is approximately 780 km² (300 square miles). A major portion of the tract is protected from public intrusion and has the typical array of habitats characterizing nonurban, nonagrarian portions of the Upper Coastal Plain of South Carolina. Because the SRP has five nuclear production reactors, of which three are currently in operation, vast quantities of water are used for cooling. These waters have been, and in some instances still are, released into a variety of aquatic habitats, including reservoirs, thermal canals, streams, and swamp deltas.

Predominant freshwater habitats include the Savannah River and five tributary freshwater streams, a 1,200-hectare (3,000-acre) reservoir system, numerous Carolina bays, and a few abandoned farm ponds and minor impoundments. The cypress-gum swamps and lowland hardwood forests bordering the river and its tributaries constitute 10% to 15% of the site. Pine plantations and natural pine stands make up about 40% of the area. Several upland hardwood stands are scattered throughout the SRP but constitute less than 4% of the site. The remainder of the SRP is composed of mixed hardwood and pine, aquatic and semiaquatic habitats, abandoned old fields, industrial complexes, and an extensive highway system. Many of the natural and affected habitats have been identified as research set-aside areas (Hillestad and Bennett, 1982).

The SRP was acquired from public lands in 1951 by the U.S. government. At that time, 30% to 40% of the area was farmed (primarily cotton and corn) and the remainder was mostly second-growth pine or hardwood forests. During the 37 years since establishment of the site, extensive environmental impact has resulted from U.S. Forest Service forest management programs that include clear-cutting. Most of the abandoned farmland has been planted in pine or is undergoing natural succession toward turkey oak–longleaf pine associations, an edaphic climax community in this region.

Extensive draining has not been done on the site since its establishment, and most lowland areas have remained undisturbed for more than a third of a century. Major aquatic alterations have resulted from thermal releases into three of the five tributary streams and from construction of the Par Pond reservoir system (Gibbons and Sharitz, 1974, 1981) and L Lake (McCort et al., 1988). Selected habitats, described below, deserve specific mention because of their uniqueness to the site or region and their importance to the herpetofauna.

Local Herpetofauna

An account of the herpetofauna of South Carolina has not been published, although checklists of coastal species have been presented (Gibbons, 1978, reptiles; Harrison, 1978, amphibians). The herpetofaunal accounts presented by Gibbons et al. (1976), Gibbons and Patterson (1978), and Gibbons and Semlitsch (1988) cover the status of SRP herpetology and are generally applicable to the South Carolina Coastal Plain. General herpetofaunal accounts applicable to South Carolina have been published in accounts of all eastern reptiles and amphibians (Cochran and Goin, 1970; Conant, 1975; Smith and Brodie, 1982) and in specific accounts of U.S. turtles (Carr, 1952; Ernst and Barbour, 1972), snakes (Schmidt and Davis, 1941; Wright and Wright, 1957), lizards (Smith, 1946), alligators (Neill, 1971), salamanders (Bishop, 1947), and frogs and toads (Wright and Wright, 1949). The most pertinent regional works are *The Reptiles and Amphibians of Alabama* (Mount, 1975) and *Amphibians and Reptiles of the Carolinas and Virginia* (Martof et al., 1980).

The South Carolina Coastal Plain has a high abundance and diversity of herpetofauna. A total of 99 species of reptiles and amphibians (16 salamanders, 25 frogs and toads, 9 lizards, 36 snakes, 1 crocodilian, 12 turtles) have been reported from the SRP since 1952 (Freeman, 1955a,b,c, 1956, 1960; Gibbons and Patterson, 1978; Gibbons and Semlitsch, 1988; Table 2.1). Because of the known or potential interaction between turtles and other species of reptiles or amphibians that live in or around aquatic habitats, the species composition of many habitats has been determined.

Habitats

This section describes the habitats where we have conducted population studies on the slider turtle, a species that appears to adapt well to a wide variety of aquatic conditions. Habitat descriptions accompany nearly every presentation of field research in the scientific literature, although the detail of presentation may vary from a brief statement to several pages. Numerous references have been made in the literature of the habitat characteristics of many of the SRP sites where population studies were and are being conducted. Because of the important influence of habitat on the behavior, ecology, and critical life history variables of this or any species, some study sites deserve detailed description. Anecdotal information relative to the selection, naming, and use of certain sites is provided to give a more thorough historical perspective.

CAROLINA BAYS

The most intensively studied population of turtles on the SRP has been at Ellenton Bay, a Carolina bay habitat that has been extremely productive for several species of turtles, including the slider. Carolina bays are among the most impressive natural wetlands in the southeastern United States, and they are finally receiving appropriate attention from wetlands ecologists and regulatory agencies that can influence their management or destruction.

These well-defined aquatic environments, confined to an area across the coastal plain regions of Georgia and the Carolinas, are the primary freshwater lentic habitats occurring naturally on the SRP (Schalles, 1979; Sharitz and Gibbons, 1982). At least 150 are present on the site (Schalles et al., 1989). The geologic origin of Carolina bays is unknown, but they are characteristically ovate in shape, are oriented in a northwest-southeast direction, and have seasonally or annually fluctuating water levels. My favorite theory of the origin of Carolina bays is the one proposed by my daughter Laura at the age of 10. Upon hearing a discussion in which a popular meteor-origin theory was rejected by someone who claimed that no meteor fragments had been found, she asked if the meteors could have been made of ice. Indeed, they could have been. Many other theories have been given for the origin of Carolina bays, but none has been convincingly confirmed or accepted (Sharitz and Gibbons, 1982).

Most bays on the SRP are temporary, filling with rainwater in the winter and drying each summer, although a few contain water throughout the year during most years. Those on the SRP have no tributary water supply, so water levels are dependent upon the interaction among precipitation, evaporation, and transpiration from aquatic plants. Some Carolina bays near swamps or streams support populations of fish that disappear during dry years and reinvade during wet ones. Carolina bay habitats are extremely productive as breeding or feeding sites for some of the herpetofauna and have been the focal point of many SRP studies (e.g., Gibbons, 1969, 1970d; Bennett, 1972; Gibbons and Coker, 1977; Gibbons et al., 1977; Gibbons and Greene, 1978; Bennett et al., 1980; Semlitsch, 1980; Semlitsch and McMillan, 1980; Gibbons and Semlitsch, 1982; Congdon et al., 1983a; Semlitsch and Moran, 1984; Semlitsch and Pechmann, 1985; Caldwell, 1987). The following Carolina bays have been used extensively in research on freshwater turtles.

ELLENTON BAY.   Ellenton Bay is a natural freshwater habitat and a typical Carolina bay. The basin, representing the high-water level of Ellenton Bay, covers approximately 10 ha (Fig. 2.4). A road embankment 5 to 6 m wide divides the bay and creates two completely separate aquatic areas. Water surface area and depth are extremely variable. The maximum depth when the basin is full is more than 2 m. In 1955-56 and again during the summers of 1968, 1981, 1985, 1986, and 1987, Ellenton Bay dried almost completely, with water remaining only in three or four small pools a few centimeters deep and 2 to

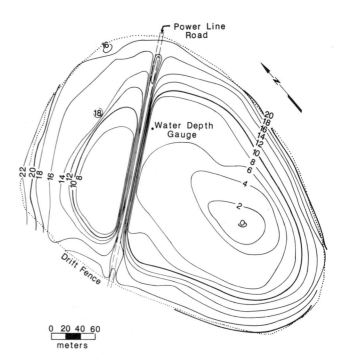

FIGURE 2.4.   Ellenton Bay, showing approximate contour intervals of the basin. Contour intervals are in decimeters, with the deepest part of the bay designated as zero.

3 m across. In 1985, 1986, and 1987 no standing water remained during early fall (Fig. 2.5). During these periods of drought, however, standing water up to 0.5 m deep normally remains beneath the thick organic crust that covers the entire lake basin. Many areas of the basin remain quite mucky during some dry spells, so that as much as a hectare of viscous mud surrounds the small area of open water.

Ellenton Bay is located near one edge of Field 3-412, which was abandoned in 1952 and has been the site of many previous ecological studies (Odum and Kuenzler, 1963; Golley and Gentry, 1964; Van Pelt, 1966). Predominant plants peripheral to the basin are dog fennel (*Eupatorium* sp.), lespedeza (*Lespedeza* sp.), and blackberry (*Rubus* sp.). The white water lily (*Nymphaea odorata*) and water shield (*Brasenia* sp.) are the most evident aquatic plants. The herpetofauna of Ellenton Bay is well known because of the many hours of field effort and the use of a variety of collecting techniques (Table 2.2). In our studies of turtles, we consider the inhabitants of Ellenton Bay and several surrounding bodies of water to be part of the Ellenton Bay System (Fig. 2.6).

I was first introduced to Ellenton Bay in the spring of 1967 when I interviewed for a job at SREL, at that time a tiny satellite research station of the University of Georgia. Michael H. Smith showed me around the SRP, taking me to a variety of aquatic habitats where I might conduct turtle studies. I remember being impressed at the opportunities for study in the streams, farm ponds, reservoirs,

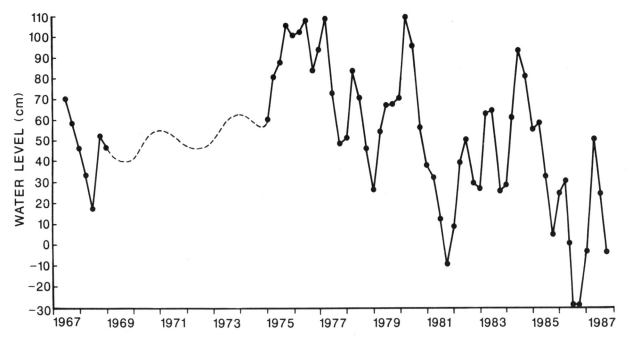

FIGURE 2.5.   Ellenton Bay water levels at the gauge. Most surface water disappears at approximately 20 cm. Negative numbers indicate water level at the gauge when standing water is beneath the organic surface layer.

Table 2.2. Vertebrates of Ellenton Bay that are potential prey or predators of turtles

Table 2.2 -- *Continued*

Fish	
Mosquito fish	*Gambusia affinis* (apparently extinct in Ellenton Bay after 1985 drought)
Amphibians	
Salamanders	
Mole salamander	*Ambystoma talpoideum*
Dwarf salamander	*Eurycea quadridigitata*
Eastern tiger salamander	*Ambystoma tigrinum*
Marbled salamander	*Ambystoma opacum*
Red-spotted newt	*Notophthalmus viridescens*
Southern two-lined salamander	*Eurycea bislineata*
Frogs and toads	
Southern leopard frog	*Rana utricularia* (= *sphenocephala*)
Southern toad	*Bufo terrestris*
Eastern narrow-mouthed toad	*Gastrophryne carolinensis*
Ornate chorus frog	*Pseudacris ornata*
Northern spring peeper	*Hyla crucifer*
Eastern spadefoot toad	*Scaphiopus holbrooki*
Southern chorus frog	*Pseudacris nigrita*
Bullfrog	*Rana catesbeiana*
Bronze frog	*Rana clamitans*
Barking treefrog	*Hyla gratiosa*
Southern cricket frog	*Acris gryllus*
Oak toad	*Bufo quercicus*
Pickerel frog	*Rana palustris*
Squirrel treefrog	*Hyla squirella*
Green treefrog	*Hyla cinerea*
Pinewoods treefrog	*Hyla femoralis*
Carolina gopher frog	*Rana areolata*
Reptiles	
Turtles	
Slider turtle	*Trachemys scripta*
Eastern mud turtle	*Kinosternon subrubrum*
Eastern chicken turtle	*Deirochelys reticularia*

Florida cooter	*Pseudemys floridana*
Stinkpot	*Sternotherus odoratus*
Common snapping turtle	*Chelydra serpentina*
Painted turtle	*Chrysemys picta*
Spotted turtle	*Clemmys guttata*
Eastern box turtle	*Terrapene carolina*
Snakes	
Carolina swamp snake	*Seminatrix pygaea*
Southern black racer	*Coluber constrictor*
Eastern coachwhip snake	*Masticophis flagellum*
Banded water snake	*Nerodia fasciata*
Florida green water snake	*Nerodia cyclopion*
Red-bellied water snake	*Nerodia erythrogaster*
Eastern garter snake	*Thamnophis sirtalis*
Eastern ribbon snake	*Thamnophis sauritus*
Eastern mud snake	*Farancia abacura*
Rainbow snake	*Farancia erytrogramma*
Eastern kingsnake	*Lampropeltis getulus*
Eastern cottonmouth	*Agkistrodon piscivorus*
Crocodilians	
American alligator	*Alligator mississippiensis* (not present after 1968)
Birds (potential predators)	
American crow	*Corvus brachyrhynchos*
Loggerhead shrike	*Lanius ludovicianus*
Red-tailed hawk	*Buteo jamaicensis*
Marsh hawk (northern harrier)	*Circus cyaneus*
Mammals (potential predators)	
Raccoon	*Procyon lotor*
Opossum	*Didelphis virginiana*
Striped skunk	*Mephitis mephitis*
Gray fox	*Urocyon cinereoargenteus*
Bobcat	*Felis rufus*

Note: Species in each taxonomic group are listed in order of perceived abundance in the aquatic habitat or in peripheral terrestrial areas.

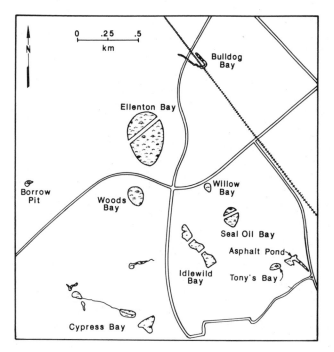

FIGURE 2.6.   The Ellenton Bay System of aquatic habitats on the SRP.

cypress-gum swamps, and even the Savannah River. But after we clawed our way through 5-foot-high blackberry bushes to reach the margin of this place called Ellenton Bay, I politely nodded that maybe turtles would be there, but I had secret thoughts that this would be one of the last places I would want to spend much time. After all, why would aquatic turtles be particularly abundant in a habitat that was known to dry up completely on occasion and never had much water even during the wet years, relative to the permanent water bodies in the region?

Nonetheless, when I arrived at SREL in July 1967, I set out a few traps at places, and the first turtle I caught was a slider turtle from Ellenton Bay. I further remember my uncertainty of the species' identity, because all of the slider turtles I had seen had been the red-eared subspecies (*Trachemys scripta elegans*) from Alabama, Mississippi, and Louisiana. I had even more reservations about my career as a turtle ecologist when, upon returning the turtle to Ellenton Bay after marking and measuring it, I arrived at the habitat to find that my first capture on the SRP had apparently crawled out of the bucket and fallen out of the pickup truck, whose tailgate was down. The turtle's code was ABC, a female that has never been seen again. At that time I decided I would carry turtles in sacks and drive with the tailgate up. Since that day, few of the thousands of turtles we have handled have escaped during transport back to their home.

My dismay at having lost my first slider turtle captured on the SRP was assuaged in part by my finding six more sliders, two mud turtles (*Kinosternon subrubrum*), and a

chicken turtle (*Deirochelys reticularia*) in traps that same week. The identity of the chicken turtle, incidentally, was even more of a mystery to me, as I had seen only one live specimen before. Carr (1952) and Conant (1958) were consulted and the species identified. At any rate, it was quickly revealed that Ellenton Bay was going to be one of the most productive turtle habitats I was working in, so my turtle collecting efforts in other areas gradually diminished for the time being, and I concentrated on this Carolina bay that surprised me by having so many turtle inhabitants. By the end of 1967 we had captured, marked, and released 380 turtles from Ellenton Bay, 286 of them being slider turtles.

In the spring of 1968, with the help of Larry Wright and a few others, we set up the first terrestrial drift fence with pitfall traps on the SRP. Our technique was primitive compared with current drift fences, but this was the prototype and was acceptable. The fence was partially a product of what was available—a lot of chicken wire and dozens of old paint buckets Du Pont (E. I. du Pont de Nemours and Company) had used and discarded. (Today we use store-bought aluminum flashing and large plastic or metal buckets that do not have dried paint in the bottom. Also, today's buckets are 10 m apart, whereas in 1967 it was acceptable to make the distance between them 30 feet.) I have since discovered that some turtles can climb chicken wire, and because our fences were intermittent around the perimeter of Ellenton Bay, we probably missed a large number of animals that simply crawled over the fences or walked through the gaps between them.

One incident that occurred during the construction of the initial Ellenton Bay drift fence also taught me that government and industrial bureaucracies might not have the same sense of humor as academics. While one of Larry Wright's friends who had been hired to help us was hammering an aluminum pole into the ground, he smashed his thumb rather severely. We assumed he would live but thought perhaps he should receive professional attention from Du Pont's medical facility on the SRP, where his thumb was satisfactorily bandaged.

My surprise came the following week when I was given a two-page form to fill out on how I would assure that this sort of accident never occurred again. I did not want to say that we would stop putting up drift fences, so I glibly wrote only one sentence: "The victim has been advised to never put his thumb between an aluminum pole and a hammer when the hammer is descending toward the pole." Who would have thought they were serious about how to avoid hitting your thumb with a hammer?

They were serious, and not just about my split infinitive. I was advised by a representative of the U.S. Atomic Energy Commission that safety was not a humorous subject on the Du Pont–run SRP and that my reply had been highly inappropriate. Furthermore, I would have to fill out the form in its entirety. This was good training for writing government documents, and I did not begrudge the time I spent explaining the extreme caution that we would now take when using potential weapons such as hammers. It was comforting to know that, on the SRP, the AEC and Du Pont were concerned with all aspects of human safety, not only with the potential dangers of making the ingredients for atomic bombs.

Had I completed a research project on Ellenton Bay after less than two years of study, I would have concluded that turtle populations in Carolina bays comprised an assemblage of species in set proportion and that they simply live from one year to the next in a stable manner. Had I conducted the study from 1969 to 1972, I would have reached completely different conclusions. The first would have been that Ellenton Bay was not where I would want to do a turtle study, for late in 1968 the bay dried up during a severe regional drought. Relatively few slider turtles lived there during the several following months.

Aquatic turtle trapping was gradually abandoned in 1968 as the water disappeared and few captures were made. In addition, we took down the drift fence in 1971 because so few turtles were being captured. What had apparently happened—although it was not quantifiable until 10 years later, when we had a complete drift fence of aluminum flashing that encircled the aquatic habitat—is that most of the slider turtles abandoned Ellenton Bay for more permanent water in the vicinity. I looked on this at the time as a catastrophic event in the lives of these turtles. Only later did I realize that slider turtles, as well as the other species in the region, are well adapted for droughts and floods and that the varying water level at Ellenton Bay was not unusual in the evolutionary history of this species (see Chapter 16).

That we caught only 27 slider turtles at Ellenton Bay between 1971 and 1974, and 481 in other parts of the SRP, is a reflection of a reduced trapping effort that was brought about by diminished returns when we did trap. There were probably more slider turtles there than revealed by the data, but there is no question that the actual numbers were far lower than they had been in the earlier years.

After 1968 the typical rains of South Carolina returned, and water levels again rose in Ellenton Bay and remained high, although it apparently took several months for the slider population to reach the earlier numbers. By the fall of 1974 I felt confident that a new drift fence would give us information on movement patterns of the turtles around the lake. But this time we would use aluminum flashing and encircle the entire system. Then we would be able to register the immigration and emigration of every individual.

Tom Murphy and Johnny Coker, who were working with me, helped me recruit 17 helpers from SREL to install what was the longest terrestrial drift fence with pitfall traps in the world. In preparation for our construction project, we asked Du Pont to provide us with 246 twenty-liter buckets that molecular sieves were shipped in, we bought approximately 1 mile of 2-foot-high aluminum flashing, and for fence stakes we acquired more than 2,000 half-inch-diameter aluminum poles that had been discarded from various reactor operations.

Tom and Johnny had modernized the drift fence technique to the point of using a tractor to dig a trench so that the fence could be placed below the ground. A 1-foot-diameter auger attached to the tractor was used to dig the bucket holes. During this operation we learned that it is best to dig the bucket holes before the fence is put in. Tom helped our understanding of this by attempting to dig bucket holes along fencing that had already been installed. We were all very smug about using modern equipment to dig the holes—until the spinning auger happened to grab a section of the fence. Before Tom could turn the motor off, the auger had ripped up 200 m of flashing and wrapped half of it around the auger like a string around your finger. None of us were amused during the four hours it took to unwrap the flashing from the auger.

The drift fence remained up and active from 1 January 1975 until 20 April 1979, when we made the decision to take it down. The exercise of checking 246 traps and removing all vertebrates every day of the year lost its appeal after about 1,500 days. I once calculated that Judy Greene alone had walked more than 1,000 miles checking the Ellenton Bay drift fence. However, the absence of the drift fence apparently created some kind of vacuum in our lives, and between Christmas and New Year's Day, 1979, we reinstalled it. It remained active until 31 December 1982, at which time Ellenton Bay had dried almost completely, and the slider turtles had again departed.

The rains returned, and by 1984 the bay had continued to hold its water level, and a few slider turtles had reinhabited it. So we reinstalled the drift fence in late December 1985. As of 1 February 1988, it was still up, despite a prolonged drought and no water in the bay. This time, though, we hope to leave the fence up, keep checking it daily, and find out the pattern of recolonization by the turtles.

WOODS BAY. Woods Bay is a small Carolina bay approximately 200 m south of Ellenton Bay. It is surrounded by hardwoods and pines and dries completely every year, but when water is present, it is known to harbor some turtles from the Ellenton Bay populations.

RAINBOW BAY. This Carolina bay is approximately 1 ha in area, has a maximum water depth of about 1 m, and dries each year during the summer (Fig. 2.7). Herbaceous plants common to the basin are bulrush (*Scirpus cyperinus*), creeping rush (*Juncus repens*), common cattail (*Typha latifolia*), and spikerush (*Eleocharis* sp.). Buttonbush (*Cephalanthus occidentalis*) and a few cypress trees (*Taxodium* sp.)

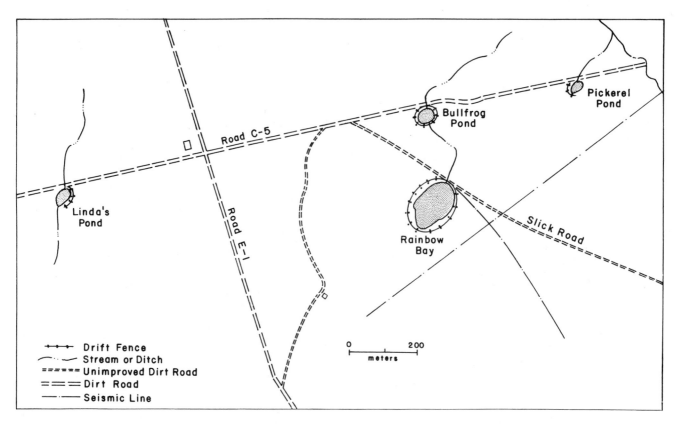

FIGURE 2.7.   The Rainbow Bay System of aquatic habitats on the SRP.

are also found in the basin. The aquatic area is surrounded by deep, well-drained sandy soil vegetated with slash pine (*Pinus elliottii*) and loblolly pine (*P. taeda*) plantations of various ages, with hardwoods along the water's edge, including sweet gum (*Liquidambar styraciflua*), water gum (*Nyssa sylvatica* var. *biflora*), water oak (*Quercus nigra*), and wax myrtle (*Myrica cerifera*). Thick vegetation, consisting of blackberry (*Rubus* sp.), honeysuckle (*Lonicera* sp.), and greenbriar (*Smilax rotundifolia*), separates the aquatic area from the surrounding upland pine plantations.

Despite its dependability in having no water during part of the year, Rainbow Bay is a highly productive herpetofaunal site. The primary research focus has been on amphibian ecology and population dynamics, but several turtle species use the aquatic habitat, and a permanent population of *Kinosternon subrubrum* is resident.

SUN BAY.   This Carolina bay was approximately 1 ha in area, had a maximum water depth of 0.35 m, and dried each year during the summer. The site was altered in June 1978 when a ditch was dug to partially drain it for construction of the Defense Waste Processing Facility. After that, the bay contained about 25% of the water volume of Rainbow Bay and dried earlier each year. During 1982 and 1983, construction continued to the point that Sun Bay now no longer contains water. Herbaceous plants in the basin of Sun Bay were similar to those of Rainbow

Bay. Cypress trees were absent. The upland habitat around Sun Bay is dominated by loblolly pine and longleaf pine (*Pinus palustris*) plantations with pockets of mixed sweet gum and oaks (*Quercus* spp.). Approximately 30% of the perimeter of Sun Bay was bordered by a 20-hectare clear-cut field planted in loblolly pine in 1976. This site was of significance to the turtle projects only because of a small permanent population of *K. subrubrum*.

FLAMINGO BAY.   This Carolina bay is approximately 5 ha in area, has a maximum water depth of 1 m, and has dried three times in the last 20 years (1968, 1981, 1986). This site may be classified as nearly permanently aquatic from the viewpoint of the amphibians and reptiles using it. The surrounding upland habitats are slash and loblolly pine plantations. The perimeter of the aquatic habitat is dominated by sweet gum, oaks, red maple (*Acer rubrum*), and wax myrtle. The basin contains buttonbush, water gum, bulrush, spikerush, lizard's-tail (*Saururus cernuus*), and American lotus (*Nelumbo lutea*). Flamingo Bay is part of the Lost Lake System (Fig. 2.8) and supports small populations of *Trachemys scripta*, *Kinosternon subrubrum*, and *Deirochelys reticularia*.

DRY BAY.   This Carolina bay contains water year-round in almost all years. Fish are normally present. The only recorded times of almost total drying were during the

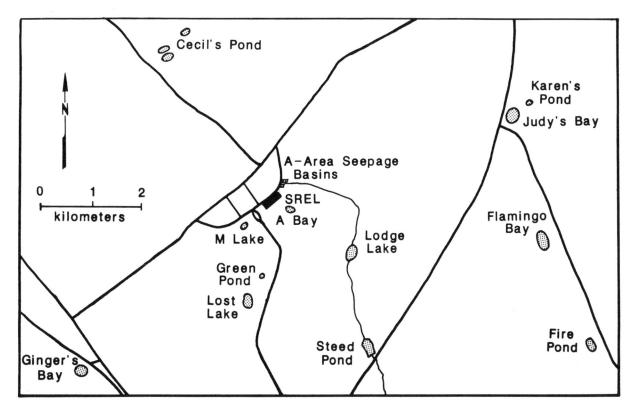

FIGURE 2.8.   The Lost Lake System of aquatic habitats on the SRP.

autumns of 1981 and 1986. A thorough description of Dry Bay is given by Sharitz and Gibbons (1982). A large number of turtles have been marked at the site and populations of *T. scripta* and *K. subrubrum* appear to be persistent.

STEEL CREEK BAY.   This large, open Carolina bay is approximately 5 ha in area. During the drought of 1981 the only water remaining was in a "gator hole" at the north end of the lake, where the water was still about 1 m deep and several fish species were present. Most of the common species of turtles found on the SRP are present in Steel Creek Bay.

LOST LAKE.   Lost Lake is a 12-hectare Carolina bay that receives effluent from an industrial facility and supports no emergent or submerged aquatic macrophytes, because of heavy concentrations of herbicides and major fluctuations in water level. Despite the lack of macrophytes, the lake supports a large population of turtles and serves as a breeding site for several species of amphibians (Bennett et al., 1980). The lake is surrounded primarily by stands of slash and loblolly pine.

The first time I went to look at Lost Lake was in 1976, when the prospect for a new building for SREL became a reality. From the "Official Use Only" topographic map of the SRP, Becky Sharitz and I had located a large body of water near where the building was to be constructed. The region was in the northwestern sector of the SRP near the administration buildings of Du Pont and the government, a part of the SRP with which most of us from SREL were unfamiliar. However, because it appeared that this would be our new home, I wanted to familiarize myself with potential turtle collecting sites that would be close by. We forgot to bring the map, though, so we tried to find the new body of water from our collective and disparate memories of where it should be. After a futile hour of tromping through pinewoods and driving around on tiny dirt roads, we returned to the lab with plans for a future trip that included the map. That was the day that we named Lost Lake.

When I finally saw Lost Lake about a week later, it turned out to be a large Carolina bay surrounded by pine trees; a flock of wood ducks flew to the other end when we arrived. Although it was apparent that this would be another good spot to collect turtles, it would be another year before I became fully aware that Lost Lake was different from most other Carolina bays in the region. Although the water was almost chest-deep in the middle, Lost Lake had no aquatic vegetation, either emergent or submerged. This feature was discovered in July 1977 on Justin Congdon's first visit to SREL, when we initiated our sampling program in Lost Lake with Don Tinkle. It was a hot day, so we waded and swam in the water to try to catch the turtles whose heads we saw out in the middle. We caught a few by hand and with a seine, which we found easy to drag through the vegetation-free water. All of us noted that when we splashed the water, it glinted bright green in the sunlight. As I remember it, the water was emerald-green but with a bizarre tint of orange that reminded me of Merthiolate. Over the next few years I asked several sources on the SRP what chemicals were deposited in the lake. I was never able to find out for sure myself, but the SREL chemical ecologists subsequently obtained the records. A major effluent in Lost Lake was uranium from the M-Area facility. To this day I have not found out what caused the bright green color in the water, though Justin thinks it was some type of herbicide.

I had two points reinforced to me with the experiences at Lost Lake, one biological and one managerial. The biological message was simply the confirmation that slider turtles can persist in places where most higher life forms might be likely to visit but not stay. The managerial point related to the attempts of individuals or organizations to acquire detailed information about the pollution of a system. Although I contacted at least a dozen different individuals, one transferring me to another, to find out what was going into Lost Lake, no one was able or willing to tell me. The conspiracy hypothesis, formed when one is greeted with what appears to be an uncooperative attitude, is that those asked are trying to hide something. This is no doubt true in many instances when industries are confronted by environmentalists, but my view of why they sometimes avoid providing the information differs from the conventional.

The reason for the hedging in some situations, such as with Lost Lake, is often because they do not know what they have released and are embarrassed to say so. The records are too voluminous to be retrieved in an effective and efficient manner, so rather than give a partial answer such as "we have dumped somewhere between 50 pounds and 10 tons of uranium into the lake you waded around in," the answer is simply never given. For some reason, an organization thinks it seems more conscientious, responsible, and environmentally concerned when it is able to say exactly how many kilograms of effluents have been released than when it is vague, as if it were untrustworthy and had something to hide.

PAR POND RESERVOIR SYSTEM

The five plutonium-production reactors on the SRP have created a variety of unusual aquatic thermal environments. A major influence of the reactor effluents on streams and ponds has been the increase in primary and secondary productivity in those and contiguous areas. Two of the reactors were placed on standby several years ago and are not operating. The resulting termination of heated effluent to some aquatic areas has created lentic and lotic postthermal habitats (Gibbons and Sharitz, 1974). Influences of thermal and postthermal environments on the biology of reptiles, amphibians, and other

species of animals and plants have been studied by SREL since the late 1960s (McCort, 1987).

An extensive man-made reservoir environment exists on the SRP because of the need to cool the reactors. The Par Pond System (Fig. 2.9) is primarily a closed loop of man-made canals and lakes, including Pond C (67 ha), Pond B (81 ha), and Par Pond (1,100 ha). Pond C temperatures may exceed 50° C during periods of reactor operation, although in some areas of the lake the temperatures remain substantially lower. Water at temperatures exceeding 35° C enters Par Pond from Pond C at the Hot Dam and disperses throughout the Hot Arm of the reservoir. The remainder of Par Pond (North Arm and West Arm) is at temperatures normal or only slightly above normal for the area. Pond B and the North Arm of Par Pond received thermal effluent from 1958 to 1964 and are now in a postthermal state.

Pond B is a one-of-a-kind reservoir in North America and possibly in the entire world. It is a 300-acre lake that received waters at temperatures that were a lot closer to the boiling point than they were to the freezing point. That does not make Pond B unique, because there are at least a few other lakes around that have been assaulted in this manner. However, the same reactor that heated the waters that entered Pond B also underwent a minor accident of some sort in the early 1960s and released an undetermined amount of radioactive materials, notably [137]cesium, which is still detectable in the sediments and biota in the 1980s. There are lakes with radioactive sediments, such as White Oak Lake at Oak Ridge, but a 300-acre lake that has first been scoured by unbelievably hot waters for many months and has then lain idle with radioactive sediments would appear to qualify as a unique environment. From this description one might imagine a sterile, unattractive habitat, yet Pond B is by far the most beautiful large lake on the SRP.

The first time I saw Pond B was in 1971, when E. Davis Parker and Mike Hirshfield began conducting a vegetational, ichthyological, and herpetological survey of the lake. One of the small islands in the lake supported a rookery of little blue herons, from which the immature fledglings rose like a swarm of white hornets around a giant nest when we approached the willow trees in a small boat with an outboard motor. This was to be the site of a fascinating study by Art Domby, Bob McFarlane, and Don Paine (Domby and McFarlane, 1978), who discovered that the young of the little blue herons had high levels of radioactivity, whereas the young of green herons that nested in the same branches were not radioactive or were only slightly so. An investigation of the phenomenon revealed that the little blue herons fed their young from fish and other aquatic animals collected along the shores of Pond B, whereas the green herons flew a short distance away to feed in a large Carolina bay that had not been affected by the release of radioactive effluent.

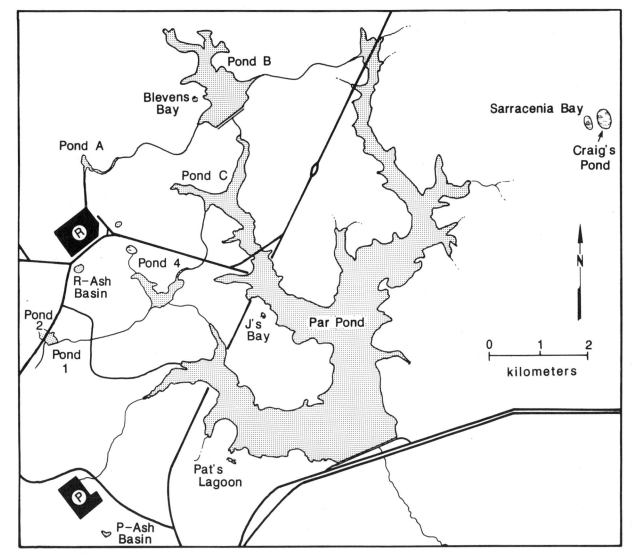

FIGURE 2.9.   The Par Pond System of aquatic habitats on the SRP.

Pond B helped reinforce our initial impressions that turtles inhabiting thermally affected bodies of water had faster growth rates as juveniles and reached larger sizes as adults. In 1971, when the first turtles from Pond B were captured, many of them had faster growth rates than those from natural habitats like Ellenton Bay and were more comparable to those from Par Pond. Today the adults in Pond B appear to be growing at rates more similar to those of turtles in typical aquatic areas such as Ellenton Bay or Risher Pond, because R reactor, from which Pond B received heated and radioactive effluents, was closed in 1964. Thus, our earliest samples were of a residual population that had presumably lived in the warm back areas of Pond B and derived the thermal benefit of faster growth. Today, after a quarter of a century, the turtles live like those in any other cool and normal body of water.

MAN-MADE AQUATIC HABITATS

One- to 3-acre (2.5- to 7.4-hectare) ponds are characteristic of this region of South Carolina for use as stocked, warm-water fishing lakes. Several such habitats were left on the SRP as holdovers from private ownership and have been focal points for research on many aquatic and semiaquatic species of herpetofauna, including freshwater turtles. In addition to the farm ponds, a variety of other man-made aquatic habitats are present on the SRP as a result of construction activities. Most have standing water during wet periods and then dry by late summer and during prolonged dry periods. Several have been used in studies with amphibians, and turtles have been captured in a few.

RISHER POND.   This small farm pond was constructed during the 1930s by damming a small stream to form a

1.1-hectare reservoir with a maximum depth of 2.5 m. Habitats peripheral to the lake are pine plantations (*Pinus taeda* and *P. palustris*) on three sides and a lowland swamp and deciduous forest on the west side below the dam. Emergent plant species around the lake include cattails (*Typha latifolia*) and rushes (*Juncus* sp.). Water levels do not vary more than a few centimeters seasonally or annually. Risher Pond was drained during the summer of 1984 in an attempt to capture turtles and was refilled within one month. The herpetofauna associated with Risher Pond are characteristic of the region.

Some old field notes I have say that on 28 July 1967, I visited an abandoned farm pond on the SRP that Bob Beyers, the SREL director, had told me about. I called it Beyers Lake at the time but found out later it was already known as Risher Pond. The biological message over the years from Risher Pond was a good one for me. It seemed intuitively obvious to the most casual observer, upon seeing the pond and comparing it with the various other aquatic habitats in the region, that this would be the place where turtles as well as all other aquatic reptiles and amphibians would thrive. The assurance of permanent water would presumably represent utopia for such animals.

Risher Pond did have populations of several species of turtles, including sliders, though the densities were actually far lower than those of the Carolina bays that were far less aquatically dependable. Likewise, we captured what seemed like, at the time, large numbers of amphibians. The reason was the encircling terrestrial drift fence and pitfall traps, not the habitat. The presence of fish in the permanent waters of Risher Pond worked against the survival success of amphibian eggs and larvae. It had not occurred to me at the time that perhaps many of these coastal plain species would be adapted to unpredictable, fluctuating aquatic habitats that varied between dry land and deep water in different years, depending on the weather, and thus would reach their maximum productivity in seemingly unsuitable habitats.

Risher Pond also had another feature that made it distinctive on the SRP. It was one of 10 habitats that were designated as SREL research set-asides. This concept, though toothless in 1967, was implemented to appease the research ecologists with the designation of particular sites as inviolate from other activities on the SRP. It was also an attempt to set aside and protect examples of each of the habitat types characteristic of the upper coastal plain region.

The research set-aside concept has had positive returns for ecologists. For example, in 1985 a power line many miles long was destined to pass over Risher Pond. To have a power line, there must be, for some reason, no vegetation between the wires and the grass. We were notified of the power line's proposed route and told that DOE would be willing to work with us to reduce the impact to our study as much as possible, even rerouting the line if necessary.

However, changing the route would have been extremely costly. In addition, the alternative route, although not passing through an SREL research set-aside, would have gone directly through a habitat where Ken McLeod of SREL was actively involved in a study on pine silviculture.

By the rules of the game, we could protest the disruption of a research set-aside, but we would have less of a case if the area were only a study site. So we agreed to allow the power line to cross Risher Pond, with the understanding that the trees around the margins would not be cut, so as to maintain the pond habitat. The more cynical members at SREL smiled knowingly and had thoughts that we would be lucky if DOE didn't drain the lake after felling the trees into it. But score one for our good faith in the integrity of some government officials. Not only did they preserve the trees in the places we requested, but they also placed large signs near the pond that say no trees should be cut in the area, in hopes that future subcontractors who are able to read will not destroy the site either.

STEED POND.   This pond (Freeman, 1960) was formed by damming a headwater stream of Upper Three Runs Creek and is part of the Lost Lake System. The mean depth was 1.5 m until the 1960s. Willows and alders grow in the major body of the pond and in surrounding low areas that seasonally flood. A mixed pine-hardwood forest surrounds the pond. The habitat has had a history of raised and lowered water levels. The dam was broken sometime before 1967, and the pond surface was less than 1 ha and the depth was seldom more than a few centimeters until 1972. The maximum aquatic area when the dam is in place is greater than 4 ha. The dam was removed again during the autumn of 1985, but too little open water remained to support many turtles.

LODGE LAKE.   This lake is a shallow flooded area in the tributary of Tim's Branch above Steed Pond. The area was apparently wooded at one time but became flooded because of beaver activity, road construction, or both. Many of the trees have fallen, so it is now a log-filled, shallow lake with a sizable population of *T. scripta*.

FIRE POND.   This abandoned farm pond from pre-SRP days harbors the typical herpetofaunal associations expected of such a habitat. It was drained in 1983 but is now partially refilled, forming a small shallow lake fed by a small stream.

DICK'S POND.   This pre-SRP farm pond is approximately 1 ha in area with a mean depth of 1.4 m and is surrounded by hardwoods and pines. *Potamogeton diversifolius* and *Sphagnum* sp. are the major submerged plants. This pond was spiked with radioactive materials for an experiment during the 1970s, but the isotopes had short half-lives and the area is no longer contaminated. Much of Ed Standora's research on thermoregulation by slider turtles was conducted at Dick's Pond.

GUS'S POND AND DEBBY'S POND.   These two lakes (Gus's Pond is the lower lake) are each about 1 to 1.5 ha in area, average 1 to 2 m in depth, and are separated by a dam. Both lakes are dystrophic. *Eleocharis acicularis* is a major submerged vascular plant species. The area is surrounded by hardwoods and pines.

Dave Clark, Debby Grosser, and I first visited the two abandoned farm ponds known as Twin Lakes in the early summer of 1968. Dave was my first undergraduate research participant at SREL, and the farm pond we named Debby's Pond became the study site for his summer project to confirm that young slider turtles are more carnivorous than adults (Clark and Gibbons, 1969). We named the other pond after Gus Chelton, who helped with the turtle projects that summer. My memories of Gus relate to his industriousness and dependability. I once asked him to construct some barrel-size turtle traps out of chicken wire, and then I left to do other things. Later that day I happened to go back to the lab where I had left him, only to find him sitting on the floor, with his back in the hallway, fixing the funnel opening on a turtle trap that stood in the doorway. I found this odd but no more so than the scene in the lab itself. Twenty-three barrel-size chicken-wire turtle traps filled the room from floor to ceiling, wall to wall. Gus noted that I had not said how many traps to make and that he had not seen me since early that morning. I was impressed by his persistence. Six months later, on 26 December 1968, I was surprised when I found that he had failed to check the newly installed Risher Pond drift fence, the only day in more than two years that the traps were not checked. Later that day my surprise turned to sorrow when I learned that Gus had been killed in an automobile accident Christmas night.

BULLDOG BAY.   This small system of streams (Fig. 2.6; not a Carolina bay) 600 m northeast of Ellenton Bay is formed primarily from seepage and runoff. It is frequently flooded because of beaver dams. Beavers are periodically eliminated from the area by SRP personnel because their burrows damage a railroad embankment. During dry years with no beavers, water is absent or limited in extent. During some years, such as 1981 during the drought, the water was more than 1 m deep for more than 1 ha and served as the refugium for many of the turtles leaving Ellenton Bay (Gibbons et al., 1983).

GREEN POND.   This artificial overflow basin for the M-Area production facility is between SREL and Lost Lake (Fig. 2.8). Only two species of reptiles have been observed in the lake: slider turtles (*Trachemys scripta*) that migrated to the habitat during a period of drought at Lost Lake, and a single American alligator of unknown origin.

Because of the variety of chemicals, detergents, and other industrial runoff materials, this is not considered an ideal habitat for herpetological investigations, although several slider turtles have been collected there.

BORROW PIT.   This pond (Fig. 2.6) is part of a system of small pools created by the excavation of sand and gravel near Ellenton Bay and is temporary in nature, often drying by late spring. The pond is about 0.2 ha in area, with a maximum water depth of 0.5 m. It is sparsely vegetated with grasses but has no trees in the basin or along its edge. It is surrounded by pine plantations and deciduous forest. A single *T. scripta* from Ellenton Bay has been captured at the site.

A-AREA SEEPAGE BASINS.   These four basins (Fig. 2.8) are 100 m north of the SREL building. They were constructed in the 1950s for containment of chemical waste, including radioactive isotopes. Although barren of emergent vegetation, they have high productivity and have the typical herpetofaunal assemblages that would be expected in normal pond habitats. Unfortunately, these basins have appreciable levels of radioactive strontium and cesium in addition to a variety of other isotopes. Their primary value for turtle research has been in experimental studies of radioactively contaminated habitats (Scott et al., 1986; also see Chapter 21).

KAREN'S POND.   This temporary pond (borrow pit) is approximately 800 m² when full, although it periodically dries. Maximum depth is normally less than 1 m. This pond does not dry in years with high rainfall (e.g., 1979). The basin of the pond has little vegetation except for a thick mat of grass that covers the bottom and the banks. The pond is encircled by mixed pine and deciduous hardwoods extending several miles to the south, east, and west. Approximately 75 m to the south is a shallow, ephemeral Carolina bay (Judy's Bay). The area north of the pond is primarily old-field habitat. Buildings and parking lots of the Savannah River Forest Station are northwest. Karen's Pond was encircled by a drift fence from July 1969 to 31 December 1970, and turtles of several species were captured.

CECIL'S POND.   I first saw Cecil's Pond from a height of 500 feet as Steve Morreale and I peered out of a helicopter in search of an aquatic habitat that might harbor radioactive turtles. Cecil's Pond is really three small farm ponds. Two are separated by a 20-foot-wide dike and receive runoff from Cecil Greene's pigpens 50 feet up the hill. There is also a third pond about 200 yards away; Mr. Greene keeps his catfish in it and his pigpen runoff out of it. The importance of Cecil's Pond to turtle research is great and began in 1982, when we convinced DOE and Du Pont that the SRP had a large population of radioactive turtles that lived in a set of unenclosed basins. They asked what we knew of turtle biology that might explain the discovery of radioactive turtles on other parts of the SRP.

This became the stimulus for our initial analyses of the extent and distance of overland travel by slider turtles, in which we learned that an appreciable number of individuals had traveled 1 to 5 km between aquatic habitats. The basins were less than 1 km away from the SRP boundary; therefore, we concluded that because turtles had the capability of traveling such a distance, radioactive individuals might be inhabiting aquatic sites on private land. Although a health hazard from these turtles was unlikely because of the relatively low body burdens of radioactivity, the political ramifications and litigation prospects were considerable if farmers discovered they had radioactive animals on their property as a consequence of the local nuclear production facility.

In a series of meetings, I was given opportunity to point out the capacity for overland travel by slider turtles and explain that our data indicated that turtles from the seepage basins might very well be residing on private property. To the credit of DOE and Du Pont, provisions were made for us to survey the local region around the seepage basins to look for off-site habitats that would support slider turtles. Although we had access to all SRP properties, the most expedient way to find off-site habitats where we did not normally conduct research was in a helicopter. After Mr. Greene's ponds were spotted from the air, we obtained permission from him to trap turtles. Although some SRP administrators were not particularly happy with our finding 3 radioactive turtles in the first 100 or so turtles we captured, it did give credence to ecologists' having certain predictive powers about the biology of these animals. It also led to our receiving funding for a project to study the distribution patterns, biological half-lives, and genetic peculiarities of radioactive turtles on the SRP.

STREAMS

Pristine blackwater streams were once characteristic of the Coastal Plain of South Carolina. Today most of the streams carry industrial, domestic, or agricultural pollutants. Upper Three Runs Creek on the SRP is unusual in having most of its headwaters on the site and therefore being essentially unaffected by agricultural runoff, domestic sewage inputs, or major industrial releases. Parts of this major tributary to the Savannah River originate in upland hardwood habitats on the SRP and in areas a few miles north. The creek traverses about 32 km (20 miles) of mostly undisturbed terrestrial habitat, including 1.6 km (1 mile) or more of cypress-gum swamp adjacent to the river. *Trachemys scripta* are present in slow-moving backwater areas, and *Pseudemys floridana* and *P. concinna* have

been found in the stream itself, though never in large numbers.

PEN BRANCH AND FOUR MILE CREEK. Pen Branch and Four Mile Creek receive effluents from C and K reactors, respectively, and the water temperatures throughout much of their main courses are too high for reptiles and amphibians when the reactors are in operation. However, certain species can be found along the corridors and backwater seepage areas whose temperatures are only slightly elevated. Both streams enter the main Savannah river swamp, and much of the heat dissipates there before the water reaches the Savannah River. *Trachemys scripta* from the associated peripheral habitats characteristically have fast growth rates and reach large body sizes, as in other thermally affected areas.

BEAVER DAM CREEK. Beaver Dam Creek receives effluent from a coal-fired power station at the heavy-water plant, but the thermal elevation diminishes as the creek approaches the river swamp and the Savannah River. Large numbers of *T. scripta* and perhaps other turtles are present, but the site has been little studied.

STEEL CREEK. This stream is 15 km (10 miles) long. It originates near P reactor and from 1954 to 1968 received effluent from L reactor. During 1984 much of the forested area of the upper reaches above the floodplain delta was cleared for construction of L-Lake, a reservoir to receive effluent upon the restart of L reactor. Thorough descriptions of the new reservoir and the impacts on Steel Creek habitats are given by Sharitz et al. (1986).

LOWER THREE RUNS CREEK. This creek originates as the overflow from Par Pond and was an original stream system on the SRP. It transported thermal effluent from 1953 to 1958, and since that time the impoundment of its upper extremity to create Par Pond has reduced stream flow considerably and altered water quality. The stream is contaminated by low levels of radioactive cesium, which are not considered to be a danger to individuals working there. Lower Three Runs is approximately 22 km (14 miles) in length from the Par Pond Cold Dam to its entry into the Savannah River, and it passes through lowland swamp forest over much of its course. *Trionyx spiniferus* is observed more commonly in the area of Lower Three Runs below Par Pond than in any other habitat on the SRP, with the possible exception of the Savannah River itself.

SAVANNAH RIVER. The Savannah River is the boundary between South Carolina and Georgia and forms the southwestern border of the SRP. This large southern river (total basin approximately 28,000 km²) receives the major tributaries of Upper Three Runs Creek, Steel Creek, and Lower Three Runs Creek. According to Bennett and McFarlane (1983), "The river gradient in the vicinity of the SRP is 0.12 m/km." The mean annual discharge at this point is 316 m³/sec (McFarlane et al., 1978, 1979). Peak flow and maximum variability in flow occur during March and April, and the lowest flow and least variability are found during the summer and autumn. The 7-day, 10-year minimum flow at the SRP site is estimated to be 160 m³/sec (5,700 cfs). At flood stage the water mass breaches the channel to form a floodplain up to 3 km wide, and the flow may approach 1,200 m³/sec. Stream velocity is approximately 0.74 m/sec at mean annual discharge and 0.65 m/sec at 7-day, 10-year low flow. The river's characteristics are currently dominated by the release of hypolimnetic water from Clarks Hill Reservoir. The principal effects have been to decrease the incidence of extreme high and low discharge and to decrease the average river temperature by 3° C.

We have trapped turtles along the river at several sites, but the majority of captures of slider turtles have been in the numerous oxbow lakes where there is no current. My impression is that river cooters (*Pseudemys concinna*) are the dominant turtle in the main channel of the river, and hundreds can be seen basking at certain times on logs along the banks over a several-mile stretch. Spiny softshell turtles (*Trionyx spiniferus*) and snappers (*Chelydra serpentina*) also seem to be more abundant in the main channel than do slider turtles. However, in backwater areas that are heavily vegetated, sliders are prevalent and can be captured in baited aquatic traps.

The oxbow lakes, of which there must be more than 50 in different stages of evolution between the Fall Line above Augusta and the Atlantic Ocean below Savannah, would be ideal sites for investigating certain movement phenomena in slider turtles. These floodplain environments with variable water levels and high primary productivity of aquatic vegetation are ideal natural habitat of the slider turtle. One of the interesting questions relates to the level of river use by sliders, as they appear to be restricted mostly to the lentic habitats along the margins. For example, it is not known how much of a barrier a large river such as the Savannah can be to this species or whether individuals traveling up or down one side or the other are more likely to use the river corridor or an overland route. Also, do slider turtles nest on the high sandbars as *P. concinna* do, or do they travel farther inland so that the emerging hatchlings are more likely to enter marsh habitat than the river itself? The investigation of this species in floodplain habitats of large rivers would be extremely informative about its natural history.

FORESTS

Approximately 4,200 ha (10,400 acres) of the SRP are cypress-tupelo and bottomland hardwood swamp forests where standing water is prevalent at certain times. Natural water levels fluctuate seasonally (highest in winter and spring; lowest in summer and autumn) and may vary more than 2 m over a year. Rapid changes of more than 1 m may occur as a result of heavy rainfalls or adjustments in reservoir levels at Clarks Hill Dam, approximately 56 km (35 miles) upstream. These habitats are used by many species of reptiles and amphibians, including turtles in open areas. The most intensively studied swamp habitat has been that bordering, and in the delta of, Steel Creek.

ISLANDS

Some of the South Carolina studies on slider turtles have been conducted on barrier islands, primarily Kiawah and Capers (Fig. 2.3). Turtles from the aquatic habitats on the islands are much larger than those from other natural habitats (Gibbons et al., 1979).

KIAWAH ISLAND.   The area of this island is about 3,200 ha, half of which is salt-marsh habitat. Other major habitats include 12 km of ocean beach, dune systems, maritime thickets, and forests that form the island's interior. The maritime thickets are characterized by closely spaced vegetation, predominantly stunted live oaks (*Quercus virginiana*), yaupon holly (*Ilex vomitoria*), and wax myrtle (*Myrica cerifera*). The interior forests are combinations of pines (*Pinus* spp.), oaks (*Quercus* spp.), magnolia (*Magnolia grandiflora*), and palmettos (*Sabal* spp.). A major influence on Kiawah Island has been the development of a recreational complex and resort. Cottages, golf courses, and blacktop roads cover more than 10% of the island.

Before development, the island had about a dozen brackish and freshwater lakes (total of 80 ha) not under tidal influence. They ranged in salinity from 0 ppt to about 17 ppt, depending upon their location on the island and upon recent rainfall. Today many of the lakes are interconnected with freshwater canal systems that also support slider turtles. In addition, many low-lying areas become flooded during wet parts of the year, creating small, shallow freshwater habitats throughout much of the forested parts of the island.

CAPERS ISLAND.   This island is about 900 ha in area and, like Kiawah, is about 50% salt-marsh habitat. Beach frontage on Capers is 5.3 km. The island vegetation is generally similar to that of Kiawah Island, although the maritime thicket community is proportionately smaller. Only one small, freshwater pond, Greene Pond, is believed to have contained water continually for the past several years. Greene Pond is less than 0.1 ha. An extensive brackish impoundment system is also present on the island. Before being breached by surf erosion several years ago, one arm of this impoundment was a large isolated

Table 2.3. Captures and recaptures of freshwater turtles used in analyses
and interpretations of life history phenomena

| Species | Michigan (Sherriff's Marsh) | | South Carolina | | Total |
	Original captures	Recaptures	Original captures	Recaptures	
Trachemys scripta	--	--	6,723	4,274	10,997
Kinosternon subrubrum	--	--	2,215	2,992	5,207
Chrysemys picta	2,693	940	10	5	3,648
Deirochelys reticularia	--	--	961	880	1,841
Sternotherus odoratus	70	3	759	224	1,056
Pseudemys floridana	--	--	434	221	655
Chelydra serpentina	61	16	311	283	671
Emydoidea blandingii	131	24	--	--	155
Malaclemys terrapin	--	--	94	16	110
Clemmys guttata	2	--	14	4	20
Pseudemys concinna	--	--	17	1	18
Trionyx spiniferus	--	--	12	--	12
Graptemys geographica	6	1	--	--	7
Total	2,963	984	11,550	8,900	24,397

Note: Numbers in this chart represent captures through 1987; however, analyses in some chapters of this book did not include captures from 1987 or part of 1986. Exact locations and habitat details are given in the text.

freshwater pond and may have been occupied by the turtles now present in Greene Pond. Numerous ditches and low-lying areas throughout the island contain water during early spring and midsummer wet periods.

Field and Laboratory Procedures

In this section, descriptions and assessments of field and laboratory techniques we have used in the study of the ecology and life history of freshwater turtles in South Carolina and Michigan are provided. Most of the techniques would also be applicable, sometimes with modifications, to terrestrial or marine species. The information is based on published reports and our own experience. It is hoped that this will answer most of the questions that may arise about methods of capturing turtles and will also indicate laboratory methods that work well for the safe manipulation of turtles and the ways of acquiring data once the turtles have been captured. My emphasis will be on nondestructive sampling, as this approach has become an important consideration with many species in today's world and the killing of individuals is not compatible with mark-recapture studies.

Methodology is considered here in the order that would be used in an ecological study of turtles, that is, first, observing or capturing the turtles, and second, taking standard field measurements, including marking individuals for future identification. Additional information on ecology of turtles includes reproduction, growth, movement, feeding habits, and other aspects of turtle biology.

COLLECTING TECHNIQUES

The first step in studying any animal in the field is to develop procedures for observing or collecting specimens. Techniques that yield high numbers of captures for some turtle species may produce few or no captures of others in the same habitat. The techniques discussed are based primarily on the field experiences of us and other investigators, primarily on the SRP and in southern Michigan over a period of 22 years (Gibbons, 1987).

The total number of original captures and recaptures through 1987, from the initiation of research on *Chrysemys picta* at Sherriff's Marsh in Michigan in 1964, is more than 24,000 (Table 2.3). Only a few individuals were collected for some of the species. They are included because the scarcity of individuals of a species in a habitat may be revealing about interspecific relationships and about the ecological character of the particular species.

Obviously, the effectiveness of a technique depends on a variety of factors, including the type of aquatic habitat, the season, and the species of turtle to be sampled. In discussing the various techniques used by turtle collectors, we will consider those that have proved effective in yielding large numbers of turtles as well as some that did not work so well. Some techniques require the presence of the investigator at the time of capture, whereas others rely on various types of traps that operate during the investigator's absence.

An important determinant of how the life history traits of a species are perceived by the investigator is sampling bias. Sampling bias can result from a variety of causes, some of which are minimized by long-term, intensive studies that use several techniques and large sample sizes. For some characteristics, replicate sampling during different years and in different localities is critical for revealing the inherent variability among individuals and populations of the species. For example, to assess population age structure in *T. scripta*, it is essential that collecting techniques be used that capture juveniles as well as adults and that adults of the two sexes have equal probabilities of capture. In many instances the use of a single collecting technique for several years at a variety of localities would not be as likely to reveal the true sex ratio or the proportions of juveniles and adults as would a single intensive effort using a variety of collecting techniques. On the other hand, a short period of observation or the restriction of observations to a single population can also lead to erroneous results. Consideration is given in Chapter 14 to how misinterpretations might occur as a result of sampling bias in a complex situation.

We have used a variety of methods to collect freshwater turtles in the study of populations in South Carolina. Different collecting techniques have often revealed information about the population structure and behavior of turtles that would not have been apparent from the use of only one technique. The two techniques that yielded the most captures of the slider turtle (*T. scripta*) were baited aquatic traps and terrestrial drift fences with pitfall traps. However, neither technique was useful in the study of some populations, such as the small population on Capers Island, where turtles were captured almost exclusively by hand.

AQUATIC TRAPS.   Baited aquatic traps are the most effective means of catching large numbers of turtles in a variety of habitats. Such traps do not work well for some species (e.g., spotted turtles, *Clemmys guttata*, or river cooters, *Pseudemys concinna*), some habitats (e.g., *T. scripta* at Capers Island), and some seasons (e.g., winter).

The designs of aquatic traps to capture turtles have been limited only by the creativity of investigators, but all designs work on the same principle. The trap has an opening that the turtle enters, because it has been either led or lured into it. Some traps are intentionally designed so that turtles can eventually escape. Others are intended to keep the turtle from escaping by flaps or funnels. My bet is that none is 100% effective in keeping all captured turtles contained. Several turtle trap designs have been reported and can be used by anyone simply by constructing a wire or net container with an opening (e.g., Legler, 1960b; Gibbons, 1968c; Iverson, 1979a).

The traps we use at SREL have steel hoops covered with treated netting and held apart by poles; a drawstring closure at one end; and a net funnel leading into the trap at the other end. The advantage of the hoop traps is that they are lightweight and can be collapsed and transported, so several can be used at one time in remote areas and, if necessary, can be set, baited, and checked by only one person. Bait is placed anywhere inside the trap, preferably anchored in some manner. The major disadvantages of these traps are that they are expensive, turtles can escape from them (on several occasions animals have been observed to enter and then leave the traps), and in some areas large alligators enter them to eat the bait, trapped turtles, or trapped fish and can destroy the traps or even drown. However, the effectiveness of hoop traps and the relative ease of transporting and setting them make them one of the most useful techniques for collecting freshwater turtles.

Fyke nets with wings can be extremely effective as unbaited hoop traps in some situations in which a large area can be blocked off. Clearing a fyke net can be difficult, because the contents of each section have to be shaken into the next smaller section until the entire contents of the net are in the terminal section. When fish, alligators, or snakes are captured in addition to turtles, the entire load can be heavy and difficult to manipulate.

An air space must be left at the top of any hoop trap, and every effort should be made to ensure that even given adverse weather conditions, such as high wind or rising water, the trap will not sink completely underwater, thus possibly drowning any trapped turtles.

BASKING TRAPS.   Generally, a basking trap consists of a square frame with floats under opposite sides. Material such as hardware cloth or welded wire is affixed to the frame to allow turtles to climb up on the frame. The inside of the frame is equipped with sheet metal so that when the turtle climbs up to bask, it slips inside the frame, which has a large net bag suspended from it. The turtle cannot swim out of the net, and the sheet metal keeps if from climbing out. Moll and Legler (1971) used basking traps in the form of a net or an enclosure attached to a preexisting basking site known to be used by turtles. When turtles were seen on the basking site, the investigators would approach rapidly in a boat, scaring the turtles from the perch and into the net. Basking traps were not used extensively in the studies on the SRP, although some captures were made in this manner. *Trachemys scripta* is a noted basker among turtles, but this behavior is greatly reduced in the warmer weather in South Carolina. In addition, the numerous basking sites in most habitats make the use of basking traps less effective. In research projects by others, basking traps were often the first traps to be discontinued (Moll and Legler, 1971; Auth, 1975).

TROTLINES.   Trotlines bearing large baited fishhooks are effective in some situations. A trotline consists of a long, relatively thick line with fishing leaders hanging from it. The leaders are armed with hooks, which are generally baited with meat, such as beef heart, chicken liver, or chicken gizzard. A disadvantage of this technique is that turtles can be injured, and if the trotline is not checked at frequent intervals, turtles may drown. An advantage is that you may catch some big fish.

TRAMMEL NETS. Trammel nets are effective in some open-water habitats with little vegetation and, preferably, low numbers of fish. They are labor-intensive, requiring regular checks to keep turtles from drowning. Another major drawback is that the researcher using trammel nets must possess a great deal of patience in unraveling twine because that seems to be how a great deal of the time is spent. Besides setting trammel nets perpendicular to the water's surface, we have had some success by draping them over and around basking sites where turtles are likely to become entangled in the net. However, imagine the problems of unraveling the net from turtles, vegetation, other debris, and the basking site itself.

SNORKELING AND SCUBA DIVING. Diving allows the researcher to invade the habitat directly, not only facilitating the collection of turtles but also allowing extended periods of observation in some situations. This, of course, depends on water clarity but has been extremely effective in sampling turtle populations in the spring runs of Florida (Marchand, 1945; Jackson, 1969; Sanderson, 1974). Diving has been used with less effectiveness in Par Pond and other habitats on the SRP, primarily because of heavy vegetation and problems with water clarity.

Snorkeling is a cheaper method of observation, requiring only a snorkel and a face mask. A pair of swim fins make a person as fast as most turtles. Scuba diving, by comparison, is much more involved, requiring a certification course that provides the appropriate training and an investment in some expensive equipment, but the benefits of extended periods of submergence in turtle habitats are obvious. Depending on the sort of data required, scuba diving or snorkeling may yield observational data unobtainable in any other manner.

MUDDLING AND NOODLING. Turtles in some populations are most effectively sampled by feeling for them with hands and feet in the mud or beneath undercut banks. This technique was particularly effective on Capers Island (Gibbons et al., 1979), being the primary means by which turtles were caught, even though other standard methods were tried without success. This technique can also be effective if a pond can be partly drained. Disadvantages of this technique can become painfully obvious if you are working in an area where cottonmouths, alligators, or snapping turtles also seek sanctuary in the mud or overhanging ledges.

DIPNETTING. Under certain conditions this collecting technique can be highly effective, depending on the amount of aquatic vegetation and the diving behavior of the turtles being sampled. On the SRP this technique has not been particularly productive in any one area, although we always seem to have a dip net with us, and several turtles are captured in this manner each year on the SRP. In conjunction with winter night collecting (see below), turtles seen beneath the surface of very cold water are slow to move and are easily captured with dip nets. The technique has proved to be the mainstay of turtle sampling efforts at Sherriff's Marsh in Michigan, where the aquatic habitat is covered with *Lemna* and *Spirodela* during the summer. In 1984 a total of 750 turtles were captured in a three-day effort involving mostly dipnetting from canoes.

WINTER NIGHT COLLECTING. During the winter of 1983–84 it was found that turtles could be easily located in the shallows of Pond B on the SRP, even though portions of the pond were partially iced over. Turtles were easily seen with flashlights as they lay on the mud bottom, where the water depth was less than 1 m. Under extremely cold conditions (C), the turtles showed no apparent aversion to the bright lights, did not move, and were captured with little or no problem with a dip net. Few observed turtles were not captured. Any small boat with a dependable light source will suffice.

SEINING. Seining is particularly effective in waters with silt or sand bottoms, few snags, and minimal aquatic vegetation. We have found a 30-foot nylon seine with 1-inch mesh and a 3-foot square bag to be the most versatile and effective overall. Obviously, certain habitat situations such as deep water, heavy aquatic vegetation, or unsavory water quality make seining less desirable than other techniques.

CAST NETS. When thrown, these large, circular, weighted nets spread out to their widest diameter and sink quickly upon contact with water. The drawstring is then pulled, causing the net to draw up on itself. With some practice, we have used this technique successfully on turtles in open-water habitats.

FLY RODS. I have seen Chuck Vincent use a fly rod to capture slider turtles swimming in a lake. The fly with a hook was cast into the water slightly beyond the turtle's shell, which was then hooked on the edge of the carapace. Several specimens were removed from the radioactive seepage basins in this manner because most other techniques would have resulted in contamination of people or equipment. A disadvantage of the technique is that individuals could be hooked in areas that might result in injury, but a more significant drawback is that most of us are not that accurate with a fly rod.

RIFLES. Shooting turtles to obtain specimens for scientific research has seldom been particularly effective anywhere. My own experience has been that even if you happen to get a good shot at a basking turtle, all of those in the vicinity disappear, including the one that you shot and may have killed, because it sinks to the bottom. Although this technique might be effective for acquiring a sample for dissection in an area where no other collecting method would be successful, a maximum sample size of one hardly seems to warrant it.

DRIFT FENCES WITH PITFALL TRAPS. All freshwater turtle species leave the aquatic environment at one time or another, even if only for the relatively short time necessary for them to lay eggs. Consequently, vital aspects of their life history and ecology will not be discovered unless an effort is made to collect them in nonaquatic situations.

The terrestrial drift fence and pitfall traps have been used for many years to sample a variety of vertebrate and invertebrate species (e.g., Imler, 1945; Gloyd, 1947; Woodbury, 1951, 1953; Storm and Pimentel, 1954; Packer, 1960; Husting, 1965; Shoop, 1968; Hurlbert, 1969; Gibbons, 1970d; Briese and Smith, 1974; Gibbons and Bennett, 1974; Randolph et al., 1976; Collins and Wilbur, 1979; Bennett et al., 1980; Brown, 1981; Wygoda, 1981). This method is based on the principle that animals traveling overland, upon encountering the drift fence, turn right or left and continue along the obstacle until they fall into a trap. The technique is outstanding for the study of turtle populations.

The basic design for a terrestrial drift fence is a straight fence extending slightly below ground with pitfall traps placed alongside the fence and buried flush with the ground at specified intervals (Gibbons and Semlitsch, 1982). Field experience has shown that the most effective material is 50-centimeter-high aluminum flashing, entrenched approximately 10 cm below the surface of the ground. This construction prevents hatchling turtles from crawling under or through the fence, and larger turtles from using a textured surface to climb over it. The flashing is sturdy enough that it cannot easily be torn or pushed down by larger vertebrates such as deer or feral pigs, making it far more practical than plastic fencing, and it does not rust or deteriorate with age, as some other fencing materials do. The most effective pitfall traps are 20-liter plastic buckets. These containers are relatively permanent and work well for long-term studies because they do not corrode, as metal ones do. Although smaller-volume traps (no. 8 cans) have been used effectively for certain species of salamanders (Shoop, 1965; Gill, 1978; Douglas, 1979), larger traps permit the capture of many

species that can easily escape from a shallow can. The 20-liter buckets are even effective for capturing adult *Chelydra serpentina* and are therefore ideal for studies of turtles.

Maintenance of drift fences and pitfall traps is essential. Vegetation alongside the fence should be mowed or cut when appropriate. New growth can be reduced in some situations by placing a heavy layer of sand on either side of the fence for a distance of 5 to 10 cm. Cracks or crevices in the soil along the fence and around the buckets should be filled to prevent escape tunnels that hatchlings might enter or fall into. Water accumulation can be prevented to some extent by drilling holes in the bottom and sides of the buckets, although bailing may be necessary in some cases. Traps must also be checked often to avoid desiccation, predation, and other problems. A frequent checking routine, or the use of wet sponges in the bottom of traps, can prevent drying and lessen heat stress during summer, although turtles are typically more resistant to desiccation and can remain in pitfall traps for longer periods of time than most other vertebrates. The probability of predation on an animal in a pitfall trap increases with time, so under most circumstances it is desirable to check traps at least once each day.

Drift fences with pitfall traps yield large amounts of data on numbers (often total population sizes), seasonality, migration patterns, diversity, and distribution patterns of many animals, including turtles. The number of captures, however, may not necessarily reflect the actual abundance of a species; as with any sampling techniques, certain biases and limitations (morphology, ecology, and behavior of a species; or fence design, maintenance, and checking frequency) must be taken into account in the interpretation of data. For example, the propensity of eastern mud turtles (*Kinosternon subrubrum*) to overwinter on land (Bennett et al., 1970) means that they are more likely to migrate across the land-water interface and be captured in greater numbers than are more aquatic species, such as the stinkpot (*Sternotherus odoratus*). Similarly, the eastern box turtle (*Terrapene carolina*) exhibits an awareness of topographic relief and an avoidance of natural pitfalls; this may be the reason that so few adults have fallen into traps. However, box turtles have not been a common species in any of the habitats where drift fences were used on the SRP, so the box turtle's awareness of topography may be more perception than reality. I suppose this would be an easily testable phenomenon.

Certain false impressions about abundance, diversity, or behavior of animals in an area also can be caused by factors such as the spatial arrangement of the drift fences in combination with the ecology of the species involved. The distance of a fence from a critical habitat, such as an aquatic breeding site or a terrestrial nesting area, might influence the number of captures of certain species. For example, if a fence is located near the water, a nesting female will probably attempt to get around by walking alongside it. However, if several meters of suitable nesting habitat lie between the water and the fence, the female may nest inside the fence rather than encounter the obstacle, even though she would have traveled farther inland had the fence not been present.

Critical, too, is the temporal aspect, not only on a seasonal or annual basis but in some instances in terms of time of day that the traps are checked (e.g., Hurlbert, 1969; Gibbons, 1970d; Semlitsch et al., 1981). Long-term studies reveal that annual disparities can be great enough to provide the potential for improper interpretations if drift fences are used to sample habitats for short periods of time (Gibbons and Bennett, 1974). Certain conclusions relating to population size or absolute abundance should be drawn with caution. However, the potential for using the technique to estimate hatchling survivorship, dispersal, migration, gene flow, and other difficult-to-obtain data in turtles has been demonstrated (Shoop, 1974; Gill, 1978; Semlitsch and McMillan, 1980; Semlitsch, 1981b; Gibbons et al., 1983) and should not be underestimated.

Drift fences with pitfall traps yield a wealth of biological information, often providing ecological perspectives that could not otherwise be obtained. Although the time and effort put into drift fence construction, maintenance, and operation are high, data accumulated are often superior to those gained by any other form of collecting, and the technique is highly cost-effective once the critical investment level has been reached. This is especially true for long-term ecological studies where continuous daily sampling by hand is impractical.

SHELL ROUNDUPS.   Turtle shells can be found around the terrestrial margins of most aquatic habitats and can be a good source of information regarding differential mortality of species, sexes, and size classes. Although all incidental shell findings are recorded in our marked populations, we routinely conduct shell roundups each winter with the assistance of as many participants as possible. Shell roundups are particularly important in establishing the age at death and the elimination of individuals from populations and are a recommended procedure for any mark-recapture program. An early experiment at Ellenton Bay was to determine the period of time necessary for shell deterioration in a field situation. We placed 20 dead slider turtles in the habitat and observed their deterioration during a period of several months. By the end of a full year most had been reduced to bony disarticulations. The purpose of this exercise was to establish that shells found during the annual turtle shell roundups were indeed from individuals that had died during the previous year. One of the advantages of the marking system for turtles (see Marking Techniques, below) is that individuals can be identified by their codes several months after death.

MISCELLANEOUS FIELD TECHNIQUES.   A variety of other techniques have also been used by us at SREL or by other investigators in the capture of turtles. As with any turtle collecting method, some of these work most efficiently for certain species or under particular conditions. Electroshocking stuns turtles (Gunning and Lewis, 1957), and several *Pseudemys floridana* and *Sternotherus odoratus* have been captured in this manner in Par Pond during the course of research on fish. Turtles develop an attitude of suspended animation when in the force field but appear unharmed by the charge from generator-powered electrical shockers mounted on boats.

The technique known at boat revving was discovered accidentally by Chaney and Smith (1950) while collecting *Graptemys* at night. They noticed that turtles were apparently attracted to the boat while the motor was running and could easily be caught by hand. During 12 hours on two successive nights, 382 *Graptemys* were collected in this manner. Sanderson (1974) used the technique to collect *Graptemys barbouri* but noticed that only certain outboard motors seemed to attract turtles. We have not used this technique successfully on the SRP, but the complete absence of any *Graptemys* species seems reason enough.

Numerous other special collecting techniques, such as the use of a carphorn (Vogt, 1978) and sounding (Carpenter, 1955), have been reported and are probably worth trying under certain circumstances.

TRACKING TECHNIQUES.   A great deal of information has been obtained in the study of turtles through the use of devices that permit an individual turtle to be followed. Sonar (Moll and Legler, 1971) and radiotelemetry (see Chapter 18) can be extremely valuable tools for following the movement of turtles, and the development of miniature systems holds great promise for future studies. The string technique (Breder, 1927), in which a spool of thread is attached to the turtle's carapace, can be extremely effective in determining terrestrial activity patterns and has even been used successfully in aquatic situations (Emlen, 1969). Tantalum tags that emit low-level gamma radiation detectable at a distance of up to 10 m have been used in the study of burrowing species such as *Kinosternon subrubrum* and resulted in the confirmation that they characteristically hibernate on land (Bennett et al., 1970; Bennett, 1972). Today the technique has the limitation that radiation health safety regulations be followed, and the paperwork can be burdensome.

Although not a method of tracking turtles by itself, the doubly labeled water technique (Congdon et al., 1982), when used with a tracking method, can be a powerful approach in the study of bioenergetics of turtles, especially terrestrial species.

LABORATORY PROCEDURES

PHOTOCOPYING.   Photocopies of the plastrons of *T. scripta* have been taken since the mid-1970s. This was initiated for two purposes. The first was to keep a photographic "fingerprint" record of each individual to solve discrepancies when marked animals were unable to be properly identified. The second was to observe ontogenetic changes in scute nonconformities and annuli growth. Photocopying is much cheaper than making a photographic film record and is highly recommended for anyone who has access to this process and is working with large numbers of marked individuals.

MEASUREMENTS.   The plastron length to the closest millimeter was measured for each individual with a plastic ruler. The level of precision provided by this approach was judged to be a sufficient measurement of body size. In most instances, measurements of specimens were made by a select few individuals to assure a level of quality control in the process. Calipers were used to measure the length of annuli on many individuals. This technique allowed determination of the relationship between the pectoral scute and plastron length and thus of the change in body size of particular individuals from one year to the next by back calculation. This approach can potentially strengthen growth-rate interpretations.

Carapace lengths were recorded initially, but the close correlation between plastron and carapace lengths for slider turtles made this measurement unnecessary for subsequent determinations of body size. The body weight was measured for more than 2,000 individuals in order to establish the relationship between plastron length and weight of the individual. On a logarithmic scale, this relationship is fairly consistent and has been used in biomass estimates of the various populations (Congdon et al., 1986).

At one time we even attempted to determine volume of individuals by the displacement of water in a large container. Attempts to make this measurement were eventually abandoned because it seemed unlikely to become a standard measure of turtle body size. In the final reckoning, plastron length was chosen as the simplest and most consistent measure of body size in slider turtles. However, it should be noted that sexual dimorphism in plastron length occurs in some species (e.g., *Kinosternon subrubrum*) and that carapace length is a more meaningful measure of body size in those species (Gibbons, 1983a).

Sex determinations were able to be made for all *T. scripta* individuals more than 100 mm in plastron length because of the elongated claws of males (see Chapter 9), and the sex of many smaller individuals was determined upon their later recapture when they had reached this size.

MARKING TECHNIQUES.   In any investigation of the natural history and ecology of turtles in which identification of individual specimens is necessary, a system must be devised so that each specimen carries a distinctive, long-lasting, unique mark that in no way hinders its normal

activity. Cagle (1939) devised a scheme for marking turtles in which each marginal scute of the carapace was assigned a number and the scute was then notched with scissors (for small, partly ossified shells) or a file. Turtles are particularly good organisms on which to conduct mark-release-recapture studies because of the permanence of the individual marks.

At SREL the marking system is based on the system of Cagle (1939; also see Kaplan, 1958; Pough, 1970; Ernst et al., 1974). Each of the 24 marginals is assigned a letter code. Because of differences in morphology, two coding systems are used—one for kinosternid turtles (with 11 marginals on each side) and the other for chelydrid and emydid turtles. Marginals that form the bridge between the carapace and plastron are not normally used in the marking system, even though they have a letter code.

Marking can be done by means of a file, power drill, or hacksaw on most specimens. A scalpel or fingernail clippers are most effective for marking hatchlings. Notches made in juvenile turtles are readily discernible after many years (more than 6 years for *K. subrubrum* and *T. scripta*), and turtles marked as adults or large juveniles clearly show the marks after more than 10 years. The notches would presumably last for the life of the individual. The marks are permanent because they are in the bony margin of the carapace and not in soft, easily regenerable tissues.

Other methods of marking turtles for identification have been developed that allow for individual identification but do not have the permanency of the notching-drilling approach. Woodbury (1956) reviewed several techniques including painting, carving, branding, and grinding. Binary-coded wires represent a recent advance in technology that promises to facilitate marking individual turtles as hatchlings.

DIET.   Turtle stomach flushing was pioneered by Legler (1977), and a restraining device was developed by Parmenter (1981) to determine the diet of turtles without harming the animal. The turtle is secured upside down in a brace with its head and neck outstretched and its mouth held open by two cables with fishhooks (see Chapter 20). The fishhooks are attached to the inside of the turtle's mandible and maxilla. A steady stream of water is flushed through a flexible plastic tube inserted through the esophagus into the stomach. A fine-mesh screen placed beneath the turtle's mouth catches the food items, while the flushed water passes out through the mouth. The entire operation requires less than five minutes per turtle. Stomach samples can be preserved in formalin for taxonomic identification. The number and dry weight of all food items can usually be obtained (Parmenter, 1980). Although the technique is presumably not something a turtle enjoys, the recapture of stomach-pumped individuals from natural habitats suggests that it does no permanent harm. In trapping specimens for stomach pumping,

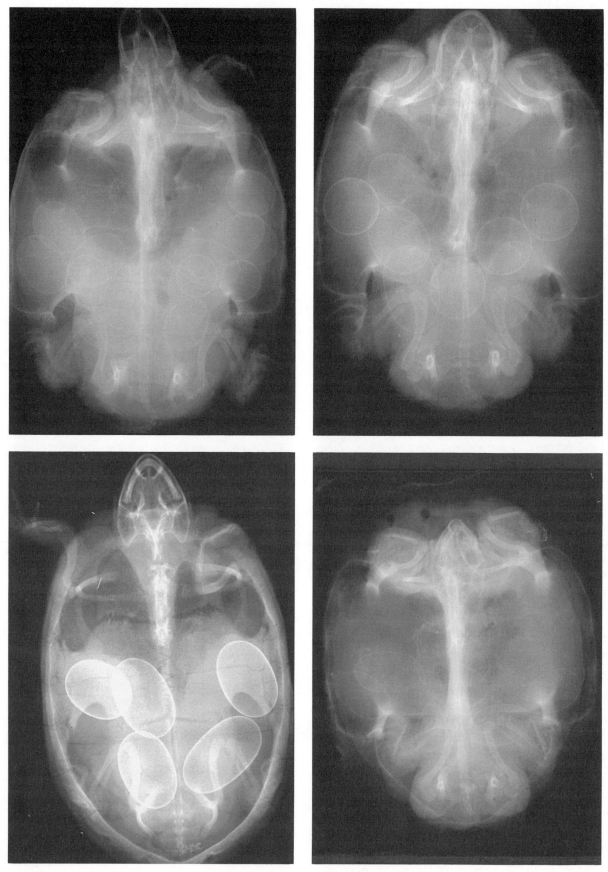

FIGURE 2.10.   X-ray photographs for determining clutch size in turtles are a consequence of the discovery in May 1976 that eggs with shells were observable despite the heavy plastron.

the bait needs to be in containers with small perforations to prevent consumption by the captured turtles (Parmenter, 1980).

REPRODUCTION.   In 1976 our turtle research at SREL received a major boost through a fortuitous and fortunate pair of incidents. On 5 May, at about the same time that Don Tinkle, Art Dunham, and I were examining a plate of x-ray photographs of lizards (*Uta stansburiana*) at the University of Michigan to determine if leg bone measurements could be made on specimens in this way, Judy Greene was picking up a female slider turtle (identification code HKN) that was digging a nest hole near Steed Pond. Later that day I talked with Judy and remarked that when looking at the lizard x rays, I had seen eggs with shells in some of them and wondered if x-ray photography would also work with turtles. She indicated that she had picked up a female turtle that obviously had eggs and would ask an x-ray technician she knew at Du Pont's medical facility to give it a try. Three days later, I was amazed to see the photograph that Judy sent, and we both knew that x-ray photography would be a major breakthrough in the study of reproduction in egg-laying species of reptiles.

X-ray photography (Fig. 2.10) is a nondestructive method of measuring clutch size that is no more disruptive to the individual than are many other facets of a population study (Gibbons and Greene, 1979). Furthermore, a female's reproductive output can be followed indefinitely as long as she can be recaptured in a gravid state; therefore, individual patterns of variation can be established. The technique is 100% accurate for determining clutch sizes, as the number of eggs in dissected females was invariably identical to the egg count first made from x-ray plates. A major advantage of the technique over dissection is that individuals in populations of permanently marked animals need not be killed.

Turtles can usually be x-rayed using nonscreened cardboard cassettes at 200 mA and 70 kV peak for 0.7 seconds at a distance of 1 m, with variations depending on the size of the turtle. This is equivalent to an adult human shoulder x-ray procedure and can be performed using standard techniques with any stationary or portable x-ray machine. Adult turtles have been reported to be less susceptible to side effects of x rays than either mammals or amphibians (Altland et al., 1951). It was concluded that the procedure has no detectable effect on developing embryos (Gibbons and Greene, 1979). Potential long-term effects on reproductive capacities of individuals undergoing multiple exposures is presently unknown.

Determinations that individuals contained eggs were also made by palpation, in which one's fingers are pushed into the abdominal cavity of a female in front of her back legs. If the turtle is held in a vertical position, shelled eggs can usually be felt. The use of oxytocin (Ewert and Legler,

1978) was extremely valuable for acquiring eggs for incubation experiments or other purposes. Dissection was used in early SRP studies, but less so in later years, to determine clutch size and maturity of the sexes.

Disclaimer for Analyses

People in general and scientists in particular are more comfortable when natural events can be identified to have consistency that leads to predictability. In fact, one of the objectives of science is to identify consistent patterns in nature. Two factors that have been antagonistic to the purpose of understanding the life history and ecology of turtles have been the natural variability inherent in many of the traits examined and the overwhelming influence that sampling biases can have in the interpretation of certain phenomena. An example is the determination of sex ratios of populations (see Chapter 14), which can vary from 2 males:1 female to 2 females:1 male. The extreme variation in perceived sex ratios has been shown to be a function of collecting biases in several instances. However, these extremes have also been observed in thoroughly sampled populations where sampling bias was minimal, indicating that sex ratios can vary significantly as a function of natural causes. The combination of these two factors can lead to major difficulties in interpreting such phenomena.

Although certain sampling biases are alleviated by large sample sizes (Table 2.3) and a long period of sampling, a different type of error has become apparent in the analysis of the SREL data base, an error that might be expected of many large dynamic data sets on which analyses are continually being made while the data base itself is continually changing. Thus, a count, a ratio, or a statistical test may be made at one time, and then a similar or even the same analysis may be made at a later time. The problem stems from the fact that the calculations made for this book were carried out over a two-year period in which more data were added for all species in most places, so it is not only conceivable but also probable that the estimates derived from the samples at different times will vary slightly. For example, the mean size of adult females from Ellenton Bay would be 187 (187.1) based on the sample through 1986, whereas if this same statistic were used in another chapter that was based on the samples through the summer of 1987, the mean size would be 188 (187.8). This would be a minor difference in the precision of the estimates but would be of no biological significance in knowing how large female slider turtles are at Ellenton Bay. Therefore, I hope that precisionists will accept this as a disclaimer for slight discrepancies in the statistics presented in different chapters of this book. Please accept my confidence that the effect on our understanding of the life history and ecology of turtles will not be jeopardized in any way.

Acknowledgments

Research and manuscript preparation were made possible by contract DE-AC09-76SROO-819 between the University of Georgia and the U.S. Department of Energy and by National Science Foundation grant DEB-79-04758.

JUSTIN D. CONGDON
J. WHITFIELD GIBBONS
Savannah River Ecology Laboratory
Drawer E
Aiken, South Carolina 29802

3

The Evolution of Turtle Life Histories

Abstract

How turtles evolved traits that are primarily related to survivorship and reproduction is explored within the framework of evolutionary theories of senescence and life history development. The evolution of a protective bony shell in the Testudines more than 200 million years ago apparently resulted in lowered mortality rates of adults, which allowed them to live long enough to have senescence deleteriously affect their reproductive capabilities. Consequently, genes that either postponed or reduced the expression of senescence were favored. A scenario is presented that suggests that turtle life history traits are more consistent with the antagonistic pleiotropy theory than with the mutation accumulation theory of senescence. Indeterminant growth, age and size at sexual maturity, clutch size, and egg size of turtles are discussed in relation to five hypotheses of the evolution of delayed sexual maturity and iteroparity.

Introduction

Turtles have been identified as being the epitome of long-lived organisms (Williams, 1957; Tinkle, 1969; Wilbur and Morin, 1988) and paragons of delayed sexual maturity, longevity, and iteroparity, that is, repeated cycles of reproduction (Wilbur and Morin, 1988). The slider turtle (*Trachemys scripta*) is one species of turtle for which the traits of extended longevity, delayed sexual maturity, and both annual and interannual iteroparity have been well documented in natural populations (Cagle, 1946, 1950; Gibbons et al., 1981, 1982; Gibbons, 1982, 1987; Gibbons and Semlitsch, 1982). Thus, turtles in general, and *T. scripta* in particular, are model organisms for an exploration of concepts related to theories of life history evolution and the evolution of longevity.

All issues related to the processes of life history evolution of either short- or long-lived organisms derive from the following question paraphrased from the insights of

Williams (1957) on the evolution of senescence. Why is it that after achieving the seemingly miraculous feat of morphogenesis, a complex metazoan is unable to perform the apparently much simpler task of merely maintaining that which is already formed? However, when the range of longevities of sexually reproducing organisms is considered, it is an inescapable conclusion that turtles do a much better job of maintaining their soma through time than do many other organisms. Among reptiles there exist relatively short-lived groups, such as most lizards and some snakes, and relatively long-lived groups, such as turtles, crocodilians, and other snakes. Although the extremes of reptile longevities represented by squamates versus turtles present an opportunity to attempt to answer the question posed above, the major emphasis in this chapter will be to examine life history traits of turtles in relation to the evolutionary theories of senescence and life histories.

To accomplish this goal it is necessary (1) to explore current concepts and theories related to the evolution of life histories and senescence that will enhance our understanding of the evolution of longevity and (2) to determine which traits are particularly pertinent to the evolution of delayed reproduction, iteroparity, and longevity of turtles.

We will not attempt to review all life history theory literature or catalog the data on turtle life history characteristics. Rather we will concentrate on features that appear to have been necessary for the evolution of longevity. We will consider how these traits arose and how they are associated with other traits within a life history. Unfortunately, the lack of complete life history data on turtles, and on long-lived organisms in general, limits inference about the evolution of longevity. Additional data will be necessary to address the problem fully. Nevertheless, the reader is referred to two syntheses of turtle life histories that have succeeded notably despite the paucity of complete life history data (Moll, 1979; Wilbur and Morin, 1988).

Although our emphasis is on turtles and their characteristic of extended longevity, comparisons with relatively shorter-lived reptiles will be made where they may enhance our understanding of the processes that led to longevity. Detailed discussions of life history evolution of lizards and snakes can be found in the following papers (Tinkle, 1969; Tinkle et al., 1970; Congdon et al., 1982; Ballinger, 1983; Dunham and Miles, 1985; Parker and Plummer, 1987; Seigel and Ford, 1987; Dunham et al., 1988a). General reviews of life history theories and concepts are outlined in articles by Stearns (1976, 1977) and Williams (1966a,b).

Turtles have several characteristics that make them good models for the study of life histories of long-lived, iteroparous species. Probably the most important is that an individual can be marked as a hatchling with a unique code that is essentially permanent throughout the turtle's lifetime. Other characteristics include the following: (1) Many turtles occur in relatively discrete populations at densities high enough to allow adequate numbers of individuals to be monitored throughout their lives; (2) eggshells are calcareous, and thus reproductive output of females can be nondestructively and repeatedly determined using x-radiography (Gibbons and Greene, 1979); (3) many turtles are of sufficient size to allow attachment of single-channel or multichannel radiotransmitters that monitor an individual's location and potentially other variables over long periods. In addition, two relatively recent nondestructive techniques—ultrasound tomography and the use of lipid-soluble gases to determine whole-body lipids—provide an opportunity to measure energy relations of turtles accurately for the first time.

Mark-recapture studies, in conjunction with some of the techniques mentioned above, have the potential to yield accurate age-specific data important to testing life history theories. Furthermore, if these studies are continued over a sufficient time, they should provide answers to questions about senescence in turtles.

Life History Traits

A life history is a suite of coevolved characteristics that directly influence population parameters. Life history traits include age-specific survivorship and reproductive output (clutch size and frequency), age at maturity, and longevity. Turtles exhibit a relatively narrow range of variation in life traits relative to lizards or snakes. For example, turtles have not evolved viviparity or complex postovipositional parental care. Whereas some aspects of turtle reproductive biology, ecology, and life history traits are relatively well known, there is a dearth of complete life history information on any given species. For example, to our knowledge only three life tables have been reported for freshwater turtles (Wilbur, 1975a; Tinkle et al., 1981; also see Chapter 15), and two of these involve the same population of *Chrysemys picta* from Michigan (Wilbur, 1975a; Tinkle et al., 1981).

The significance of demographic studies in testing predictions of life history theories stems from the following realization: Life history traits, like other phenotypic characteristics, evolve because they endow their possessors with higher individual fitness than alternate traits possessed by conspecifics within a population. In field studies, fitness can best be measured in terms of relative reproductive success, which largely depends on traits such as age and size at maturity, the proportion of assimilated energy devoted to reproduction, survivorship of offspring to reproductive age, and survivorship of individuals from one reproductive period to the next. These characteristics are exceptionally difficult to determine, and the problem is compounded because the necessary scrutiny of individuals of long-lived species must by definition be of long duration. In fact, the following observation about reptiles and amphibians may have arisen with turtles in mind: ". . . in the larger forms the life-cycle is so easily modified by diapause, diet, temperature, and the like that individuals probably age at rates so different as to be beyond the access of actuarial statistics except in an experiment of intolerable length" (Comfort, 1979).

Senescence and Life Histories

In simplest terms, senescence is the process of becoming old. The process of aging is identified by the accumulation of physical and physiological traits that reduce the effectiveness of the individual in some manner related to reproduction or survival. We concur with the assumption made by Williams (1957) that expression of traits related to senescence is unavoidable and is, in most if not all cases, opposed by natural selection. Two not mutually exclusive evolutionary theories of aging provide a potential answer to the question posed earlier about the difficulty organisms have in maintaining their soma.

The theory of mutation accumulation refers to the accumulation of alleles arising through mutation that have deleterious effects expressed late in life, a time when natural selection has minimal effect on reducing their frequency of expression (Bidder, 1932; Haldane, 1941; Medawar, 1952; Edney and Gill, 1968). Proponents of the mutation accumulation theory argue that the ability of natural selection to influence the frequency of mutations leading to senescence is weak, because most individuals in natural populations die of extrinsic causes before traits of senescence are expressed. In cases where deleterious effects of aging are expressed, Medawar (1952) hypothesized the existence of modifier genes (age-of-onset modifiers) that would suppress the expression of senescence traits as long as possible.

According to the theory of antagonistic pleiotropy, genes that are favored by selection early in life, when natural selection has the greatest impact, have cumulative deleterious effects later in life, when natural selection is less effective at postponing or masking their expression (Williams, 1957, 1966a). Williams (1957) envisioned pleiotropy to result when the same genes have different effects on fitness at different ages because of changes in the somatic environment. Eventually, as the cumulative effects of pleiotropic genes become expressed earlier and begin to interfere with an earlier, and thus larger, portion of the total reproduction of the individual, opposition by natural selection to further accumulations would increase. There is no apparent reason that selection for age-of-onset modifiers (Medawar, 1952) could not function to modify pleiotropic genes (Mertz, 1975). The more important a gene is in the expression of senescence, the more strongly selection should act through modifiers to reduce or delay unfavorable effects (Williams, 1957). As suppres-

sion of the deleterious effects is realized, selection pressure for further reduction would diminish so that complete suppression would be difficult.

Williams extended his argument by stating, "Senescence should always be a generalized deterioration, and never largely due to changes in a single system." In many organisms the deterioration associated with aging occurs throughout most body systems and thus appears to result from the action of many genes. However, recent work on fruit flies (*Drosophila*) suggests that in some cases delayed senescence may be under the control of a single factor (Luckenbill et al., 1987). Rose and Charlesworth (1980, 1981) examined long-lived stocks of *Drosophila* for evidence of accumulated mutations, but their data supported the trade-offs predicted by antagonistic pleiotropy. However, Service et al. (1988) found evidence that mutation accumulation and antagonistic pleiotropy were involved in the evolution of senescence in *Drosophila*. Further expansion, development, and clarification of senescence theories have been made by Charlesworth (1980), Hamilton (1966), Kirkwood (1985), and Rose and Hutchinson (1987).

Life span has been both extended (*Drosophila*—Clark and Maynard Smith, 1955; Wattiaux, 1968) and reduced (*Tribolium*—Sokal, 1970; Mertz, 1975) by selection experiments. In general, age at sexual maturity is correlated with life span (Cutler, 1978). We propose that the correlation of age at sexual maturity with life span is more consistent with the antagonistic pleiotropy theory of senescence than with the mutation accumulation theory. If accumulation of random mutations causes senescence, then age-of-onset modifiers or genes that reduce expression of the accumulated mutations would operate randomly with regard to age. Therefore, modifier genes would not necessarily be restricted to acting directly on the expression of genes associated with a particular ontogenetic stage. However, assuming antagonistic pleiotropy, both age-of-onset and suppression genes would only modify the expression of genes involved in both early and late life processes. It is hard to envision modifier genes, acting on critical metabolic processes necessary at all ages, that could be precise enough to suppress the expression of traits late in life without also modifying their expression early in life.

We propose the following scenario, which seems particularly appropriate in a chapter on turtles, based on the original example of pleiotropic effects of genes related to calcium metabolism presented by Williams (1957). In a turtle, a mutation occurs that has a favorable effect on calcium metabolism, resulting in rapid growth, attainment of sexual maturity, and increased protection due to faster shell development. Later in life, the gene promotes calcification of connective tissue in arteries. Senescence, in this example, is the result of two opposing selective forces. The first is driven by a high probability of mortality of adults to favor rapid growth and early attainment of sexual maturity at the expense of vigor later in life. The second selective force results because protection afforded by the shell allows adults to survive long enough to become harmed by calcification of arteries. In older individuals selection would favor age-of-onset modifiers and suppression genes that modify arterial calcification. Perfect modification would be restricted to gene expression related to calcification of arteries that occurs late in life. However, in a less precise natural system, the modifiers also exert a negative influence on calcium metabolism early in life. Modifications that influence the early expression would result in reduction of growth, postponement of sexual maturity, and a delay in protection provided by shell calcification.

From the above discussion, two considerations appear important if we are to understand the evolution of life histories of long-lived organisms. First, we must identify how traits or conditions arise that allow an organism to break the barrier of high extrinsic adult mortality and subsequently experience higher relative reproductive contribution later in life. Breaking this barrier appears to be a critical step in the evolution of longevity because under conditions of high extrinsic mortality of adults, natural selection seems to be biased in favor of youth over old age whenever a conflict of interest exists (Medawar, 1952; Williams, 1957). Age at death is important only insofar as it influences births or, more precisely, the proportion of early versus later births of individuals. Second, we need to identify how life history alternatives result in traits that are presently maintained and associated with long-lived organisms.

Mechanisms for Reducing Adult Mortality

Organisms may experience low adult mortality under the following conditions: domestication (horses, dogs, cats), armor (turtles); flight (birds, bats); noxiousness or poisonousness (plants, snakes); aggressiveness (carnivores); size (elephants, whales); sociality (primates); encephalization (primates); cryptic coloration (lizards, snakes). On occasion, specific environmental conditions in which predators are few or absent (e.g., certain insular settings) can result in reduced adult mortality. Of these traits or conditions, those that appear to be associated with longevity fall into three categories that lie along a gradient of increasing apparent costs: (1) no costs should result from domestication or living on islands in the absence of predators; (2) minimal costs might result from being cryptic, secretive, noxious, or poisonous; and (3) large costs should result from the development and maintenance of armor, flight, aggressiveness, or intelligence. Animals that become domesticated and are not used for food (pets such as dogs, cats, and horses) and prey species that colonize islands

could abruptly begin living long enough for the expression of senescence traits to become a cause of mortality. A striking example of extended longevity within a group involves insular populations of the gecko *Hoplodactylus duvauceli*) that were marked in 1956 and 1959; individuals recaptured in 1968 had minimum ages of 13 and 19 years (Barwick, 1982). These geckos live longer and take longer (up to 7 years) to reach sexual maturity than do closely related species on the mainland. In this case, extended longevity bears no apparent costs to the animals involved because the initial change was strictly environmental.

In contrast, adult mortality can be reduced as a consequence of changes in the species itself. Animals that adopt behaviors such as reduced activity to escape predation may incur indirect energy costs associated with restricted resource acquisition due to reduced time and activity budgets. Alternatively, energy costs are directly involved in synthesis of noxious or toxic chemicals used for defense from predators. Animals that adopt armor, flight, aggressiveness, or intelligence to reduce mortality, however, may invest a relatively large amount of energy and time that could result in postponement of sexual maturity.

Fossil records indicate that armor has been a trait of turtles since they arose in the Triassic period about 200 million years ago. The shells of turtles certainly reduce their vulnerability to many predators, accidental injuries, and adverse environmental conditions. Yet, even the shell of a relatively small adult turtle may have required a major investment in time and energy to become fully functional in a protective sense. However, even relatively small-bodied turtles may live up to twice as long as some crocodilians (Comfort, 1956). The records of great delays in longevity (Swingland and Lessells, 1979; Gibbons and Semlitsch, 1982; Congdon et al., 1983b; Turner and Berry, 1986) and sexual maturity (Gibbons et al., 1981; Congdon et al., 1983b, 1987; Turner et al., 1987) that have been reported for turtles in the wild may both be associated with the investment required to obtain a maximum ambit of protection from armor.

For individuals, the shell's effectiveness increases with body size and increased calcification that occurs with age. Thus, the shells of modern turtle species appear to function more effectively in the protection of adults than of hatchlings and juveniles. However, as long as the increase in reproduction later in life compensates for the decrease in early reproductive success of individuals that delay reproduction, any benefit derived from even small increases in protection from the shell early in life would also be strongly favored.

It may seem unlikely that the intermediate stages of shell development would be effective against the array of large predators that existed and still exist on most continents. However, for armor to evolve, it would have to be effective not against all predators but against only those responsible for a biologically significant portion of the mortality. Thus, it seems most likely that specialized armor would evolve today only in isolated settings with predator types reduced to one or a few of a specific type.

One problem that arises in the consideration of many evolutionary phenomena is that current traits are reflective of former conditions, so their function is no longer in the original context. A modern paradox exists with turtles in this regard. In contrast to an increase in survivorship associated with larger size, a special case exists when man acts as a major, highly selective predator. Ironically, the large body size and high fecundity of some turtles have resulted in increased death rates of adults and, in some species, of the embryos as well. A decrease in the protection that may have resulted from large body size has certainly increased rapidly in relatively recent times with the advent of commercial exploitation of eggs and meat of turtles in many regions of the world (King, 1982; Ross, 1982).

Indeterminant Growth

An early hypothesis advanced for fish (Bidder, 1932), but also applicable to turtles, suggested that senescence in vertebrates is caused by growth mechanisms that continue to operate after growth of the organism has ceased. Therefore, species that exhibit indeterminant growth would not exhibit traits of senescence, whereas those with determinant growth would. Subsequently, observations made on small teleost fishes indicated that senescence does occur even though growth continues past the onset of reproduction (Gerking, 1957). Although the hypothesis of Bidder (1932) was not supported as an all-or-none process, the association of a more rapid senescence rate with determinant growth has been documented (Comfort, 1956). These observations seem consistent with the aforementioned predictions of Medawar (1952) and Williams (1957).

Following the arguments of Bidder (1932), Comfort (1956), and Williams (1957), indeterminant growth can function within a population of turtles in a variety of ways to allow natural selection to oppose senescence by increasing the proportion of reproductive success, and in some cases the quality of offspring, that results from late reproduction. Some of the ways that larger body size may increase a turtle's reproductive output later in life have been well documented: for females, increased clutch size (Cagle, 1950; Moll and Legler, 1971; McPherson and Marion, 1981a; Tinkle et al., 1981; Gibbons et al., 1982; Congdon et al., 1983a, 1987; also see Chapter 9) and increased size or quality of eggs and thus neonates (Tucker et al., 1978; Congdon and Tinkle, 1982a; Congdon et al., 1983a; Congdon and Gibbons, 1985, 1987); for males, greater protection during terrestrial excursions in search of females for mating (Gibbons, 1986). In addition, increased survivorship associated with larger size of adults has often been suggested, but not documented, in turtles.

A pattern contrary to expectation seems to exist in data on the relationships among reproductive characteristics, age, and body size within populations of adult slider turtles (*T. scripta*). The slider turtle and many other turtle species as well exhibit indeterminant growth (but see Andrews, 1982). Therefore, the size of a growing individual must be correlated with its age (i.e., because growth takes time, individuals become older as they grow larger). The relationship between time and growth suggests that age and body size should be related. However, among slider turtles, clutch size is more strongly correlated with body size than with age (Gibbons, 1982). A possible explanation is suggested for this apparent discrepancy when growth rates of juveniles are considered. Growth rates of juvenile turtles and most other organisms are higher than those of adults. In addition, the variation among individuals in the growth rate of juveniles is apparently greater than in that of adults. Variation in both juvenile growth rates and ages at maturity apparently causes most of the differences in body size of adults. Furthermore, a large portion of this variation may persist in the population because growth rates among adults are low, and variation in growth rates of adults is not related to body size. Thus, the positive relationship between body size and age of sliders should be primarily considered an individual trait and only secondarily, if at all, a population trait. It follows then that indeterminant growth of an individual, operating through increased survivorship or increased reproduction associated with larger body size, should be viewed as a mechanism that may enhance natural selection for longevity by increasing the proportion of late versus early births of individuals. Therefore, we predict that indeterminant growth should be most prevalent in, but not an exclusive trait of, longer-lived species.

Theories of Life History Evolution

The papers of Fisher (1930), Svardson (1949), Cole (1954), Lack (1954a), and Williams (1957, 1966a,b) are examples of early contributions toward our understanding of the relationships between natural selection and life history traits. Over the past 20 years there have been many additions to the literature on life history evolution. The following is a partial list of contributions that are central to our current level of understanding of life history evolution: Lewontin (1958), Williams (1966a,b), Istock (1967), MacArthur and Wilson (1967), Murphy (1968), Tinkle (1969), Emlen (1970), Gadgil and Bossert (1970), Pianka (1970, 1972), Tinkle et al. (1970), Mertz (1971), Charnov and Schaffer (1973), Schaffer (1974a,b), Taylor et al. (1974), Hirshfield and Tinkle (1975), Schaffer and Gadgil (1975), Nichols et al. (1976), Stearns (1976, 1977), Armstrong and Gilpin (1977), Case (1978), Maynard-Smith (1978), Whittaker and Goodman (1979), Charlesworth (1980), Stearns and Crandal (1981), Congdon et al. (1982), Goodman (1982), Lande (1982), Ballinger (1983), Caswell (1983), Dunham and Miles (1985), Stearns and Koella (1986). Many of these were certainly influenced by the original insights of Williams (1966a,b).

Two major selective factors have been explicated in most theories of life history evolution: resource availability (r- and K-selection—Dobzhansky, 1950; MacArthur and Wilson, 1967; Pianka, 1970, 1972) and the demographic environment or pattern of age-specific survivorship (demographic and bet-hedging theories—Williams, 1966a,b; Murphy, 1968; Stearns, 1976, 1977). Both theories attempt to predict whole suites of life history attributes based on a single selective factor, and attempts to test them have met with various results. Some problems associated with these attempts are that (1) there is a lack of sufficient data on life history traits and on environmental parameters such as resource levels (Stearns, 1976, 1977), (2) dramatically different selective forces may give rise to similar life history traits (Wilbur et al., 1974), and (3) most populations are not stable with respect to either resource levels or demographic environment.

The latter problem points out that for any life history study of animals to be successful, it must continue long enough to address the following issues. First, variation in life history traits among individuals within populations must be identified. An emphasis on variation among individuals represents a shift from traditional demographic studies on identifying the mean values of age-specific survivorship and reproduction. To identify variation among individuals, a mark-recapture study must continue long enough to follow individuals from early age classes to sexual maturity and beyond. A study of this nature on turtles is by definition long-term, because turtles do not mature early in life and are long-lived. Personnel, logistic, and funding problems associated with a long-term study are the primary reasons that most data on long-lived organisms are size-specific rather than age-specific. Miller (1976) made a cogent plea for the study of long-lived organisms, and Wilbur (1975a) stated that one of the most serious gaps in the study of life histories in general is the lack of data on long-lived iteroparous organisms. Weins (1977), Tinkle (1979), and Kephart and Arnold (1982) have emphasized the necessity of long-term studies that closely monitor populations while paying special attention to variation in individual and population attributes. Other notable contributions include the long-term studies of Tinkle (1967) and Dunham (1982) on lizards; Clutton-Brock et al. (1982) on red deer; Kephart and Arnold (1982) on snakes; and Stickel (1950, 1978), Gibbons et al. (1981, 1982), Gibbons (1982), and Congdon et al. (1983b,

1987) on turtles. Many of the chapters that follow should add to this foundation.

Hypotheses for Delayed Sexual Maturity and Iteroparity

Given the earlier statement that turtles are the paragons of delayed sexual maturity, longevity, and iteroparity (Wilbur and Morin, 1988), five evolutionary hypotheses warrant consideration:

1. Delayed maturity results in a gain in fecundity (Tinkle, 1969; Gadgil and Bossert, 1970; Wiley, 1974; Schaffer and Elson, 1975; Bell, 1977).
2. Delayed maturity results in an increase in survival of offspring (Hirshfield and Tinkle, 1975).
3. Delayed maturity results in a reduction in the cost of reproduction (sensu lato Tinkle, 1969).
4. Whether organisms mature early or late, iteroparity will be favored if adult survival rates are high relative to juvenile survival rates (Murdoch, 1966; Cody, 1971; Charnov and Schaffer, 1973).
5. Iteroparity will be favored if variation in the success of reproductive attempts is high (Holgate, 1967; Murphy, 1968; Stearns, 1976).

AGE AT MATURITY

The point at which a turtle reaches sexual maturity is probably an integration of sex, age, and body size. In addition, habitat quality and the nutritional state of turtles can affect the variation in age and body size at sexual maturity (Barney, 1922; Hildebrand, 1929; Parmenter, 1980; Gibbons et al., 1981). The models developed by Stearns and Crandal (1981) and Stearns and Koella (1986) demonstrate the need to identify the sources of variation of adult body size of females within a population and the relationship between age and body size at sexual maturity.

Among the smaller turtle species there is a strong correlation of the width of the pelvic canal opening and egg width (Tucker et al., 1978; Congdon and Tinkle, 1982a; Congdon et al., 1983a; Congdon and Gibbons, 1987). If pelvic aperture constrains the size of an egg that can be produced, this constraint may set the minimum size a female must attain to produce an egg large enough to contain sufficient material for embryogenesis and yolk reserves for the hatchling (Congdon, 1989; also see Chapter 8). Some support for this possibility can be found in the geographic comparisons of egg size in *Chrysemys picta* (Mitchell, 1985a).

Some confusion exists about the pattern of interaction of body size and age at sexual maturity among turtle species. It has been reported that sexual maturity is attained earlier in smaller species (Bury, 1979) and that age at sexual maturity in turtles is not correlated with body size (Moll, 1979). Resolution of the conflicting reports about the relationships between age at maturity and body size will require additional data and careful analysis and may be confounded by the extreme interpopulation variation observed within some species (Gibbons et al., 1981). Males mature in many species at smaller sizes than do females, in other species at sizes similar to those of females, and in a few species at larger sizes than those of females (Bury, 1979). These different patterns in the sexes of body size at maturity are most likely related to mating tactics and territoriality of the species. *Trachemys scripta* mature at larger sizes in some tropical areas (Moll and Legler, 1971) than they do in temperate areas (Cagle, 1950; Gibbons, 1982). Gibbons et al. (1981) compared ages and sizes at maturity of males and females in thermally altered versus natural habitats. They concluded that male *T. scripta* mature at a fixed size regardless of age and that females mature at a fixed age regardless of size.

CLUTCH FREQUENCY

Clutch frequency in turtles has almost always been determined indirectly. Indirect methods commonly involve sampling adult females from a population and finding that the number of large ovarian follicles greatly exceeds the mean number of oviductal eggs, or that large follicles remain in the ovary even after one clutch is known to have been laid. A more direct determination comes from finding multiple sets of corpora lutea in the ovary (Cagle, 1950; Legler, 1960a; Powell, 1967; Gibbons, 1968d; Moll and Legler, 1971; Christiansen and Moll, 1973; Moll, 1973; Shealy, 1976). Ernst (1971b) and Moll (1973) correctly pointed out that no observed second clutches had been reported for *Chrysemys picta* until the early 1970s. Wilbur (1975) emphasized this void of data for Michigan populations, and other authors (Legler, 1954; Gemmell, 1970) have expressed doubts of second clutches (but see Snow, 1980, and Tinkle et al., 1981).

Gibbons (1982) presented data from a long-term study of three species of turtles in South Carolina, suggesting that in some cases clutch frequency may be a more important source of variation in annual fecundity than is clutch size. Until recently, determining clutch frequency for a population of freshwater turtles consisted primarily of demonstrating whether some individuals produced more than one clutch annually. Gibbons and Greene (1978) reported that some adult *Deirochelys reticularia* might not reproduce every year. Since then, evidence that female turtles may skip reproduction some years has been reported for *Gopherus polyphemus* (Auffenberg and Iverson, 1979; Landers et al., 1980), *Chrysemys picta* (Tinkle et al., 1981), *Emydoidea blandingii* (Congdon et al., 1983b), and *Chelydra serpentina* (Obbard, 1983; Congdon et al., 1987).

Bull and Shine (1979) discussed the possible signifi-

cance and evolution of iteroparity, in which reproduction occurs in some individuals in the population every year but other individuals reproduce less often. They called this behavior "low frequency of reproduction" (LFR) and suggested that it would most often be found in animals incapable of producing more than one clutch per year and having some accessory activity associated with reproduction (e.g., breeding migrations, egg brooding, or bearing live young). The turtle species mentioned above exhibit no known accessory activity as defined by Bull and Shine (1979), and studies of *Chrysemys picta* (Tinkle et al., 1981), *Kinosternon subrubrum* (Gibbons, 1983), *D. reticularia* (Gibbons, 1969), and *T. scripta* (see Chapter 9) indicate that some individuals can produce two clutches per year. Some important goals of future research will be to identify the proximate causes of clutch frequency (Congdon and Tinkle, 1982a) and to clarify how age, age at maturity, and body size relate to the frequency that individuals in a population have second clutches or skip reproduction. These data are critical to testing models that relate fecundity to the evolution of age at maturity (hypotheses 1, 2, and 3) and to defining the type of iteroparity (clutch interval) that occurs in turtles (hypotheses 4 and 5).

CLUTCH SIZE AND FECUNDITY

An animal can increase immediate or annual fecundity in two ways: (1) by increasing clutch size with body size or age and (2) by increasing clutch frequency with body size or age. Lifetime fecundity can be increased by extending reproductive life without increasing annual fecundity. If larger body size of females is associated with increased age, then increased fecundity with age has often been demonstrated in reptiles as well as other organisms (hypothesis 1) through the positive correlation of larger clutch sizes with larger body sizes (Gibbons et al., 1982; Congdon and Gibbons, 1985). However, the assumption that body size and age are positively correlated in turtles has recently been questioned (see Indeterminant Growth, above).

EGG SIZE

Whereas a positive relationship of clutch size to body size frequently occurs in reptiles, a relationship between egg size and body size (or age?) occurs less often. Within most lizard species, clutch size, but not egg size, increases with body size (but see Stewart, 1979). However, in some species of turtles both clutch size and egg size increase with body size of females (hypotheses 1 and 2; *Chrysemys picta*—Congdon and Tinkle, 1982a; *Chelydra serpentina*—Congdon et al., 1987; *T. scripta*—Congdon and Gibbons, 1983). In no other species of turtles examined is the increase in egg size as pronounced as in *D. reticularia* (Congdon et al., 1983a; Congdon and Gibbons, 1987), in which approximately 75% of the increase in clutch mass associated with increased body size results from increased egg size. Egg size has been shown to be positively related to body size of hatchlings (Congdon et al., 1983a; also see Chapter 8). Although it has not been documented, larger hatchlings are believed to have higher survivorship than do smaller hatchlings. Therefore, increased egg size should be viewed as a mechanism by which animals with indeterminant growth can increase the quality of their offspring that are produced later in life. The relationship of egg or offspring size to body size and age must be well documented to test hypothesis 2. In addition, data on the relationships among egg size, clutch size, body size, age at sexual maturity, and age of reproductive adults are necessary to determine if there are interactions among the benefits proposed in hypotheses 1 and 2.

The development of hypotheses 3, 4, and, by logical extension, 5 can generally be traced to the attempt by Cole (1954) to discover how great an increase in fitness (defined as r) is caused by reproducing more than once (iteroparity) rather than only once (semelparity) in a lifetime. In Cole's model the population age structure was assumed to be stable, and there was no mortality except that semelparous organisms died immediately after reproduction (i.e., the value of r depends on fecundity and age at maturity only). Murdoch (1966) criticized Cole's result as being too simplified. Gadgil and Bossert (1970) assumed that there was juvenile but no adult mortality, whereas Bryant (1971) assumed that adult and juvenile mortalities were equal. Charnov and Schaffer (1973) compared annual and perennial populations and emphasized the importance of keeping mortality of juveniles and adults separate. They concluded that the absolute gain in intrinsic population growth rate achieved by iteroparity was equivalent to adding to the average clutch size the number of individuals that is equal to the ratio of adult mortality rate to juvenile mortality rate. Thus, they predicted that iteroparity would be favored when adult survivorship is high relative to that of juveniles (hypothesis 4). Holgate (1967) and Murphy (1968) pointed out the problems an organism faces when juvenile mortality is highly variable and when there is a high probability that any given reproductive event may result in total failure (hypothesis 4).

SURVIVORSHIP AND LONGEVITY

Two studies have documented nest survivorship in freshwater turtles over six years in *Emydoidea blandingii* and over eight years in *Chelydra serpentina* (Congdon et al., 1983b, 1987). Nest mortality in Blanding's turtles ranged from 42% to 93%, with a mean of 67%, and in snapping turtles it ranged from 30% to 100%, with a mean of 70%. The primary predators of nests of both species are raccoons (*Procyon lotor*) and red foxes (*Vulpes vulpes*). Adults of both

species of turtles are seldom harmed by either predator.

Mortality rates of juvenile turtles are poorly known, despite their importance in population dynamics (Wilbur and Morin, 1988). Cumulative survivorship of a cohort of 125 *T. scripta* hatchlings to age 4 was 0.18; however, the majority of the mortality occurred between hatching and the end of the first year in the aquatic habitat (see Chapter 15).

Survivorship of adult turtles in most cases is high. Reports of annual survivorship include *Chelydra serpentina*, .93 to .97 (Galbraith and Brooks, 1987); *Chrysemys picta*, .76 to .83 (Wilbur, 1975a); *Geochelone gigantea*, .84 to .98 (Swingland and Lessells, 1979); *Terrapene carolina*, .85 to .94 (Stickel, 1978; Williams and Parker, 1987); *T. ornata*, .78 (Blair, 1976, in Wilbur and Morin, 1988); *Trachemys scripta*, .81 to .84 (see Chapter 15); and *Xerobates agassizii*, .98 (Turner and Berry, 1986). Although these survivorship rates are remarkable, it has been pointed out that even with annual survival rates of 90%, only 1 in 100 turtles would be alive after 44 years (Wilbur and Morin, 1988).

Although data on the relative survivorship of adults and juveniles are scarce, mortality rates of embryos in the nest and of first-year hatchlings are apparently much higher and more variable than those of adults (*Chrysemys picta*—Tinkle et al., 1981, and Wilbur, 1975a; *E. blandingii* and *Chelydra serpentina*—Congdon et al., 1983b, 1987; *T. scripta*—see Chapter 15). Thus, it appears that mortality of eggs, embryos, and juveniles is high relative to that of adults (hypothesis 4), and in the case of eggs and embryos mortality is probably more variable (hypothesis 5).

Little data exist on the longevity of turtles and on the survivorship of various age classes. Gibbons and Semlitsch (1982) have estimated that *Trachemys scripta* live to approximately 30 years of age, and individuals greater than 30 years old have been documented for populations of *Terrapene carolina* (Oliver, 1955; Stickel, 1978) and *T. ornata* (Blair, 1976). Data from the study by Woodbury and Hardy (1948) of the desert tortoise (*X. agassizii*) and past studies of Blanding's turtles (*E. blandingii*) on the E. S. George Reserve (Sexton, 1959a,b; Wilbur, 1975a,b; Congdon et al., 1983b) indicate that longevity may exceed 60 years in nature.

Because these studies clearly document that turtles can live a long time, it is appropriate to ask whether there is any substantive evidence for senescence in turtles. Moll (1979) and Dunham et al. (1988a) cite reports of senescence in three species of turtles: *Deirochelys reticularia* (Gibbons, 1969), *Terrapene ornata* (Legler, 1960a), and *Trachemys scripta* (Cagle, 1946). Cagle (1944c) examined 183 female *T. scripta* ranging from 70 to 260 mm in plastron length that had follicles greater or equal to 15 mm in diameter, and 138 females from 70 to 230 mm in plastron length that had follicles less than 15 mm in diameter. Cagle (1944c) stated: "It has been commonly assumed that fishes and reptiles remain reproductively active throughout their lives. The repeated observation of senile turtles has indicated that this is not true for the species considered here. Of 183 females examined, 7, ranging in size from 210 to 220 mm. and apparently of great age, contained senile ovaries." No explanation of the criteria used to make this assumption was given. Gibbons (1969) stated: "The absence of enlarged follicles in four of the five specimens [of *D. reticularia*] greater than 180 mm suggests the possibility of senility or a reduced reproductive rate in older individuals." However, it should be noted that a later assessment (Gibbons and Greene, 1978) based on an additional decade's worth of data and the use of x-radiography was that some females were not reproductively active in some years but were in subsequent ones. Legler (1960a) stated that for *Terrapene ornata* "one ovary may become senile in old females before its partner does; this may explain the occasional absence or atrophy of one ovary in large females that I have examined." Cagle, Gibbons, and Legler apparently assumed that size and age are correlated, an assumption that has been questioned in an analysis of *Trachemys scripta* (Gibbons, 1982). We conclude that in each of the above cases there was no compelling reason to evoke senescence as the cause of the absence of reproduction in a turtle in a given year.

Summary

A life history is a suite of coevolved characteristics that directly influence population parameters. Because turtles are among the longest-lived vertebrates, concepts related to senescence are of obvious interest because they may have had substantial impact on life history evolution. Two evolutionary theories of senescence—mutation accumulation and antagonistic pleiotropy—were examined for aspects that seemed important to life histories. Factors, such as age at death and indeterminant growth, that influence the ratio of early births to late births by females appear to be critical to the evolution of longevity. A positive correlation between age at maturity and estimates of longevity among species would appear to be more consistent with the antagonistic pleiotropy theory than with the mutation accumulation theory. However, both processes may play a role in determining the absolute life span of individuals. The protective shell, which has been present in fossil turtles since the Triassic period, about 200 million years ago, appears to have played a central role in allowing turtles to evolve longevity by (1) decreasing adult deaths due to extrinsic causes, (2) increasing the proportion of late births relative to early births, (3) allowing more adults to live long enough for senescence traits to become implicated in their deaths, and (4) permitting natural selection to act on age-of-onset modifiers, and suppression genes to act on traits of senescence. Indeterminant growth may also have been an important mecha-

nism allowing older, and thus larger, turtles to increase their reproductive output and, for some species, the quality of their offspring. However, variation in reproductive characteristics of *T. scripta* is more strongly correlated with body size than with age. Because body size plays an important role in determining the annual and lifetime reproductive output of turtles, and because age is implicated in almost all theories of life history evolution, the cause of the apparent discrepancy between individual and population traits in some turtles needs investigation.

At present, theories (r- and K-selection, demographic, and bet-hedging) that attempt to predict associations of life history characteristics based on a single selective factor have not been notably successful. More-specific theories that attempt to predict the direction of selection on a single trait (such as age at sexual maturity, iteroparity, or quality of young) seem to hold more promise. Turtles appear to have many traits that make them good models for tests of these theories:

1. Turtles can be individually marked, and the mark is relatively permanent throughout their lives.
2. They occur at population densities that provide adequate numbers of marked individuals and are still manageable in field situations.
3. For many species, early ages can be determined from growth rings laid down in their shells.
4. Turtles reproduce more than once in their lifetimes, and some reproduce more than once in a single season.
5. Both clutch size and egg size increase with body size in some species.
6. All turtles produce eggs with calcified shells that allow their reproductive output to be determined nondestructively and repeatedly by x-radiography.

Recent advances in the area of ultrasound tomography, telemetry, and the use of lipid-soluble gases to determine whole-body lipid levels should help answer questions about age-specific resource allocation patterns that are important in understanding life histories.

Many estimates of survivorship of adults are greater than .90, and some estimates are as high as .97. Even with survivorships of .90, only 1 in 100 turtles would be alive after 44 years. Reliable records of turtles living more than 60 years in the wild indicate that adult survivorships are indeed that high or higher. For some species, reproductive life span may exceed 30 years; however, there are apparently no convincing data that reproductive senility occurs in turtles. Several factors make it extremely difficult to collect reliable evidence for senility in turtles. First, even with high adult survivorships, few very old individuals will exist in a population, so the potential source of data is low. Second, turtles are not social animals, so they cannot affect the fitness of their offspring after the first year of life. Therefore, natural selection should favor postponement of senescence in an individual only during its reproductive life, and reproductive failure and death should be closely linked in time. Third, variability in clutch size and clutch frequency due to proximate causes such as resource availability would affect all age groups and, because the number of old individuals is small, might mask variations in reproductive parameters that are due to senescence.

We believe that long-term field research documenting variation in life history characteristics of turtles both within and among individuals will continue to provide new insights into life history processes of long-lived organisms. Such insights can become the basis for tests of current life history theories and will eventually lead to the develop-

ment of new theories based on a more comprehensive understanding of life history processes.

Acknowledgments

We thank the following individuals for comments and discussions that improved early drafts of this manuscript: John Aho, Roger Anderson, Robert Fischer, Trip Lamb, and David Scott. Research and manuscript preparation were aided by National Science Foundation grants DEB-79-06031 and BSR-84-00861 to Justin D. Congdon and DEB-79-04758 to J. Whitfield Gibbons, as well as contract DE-AC09-76SROO-819 between the University of Georgia and the U.S. Department of Energy.

Taxonomic
Status and
Genetics

CARL H. ERNST
Department of Biology
George Mason University
4400 University Drive
Fairfax, Virginia 22030

4

Systematics, Taxonomy, Variation, and Geographic Distribution of the Slider Turtle

Abstract

The slider turtle, *Trachemys scripta*, has had a controversial nomenclatural history. Although it was originally separated from the genera *Chrysemys* and *Pseudemys*, subsequent taxonomists at one time considered all three to be congeneric, placing them in the genus *Chrysemys*. The genus has been subdivided more than once to form the *Pseudemys* complex (including slider turtles) and *Chrysemys picta*. Recent work suggests that the slider turtle is indeed different from the other genera, thus warranting resurrection of *Trachemys*. In spite of the nomenclatural stability currently enjoyed by the genus, the presence of 14 presumed subspecies on two continents, coupled with extreme variation in morphology and behavior, suggests the need for more systematic work in this group.

Introduction

The slider, *Trachemys scripta*, is probably the best-known turtle in the world, because of its popularity in the North American and European pet trade and its frequent use as a subject of physiological and ecological studies. Despite this familiarity, it has had a controversial taxonomy, at least at the generic level. In the following chapter, discussion of its systematic position is presented, along with a description and analysis of geographic variation.

Systematics

Trachemys scripta, with many of the other semiaquatic turtles in North America, belongs to the family Emydidae. This family is the largest and most diverse of living turtles, with 33 genera and almost 90 species (the exact number is debatable). Emydids are found in the Americas, Europe,

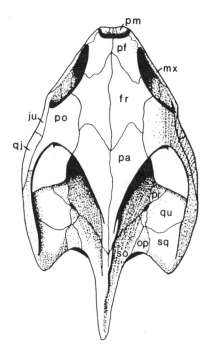

FIGURE 4.1. Dorsal skull bones of *Trachemys scripta: fr*, frontal; *ju*, jugal; *mx*, maxillary; *op*, paroccipital; *pa*, parietal; *pf*, prefrontal; *pm*, premaxillary; *po*, postorbital; *pr*, pro-otic; *qj*, quadratojugal; *qu*, quadrate; *so*, supraoccipital; *sq*, squamosal. (Drawing by Evelyn M. Ernst)

northern Africa, Asia, Indonesia, and the Philippines. Fossils indicate that the family was formerly more widespread in Europe and Asia. The oldest known fossils are from Paleocene deposits in Saskatchewan (Russell, 1934) and Eocene deposits in Europe, North America, and Asia (Romer, 1956).

Emydid turtles share several osteological characters. The skull is relatively small and is similar to that of tortoises (Testudinidae). The temporal region is widely emarginated posteriorly, so the squamosal is not in contact with the parietal (Fig. 4.1). The frontal bone enters the orbit, and the postorbital is wider than in the Testudinidae. The maxilla and quadratojugal are separated, and the quadrate is open posteriorly so as not to completely surround the stapes. A splenial bone is usually absent but may be present and vestigial. Additional diagnostic characters and descriptions are given by McDowell (1964) and Bramble (1974).

There is much diversity among members of the Emydidae, but two major groupings are generally recognized: the subfamilies Batagurinae, or Old World pond turtles, and Emydinae, or New World pond turtles, including the slider turtle (McDowell, 1964).

The subfamily Emydinae includes 10 genera and 34 species. With the exception of the genus *Emys,* which occurs in Europe, northern Africa, and the Middle East, emydines range from Canada to central South America and the West Indies. Emydine turtles have the angular

bone of the lower jaw in contact with Meckel's cartilage. The basioccipital is narrow, is separated from the paracapsular sac and pterygoid, lacks a lateral tuberosity, and does not form the floor of the tympanic cavity. Emydines also have a double articulation between the centra of cervical vertebrae V and VI, and the suture between the 12th marginal scutes and 5th vertebral scute lies over the pygal bone, not over the suprapygal.

McDowell (1964) and Bramble (1974) recognized two generic complexes within the subfamily Emydinae. The more primitive of these, the *Clemmys* complex, includes the genera *Clemmys, Emydoidea, Emys,* and *Terrapene.* The plastron of *Clemmys* is rigid, but that of the other three genera is hinged and movable. *Clemmys* is thought to be ancestral to the hinged forms, of which *Emys* is most primitive, *Emydoidea* intermediate, and *Terrapene* the most derived (Bramble, 1974). These turtles have the triturating surfaces of the jaws narrow and ridgeless, with the upper triturating surface lacking portions of the palatine or the pterygoid bone. The orbitonasal foramen is small. The interorbital region is coarsely sculptured, and the postorbital bar is relatively wide. The jugal bone does not touch the palatine. On the plastron the humeropectoral seam crosses the entoplastron. The cervical vertebrae are not elongated in *Clemmys, Emys,* and *Terrapene,* but they are in *Emydoidea,* in which also the cervical extensor muscles are hypertrophied. Musk glands are present in all four genera.

The second generic complex, the *Chrysemys* complex, includes the freshwater genera *Chrysemys, Deirochelys, Graptemys, Pseudemys, Trachemys,* and the brackish-water genus *Malaclemys.* All have a rigid plastron with the humeropectoral seam crossing posterior to the entoplastron. The triturating surface of the jaw is usually broad (narrow in *Deirochelys*), with or without ridges, and with the upper surface composed of portions of the palatine or the pterygoid (except in *Deirochelys*). The nasopalatine foramen is usually much larger than the posterior palatine foramen (not as large in *Deirochelys*). Coarse sculpturing is absent from the interorbital region of the skull, and the postorbital bar is narrow. The jugal is in contact with the palatine. Except in *Deirochelys,* the cervical vertebrae are not elongated, nor are the cervical extensor muscles hypertrophied. Musk glands are absent. A good general summary of the *Chrysemys* complex is presented by Obst (1985).

Trachemys Agassiz, 1857 (Slider Turtles)

The slider turtles were first assigned to the genus *Testudo,* a catchall grouping of turtles (Lacépède, 1788-89; Schoepff, 1792), and later placed with other freshwater emydid turtles in the nebulous genus *Emys* by Gray (1831). There they remained until 1857, when Agassiz separated the sliders from the cooters and the painted turtle. He proposed that sliders be placed in the genus *Trachemys* (including the species group *scripta* and all West Indian and neotropical species), the cooters in *Pseudemys* (including the *floridana*, *concinna*, and *rubriventris* species groups), and the painted turtle in *Chrysemys* (*picta*). This arrangement gained little support, and Cope (1875) placed the sliders with the cooters in the genus *Pseudemys*. However, Boulenger (1889) combined sliders, cooters, and the painted turtle under the name *Chrysemys*. Boulenger's designation was not readily accepted, and the designation of *Pseudemys* and *Chrysemys* proposed by Cope (1875) prevailed until 1964.

McDowell (1964) revised the emydine genera on the basis of cranial, lower jaw, and foot morphology and included in *Chrysemys* the painted turtle and the cooter and slider turtles of the genus *Pseudemys* (sensu Cope, 1875). He concluded that the placement of both the cooters and the sliders in the genus *Pseudemys* was unnatural because *Pseudemys* is more divergent from *Trachemys* than is *Chrysemys picta*. He concluded that all of these turtles should either be assigned to the genus *Chrysemys* (sensu Boulenger, 1889) or be placed in three separate genera, *Pseudemys*, *Trachemys*, and *Chrysemys* (as proposed by Agassiz, 1857). McDowell compromised by suggesting subgeneric status for the three groups under the genus *Chrysemys*. Similarities in the choanal structure of *C. picta* and various species of *Pseudemys* upheld both the placement of *Pseudemys* within the genus *Chrysemys* and McDowell's subgeneric distinctions (Parsons, 1968). Zug (1966) found little difference in the penial structure of *C. picta*, *P. nelsoni*, *P. floridana*, and *P. concinna*, strengthening the inclusion of *Pseudemys* in *Chrysemys*.

On the basis of the anatomical data presented by McDowell (1964), Zug (1966), and Parsons (1968), some researchers accepted a polytypic, all-inclusive *Chrysemys* (Weaver and Rose, 1967; Ernst and Barbour, 1972; Conant, 1975; Obst, 1985). However, other investigators sharply criticized this arrangement (Holman, 1977; Legler, pers. com.). There was relatively little opposition to the subgeneric arrangement of McDowell (1964), except by Weaver and Rose (1967), but there was strong disagreement with the treatment of sliders, cooters, and painted turtle as congeners.

Rose and Weaver (1966) and Weaver and Robertson (1967) did not accept the validity of *Trachemys*. Rose and Weaver reported that the Pliocene fossil *Chrysemys carri* (= *P. caelata* Hay) from Florida had a shell like a *Pseudemys* (*P. nelsoni*) but a mandible nearly identical to that of *Trachemys scripta*, thus showing the two groups to be identical. They concluded that the correct generic designation would be the older name *Pseudemys* Gray, 1855. However, Jackson (1976) has shown that the mandible of *C. carri* (= *P. caelata* Hay) more closely resembles that of either *P. floridana* or *P. concinna*. Rose and Weaver (1966) also described another Pliocene fossil, *Chrysemys williamsi*, as

intermediate between *Pseudemys* and *Trachemys*, but its description was based on incomplete shells.

Holman (1977) expressed doubts about the status of McDowell's (1964) all-inclusive genus *Chrysemys*. Holman pointed out that under McDowell's concept, as many as four species may occur in the same water body in the southeastern United States (e.g., Reelfoot Lake, Tennessee), but there are no records of hybridization between *Chrysemys picta* and other species of *Chrysemys* (sensu McDowell, 1964). However, hybrids have been reported within the subgenus *Pseudemys*: *C. floridana* × *C. concinna* (Smith, 1961; Mount, 1975; Fahey, 1980) and *C. floridana* × *C. rubriventris* (Crenshaw, 1965). Recent studies on host-parasite relationships by Ernst and Ernst (1980) and protein electrophoresis by Vogt and McCoy (1980) have indicated that the species of *Pseudemys* (sensu Cope, 1875) and *Chrysemys picta* represent separate evolutionary lineages. Ward (1984), Seidel and Inchaustegui Miranda (1984), and Seidel and Smith (1986) have returned to the three-genus arrangement of Agassiz (1857): *Trachemys*, *Pseudemys*, and *Chrysemys*.

Seidel and Smith (1986) presented a survey table of shared-unshared character states in *Graptemys* (including *Malaclemys*), *Trachemys*, *Chrysemys*, *Pseudemys*, and *Deirochelys* as evidence to support the partitioning of *Pseudemys* (sensu Cope, 1875) into the genera *Pseudemys* (cooters) and *Trachemys* (sliders). As is revealed in the table, many of the shared characters that were previously cited as evidence for recognition of an all-inclusive *Chrysemys* or *Pseudemys*, which includes both sliders and cooters, are also present in *Graptemys*. *Chrysemys* and *Pseudemys* share only 9 character states, and *Graptemys* and *Trachemys* share 19. When all available data sets are considered, divergence among *Trachemys*, *Pseudemys*, and *Chrysemys* appears to be as great as their collective distance from *Graptemys*. Also, the apparently complete reproductive isolation between these groups (see above) supports this conclusion. For these reasons the slider turtle is considered to belong to the genus *Trachemys*, *T. scripta*, by most authors in this book. The reader is referred to Seidel and Smith (1986) and Chapter 5 for a more comprehensive discussion.

Turtles of the genus *Trachemys* are predominantly freshwater in habitat preference (Morreale and Gibbons, 1986) but may enter brackish coastal waters. Five extant species are included: *T. decussata*, *T. stejnegeri*, and *T. terrapen* of the West Indies; the South American *T. dorbigni*; and *T. scripta* of the New World mainland from North America to northern South America.

All have elongated oval carapaces (to about 60 cm in greatest straight-line length; Obst, 1985) that are strongly serrated posteriorly. A vertebral keel is usually present, as is also a series of low longitudinal ridges, which give the carapace a rugged appearance. The seams that separate the vertebral scutes alternate with those separating the pleural scutes; they are never aligned, as occurs in some

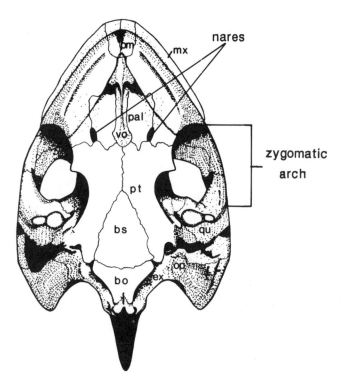

FIGURE 4.2.   Ventral skull bones of *Trachemys scripta: bo,* basioccipital; *bs,* basisphenoid; *ex,* exoccipital; *mx,* maxillary; *op,* paroccipital; *pal,* palatine; *pm,* premaxillary; *pt,* pterygoid; *qu,* quadrate; *vo,* vomer. (Drawing by Evelyn M. Ernst)

populations of *Chrysemys picta.* The plastron is broad and posteriorly notched, lacks a movable hinge, and is firmly united to the carapace by a well-developed bridge. The cranium is relatively shallow anterior to the basisphenoid (30% to 34% of the condylobasal length), and the zygomatic arch and narial openings are relatively narrow (Fig. 4.2). The orbits are located anterolaterally. The pterygoid often extends posteriorly to near the exoccipital, and the crista praetemporalis is larger than in most emydines. The maxilla does not touch the squamosal. The triturating surface of the maxilla is broad, with a medial ridge that lacks tuberculate denticles. Also, no cusps or serrations occur on the outer cutting edge of the upper jaw, but there is a shallow medial notch. The triturating surface of the lower jaw is also narrow and lacks tuberculate denticles. The lower surface of the dentary is rounded when viewed from the front (it is flat in *Pseudemys*). Three phalanges occur in the fifth toe.

Trachemys scripta (Schoepff, 1792)

DIAGNOSIS

A medium-sized to large emydine (adults have carapaces 20–60 cm; Obst, 1985) with a prominent patch (or patches) of red, orange, or yellow on each side of the head and a rounded lower jaw. Because the species consists of several subspecies, the following description is general.

The oval carapace is weakly keeled and has a slightly serrated posterior rim. A series of low longitudinal ridges or wrinkles may lie along the pleural scutes. The carapace is highest at the third vertebral scute and broadest at the level of the eighth marginals. The cervical scute is rectangular or slightly triangular in shape; it may be narrow or broad, and the anterior margin is indented past the rims of the adjacent marginal scutes. The first vertebral scute is either longer than broad or as long as broad. The posterior four vertebrals are usually broader than long. Vertebral I has straight parallel sides. The sides of vertebrals II through IV converge to points where they meet the seams separating the pleural scutes; the sides of vertebral V diverge toward the rear. Four pleural scutes are present on each side. Pleural I is the broadest, pleural II the highest, and pleural IV the smallest. Twelve marginal scutes border the carapace on each side. The anterior marginals are flared, those most posterior are serrated, and those lying along the sides are only slightly flared in adults. The marginals above the bridge are the lowest.

The carapace is olive to brown, with yellow markings that vary geographically from stripes and bars to reticulations or ocelli. The markings on the marginal scutes also are variable but usually take the form of a dark blotch partly surrounded by a light band. Melanism is prevalent in the older males of some populations (see Chapter 19).

Carapacial bones (Fig. 4.3) consist of 7 to 9 (usually 8) middorsal, hexagonal-shaped neurals with their shortest side anterior (neural I may be tetragonal in some individuals, and occasionally the other neurals may be octagonal or heptagonal); 8 pairs of costals; and 11 pairs of pe-

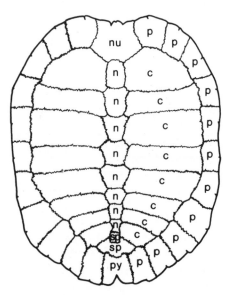

FIGURE 4.3.   Carapacial bones of *Trachemys scripta: c,* costal; *n,* neural; *nu,* nuchal; *p,* peripheral; *py,* pygal; *sp,* suprapygal. (Drawing by Evelyn M. Ernst)

ripherals. Ten dorsal vertebrae are firmly united dorsally with the carapace, but the two sacral vertebrae are not, although the anterior-most is connected to the ilia of the pelvic girdle via ribs.

The large hingeless plastron is slightly broader anteriorly than posteriorly. It is convex anteriorly but bears a shallow posterior notch. The bridge is broad, usually measuring 33% to 40% of the carapace length. The usual plastral scute formula is

$$\text{abdominal} > \text{anal} > \text{femoral} > < \text{gular}$$
$$> < \text{pectoral} > \text{humeral}$$

but much variation occurs. There are large axillary and inguinal scutes on the bridge. The plastron is yellow in ground color and exhibits a pattern that varies geographically from no pattern or only a single blotch on each scute to an extensive pattern covering most of the plastron. Bridge markings vary from dark blotches to elongated black bars.

The plastron is extensively sutured to the carapace along the broad bridge. The axillary and inguinal buttresses are moderate in length and well developed. The axillary is ankylosed to the first costal bone, the inguinal to the fifth costal. The large entoplastron is situated anterior to the humeropectoral seam and is covered by both the gular and the humeral scutes (Fig. 4.4).

The rounded head is moderate in size, with a protruding snout (more so in males of some tropical subspecies) and a medially notched upper jaw. The dorsal surface is flattened or concave and is covered with smooth skin. The supratemporal and orbitomandibular stripes are conspicuous; a postorbital stripe of red, orange, or yellow is usually present; and a prefrontal arrow is formed as the supratemporal stripes pass forward from the eyes to meet a median saggital stripe on top of the snout. A dark stripe runs through the greenish-to-yellow eye, and the tomia are usually yellow.

The skull is shortened and extensively emarginated posteriorly and behind the maxilla. The supraoccipital is elongated, unflanged, and pointed. The maxilla and quadratojugal are usually separated by the jugal. Nasal bones are absent. The triturating surfaces of the jaws are narrow and lack elaborate serrations, but a median ridge does occur on the maxilla. There is no corresponding ridge on the lower jaw. The orbit has a larger diameter than the tympanum (Fig. 4.5).

The neck is olive to brown, with cream-colored-to-yellow stripes. A Y-shaped mark is usually present on the chin, and ocelli may occur on both the chin and the jaws. The limbs are also olive to brown, and the forelimbs bear a variable pattern of light stripes, whorls, or ocelli, whereas the hind limbs bear stripes or dots. The posterior surface of the thigh usually has a pattern of yellow vertical bars on each side of the tail. The first and fifth toes on all feet have

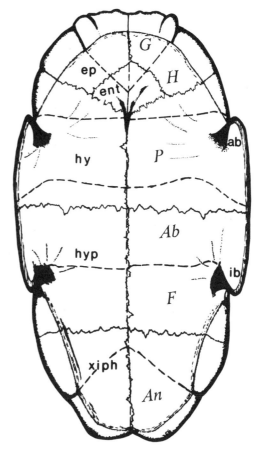

FIGURE 4.4. Plastral bones of *Trachemys scripta* (dorsal view): *ab*, axillary buttress; *ent*, entoplastron; *ep*, epiplastron; *hy*, hyoplastron; *hyp*, hypoplastron; *ib*, inguinal buttress; *xiph*, xiphiplastron. Dashed lines show position of plastral scutes: *Ab*, abdominal; *An*, anal; *F*, femoral; *G*, gular; *H*, humeral; *P*, pectoral. (Drawing by Evelyn M. Ernst)

two phalanges each, whereas the other three toes have three phalanges each. The toes are webbed.

Adult males are smaller and may have elongated, curved foreclaws (or an elongated snout in tropical populations) and long, thick tails, with the vent posterior to the

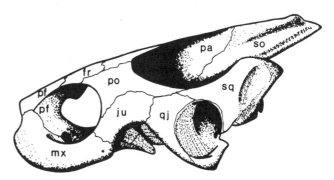

FIGURE 4.5. Lateral skull bones of *Trachemys scripta*: *fr*, frontal; *ju*, jugal; *mx*, maxillary; *pa*, parietal; *pf*, prefrontal; *po*, postorbital; *qj*, quadratojugal; *so*, supraoccipital; *sq*, squamosal. (Drawing by Evelyn M. Ernst)

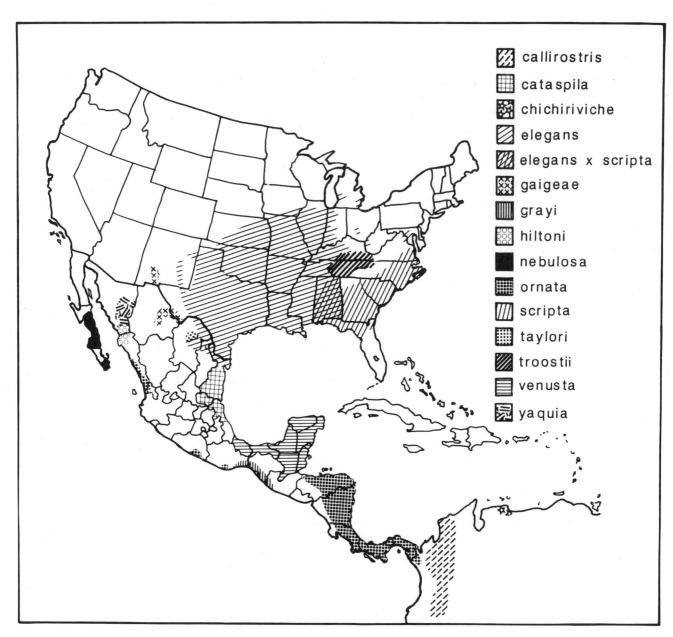

FIGURE 4.6.   Distribution of the various subspecies of *Trachemys scripta*.

carapacial rim. The karyotype contains 50 diploid chromosomes, 26 macrochromosomes (16 metacentric, 6 submetacentric, and 4 telocentric), and 24 microchromosomes (Stock, 1972; Killebrew, 1977).

DISTRIBUTION

Trachemys scripta occurs in the United States from southeastern Virginia south to northern Florida and west to Kansas, Oklahoma, and New Mexico; thence it ranges through Mexico and Central America to Venezuela (Fig. 4.6).

Formerly, juvenile *T. scripta* appeared in great numbers in the baby-turtle trade. In fact, at one time it was the

most popular pet turtle in North America and Europe. It is a hardy species that does well in captivity and, to the chagrin of some pet owners, may grow to be large. Consequently, many have been released into water bodies well beyond the species' natural range, and in those areas that have a sufficiently long summer in which its eggs can fully develop, *T. scripta* has become established. Populations of introduced sliders have been reported from Michigan, Pennsylvania, New Jersey (Ernst and Barbour, 1972; Conant, 1975; Manchester, 1982), and even Great Britain and Japan. A large reproducing colony outside the species' natural range occurs in the ponds of the United States National Arboretum in Washington, D.C. The taxonomy of some of these introduced populations can be

FIGURE 4.7. *Trachemys scripta scripta*. (Photo by Roger W. Barbour)

FIGURE 4.8. *Trachemys scripta elegans*. (Photo by Roger W. Barbour)

quite confusing. If more than one subspecies has been released at the same site, the resulting intergradation can produce individuals with unusual pigment patterns (Ernst and Jett, 1969).

Although *T. scripta* prefers quiet waters with soft bottoms, an abundance of aquatic vegetation, and suitable basking sites, the species occupies most freshwater habitats within its range (Morreale and Gibbons, 1986). In the tropics, *T. scripta* occupies fluvial waterways more often than it does in North America.

GEOGRAPHIC VARIATION

Trachemys scripta has been recognized as the most variable of all turtles; 14 subspecies have been described and named. *Trachemys scripta scripta* (Schoepff, 1792), with a maximum size (carapace length) of 28 cm, ranges from southeastern Virginia to northern Florida. It has a wide vertical yellow bar on each pleural scute, a conspicuous yellow postorbital blotch that may join a neck stripe (Fig. 4.7), and a yellow plastron, which usually has ocelli or smudges only on the anterior-most scutes.

T. s. elegans (Wied, 1839), maximum size 28 cm, occupies the Mississippi Valley from Illinois to the Gulf of Mexico. It has a wide red postorbital stripe, narrow chin stripes, a transverse yellow bar on each pleural, and a plastral pattern consisting of a dark blotch or an ocellus on each scute (Fig. 4.8).

T. s. troostii (Holbrook, 1836), maximum size 21 cm, occurs in the upper portions of the Cumberland and Tennessee rivers, from southeastern Kentucky to northeastern Alabama. It has a narrow yellow postorbital stripe (Fig. 4.9), broad chin stripes, a transverse yellow bar on each pleural scute, and a plastral pattern of ocelli or small black smudges.

T. s. gaigeae (Hartweg, 1939), maximum size 22 cm, is

found in the Rio Grande (Big Bend and above) and Río Conchos drainages of Texas, New Mexico, Chihuahua, and Coahuila. It has a reticulate carapacial pattern, often with small ocelli, and an oval, black-bordered red-to-orange spot behind the eye and well separated from it (Fig. 4.10). The chin is striped medially, with the lateral stripes shortened to ovals that are almost ocelli, and a plastral pattern that varies from a large blotch on each scute to a large dark central figure spreading out along the transverse seams.

T. s. taylori (Legler, 1960b), maximum size 22 cm, occurs only in the Cuatro Ciénegas Basin of Coahuila, Mexico. It resembles *T. s. elegans* and has a supratemporal stripe that terminates abruptly on the neck behind an expanded red, very elongated postorbital stripe; an extensive black plastral pattern with all parts interconnected; small, scattered, elongate or ovoid dark spots on the

FIGURE 4.9. *Trachemys scripta troostii*. (Photo by Roger W. Barbour)

FIGURE 4.10. *Trachemys scripta gaigeae*. (Photo by Roger W. Barbour)

FIGURE 4.11. *Trachemys scripta venusta*.

carapace; and the pectoral midseam longer than that of the gular.

T. s. cataspila (Günther, 1885), maximum size 22 cm, occurs on the Gulf coastal plain of Mexico from northern Tamaulipas to the vicinity of Punta del Morro, Veracruz. The yellow supratemporal stripe is wide on the temples, and it has dark-centered ocelli on the pleurals and marginals, and a medial plastral figure that does not extend along the interanal seam to the rear edge of the anals.

T. s. venusta (Gray, 1855), maximum size 48 cm, ranges from the city of Veracruz, Mexico, through Honduras (including the Yucatán Peninsula) in Atlantic and Gulf drainages. The dark-centered ocelli on the pleural scutes are very large (Fig. 4.11a), its supratemporal stripe reaches the eye, and the seam-following plastral pattern is extensive (Fig. 4.11b).

T. s. yaquia (Legler and Webb, 1970), maximum size 31 cm, inhabits the lower portions of the Sonora, Yaqui, and Mayo drainages in Sonora, Mexico. The postorbital mark is yellowish orange and only moderately expanded, the pleural scutes have only poorly defined ocelli with jagged black centers, and the medial plastral mark is extensive but faded in adults.

T. s. hiltoni (Carr, 1942), maximum size 28 cm, is restricted to the Río Fuerte drainage in Sonora and Sinaloa, Mexico. The orange postorbital portion of the supratemporal stripe either is isolated anteriorly and posteriorly or is connected posteriorly with a narrow orbital stripe; there are black smudgelike spots on the upper and lower surfaces of each lateral and posterior marginal scute and some pleural scutes; and the plastron has a dark central blotch surrounding a narrow yellow medial area.

T. s. nebulosa (Van Denburgh, 1895), maximum size 37 cm, occurs in freshwater bodies in southern Baja California, Mexico. The orange or yellow supratemporal stripe does not reach the eye and ends as a large oval postorbital spot well behind the eye; the carapace usually lacks ocelli but may have a pattern of black spots and irregular light marks; and the plastron bears a series of smudgelike medial blotches.

T. s. ornata (Gray, 1831), maximum size 38 cm, occurs on the Pacific coastal plain of Mexico from northern Sinaloa to central Oaxaca at low altitudes, and from Guatemala through Central America to Colombia. The orange postorbital stripe usually starts at the orbit, is expanded over the temple, and continues to the neck; the carapace has dark-centered ocelli on the pleurals; and the plastral pattern consists of four concentric, faded medial lines that do not extend to the anal notch.

T. s. grayi (Bocourt, 1868), maximum size 60 cm (Obst, 1985), occurs from the Pacific coastal plain of Tehuantepec, Mexico, southeastward to Departamento La Libertad, Guatemala (Fig. 4.12a). The yellow supratemporal stripe reaches the eye, all head stripes are narrow, the carapace has dark-centered ocelli on the pleurals and marginals, and the plastral figure is diffused, fragmented, and faded in adults (Fig. 4.12b).

FIGURE 4.12. *Trachemys scripta grayi: a*, male with elongated snout; *b*, plastron.

FIGURE 4.13. *Trachemys scripta callirostris*. (Photos by Roger W. Barbour)

T. s. callirostris (Gray, 1855), maximum size 25 cm, lives in the Caribbean drainages of Colombia and Venezuela. It is easily recognized by these characters: the large number of ocelli on the underside of the snout and on the upper and lower jaws; the broad, reddish, parallel-sided supratemporal stripe well separated from the orbit (Fig. 4.13*a*); the pattern of ocelli on the carapace; and the extensive pattern of dark lines that cover most of the plastron (Fig. 4.13*b*).

T. s. chichiriviche (Pritchard and Trebbau, 1984), maximum size 32.5 cm, inhabits the small coastal drainages between the Río Tocuyo and Morón in northern Venezuela. It also has ocelli on the chin but has a brownish red wedge-shaped supratemporal stripe well separated from the orbit (Fig. 4.14*a*), oval or irregular black pleural blotches, and a narrow dark pattern along the plastral midseam (sometimes diffuse in adults, Fig. 4.14*b*).

Several additional populations may eventually be designated as subspecies. Moll and Legler (1971) reported the following areas with populations that represent unnamed forms: (1) Río Nazas drainage of Durango and

Coahuila, Mexico; (2) *aguadas* and cenotes in the northern half of the Yucatán Peninsula; (3) region of Cabo Gracias a Dios, Nicaragua, to the Isthmus of Panama and the Río Atrato of Colombia; (4) Lakes Managua and Nicaragua and their tributaries; and (5) Río Terraba of Costa Rica to the Río Bayano and Chucunaque drainages of eastern Panama. (See Chapter 7.)

Three combinations of sexually dimorphic characters occur in male *T. scripta* from the various subspecies (see Moll and Legler, 1971). Males of the North American races *scripta, elegans,* and *troostii* have elongated foreclaws but lack an elongated snout. Male *gaigeae* and *taylori* have neither the snout nor the foreclaws elongated. Males of the other nine subspecies have elongated snouts but lack elongated foreclaws. In view of this variability in dimorphic characters, as well as the differences in size and in carapace, plastron, and head patterns, it is possible that two or more species are involved in this variable group. In addition, two courtship patterns exist, depending on whether the males possess elongated foreclaws. If elongated foreclaws are present, as in subspecies like *T. s.*

elegans, the male swims to a position in front of the female, turns to face her, extends his forelegs with palms outward, and strokes her face with his foreclaws (Jackson and Davis, 1972). If the male lacks elongated foreclaws, as in subspecies like *T. s. taylori,* he does not swim in front of the female but instead pursues her and vigorously bites the posterior rim of her shell, her hind legs, and her tail (Davis and Jackson, 1973). No courtship function has been ascribed to the long snout of the neotropical forms, but it could be assumed that such a function might exist in such a sexually dimorphic character.

FIGURE 4.14. *Trachemys scripta chichiriviche.*

Key to the Subspecies of *Trachemys scripta*

1a. Supratemporal light stripe does not reach the orbit →2
 b. Supratemporal light stripe reaches the orbit →6
2a. Pleural scutes with reticulate pattern of light lines; large, black-bordered orange postorbital spot →*gaigeae* (Fig. 4.10)
 b. Pleural scutes with pattern of ocelli or dark spots; postorbital orange or red mark either small and isolated or large and elongated →3
3a. Postorbital blotch small and isolated →*hiltoni*
 b. Postorbital blotch large and elongated posteriorly →4
4a. Each pleural scute with a dark spot →*nebulosa*
 b. Each pleural scute with a dark-centered ocellus →5
5a. Plastral figure a broad series of concentric dark lines; postorbital red stripe approximately parallel-sided →*callirostris* (Fig. 4.13)
 b. Plastral figure narrow, clustered tightly about midline; postorbital red stripe strongly wedge-shaped with the pointed end anteriad →*chichiriviche* (Fig. 4.14)
6a. Pleural scute pattern consisting predominantly of transverse light bars →7
 b. Pleural scutes with ocelli →9
7a. A conspicuous yellow postorbital blotch that turns downward anteriorly; a mostly immaculate plastron with dark marks restricted to the anterior scutes →*scripta* (Fig. 4.7)
 b. Red or yellow postorbital stripe does not turn downward anteriorly; each plastral scute with a dark ocellus or blotch →8
8a. Wide red postorbital stripe; narrow chin stripes →*elegans* (Fig. 4.8)
 b. Narrow yellow postorbital stripe; broad chin stripes →*troostii* (Fig. 4.9)
9a. Broad red postorbital stripe ending abruptly on the neck →*taylori*
 b. Red, yellow, or orange postorbital stripe continuing along neck →10

10a. Dark-centered ocellus in posterolateral corner of second pleural; medial chin stripe interrupted before forking posteriorly →*cataspila*

   b. Ocellus on second pleural positioned posterocentrally or posteromedially; medial chin stripe may not be interrupted before forking posteriorly →12

11a. Pleural ocelli large and light-centered →*venusta* (Fig. 4.11)

   b. Pleural ocelli small and dark-centered →12

12a. Pleural ocelli poorly developed, with irregularly shaped dark centers; plastral pattern indistinct →*yaquia*

   b. Pleural ocelli well developed, with round dark centers; plastral pattern distinct →13

13a. Postorbital stripe orange to red, expanded over the temple; pleural ocelli with branching interconnections; plastral pattern consisting of four concentric medial lines; medial chin stripe interrupted posteriorly →*ornata*

   b. Postorbital stripe yellow, little expanded over the temple; pleural ocelli without branching interconnection; plastral pattern diffuse and fragmented in older individuals; medial chin stripe forked posteriorly →*grayi* (Fig. 4.12)

Conclusion

Although the taxonomic status of the genus *Trachemys* appears to have stabilized for now, much work remains to determine the validity of present subspecific designations. The extreme variation exhibited by this adaptable group of turtles, both morphologically and behaviorally, surely warrants further investigation.

MICHAEL E. SEIDEL
Department of Biological Sciences
Marshall University
Huntington, West Virginia 25701

DALE R. JACKSON
Florida Natural Areas Inventory
The Nature Conservancy
254 E. Sixth Avenue
Tallahassee, Florida 32303

5

Evolution and Fossil Relationships of Slider Turtles

Abstract

Slider turtles belong to the genus *Trachemys,* which includes *T. scripta* and four insular species endemic to the Caribbean region. Based on overall comparisons of morphology, biochemistry, and ecology, sliders appear most similar to map turtles, genus *Graptemys.* However, phylogenetic analysis suggests that sliders, map turtles, cooters (*Pseudemys*), and terrapins (*Malaclemys*) are all closely related and form a monophyletic group (clade). This relationship, as well as similarities between sliders and painted turtles (*Chrysemys*), is supported by electrophoretic evidence. Fossil skulls recently assigned to *Trachemys* have contributed to our knowledge of the evolutionary history of sliders. Based on available fossil material, three extinct species of *Trachemys* are tentatively considered to be valid: *T. idahoensis* Gilmore from late Pliocene, and *T. inflata* Weaver and Robertson and *T. hillii* (Cope) from the Upper Miocene. *Trachemys inflata* is a highly specialized form that appears divergent from the lineage leading to extant *Trachemys.* The progenitor of modern trachemyne species was probably an early Pliocene form similar to *T. idahoensis* or *T. hillii.* The relationship of this ancestor to *Chrysemys, Graptemys,* and *Pseudemys* remains undetermined.

Introduction

Although the taxonomy of slider turtles has received considerable attention (see Chapter 4), most work has focused on the alpha level, with emphasis on descriptions of new subspecies or generic identifications. Theories on the evolution of *Trachemys scripta* are few. This is, in part, due to the uncertain relationships of many Mesoamerican populations and the often confused taxonomy of closely related species in the West Indies. Recently, however, some of these taxonomic problems have been resolved (Seidel and Inchaustegui Miranda, 1984; Seidel and Adkins, 1987; Seidel, 1988; also see Chapter 7). The extensive variability of diagnostic characters in sliders makes it difficult, and in some cases nearly impossible, to identify homologies or homoplasies (convergent character states). Morphological convergence resulting from similar feeding strategies (herbivory versus omnivory) and habitat selection (fluviatile versus lentic) appears to be common in *Trachemys* and related forms (Jackson, 1977, 1978a). Unfortunately, much more work is needed in this area, and there remain more questions than answers. Nevertheless, the following discussion presents theories on the origin and phylogeny of sliders, based on our current understanding of their taxonomy and fossil record.

Trachemys and Related Extant Genera

As noted by Ernst (see Chapter 4), slider turtles are assigned to the subfamily Emydinae, genus *Trachemys* (formerly and occasionally still included in *Pseudemys* sensu lato or *Chrysemys* sensu lato), which includes *T. scripta*, *T. decussata*, *T. decorata*, *T. terrapen*, and *T. stejnegeri* (Seidel and Smith, 1986). *Trachemys scripta dorbigni* (South America) and *T. s. gaigeae* (Texas and New Mexico) have been elevated to species by some recent authors (Dixon, 1987; Ernst, pers. com.). *Trachemys scripta* is the only extant mainland species and is widely distributed from the United States to lower South America. The other four species are endemic to the Greater Antilles and adjacent West Indian islands. The taxonomic position of trachemyne turtles has been controversial for the past 20 years, resulting in their inconsistent assignment to the genus *Pseudemys* (which includes cooters and red-bellied turtles) or the composite genus *Chrysemys* (which also includes painted turtles). Recently, Seidel and Smith (1986) reviewed these genera and presented evidence that sliders (*Trachemys*) are a natural, monophyletic group. The following combination of shared character states distinguishes them from cooters (*P. concinna* and *P. floridana*), red-bellied turtles (*P. rubriventris*, *P. nelsoni*, and *P. alabamensis*), and painted turtles (*C. picta*): adult carapace rugose, notched and serrated posteriorly (sensu Weaver and Robertson, 1967), and usually keeled; ventral surface of lower jaw rounded, and upper (alveolar) surface usually narrow and without a conspicuous symphyseal ridge; tuberculate denticles absent from alveolar surface of upper jaw; cutting surface of upper jaw uncusped and medially forming an angle or shallow notch; cranium shallow anterior to basisphenoid (30% to 40% of condylobasal length); and zygomatic arch and narial opening relatively narrow. In addition to finding close relationships among *Trachemys*, *Pseudemys*, and *Chrysemys*, a number of authors have recognized affinities of these genera with *Graptemys* (*Malaclemys* sensu lato) and *Deirochelys* (Loveridge and

Williams, 1957; McDowell, 1964; Zug, 1971; Bramble, 1974; Jackson, 1978a; Dobie, 1981; Frair, 1982; Ckhikvadze, 1984). A survey of shared-unshared character states in these turtles (including morphology, biochemistry, and ecology) is presented in Table 5.1. A strictly phenetic comparison based on these characters indicates that sliders (*Trachemys*) and map turtles (*Graptemys*) are most similar, with 19 character states in common. No karyologic variation has been observed in the Emydinae (Bickham and Baker, 1976a,b; Killebrew, 1977).

In the past decade there has been a major shift in systematics from the evolutionary and phenetic approaches to the phylogenetic (or cladistic) approach. Rather than defining genealogical relationships by overall similarity, phylogenetics involves the identification of homologous structures and the evolutionary direction (polarity) of characters from a primitive (plesiomorphic) to a derived (apomorphic) state (for a review, see Wiley, 1981). Those groups that share the greatest number of derived character states (synapomorphies) are presumed to have an exclusive common ancestor and are thus joined as sister taxa in a branching tree. In determining polarity, character states are sometimes identified as primitive if they are the most common or if they appear in fossils. More often, however, primitive states are identified by their presence in a closely related, extant taxonomic out-group (see Watrous and Wheeler, 1981). This purely phylogenetic approach has seldom been applied in systematic studies of *Trachemys*, in spite of the relatively large suite of characters reported (Table 5.1). Based on fossil evidence and extant morphology, *Deirochelys* (the chicken turtle) is a logical out-group for analyzing the phylogeny of *Trachemys*, *Pseudemys*, *Chrysemys*, and *Graptemys*. Although aspects of the head and neck morphology of chicken turtles are highly derived for specialized feeding, *Deirochelys* presumably diverged from a *Chrysemys-Pseudemys-Trachemys*–like ancestor (perhaps in the Oligocene) and has retained a number of characters shared with extant species of that group (Jackson, 1978a). Electrophoretic data also support a close relationship among *Deirochelys*, *Trachemys*, *Pseudemys*, *Chrysemys*, and *Graptemys* (Frair, 1982; Seidel, pers. obs.). Most of the character states identified in *Deirochelys* (Table 5.1) are also present in *Clemmys*, a genus of emydines often considered generalized and primitive (Bramble, 1974; Ward, 1980). When *Deirochelys* is the designated out-group, nine characters are synapomorphic between *Trachemys* and *Graptemys*, and nine are synapomorphic between *Trachemys* and *Pseudemys* (Table 5.1). *Trachemys* and *Chrysemys*, which have often been viewed as closely related (congeneric) taxa, are joined by only two synapomorphies. A phylogenetic tree based on these character polarities indicates an unresolved trichotomy among *Trachemys*, *Pseudemys*, and *Graptemys* (Fig. 5.1). *Chrysemys*, which has a greater number of plesiomorphic states (18, Table 5.1), appears as an earlier divergent lineage. This agrees with

Table 5.1. Adult character states of some emydine turtles

Character state	Graptemys (Malaclemys)	Trachemys	Chrysemys	Pseudemys	Deirochelys
Cranium and mandible (McDowell, 1964)					
1. Cranium short and deep	-	-	-	+	-
2. Thick anterior border of inferior parietal process	+	-	-	-	-
3. Mandible flattened ventrally	-	-	-	+	-
4. Tuberculate denticles prominent on alveolar surface	-	-	-	+	-
5. Alveolar surfaces nearly flat (median ridge absent)	+	-	-	-	+
6. Alveolar surface of lower jaw usually narrow	-	+	+	-	+
7. Anterior cusp absent from median ridge of upper jaw	+	+	-	-	+
8. Posterior palatine foramen large relative to nasopalatine fenestra	-	-	+	-	+
9. Posterior pterygoid near to or contacting exoccipital	+	+	-	-	+
Carapace and appendages (Hay, 1908; McDowell, 1964; Zug, 1971; Ernst and Barbour, 1972; Dobie, 1981)					
10. Carapace with median keel	+	+	-	+	-
11. Carapace with longitudinal rugosities	+	+	-	+	+
12. Posterior marginals (peripherals) usually serrate and/or notched	+	+	-	+	-
13. Vertebral scute I usually not constricted anteriorly	+	-	+	-	+
14. Lateral edges of nuchal bone usually overlapped broadly by first pleural scutes	+	+	-	+	-
15. Anterolateral border of vertebral scute I confined to nuchal bone	+	+	-	+	-
16. Female carapace length < 250 mm	-	-	+	-	+
17. Adult females often larger than twice the size of males	+	-	-	-	-
18. Never more than three phalanges on fifth toe	-	+	+	-	+
Penial morphology (Zug, 1966)					
19. Plica media spade-shaped	-	+	+	+	+
20. Lateral folds of plica media thick and sulcus weakly defined	-	-	+	-	+
Isozymes (Vogt and McCoy, 1980)					
21. Slow (cathodal) electromorphs for lactate dehydrogenase	-	-	+	-	
22. Medium-fast (anodal) electromorph for plasma protein	-	-	+	+	
Choanal structure (Parsons, 1960)					
23. Flap (rarely a ridge) along lateral choanal margin	+	+	+	-	-
Endoparasites (Ernst and Ernst, 1980)					
24. High diversity of monogenetic trematodes	-	+	+	+	
25. High diversity of acanthocephalans	-	+	-	+	
26. Cestodes present	+	+	-	+	
Ecology (Cagle and Chaney, 1950; Jackson, 1978a; Bury, 1979)					
27. Feeding habits mostly herbivorous	-	-	-	+	-
28. Often demographically dominant to sympatric emydines	+	+	-	-	-
Frequency of shared character states					
Trachemys	19				
Chrysemys	7	12			
Pseudemys	12	17	9		
Frequency of presumptive synapomorphies					
Trachemys	9				
Chrysemys	1	2			
Pseudemys	9	9	3		
Frequency of presumptive plesiomorphies	9	12	18	6	

Note: Matrix summarizes the numbers of character states shared between genera (modified from Seidel and Smith, 1986). Character states indicate what is typical of most, but not necessarily all, species in a genus, and polarities are determined by out-group comparisons with *Deirochelys.* Abbreviations: +, present; -, absent.

the phylogenetic position of *C. picta* illustrated by Weaver and Rose (1967) and with the conclusion of Ward (1980) that *Chrysemys* preceded the appearance of *Pseudemys* and *Trachemys.*

Obviously there are alternative phylogenetic theories if different taxonomic out-groups are designated, if characters are weighted, or if subsets of characters are used. For example, if only cranial characters are considered, *Trachemys* and *Chrysemys* appear to be closely related (sister taxa) because they are more generalized (Loveridge and Williams, 1957; McDowell, 1964). The cranium of *Pseudemys* is deep, with large orbits and broad, tuberculate, alveolar surfaces for processing vegetation. Pritchard and Trebbau (1984) implied that the specialized feeding

apparatus of *Pseudemys* is derived from a generalized ancestral stock of *Trachemys.* Skulls of adult female *Graptemys* may be even more specialized. In some species the crania are disproportionately large and very wide, with broad alveolar surfaces adapted for molluscivory. McDowell (1964) proposed that *Graptemys* (= *Malaclemys* auct.) is a highly derived genus, perhaps from trachemyne stock. Dobie (1981) proposed that *Graptemys* and *Malaclemys* arose from a pseudemyne-trachemyne stock. Dryden (1985) reported that *Malaclemys* and *Graptemys* form a monophyletic unit based on cranial and postcranial characters, as do *Chrysemys, Trachemys,* and *Pseudemys.* If fossil *Graptemys* from the Oligocene reported by Loomis (1904) and Clark (1937) are correctly assigned, the origin (diver-

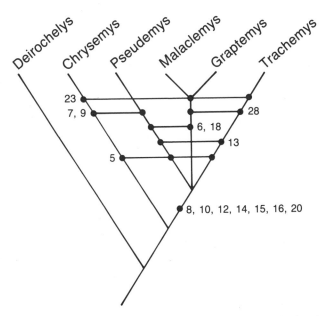

FIGURE 5.1. A theory on the phylogeny of *Trachemys* and related genera of emydines. Numbers (identified in Table 5.1) refer to synapomorphies or possible homoplasies (convergent states), as indicated by lines cutting across lineages.

gence) of this genus would have occurred quite early, probably before the origin of a trachemyne line. Some of the trophic-related character states as well as others (e.g., notched marginal scutes and underlying peripheral bones) in these turtle genera may be homoplasous. However, if all available characters are considered equally (Table 5.1 and Fig. 5.1), the precise relationship of *Trachemys* to *Graptemys* and *Pseudemys* is unclear.

Trachemys Fossils

A major limitation of the fossil record in defining the evolutionary history of *Trachemys* has been the absence of skulls of extinct forms. Until recently, only two fossil emydid skulls from North America had been reported (Hay, 1908; Gilmore, 1933), and the identities of these were ambiguous. The conclusions drawn by McDowell (1964) almost entirely from cranial characters have, therefore, been nearly impossible to apply to fossil species whose taxonomy has been based primarily on shell morphology. However, the report by Jackson (1988) of previously unrecognized skull material from the Florida Pliocene has allowed reanalysis of some of these problems. Probably owing to their abundance in the Pleistocene of Florida and Texas and their ease of recognition, fossils of the *T. scripta* group have been known longer and studied more extensively than those of most other emydine turtles (Table 5.2). Hay (1908, 1916) assigned eight extinct species from Florida and Texas Pleistocene deposits to this group: *T. euglypha* (Leidy), *T. sculpta* Hay (1908), *T. jarmani* Hay (1908), *T. petrolei* (Leidy), *T. bisornata* (Cope),

T. trulla Hay (1908), *T. delicata* Hay (1916), and *T. nuchocarinata* Hay (1916). Weaver and Robertson (1967) correctly placed six of these names in synonymy with *T. scripta* and incorporated them, as well as other Florida material, in their new combination, *T. s. petrolei*. However, the validity of *T. s. petrolei* and subspecific designation of fossil *Trachemys* in general is questioned by Jackson (1988). The remaining two names represent fossils incorrectly assigned to *Trachemys*: *T. nuchocarinata* = *Terrapene carolina* (Auffenberg, 1958) and *T. jarmani* = *Pseudemys nelsoni* (Jackson, 1978b). The only other *Trachemys* recognized by Hay (1908) was *T. hillii* (Cope), presumably from the Upper Miocene of Kansas (exact stratigraphic position uncertain). This species was expanded by Adler (1968b) to include Galbreath's (1948) *Chrysemys limnodytes*. Two Pliocene (Blancan) fossils, believed to be in the *Trachemys* group, have been described: *T. platymarginata* from Florida (Weaver and Robertson, 1967) and *T. idahoensis* from Idaho (Gilmore, 1933; Zug, 1969; Jackson, 1988). Finally, the oldest stratigraphically fixed fossil turtle that can be definitely assigned to *Trachemys* is *T. inflata*, reported from the Upper Miocene of Florida (Weaver and Robertson, 1967).

Whereas the Pleistocene may provide information on the former distribution of *T. scripta* and development of geographic variation (subspeciation), we must look back to the Pliocene for information on the evolution of *Trachemys*. Weaver and Robertson (1967) correctly assigned *T. platymarginata* to the *T. scripta* complex, but they believed that no skull material of *T. platymarginata* was available. Jackson (1988) recently reported cranial fragments identifiable to this species. The skull of *T. platymarginata* shares many features of *Trachemys* with *T. scripta*, its probable descendant. However, Jackson noted that some morphological features of *T. platymarginata* suggest a more exclusively herbivorous diet than that of the omnivorous *T. scripta*. The discovery of skulls of *T. platymarginata* allows analysis of its relationships to other species. Aside from the report by Rogers (1976) of fossil *Trachemys* shell fragments from Texas, the only other Blancan turtle that

Table 5.2. Geologic timetable of Upper Cenozoic era, with occurrence of fossil and extant forms of *Trachemys*

Epoch	Time, beginning of period to present (millions of years)	Species
Recent	0.01	*T. scripta*
		T. decussata
		T. decorata
		T. stejnegeri
		T. terrapen
Pleistocene	2	*T. scripta*
		T. stejnegeri
Pliocene	4	*T. idahoensis*
Upper Miocene	7	*T. hillii*
		T. inflata

is potentially a member of the *T. scripta* group is *T. ida-hoensis* Gilmore (1933) from the Pliocene of Idaho. The holotype of this species is an entire (though partially crushed) shell, a well-preserved skull, and much of the postcranial skeleton. The shape of the nuchal scute underlap (longer than wide) and the absence of bosses on the carapace clearly distinguish the shell from that of *Graptemys*. Previous authors (Gilmore, 1933; Rose and Weaver, 1966) associated *T. idahoensis* with the *P. rubriventris* lineage on the basis of similarly broad alveolar surfaces of jaws. However, broad triturating surfaces have occurred in the *T. scripta* lineage in the past as well, specifically in *T. platymarginata*. Zug (1969) correctly noted that other cranial characteristics, as well as the geographic distribution of *T. idahoensis*, are actually more similar to *T. scripta*'s than to those of the *P. rubriventris* lineage. From such lines of evidence, Jackson (1988) concluded that *T. platymarginata* is synonymous with *T. idahoensis*, which is viewed as a widespread species of Pliocene *Trachemys*.

Clearly *T. idahoensis* could not have been the progenitor of the *Trachemys* line. It appears too late in the fossil record and already shows most of the diagnostic characteristics of northern populations of modern *T. scripta*, such as the doubly toothed peripheral bones. *Trachemys hillii* (Cope), as expanded by Adler (1968b), presumably is known from Upper Miocene strata in Oklahoma and Kansas (Cope's collections were subject to little stratigraphic control). Adler (1968b) noted a number of similarities between *T. hillii* and *T. scripta*, including slight notching of the posterior peripheral bones, and speculated that the fossil may be ancestral or closely related to *T. scripta*. The Upper Miocene *T. inflata* (Weaver and Robertson, 1967), still known only from peninsular Florida, remains ambiguous. Until contradictory material is discovered, the interpretation by Weaver and Robertson (1967) that "it was a specialized or aberrant species characterized by an extreme development of *Trachemys* features and not representative of the main evolutionary sequence leading to recent *T. scripta*" must stand. *Trachemys inflata* may represent a pre-Blancan isolate from *T. idahoensis* stock that, perhaps in response to unique environmental circumstances, developed a massive, highly sculptured shell. It seems reasonable to assume that the progenitor of all trachemynes was a form similar to *T. idahoensis* and *T. hillii*. Whether this ancestor shared a closer relationship with the *Chrysemys*, *Graptemys*, or *Pseudemys* line remains undetermined. Of further interest are the relationships of these modern genera to possibly ancestral turtles assigned to the early Cenozoic North American genus *Echmatemys*.

Little or no information on the origin of *Trachemys* in the West Indies, Mesoamerica, or South America can be obtained from the fossil record. Tertiary remains of terrestrial and freshwater vertebrates are virtually absent from the Caribbean islands. Whether this implies that habitation did not occur until the Quaternary period

(Pregill, 1981a) or simply reflects a lack of conditions suitable for fossilization is subject to controversy (Poinar and Cannatella, 1987). The only report of fossil *Trachemys* in the West Indies is that of a plastral fragment, presumably *T. stejnegeri*, from the late Pleistocene of Puerto Rico (Pregill, 1981b). This supports the belief (Seidel, 1988) that *Trachemys* did not occur in the Greater Antilles until late Pliocene or early Pleistocene. The fossil record of *Trachemys* from Central and South America consists of a single late Pleistocene specimen from Panama (Gazin, 1957). This is congruent with theories, based on reproductive cycles and nesting habits, that *T. scripta* is a recent (perhaps Pleistocene) colonizer of the tropics (Moll and Legler, 1971; Pritchard and Trebbau, 1984).

For information on the evolution of modern *T. scripta* and its northern races, we can look again at fossils from the Pliocene of Florida and Idaho (*T. idahoensis*). Jackson (1988) noted that additional series of fossil *Trachemys* from the Pliocene of Nebraska (J. A. Holman, pers. com.), Kansas (Zug, 1969), and Texas (Rogers, 1976) share many characteristics with *T. idahoensis* and proposed that all Pliocene trachemyne fossils represent a single widespread species. With regard to subtle morphological differences, *T. idahoensis* from Idaho through Texas more closely resembles the northern and western *T. s. elegans*, whereas *T. idahoensis* from Florida shows more similarities to the southeastern *T. s. scripta* (Jackson, 1977). Thus the inclusive chronospecies, *T. idahoensis*, exhibits a pattern of geographic variation not unlike that of modern *T. scripta*.

A look at early Pleistocene fossils of *T. scripta*, presumably descended from and possibly conspecific with *T. ida-hoensis*, shows a similar pattern of geographic variation. Unfortunately, the diagnoses for modern subspecies of *T. scripta* rely mostly on color pattern, making comparisons with the fossils difficult. However, the osteological characters used by Preston (1966) to distinguish temperate forms have some value, particularly the development of a middorsal keel and relief of the nuchal lamina (though some intrasubspecific variation is evident). It is also difficult to ascertain subspecific differences when the two most widespread North American subspecies, *T. s. scripta* and *T. s. elegans*, have a broad range of intergradation (Davidson, 1971; Conant, 1975). Nonetheless, carapaces of *T. scripta* from Irvingtonian deposits in Florida and Texas appear to differ osteologically in the same way that the subspecies *T. s. scripta* and *T. s. elegans* differ in these regions today (Jackson, 1988). It appears that these two modern subspecies became established no later than early Pleistocene, a process that may have begun in the Pliocene.

Biochemical Evidence

Electrophoretic analyses of *Trachemys* have been reported by Dessauer et al. (1957), Ramirez and Dessauer (1957),

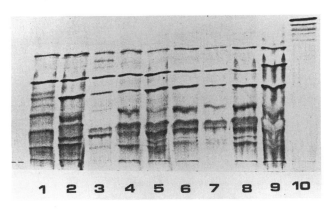

FIGURE 5.2. Electrophoregram of skeletal muscle proteins from *Pseudemys concinna* (1), *Chrysemys picta* (2), *Graptemys geographica* (3), *Trachemys scripta elegans* (4, 5, 6), *T. s. scripta* (7), *T. s. venusta* (8, 9), and protein standard (10) separated by isoelectric focusing.

Zweig and Crenshaw (1957), Kaplan (1960), Bueker (1961), Leone and Wilson (1961), Dozy et al. (1964), Sheeler and Barber (1965), Manwell and Schlesinger (1966), Masat and Dessauer (1968), Vogt and McCoy (1980), Frair (1982), Rose and Dobie (1983), Scribner et al. (1984a, 1986), Sites et al. (1984), Alonso Biosca et al. (1985), and Seidel and Adkins (1987). On cellulose acetate, electrophoretic protein patterns of *Deirochelys*, *Trachemys*, *Chrysemys*, and *Graptemys* were found to be more similar to each other (*Pseudemys* was not examined) than to other emydines (Frair, 1982). Starch gel analysis of polymorphic lactate dehydrogenase and general protein indicated no variation between *Graptemys* and *Trachemys*, whereas unique bands appeared in *Chrysemys* and *Pseudemys* (Vogt and McCoy, 1980). Profiles of protein banding patterns separated by isoelectric focusing also reveal greater similarities among *Pseudemys*, *Chrysemys*, *Graptemys*, and *Trachemys* (Fig. 5.2) than among other members of the Emydinae (Seidel, pers. obs.). Although previous biochemical studies confirm the close relationship of these genera, they add relatively little to the understanding of the phylogeny of *Trachemys*. There is clearly a need for a broad electrophoretic analysis of the Emydinae based on a large number of protein systems and genetic loci.

Some information on biochemical relationships within *Trachemys* is presented by Seidel and Adkins (1987). From isoelectric focusing, these authors described relationships among several subspecies of *T. scripta* and trachemyne species from the West Indies. They detected variation in the occurrence of nine protein bands (electromorphs in liver, heart, kidney, or skeletal muscle), eight of which were identified as apomorphies by out-group comparisons to *P. nelsoni*. No electrophoretic character was found to be synapomorphic among all West Indian species examined, whereas *T. decussata* and *T. terrapen* shared a unique apomorphy with *T. scripta*. This suggests that the insular

forms of *Trachemys* may not be monophyletic and have perhaps originated independently from more than one *T. scripta*–like ancestor. *Trachemys s. callirostris* (from South America) appeared highly divergent from West Indian species as well as from the races of North American *T. scripta* examined. On morphological grounds, Williams (1956) defined *T. s. callirostris* as a very distinct form and recognized two major groups in *T. scripta*: a *scripta* group including the northern races and an *ornata* group of Middle and South America. Weaver and Rose (1967) also separated Middle American forms (which they elevated to *T. ornata*, *T. callirostris*, and *T. gaigeae*) from northern races of *T. scripta*. However, that interpretation has been criticized by Legler (see Chapter 7) and Moll and Legler (1971), who consider all mainland *Trachemys* to be conspecific. Preliminary biochemical observations suggest that both the West Indian species complex and *T. scripta* are paraphyletic or polyphyletic groups. The phylogeny and taxonomy of the former are discussed in detail by Seidel (1988). One could argue that several races of *T. scripta* should be elevated to species rank, but the existence of 16 modern species of trachemynes, as suggested by Ward (1984), seems unlikely. Additional comparisons of *Trachemys* throughout Central and South America (see Chapter 7) are necessary before a thorough taxonomic revision or phylogeny of the *T. scripta* complex can be proposed.

Concluding Remarks

Our present knowledge of the origin and evolutionary relationships of slider turtles remains incomplete. Available morphological, paleontological, and biochemical information indicates that *Trachemys* arose during or prior to the Miocene from a generalized *Chrysemys-Pseudemys*–like ancestor. Subsequent radiation resulted in several Miocene and Pliocene forms broadly distributed in temperate North America. Multiple dispersals, followed by isolation of *Trachemys* in the neotropics during the early Pleistocene, have resulted in divergence of Central and South American *T. scripta* as well as several species in the West Indies.

Acknowledgments

We appreciate comments by James L. Dobie and John M. Legler on the original version of the manuscript. Manuscript preparation was aided by contract DE-AC09-76SROO-819 between the U.S. Department of Energy and the Institute of Ecology of the University of Georgia. The paleontological analysis formed part of a dissertation submitted to the University of Florida by Dale R. Jackson, who thanks W. Auffenberg and S. D. Webb for their guidance as committee members.

MICHAEL H. SMITH
KIM T. SCRIBNER
Savannah River Ecology Laboratory
Drawer E
Aiken, South Carolina 29802

6

Population Genetics of the Slider Turtle

Abstract

Genetic data necessary for defining population structure in *T. scripta* were collected through starch gel electrophoresis, which permits visualization of Mendelian inherited gene products (proteins) found in various body tissues. The available genetic data are summarized, and documentation is given that populations are not genetically homogeneous temporally, spatially, or among demographic subgroups. The slider turtle appears to be one of the most genetically variable vertebrates. Possible explanations are given for the existence of both spatial genetic differentiation and high dispersal rates among populations of *T. scripta*. Dispersal, stochastic events, and natural selection interact to produce a series of populations that are in a state of dynamic disequilibrium and are dramatically affected by environmental conditions such as droughts. The suggestion is made that the observed genetic disequilibrium may occur generally in vertebrates, especially those with short life cycles, resulting in more opportunities for rapid genetic changes to local environmental differences. The influence of genetics, environmental factors, and their interactions on population dynamics needs to be evaluated within a regional context to obtain a better understanding of the genetically dynamic nature of this species.

Introduction

The slider turtle (*Trachemys scripta*) is a long-lived species that has been extensively studied on the Savannah River Plant (SRP) for the last 20 years. Many aspects of its population biology are associated with its longevity, long generation time, and overlapping generations (Gibbons and Semlitsch, 1982; Gibbons, 1987). These characteristics make populations relatively slow to respond to environmental pressures for evolutionary change, because they increase the length of time needed for the population to turn over. These demographic parameters are well documented for a number of populations on the SRP. Populations occur in a variety of natural and disturbed habitats and vary in their age structures, reproductive characteristics, and growth patterns (Gibbons et al., 1981; Gibbons and Semlitsch, 1982). The genetic characteristics of populations on the SRP are less well known (Scribner et al., 1986), but the pattern for both the genetic and the demographic characteristics is one of strong interpopulational differentiation over the SRP (Gibbons et al., 1981; Congdon and Gibbons, 1983; Congdon et al., 1986; Scribner et al., 1986). Significant differences are observed even though the distances between suitable habitats are often relatively small and turtles frequently disperse between them (Gibbons, 1970d; Morreale et al., 1984). Further quantification of the intra- and interpopulation genetic variation is a logical extension of previous work and is needed to understand the microgeographical differentiation of this species within its patchy environment (Levins, 1968).

Genetic differentiation can also be found among various subgroups within a population (e.g., males and females, or young and old), which are often assumed to be genetically equivalent. In other words, the populations are frequently assumed to be panmictic, with the subgroups having the same allelic and genotypic frequencies. For a number of vertebrates this is clearly not the case. Allele frequencies and/or heterozygosities vary according to age (Tinkle and Selander, 1973; Chesser et al., 1982; Scribner et al., 1985; Al-Hassan et al., 1987), sex (Manlove et al., 1975), sex ratios (Simanek, 1978), or body size (Avise and Smith, 1974; Smith and Chesser, 1981; Feder et al., 1984). Such genetic heterogeneity within populations is not normally expected for long-lived vertebrate species exhibiting high vagility and where extensive interbreeding is expected to occur within the population. In addition to the intrapopulational breeding structure, populations interact with others in adjacent areas through dispersal and gene flow. This exchange not only adds or subtracts numbers from the population through immigration and emigration (Lidicker, 1975) but also influences the genetic characteristics of the resulting offspring. A species with high dispersal rates should be characterized by genetic homogeneity over space and among the demographic units within populations unless some other factor or factors, such as strong selection or drift, are acting concurrently. Such a high degree of genetic variation within and among populations may be common, and the approach to genetic equilibrium may be slow in a long-lived species such as *T. scripta*. Environmental perturbations, which may promote large-scale dispersal, local selection, or extreme fluctuations in population size, may prevent equilibrium from ever being attained. The first step in understanding such a potentially dynamic system is to document the existing spatial genetic pattern of the populations.

Genetic data necessary for defining population struc-

ture in *T. scripta* were collected through starch gel electrophoresis (Scribner et al., 1986). This technique allows for the visualization of Mendelian inherited gene products (proteins) found in various body tissues. Samples such as blood, liver, and muscle were taken from dissected turtles, or blood and tail muscle were obtained from live turtles that were then released. Variation in general proteins and metabolic enzymes was quantified on starch gels using appropriate stains. With this method, a series of bands are produced, which are interpreted using existing literature on biochemical variation and information on protein quaternary structure. Data consist of allelic and genotypic frequencies and heterozygosities for a number of loci. Single-locus heterozygosity (h) is a measure of the proportion of individuals in a sample that received a different allele from each parent. Multilocus heterozygosity (H) is the average of the single-locus heterozygosities. Available demographic data were taken during mark-release studies or from dissected turtles (Scribner et al., 1986).

Our objective is to summarize the available genetic data for *T. scripta* and to document how the genetic characteristics vary among populations at various times and among demographic subgroups within populations. Specifically, we want to illustrate how the genetic characteristics vary (1) over space as a function of geographical distance among collecting sites, (2) over years, or (3) among turtles of differing ages or sexes. Nineteen loci have been studied for variation in 16 populations, and 1 additional locus was analyzed for only 4 populations (Table 6.1). Collecting sites were on or near Aiken, South Carolina, on the SRP (Fig. 6.1). These data for populations within the Lost Lake System (1 = Seepage Basin, 2 = Lost Lake, 3 = Steed Pond, and 4 = Lodge Lake), Par Pond, and Oxbow Lakes have been previously published (Scribner et al., 1984b, 1986). Data from all 19 loci for Cecil's Pond, Pond B, Ellenton Bay, and Steel Creek are reported here for the first time.

Trachemys scripta appears to be genetically more variable than the majority of reptiles and vertebrates in general (Nevo et al., 1984). Genetic variability is often reported as H. Reptiles have an H of .060 ± .053 (SE), and *T. scripta* has an H of .127 ± .045 (Table 6.1). The overall estimate for reptiles contains data for very few turtles: *Sternotherus odoratus*, $H = .080–.138$ (Seidel et al., 1981); *Caretta caretta*, $H = .019–.022$; and *Chelonia mydas*, $H = .000–.135$ (Smith et al., 1977; Bonhomme et al., 1987). Additional multilocus studies in turtles have been conducted using electrophoretic techniques without estimating H (Crenshaw, 1965; Karig and Wilson, 1971; Merkle, 1975; Vogt and McCoy, 1980; Seidel and Lucchino, 1981; Sites et al., 1981; Derr et al., 1987; Seidel and Adkins, 1987). The percent polymorphic loci (P) and alleles per locus (A) also tended to be high in *T. scripta* (Table 6.1). These estimates of genetic variability would be expected to change if additional loci were studied (Gorman and Renzi, 1979). How-

Table 6.1. Measures of the variability for 19 loci in *Trachemys scripta* on or near the Savannah River Plant

Locus (abbreviation)	Allele designations[a]	Number of alleles	Mean single-locus heterozygosity (h)[b]	Number of populations	F_{st}[c]
Creatine kinase (*Ck*)-1	100	1	.000	16	.000
Ck-2	100	1	.000	16	.000
Ck-3	100	1	.000	16	.000
Glucose phosphate isomerase (*Gpi*)-1	100,105,98[d]	3	.489	16	.022
Fumarase (*Fh*)	100	1	.000	16	.000
Isocitrate dehydrogenase (*Icd*)-1	100,104,94	3	.332	16	.057**
Icd-2	100,109,95	3	.273	16	.083**
Lactate dehydrogenase (*Ldh*)-1	100	1	.000	16	.000
Ldh-2	100,88	2	.004	16	.059**
Malate dehydrogenase (*Mdh*)-1	100,92,85,78	4	.648	16	.025
Mdh-2	100,58	2	.014	16	.018
Malic enzyme (*Mod*)-1	100,94	2	.006	16	.074**
Mod-2	100,115	2	.395	16	.026
Mannose-6-phosphate isomerase (*Mpi*)	100,91,110	3	.042	16	.136**
Nucleoside phosphorylase (*Np*)	100,112,89	3	.026	16	.022
Peptidase (*Pep*)-1	100	1	.000	4	.000
Phosphoglucomutase (*Pgm*)-1	100,107,92	3	.105	16	.032*
6-Phosphogluconate dehydrogenase (6-*Pgd*)	100,112,89	3	.535	16	.089**
Protein (general; *Pt*)-2	100,86	2	.089	16	.038*
Mean		2.33 ± 0.23 (*A*)	.127 ± .045 (*H*)		.048**

Abbreviations: *A*, alleles per locus; *H*, multilocus heterozygosity; *h*, single-locus heterozygosity.
[a]Alleles are listed from left to right in terms of their frequencies across populations with the common allele as 100.
[b]Percent polymorphic loci (*P*) at the .01 level of significance = 57.9 and at the .05 level of significance = 47.4.
[c]Measure of divergence at individual loci among populations (Nei, 1978).
[d]Only one turtle was observed with this allele.
*$p \leq .05$ for test of $F_{st} = 0$.
**$p \leq .01$.

ever, the conclusion that *T. scripta* is a highly variable vertebrate is likely to be correct (Nei, 1978). Seidel et al. (1981) have suggested that differences in *H* among turtle taxa are related to the propensity for both aquatic and terrestrial existence, with habitat generalists having high *H*. The high variability of this species makes it ideal for population-level studies.

Multilocus heterozygosity showed significant differences among locations with the value for Par Pond 3 (*H* = .105) being only 55% of that for Oxbow Lake 3 (*H* = .190), which was the highest value recorded. Large differences in *H* occurred even over short distances within the continuous aquatic habitat of the Par Pond Reservoir (Fig. 6.1). The lowest *H* within the reservoir was only 67% of the highest value. Such differences are normally seen only over larger geographical distances in vertebrates and imply microgeographical structuring. There was also significant differentiation in allele frequencies among the samples for *Icd*-1, *Icd*-2, *Ldh*-2, *Mod*-1, *Mpi*, 6-*Pgd*, *Pgm*-1, and *Pt*-2, which included all of the highly variable loci (*h* > .100) except *Gpi*-1, *Mdh*-1, and *Mod*-2 (*F* statistics, Table 6.1). The spatial heterogeneity was also significant when considered across all loci (*F_{st}* = .048). The observed levels of genetic heterogeneity suggest that

the samples are not panmictic but rather represent disjunct breeding groups. The number of populations on the SRP cannot be determined from these data but is probably quite large. Locations that are close together can have turtles with significantly different genetic characteristics (e.g., 6-*Pgd*, Fig. 6.1). Thus, populations are structured on a microgeographical scale, and the causes and consequences of this structure could be important in influencing the population dynamics of this species.

Dispersal is an important process in determining gene flow among local populations. When gene flow is high and random with respect to the genotypes of the dispersing individuals, the probability of differentiation is low (Crow and Kimura, 1970; Brown, 1985). The amount of movement and presumably gene flow between local populations of *T. scripta* and related species seems quite high (Gibbons, 1970d; MacCulloch and Secoy, 1983b; Morreale et al., 1984; Parker, 1984). One consequence of high amounts of gene flow should be that allele frequencies of adjacent populations are similar and show positive correlation. There is a trend for significant spatial autocorrelation between allele frequencies at interpopulational distances up to 6 km (Fig. 6.2). The influence of gene flow becomes negligible at interlocation distances of 6 to 8 km.

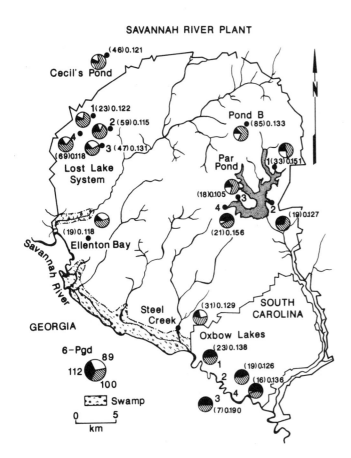

SAVANNAH RIVER PLANT

FIGURE 6.1. The locations of 16 sampling sites for *Trachemys scripta* on the Savannah River Plant are given as solid dots. Sample sizes are given in parentheses followed by multilocus heterozygosity (*H*). The proportions of the circles shaded differentially indicate the frequencies of the three alleles for 6-phosphogluconate dehydrogenase in 1983.

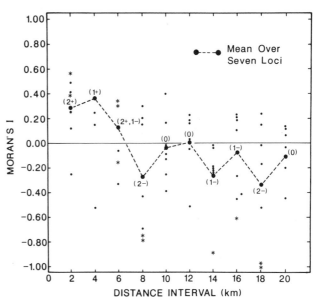

FIGURE 6.2. Results of spatial autocorrelation (Sokal and Oden, 1978) with Moran's *I* given for various intervals of distance between turtle sampling sites (Fig. 6.1). *I* is a type of correlation coefficient and varies from −1 to +1, with the sign indicating the direction of association. *I* was calculated from the common allele frequencies for the seven most variable loci listed in Table 6.1. The numbers in parentheses indicate the number and direction of significant associations for particular loci. Significance ($p \leq .05$) for *I* is indicated by asterisks.

The degree of spatial autocorrelation does not decrease until the interlocation distances exceed 4 to 6 km. Gene flow is of a magnitude such that samples taken within 4 km of each other are genetically homogeneous. Effective gene flow appears to be occurring over greater distances than the observed mean individual dispersal distance among the locations of the Lost Lake System ($\bar{x}$ = 1.84 km; Morreale et al., 1984). The distance of positive association should be strongly influenced by the type of intervening habitat as well as by other factors that influence dispersal of turtles; it represents the cumulative effects of gene flow averaged over many generations and is much greater than the mean dispersal distance observed during any one generation.

Significant spatial autocorrelation and differentiation seem contradictory, and perhaps a conclusion of relatively high gene flow among local populations is erroneous. For example, large amounts of movement between local populations may not result in gene flow, because individuals may not breed in the new populations that they enter.

Additional evidence for relatively high gene flow is seen in a high prevalence of occurrence of alleles across all 16 locations (Fig. 6.3). Alleles with only moderate frequencies are found in relatively high proportions of the populations. Only one individual per generation need disperse

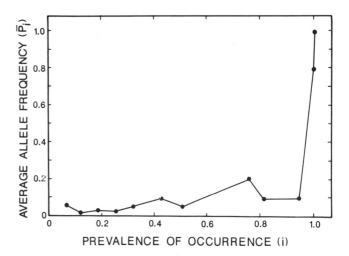

FIGURE 6.3. The unweighted mean frequency of an allele ($\bar{P}_i$) over the 16 samples (Fig. 6.1) as a function of the proportion of the samples in which it occurred (*i*), as calculated in Slatkin (1981).

Table 6.2. Frequencies of alleles for four variable loci at four locations from which turtles were sampled during 1974 and 1983

		Locations										
		Lost Lake			Steel Creek			Oxbow Lakes			Ellenton Bay		
Locus	Allele	1974	1983		1974	1983		1974	1983		1974	1983	
Gpi	105	.000	.106		.115	.167		.065	.152		.188	.028	
	100	.704	.670	*	.692	.617	NS	.677	.565	NS	.609	.694	*
	98	.296	.223		.192	.217		.258	.283		.203	.278	
Pgm-1	107	.135	.043		.154	.067		.000	.065		.097	.028	
	100	.865	.957	*	.846	.933	NS	.988	.935	*	.903	.972	NS
	92	.000	.000		.000	.000		.032	.000		.000	.000	
Icd-2	109	.000	.053		.000	.050		.000	.023		.000	.139	
	100	1.000	.766	**	1.000	.883	NS	.929	.841	NS	.100	.556	**
	95	.000	.181		.000	.067		.071	.136		.000	.306	
6-Pgd	112	.037	.125		.038	.161		.000	.474		.000	.167	
	100	.815	.569	*	.692	.571	NS	.883	.526	**	.438	.536	*
	89	.148	.306		.269	.268		.117	.000		.563	.278	

Note: Significant differences were found in allele frequencies between years in 8 of 16 tests. Abbreviations: Locus abbreviations are given in Table 6.1; NS, $p > .05$.
*$p \leq .05$.
**$p \leq .01$.

between populations to maintain their qualitative equivalence (Wright, 1931), although many more are needed to maintain quantitative equivalence of allele frequencies (Allendorf, 1983). Figure 6.3 presents results similar to those of a simulation model using a migration rate (mN; Slatkin, 1981) of approximately 1.25 to 5 per generation, where N is the number of individuals in the population, and m is the proportion that disperses or migrates. The migration rate can also be calculated from the F_{st} value for each locus or from the overall mean of all loci (.048, Table 6.1); mN is 4.21 per generation, using this method (Wright, 1943). The approximate concordance of these estimates of mN and their large values indicate relatively high gene flow among turtle populations that occur even among discontinuous aquatic habitats. These estimates are averages for the populations, and the rates are probably much higher for some sex-age classes than for others (Morreale et al., 1984; Parker, 1984).

The existence of spatial genetic differentiation among samples, in spite of evidence for high dispersal rates, requires further explanation. Genetic differences could arise by chance in small populations or during severe fluctuations in numbers of effective breeders and then be amplified by drift during subsequent population expansion. These differences, once established in a local population, could require many years of random mating and dispersal to ameliorate, although the local populations could each be in approximate Hardy-Weinberg equilibrium. Populations on the SRP could contain many local subunits that deviate from the mean genetic characteristics of the populations throughout the region, though deviations could continually move toward the average condition by random mating and dispersal within the effective dispersal

distance. There is evidence that the genetic characteristics of populations of *T. scripta* are in a state of change on the SRP.

The genetic characteristics of populations on the SRP change over time. Four populations were sampled in 1974 and 1983 for a limited set of loci (Scribner et al., 1984b, 1986). Four of these loci exhibited sufficient variability to warrant testing for significant temporal differences in allele frequencies. Three of the four populations showed significant temporal variations in allele frequency (Table 6.2). Differences are too great for these effects to be interpreted as being caused by chance alone (Sokal and Rohlf, 1969). The genetic characteristics of these populations were temporally transient over this period.

Temporal variation has also been observed for *T. scripta* populations over much shorter intervals. A large number of *T. scripta* were sampled from Pond B during 1983 and 1984 to test for significant temporal shifts in genetic characteristics and changes associated with age for the 19 loci listed in Table 6.1. Younger and older turtles have fewer alleles per locus than those of intermediate ages (A, Table 6.3). The trend for H is different, with the most homozygous turtles being the youngest, whereas the most heterozygous ones are the oldest (2, 3, and 4 years of age, $H = .114$; 4 to 7+ years of age, $H = .144$). The common allele frequencies for the 2 loci chosen to illustrate the maximum differences over age classes were both significantly different, the heterogeneity being due to the differences in the turtles of the 2- and 3-year-old classes. The mean F_{st} associated with age (.050, Table 6.3) is slightly larger than that across the 16 populations (.048, Table 6.1).

Data were also collected from Lost Lake and Steed

Table 6.3. Selected age-specific genetic characteristics for five age classes of *Trachemys scripta*

Age (years)	Number of turtles	Mean multilocus heterozygosity[a]	Mean alleles per locus (A)[b]	Common allele frequency[c] 6-Pgd	Common allele frequency[c] Mdh-2
2,3	12	.115	1.67	.364	.800
4	26	.113	1.89	.690	.455
5	19	.133	1.78	.611	.306
6	14	.158	1.83	.500	.500
7,7+	12	.144	1.66	.773	.409

Note: Turtles were collected in Pond B during 1983 and 1984. Loci abbreviations are given in Table 6.1.

[a]$p = .005$ for significant age effects with chi-square test.

[b]$p = .006$ for significant age effects with chi-square test.

[c]Average $F_{at} = .050$ for the variable loci (Table 6.1) measures differentiation due to age; $p \leq .05$ for significant age effects for both loci with chi-square test.

Pond during the same two years, with a highly significant difference in allele frequencies observed between years (mean $F_{st} = .048$ and .065, respectively). These F_{st} values were calculated without including data from recaptured animals in 1984. Thus, processes within populations result in intrapopulational variances as great as the variance among populations on the SRP. The temporal differences in allele frequencies observed between years in Pond B suggest that the population showed significant evolutionary change over this year, probably because of recruitment of young or the effects of immigrants on the breeding structure. Demographic processes may be equally important to both inter- and intrapopulational differentiation.

The data from Lost Lake and Steed Pond in 1983 and 1984 provide further evidence of disequilibrium. During the first year, the populations exhibited significant deviation in expected Hardy-Weinberg genotypic proportions for three of six variable loci at one location and for three of six loci at the second location. These deviations were not observed in the second year. This difference may be the result of habitat loss, dispersal, and subsequent reproduction among turtles that had previously occupied different locations. In 1981 a large number of turtles from the peripheral ponds moved into the Lost Lake System because of a severe drought in the area. Turtles collected during 1983 exhibited significant deviations from Hardy-Weinberg equilibrium, all in the direction of heterozygote deficiencies, which would be predicted if turtles from populations with differing allele frequencies had been combined in one sample (Wahlund Effect; Wahlund, 1928). The second year's sampling included 2- and 3-year-old turtles that were produced during the drought. The populations were all in Hardy-Weinberg equilibrium during this second year because of the recruitment of these two cohorts.

During droughts, turtles probably move to areas with permanent water and remain there until favorable conditions reoccur (Gibbons et al., 1983). The relatively rapid reestablishment of equilibrium suggests that many of the 1983 immigrants emigrated from the Lost Lake System in 1984. Similar movements were probably occurring at Pond B, because the changes there also took place during and after the drought. Even though turtles often occur in discontinuous habitats, their populations are highly dynamic, and animals are interchanged, especially during periods of habitat loss.

Although turtles are known to make frequent movements between populations (Morreale et al., 1984; Parker, 1984), the genetic data show that these populations have different allele frequencies at a number of loci. One way to explain this seeming contradiction is to assume that the dispersers are not a random genetic subset of the turtles that are in these populations (Brown, 1985). The latter phenomenon can alter the conclusion that large amounts of dispersal cause allele frequencies to be essentially the same through space. However, there is no evidence that nonrandom dispersal by genotype occurs in turtles, so other factors are probably involved in explaining the spatial heterogeneity of allele frequency in *T. scripta*.

Low effective population size (N_e) is usually implicated as a principle cause of stochastic changes in allele frequency (Wright, 1969, 1970). Effective population size is a function of the number of individuals that actually contribute reproductively to the next generation (Crow and Kimura, 1970), and such things as sex ratio and variability in reproductive output can dramatically reduce N_e. Many turtles may breed, but if their offspring do not survive to the next generation for some reason, even chance, then they are not a part of the effective breeding population. The actual situation for breeding turtles may involve high variance in reproductive output because predators often eliminate entire clutches from some females (Congdon et al., 1983b). In any one year the eggs of a relatively small proportion of the adult females may survive. It could be a matter of chance that predators find some eggs and not others. Stochastic change is possible when a small number of a surviving cohort eventually breed and disproportionately influence the allele frequency and heterozygosity of the population. Under such circumstances a population could be different from adjacent ones for a number of years before dispersal and reproduction eliminated or greatly reduced the interpopulational genetic differences. The high heterozygosity of *T. scripta* indicates that low N_e is not expected as a general rule but could periodically occur.

Selection could also be involved in determining some of the genetic differences within and among populations. Selection is difficult to prove in natural populations, but some of the data for *T. scripta* suggest its effect. Two-, 3-, and 4-year-old turtles are significantly less heterozygous than older turtles in Pond B, a stable reservoir that supports a large turtle population. The Pond B population should be more resistant to chance fluctuations and be in approximate equilibrium with all subgroups having similar genetic characteristics. The source and mechanism for the selection are not known, but two other vertebrates on the SRP show similar changes in *H* (Smith and Chesser, 1981; Cothran et al., 1983), and there are a number of vertebrates that show age- or size-related changes in allele frequencies (e.g., Tinkle and Selander, 1973; Feder et al., 1984; Chesser and Smith, 1987). If additional sampling shows size- or age-related genetic changes to be common and their pattern of change similar across a series of turtle populations, then selection associated with some life history trait would be strongly suggested. The lower *H* in the young classes in Pond B is opposite of that expected if dispersal and subsequent reproduction are the cause of the age-related differences.

Regardless of whether the changes in the frequencies of the genetic characteristics are brought about stochastically or in a deterministic manner, there are consequences for the genetic quality of the offspring of turtles that are dispersing among genetically different populations. When allele frequencies differ significantly at a number of loci, as appears to be the case for *T. scripta* (Table 6.2), dispersing individuals are likely to breed with others that have different alleles in their genome. The offspring from matings involving a disperser and a resident are likely to be more heterozygous than those from matings between two residents in the same population. The latter type of mating probably involves more inbreeding than matings involving a disperser. Inbreeding is not necessarily detrimental (Shields, 1982), but it does change *H*, which is correlated with a number of functional traits in vertebrates (Mitton and Grant, 1984). As the ratio of inbred and outbred matings and/or the ratio of highly heterozygous and less heterozygous turtles in the population change, the functional properties of the populations are also likely to change (Smith et al., 1978). The result is the same if turtles from a population's subgroups have significantly different allele frequencies and breed

with one another. These subgroups might be composed of animals of different cohorts, ages, or sexes.

For our purposes many of the correlates of *H* are components of, or have direct effects on, secondary productivity. The best-studied animal in this regard is the white-tailed deer on the SRP. Antler growth and number of spikes both increase in the most heterozygous males (Smith et al., 1982; Scribner et al., 1984b; Scribner and Smith, n.d.). The most heterozygous females are the largest within each age class, have faster-growing fetuses, breed later in the season (Cothran et al., 1983), tend to have twins rather than single offspring (Chesser and Smith, 1987), have higher levels of body fat prior to conception, and lose body fat at slower rates during pregnancy (Cothran et al., 1987). Other vertebrates also show changes in reproductive rate, growth rate, and/or body size correlated with increasing *H* (Smith et al., 1975; Smith and Chesser, 1981; King, 1985). Basal metabolism and morphological asymmetry are also correlated with *H* in amphibians and reptiles (Mitton and Grant, 1984). The changes in heterozygosity with age in the Pond B turtles (Table 6.3) might also be due to a correlation with body size, which also increases with age. However, sample size will need to be increased to reliably separate the effects of age and body size on *H*. Heterozygosity-correlated changes in secondary productivity might be expected in all vertebrates if the cause is decreased maintenance metabolism in the most heterozygous animals (Garton et al., 1984). If energy intake is the same in animals of differing heterozygosities, then the most heterozygous ones would have more energy for growth and reproduction.

If size does change as a function of *H*, then size would have a profound effect on the number of eggs laid by breeding females and probably the reproductive rate of the local populations. Body size is the most important correlate of clutch size within a species of turtle (Gibbons, 1982; Congdon and Gibbons, 1983, 1985). Thus, the interaction of genetically different populations could alter the heterozygosity of resulting offspring and their reproductive contribution to these populations. A small difference in female body size of 10% to 20% within an age class could result in a much larger impact on the numbers of turtles in a population. The potential impact of genetics on the demography of turtles has yet to be studied, but density is correlated to *H* in old-field mice (Smith et al., 1975). Studies on the effects of genetic variability on the density and demography of *T. scripta* are needed.

In summary, populations of *T. scripta* are not genetically homogeneous over the SRP, over years, or among demographic units. The amount of heterogeneity in allele frequency due to demography within a single population is as great as that among turtles from the 16 locations on the SRP. The overall amount of heterogeneity is especially.

surprising, considering the relatively small distances and short time periods considered in this study. In addition, gene flow appears to be relatively high and might be expected to result in homogeneous allele frequencies among populations. The results of stochastic processes might be amplified through population expansion or differential reproductive success of certain turtles, and reversal of the resulting genetic disequilibrium through gene flow might take many generations. Thus, dispersal, stochastic events, and natural selection may all be interacting to produce a series of populations that are in a state of dynamic disequilibrium, which can be dramatically affected by environmental conditions such as droughts.

Trachemys scripta presents an interesting situation in which to study the interaction of these processes, and the effects observed in this study may be occurring generally in many vertebrates with a shorter life cycle, which results in more opportunities for rapid genetic changes. These short-term evolutionary changes could have direct effects on population processes by altering the functional properties of individuals. The importance of genetics, environmental factors, and their interactions to population dynamics of *T. scripta* needs to be evaluated within a regional context to obtain an understanding of changes or differences in density within and among populations.

Acknowledgments

Research and manuscript preparation were made possible by contract DE-AC09-76SROO-819 between the University of Georgia and the U.S. Department of Energy and by National Science Foundation grant DEB-79-04758.

JOHN M. LEGLER
Department of Biology
University of Utah
Salt Lake City, Utah 84112

7

The Genus *Pseudemys* in Mesoamerica: Taxonomy, Distribution, and Origins

Abstract

Pseudemys is the most diverse and wide-ranging genus in an emydine group that includes *Graptemys*, *Chrysemys*, and *Malaclemys*. *Pseudemys scripta* (Schoepff) 1792 is treated as a polytypic species with 17 or 18 subspecies and a latitudinal range of 77 degrees. At least 12 subspecies occur in Mesoamerica. This study is based on 2,308 specimens; 29 variables were analyzed. Brief accounts of taxonomy and distribution are given for each subspecies. Populations in the Río Nazas of northern Mexico and the Lago de Nicaraqua are described as new. All matters pertaining to distribution are considered by natural drainage systems and their recent histories. The distribution of *P. scripta* in Mesoamerica is explained as a series of dispersal events ranging from simple dispersal along coastal plains to headwater dispersal across continental divides. Distributions appear to be largely natural, but humans could have caused or influenced almost any of the events hypothesized.

Pseudemys scripta has crossed the Mesoamerican landmass five times, as follows: from the Atlantic to the Pacific via the Rio Grande and the interior basins of northern Mexico, via the Isthmus of Tehauntepec, via the Río San Juan and Lake Nicaragua, and via the Isthmus of Panama; and from the Pacific to the Atlantic, from the Río Tuira of Panama to the Río Atrato of Colombia. Relatively recent colonization and differentiation of *P. scripta* in Mesoamerica is proposed (Pleistocene or later). The following three groups of *scripta*-like taxa are proposed: the three subspecies in the United States; Mesoamerican populations; and Antillean populations. In the U.S. subspecies, males are much smaller than females and have greatly elongated foreclaws, which are used in a complex Liebespiel. Mesoamerican populations lack these sexually dimorphic characters and the Liebespiel. The dimorphic characters and the courtship behavior exhibited by U.S. subspecies are considered to be precopulatory isolating mechanisms in a zone where more than one species of *Pseudemys* (plus other striped emydines) are sympatric. *Pseudemys scripta* is the only striped emydine south and west of the Rio Grande.

Introduction

The Northern Hemisphere emydine genera *Graptemys*, *Malaclemys*, *Pseudemys*, and *Chrysemys* seem to be closely related (the *Chrysemys* complex of McDowell, 1964). I refer to this assemblage hereinafter as the *Chrysemys* group; the group excludes *Deirochelys*, and I consider *Chrysemys* to be monotypic (*Chrysemys picta*). These genera share most of the following characters: pale stripes on the soft skin; a pattern of pale ocelli, whorls, or vertical bars on the lateral scutes; a dusky, usually concentric plastral figure; distinct and extreme patterns of sexual dimorphism (adult size, foreclaws, head size, melanism); mating behavior often complex; regular thermoregulatory basking (Moll and Legler, 1971; Ernst and Barbour, 1972; pers. obs.). *Pseudemys* is the most diverse and widely distributed of these genera. One of its species, *Pseudemys scripta*, is remarkable in ranging over 77 degrees of latitude and nearly encompassing the latitudinal range of all other New World emydines (*Emydoidea* and parts of *Clemmys* and *Chrysemys* being the exceptions).

The objective of this study was a stable, natural classification of *Pseudemys scripta*. My emphasis was on taxonomic research and zoogeography rather than on nomenclatural change. This account is prepared as general information, not as a scientific monograph. My approach to this problem has been deliberate in the interest of thoroughness; this has made the work of compilers difficult. We must all be grateful to Hobart and Rosella Smith (1979) for the arduous job of compiling keys, synonymies, and references to the turtles of Mexico. I have concentrated on relationships and zoogeography.

In my early days as a student I heard dark mutterings and witnessed a lot of hand waving about "difficult" taxonomic groups and about not having enough "material." A "difficult group" seemed to have the following characteristics: (1) no one knew much about it, (2) one couldn't learn much about it by looking in specimen jars, (3) finding and studying the animals required a lot of work. In the case of turtles, systematic research often involves starting almost de novo by gathering the necessary collections. I did so for Mesoamerican *Pseudemys*.

In 1958 Wendell L. Minckley and I visited the basin of Cuatro Ciénegas, Coahuila, in search of an aquatic box turtle (*Terrapene coahuila*) and found that most of the aquatic organisms in the basin were endemic (Minckley, 1969). Among these was *Pseudemys scripta taylori*. This taxon was obviously part of the "*scripta* series" we knew in the United States, but relating the new taxon to the rest of the group was an ordeal because *Pseudemys scripta* had not been adequately studied. It was soon evident that *P. scripta* extended far into Mesoamerica. I date the present study from that time (Legler, 1960b).

The "problems" of generic nomenclature are not addressed here. Seidel and Smith (1986) provide the most recent review of the subject. This study deals with the group I recognize as a single polytypic species, *Pseudemys scripta* (Schoepff) 1792, as outlined in Moll and Legler (1971).

Materials and Methods

The study is based on 2,308 specimens for which complete data were available (Table 7.1). The 29 variables analyzed were carapace length (as a raw datum), 3 stripe character states, and 25 measurements expressed as percentages of carapace length. Early hypotheses were formed with the aid of simple descriptive statistics before the advent of computers. Multidiscriminant analysis was used in the final stages; in nearly all cases the early hypotheses were congruent with the final analyses. Computer analysis saved time but produced no surprises.

DATA STORAGE

All data used in this study have been stored (raw and transformed) in ASCII files at the University of Utah.

Table 7.1. Summary of specimens examined

Population	Male	Female	Immature	Total
Pseudemys scripta				
scripta	12	14	19	45
troosti	5	5	5	15
elegans	106	73	279	458
elegans/taylori	6	6	7	19
taylori	51	62	15	128
gaigeae	16	23	11	50
hartwegi	7	13	14	34
hiltoni	30	14	10	54
nebulosa	7	5	7	19
yaquia	15	5	5	25
ornata	17	21	11	49
grayi	13	22	22	57
elegans/cataspila	2	2	0	4
cataspila	44	17	15	76
venusta	224	238	108	570
emolli	31	36	39	106
GDULCE	5	25	24	54
CAPAC	46	48	32	126
Río Atrato	0	1	1	2
callirostris	1	2	22	25
dorbigni	0	2	4	6
P. felis	6	4	10	20
P. malonei	6	12	0	18
P. granti	7	6	8	21
P. terrapen	18	12	20	50
P. vicina/decorata	3	5	2	10
P. decorata	6	4	14	24
P. vicina	16	8	14	38
P. decussata				
angusta	10	6	0	16
decussata	66	87	38	191
plana	4	2	2	8
P. concinna	5	6	12	23
P. floridana	6	3	5	14
P. nelsoni	3	3	4	10
Total	794	792	779	2,365

These files and the collections of specimens will be available to other workers when the study is completed. The data used in this study can be tested or reinterpreted with a minimum of effort. Specimens and data now at UU will eventually be transferred to one or more public museums.

MEASUREMENTS

Terminology for scutes and bones follows Moll and Legler (1971). Measurements were designed to express what I could detect with ordinary human senses and to be repeatable. Measurement techniques are shown in Figure 7.1. Basic measurements express the size of the smallest rectilinear box into which the shell would fit. A videotape describing turtle measurements is available from the author (Legler, 1982). Data were rejected for any structure that was broken or anomalous.

The following is a list of measurements, other data, and their abbreviations: LC, length of carapace; WC, width of carapace; LP, length of plastron, maximal; WPHP, width

of plastron, humeropectoral seam; WPMF, width of plastron, midfemoral scute; HT, height of shell, maximal; GUL, length of gular scute; HUM, length of humeral scute; PEC, length of pectoral scute; AB, length of abdominal scute; FEM, length of femoral scute; AN, length of anal scute; LC1, length of C1 (first central scute); LC2, length of C2; LC3, length of C3; LC4, length of C4; LC5, length of C5; WC1A, width of C1, anterior; WC1P, width of C1, posterior; WC2, width of C2; WC3, width of C3; WC4, width of C4; WC5, width of C5; WH, width of head, maximal, at tympanum; FING, length of ungual phalanx, third digit, manus; BR, length of bridge (mean of right and left); POSEYE, postorbital stripe connected to eye? (+ or −); POSNCK, postorbital stripe connected to neck stripe? (+ or −); MANDNCK, mandibular stripe connected to neck stripe? (+ or −).

STATISTICAL ANALYSIS

Final analysis was done with various BMDP statistical software programs (Version 1982) on a mainframe computer (see Dixon, 1983). The programs most used were BMDP7M, stepwise discriminant analysis; BMDP3D, comparison of two groups with t tests; and BMDP7D, description of groups with histograms and analysis of variance. BMDP7M will not tolerate incomplete data sets. Missing data points resulted mainly from the rejection of measurements from broken or deformed parts. Missing data were estimated with BMDPMD. Spot checks of estimated data corresponded almost exactly to my own interpolative method of estimation with specimens ranked by population, sex, and carapace length. My own tolerance of estimated data was inversely proportional to the need for specimens in the sample. Percentages of estimated values higher than 10% were tolerated only to avoid eliminating a population from the analysis. The alternative was to reject the character; this accounted for the removal of several characters from the original data base. Thus it was possible to use the same combination of characters for all populations of *Pseudemys* considered.

Analyses of adults were done separately by sex; the analysis was repeated for all adults if the results were not significantly different between sexes (this was common). Statistical comparisons of immature specimens have been avoided in recent turtle studies (Berry, 1978; Iverson, 1981). I used juveniles in some analyses because (1) some former studies of *Pseudemys scripta* (Müller, 1940; Williams, 1956) were based substantially on young turtles and (2) at least some juveniles are available from nearly all geographic regions, whereas there are many gaps in the availability of adults. Carapace length and finger length were excluded from the analysis of juveniles.

Data on stripes were "yes or no" character states: connection of postorbital stripe to the eye or to a neck stripe (expressing degree of isolation of postorbital mark), and

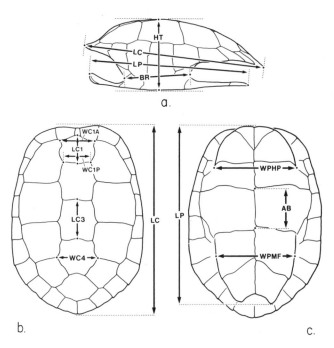

FIGURE 7.1. *a–c*, lateral, dorsal, and ventral views of a *Pseudemys scripta* shell, showing method of measurement. Note that a single measurement expressed the mean length of right and left plastral scutes. Width of central scutes was measured from points common to three scutes. Central lengths were measured along the midline. Carapace and plastron lengths were maximal and measured in a plane usually tangential to the true frontal plane. *AB*, length of abdominal scute; *BR*, length of bridge; *HT*, height of shell, maximal; *LC*, length of carapace; *LC1*, length of C1 (first central scute); *LC3*, length of C3; *LP*, length of plastron; *WC1A*, width of C1, anterior; *WC1P*, width of C1, posterior; *WC4*, width of C4; *WPHP*, width of plastron, humeropectoral seam; *WPMF*, width of plastron, midfemoral scute.

connection of mandibular stripe to a neck stripe. These character states were recorded for each of the pertinent stripes on each side but were ultimately expressed in a manner that indicated a connection was present on one or both sides. These stripe character states, although qualitatively different from body measurements, were included in the multidiscriminant analyses because (1) they are important in my own visual discrimination of the populations and (2) they are probably used by the turtles in the same way (see Conclusions, below).

Measurements were also made of isolated stripes or expansions of the postorbital stripe whether isolated or not. These were not used in the main analysis because they were not available for some populations. However, they were useful in diagnosing some subspecies.

On all BMDP7M plots there are outliers that distort the cluster and the mean. Outliers were removed if they resulted from anomaly or error, but most outliers were normally exceptional individuals (e.g., the largest *P. s. venusta*, the smallest male *P. s. cataspila*, etc.). Such specimens were left in the data base.

LOCALITIES

Specific localities (although they exist) are avoided in this chapter; distributions are couched in the context of drainage systems and known place names on easily available maps. Latitudes (N) and longitudes (W) are abbreviated for easy reference. In a few cases, actual coordinates are given (e.g., lat. 11-4, long. 68-15), but more often a single meridian or parallel is given to signify where that line intersects the coastline or stream in question. The easiest way to actually locate localities is on World Aeronautical Charts (WAC) or Operational Navigational Charts (ONC), both of which are 1:1,000,000. Most of the Mexican localities are listed in Smith and Smith (1979).

Mesoamerica, for purposes of this study, begins just south of the U.S.-Mexican border and extends approximately to the Río Atrato of northern Colombia. The northern political boundaries are congruent with a major faunal transition.

COLOR AND PATTERN

STRIPES.   Pale stripes on the soft skin range from yellow to cream. They are most regular and evident on the head and neck. The stripes appear in all members of the *Chrysemys* group and seem to be homologous within that group. Similar stripes in other emydids may have evolved independently (e.g., *Ocadia*).

Stripes vary in distinctness by virtue of width, degree of contrast with ground color, and the extent to which they are outlined in black. Between the main or primary stripes there are lesser numbers of secondary and tertiary stripes.

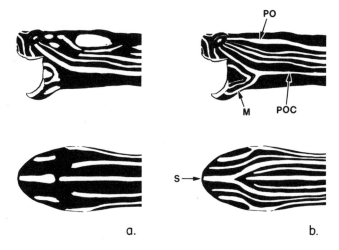

FIGURE 7.2.   Head striping in *Pseudemys*: *a*, lateral and ventral views of derived conditions; *b*, lateral and ventral views of hypothesized ancestral condition of continuous stripes. All stripe patterns in *Pseudemys* can be derived by interruptions, obliterations, and fusions of the stripes shown here. Stripes mentioned in the text are identified: *M*, mandibular; *PO*, postorbital; *POC*, primary orbitocervical; *S*, symphyseal.

The basic and presumably ancestral pattern is that of unbroken, parallel stripes, extending from the face, snout, and mouth to the base of the neck (Fig. 7.2). Substantial modification of this plan occurs when stripes fuse with other stripes or are fragmented, when isolated parts assume various shapes, and when stripes or derived fragments acquire a color other than some shade of yellow (usually red or orange). The degree of pattern fragmentation is low in *P. s. scripta*, *P. s. elegans*, and *P. s. ornata* and very high in *P. s. callirostris*. A survey of stripe patterns appears in Table 7.2.

Isolated, brightly colored, or otherwise distinctive marks in the temporal region seem always to be modifications of the postorbital stripe. In some populations (e.g., *P. s. venusta*) the widened primary orbitocervical becomes the dominant mark on the side of the head. The pale stripes and the dark background can undergo vast ontogenetic changes, becoming completely obliterated or obscured through melanism or fading. Fading reaches its extremes in the Antillean populations but is important also (especially on the throat) in *nebulosa* and other Mesoamerican populations. Extremes of melanism and fading are characteristic of U.S. and Antillean populations but are rare in Mesoamerica. Despite the potential for ontogenetic change, the connections of the stripes do not change with age, and if visible at any stage, they are easily quantifiable and useful.

Stripes may have evolved initially as disruptive markings. Modifications in the basic patterns later evolved as species-specific combinations that may serve as premating isolating mechanisms in zones of sympatry (see Con-

Table 7.2. Stripe patterns in 18 populations of *Pseudemys scripta*

Taxon	Color of POM	N	Eye	Neck	Mand.	Sym.	PI
elegans USA	Red	97	98.6	35.7	84.1	97.1	.789
elegans Rio Grande	Red	154	58.9	6.3	56.8	100.0	.555
taylori	Red	101	27.1	10.4	0.0	86.9	.311
gaigeae	Br. orange	50	0.0	0.0	54.5	100.0	.386
hartwegi	Dk. or. yellow	34	0.0	35.5	0.0	33.3	.172
hiltoni	P. dusky or.	54	17.8	15.6	46.3	50.0	.324
nebulosa	P. dusky or.	18	0.0	0.0	66.7	33.3	.250
yaquia	P. or. yellow	25	76.0	100.0	16.0	68.0	.650
ornata	P. or. yellow	5	40.0	60.0	20.0	80.0	.500
grayi	P. yellow	58	96.9	97.0	9.1	70.0	.683
cataspila	P. or., dk. or. yellow	74	44.3	74.3	24.3	64.9	.520
venusta	P. or. yellow	570	90.9	96.5	15.7	41.8	.615
emolli	P. or. yellow	106	27.4	83.3	17.9	90.5	.548
GDULCE	P. or. yellow	54	100.0	96.2	3.8	38.5	.596
CAPAC	P. or. yellow	126	98.2	97.3	49.6	32.4	.694
Río Atrato	Brick red (1)	2	100.0	100.0	100.0	0.0	.750
callirostris	Reddish or.	25	0.0	47.8	0.0	0.0	.120
dorbigni	Or. yellow (2)	5	80.0	100.0	40.0	100.0	.800

Note: Color of postorbital mark (POM) or expansion and stripe connections is as follows: eye and neck--frequency with which postorbital stripe enters the orbit or joins a neck stripe; "mand." and "sym." indicate whether mandibular stripe and symphyseal stripes join neck stripes. Frequencies apply to joined condition on one or both sides. Ergo data for *hartwegi* show that postorbital mark is always isolated from eye on one or both sides and that symphyseal stripe joins a neck stripe on one or both sides in 33% of specimens examined. PI = pattern integrity, a general expression of disruption of the ancestral pattern of continuous stripes ([sum of four frequencies]/400). Most stripes are broken in *callirostris* (.120), and relatively few are broken in *venusta* (.615). (Personal observation except (1) = Medem, 1962, and (2) = Freiberg, 1967b.) Abbreviations: p., pale; dk., dark; br., bright; or., orange.

clusions, below). However, the distinctive stripe patterns in Mesoamerican populations of *P. scripta* are probably nonadaptive.

SHELL PATTERN. Although shell patterns can be used to characterize populations, they are not easy to quantify and were not used in the statistical analysis.

Carapace. The basic carapace pattern consists of ocelli on the lateral and marginal scutes and a variable pattern on the central scutes. The pale marks of the carapace range from yellow through pinkish orange to dark orange. The lateral ocelli vary in shape but are usually vertical ellipses. Ocelli consist of two to four concentric rings that vary in their distinctness; there may be one or more side branches in various directions from the peripheral ring. The outermost ring normally becomes the most prominent ring. The ocellar center often becomes a dark bull's-eyelike figure.

There are four lateral ocelli on each side. Each is centered over an intercostal osseous suture, placing it usually on the posterior half of a lateral scute. There are eight costal bones. If we count the nuchal-costal suture as the first intercostal suture (IC1), then the ocelli are centered on even-numbered intercostal sutures. This seems to be constant. The centers of the ocelli vary in their juxtaposition to interlaminal seams because the seams vary in their juxtaposition to the sutures.

Two extremes of carapace pattern are the unmodified ocellar pattern of many Mesoamerican *scripta* and the ver-

tically barred pattern of U.S. *P. scripta. Pseudemys s. elegans* usually has four vertical bars, each of which occurs near the center of a lateral scute and is oriented over the approximate center of an underlying costal bone (i.e., C1, C3, C5, C7). The vertical bars are modifications of the ocellar pattern. In fact, ocelli *and* bars can be observed in many *elegans*. It is clear that the vertical bars are derived from the anterior parts of the ancestral ocelli.

The marginal ocelli are in two series: supramarginal and inframarginal. They are clearly centered on the intermarginal seams. Those on the superior surfaces show a variation and modification similar to the principal lateral ocelli; those below are less complex and more like the plastral pattern. Marginal ocelli seem to be only slightly modified in derived carapace patterns, such as in *P. s. elegans.*

The most common feature of the central scute pattern is a pair of parenthetical marks, one on either side of the middorsal line. These marks may connect in two longitudinal series or form a completely separate pair of marks on each scute. In populations with complex patterns, there is commonly an intricate pattern of triangles, rhomboids, or irregular polygons between the parenthetical marks. A series of straight marks on and parallel to the middorsal line may be emphasized to form a middorsal stripe. Anywhere on the carapace, as on the soft skin, the pattern can be altered and complicated by the intercalation of other pale lines. Some shells have a confusing reticular appearance.

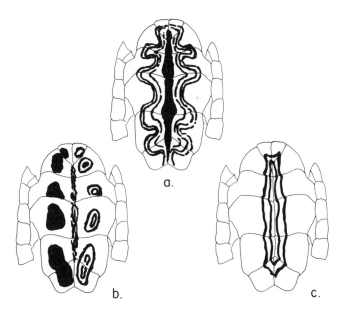

FIGURE 7.3. Plastral pattern in *Pseudemys scripta*. *a*, full "*Chrysemys*" pattern. *b* and *c*, two derived conditions: *b*, composite figure showing isolated whorls on one side and isolated whorls overlaid by solid blotches on the other side; *c*, reduced plastral pattern (e.g., *hartwegi*). Whorls and blotches in *b* occur in *elegans*, *hiltoni*, and *nebulosa*; the whorls are present at hatching, and the blotches develop later.

Plastron. The basic plastral pattern in *P. scripta* is a dusky, concentric figure, usually lacking sharply defined edges, that is greater than half the plastral area (Fig. 7.3). Whorls or fingerlike projections extend laterally along the interlaminal seams. This basic pattern is most easily seen in juveniles. Some modifications of this pattern are isolation of some or all of the seam-following whorls (e.g., *P. s. elegans*, *P. decorata*), loss of lateral whorls and narrowing (e.g., some *P. s. venusta*), and extreme fading (e.g., *P. s. scripta*, *P. terrapen*). The concentric pattern remains visible throughout life in *Chrysemys picta* and *P. s. venusta* with only minor change. Secondary deposition of melanin causes striking changes in some populations, but these changes occur over the concentric pattern. In *P. s. elegans* (rarely in *P. s. scripta*) the isolated whorls are overlaid by solid blotches of melanin, some of which can be seen in a shed scute. The dusky whorls remain clearly visible in the soft tissue beneath the scute, but only if the scute can be removed. This explains the solid black fingerprintlike smudges seen in the subspecies *elegans*, *hiltoni*, *nebulosa*, and sometimes *scripta*. A full concentric pattern is here regarded as ancestral; it occurs in all genera of the *Chrysemys* group, all other plastral patterns can logically be derived from it, and it appears in the young of nearly all species of *Pseudemys*.

The ancestral *P. scripta* had a pattern of unbroken yellow stripes on the head and neck, an ocellar carapace pattern, and a dusky, concentric plastral pattern. This

pattern is more common in Mesoamerica than elsewhere in the broad range of *P. scripta*.

Results and Discussion

Pseudemys scripta is aquatic. All matters pertaining to geographical distribution are considered by natural drainage systems and their recent histories. Analysis began with the assumption that each drainage system could contain a distinctive population. Progressive amalgamation of smaller populations, assisted by multidiscriminant analysis, formed the assemblages here defined as subspecies.

ACCOUNTS OF SUBSPECIES

There are 17 or 18 subspecies of *Pseudemys scripta*; 17 are considered below. Two are described as new herein. Populations on the Pacific Coast of Central America (CAPAC) may be named when their status is resolved. Mexico has the greatest diversity, with 11 subspecies. My personal knowledge of the three South American subspecies is slight, based on a total of 31 specimens; by comparison, my knowledge is substantial for all populations north and west of the Río Atrato in Colombia. Mesoamerican populations are considered in four geographic groups: the Northern Isolates; the Gulf Coast–Caribbean series; the Pacific Coast series; and the Lake Nicaragua–Pacific series, from Lake Nicaragua and the Pacific Coast of Central America southward to the Isthmus of Panama. South American populations are included simply for completeness.

The following brief accounts of subspecies give current subspecific epithet, literature reference to type description, type locality, a brief statement of geographic distribution, and any qualifying or supporting information necessary to the account. Note that the designation and description of *P. s. hartwegi* is formalized. Figure 7.4 shows the geographic ranges of the subspecies discussed; the map is diagrammatic and does not show individual localities. Smith and Smith (1979) had access to all of the material in my data base. Their localities are accurate to 30 minutes of longitude or latitude (± about 50 km at the Tropic of Cancer).

UNITED STATES POPULATIONS. These three subspecies form a natural group that has differentiated within the United States (excluding *P. s. gaigeae*; see USASCRIP in Conclusions, below). They are not considered in any detail here except to compare them with Mesoamerican populations. Satisfactory summaries of knowledge appear in Pritchard (1979), Ernst and Barbour (1972), and Carr (1952).

P. s. scripta (Schoepff), 1792:16.

Type locality: Restricted to Charleston, South Carolina (Schmidt, 1953).

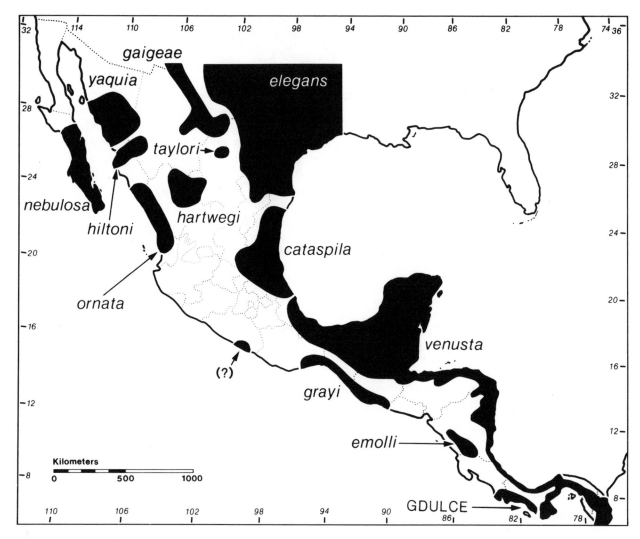

FIGURE 7.4.   Distribution of the subspecies of *Pseudemys scripta* in Mesoamerica. The ranges shown are diagrammatic and approximate. No attempt is made to show the U.S. distribution of *elegans*, *scripta*, and *troosti*.

Distribution: Eastern coastal plain, Virginia to northern Florida.

P. s. troosti (Holbrook), 1836:55.
    Type locality: Cumberland River, Tennessee.
    Distribution: Upper parts of Cumberland and Tennessee rivers from extreme southwestern Virginia to extreme northeastern Alabama.

P. s. elegans (Wied), 1839:213.
    Type locality: Fox River, New Harmony, Indiana.
    Distribution: In Mexico, the lower Rio Grande and its tributaries. Elsewhere, the Mississippi drainage from southern Michigan to the Gulf of Mexico (eastward to Ohio, Kentucky, Tennessee, and Alabama; westward to Nebraska, Kansas, Oklahoma, and Texas); Gulf drainages between New Orleans and Brownsville; the Pecos drainage.

NORTHERN ISOLATES.

P. s. taylori Legler, 1960b:73–84.
    Type locality: 16 km south of Cuatro Ciénegas, Coahuila, Mexico.
    Distribution: Basin of Cuatro Ciénegas, Coahuila.

P. s. gaigeae Hartweg, 1939:1.
    Type locality: Boquillas, Rio Grande, Brewster County, Texas.
    Distribution: Upper Rio Grande above the Big Bend region and Río Conchos drainages of Texas, New Mexico, Chihuahua, and Coahuila.

P. s. hartwegi (see below).
    Distribution: Río Nazas drainage of Durango and Coahuila.

Life History and Ecology of the Slider Turtle

GULF COAST–CARIBBEAN SERIES.

P. s. cataspila (Günther), 1885:4.

Type locality: Restricted to Tampico, Tamaulipas, Mexico (Smith and Smith, 1979).

Distribution: Río San Fernando drainage of Tamaulipas (mouth at lat. 24-45) southward to Punta del Morro (lat. 19-55).

Remarks: Little suitable habitat for *Pseudemys* exists between the Río San Fernando and Brownsville. Four juveniles from La Laca (lat. 25-6, long. 98-7) show a great range of variation that includes characters of both *elegans* and *cataspila*.

P. s. venusta (Gray), 1855:24.

Type locality: Honduras or British Honduras (see Smith and Smith, 1979:495).

Distribution: From the beginning of the coastal plain just south of Punta del Morro southward through the lowlands of Veracruz, Oaxaca, and Tabasco to the base of the Yucatán Peninsula; thence across and around the Yucatán Peninsula through northern Guatemala, Quintana Roo, and British Honduras; thence eastward along the Caribbean coast of Guatemala, Honduras, Nicaragua, Costa Rica, and Panama. The population in the Río Chagres drainage (studied by Moll and Legler, 1971) is here included in *venusta*. Populations on the Pacific side of Panama are still under investigation.

Remarks: It is possible that *venusta* has colonized the Pacific coast of Panama and Costa Rica northward to the Golfo Dulce. The population in the Río Atrato of Colombia is placed in *venusta*.

PACIFIC COAST SERIES.

P. s. hiltoni Carr, 1942:1.

Type locality: Guirocoba, Sonora, Mexico, 453 m.

Distribution: Río Fuerte drainage of Sonora and Sinaloa.

P. s. nebulosa (Van Denburgh), 1895:84.

Type locality: Los Dolores, Baja California Sur, Mexico.

Distribution: Baja California Sur southward from San Ignacio.

P. s. yaquia Legler and Webb, 1970:157–168.

Type locality: Río Mayo, Conicarit, Sonora, Mexico.

Distribution: Sonora, Yaqui, and Mayo drainages in Sonora.

P. s. ornata (Gray), 1831:30.

Type locality: Mazatlán, Sinaloa, Mexico.

Distribution: From Culiacán, Sinaloa, southward to the region of Cabo Corrientes.

Remarks: A population near Acapulco may be *ornata* but is not considered in this work. The range of *ornata* may extend northward into the Río Sinaloa drainage.

P. s. grayi (Bocourt), 1868:121.

Type locality: Río Nagualate, Guatemala.

Distribution: From the region of Salina Cruz, Oaxaca, southeastward the coastal lagoons of Oaxaca and Chiapas, along the Pacific coast of Guatemala to just east of Acajutla, El Salvador.

Remarks: *P. s. grayi* seems to flourish in coastal lagoons.

LAKE NICARAGUA–PACIFIC SERIES.

P. s. emolli (see below).

Distribution: Drainage of Lago de Nicaragua and Lago de Managua in Nicaragua and adjacent Costa Rica; an indeterminate distance down the San Juan River.

Remarks: Populations at the source of the San Juan just north of San Carlos are clearly *emolli*; populations near the mouth are clearly *venusta*.

GDULCE (abbreviation for "Golfo Dulce").

Distribution: From the region of Puerto Cortés and Palmar Sur, Costa Rica, definitely to Horconcitos, Panama, on the Golfo de Chiriquí; most closely related to *venusta*.

Remarks: The taxonomic position of this population is still under study.

CAPAC (abbreviation for "Central America Pacific").

Distribution: Pacific side of Panama from the Azuero Peninsula at least to the Isthmian region.

Remarks: This population is under study.

SOUTH AMERICAN POPULATIONS.

P. s. callirostris (Gray), 1855:25.

Type locality: Río Magdalena, Colombia (restricted; see Müller, 1940).

Distribution: Río Magdalena, Río Cauca, and their combined deltas in Colombia eastward to eastern Falcón Province, Venezuela (near Puerto Cabello).

P. s. chichiriviche Pritchard and Trebbau, 1984:37–38.

Type locality: Lago de Tacarigua, Falcón, Venezuela (lat. 11-4, long. 68-15).

Distribution: Small coastal river systems between the Río Tocuyo in Falcón and Morón, Carabobo, Venezuela.

Remarks: No specimens of *P. s. chichiriviche* have been examined.

P. s. dorbigni (Duméril and Bibron), 1835:272.

Type locality: Buenos Aires.

Remarks: I am provisionally placing all remaining populations of South American *P. scripta* in the synonymy of *P. s. dorbigni*.

NEW TAXA.

Pseudemys scripta hartwegi new subspecies
  (Fig. 7.5, Tables 7.2–7.6)

P. s. gaigeae; Hartweg, 1939 (part).

FIGURE 7.5. *a* and *b*, ventral and dorsal views of holotype of *Pseudemys scripta hartwegi* new subspecies, UU 3802, carapace length 95 mm; *c, P. s. gaigeae*, immature female, KU 51205, Río Conchos, 1.6 km northwest of Ojinaga, Chihuahua; *d, P. s. hartwegi*, male paratype, MSU 1140. Both heads are slightly larger than life.

P. s. hartwegi Legler nomen nudum; Smith and Smith, 1979:469.

I first became aware of this taxon in 1959; a description was prepared but was consistently delayed as studies of *Pseudemys* progressed. Hobart Smith and I agreed to the inclusion of this taxon in the work on Mexican turtles (Smith and Smith, 1979:469). It was included as *Pseudemys scripta hartwegi* Legler nomen nudum, in a manner that

would ensure the name was available for my use at a later date.

Holotype: UU 3802, immature; carapace length 95 mm; Río Nazas, 1.2 km east of Presa Lázaro Cardenas, Durango, Mexico. Collected by Roger Conant, 2 October 1961. Whole specimen in alcohol.

Paratypes: Total of 29 specimens, all from Río Nazas drainage. Coahuila: MCZ 4550 female (shell only), 4551 three juveniles, San Pedro [de las Colonias]; USNM

Table 7.3. Relative proportions of head stripes for two new taxa, *Pseudemys scripta emolli* and *Pseudemys scripta hartwegi*, compared with those of their nearest geographic neighbors

Taxon	LPO/LC	WPO/LC	LMS/LC	WPO/LPO	LMS/LPO
elegans	0.13 ± 0.022	0.04 ± 0.007	0.11 ± 0.019	0.31 ± 0.073	0.78 ± 0.163
taylori	0.12 ± 0.015	0.03 ± 0.009	0.10 ± 0.012	0.27 ± 0.054	0.83 ± 0.085
gaigeae	0.08 ± 0.013	0.04 ± 0.008	0.10 ± 0.020	0.49 ± 0.085	1.42 ± 0.378
hartwegi	0.12 ± 0.014	0.05 ± 0.012	0.05 ± 0.012	0.44 ± 0.089	0.47 ± 0.093
hiltoni	0.07 ± 0.008	0.03 ± 0.008	0.09 ± 0.016	0.43 ± 0.084	1.33 ± 0.259
nebulosa	0.06 ± 0.007	0.03 ± 0.013	0.10 ± 0.024	0.45 ± 0.170	1.60 ± 0.378
venusta	0.11 ± 0.018	0.03 ± 0.007	0.09 ± 0.017	0.25 ± 0.037	0.82 ± 0.185
emolli	0.06 ± 0.027	0.03 ± 0.009	0.09 ± 0.016	0.56 ± 0.129	1.61 ± 0.394
GDULCE	0.11 ± 0.018	0.04 ± 0.009	0.09 ± 0.015	0.30 ± 0.044	0.86 ± 0.081
CAPAC	0.11 ± 0.012	0.03 ± 0.007	0.09 ± 0.017	0.27 ± 0.051	0.89 ± 0.173

Note: Mean and one standard deviation are given. Abbreviations: LC, carapace length; LPO, length of postorbital mark; WPO, width of postorbital mark; LMS, length of mandibular stripe.

Table 7.4. Comparison of *Pseudemys scripta hartwegi*
new subspecies with *P. s. gaigeae* Hartweg

Pseudemys scripta gaigeae	*Pseudemys scripta hartwegi*
1. Gular and pectoral scutes shorter, 12% and 16% of carapace length, respectively (see Table 7.5).	Gular and pectoral scutes relatively longer, 14% and 19% of carapace length, respectively.
2. Abdominal scute the longest scute of plastron, anal scute second longest in 95% of specimens.	Anal scute longest or anal and abdominal scutes subequal in length.
3. Plastral pattern more or less continuous from gular scute to anal scute, consisting of two or more concentric lines (distinct at least in young) and distributed about equally on anterior and posterior halves of plastron.	Plastral pattern concentrated chiefly on posterior half of plastron (behind pectoro-abdominal seam); small markings on pectorals, humerals, and gulars, if present, usually isolated from rest of pattern; pattern lacks distinct concentric arrangement (except in juveniles).
4. Middorsal keels obtuse or wanting, occasionally distinct in young.	Middorsal keels ordinarily distinct and black on posterior halves of first four central scutes (all ages).
5. Radial corrugations on central scutes indistinct or wanting in adults.	Radial corrugations on central scutes usually distinct in adults.
6. A dark spot on each of first three lateral scutes (and usually on the fourth) slightly less distinct in adults than in young.	Dark spots on lateral scutes obscure or wanting.
7. Dark spots on upper and lower surfaces of marginals obscure, tending to be pale-centered; those of upper surfaces much less distinct than spots on laterals.	Dark spots on upper and lower surfaces of marginals bold, solid, and frequently pale-bordered, contrasting sharply with ground color.
8. Postorbital mark (an isolated, black-bordered portion of postorbital stripe) relatively small, often pointed behind, in shape of teardrop.	Postorbital spot relatively large, usually not pointed behind, more nearly in shape of perfect oval.
9. Symphyseal stripe forked behind, one or both rami continuous with a ventral longitudinal neck stripe.	Symphyseal stripe not forked behind but separated by a black border and usually a hiatus from other ventral, longitudinal neck stripes; posterior end flanked by a pair of spots in some specimens.
10. Mandibular stripe forming a Y with a stripe from lower orbital border to neck or continuous with a separate neck stripe in 55% of specimens; mandibular stripe longer than postorbital mark in 97% of specimens.	Mandibular stripe short, ovoid, not linear, never continuous with any other stripe; half or less than half the length of postorbital mark in all specimens.

Note: Descriptions are based on all specimens examined.

105265, 105267–68 males, 105266, 105269 females, 21 km west of San Pedro [de las Colonias]; KU 29357 juvenile, 8 km south of San Pedro de las Colonias. Durango: USNM 103760 female, Río Nazas; UU 17583, 4700–4701 females, 3848–49, 4702 juveniles, from the type locality; USNM 60921 juvenile, Lerdo; AMNH 67494 juvenile,

24 km southwest of Lerdo; UU 4703–5 females, 4706–7 males, 16 km north-northwest Rodeo; MSU 1137–40 females, 1141 male, 2.4 km northwest of Nazas.

Diagnosis: A subspecies of *Pseudemys scripta* closely related to *P. s. gaigeae* and distinguished by the following combination of characters: anal lamina usually longer than abdominal; plastral pattern brown, relatively narrow, concentrated posterior to pectoro-abdominal seam; carapace pattern chiefly indistinct except for bold, circumferential series of dark-centered ocelli, one on each marginal scute; and isolated stripe on mandibular ramus half or less than half as long as isolated postorbital mark. *Pseudemys s. hartwegi* has the shortest mandibular stripe of any subspecies of *P. scripta* other than *callirostris*. See Table 7.4 for a detailed comparison with *P. s. gaigeae*.

Distribution: Río Nazas drainage of Durango and Coahuila.

Remarks: The type locality is in the tail water below and within sight of the dam itself. This section of the river has a gallery forest of mature Mexican cypress (*Taxodium mucronatum;* Conant, 1963). The subspecies may be nearing extinction in the vicinity of San Pedro de las Colonias. A large female (274 mm, UU 17583) obtained 26 May 1976 at the type locality contained 48 enlarged ovarian follicles in three sets (no corpora lutea).

Etymology: Named in honor of Norman E. Hartweg (1904–64), who made the first efforts in modern taxonomic studies of Mesoamerican chelonians.

Pseudemys scripta emolli new subspecies
(Fig. 7.6, Tables 7.2, 7.3, 7.6, 7.7)

Holotype: UU 6728 immature female, original number FVN 370; carapace length 194 mm; Río Tepetate, 2.5 km northeast of Granada, Granada Province, Nicaragua. Collected by E. O. Moll and F. V. Nabrotzky, 16–18 May 1964. Whole specimen in alcohol.

Allotype: UU 6765 male, original number FVN 369; carapace length 179 mm; same data as holotype.

Paratopotypes: UU 6731, 6733 immature females; same data as holotype.

Paratypes: Total of 103 specimens (38 females, 30 males, 35 immature of all stages), all from Lago de Nicaragua–Río San Juan drainage (Nicaraguan specimens 11 April–1 July 1964), as follows: UU 6712–27, 6729–30, 6732, 6734–64, 6766–73, 13026, several localities near Los Cocos, Granada Province (including Río Tipitapa, Río Moguana, and the lakeshore); UU 6791–6800, El Morillo, Río San Juan Province (15 km north of origin of Río San Juan); UU 6774–76, 6778–85, 6788–90, Río El Limón, 2.4 km southeast of La Virgen, Rivas Province (abreast of Isla Omotepe); UU 6695–6711, Rancho El Paraíso, 16 km east of Managua, Managua Province (short unnamed stream draining to Lago de Managua); UU 6777, 6786–87, Río Sapoá, Peñas Blancas, Guanacaste Province, Costa Rica, 22 August 1961.

Table 7.5. Comparison of *Pseudemys scripta hartwegi* with nearest geographic
neighbors for various scute lengths and widths

Taxon	GUL	PEC	AB	AN	WC1A	WC1P
elegans	.16 ± .014	.13 ± .018	.24 ± .018	.20 ± .019	.15 ± .028	.15 ± .014
taylori	.12 ± .010	.14 ± .014	.23 ± .016	.20 ± .016	.20 ± .023	.15 ± .014
gaigeae	.12 ± .010	.16 ± .016	.23 ± .015	.20 ± .013	.20 ± .023	.16 ± .013
hartwegi	.14 ± .010	.19 ± .008	.20 ± .016	.20 ± .013	.21 ± .013	.13 ± .007
hiltoni	.12 ± .012	.14 ± .017	.23 ± .013	.15 ± .020	.14 ± .021	.14 ± .009
nebulosa	.12 ± .010	.15 ± .019	.22 ± .015	.16 ± .020	.15 ± .021	.12 ± .007

Note: Measurements are expressed as percentages of carapace length. Mean and one standard deviation are given.
Abbreviations: GUL, PEC, AB, and AN = length of gular, pectoral, abdominal, and anal scutes; WC1A and WC1P
= width of first central scute, anterior and posterior.

Table 7.6. Adult size (carapace length, mm) in *Pseudemys scripta*

Taxon	Males					Females				
	N	Max.	Min.	Mean	Med.	*N*	Max.	Min.	Mean	Med.
elegans	102	214	90	156	126	71	257	107	204	179
taylori	51	179	90	127	124	60	218	93	167	174
gaigeae	16	173	115	140	137	23	220	135	179	183
hartwegi	7	149	124	139	140	14	298	120	177	162
hiltoni	28	320	158	244	253	14	351	207	284	287
nebulosa	7	324	176	227	219	5	285	235	266	273
yaquia	15	268	162	223	230	5	309	241	284	289
ornata	16	359	126	201	193	15	353	153	249	241
grayi	11	278	151	207	198	17	395	209	297	308
cataspila	44	312	125	242	245	16	314	168	273	280
venusta	195	341	110	192	205	213	424	162	232	254
emolli	31	296	162	201	200	36	372	184	286	294
GDULCE	5	187	161	175	178	25	305	218	256	249
CAPAC	43	234	139	182	185	48	320	161	234	233

Note: Number of specimens, maximum (max.), minimum (min.), mean, and median (med.) are given for adults of
each sex (specimens examined this study). See text for explanation of GDULCE and CAPAC populations.

Table 7.7. Comparison of *Pseudemys scripta emolli* with nearest geographic
neighbors for various scute and shell measurements

Taxon	LP	WPMF	GUL	FEM	LC5	WC5
venusta	.92 ± .027	.43 ± .021	.14 ± .014	.13 ± .017	.17 ± .017	.22 ± .017
emolli	.90 ± .026	.40 ± .016	.13 ± .013	.13 ± .014	.18 ± .015	.24 ± .017
GDULCE	.94 ± .022	.44 ± .016	.14 ± .011	.14 ± .008	.18 ± .017	.23 ± .010
CAPAC	.93 ± .033	.44 ± .020	.15 ± .014	.15 ± .012	.16 ± .015	.22 ± .015

Note: Measurements are expressed as percentages of carapace length. Mean and one standard deviation are given.
Abbreviations: LP, length of plastron; WPMF, width of plastron, midfemoral; GUL, length of gular scute; FEM, length
of femoral scute; LC5 and WC5, length and width of fifth central scute.

FIGURE 7.6. *a* and *b*, ventral and dorsal views of holotype of *Pseudemys scripta emolli* new subspecies, UU 6728, carapace length 194 mm. *c–h*, lateral and ventral views of heads: *c* and *d*, *P. s. emolli*, female paratype, UU 6697, anterior half of bilobate postorbital mark pale orange, posterior half pale yellow; *e* and *f*, *P. s. emolli*, male paratype, UU 6707; *g* and *h*, *P. s. venusta*, female, UU 6183, 8.8 km northwest of Puerto Cabezas, Zelaya, Nicaragua, thin postorbital stripe uniformly dark orange. Photos are from color transparencies of live turtles. All heads are approximately × 0.75.

Diagnosis: A subspecies of *Pseudemys scripta* closely related to *P. s. venusta* and distinguished from other Central American *P. scripta* by the following combination of characters: a wide postorbital stripe with a constriction at level of tympanum (forming a bilobate figure), or the constriction complete, forming a short isolated postorbital mark approximately half as wide as long; postorbital mark or stripe usually (73%) isolated from eye but connected (83.3%) posteriorly to a neck stripe; mandibular stripe isolated (82.1%) but relatively long, much longer (mean = 1.61 times) than isolated postorbital mark (or part of postorbital anterior to constriction). Symphyseal stripe usually (90.5%) connected to neck stripes, plastron relatively short (0.90 × LC), posterior plastral lobe relatively narrow (0.40 × LC).

Comparisons: Overall differences in appearance between *Pseudemys scripta emolli* and *P. s. venusta* from the Caribbean coast of Nicaragua (between Puerto Cabezas and Bluefields) are most evident in color and pattern of the head, neck, and shell. In the following brief comparison, the characters stated are for *emolli*, whereas those in brackets are for *venusta:* pattern of carapace dominated by ocelli with large dark brown centers and usually a single pale orange peripheral ring, lacking contrast in general [pattern of carapace with more contrast, dark ocellar centers smaller and surrounded usually by more than one pale orange ring]; little or no pattern on central scutes [pattern on central scutes bold, bright, and often complex]; side of head dominated by wide postorbital stripe that is bilobate and often bicolored, the anterior part pale orange and the posterior part pale yellow [postorbital stripe narrow, continuous, and uniformly dark or dull orange]; postorbital stripe chiefly wider than primary orbitocervical [postorbital narrower than primary orbitocervical]; plastral pattern at least slightly reduced in extent and contrast; usually a bowlike figure on the gular scutes, isolated from main plastral pattern or connected to it by a narrow isthmus [plastral pattern extensive and contrasting, continuous from anal to gular regions].

Etymology: The taxon is named for Prof. Edward O. Moll, Eastern Illinois University, my former student, coworker, and companion in Central America and now a prominent chelonian biologist.

Distribution: Lago de Nicaragua, Lago de Managua, lakes and streams connecting the two main lakes, short drainages flowing into the lakes from Nicaragua and extreme northern Costa Rica; an indeterminate distance from Lago de Nicaragua down the Río San Juan. We saw *Pseudemys* in the Laguna Masaya (18 km west northwest of Granada). Populations at the source of the Río San Juan just north of San Carlos are clearly *emolli;* specimens in the San Juan delta near the mouth are clearly *venusta*.

Remarks: The Río Tipitapa flows from Lago de Managua to Lago de Nicaragua and receives many small tributaries in the isthmus between the lakes. Most of the specimens come from this isthmus and the region on the northwest shore of Lago de Nicaragua between Granada and the mouth of the Río Tipitapa. The type locality is a small mud-bottomed creek draining cleared pastureland, reached by driving 1.5 km northwest on the beach from the former Colegio Centro América.

Turtles in the lake were in warm (33° to 35° C) shallow water near the shore, and most were caught by hand. Numerous turtle tracks were visible in the sand between the water and the dense low vegetation on the shore; natives said that turtles came out at night to eat on land (unconfirmed). The turtles may have been seeking relief from the warm receding water. By cutting down the dense vegetation and going through the moist humus at its base, E. O. Moll and F. V. Nabrotzky found 111 *Kinosternon scorpioides* and 7 juvenile *P. s. emolli* buried in an area approximately 4.5 m square; the turtles seemed to be estivating. Some of the larger female *P. s. emolli* from the lakeshore had broad heads and well-developed crushing surfaces on the jaws.

There is a tendency to melanism in the males of this subspecies, but there are no noticeable melanistic tendencies in the females.

SPECIES VERSUS SUBSPECIES

This study regards *Pseudemys scripta* as a polytypic, monophyletic species despite its immense amount of variation and extensive geographic range. Some recent reviews have used this conservative approach (Smith and Smith, 1979), and others have considered one or more of the taxa to be full species (Weaver and Rose, 1967; Ward, 1984). The groups defined by clustering and my own a priori assumptions fit what most biologists would call subspecies. On the other hand, the Northern Isolates are certainly as distinct as many full species, their distinctness being partly due to genetic drift. Similarities of these subspecies to others in the north suggest that gene flow occurred in the past. The potential for gene flow exists nearly everywhere else by virtue of more or less continuous aquatic environments or a nearly continuous coastal plain. In general, all populations of *P. scripta* share enough characters at some stage of ontogeny to suggest that they have common ancestry.

All known stripe and plastral patterns can be derived logically from a hypothetical ancestral pattern. The most radical departures from the ancestral pattern (e.g., the stripes of *P. s. callirostris* and the virtually patternless shell of *P. terrapen*) may have resulted from the founding of populations by a few individuals or one gravid female.

ZOOGEOGRAPHY AND PHYLOGENY

DISPERSAL. The distribution of *Pseudemys* in Mesoamerica requires an understanding of dispersal. Dispersal can be active or passive and can involve movement within or between drainage systems. Dispersal within a system can be upstream or downstream; the latter is ipso facto passive, the former active. Floods are regular and predictable in any true drainage area (excluding spring creeks). Although turtles have ways of staying in place during floods (Moll and Legler, 1971), some are surely displaced downstream and some are displaced to the sea. If this involves displacement over barriers to upstream migration (e.g., falls or rapids), permanent range expansions may result. Being carried to sea in a flood does not necessarily involve swimming in salt water; floods cause considerable dilution in coastal areas, and floods discharge mats of flotsam (usually aquatic vegetation) upon which various animals can be supported. Carr (1952) mentions saltwater tolerance of *P. concinna*. *Pseudemys s. grayi* occurs at least occasionally in brackish water.

Turtles discharged from a flooded river can come ashore at some distance from the mouth of the river and move along a coastal plain to the mouth of another river. The process is easier and faster if coastal swamps or lagoons exist. This is the simplest mode of dispersal wherever rivers and coastal plains exist. I refer to it as mouth-to-mouth dispersal, and it is the principal explanation for the coastal distributions considered here.

Dispersal between drainage systems is more difficult to explain when exchanges must occur across a divide. Stream piracy is commonly invoked to explain shared fish faunas in adjacent headwaters. This may involve the actual capture of a tributary in one catchment by headwater erosion of a tributary in another, or the natural damming and actual diversion of part of one drainage to another (e.g., by a lava flow or by an earthquake). Changes in water level during long-term dry cycles cause isolation by creating internal drainage systems.

All these events seem to have occurred in northern Mexico over a period of about 30 million years; some are as recent as Pleistocene. Rarely is there historic evidence of a drainage change in progress or one that is poised to happen (Brand, 1937). Various hypotheses and corroborations have been used to explain the distribution of fishes. These hypotheses do not differ greatly from the basics laid down by Meek (1904). Fish species sharing adjacent headwaters are logically explicable only in this manner; fish cannot survive out of water, and dispersal far upstream from the sea is rare. Minckley et al. (1986) provide the most recent summary of these phenomena in Mexico.

Turtles are pulmonate quadrupeds and can move between streams across terrestrial barriers; they can survive for several days out of water, within certain limits of temperature and humidity. Females predictably nest on land. Also, in a drying stream, movement of turtles from one pool to another is expected. However, turtles do not climb cliffs. None of the foregoing reasons for walking on land can account for the movement of turtles from stream to stream in canyon country (even though the distances are short). Large birds of prey (*Haliaeetus* spp.) could pick up a *Pseudemys* and drop it in another drainage system; eagles of this genus commonly pick up live turtles in northern Australia (pers. obs.) and in Africa (Clayton White, pers. com.). A gravid female on land for the purpose of nesting would be the most likely candidate for this scenario. Introduction by humans is mentioned below.

DRAINAGE HISTORY IN NORTHERN MEXICO.   This subject is treated separately because it bears on the origin of several subspecies. The literature has been thoroughly and recently reviewed by Minckley et al. (1986) and Smith and Miller (1986). These authors and others cited by them corroborate most of the remarks that follow. The physiographic features mentioned and the hypothesized dispersal routes are clearly seen on any small-scale topographic map (e.g., U.S. Department of Commerce ONC charts, 1 : 1,000,000).

The present Rio Grande was once two rivers. The two main tributaries of the lower Rio Grande were the Pecos River and another tributary eroding upstream through the Big Bend region southeast of El Paso. The Pecos River also eroded headward and eventually captured parts of other streams (the Canadian River and perhaps other Gulf streams). At some stage the Río Conchos joined the Big Bend tributary; it seems clear that this confluence occurred before the Río Conchos acquired its southern headwaters.

The upper Rio Grande flowed from the San Juan Mountains of southern Colorado southward to interior drainage systems in New Mexico, Texas, and adjacent Mexico; this internal system received contributions also from the east face of the Sierra Madre Occidental. There was a large lake or series of lakes in this region in the Pleistocene. The lower Rio Grande captured the upper Rio Grande and parts of the internal systems in mid-Pleistocene times. Subsequently the entire Rio Grande has flowed to the sea.

There is a large arid area, just south of the U.S.-Mexican border, that contains many dry basins and internal drainage systems. Most of the latter are now dry except in times of heaviest rainfall; a few (e.g., the Río Nazas, Río Aguanaval, and Río Casas Grandes) still flow in places and have fluctuating terminal lakes. All of these basins and drainages contained more water at times in the Pleistocene. The area extends southward approximately to 24 degrees (southern extent of Río Aguanaval), is bounded generally by the Sierra Madre Occidental and the Sierra Madre Oriental, and extends northward to the Rio Grande and at least to the basins (pluvial Lake Palomas) just south of Columbus, New Mexico. This region is termed the central Mexican interior basins by Smith and Miller (1986) and is hereinafter called the interior basins for brevity.

The former confluence of basins and drainages within the northern central region of Mexico—with each other, with the upper Rio Grande and Río Conchos, and with the lower Rio Grande—is generally accepted (although weak in detail). I interpret the evidence as follows. These drainages were all interconnected at some time during the Pleistocene in a manner that permitted exchange of aquatic faunas or gene flow between existing populations. These drainage connections were not all concurrent; they probably occurred in a stepwise fashion as basins overflowed and as low-gradient streams altered their courses or were captured by others.

The ancestral stock of *gaigeae/hartwegi* evolved in this interior basin system. Accounting for the presence of these ancestors in the system is an unsolved zoogeographic problem. Aquatic organisms could have entered this system via the following routes: (1) via drainage exchanges between the upper Rio Grande and the Pecos River, (2) by migration up the Rio Grande, (3) via the Torreón basin. There is evidence that fishes have dispersed via all of these routes. Route 3 involves the fewest assumptions for turtles.

Just north of Torreón there is a corridor that extends eastward toward Saltillo. This corridor includes the western extent of the range of *hartwegi* (Río Nazas at San Pedro de las Colonias). The corridor is the route of a railroad; just south of Reata the line branches with one track going to Monterrey and another running northward to Monclova. Drainage exchanges could have occurred between the Nazas and the Río San Juan drainage 40 to 50 km northwest of Monterrey or with the Río Salado drainage 95 km northwest of Monterrey. *Pseudemys* could have entered the Río Nazas drainage this way. This may be the route attributed to Arellano (1951) by Conant (1963).

It seems likely that the southernmost Río Conchos tributaries were once confluent with the interior drainages (pers. obs.). Tributaries flowing to the interior basins are narrowly separated from those of the Río Florido approximately 65 km south of Jiménez, Chihuahua. The Mapimían channels are now dry, but they are unquestionably on the general drainage that terminates in lakes near Torreón. The headwaters of the Río Nazas come into close proximity with other Río Florido (Conchos) tributaries approximately 60 km upstream from the Presa El Palmito (= P. Lázaro Cardenas), where tributaries of both systems seem to drain the same small valley.

It is also clear that waters of the interior basins were captured by headwaters of high-gradient Pacific streams in several places. (Whether or not the internal streams were concurrently or directly connected to the Rio Grande is not an issue.) This has resulted in the dispersal of fishes into the Pacific streams, either directly from the interior drainages or in a stepwise fashion southward along the Continental Divide from headwater to headwater. Stream piracy across the Continental Divide is well documented in two places: The Río Papigóchic was formerly a Casas Grandes tributary and now flows to the Río Yaqui; the Río Tunal was formerly a tributary of the Nazas and now flows to the Río Mezquital.

NORTHERN ISOLATES.   Three subspecies occur in northern Mexico, each in a separate drainage that flows to the Rio Grande or has been isolated from that drainage. The Northern Isolates are distinct but probably as closely related to one another as each is to the ancestral stock. The ancestry of these three populations can be traced to the lower Rio Grande. (See Fig. 7.7 for a summary of hypothesized dispersal routes.)

Pseudemys scripta taylori occurs only in the basin of Cuatro Ciénegas. Periodic past isolation of the basin (Minckley, 1969) has produced many endemics in the aquatic biota. The basin presently drains (via the Río Nadadores) to the Río Salado system with its mouth on the lower Rio

Grande at Falcon Reservoir. Typical *P. s. elegans* occurs everywhere else in the Río Salado drainage.

Pseudemys s. taylori is one of four aquatic turtles in the basin: The distinctiveness of *Terrapene coahuila* suggests that its isolation was ancient; *Trionyx ater* is endemic and sometimes hybridizes with *Trionyx spiniferus*, a recent entrant to the basin. *Pseudemys s. taylori* probably evolved in isolation from an ancestral stock during the Pleistocene; the ancestral stock probably gave rise also to *elegans* and *cataspila* during the time that *taylori* was isolated. Although *taylori* is one of the most distinctive subspecies of *P. scripta*, it now intergrades with *P. s. elegans* where the two meet immediately outside the basin (Legler, 1963; pers. obs., 1976).

Pseudemys s. gaigeae and *P. s. hartwegi* were seemingly derived from a common ancestor in the interior basins. The ancestral stock probably entered the interior basins from the Río Salado or the Río San Juan drainage via the corridor east of Torreón and the Río Nazas (Fig. 7.7). This stock may have ranged northward to lat. 27 in wetter times. Increased aridity isolated the stocks that eventually became *gaigeae* and *hartwegi*. Subsequently, *P. s. gaigeae* differentiated in the northern part of the system, which became the headwaters of the Río Conchos (and provided a route to the Rio Grande). *Pseudemys s. hartwegi* differentiated in the south and survived only in the Nazas drainage. The subspecies has become extinct in the Laguna Viesca since 1960 (based on clear photos by John Iverson of specimens at Baylor University). My own explorations indicate that *Pseudemys* did not occur in the Río Aguanaval, Río Carmen, Río Santa María (*Chrysemys picta* occurs there), Río Casas Grandes, or Laguna Bavícora in 1961. Aridity and the increased use of water for irrigation may have placed *hartwegi* populations in danger everywhere except in the immediate region of the Presa El Palmito.

GULF COAST–CARIBBEAN SERIES.   *Pseudemys s. cataspila* ranges from the Río San Fernando (145 km south of Brownsville) to Punta del Morro, Veracruz. Punta del Morro is a well-known headland; it interrupts the coastal plain for about 25 km at lat. 19-55. The distributions of many neotropical species end just south of Punta del Morro, and it is seemingly a barrier of long standing.

Pseudemys s. venusta extends southward from Punta del Morro as a virtually continuous population to Isthmian Panama and the Río Atrato of northern Colombia and is clearly the most wide-ranging subspecies of *P. scripta*. *Pseudemys s. venusta* has an extensive range by virtue of occurring chiefly on a nearly continuous coastal plain. Gene flow is probably unimpeded over most of this range. Within *venusta* there are populations that are distinctive when considered alone but are parts of a cline in the context of the total sample. This is a more conservative treat-

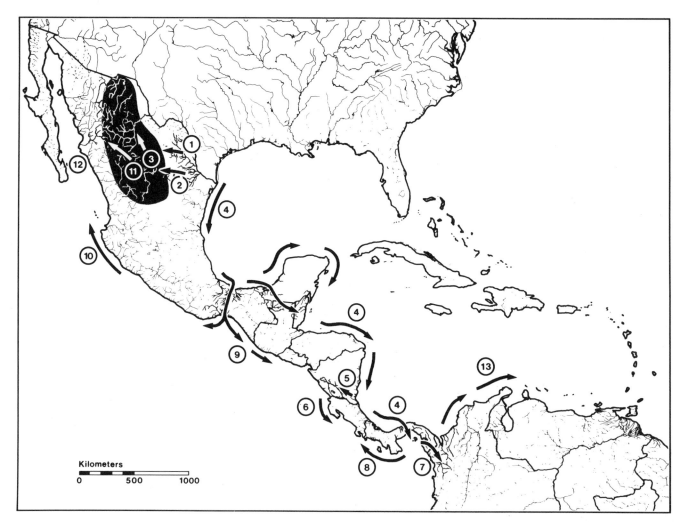

FIGURE 7.7.   Hypothesized dispersal events and routes for ancestral stocks of *Pseudemys scripta* in Mesoamerica. The numbered events are neither concurrent nor chronological. The shaded area in northern Mexico shows the approximate extent of the interior basin region discussed in the text. *1*, isolation of *taylori* in basin of Cuatro Ciénegas; *2*, invasion of interior basins by *hartwegi/gaigeae* ancestral stock; *3*, isolation of *gaigeae* in interior drainages later captured by Río Conchos; *4*, coastwise dispersal of *cataspila* and *venusta* through Gulf coastal plain, around and across Yucatán Peninsula, and thence to Isthmian Panama; *5*, isolation of *emolli* in Nicaraguan lakes via Río San Juan; *6*, possible dispersal from Lake Nicaragua to Golfo Dulce region; *7*, colonization of Río Atrato via Río Tuira; *8*, coastwise dispersal of *venusta* to colonize Pacific coast of Central America; *9*, ancestral stock crosses Isthmus of Tehuantepec to found Pacific coast of Mexico and gives rise to *grayi; 10*, northward dispersal of Pacific stock; *11*, Río Fuerte founded by ancestors in the interior basins; *12*, *hiltoni* crosses Gulf of California; *13*, possible coastwise dispersal of *venusta*-like stock to account for origin of *callirostris*.

ment than that expressed in Moll and Legler (1971).

Isolated aquatic habitats on the Yucatán Peninsula range from cavernous cenotes to small sinkholes, lakes of various sizes, and muddy *aguadas*. *Pseudemys* occurs in most of these, but populations flourish only in the more exposed habitats. Limestone sinks in intermediate stages of senescence are spectacular in their potential for isolation. Near Libre Unión, I observed breeding populations of *P. scripta* in small pondlike habitats (with aquatic vegetation and earthen shoreline) that were surrounded by vertical rock walls at least 12 m high (the crowns of ma-

ture palms were below ground level). Turtles colonize these holes by simply falling in. The chances of overland escape are virtually zero.

Underground water connections in Yucatán could be significant in turtle dispersal. I observed medium-sized tarpon and *P. scripta* in some small cenotes where water was welling up to the surface. These had small surface exposure (less than 15 m²) and were deeper than I could see in crystal-clear water; an underground connection to a larger aquatic system probably existed (and this was the opinion of the natives).

The distribution of *Pseudemys scripta* extends around and across the base of the Yucatán Peninsula. From Quintana Roo to Colón, Panama, the coastal plain is constricted in places (e.g., Omoa and Trujillo, Honduras), and there are some areas from which specimens are unknown (e.g, Coclé del Norte to Colón, Panama), but in no case do these exceptions refute the concept of a single subspecies with a wide range. It may be that *Pseudemys* actually skips some of these drainages.

Pseudemys is common in the Chagres drainage of Panama and occurs across the Isthmus, in suitable habitats, most of which have been altered by humans. Eastward from the Port of Panama, *Pseudemys* occurs in short coastal drainages and the Río Bayano. There are no records for the Tuira-Chucunaque system with its mouth in the Gulf of San Miguel, but I think it is probable that *Pseudemys* occurs in this basin and has colonized the Río Atrato from there (I could establish no evidence for the occurrence of *Pseudemys* on the San Blas coast of Panama, east of Colón). The headwaters of the Tuira interdigitate with those of the Río Atrato; it is possible to portage dugouts between these rivers in the wet season (Colombian natives, pers. com.).

ORIGIN AND RELATIONSHIPS OF *PSEUDEMYS SCRIPTA* EMOLLI. The relationships of *Pseudemys scripta emolli* are shown in Fig. 7.8. There is no reason to doubt its close relationship to *venusta* and its origin from a *venusta*-like stock via migration up the Río San Juan. The Río San Juan drains Lago de Nicaragua, which in turn drains Lago de Managua. The route of the Río San Juan passes through low mountain ranges about midway between the lake and the mouth. The nature of the Río San Juan has changed within historic times. "Rapids" are shown in the area where the river passes through the higher elevations. Parallel to the course of the Río San Juan, but chiefly to the south, there is a clear route from the Atlantic Lowlands to Lago de Nicaragua; Puerto Viejo, Costa Rica, lies in this lowland corridor. The corridor extends narrowly along the south shore of the lake to just north of Rivas (abreast of Isla Zapatera).

The populations to the southeast on the Pacific coast are an unsolved problem. The Golfo Dulce–Golfo de Chiriquí population is more closely related to *venusta* than to either *emolli* or CAPAC (Fig. 7.8). For this reason it is provisionally treated as a disjunct population of *venusta*.

Populations on the Pacific coast of Panama are noticeably paler and less contrasting in all color and pattern than is *venusta* in the Chagres drainage of the Isthmus. Nothing in the computer analysis expresses this pallor, and I therefore regard the matter as unresolved.

We were unable to collect or otherwise establish the presence of *Pseudemys* in the Golfo de Nicoya region in August 1961. *Pseudemys scripta* is common at Palmar Sur (350 km south of Lago de Nicaragua) in lowland country

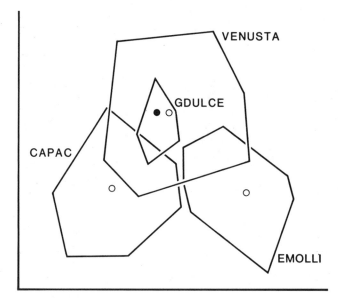

FIGURE 7.8.   Plots of adults of *P. s. emolli* ($N = 67$) and their nearest geographic neighbors, *P. s. venusta* ($N = 411$) and two populations on the Pacific side of Costa Rica and Panama, GDULCE ($N = 30$), and CAPAC ($N = 94$). Plots are based on 29 characters (length of carapace, 25 measurements of shell expressed as percentages of carapace length, and 3 stripe characters). Polygons show total dispersion of individuals; dots show population means (the mean for GDULCE is a solid dot). The first (horizontal) and second (vertical) canonical axes account for .457 and .377 of the variation, respectively. This plot tends to corroborate these hypotheses: *emolli* was derived from a *venusta*-like stock; GDULCE is phenetically closer to *venusta* than to either of the other populations (and could be regarded as a disjunct population of *venusta*).

where bananas are grown. The area was formerly laced with streams draining to the Río Térraba near its delta. The turtles are common in oxbows resulting from the realignment of streams for banana growing. The Río Térraba is fast and gravel-bottomed; the only suitable *Pseudemys* habitats in the river itself are man-made (barge harbors, etc.). Presumably the population is more or less continuous along the Golfo de Chiriquí. This population is termed GDULCE in Fig. 7.8.

There are several ways to explain the presence of *venusta* in the Golfo Dulce region: (1) dispersal of a pre-*emolli* stock by coastwise migration from Lago de Nicaragua or by waifs from an overflow of the Nicaraguan lakes; (2) successive waves of colonization from a Panamanian Isthmus stock, with *venusta* crossing the Isthmus of Panama, dispersing up the Pacific coast to the Golfo Dulce, and then differentiating only between the Azuero Peninsula and the Panamanian Isthmus; (3) human introduction by aboriginals or banana growers from the Atlantic side (see Epilogue, below).

The first hypothesis is the most attractive. Overflow of the lakes could easily occur into the Pacific Ocean between Puerto Somoza and Rivas if the Río San Juan were blocked (there is a history of earthquakes in the region). On the other hand, large gaps in the coastal plain south of San Juan del Sur and the seeming lack of *Pseudemys* near the Golfo de Nicoya argue against coastwise dispersal.

The following turtles occur in sympatry with *P. scripta* near the origin of the Río San Juan at El Morillo: *Kinosternon scorpioides*, *K. leucostomum*, *Rhinoclemmys funerea*, and *Chelydra serpentina*. The last three are primarily Atlantic species. *Rhinoclemmys funerea* is unknown from the Pacific side (and I strongly doubt its occurrence there); *Chelydra* and *K. leucostomum* both begin a Pacific distribution south of Lago de Nicaragua. *Chelydra* is known from the Golfo de Nicoya region, Tilarán, and the Palmar Sur region on the Pacific side of Costa Rica (chiefly pers. obs.; also E. H. Taylor and Jaime Villa, pers. com.). *Kinosternon leucostomum* occurs at Palmar Sur (UU 8678–79) but is rare. Except for rare occurrence in the Río Chagres drainage, *K. scorpioides* is completely Pacific in its distribution (and is the common species of *Kinosternon*) northwestward to the latitude of Lago de Nicaragua; thence it occurs commonly on both sides of Central America (UU collection; Iverson, 1986). Ergo, of the five species at El Morillo, three seem to have crossed the Central American landmass via the Río San Juan corridor, and one (*R. funerea*) has reached only as far as the lake.

Because *Pseudemys* shows essentially the same pattern as *Chelydra* and *K. leucostomum*, hypothesis 1 seems to be the most parsimonious explanation of the Golfo Dulce population. However, this does not explain why the population is more closely related to *venusta* than to *emolli*. Perhaps the Golfo Dulce population was founded by *venusta*, from the lakes, before the lake populations differentiated. Hypothesis 2 involves too many assumptions to warrant serious discussion at present.

PACIFIC POPULATIONS OF MEXICO AND GUATEMALA. Distributions on the Pacific side of Mexico and Guatemala are discontinuous and more complex. A *venusta*-like Gulf Coast population in Veracruz probably founded the Pacific coast by crossing the Isthmus of Tehuantepec. Certainly this explains the origin of *grayi*. It is presently the only logical way to account for other Mexican Pacific populations (except *hiltoni*)—by coastwise dispersal, north and west of the Isthmus of Tehuantepec.

Pseudemys s. yaquia occurs in the Río Sonora, Río Yaqui, and Río Mayo. *Pseudemys s. ornata* occurs on the continuous coastal plain from Culiacán, Sinaloa, to the region just north of Cabo Corrientes, Jalisco (lat. 21-0). It may occur from Los Mochis to Culiacán, but no specimens are known. Between Cabo Corrientes and Puerto Angel, the coastal plain is broken; *ornata*-like *scripta* occur near Acapulco, but their status is not considered here. There may be other isolated populations in short pieces of coastal plain (e.g., Manzanillo, Colima, lat. 19-0; Chila, Oa-

xaca, long. 97-0). Duellman (1961) gave no records for *Pseudemys* from the coast of Michoacán or from the Balsas-Tepalcatepec Basin.

Pseudemys s. grayi is known near the mouth of the Río Tehuantepec, but its range may begin to the west at Majada Villalobos. It is most common in the Pacific coastal lagoons beginning just east of Salina Cruz and extending through Chiapas and Guatemala (type locality, long. 91-33) to extreme western coastal El Salvador (long. 89-40), where lava flows from Ilopango and other volcanoes form an impassible headland. There are specimens from Laguna Muchacha, Jutiapa Province, Guatemala (long. 90-10, UU collection).

A small stretch of coastal plain, containing the mouth of the Río Lempa, begins immediately east of La Libertad and extends to a small basin containing the Laguna Olomega (long. 88-04). A headland separates this basin from the principal coastal plain surrounding the Golfo de Fonseca. The Laguna Olomega has satisfactory habitat for *Pseudemys*, but observation and collecting effort convince me that sliders do not occur there. There are no records of *Pseudemys* from the coastal plain of the Golfo de Fonseca. Although this coastal plain is clearly continuous with a lowland corridor extending from La Canoa (lat. 13, long. 87) southeastward to Lago de Managua, *Pseudemys* are known only from the lake. We have been to Chinandega, Nicaragua, and were unable to establish any information to suggest that *Pseudemys* occurred there.

The distribution of *P. s. grayi* therefore stops at Acajutla. All Central American populations of *P. scripta* to the south and east are independent derivatives of *venusta*-like stocks on the Atlantic side (see below).

The relationship of *venusta* to *grayi* deserves special comment. The populations are narrowly separated. They do not occur sympatrically (despite the comment of Bogert, 1961). M. Alvarez del Toro (Smith and Smith, 1979) keeps the two subspecies together in the same zoo ponds in Tuxtla Gutiérrez; the subspecies ignore each other and do not interbreed. These taxa may be incipient species, but it remains to be seen what would happen if they occurred in natural sympatry.

Pseudemys scripta yaquia, *P. s. ornata*, and *P. s. grayi* comprise a natural series of closely related subspecies. This series is interrupted by the range of *hiltoni* in the Río Fuerte. There is no completely satisfying explanation for the presence of *hiltoni* in this coastal series. The juxtaposition of *yaquia*, *hiltoni*, and *ornata* may represent the termini of a long chain of subspecies.

The following discussion and hypotheses stipulate the following basic findings of this study (Fig. 7.9): (1) *P. s. hiltoni* and *nebulosa* are more closely related (phenotypically similar) than any other two subspecies of *P. scripta*, and any scenario applicable to one must be applicable to the other; (2) *yaquia*, *ornata*, and *grayi* are more closely related inter se and to *venusta* than any is to *hiltoni*/*nebulosa*;

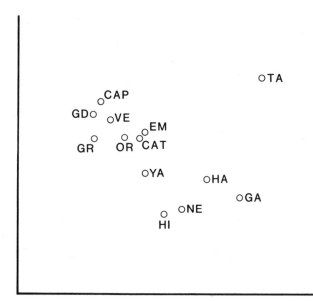

FIGURE 7.9. Plots of adult population means for 13 subspecies of *Pseudemys scripta* in Mesoamerica on the first (horizontal) and second (vertical) canonical axes. Plots are based on the same characters as in Figure 7.8. The first and second canonical axes account for .402 and .211 of the variation, respectively. Abbreviations of subspecies as follows: *CAP*, CAPAC; *CAT, cataspila; EM, emolli; GA, gaigeae; GD,* GDULCE; *GR, grayi; HA, hartwegi; HI, hiltoni; NE, nebulosa; OR, ornata; TA, taylori; VE, venusta; YA, yaquia.*

(3) *hiltoni/nebulosa* is more closely related to *hartwegi/ gaigeae* than to the *yaquia/ornata/grayi* group; (4) the ancestral stock of the *yaquia/ornata/grayi* group reached the Pacific coast via the Isthmus of Tehuantepec. If these taxonomic judgments are incorrect, the hypotheses are necessarily weakened or refuted.

Freshwater fishes in Pacific coast drainages show close relationships to species of the Rio Grande. This can be explained by headwater exchanges with interior basin streams (see Drainage History, above). Many such instances are well substantiated (Meek, 1904; Minckley et al., 1986; Smith and Miller, 1986).

Exchanges between the Río Fuerte and interior basin streams are not mentioned in the literature, and I can see no really good possibilities for this on any map. All of the known drainage exchanges have occurred north (Yaqui-Guzmán) or far south (Nazas-Mezquital) of the Río Fuerte. Headwaters of the Río Fuerte lie close to those of the Río Conchos and the Río Nazas, but in all cases this is in rugged canyon country (e.g., near Creel, Chihuahua). The ancestors of *hiltoni/nebulosa* probably crossed these barriers, but I cannot explain how (see Dispersal, above).

The following hypotheses are presented more or less in the order of their likelihood and parsimony:

1. The ancestors of *hiltoni* reached the Río Fuerte by crossing the divide from the interior basins—from

what is now the Río Nazas or the Río Conchos. The part of this ancestral stock that remained in the interior basins gave rise to *gaigeae* and *hartwegi* (or had already done so). *Pseudemys s. hiltoni* differentiated in the Río Fuerte. If an *ornata*-like population was already present in the Fuerte, it was assimilated by *hiltoni.* Pacific populations in streams flanking the Río Fuerte remained unaffected. If *ornata*-like stocks had not already colonized the Pacific coast, they either bypassed the Fuerte drainage or were assimilated by *hiltoni* if they entered the river.

2. Drainage exchanges between the Río Nazas and the Río Mezquital are well documented. The mouth of the Mezquital (= Río San Pedro) is at Tuxpan, Nayarit, well within the present range of *ornata.* Drainage exchanges between the Yaqui and the Guzmán system (later Rio Grande) are also well documented; exchanges between Yaqui and Conchos headwaters are likely. Although I propose that the ancestors of *hiltoni/nebulosa* were already substantially differentiated from a fully striped *venusta/ ornata*-like ancestor, a fully striped ancestral stock in the interior basins could have independently given rise to *P. s. yaquia* (via the known Papigóchic capture) and to *P. s. ornata* via the Tunal-Mezquital exchange. At some later time, after the differentiation of the *gaigeae/hartwegi* stock, ancestors of *hiltoni/ nebulosa* colonized the Río Fuerte, where they either replaced an existing population or colonized an unoccupied river. No coastal barriers exist between the Río Sonora and the Río San Pedro at Tuxpan.

3. The Río Fuerte is a new drainage system that originated after an *ornata*-like ancestor had colonized the Mexican Pacific coast from the south. This suggestion, although not frivolous, is absolutely without substantiation. But it would solve nearly all the problems.

BAJA CALIFORNIA. *Pseudemys s. hiltoni* and *P. s. nebulosa* are so closely related that it is necessary to invoke a crossing of the Gulf of California to explain their distribution. However, neither the means of crossing nor its direction are clear at this time. The distance from the mainland to the peninsula is about 135 km. If *Pseudemys* could reach the Antilles (200 km, Yucatán to Cuba; 150 km, Key West to Cuba), they could probably traverse the Gulf of California. The Río Fuerte does not seem to be the kind of river that would discharge island-size mats of floating vegetation, but surely there is flotsam of some kind crossing the Gulf of California.

The following authors have alluded to the possibility of human introduction of *P. scripta* into Baja California: Conant (1963); Smith and Smith (1979); R. Murphy (1983, Indians and Jesuit priests mentioned). The idea is attractive in its simplicity but is difficult to prove. If humans carried *Pseudemys* to Baja California, it seems that they would also have carried *Kinosternon*. That genus is less desirable as food but is edible; it is also used medicinally (pers. obs. in Chihuahua and Durango).

According to R. Murphy (1983), what is now the Cape region of Baja, California, broke away from the Mexican west coast in the Miocene (13 million years B.P.). Several things argue against this history for *Pseudemys*. *Pseudemys s. hiltoni* and *P. s. nebulosa* are too similar to have been isolated that long. If *Pseudemys* was present on a detached piece of the continent, it is probable that *Kinosternon* would also be present. Baja California is one of two Mesoamerican mainland places where *Pseudemys scripta* is not sympatric with a *Kinosternon* (Cuatro Ciénegas is the other). *Kinosternon* is the more likely to survive aridity because it can burrow and utilize seasonal rain pools. On the other hand, by using the Miocene scenario, we could derive *hiltoni* from ancestors in Baja California. However, this would be incongruent with most of what is proposed in this chapter.

ISLAND DISTRIBUTION. *Pseudemys scripta* colonized the Antilles in the same relatively recent period discussed for mainland species. It has prospered in the Antilles and differentiated there. My own work on Antillean *Pseudemys* will be published elsewhere. It seems probable that more than one colonization occurred. It is possible that parts of Central America and South America were also colonized from the Antilles. There are no freshwater turtles of any other kind in the Antilles proper. *Kinosternon leucostomum* occurs with *Pseudemys s. venusta* on Great Corn Island (Nicaragua). *Pseudemys* does not occur on Escudo de Veraguas and other islands off the Panamanian coast near Almirante. Only *Kinosternon leucostomum* occurs on Isla Pinos off the San Blas coast of Panama.

SOUTH AMERICA. The distribution of *Pseudemys* in South America is spotty. I have no scientific experience with this vast area except for northern Colombia. There are three natural ways to explain these spotty distributions: (1) *Pseudemys* occurs in most lowland aquatic habitats and remains chiefly undiscovered; (2) distributions are so recent that populations still exist as small founding colonies; (3) *Pseudemys* has been less successful in South America because aquatic niches there are occupied chiefly by pleurodires. The most recent review of *Pseudemys* in South America is by Pritchard and Trebbau (1984).

SUMMARY OF MAJOR ZOOGEOGRAPHIC EVENTS. *Pseudemys scripta* has crossed the Mesoamerican landmass in five places (Fig. 7.7): (1) from the Gulf of Mexico to the Pacific coast of Mexico via the Rio Grande and interior basins of northern Mexico; (2) from the Gulf of Mexico to the Pacific coast at the Isthmus of Tehuantepec; (3) from the

Caribbean coast to the Pacific coast via the Nicaraguan lakes–Río San Juan corridor; (4) from the Atlantic coast to the Pacific coast at the Isthmus of Panama; and (5) from the Pacific to the Atlantic between the Río Tuira and Río Atrato in northern Colombia. In four of these instances, the dispersal route remains open and is an actual or potential route of gene flow. The Isthmus of Tehuantepec is now a barrier.

OVERALL RELATIONSHIPS

A broad comparison of all *Pseudemys scripta*–like species will serve to place the foregoing remarks in perspective. All of my work suggested that three major groupings existed: the subspecies in the United States, the Antillean taxa, and all Mesoamerican taxa, including those immediately south of the Rio Grande in northern Mexico. To test this idea, 31 definable populations (including all Antilles taxa) were plotted together with BMDP7M: once for all adults (29 characters) and once for all subadults (27 characters, LC and FING omitted). The population clusters were tightly packed and served only to assess relationships between groups of populations (not to scrutinize relationships among taxa). The groupings were as hypothesized above. The populations were then reamalgamated into three large groups designated USASCRIP—*elegans*, *scripta*, and *troosti;* ANTISCRIP—all Antillean populations; and MESOSCRIP—all mainland populations of *Pseudemys scripta* south (and west) of the lower Rio Grande. Plots for nonadults and adults showed essentially the same results.

The plots for adults are shown in Figure 7.10. Note that MESOSCRIP slightly overlaps both USASCRIP and ANTISCRIP and that the last two groups do not overlap at all. This strongly suggests the following: (1) the relationship of any one group to any other is of approximately equal magnitude; (2) Antillean species are part of the *P. scripta* group, regardless of their taxonomic designation; (3) the differences between MESOSCRIP and USASCRIP are real. The clustering suggests that Antillean populations are more closely related to each other than any is to USASCRIP or to MESOSCRIP (even though Antillean stocks could have been established by separate and distinct invasions from different mainland stocks).

MESOSCRIP constitutes a natural group composed of all the mainland *Pseudemys* south and west of the Pecos–lower Rio Grande, including all South American populations. The difference between USASCRIP and MESOSCRIP is great enough to consider them as different groups of the same polytypic species. The remainder of this report deals with this seeming paradox.

SEXUAL DIMORPHISM AND SYMPATRY

SYMPATRY. *Pseudemys scripta* occurs in microsympatry with *Pseudemys concinna* in the Pecos River and in the tribu-

All adults (1494)

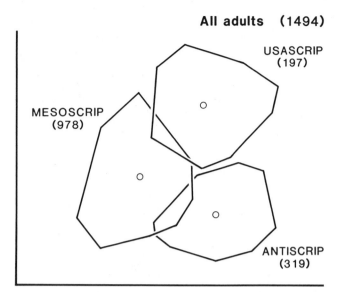

FIGURE 7.10. Canonical plots of all adult *Pseudemys scripta* group specimens ($N = 1,494$). All populations in the United States, Mesoamerica (including South America), and the Antilles were first plotted; these formed three basic clusters. Populations in these clusters were then amalgamated into the three groups shown here. The first (horizontal) and second (vertical) canonical axes account for .753 and .247 of the variation, respectively. USASCRIP includes the three subspecies in the United States; ANTISCRIP includes all known Antillean taxa; MESOSCRIP includes all mainland populations south and west of the Rio Grande. *N* is parenthetical. Plots are based on the same characters as in Figure 7.8.

taries of the lower Rio Grande below Del Rio, Texas. ("Microsympatry" refers to sympatry in which the species occur in close enough proximity to be aware of each other's presence through seeing, smelling, touching, etc.) This is supported by specimens in collections, and I have personally observed the two species within 1 m of one another in clear water at several places in the mentioned drainages (*Chrysemys picta* also occurs in the Upper Pecos, but not necessarily with the two *Pseudemys*). Lower Rio Grande tributaries may extend as far south as lat. 27 (Río Sabinas) in Coahuila and lat. 25-30 in Nuevo León and Tamaulipas.

The Pecos–lower Rio Grande drainage marks the western and southern extremes of intrageneric sympatry for *Pseudemys*. Northward and eastward in the Mississippi drainage, in the Gulf drainages, and along the eastern coastal plain of the United States, *Pseudemys scripta* occurs almost always with at least one other species of *Pseudemys* and sometimes with more than one other species. *Chrysemys picta* and several species of *Graptemys* also occur in this zone of sympatry. It is therefore possible to have at least two species of *Pseudemys* plus at least one other emydine genus occurring in microsympatry. This sympat-

ry reaches its peak in the southeastern United States east of the Mississippi. All of these turtle species have stripes on the head and neck, and all lack mental glands and musk glands (Waagen, 1972; Winokur and Legler, 1975).

South and west of the Pecos–lower Rio Grande there is no emydine sympatry. *Pseudemys scripta* is the only emydine, the only basking turtle, and the only turtle with stripes in all of Mesoamerica and South America. There are a few exceptions. *Chrysemys picta* occurs (naturally) in the Río Santa María of Chihuahua (no *Pseudemys*). In parts of Central America (e.g., the San Juan Delta, the region of Almirante, Panama), *Pseudemys scripta* shares basking logs with *Rhinoclemmys funerea* (pers. obs.); this phenomenon is local and uncommon (*R. funerea* is more characteristic of forest pools and commonly feeds on land at night; *Pseudemys* is chiefly riverine and feeds only in the water). This is the closest sympatric relationship that *Pseudemys* has anywhere in Mesoamerica to the best of my knowledge.

SEXUAL DIMORPHISM AND MATING.   Of 38 mensural characters analyzed, 28 were sexually dimorphic (determined with *t* tests at the .05 level). Some of these are easily understandable in terms of adaptive value for reproduction (e.g., height). Others are certainly associated with allometric changes occurring with larger size (e.g., widths of central scutes). But many are not well understood. These statements apply to most kinds of turtles.

This discussion concentrates on sexual dimorphism in adult size, foreclaw length, and shape of snout in profile. Sexual dimorphism in these characters can be demonstrated statistically in all *Pseudemys scripta*. However, this dimorphism is so extreme in some subspecies that statistics are scarcely necessary to express it.

Adult size.   Table 7.6 gives carapace length for all specimens of *scripta* I have examined, in terms of extremes, mean, and median for each sex. Obst (1985) gives some adult sizes that exceed any I have seen (almost 500 mm for *venusta*, 600 mm for *grayi*) and should be substantiated in terms of museum numbers (it is possible that the measurements are actually of *Dermatemys*).

There is extreme sexual dimorphism in adult size in the three U.S. subspecies of *P. scripta*. Males mature at a much smaller size than females and never become as large as females; the chances of a mating pair's being the same size are low. By comparison, there is much less size dimorphism in Mesoamerica. Although most females are larger than most males, males often grow as large as females, and the chances of a male's being as large or larger than a female are good (Moll and Legler, 1971). Males of *P. s. elegans* are contrasted to males of all Mesoamerican populations in Figure 7.11.

Foreclaw length.   The terminal (ungual) phalanges of the manus are greatly elongated in males of 12 of the

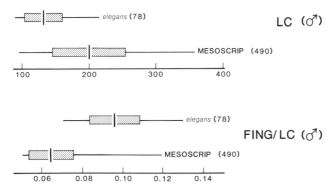

FIGURE 7.11.   Sexually dimorphic characters in *Pseudemys scripta*. Males of *P. s. elegans* (representing USASCRIP) are plotted against males of all Mesoamerican populations (MESOSCRIP) for carapace length (LC) and for length of third ungual phalanx of manus (FING), expressed as a percentage of carapace length. Vertical and horizontal lines represent the mean and the extremes, respectively. Rectangles represent one standard deviation of the mean.

17 species in the *Chrysemys* group (not in *Malaclemys;* not in 4 of 9 *Graptemys* species). This character is expressed by length of the ungual phalanx of the third digit in the analysis. This is a male secondary sexual characteristic. Within *Pseudemys scripta* (sensu stricto), long foreclaws occur in the three U.S. subspecies and not in the other subspecies. The phenotype is rarely and irregularly expressed in Mesoamerica. Males of Antillean species have elongated foreclaws.

Shape of snout in profile.   Males of all *Pseudemys scripta* have a narrower head and a more pointed snout than females. This is only a statistically demonstrable tendency in U.S. *scripta;* it is extreme in Mesoamerica. Mature males have long, pointed snouts. There is variation, and some subspecies have distinctive profiles. The snout may become bulbous and bosslike with age (e.g., *hiltoni*). Skulls of old large males have a raised, thickened ridge on the upper edge of the narial aperture. Unfortunately, the development and shape of the snout is not expressed by any character recorded in this study. Because a narrowing of the head seems to accompany snout elongation, relative head width is used to characterize snout shape.

Mating.   *Pseudemys scripta elegans* has an elaborate courtship behavior. The male overtakes a female and positions himself in front of her. He then titillates her by rapid vibration of his elongated foreclaws near her face and also by some rapid movements of the head. This complex Liebespiel was first noted by Taylor (1933). Jackson and Davis (1972) gave a thorough description of mating in *P. s. elegans* and suggested that titillation has evolved to replace biting as a means of immobilizing the female and that modifications in the complex Liebespiel could produce distinctive patterns within "the genus or subfamily."

Courtship involving titillation (and probably rapid head movements) occurs in the 12 *Chrysemys* group species that have elongated foreclaws (Carr, 1952; Ernst and Barbour, 1972; Jenkins, 1979; pers. obs.), including the 3 U.S. subspecies of *P. scripta*. It seemingly does not occur in taxa that lack the elongated foreclaws; this includes all Mesoamerican *P. scripta*. Evidence from observed matings is as follows: Davis and Jackson (1973), male *P. s. taylori* with captive females of *P. s. elegans* and *Chrysemys picta*, direct approach with biting; Moll and Legler (1971), *P. s. venusta* in Panama, two natural matings, rear approach and mounting without foreplay; personal observation (with binoculars from a cliff), natural mating, *P. s. hiltoni* male following female and mounting periodically, no face-to-face Liebespiel; personal observation (Taronga Park Zoo, Sydney, Australia), 250 mm male *P. s. dorbigni* courting female *P. s. elegans* (also being courted typically by male *elegans*), no titillation, direct approach with cloacal sniffing and trailing.

The function of elongated foreclaws is seemingly clear, but there is no demonstrable function for the elongated snout. It may permit sexual recognition by head profile in populations where males and females do not differ predictably in size. The snout could also be an erotic prod used in mating.

CONCLUSIONS.   The following points summarize my conclusions on sexual dimorphism and sympatry (Fig. 7.12).

1. All USASCRIP (*elegans, scripta, troosti*) share three derived characters:
   a. Males have greatly elongated foreclaws.
   b. There is an elaborate courtship in which the long claws are used.
   c. Males are significantly smaller than females.
2. All MESOSCRIP lack those characters. They have no elongated foreclaws and no elaborate courtship, and the sexes are more or less the same size.
3. Males of MESOSCRIP have a pointed, elongated snout that is not present in USASCRIP.
4. Because the elongated snout of MESOSCRIP is a phenotypic tendency in USASCRIP, and the distinctive phenotypes of USASCRIP show up as occasional variants in MESOSCRIP (pers. obs.), it can be hypothesized that selective factors acting on these phenotypes in the two groups are different.
5. All USASCRIP occur sympatrically with other striped emydines of the *Chrysemys* group in some parts of their ranges. South of lat. 38 this is usually a microsympatric association with another species of *Pseudemys* and at least one other species of striped emydine of the *Chrysemys* group. The elongated foreclaws, the sexual size dimorphism, and the Liebespiel are precopulatory isolating mechanisms that

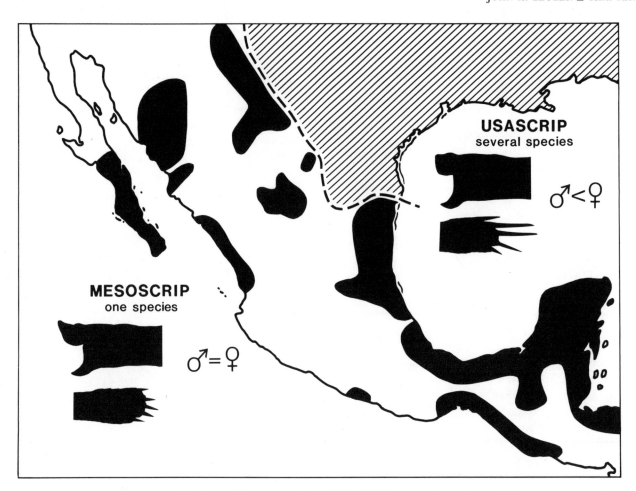

FIGURE 7.12.   Map showing distributions of Mexican species (MESOSCRIP) and a diagonally shaded area indicating where more than one species of *Pseudemys* (USASCRIP) occurs. South and west of the Rio Grande, *Pseudemys scripta* is the only emydine and the only turtle with stripes. In the area of sympatry, males are smaller than females, lack a pointed snout, and have elongated foreclaws. In the area of nonsympatry, males are about the same size as females, have a pointed snout, and lack the elongated foreclaws.

have been selected for in this zone of sympatry where many striped species occur.

6. These sexually dimorphic characters do not have a high selective advantage in MESOSCRIP. There is virtually no emydine sympatry in the entire range of MESOSCRIP; *Pseudemys* is the only striped aquatic turtle and the only basking emydid in the entire region. *Pseudemys* can mate without chance of error.

TIME OF ORIGIN

The Northern Isolates and the subspecies *hiltoni* and *nebulosa* have differentiated more than other subspecies of *Pseudemys scripta* (perhaps to the point logically expected in full species). I attribute much of this differential divergence to isolation and genetic drift. In known instances of secondary overlap (e.g., *taylori* and *elegans*), interbreeding

occurs (this has simply been noted, not studied). This secondary overlap has not resulted in character displacement, and no isolating mechanisms seem to have evolved (but see discussion of *grayi* and *venusta* in Pacific Population of Mexico, above). Differentiation in the other subspecies is closer to that expected in geographic races. An intensive ecological study by Moll and Legler (1971) showed few life history modifications when populations in Panama were compared with those of *elegans* in the United States.

All that I have learned of the relationships and ecology of Mesoamerican *Pseudemys scripta* bespeaks relatively recent colonization and differentiation. The origin of some populations in Mexico can be logically associated with Pleistocene events. I conclude that it is unnecessary to invoke Tertiary events to explain what we see in *Pseudemys scripta*. It is more reasonable to think in terms of recency than of antiquity.

Epilogue

Although the distribution of *Pseudemys scripta* has the appearance of being largely natural and congruent with fairly recent drainage histories, there is no zoogeographic scenario presented here that could not have occurred as a result of human introduction. All *Pseudemys* are bright and attractive as juveniles (witness the German, *"Schmuck . . ."* = jewel; Obst, 1985), but they become less attractive and more difficult to keep as they grow larger. Disenchanted turtle owners commonly release their pets (usually *P. s. elegans*). This has probably happened in every state of the United States, in the Canal Zone, and sporadically on all other continents except Antarctica. Turtles are commonly carried and used by humans for food; this practice occurs now (pers. obs.) and certainly occurred in prehistoric times (Tamayo and West, 1964). Human introduction is a serious alternative hypothesis for the dispersal of *P. s. nebulosa*, some Antillean populations, and some South American populations.

Acknowledgments

Although this study is largely my own work, I have received a significant amount of help. To prepare a complete list of names spanning 30 years of work is presently impossible. The following remarks are lamentably cursory; they mention only the principals. For assistance with field work and companionship I thank Raymond Lee, James S. Peebles, James L. Christiansen, Robert G. Webb, Robert Bolland, Frank Nabrotzky, Nowlan K. Dean, Edward O. Moll, and Roger Conant. Substantial financial aid was received in grants from the following agencies and institutions: National Science Foundation, American Philosophical Society, and University of Utah Research Committee.

All of the field work for this study involved living and working in Mesoamerican and Caribbean countries where we were aliens. We were always treated with courtesy, generosity, and respect, even at times of profound political uncertainty (some of which involved our home country). Specifically I thank the various governments, institutions, and landowners for permission to travel, collect, and export specimens. Notable among individuals who assisted us in these matters were Prof. Alvaro Wille, Universidad de Costa Rica; the late Dr. Marshall Hertig, Gorgas Memorial Laboratory, Panama; Dr. L. G. Clark, University of Pennsylvania (in Nicaragua); the United Fruit Company; the Standard Fruit Company; the Instituto Tropical de Investigaciones Científicas, San Salvador; Dr. and Mrs. David M. Pendergast, Royal Ontario Museum (in British Honduras).

For assistance with data and manuscript preparation I thank Katrina Heiner Childs, Maurine Vaughan, Laura Eberhardt-Morehead, Gloria Cuellar, and Cameron S. Denning. Kerry S. Matz prepared all of the artwork. For assistance with the entirely new world of computers and computer analysis I thank Steve Fullerton, Doug Hendry, and John Iverson. Dan Holland helped with the first agonizing steps in using a mainframe BMDP computer program. Special thanks to James F. Berry for enduring hours of telephone queries on multidiscriminant analysis. Dale R. Jackson and George R. Zug provided rigorous, cordial reviews of the manuscript.

I am especially grateful to my family, who accompanied me on many expeditions and permitted me to spend most of our extra money on such scientific trips. Austin F. Legler learned to catch turtles and to tell time on the same trip to Yucatán.

Reproduction
and Growth

JUSTIN D. CONGDON
J. WHITFIELD GIBBONS
Savannah River Ecology Laboratory
Drawer E
Aiken, South Carolina 29802

8

Turtle Eggs: Their Ecology and Evolution

Abstract

The state of knowledge about eggs of the slider turtle is pre-sented, based on a general review of the literature and on data acquired in studies in South Carolina. Features of turtle eggs that appear critical to understanding how they protect and fuel the embryo are discussed. These include determina-tion of the amount of energy a female dedicates to each egg and to the entire clutch and determination of the time over which energy is harvested, stored, and allocated. The impor-tance of nest site selection by females and the environmental factors of soil moisture, texture, and temperature is dis-cussed. Consideration is also given to the composition of the shells, yolk, and albumen of eggs in the context of protecting and fueling the developing embryo and hatchling. Ideas that are considered critical to understanding the evolution and current function of turtle eggs are discussed, and key ques-tions that must be answered are presented.

Introduction

Many of the divergences in the natural and life histories of present-day amphibians and reptiles can be traced to the differences in their eggs. Primitive reptiles, the romeriid captorhinomorphs, apparently produced a relatively naked amniotic egg similar to the eggs of present-day amphibians that develop in terrestrial nests and produce a miniature adult rather than a larval stage (Carroll, 1969). The latter similarity suggests that, compared with aquatic amphibians, primitive reptiles had a longer develop-mental time within the egg and required greater amounts of egg yolk to provide the material and energy reserves to support the developing embryo until it hatched from the egg, and possibly for some time after. Reptile eggs have since developed a shell that helps to shield the egg's con-tents from its environment.

The eggshells of present-day reptiles may have evolved to protect the egg's contents from desiccation, bacteria, fungi, and arthropod predators (Gray, 1928; Needham, 1931; Carroll, 1969; Packard and Packard, 1980). Eggshells of contemporary reptiles exhibit a wide range in type, texture, and configuration (Agassiz, 1857; Giersberg, 1922; Erben, 1970; Packard et al., 1977; Ewert, 1979; Packard and Packard, 1979; Sexton et al., 1979; Packard, 1980; Ferguson, 1982, 1985; Lamb and Congdon, 1985; Allison and Greer, 1986; Packard and Hirsch, 1986). Two major features of reptile eggs separate them from those of aquatic amphibians: (1) a much larger proportion of yolk and (2) a highly developed calcareous shell. These features combine to make the eggs of reptiles more resistant to desiccation and better able to fuel a longer developmental period and provide nutritional support for the hatchling after it leaves the egg.

In contrast to both lizards and snakes, there are no known viviparous turtles, nor are any turtles known to routinely delay laying eggs after they have been ovulated. Therefore, the shelled egg represents, in essence, the first environment that every turtle embryo is exposed to, and that environment is soon totally independent of the parent. The eggshell's role of protecting the embryo, a vulnerable stage in a turtle's life history, may thus be partially analogous to the role played by the carapace and plastron of adult turtles. Turtle eggs must provide all aspects of an embryo's needs from the time the eggs are independent of the female until the hatchling leaves the nest, a period that may exceed one year (Goode and Russell, 1968; Gibbons and Nelson, 1978). In addition, recent investigations indicate that the egg acts as a container of material for preovulatory parental investment in care (Kraemer and Bennett, 1981; Congdon et al., 1983a,c; Congdon and Gibbons, 1985; Wilhoft, 1986). The amount of preovulatory parental investment in care is not trivial. At least 50% of the contents of a turtle egg may remain in the form of hatchling fat bodies or residual material in the yolk sac. The residual yolk provides material and energy for maintenance, and possibly growth, of hatchlings after they leave the egg. Thus, the attributes of turtle eggs, and indeed all reptilian eggs, make them excellent subjects for examining the concepts of parental investment and optimal egg size.

The purposes of this chapter are (1) to place our knowledge of the eggs of *Trachemys scripta* in relation to knowledge about other turtle eggs, (2) to review and consolidate information about turtle eggs, (3) to identify the features that seem critical to our understanding of how turtle eggs protect and provide for their embryos in various nest environments, (4) to review and develop ideas that will increase our understanding of the evolution and present function of turtle eggs, and (5) identify areas in which our knowledge of turtle eggs is lacking and to pose important questions that remain to be answered. Progress toward these goals will require a review of material on egg components and developmental processes related to hatchling

viability and quality. In addition, it will require consideration not only of the egg itself but also of the timing and variation of investment in eggs; the nesting behavior of females related to nest site selection, the range of variation in the microenvironments within and among nests, and how environmental variation affects the survivorship of eggs and hatchlings; and the relationship between levels of preovulatory parental investment and survivorship of hatchlings. This chapter will not attempt to review all that is known about egg sizes or developmental stages of embryos. For viewpoints on other aspects of reptilian egg biology, see the following reviews and key papers: embryo development (Agassiz, 1857; Rathke, 1848); turtle eggs (Ewert, 1979, 1985; Miller, 1985); eggs, reproduction, and life histories of turtles (Wilbur and Morin, 1988); physiological ecology (Packard et al., 1977); evolution of the cleidoic egg (Packard et al., 1980); function of crocodilian eggs (Webb et al., 1987); crocodile egg chemistry (Manolis et al., 1987); the adaptive value of lipids in biological systems (Hadley, 1985); and lipid analysis (Christie, 1982).

Development of Eggs

The amount of energy available for production of eggs can come from resources harvested and sequestered during the period that the eggs are being produced or from energy and material stored previously. To understand reproduction in turtles, it is necessary to know the total amount of energy allocated to each clutch of eggs, the amount allocated to each egg, the time over which the energy was harvested and allocated, and the relative contributions of stored versus directly harvested energy for each clutch.

In *Chrysemys picta*, follicle sizes are smallest in the ovaries just after the nesting season, with substantial follicle enlargement taking place from late August through October (Ernst, 1971d; Congdon and Tinkle, 1982b). On average, the set of largest follicles found in females in October represented 50% of the energy of a complete clutch of eggs that would be laid during May and June of the following year. Energy allocated to follicle enlargement during the summer and early fall months was presumably obtained directly from harvested resources because stored lipids in females also increased during this period. The additional 50% of the energy to complete follicle enlargement prior to ovulation was allocated between spring emergence in late-March through mid-May when nests for first clutches were initiated (Congdon and Tinkle, 1982b).

The energy allocated to follicles during spring presumably came entirely from stored body lipids because the decrease in lipid levels of females during the period was almost equivalent to the increase in lipids in follicles (Congdon and Tinkle, 1982b). In addition, examination of growth in *C. picta* from Michigan and Pennsylvania indicated that little or no growth, and presumably feeding activity, was taking place before June (Sexton, 1959a, 1965; Ernst, 1971a). A similar pattern of follicle development during late summer has been observed in *Sternotherus odoratus* in Alabama, where follicles were fully developed (ovulatory size) between August and December, with ovulation occurring during late April of the following year (McPherson and Marion, 1981a).

The minimum interval between the first and second clutches of *C. picta* in Michigan and *T. scripta* in South Carolina is approximately 12 days (Gibbons and Greene, unpub. data). This short interval indicates that (1) ovulation of a subsequent clutch of eggs can occur shortly after a clutch has been placed in a nest and (2) the follicles for the second clutch develop at the same time as those for the first clutch and, if necessary, complete development during the time the eggs for the first clutch are in the oviducts. In species in northern latitudes, energy for the second clutch probably comes primarily from stored lipids, because feeding activity would still be minimal during the period of egg development. In turtles from more southern latitudes, such as *T. scripta*, proportionally more energy in subsequent clutches may come directly from harvested energy rather than stored reserves; however, the relative contributions of the energy sources have not been documented.

Turtle Nests and Nest Site Selection by Females

Nests of many, and probably most, freshwater turtles are placed in areas that are exposed to full sunlight during some portion of the day. Nests are usually constructed in sandy to loam soils with little vegetation cover. Disturbed areas such as road banks, railroad grades, dikes, levees, and dams seem to be favored for nesting (Burger, 1977; Obbard and Brooks, 1980, 1981a; Petokas and Alexander, 1980; Seigel, 1980a; Snow, 1982; Congdon et al., 1983b, 1986; Obbard, 1983; Schwarzkopf and Brooks, 1987). Freshwater turtles generally dig flask-shaped nests in well-drained soils with their hind feet. Both within and among species the size of the nest and the number of eggs placed in the nest are in general positively related to the body size of the female (Congdon and Gibbons, 1985). Some turtles such as *S. odoratus* may deposit their eggs in muskrat mounds (Carr, 1952) or rotting stumps of trees but in some instances may only partially bury them or leave them entirely exposed (Risley, 1933; Ewert, 1979). Some species of the genus *Rhinoclemmys* cover their eggs with leaves (Medem, 1962; Moll and Legler, 1971). It seems logical that eggs in poorly covered nests will most often be in habitats that are shadier and more moist than the sites of covered nests, and in most if not all cases the eggs should have relatively impermeable rigid shells.

Temperature and soil moisture are major variables in the nest microenvironment and have been shown to be important in determining the ultimate survivorship and quality as well as the sex of developing embryos (Pieau, 1972,

1982; Bull, 1980, 1983; Bull and Vogt, 1981; Mrosovsky, 1982; Caudle, 1984; Packard et al., 1985; Congdon et al., 1987). Both of these factors, in conjunction with the number and possibly the size of eggs in a nest, have been shown to influence the rate of development and total incubation time before emergence from the egg. However, arguments that larger eggs of the terrestrial box turtle, *Terrapene carolina*, represent an adaptation for incubation and egg development in terrestrial environments (Packard et al., 1985) are not logical, because the eggs of most aquatic species also incubate and develop in terrestrial situations.

We suggest that the following scenario, modified from Wilbur and Morin (1988), is more likely. The relatively larger eggs of terrestrial turtles, compared with those of aquatic species with similar body size, may result from the requirements of hatchlings after they leave the nest. Hatchlings of aquatic species move to highly productive habitats containing high densities of aquatic insect adults and larvae. Thus, in such habitats hatchlings can attain a positive energy balance in a relatively short time. We do not agree with Wilbur and Morin (1988) that the speed and maneuverability of aquatic hatchlings, relative to terrestrial hatchlings, play a major role in their ability to attain a positive energy balance. In contrast to the productive environment encountered by hatchlings of aquatic turtles, hatchlings of terrestrial species emerge into an environment in which the distribution of prey is less dense and probably more clumped. These factors probably result in terrestrial turtles' being more herbivorous and less able to attain a positive energy balance in as short a time as do aquatic hatchlings. Thus, we propose that for terrestrial turtles (1) larger energy stores are provided by the parent and result in larger eggs and possibly larger hatchlings, (2) the ability to make longer movements among resource patches is enhanced by larger body size, and (3) a slightly larger body size may be necessary for increased gut length and volume related to herbivory.

A third feature of the nest environment that is less studied but may also be important is gas exchange between the embryos and the nest's surroundings. To what degree the female can ascertain the present conditions of the nest site or predict the future nest microenvironment to which her eggs will be exposed is not known but is certainly important to our understanding of turtle reproduction.

Both the depth of a nest and the egg's position within a nest determine the microenvironment of each egg. Eggs in shallow nests or at the top of nests would be expected to be exposed to larger diel and longer-term temperature variations than those deeper in the soil (Figs. 8.1 and 8.2). For example, temperatures at the surface of the soil exposed to full sunlight in South Carolina during late summer can reach daytime highs of more than 40° C, whereas those at 10 to 15 mm below the surface might not reach 35° C.

The lower thermal limit for turtle eggs incubated at relatively constant temperatures is approximately 22° C.

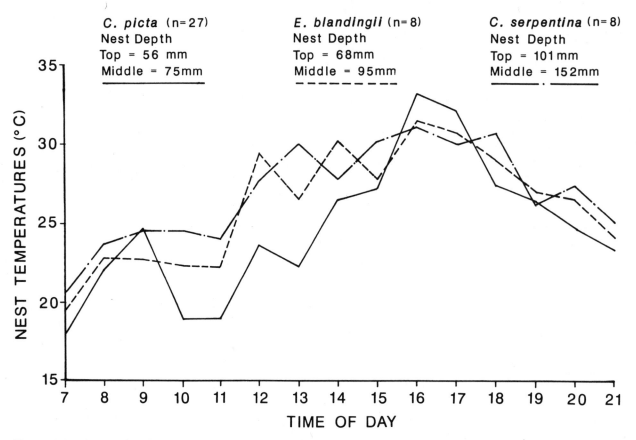

FIGURE 8.1.   Average hourly temperatures over the entire incubation period taken from the center of nests of three species of turtles on the E. S. George Reserve in southeastern Michigan.

Below this temperature turtles such as *Chelonia mydas* (Bustard and Greenham, 1968; Bustard, 1971), *Chelydra serpentina* (Ewert, 1979), and *Chrysemys picta* (Ream, 1967) failed to develop. Minimum incubation temperature for turtles of the genus *Trionyx* may be closer to 25° C (Ewert, 1979). The thermal maximum above which turtle embryos cease development and die appears to be approximately 33° C (Yntema, 1960; Ewert, 1979). However, turtle embryos are certainly able to withstand short periods with temperatures below and above these thermal limits. Nest temperatures below the lower extremes may be common during the early portion of nesting seasons, but with the exception of very shallow nests, it is difficult to envision conditions in which eggs would be commonly exposed to temperatures above the upper lethal limits (Fig. 8.1).

Composition and Function of Eggshells

Eggshells of contemporary turtles are composed of two membranes of dense fibrous material that is thicker than that found in bird eggs (Schmidt, 1943; Young, 1950; Packard and Packard, 1979). The inner shell membrane lies next to the albumen, and the outer shell membrane lies next to the inorganic crystalline layer (Fig. 8.3). The membranes are so closely apposed that they cannot be visually distinguished except at the white patch, or air cell, that forms between them at the top of the egg (Einem, 1956; Ewert, 1979; Packard and Packard, 1979). The eggshell and membranes associated with the air cell contain 26% less water than do the membranes from translucent areas of the egg (Thompson, 1985). Thus, the air cell is apparently an area of regional drying that is related to gas exchange required by respiration of the developing embryo (Thompson, 1985).

The inorganic portion of eggshells of both fossil and contemporary turtles is composed primarily of calcium carbonate ($CaCO_3$) in the form of aragonite (orthorhombic $CaCO_3$). The eggs of most other squamates and birds are calcite (Erben, 1970; Erben and Newesley, 1972; Solomon and Baird, 1976; Ferguson, 1982, 1985; M. Packard et al., 1982; Hirsch, 1983). Variation in the relative amounts of calcite and aragonite reported for eggshells of captive sea turtles (*Chelonia mydas*—Solomon and Baird, 1976) and pythons (Solomon and Reid, 1983) indicates that (1) reptiles may alter the type of crystals formed in their eggshells in response to conditions that exist in farms or zoos, and (2) reptiles have some physiological capability of producing the crystal type that is atypical for their group. These two factors suggest that if there is a function-

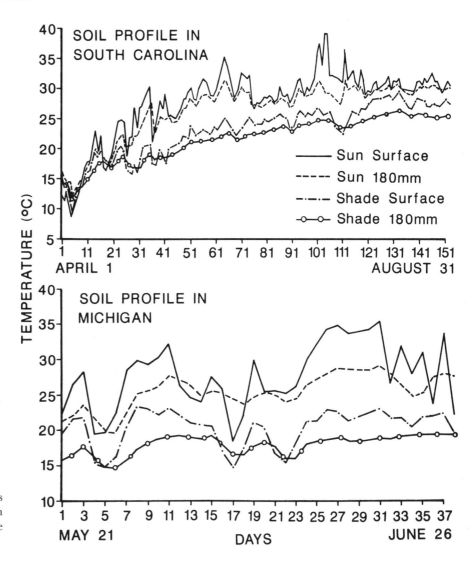

FIGURE 8.2.   Soil temperature profiles in full sun and shade from the Savannah River Plant in South Carolina and the E. S. George Reserve in Michigan.

al difference in the type of eggshell crystals, natural selection could act upon variability in the trait.

Among the amniote eggs of contemporary reptiles, there are three main types of eggshells, based on the degree of calcification: (1) parchmentlike—a shell with little or no calcareous material (found in snakes and lizards), (2) flexible calcareous—a shell that ranges from a weakly defined calcareous layer to a discrete calcareous layer of loosely arranged shell units that do not interlock, and (3) rigid—a shell that has a thick calcareous layer with well-defined shell units that interlock. As a general rule, shell units of flexible eggshells are wider than tall and have distinct pores that penetrate to the underlying shell membranes, whereas shell units of rigid eggshells are taller than wide and have pores that are less structured than those of flexible-shelled eggs. Modern turtles have flexible calcareous or rigid eggshells (Ewert, 1979). Carettochelyids, chelids, dermatemydids, kinosternids, testudinids, and trionychids produce rigid-shelled eggs, and cheloniids, chelydrids, and dermochelyids produce flexible-shelled

ones. Within the emydids and pelomedusids, eggshell type varies among species (Ewert, 1979, 1985; M. Packard et al., 1982).

Eggshells of six species of emydid turtles with flexible-shelled eggs ranged from 15.8% to 20.6% ($\bar{x} = 19.2\%$) of the total dry mass of the eggs, with eggshells of *Trachemys scripta* averaging 18.6% (Congdon and Gibbons, 1985). Eggshells of *Clemmys marmorata*, an emydid turtle with brittle-shelled eggs, averaged 39.6% of the total dry mass of eggs. Five turtle species with brittle-shelled eggs had eggshells that averaged 40.8% of the total dry mass of eggs. The proportion of total egg dry mass in eggshells of the two eggshell categories was significantly different (Congdon and Gibbons, 1985).

The total amount of inorganic material found in the flexible eggshells of four species of turtles ranged from 35.9% to 39.3% and averaged 38.0% by dry mass (Lamb and Congdon, 1985). Eggshells of *T. scripta* averaged 39.3% inorganic ash by dry mass, and the inorganic ash in the shell averaged 7.4% of the total dry mass of the egg.

a.

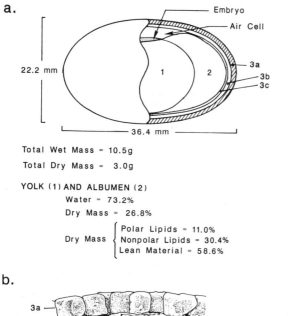

Total Wet Mass = 10.5g
Total Dry Mass = 3.0g

YOLK (1) AND ALBUMEN (2)
    Water = 73.2%
    Dry Mass = 26.8%

    Dry Mass { Polar Lipids = 11.0%
              Nonpolar Lipids = 30.4%
              Lean Material = 58.6%

b.

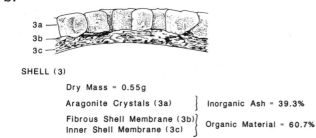

SHELL (3)

    Dry Mass = 0.55g
    Aragonite Crystals (3a)   } Inorganic Ash = 39.3%
    Fibrous Shell Membrane (3b) }
    Inner Shell Membrane (3c)   } Organic Material = 60.7%

FIGURE 8.3. Schematic diagram of a typical *Trachemys scripta* egg.

Among five species with rigid eggshells, inorganic material ranged from 50.4% to 52.9% and averaged 51.8% by dry mass. The inorganic portion (approximately 22%) of the eggshell of the sea turtle *Chelonia mydas* (Solomon and Baird, 1976) was notably lower than the portions reported above for freshwater and terrestrial turtles. Whether the low inorganic level is normal for sea turtles is difficult to say at this time, because eggshells of sea turtles represent a distinct subgroup of flexible-shelled eggs in which (1) the shell units are smaller and less distinct, (2) the crystallites of aragonite are larger and more variable in size, and (3) the pores are not distinct, but numerous spaces penetrate the inorganic layer (Baird and Solomon, 1979; M. Packard et al., 1982; Hirsch, 1983). Also, the turtles were raised in captivity, which may have influenced the amount of inorganic content in their eggshells and the type of the calcium carbonate crystals formed as well (see the discussion of eggshell crystals above).

The reason that turtles are the only group of reptiles that produce eggshells made from aragonite rather than calcite crystals is unknown. It may be that the use of aragonite crystals is a primitive trait that arose early in the evolution of turtles. In contrast, the different eggshell types found among turtles may be the result of selection pressures that are associated with different nest microenvironments, although ecological correlates of eggshell types with present-day nest environments have not been identified and are not readily apparent. For example, eggs of some crocodilians are placed in nests in sandy soils or in nests constructed of decaying vegetation. Similar substrates can be found in turtle nests, and indeed some turtles lay their eggs in alligator nest mounds (Deitz and Jackson, 1979; Kushlan, 1980). Regardless of crystal or eggshell type, it is apparent that the shells of reptile eggs protect the egg's initial contents and the developing embryo from a range of biotic and abiotic dangers.

Egg Component Studies and Data Reporting

Comparisons of egg or body components among studies are sometimes confounded by the lack of uniform techniques for determining the amounts of materials that make up the egg. In addition, there is a lack of uniform reporting of actual values and the way that proportions of egg components are expressed. Some of these differences result because the types of questions being asked vary, and different techniques will remain in use. However, some of the problems could be avoided with a few basic rules for extracting lipids and for reporting data. We will attempt to standardize the reporting of certain data from egg component studies.

Two general classes of lipids exist that differ in their solubility in organic solvents. Polar lipids are combinations of nonpolar fatty acid chains associated with a polar functional group such as phosphate or sugars. Polar lipids are generally extractable in a highly polar solvent such as methanol, ethanol, or chloroform (Christie, 1973). Nonpolar lipids such as triglycerides or cholesteryl esters are soluble in a less polar solvent such as ether, hexane, benzene, or cyclohexane but may also be extracted in a slightly more polar solvent such as chloroform or diethyl ether (Christie, 1973).

The choice of extraction technique should be made based on the questions asked. Polar lipids are usually associated with cell membranes and other structural components of animals such as myelin sheaths of nerves, whereas nonpolar lipids are generally associated with lipid reserves of animals. Therefore, if questions are asked about annual cycling of lipid stores of an animal, nonpolar solvents should be used so that extraction of polar lipids associated with body structures is minimized.

The choice of extraction techniques used for eggs is not quite as clear. Because triglycerides are the traditional storage lipids in adults, some authors have focused on nonpolar lipids in eggs to estimate parental investment in care (Kraemer and Bennett, 1981; Congdon et al., 1983a,c; Congdon and Gibbons, 1985). However, ques-

Table 8.1. Characteristics of *Trachemys scripta* and eggs

Plastron length at sexual maturity (mm)	Eggs								
	Length (mm)	Width (mm)	Length-width ratio	Wet mass (g)	Percent water[a]	Clutch size	N (eggs; clutches)	Region	Reference
--	36.4	22.2	1.64	10.5	72.2	7.1	489; 88	South Carolina	6
207	36.4	21.4	1.70	9.8	--	6.1	--; 42	South Carolina	4
150	36.0	22.9	1.57	11.0	--	9.6	--; 23	South Carolina	4
--	36.0	22.6	1.59	10.9	74.4	8.7	--; 33	South Carolina	5
240	42.2	28.2	1.50	20.7	--	17.4	87; --	Panama	3
205	34.3	23.2	1.48	10.8	--	10.2	--; 43	Virginia	7
158	36.2	21.6	1.68	9.7	--	9.3	221; 67	Illinois	1
159	37.7	22.6	1.67	11.1	--	7.0	406; 129	Louisiana	2
194	38.1	22.6	1.68	11.8	--	12.0	373; --	Southern Mexico	8
$\bar{X}$ 187.6	37.0	23.0	1.60	11.8		9.7			

References: 1, Cagle, 1944; 2, Cagle, 1950; 3, Moll and Legler, 1971; 4, Congdon and Gibbons, 1983; 5, Caudle, 1984; 6, Congdon and Gibbons, 1985; 7, see Chapter 11; 8, see Chapter 13.

[a]Water as a percentage of total egg wet mass, including shell.

tions remain about the ability of yolk reserves to be used for growth of hatchlings, so information about the polar lipids in eggs is also important (Caudle, 1984; Wilhoft, 1986). Thus, we recommend that both polar and nonpolar solvents be used in future studies of egg components so that the amount of both lipid classes can be determined. In addition, we recommend that, because of the variety of eggshell types among turtle species, the eggshell be removed prior to lipid extraction. Minimum data reported should include (1) the clutch size, body length, and wet mass of females producing the eggs; (2) the length, breadth, and total wet mass of fresh eggs; (3) the dry mass of shell and egg components as well as the masses of polar and nonpolar lipids and lean dry material; and (4) the percentages of each component.

Among populations of the slider turtle (*Trachemys scripta*), sexual maturity of females is attained at a plastron length (PL) ranging from 150 to 240 mm (Cagle, 1950; Moll and Legler, 1971; Gibbons et al., 1982; Congdon and Gibbons, 1983). Females reproduce at PLs ranging from 150 mm to more than 325 mm (Moll and Legler, 1971; Gibbons et al., 1982). Adult females from populations in the southeastern United States had PLs that ranged from 150 to 277 mm (Congdon and Gibbons, 1983). Among those females, egg wet mass and egg width, but not egg length, increased significantly with body size. When mean values were included for populations from the tropics (Table 8.1), essentially the same pattern persisted. Relationships of egg wet mass and egg width to body size were marginally significant, but egg length was not.

In a tropical slider population, egg length was used to explore the relationships of egg size to body size among turtles (Moll and Legler, 1971). The data presented in Table 8.1 and from Congdon and Gibbons (1983) indicate that egg width and egg wet mass exhibit stronger relation-

ships with body size of *T. scripta* than does egg length. Similar results have been found for both *Chrysemys picta* (Congdon and Tinkle, 1982b) and *Deirochelys reticularia* (Congdon et al., 1983a). It is a common observation among many groups of reptiles that clutch size increases as body size of females increases (Carpenter, 1960; Semlitsch and Gibbons, 1978; Dunham and Miles, 1985; Dunham et al., 1988a; Wilbur and Morin, 1988). Less frequently reported are incidences in which egg or neonate size increases with body size of females (Caldwell, 1959; Ewert, 1979; Moll, 1979; Stewart, 1979). Tucker et al. (1978) documented that egg size increased with body size in the painted turtle (*C. picta*) and suggested that egg size might be constrained by the size of the pelvic opening through which the eggs must pass. Since that time, evidence supporting pelvic constraint of egg size has been reported for *C. picta* and *D. reticularia* (Congdon and Tinkle, 1982b; Congdon et al., 1983a; Congdon and Gibbons, 1987).

In a study of three species of emydid turtles (*C. picta*, *D. reticularia*, and *T. scripta*), we found that pelvic constraint on egg size among the species appeared to be related to body size (Congdon and Gibbons, 1987). In two small-bodied species (*C. picta* and *D. reticularia*), egg size increased from the smallest to the largest gravid females, and the slopes of the lines relating egg size and pelvic opening width to body size were essentially equal. In contrast, eggs of female *T. scripta* increased with body size only slightly, relative to eggs of the other two species, and the slope of the line relating pelvic width to body size was five times steeper than the line relating egg width to body size. The constraint on egg size due to pelvic opening size in *C. picta* and *D. reticularia* apparently resulted in a situation that is not in accord with that predicted by optimal-egg-size models; that is, substantially more of the variation in reproductive output was due to variation in egg size than was found in *T. scripta,* where pelvic constraint did not exist.

Characteristics and Components of Turtle Eggs

Of the 12 species with oblong eggs that are described in Figure 8.4, 9 (75%), including *T. scripta,* had egg length-width ratios of 1.6 or 1.7. Only one large-bodied species (*Pseudemys concinna,* 1.5) and 2 small-bodied species (*Clemmys marmorata* and *Chrysemys picta dorsalis,* 1.9) had egg measurement ratios other than 1.6 or 1.7. The only pattern that is apparent in relation to egg shape (i.e., whether the eggs are round or oblong) is that only those turtles with relatively large body size have round eggs. The wet mass of *Gopherus polyphemus* eggs was approximately four times the wet mass of the largest of all other eggs. Water averaged 68.8% of the wet mass of all turtle eggs (Table 8.2).

The components of turtle eggs, and probably all reptile eggs, provide material and energy for two distinct, albeit continuous, aspects of early development. First, energy

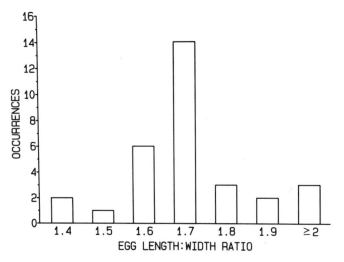

FIGURE 8.4. Frequency histogram of the ratio of egg length to egg width of 12 species of turtles with oblong eggs. Data are from Ewert (1979) and Congdon and Gibbons (1985).

Table 8.2. Egg characteristics of various species of turtles

Family and species	Eggs					
	Length (mm)	Width (mm)	Wet mass (g)	Percent water[a]	Clutch size	N (eggs; clutches)
Intermediate-shelled eggs						
Chelydridae						
Chelydra serpentina	--	25.8	9.6	68.3	23.6	73; 44
	--	--	9.4	72.6	--	139; 22
	--	--	10.4	70.6	44.5	400; 9
	27.2	11.2	--	34.0	--	--; 230
Flexible-shelled eggs						
Emydidae						
Chrysemys picta dorsalis	--	--	6.9	74.4	--	13; --
	17.3	33.2	6.2	66.5	--	5; 1
C. p. marginata	17.5	29.8	4.1	--	7.6	398; 77
Deirochelys reticularia	20.8	34.8	9.1	70.7	8.0	110; 13
Emydoidea blandingii	23.2	37.6	11.3	--	10.0	132; 20
Malaclemys terrapin	--	--	7.3	68.9	--	21; 7
Pseudemys concinna	23.9	36.4	12.0	72.8	--	15; 1
P. floridana	23.2	36.2	11.5	72.0	11.5	89; 11
Terrapene carolina	20.7	35.6	9.0	67.9	3.4	25; 8
Trachemys scripta	22.2	36.4	10.5	72.2	7.1	489; 88
Rigid-shelled eggs						
Emydidae						
Clemmys marmorata	19.1	37.3	8.3	71.2	--	6; 2
Testudinidae						
Geochelone yniphora	44.5	--	42.8	65.3	--	4; 1
Kinosternidae						
Kinosternon flavescens	16.6	26.9	4.3	65.9[a]	4.9	52; 10
K. subrubrum	15.6	26.2	3.9	61.2	3.4	66; 19
Sternotherus odoratus	15.5	27.1	4.0	64.5	4.5	36; 9
Trionychidae						
Trionyx ferox	--	26.7	10.4	70.7	--	15; 1

Sources: Lynn and von Brand, 1945; Obbard, 1983; Congdon and Gibbons, 1985; Wilhoft, 1986.

[a]Water as a percentage of total egg, including shell.

Table 8.3. Characteristics of dry components of *Trachemys scripta* eggs

Total mass	Mass	Shell		Lipids			Egg lean dry mass	Reference
		% of total egg	Yolk mass	Mass	% of yolk	% of total egg		
3.24	--	--	--	0.96[a]	--	29.5[a]	2.28[c]	1
3.13	0.54	18.0	2.78	1.01[b]	40.7[b]	33.4[b]	1.77[e]	2
2.90	0.55	18.8	2.35	0.71[a]	30.4[a]	24.8[a]	1.64[d]	3

Note: Mass is given in g.
References: 1, Congdon et al., 1983c; 2, Caudle, 1984; 3, Congdon and Gibbons, 1985.
[a]Includes nonpolar lipids only.
[b]Includes polar and nonpolar lipids.
[c]Includes polar lipids and shell.
[d]Includes polar lipids.
[e]Includes no polar lipids.

and material are used within the egg for development and maintenance of the embryo, and, second, energy and material remaining in the hatchling yolk sac are used for maintenance and possibly for growth of the hatchling. The distinction between the two components of energy utilization is important in understanding the function of the reptilian egg (Kraemer and Bennett, 1981; Congdon et al., 1983a,c; Congdon and Gibbons, 1985; Wilhoft, 1986).

Eggs of *T. scripta* from South Carolina average 10.5 g in wet mass and 3.0 g in dry mass (Fig. 8.3, Table 8.2). The dry mass of the shell (0.55 g) averages approximately 18% of the dry mass of the egg (Table 8.3). Polar lipids (Caudle, 1984) and nonpolar lipids (Congdon and Gibbons, 1985) make up approximately 11% and 30% of the dry mass of the egg, respectively. The proportion of nonpolar lipids in the yolks of turtle eggs ranges from 23% (*Chelydra serpentina*) to 34% (*D. reticularia*) among species (Table 8.4).

The most complete analysis of the components of turtle eggs has been done on the snapping turtle (*C. serpentina*—Wilhoft, 1986). Wilhoft's study is unique in that, as far as we know, it is the only study that provides complete information on the proportions of polar and nonpolar lipids in turtle eggs. In the egg yolk of *C. serpentina*, 12.3% of the lipids are polar and 21.5% are nonpolar. Data on the polar lipids left in hatchling yolk sacs were not reported, but it would be interesting to know if proportionally more of the polar lipids, relative to the nonpolar lipids, are used during development. Wilhoft's statement that "for turtle eggs, the total extractable lipids as well as protein should be considered as total storage energy [for the hatchling]" should be carefully examined. First, if the question is related to total support of all immediate needs of the hatchling (e.g., maintenance, tissue maturation, and growth), then the statement may be valid if only the material in the yolk sac is considered. If lipids are also extracted from the body of the hatchling, using polar solvents (Wilhoft, 1986), then structural lipids from the hatchling bodies are

included as stored energy. If the question is asked just about support of maintenance for the hatchling, rather than tissue maturation or growth, then the nonpolar lipids are probably a better index of storage energy.

Two other aspects of turtle eggs—eggshell type and whether the hatchlings delay emergence from the nest—are apparently related to the relative proportions of egg yolk components. Because turtle eggs have two distinct shell types, it is necessary to examine egg components of each group for differences (Tables 8.2 and 8.4). The slope (0.41) of the line relating eggshell dry mass to the amount of nonpolar lipids in eggs with flexible shells was more than twice as steep as the slope (0.15) of the line for eggs with rigid shells (Congdon and Gibbons, 1985). The increased slope resulted from the combination of less inorganic material in the shells of flexible-shelled eggs (Lamb and Congdon, 1985) and a higher proportional yolk lipid content (33%) relative to yolks from eggs with rigid shells (26%; Congdon and Gibbons, 1985).

Two notable exceptions to the general comparison of lipid levels with shell types are *Terrapene carolina* (25.8% yolk lipids), which has a flexible-shelled egg, and *Kinosternon subrubrum* (31.6% yolk lipids), which has a rigid-shelled egg. Both are more similar in proportional yolk lipids to turtles with opposite eggshell types (Table 8.4; Congdon and Gibbons, 1985). Two apparent differences in these exceptions that may be important in determining lipid levels in their eggs is that *T. carolina* is the only terrestrial turtle with flexible-shelled eggs that was examined by Congdon and Gibbons (1985), and *K. subrubrum* is the only turtle examined that has rigid-shelled eggs and hatchlings that overwinter in the nest. Why the difference in eggshell type and lipid levels in turtle eggs should have any association remains an open question. However, it seems likely that differences in eggshell type are related to differences in water exchange between the egg and its environment (see Water Relations of Turtle Eggs during Development, below). An additional factor may be the length of time that the hatchling spends in the nest.

Table 8.4. Characteristics of dry components of eggs of various species of turtles and other reptiles

Family and species	Total dry mass	Shell dry mass	Nonpolar lipids			Egg lean dry mass	Region	Reference
			Mass	% of total egg	% of yolk			
Intermediate-shelled eggs								
Chelydridae								
Chelydra serpentina	2.59	0.77	0.60[a]	16.2	33.8[a]	1.22[b]	New Jersey	7
	3.04	--	0.45	14.6	--	2.59[c]	Michigan	3
	3.05	0.71	0.55	18.0	23.5	1.78[d]	North Carolina	5
Flexible-shelled eggs								
Emydidae								
Chrysemys picta	2.07	0.41	0.54	26.4	33.0	1.11[d]	Georgia	5
	1.78	--	0.32	22.7	--	1.11[c]	Michigan	3
	1.86	--	0.42	22.8	--	1.44[c]	Wisconsin	3
Deirochelys reticularia	2.46	0.49	0.62	25.2	31.5	1.35[d]	South Carolina	2
	2.80	0.54	0.73	26.2	32.4	1.52[d]	South Carolina	5
Emydoidea blandingii	3.55	--	0.55	15.6	--	3.00[c]	Michigan	3
Graptemys geographica	2.51	--	0.40	15.9	--	2.11[c]	Michigan	3
G. ouachitensis	2.56	--	0.62	24.4	--	1.94[c]	Wisconsin	3
Malaclemys terrapin	2.24	--	--	--	26.4	--	New Jersey	1
Pseudemys concinna	3.24	0.51	0.76	23.3	27.7	1.97[d]	South Carolina	5
P. floridana	3.41	0.60	0.80	23.7	29.0	1.96[d]	South Carolina	5
Terrapene carolina	2.94	0.60	0.59	20.6	25.8	1.70[d]	South Carolina	5
Trachemys scripta	3.24	--	0.96	29.5	--	2.28[c]	South Carolina	3
	2.90	0.55	0.71	24.8	30.4	1.64[d]	South Carolina	5
Rigid-shelled eggs								
Kinosternidae								
Kinosternon flavescens	1.65	--	0.43	26.1[a]	--	1.22[c]	Texas	6
K. subrubrum	1.53	0.67	0.27	17.7	31.6	0.59[d]	South Carolina	5
Sternotherus odoratus	1.41	0.58	0.21	15.4	25.8	0.62[d]	South Carolina	5
	1.94	--	0.23	11.8	--	1.71[c]	Michigan	3
Trionychidae								
Trionyx ferox	3.05	0.96	0.58	19.2	28.0	1.51[d]	Georgia	5
Crocodylidae								
Alligator mississippiensis	20.10	7.10	5.20	26.0	40.0	7.80[d]	Florida	8
Anguidae								
Gerrhonotus coeruleus	0.20	--	0.08	--	--	≈0.02	California	4
Colubridae								
Nerodia rhombifera	3.52	--	1.15	--	--	≈0.31	Oklahoma	3

Note: Mass is given in g.

References: 1, Ricklefs and Burger, 1977; 2, Congdon et al., 1983a; 3, Congdon et al., 1983c; 4, Stewart and Castillo, 1984; 5, Congdon and Gibbons, 1985; 6, Long, 1985; 7, Wilhoft, 1986; 8, Congdon and Gibbons, 1989b.

[a] Includes polar and nonpolar lipids.

[b] Includes no polar lipids.

[c] Includes polar lipids and shell.

[d] Includes lean polar lipids.

Hatchlings of *T. scripta* and a number of other species of turtles delay emergence from the nest (Bleakney, 1963; Goode and Russell, 1968; Gibbons, 1969; Gibbons and Nelson, 1978; Breitenbach et al., 1984). As a result, hatchlings that delay emergence are exposed during the first months of life to an environment that differs from that for hatchlings that emerge a short time after hatching. Preliminary data indicate that hatchlings that emerge from the nest upon hatching move to nearby aquatic habitats where they may forage until cold weather and remain during their first winter. In contrast, hatchlings that do not emerge from their nests spend their first winter in terrestrial nest cavities (Hartweg, 1944, 1946; Woolverton, 1961, 1963; Breitenbach et al., 1984). A comparison of the lipid levels of eggs of turtle species whose hatchlings overwinter in the nest versus those of turtles that emerge upon hatching indicated that eggs of species with hatchlings that overwinter in the nest have a higher proportion of lipids (Congdon et al., 1983c; Congdon and Gibbons, 1985).

Two major features of these environments may be important in influencing the proportion of lipids in eggs and in the yolk reserves of hatchlings. First, hatchlings that emerge from a nest are exposed to water as soon as they reach an aquatic habitat during late summer or fall. Second, hatchlings that remain in the nest in northern latitudes have the potential to be exposed to temperatures below the freezing point of water (Woolverton, 1963; Breitenbach et al., 1984). Hatchlings remaining in nests and metabolizing lipids would benefit from the amount of metabolic water produced whether they were in nests in southern or northern climates. Hatchlings at either latitude may require metabolic water to survive the extended time in the nest; however, the need for water as well as the amount of lipids metabolized at higher latitudes during winter would be low. In fact, desiccated tissue would be slightly more resistant to freezing than would well-hydrated tissues. In addition, hatchlings that delay emergence from the nest may use metabolic products of the additional lipids in the eggs to synthesize antifreeze compounds during winter. Although preliminary data do not indicate that hatchling *Chrysemys picta* (Breitenbach et al., 1984) can withstand temperatures below the supercooling limits of vertebrates (Lowe et al., 1971), further study is needed to determine the way egg components influence hatchling survival of winter temperatures in nests less than 10 cm below the surface at cold temperate latitudes.

Gas Exchanges among Embryo, Egg, and Nest

Gas exchanges between the embryo and the egg probably proceed from simple diffusion that is enhanced briefly by development of the vitelline circulation and subsequently by the allantoic circulation (Fisk and Tribe, 1949; Patten, 1958; Romanoff, 1967). Within a few days after eggs are first laid, their translucent shells begin to develop an opaque white patch at the top of the egg. This patch forms by partial drying of the shell and underlying membranes. Conductance of gases across the shell is low initially but increases as the opaque patch develops (Thompson, 1985). The increase in conductance is concomitant with increasing demands for gas exchange made by the developing embryo. Oxygen consumption by *T. scripta* embryos was higher for those incubated at 30° C through the seventh week than for those incubated at 26° C or 34° C (Fig. 8.5). However, during the seventh week, oxygen consumption rates were highest in embryos incubated at 26° C, followed by those incubated at 30° C and 34° C (Fig. 8.5).

These results seem to indicate that the rapid growth of embryos during the final stages of embryogenesis is inhibited by higher incubation temperatures. Oxygen consumption in the eggs of *Emydura macquarrii* increased 10 times, from almost 0.01 to approximately 0.1 cm³/h (STP), during approximately the first third of development, and then 5 times, to 0.5 cm³/h (STP), during approximately the second third of development. From 60% to 75% of the developmental period, oxygen consumption increased approximately 2.2 times, to 1.1 cm³/h (STP), whereupon it leveled off and then dropped slightly before the hatchling emerged from the egg (Thompson, 1985). The periods of development represented as percentages of the total developmental period roughly correspond to the developmental stages of tissue formation, organogenesis, and embryonic growth.

If developmental problems resulting from restricted gas

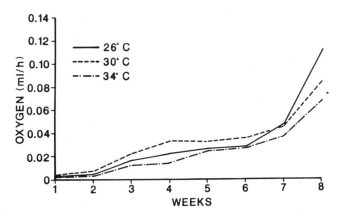

FIGURE 8.5.   Oxygen consumption rates of *Trachemys scripta* eggs incubated at three temperatures.

exchange between the nest cavity and the surrounding soils occur, they should be most pronounced in the deepest nests, in nests laid in the most claylike soils, and in nests containing the largest mass of eggs late in development. For example, nests of *Chelonia mydas* with eggs that were within two weeks of hatching had oxygen levels 3% to 9% lower than the level in atmospheric air, and CO_2 levels increased 70 times, to 0.03% (Ackerman and Prange, 1972; Prange and Ackerman, 1974). The changes from atmospheric air were presumably caused primarily by the metabolic activities of the developing embryos, because the nests of *C. mydas* are usually in coarse sand, which may have relatively low microbe densities and resulting metabolic demands.

Nest plugs of *Chrysemys picta* constructed in clay soils have the consistency of a thick milkshake as a result of the female's voiding water onto the hard soil during the digging process (pers. obs.). Eggs of the tortoises *Chelodina longicollis* and *C. expansa* are sometimes placed in puddles of clay that harden and encase the eggs and subsequently the hatchlings (Goode and Russell, 1968). The effect of this encasement on gas exchange with the soil is unknown, but it can substantially delay emergence of the hatchling until rain softens the surrounding soil.

Another unexplored but potential problem with gas exchange in nests may occur for hatchlings that overwinter in nests where the ground freezes and snow cover is substantial (Breitenbach et al., 1984). Certainly much experimental work is needed to determine how nest site selection by the female might be translated into subtle effects on the quality and survival of her hatchlings.

Water Relations of Turtle Eggs during Development

Perhaps the best-documented manner in which eggshells of turtles differentially isolate the developing embryos from the external environment is the response of rigid and flexible eggshells to hydric conditions of the incubation

Table 8.5. Characteristics of hatchling *Trachemys scripta* incubated on substrates with different levels of hydration

Substrate	Carapace length (mm)	Wet mass	Dry mass	Yolk sac		Lipids			
				Dry mass	% lipids	Dry mass of soma lipids	% of soma mass	% of total hatchling mass	% of egg
Dry	28.7	6.72	2.30	1.04	34.5	0.24	19.0	26.1	59.5
Moist	30.9	7.73	2.27	0.64	39.3	0.34	20.9	25.8	57.5
Wet	31.2	8.04	2.14	0.48	40.8	0.32	19.9	24.5	52.0

Source: Caudle, 1984.

Note: Mass is given in g. Hatchlings were incubated on vermiculite that contained 19% water (dry), 40% water (moist), and 58% water (wet) by mass.

substrate. To a large extent the amount of isolation depends on the degree of calcification of the eggshell and the associated changes in shell morphology. Flexible-shelled eggs incubated on relatively moist substrates (approximately −150 kPa) absorb water (Cunningham and Hurwitz, 1936; Cunningham and Huene, 1938; Dmi'el, 1967; Tracy et al., 1978; Packard et al., 1980, 1981a,b, 1983, 1985, 1987; G. Packard et al., 1982; Morris et al., 1983; Gettinger et al., 1984; Packard and Packard, 1984a,b, 1986; Ackerman et al., 1985a,b; Gutzke and Packard, 1985; Gutzke et al., 1987; Thompson, 1987) and increase in mass over the first third to half of incubation. Flexible-shelled eggs incubated on relatively dry substrates (drier than −750 kPa) lose water, and thus mass, continually over the incubation period (Morris et al., 1983).

Position also affects water relations of flexible-shelled eggs. Not all eggs within turtle nests are in contact with the substrate. Those at the center of the nest may be entirely suspended by contact with other eggs and exposed to a hydric environment different from that of the eggs in contact with the substrate (Packard et al., 1981a). Position is obviously more important in nests of turtles that produce large clutches of flexible-shelled eggs (e.g., *Chelydra serpentina* and some sea turtles) and less important in species that produce small clutches (e.g., *Terrapene* spp., *Chrysemys picta marginata, Gopherus* spp.). However, even in nests of species with moderate-sized clutches of eggs (e.g., *Trachemys scripta* and *C. picta bellii*), eggs lowest in the nest appear to be better hydrated (Cagle, 1937; Carr, 1952; Legler, 1954; Ewert, 1979). Thus, if there is an adaptation to conserve water in relation to position, it would not necessarily be most likely to occur in species with large clutches of eggs but could also occur in small-bodied species that have relatively shallow nests.

In contrast to the mass of flexible-shelled eggs (Packard et al., 1979a, 1981a), the mass of eggs with rigid shells is relatively independent of position in the nest or of substrate moisture potential. The independence from substrate moisture potential by rigid-shelled eggs may be the factor that allows some turtles to bury their eggs only partially.

In eggs with flexible, porous shells, survivorship and development of embryos are influenced by the hydric environment of the incubation substrate because there is water exchange between the egg and the environment. In general, developmental abnormalities and mortality of embryos increase in eggs incubated on extremely dry substrates (Caudle, 1984). The degree of hydration of the incubation substrate influences the body size and mass that *T. scripta* hatchlings attain before leaving the egg (Table 8.5). Hatchlings that emerged from eggs incubated on wet substrates averaged 2.5 mm (8%) larger and 1.3 g (16%) heavier in wet mass than those incubated on dry substrates. However, the dry mass of hatchlings incubated on dry substrates averaged higher for both hatchling body (0.16 g, 9%) and yolk sac (0.56 g, 46%). The dry mass figures indicate that hatchlings incubated on wet substrates have grown earlier in the incubation period and converted more of the original egg mass to hatchling tissues. As a result, these hatchlings experienced higher maintenance costs that were concomitant with earlier growth and larger size. In contrast, hatchlings incubated on dry substrates had a higher dry mass upon hatching because they grew less rapidly, they had smaller maintenance costs, and more of their mass was composed of original yolk material.

In summary, embryos incubated in moist environments use more of the egg material, hatch at larger sizes, and have smaller yolk stores (Tracy et al., 1978; Packard et al., 1980, 1981a,b, 1983, 1985, 1987; G. Packard et al., 1982; Morris et al., 1983; Gettinger et al., 1984; Packard and Packard, 1984a,b, 1986; Ackerman, 1985a,b; Gutzke and Packard, 1986; Gutzke et al., 1987; Thompson, 1987). In contrast to embryos in flexible-shelled eggs, survivorship and growth patterns of embryos that develop inside rigid-shelled eggs tend to be relatively insensitive to the hydric conditions of the incubation substrate (Packard et al., 1979a, 1981a).

Eggs of *C. picta* contained an average of 104.8 mg of calcium, with 0.1 mg, 7.1 mg, and 97.6 mg found in the albumin, yolk, and eggshell, respectively (Packard and Packard, 1986). Calcium used for development of the embryo came from both the yolk and the eggshell and was influenced by hydric conditions during development (Packard et al., 1984a,b, 1985; Packard and Packard, 1986). Embryos incubated on wet substrates obtained most of their calcium from the eggshell (56%) and the egg yolk (40%). Less than 1 mg of calcium remained in the yolk reserves of hatchlings incubated on either wet or dry substrates (Packard and Packard, 1986).

The conclusion that the calcium level in yolk reserves of hatchlings could not support the growth of soft tissue (Packard and Packard, 1986) seems unfounded. If we assume that the calcium content in muscle tissue of a *C. picta* hatchling weighing 4 g is similar to that of a fish (0.43 mg calcium/g wet mass of muscle; Agnedal, 1967), then the hatchling could add approximately 2 g (50% of its body mass) before depleting the calcium in the yolk reserves. Whether hatchlings do use yolk reserves for growth remains to be demonstrated. Yolk reserves available to hatchlings (Kraemer and Bennett, 1981; Congdon et al., 1983a,c; Wilhoft, 1986) are used by the hatchling for maintenance metabolism and may also be used to promote tissue maturation and growth of soft tissue, but probably not growth of skeletal tissue.

Hatchlings resulting from embryos that either developed earlier or developed more completely by delaying emergence from the egg should have more tissue mass developed or more mature tissues. Because the egg is a closed system in terms of chemical potential energy, the maintenance costs associated with a greater tissue mass or with maintaining an equivalent tissue mass for a longer time should be higher and, by definition, should result in less residual yolk at the time of hatching. Thus, the larger yolk stores in smaller hatchlings may be beneficial (relative to a similarly small hatchling with lower reserves) but should not be considered an adaptation. Rather, the larger stores are the result of constraints on the developmental processes that took place within the egg. This view is supported by the evidence of improved running speed on land and swimming speed in water of hatchling snapping turtles that were incubated on wet, rather than dry, substrates (Miller et al., 1987).

The pattern of changes in turtle hatchling characteristics in response to variation in the incubation environment appears to be a general pattern in reptiles (Muth, 1980; Andrews and Sexton, 1981; Stewart and Castillo, 1984; Gutzke and Packard, 1986). Turtle eggs incubated at lower temperatures take longer to hatch than those incubated at higher temperatures. However, species vary considerably in the length of incubation (Ewert, 1979, 1985). Slider turtle eggs can complete the incubation process in approximately two to three months, depending upon the temperature, although variability can be high at any temperature regime (e.g., days to emergence from egg in laboratory experiments ranged from 67 to 104 [$\bar{x} = 81$; $N = 27$] at temperatures of 29°–31° C).

Eggs and Evolutionary Concepts

In preparation for reproduction, a female must make three major "determinations": (1) the total amount of energy available for present reproduction, (2) the quantity of energy to be allocated to each offspring, and (3) the number of individuals that can be produced by the present level of investment in each offspring. The three determinations fall roughly into the conceptual categories of reproductive effort (RE), parental investment (PI), and optimal egg size (OES).

Within overall life history theories is a subset of models that describe how an organism should apportion its finite resources among the competing compartments of maintenance, growth, and reproduction. Central to these theories is the concept of reproductive effort, or that portion of an animal's resource budget that is allocated to reproduction (Fisher, 1930; Hirshfield and Tinkle, 1975), a concept that does not directly pertain to egg size or quality.

All of the energy allocated to each individual turtle hatchling is contained within the egg. Because of this, the concepts of parental investment and optimal egg size are more tightly coupled for turtles than for mammals and birds, which provide extended parental care such as guarding and feeding of young. Thus, for turtle eggs it is important to separate the investments made for embryonic development from those made for fueling the hatchling after it leaves the egg (Table 8.6).

The interactions between determinants of offspring numbers and size or quality of offspring have been considered for some time (Darwin, 1859). More recent considerations have centered on the idea that organisms should invest in offspring at the level that maximizes the fitness of the parents (Lack, 1947, 1948, 1954b, 1968; Svardson, 1949; Williams, 1966a). There are presently two major categories of evolutionary theories (i.e., optimality or canalization theories and developmental plasticity theories) that attempt to explain the range of variation in egg size either within or among females. Morphological constraint on egg size has also been offered to explain some of the variation in turtle egg size.

Optimal-egg-size models (Williams, 1966; Smith and Fretwell, 1974; Brockelman, 1975; Parker and Begon, 1986) attempt to describe the relationships and interactions between egg size and number. The models make the

Table 8.6. Percent lipids found in various species of hatchlings upon leaving egg

Species	Nonpolar lipids	Total lipids
Chelydra serpentina	12.9	29.2
Chrysemys picta	14.7	--
Deirochelys reticularia	27.4	--
Emydoidea blandingii	14.7	--
Trachemys scripta	--	24.5

following assumptions: (1) Parents have a limited amount of resources and energy available for a given reproductive bout; (2) a minimum amount of energy is required to produce viable offspring; and (3) the gain in fitness of offspring is not linear with the amount of parental investment, that is, there is a level at which a given investment in offspring results in large gains followed by a level of investment for which minimal or no increase in the fitness of offspring occurs (also see Pianka, 1974; Schaffer and Gadgil, 1975). If the first assumption is true, it follows that as the amount of energy invested in individual offspring goes up, the number of individuals produced must be reduced. However, if some factor other than absolute energy availability exists (e.g., morphological constraints such as volume of a turtle's body cavity or size of the pelvic opening), then results inconsistent with predictions from OES models can be obtained.

A major prediction from OES theory is that within a population the amount of variation in reproductive output among females should result primarily from variation in the number of offspring produced and secondarily from variation in egg size. One problem is that the actual level of variation in reproductive output due to variation in egg size that is acceptable under OES models has not been defined in either relative or absolute terms.

In contrast to OES theory, other investigators have proposed that natural selection should favor developmental plasticity that results in a range of reproductive characteristics when environmental variability is unpredictable (Robertson, 1971; Capinera, 1979; Kaplan, 1980; Cooper and Kaplan, 1982; Caswell, 1983; Kaplan and Cooper, 1984). Within these models, variation in egg size should occur within a single reproductive bout or among reproductive bouts within a single year (Kaplan and Cooper, 1984). We expect that there are life history traits and environmental conditions that could result in either strategy, and the existence of support for one theory does not necessarily refute the other.

Regardless of the type of reproductive tactic used by females, two factors must be considered when attempting to understand the functions and evolution of the eggs of turtles and probably all reptiles. It has been argued that the eggs of turtles and other reptiles should be viewed as two distinct components of a single system in which energy is allocated by the female for (1) embryogenesis and (2) extended parental care in the form of yolk reserves that remain in the egg after hatching (Kraemer and Bennett, 1981; Congdon and Tinkle, 1982b; Congdon et al., 1983a,c; Troyer, 1983; Wilhoft, 1986; Congdon and Gibbons, 1987; Congdon and Gibbons, 1989b). Considering turtle eggs as a two-component system points out some problems with existing definitions of parental investment. Specifically, PI should identify how the investment is to be used by the offspring and at what developmental period the investment is made by the parent.

Trivers (1972) defined parental investment as "any investment by the parent in an individual offspring that increases the offspring's chance of surviving (and hence reproductive success) at the cost of the parent's ability to invest in other offspring." This definition was modified (Trivers, 1985) and stated as "anything done for the offspring, including building it, which increases the offspring's reproductive success at a cost to the remainder of the parent's reproductive success." Both statements yield essentially the same definition of PI. For both, the benefit to the parent is measured in units of reproductive success of the offspring that receive the PI, and the cost to the parent is in units of reduced reproductive success of future or other offspring.

We find two problems with Trivers' definition. First, both categories of investment, that used for embryogenesis and that used for fueling the developed hatchling, fall under the overall category of PI. The definition is adequate for attempts to model optimal egg size in which it is assumed that all of the PI is used to make a larger offspring (Parker and Begon, 1986) rather than providing it with post-hatching reserves. We suggest that by lumping together both categories of investment in an egg, Trivers' definition obscures important ecological and evolutionary questions about distinct processes that proceed in different ways toward the common goal of making a successful offspring. Second, we suggest that if all energy allocated to a single egg is to be considered PI, the trade-off between offspring that is implicit in Trivers' first definition is very narrow; i.e., there is no trade-off between competing offspring but rather only a "decision" to make offspring A rather than make offspring B. We at least need new terminology to distinguish between the two energy compartments that make up reptile eggs.

For the rest of the discussion of PI in reptile eggs, we will separate the investments made by the parent into (1) the energy invested in making a complete embryo (PIE) and (2) the energy invested by the female for parental care (PIC), that is, energy in excess of that needed to produce a complete hatchling (either hatching from an egg or the product of live birth), in the form of a yolk sac or hatchling fat bodies, that is used by the hatchling after it leaves the egg. We assume that a portion of the energy allocated to an egg by the female is done expressly to fuel the hatchling. Because data on turtles and other reptiles indicate that the material, lipids, or energy left in the yolk sac when the hatchling leaves the egg or is born usually exceeds 50% of the original energy in the egg, this investment is far from trivial (Kraemer and Bennett, 1981; Congdon and Tinkle, 1982b; Congdon et al., 1983a,c; Troyer, 1983; Stewart and Castillo, 1984; Wilhoft, 1986; Congdon and Gibbons, 1989b). This assumption could be shown to be incorrect by demonstrating that hatchlings incubated under what could be considered optimal conditions hatched with no residual yolk sac and formed no fat bodies. In this case all of the material in the egg would be in the form of hatchling tissues or waste products (i.e., all of the material in the egg would be used for embryogenesis).

The second problem of terminology associated with PI is that of identifying the portion of the developmental process during which PIC is made. Parental investment in care should be identified as investments made before ovulation, during intrauterine development, or after gestation or egg laying (Kaplan, 1980; Congdon and Gibbons, 1985; Congdon and Gibbons, 1989b). These distinctions are important because not all options are open to parents at each stage of development. For example, pre-ovulatory PIC is made before the egg is ovulated and fertilized; therefore, matching unequal investment to differences in the complete genotype of the offspring is impossible. Investment during the intrauterine period or after birth of individuals allows the parent to invest selectively and unequally in its offspring in such a way that the parent's fitness is enhanced at the expense of some of her offspring's.

Eggs of the Slider Turtle: An Overview

Based on our own and other studies on slider turtles and other freshwater species, egg development in the slider turtle proceeds in the following manner. The follicles of an adult female are smallest following ovulation of the last clutch during the egg-laying season and begin to enlarge during late summer or early fall. Most or all of the energy allocated to the first clutch during the egg-laying season comes from that harvested during the previous summer and fall. Two or more clutches may be laid by an individual female in a single season, with a minimum of approximately two weeks between clutches. Energy for clutches subsequent to the first one is presumed to be acquired primarily from that harvested during the egg-laying season, but documentation for this hypothesis is lacking. Sliders, like most other species of turtles, construct nests in sites that are exposed to sunlight during a portion of the day. Soil temperatures, moisture, and texture are critical to incubation rate, embryo survivorship, and even sex ratio within the clutch and can be influenced to some degree by the female through choice of nest site location and depth of the nest. However, whether the female takes a conscious or inherent role in such determinations is yet to be demonstrated.

The composition and construction of the eggs of slider turtles are characteristic of the order Testudinata. The eggshell of turtles is composed of calcium carbonate in the form of aragonite rather than calcite, as in most other reptiles and birds. However, the eggshells of some turtles, such as the slider, are flexible, whereas some species have rigid eggshells with interlocking units. The variations in structure of flexible and rigid eggshells do not follow phylogenetic lines but may be associated with nest site substrates. However, the evolution of eggshell types of turtles as an adaptation to particular nest site characteristics has not been satisfactorily demonstrated. The eggshell of the slider turtle constitutes approximately 18% of the dry mass of the egg and is similar to that of other species that produce flexible-shelled eggs. Among species with rigid-shelled eggs, the shell may make up more than a third of the total egg dry mass. A major difference associated with shell types is in the patterns of growth and development of embryos in response to varying amounts of soil moisture. Embryos from rigid-shelled eggs are not appreciably affected by substrate moisture conditions, whereas hatching size of embryos from flexible-shelled eggs is significantly larger in moist substrates.

The harvesting and storage of energy by female turtles, and the timing and proportional allocation of lipid reserves to eggs, are critical to understanding the evolution of hatchling development. The lipid component of turtle eggs can be partitioned into polar and nonpolar lipids. Both types should be determined if possible when considering egg components. In addition, the clutch size, female size, and wet and dry mass of the shell and other egg components should be determined when addressing questions of parental investment.

The eggs and hatchlings of many species of turtles remain in the nest for several months after incubation is complete. Eggs of species such as the slider turtle that have hatchlings that delay emergence from the nest have higher proportions of lipids. One suggestion for these higher lipid reserves is that they may be used in some way to synthesize antifreeze compounds in winter.

The concepts of reproductive effort, parental investment, and optimal egg size all center around how individual females allocate energy within and among clutches. Research with turtles has permitted challenges to and reconsideration of some life history models (e.g., optimal egg size and morphological constraint). We consider turtles to be ideal organisms for addressing a number of evolutionary concepts regarding eggs because of the group's consistency in total oviparity and long incubation period, extreme iteroparity, and lack of post-ovipositional parental care in natural situations. We anticipate great strides during the next few years by turtle biologists interested in eggs and evolutionary concepts.

Acknowledgments

Research and manuscript preparation were made possible by contract DE-AC09-76SROO-819 between the University of Georgia and the U.S. Department of Energy and by National Science Foundation grants DEB-79-04758 to J. W. Gibbons and DEB-79-06031 and BSR-84-00861 to J. D. Congdon.

J. WHITFIELD GIBBONS
JUDITH L. GREENE
Savannah River Ecology Laboratory
Drawer E
Aiken, South Carolina 29802

9

Reproduction in the Slider and Other Species of Turtles

Abstract

Reproductive aspects are considered for the slider turtle (*Trachemys scripta*) and other freshwater species, based on samples from the Savannah River Plant in South Carolina. Most males attain maturity at plastron lengths between 90 and 110 mm in all populations, whereas the size at maturity in females is less than 160 mm in some populations and greater than 200 mm in others. Clutch size varies seasonally and among habitats, but most of the variability can be explained as a function of body size. Age of the female per se is not directly correlated with body size. The seasonal timing of nesting is discussed, and clutch frequency is identified as an important measurement in the study of turtle populations.

Introduction

Among the critical life history traits of a species are those associated with reproduction. Several reviews of reproductive characteristics in turtles have been presented in recent years (e.g., Ernst and Barbour, 1972; Moll, 1979; Gibbons et al., 1982), but different conclusions have been reached, sometimes for the same species, about generalizations that are applicable to turtles as a group. For example, the clutch sizes of *Chrysemys picta* have been reported to be larger in northern latitudes (Powell, 1967; Moll, 1973), to show no significant difference with latitude (Christiansen and Moll, 1973), and to show significant variation within a single geographic region (Gibbons and Tinkle, 1969). Clutch size has been reported to be correlated with body size in *T. scripta* (Cagle, 1944c, 1950; Gibbons, 1970b; Tinkle et al., 1981; Gibbons et al., 1982), whereas the seemingly similar *C. picta* has been reported as having no correlation between clutch size and body size (Cagle, 1954; Gibbons and Tinkle, 1969).

Similar contradictions among species exist in the literature for relationships between latitude and maturity. *Trachemys scripta* (Cagle, 1950) and *Kinosternon subrubrum*

(Gibbons, 1983a) have been reported to show no relationship between latitude and size at maturity, whereas *C. picta* (Cagle, 1954; Christiansen and Moll, 1973; Moll, 1973) and *Sternotherus odoratus* (Tinkle, 1961) have. Clutch frequency has been reported as having a consistent relationship with latitude, being higher in the southern United States than in northern areas (Gibbons, 1983a), but this information is available for only three species.

One explanation for the discrepancies in these types of generalizations could be that species actually do vary from each other, although by definition this cannot be the case within a species. A more likely explanation is that the variability in reproductive traits is high when viewed from a long-term perspective, so that geographic trends can be confounded by the timing of local environmental conditions.

Our purpose in this chapter is to examine reproductive phenomena in the slider turtle (*T. scripta*) and other freshwater species on the Savannah River Plant (SRP) in South Carolina. Our information on the reproductive patterns of these species is based on previous publications and more-recent data. We will identify some of the critical lines of inquiry about turtle reproduction and where empirical efforts might best be placed at this time.

The general reproductive cycle of *T. scripta* is similar to that of most other temperate zone turtles (Carr, 1952; Ernst and Barbour, 1972; Moll, 1979). However, a long-term research effort can reveal details of reproductive patterns and relationships that might be difficult to ascertain over a shorter period. For example, establishing the interactive relationship of clutch size with body size, age, and year in a long-lived species would be beyond the normal expectations of a doctoral dissertation or a three-year grant from the National Science Foundation. The availability of radiograph (x-ray) facilities has allowed us to determine the intraindividual variability in clutch size by keeping populations of marked individuals intact so that subsequent clutches of particular females could be monitored. Furthermore, because of drift fence enclosures at certain sites, we have information on clutch frequency, a difficult determination to make without dissection and examination of corpora lutea.

To be sure, our understanding of the complexity of reproduction and its shaping by natural selection has room for improvement, but collectively the data provide a picture of reproductive plasticity in *T. scripta* and other species of freshwater turtles, suggest relevant questions that bear attention at this time, and perhaps provide an explanation for why generalizations have been difficult to make. The material presented is basic descriptive information that should be a reliable source for comparisons of reproductive characteristics with the same or different species from other regions.

The following sections present information we have gathered regarding reproductive characteristics of several freshwater species and supplements our earlier publications, which were based on smaller sample sizes and shorter-term observations. Reproductive information on turtle species that inhabit the SRP has been published by us previously on *T. scripta* (Gibbons, 1970b; Gibbons et al., 1981; Congdon and Gibbons, 1983), *K. subrubrum* (Gibbons, 1983a), *Deirochelys reticularia* (Gibbons, 1969; Gibbons and Greene, 1978; Congdon et al., 1983a), *S. odoratus* (Gibbons, 1970d), *Pseudemys floridana* (Gibbons and Coker, 1977), *Chelydra serpentina* (Congdon et al., 1987), and combinations of the above and other species (Gibbons et al., 1978b; Gibbons and Greene, 1979; Gibbons, 1982; Gibbons et al., 1982; Congdon and Gibbons, 1985; Congdon and Gibbons, 1987). In most instances our original conclusions have not been modified by the augmentation, but in a few instances they have. We have tried to address the basic questions that should be answered about selected reproductive traits before more esoteric considerations are undertaken. We have also identified in our own studies some enormous gaps about reproduction in turtles that should be filled if we are to have a complete understanding of reproductive output, cycles, and associated processes.

Attainment of Maturity

SEXUAL MATURITY IN MALES

The age and size at which males attain maturity in a marked population can be identified more effectively and with greater precision than those for females because of the expression of maturity in secondary sexual characteristics such as elongation of the preanal portion of the tail. The elongation of the foreclaws in *T. scripta* has been demonstrated by Cagle (1948b) to have a direct relationship with gonadal development indicative of the attainment of sexual maturity. Therefore, foreclaw length relative to body size of an individual can be used to determine whether a male is approaching maturity or is mature.

Male *T. scripta* on the SRP begin to show secondary sexual characteristics, and most presumably reach maturity, at a plastron length of around 100 mm. The foreclaws increase in length from approximately 6 mm at a plastron length of 100 mm to 12 mm at a plastron length of 120 mm (Fig. 9.1). In juveniles and females, claw length increases approximately isometrically at a rate of 0.5 mm for each centimeter increase in plastron length (Figs. 9.2 and 9.3). Once males have attained maturity, the claws presumably increase isometrically with body length at a rate that is not significantly different from that of juveniles or females, but because of the high variability observed (Fig. 9.1), a definitive statement about the rate of increase is difficult to make.

Although individual growth rates, maximum body size,

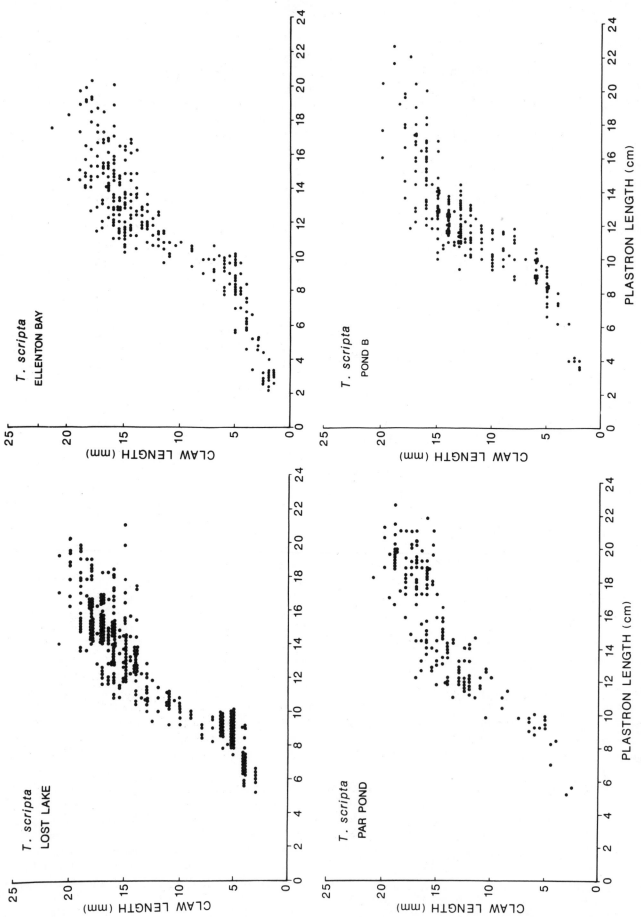

FIGURE 9.1. Relationship between body size (plastron length) and a secondary sexual characteristic (claw length) in male *T. scripta* from four SRP populations.

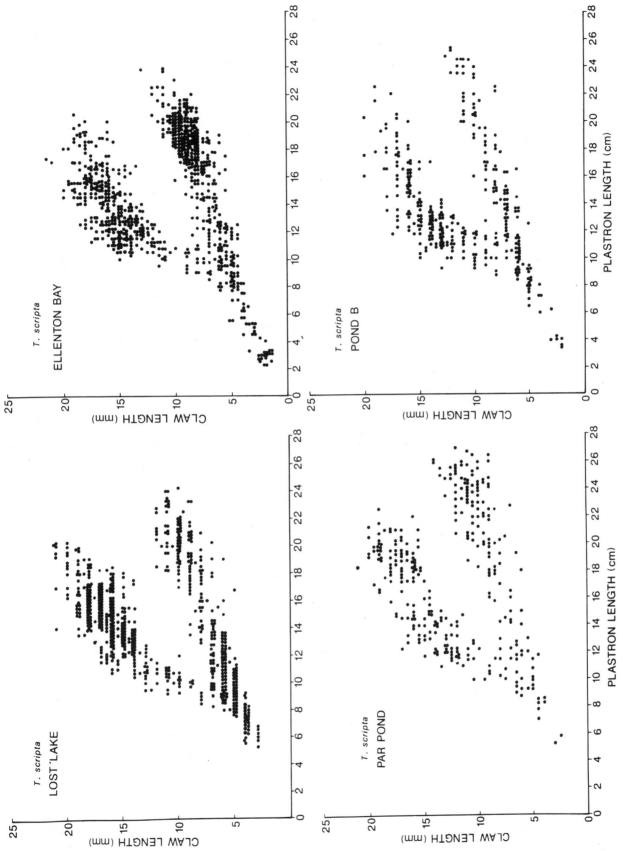

FIGURE 9.2. Relationship between body size (plastron length) and claw length to determine size at maturity in male *T. scripta* from four SRP populations. Incipient maturity is expressed by claw elongation in males that are 9 to 11 cm in plastron length, at which point they begin to diverge from females.

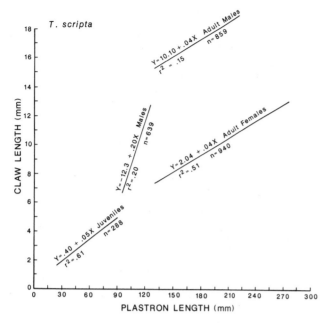

FIGURE 9.3. Regression equations of the relationship between body size and claw length of *T. scripta* from the SRP. Slopes are similar for juveniles less than 9 cm in plastron length, adult males, and adult females. The slope during the period that males reach maturity (labeled "Males") is much steeper, indicating the rapid elongation of claws.

and age of males at maturity vary among some regional populations of *T. scripta* (Gibbons et al., 1981), the claw length–body length regression relationships are similar among populations (Figs. 9.1 and 9.2). However, the exact size at which maturity is reached among different individuals varies considerably within and among populations, as is seen by the examination of the proportions judged mature and immature in samples of males from Ellenton Bay ($N = 182$) and Par Pond ($N = 195$) ranging from 80 to 130 mm in plastron length (Table 9.1). Virtually all males in both populations have reached maturity by the time they have reached a plastron length of 110 mm.

SEXUAL MATURITY IN FEMALES

Sexual maturity in females can be defined as the capability for producing eggs during the next breeding season and can be confirmed by the presence of oviductal eggs, corpora lutea in the ovaries, or enlarged preovulatory follicles of sufficient size to be ovulated during the nesting season. All of these have been used as indicators in studies with female turtles. Observations of copulation, stored sperm in the oviduct, or female cloacal smears containing viable sperm would also be reliable indicators of maturity. Because of an effort to maintain the integrity of the marked populations on the SRP, few dissections were made of individuals from the study populations. At the time, the only method available for documenting immaturity in an individual was by examination of the condition of the ovaries. Future efforts may apply the technique of laparoscopy to examine ovaries. The development of the x-ray technique (Gibbons and Greene, 1979) has aided greatly in the confirmation that females are gravid, because the palpation technique creates uncertainty in many instances.

X-ray photographs in a large number of individuals (377) of *T. scripta* from Ellenton Bay (and other natural populations) and Par Pond (and other thermal areas), complemented by a limited number of dissections of turtles from these populations, give some indication of the size at which maturity is reached by *T. scripta* females (Fig. 9.4). An important observation is that females in the two populations reach maturity at dramatically different body sizes, those from natural areas being approximately 160 mm in plastron length, and those from thermal areas around 200 mm. Therefore, in contrast to males, females cannot be said to have a characteristic size at maturity in the region. It should be noted that the proportion of mature females that are mature at 14 to 15 cm in the nonthermal areas is deceptive and is much lower than it appears. Numerous x rays have been taken of individuals at this size that did not contain eggs but were not included on the graph. Thus, a plastron length of 160 mm is considered to

Table 9.1. Proportions of size classes of *Trachemys scripta* from Ellenton Bay and Par Pond judged to be immature or mature males

Location	Plastron length (cm)					
	8	9	10	11	12	13
Ellenton Bay	.03 (10)	.72 (18)	.94 (34)	.98 (52)	1.0 (65)	1.0 (3)
Par Pond	.36 (11)	.45 (20)	.82 (34)	.96 (67)	.98 (56)	1.0 (7)

Note: Judgment of turtles as males was based on an allometric increase in foreclaw length as a secondary sexual characteristic. An individual with a claw-length/body-length ratio less than .07 was considered to be immature based on the ratios of individual females and small juveniles, none of which exceeded .07. Numbers indicate proportion of sample showing foreclaw elongation. Sample size is indicated in parentheses.

be the size at which a majority of the females from most nonthermal areas attain maturity.

Age at Maturity

In male *T. scripta*, size appears to be more important than age in the determination of sexual maturity, whereas in females, age is apparently more critical, although the variability among individuals is extreme. If the secondary sexual characteristic of lengthening of the foreclaws is used as an indication of maturity, most males in Ellenton Bay approach or reach maturity during their third to fifth years, and those from Par Pond mature as early as their second year. Almost all have attained maturity by their fourth year.

Age at maturity of females also appears to be highly variable among individuals within a population, although some of the larger rapid-growth females from Par Pond appear to reach maturity at slightly younger ages than those from Ellenton Bay (Fig. 9.5). However, compared with the size disparity, age is relatively similar between the Ellenton Bay and Par Pond populations. The complexity of the interaction between age, size, maturity, and other life history traits continues to be one of the most perplexing problems in the study of turtles. Additional field studies on a variety of species and populations will be

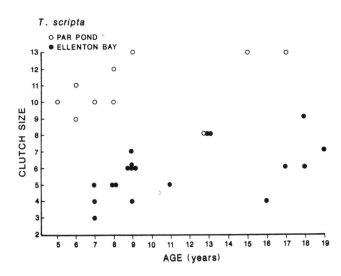

FIGURE 9.5. Relationship between age and clutch size of *T. scripta* from Ellenton Bay and Par Pond. The slopes are not significantly different from zero.

necessary to resolve many of the questions related to these interactions.

Reproductive Cycle

Mature males of *T. scripta*, as well as most other species of freshwater turtles in temperate regions, can apparently be sexually active in the spring and the fall and possibly during warm periods in winter. Documentation of spring reproductive activity has been provided by Gartska (pers. com.) for *T. scripta* in northern Alabama, but he observed no evidence to support fall or winter reproduction. Laboratory observations of courtship have been made in October, November, and December (Davis and Jackson, 1970; Jackson and Davis, 1972). Courtship behavior has been observed in *T. scripta* from South Carolina in October (Lovich, pers. com.), December (Hinton, pers. com.), and January (Gibbons, pers. obs.). Copulation has been observed in December (Lovich, pers. com).

It seems surprising that this important aspect of the reproductive cycle of this common species has not been determined more thoroughly, particularly in our studies in South Carolina. Part of the difficulty in determining male reproductive cycles is that field observations are only happenstance, so experimental enclosure studies or dissections are usually necessary. The association of slider turtles with habitats having dense, floating vegetation unfortunately precludes many of the serendipitous observations of courtship that might be possible in clear, open waters. We will not attempt to list all of the anecdotal observations of courtship that have been made on different species, because a solid understanding of the male reproductive cycle will best come from a definitive study undertaken for this purpose.

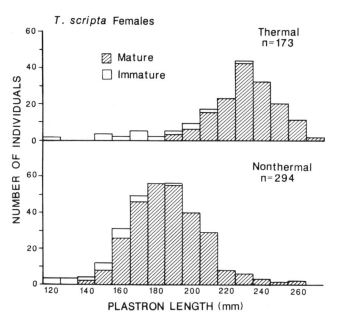

FIGURE 9.4. Size at maturity in female *T. scripta* from two types of areas on the SRP. Several nonthermal habitats are included, but most specimens were from Ellenton Bay. Most of the thermal-habitat specimens were from Par Pond. Maturity was confirmed by dissection in a few instances but by x ray in most. All immature animals were judged to be so on the basis of dissection (absence of enlarged follicles, and undeveloped ovaries and oviducts).

Table 9.2. Proportion of females of six species of turtles nesting during each month at Ellenton Bay

Species	N	J	F	M	A	M	J	J	A	S	O	N
							Month					
T. scripta	81				.07	.52	.37	.04				
K. subrubrum	296				.04	.44	.33	.18	.01			
P. floridana	39					.23	.64	.08	.05			
S. odoratus	41				.49	.39	.12					
C. serpentina	9					.89	.11					
D. reticularia	97	.01	.14	.37	.05				.13	.24	.01	.02

Note: Figures are based on x-ray data from 1976 to 1987. No females of any species nested during December.

From dissection studies we can be confident that painted turtles (*Chrysemys picta*) in northern habitats mate in the spring, soon after the conditions become warm enough for aquatic activity (Gibbons, 1968d; Ernst, 1971d), although *C. picta* have been observed in courtship in the fall in Michigan (Gibbons, pers. obs). The evidence appears to be growing that mating can occur in the fall and spring in other freshwater species. McPherson and Marion (1981b) documented that *Sternotherus odoratus* males are reproductively active in both fall and spring.

Ovulation

Female turtles of some species, and probably most or all, including *T. scripta,* can retain viable sperm for at least part of a year and up to several years (Barney, 1922; Hildebrand, 1929; Ewing, 1943; Hattan and Gist, 1975; Ehrhart, 1982; Gross and Gartska, 1984). Thus, mating may occur several weeks or months prior to ovulation, fertilization being achieved with sperm that is held in the oviducts. Ovulation occurs in the spring, and the fertilized eggs are shelled in the oviducts. Oviposition occurs several days after ovulation, when the eggs have been shelled and environmental conditions are suitable. Additional clutches in some freshwater species may be deposited within 2 to 4 weeks of a preceding one (Gibbons et al., 1982). Although warm weather persists for several months after the initiation of nesting in South Carolina, clutches are generally not deposited after midsummer by most species.

A major exception to the nesting chronology of all other North American turtles in areas where winter weather occurs is that of the chicken turtle (*Deirochelys reticularia*). This species nests in fall, winter, and early spring, when nesting by other species does not occur (Gibbons and Greene, 1978; Table 9.2). Ovulation in all species presumably occurs shortly before the eggs are shelled and laid, although the evidence for the timing of events is based on relatively limited information. No one has reported the presence of unshelled eggs as a common occurrence in the oviducts of turtles, despite the hundreds of turtles that have been dissected (e.g., Cagle, 1950; Dobie, 1971; Ernst, 1971d; Moll and Legler, 1971), suggesting that the eggs are shelled in the oviducts immediately after ovulation. Additionally, shelled oviductal eggs have not been reported to occur with any regularity in turtles except during the prescribed nesting season, which seems to be evidence that ovulation is initiated just before nesting.

Clutch Size

Clutch size and the influential variables (particularly body size) that are associated with it have been the most thoroughly examined reproductive traits in turtles as a group. Thorough listings of clutch sizes of turtles have been given in a variety of review papers and general works (e.g., Carr, 1952; Ernst and Barbour, 1972; Moll, 1979), and subsequent detailed studies have been made for some species (e.g., Gibbons et al., 1978b; Tinkle et al., 1981; Congdon and Tinkle, 1982b; Gibbons, 1982; Gibbons et al., 1982; Gibbons, 1983a; Frazer and Richardson, 1986). Clutch size in *T. scripta* on the SRP has ranged from 2 to 18 ($N = 282$). A wide range of variability has been observed in other regions, such as Virginia, Mexico, and Panama (see Chapters 11, 12, and 13). However, the important task is not simply to identify how species vary among or within themselves but to explain why the mean and variance in clutch size are what they are for a species. The first step in this process is to establish the relationships that exist between clutch size and other factors, such as body size, age, egg size, clutch frequency, phylogenetic relationships, nesting habits, climate, and local environmental conditions. We will address some of the relationships with data from x rays and dissections of individuals from the SRP. However, much of the issue remains unresolved because of the high variability and presumably because clutch size is influenced by all of these factors to some degree.

RELATIONSHIP BETWEEN CLUTCH SIZE AND BODY SIZE

Although clutch size has been documented to vary as a function of body size in some species of turtles (e.g., Cagle,

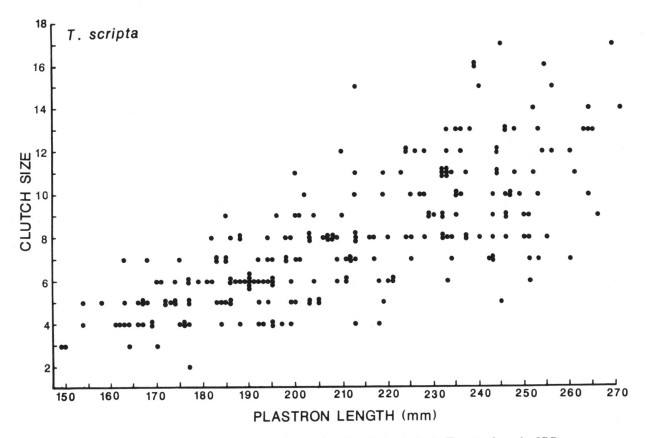

FIGURE 9.6.   Relationship between plastron length and clutch size in *T. scripta* from the SRP.

1950; Tinkle, 1961; Gibbons et al., 1982; Gibbons, 1983a; Georges, 1985), the observation has not been universal (e.g., Cagle, 1954; Gibbons and Tinkle, 1969; Tinkle et al., 1981; Frazer and Richardson, 1986). We define a clutch as the maximum number of shelled oviductal eggs being carried by an individual on a nesting excursion. The clutch may be distributed in more than one nest (Moll, 1980) or may even be retained for several months (Gibbons and Greene, unpubl. data for *D. reticularia*).

Data from five species from the SRP for which we have sufficient information categorically demonstrate that larger individuals of each species are more likely to have more eggs in a clutch (Gibbons et al., 1982). Although the regression relationships vary among the species, each shows a significant positive relationship between body size and clutch size.

In every species examined, the clutch size–body size relationship is highly variable (r^2 range is .03–.67 for Pearson's correlation coefficient and .03–.59 for Spearman Rank; Gibbons et al., 1982), with the larger size classes of species usually having individuals with clutches that ranged from low to high numbers. Smaller individuals practically never have large clutches. However, the positive relationships between clutch size and body size are statistically significant for each species on the SRP, a fact attributable in some instances to the large sample

sizes (Gibbons et al., 1982). The even larger sample sizes in subsequent analyses do not substantially alter any of the conclusions drawn about these relationships.

The comparison of a linear measurement versus mass as a measure of size has little effect on the interspecies comparisons (Gibbons et al., 1982; Figs. 9.6 and 9.7). Body size is a factor no matter how size is measured, although the sample size required to demonstrate this convincingly would probably vary for the two measurements.

RELATIONSHIP BETWEEN CLUTCH SIZE AND HABITAT

Differences in clutch size between populations of a species in a region have been reported for *C. picta* (Gibbons and Tinkle, 1969) and *T. scripta* (Gibbons, 1970b). The mean clutch size at Ellenton Bay ($\bar{x} = 6.1$, $N = 73$) is significantly smaller ($p < .01$) than that at Par Pond ($\bar{x} = 10.2$, $N = 48$, ANOVA). However, when the effect of body size is removed by covariate analysis, clutch sizes in the two habitats are not significantly different. The ecologically pertinent point is that although turtles in Par Pond display significantly higher secondary productivity in growth rates and body size than those in Ellenton Bay (Gibbons, 1970b), this productivity is not realized in clutch size beyond the extent expected from an increase in body size. We have proposed earlier (Gibbons et al., 1982)

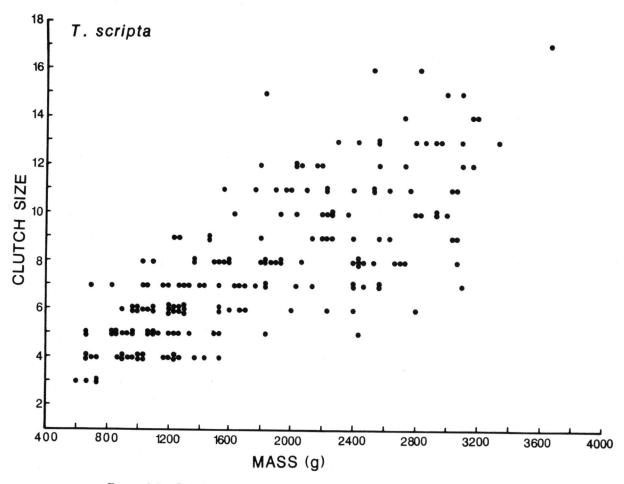

FIGURE 9.7.   Relationship between mass and clutch size in *T. scripta* from the SRP.

that maximum clutch size is limited by the female's body size. We consider this to be a form of morphological constraint to reproductive output by an individual, because limits on the number of eggs of a given size are set by the shell casing. The issue of clutch size and optimal egg size has been discussed in depth by Congdon and Gibbons (1987) and in Chapter 8.

ANNUAL VARIATION IN CLUTCH SIZE

Mean clutch size of individuals in populations of turtle species has been reported to remain the same in different years despite environmental differences among years (Gibbons, 1982). We used covariate analysis to compare *T. scripta* ($N = 71$) from Ellenton Bay during four years. No significant difference in the mean clutch size of an average-sized female was observed among years. However, a highly significant interaction between plastron length and year was observed; that is, the slopes of the lines relating clutch size and body size were not parallel among years.

SEASONAL DIFFERENCES IN CLUTCH SIZE

It has been suggested that some turtles have smaller clutches during the latter part of the nesting season (Gibbons et al., 1982; Gibbons, 1983a), although Kaufmann (1975) gave solid evidence of increasing clutch size in successive nestings of *Caretta caretta* in Colombia. A comparison of early nesting and late nesting in *T. scripta* indicates that mean clutch size does differ seasonally at Ellenton Bay (April, 8.7; May, 5.8; June, 6.3; July, 4.7), being smaller at the end of the egg-laying season. However, mean plastron length (mm) also decreased (April, 194.3; May, 183.3; June, 183.0; July, 179.0). No explanation is readily available for why larger females of a turtle species might lay eggs earlier than smaller ones. However, decreasing clutch size as a consequence of smaller mean body size of females in some species during the nesting season appears to be a real phenomenon in some situations. The issue bears further scrutiny for other species for which large data sets are available.

In examining the first and second clutches of a year in six *T. scripta* from Ellenton Bay, the second clutch was smaller in four instances (mean difference = 2.3 eggs) and higher in two (mean difference = 1.0 egg). Variability in successive clutches has also been observed in *K. subrubrum* (Iverson, 1979b; Gibbons, 1983a), but no clear trend in increase or decrease is apparent.

RELATIONSHIP BETWEEN CLUTCH SIZE AND AGE

Although age of a female turtle may indirectly affect clutch size because of the obvious positive relationship between body size and age, age per se has no clear relationship with the number of eggs (Gibbons, 1982). The additional data collected since publication of the paper by Gibbons (1982) does not alter our conclusion (Fig. 9.5).

INDIVIDUAL VARIABILITY IN CLUTCH SIZE

Multiple egg counts of individual turtles have been used to show that variability within an individual is as great as that among individuals, if body size is accounted for (Gibbons et al., 1982). In 12 individual *T. scripta* from Ellenton Bay for which x rays of clutch size were available for two or more reproductive events, the intraindividual variability in clutch size was as great as the variability among individuals ($F = 0.817$; $p = .63$; df = 11, 19; ANCOVA).

Timing of Nesting

In South Carolina, *T. scripta* females lay their eggs predominantly from mid-April to mid-July, the peak being in late May to early June (Table 9.2). Ovulation and shelling of the eggs presumably occurs less than a week before nesting, according to a comparison of dates of nesting females and of aquatically captured individuals without oviductal eggs. The radiographs of individuals with unshelled eggs prior to a later known nesting date also provide evidence of the length of time that eggs are retained, and the time between successive drift fence captures of nesting females is indicative of the ovulation cycle. The absence of oviductal eggs in a significant proportion of the population at a particular time period is also informative about the seasonal timing of ovulation.

The initiation of nesting varies annually and is at least partially controlled by temperature in early spring. As is always true in trying to tie animal activities to environmental conditions, the approach of the observer is to select a particular component of some quantifiable variable that seems important. Temperature is clearly critical for a reptile that is leaving the water to lay eggs, and there should be little argument that below a certain temperature turtles will not nest. Water temperature, some photoperiod feature, or both might be the cue for ovulation itself. The air temperature would presumably be the cue for travel to the nesting site. Despite observational data from many years,

establishing precise relationships between egg laying and environmental variables must come ultimately from experimental efforts.

Clutch Frequency

How often individuals lay eggs within and among years is a critical population characteristic for consideration of the life history of a species. The most thorough information on nesting frequencies of turtles has been obtained for some of the sea turtles, some of which nest multiple times within a year but apparently not in consecutive years (Carr and Carr, 1970; Kaufmann, 1975). Comparable information on freshwater or terrestrial species is minimal (Gibbons, 1982; Lovich et al., 1983).

Slider turtles are known or thought to be capable of laying more than one clutch per year in some localities and situations (Cagle, 1950; Moll and Legler, 1971; Gibbons, 1983a). The factors influencing the number of clutches per year or the frequency among years are not known with certainty, but the clutch frequency, interacting with clutch size and egg size, would presumably reflect the availability and acquisition of environmental resources by turtles. The determination of what factors govern a female turtle's reproductive effectiveness would contribute to the study of the evolutionary ecology of the group. Clutch frequency is a key variable in such determinations. On the SRP, individuals of three species of turtles are known to have laid more than one clutch in a season. A measure of clutch frequency of *T. scripta* at Ellenton Bay is given in Chapter 15.

Conclusions

Turtle studies on the SRP reveal the high level of variability in some reproductive characteristics and demonstrate consistent trends and patterns in others. A positive relationship clearly exists between clutch size and body size of turtles, although the variance may be high, and both clutch size and frequency vary greatly as a function of factors other than body size. Thus, clutch size varies among years, seasons, and habitats, although body size is an overriding influence that explains the greatest portion of the variance. A tendency toward gradual reduction in clutch size during an egg-laying season is suggested for some species, but a more careful look at this phenomenon is needed. The variability observed among successive clutches of the same individual indicates the importance of factors other than body size.

The variability and inconsistency observed in the relationship between clutch size and body size in turtles are presumed to be a function of two primary factors: (1) the female's body size, which sets an upper limit on the number of eggs of a given size that can be carried; and (2) previous resource acquisitions, which vary spatially (at both the habitat and the microhabitat levels) and temporally (both seasonally and annually), so that a particular female can realize a maximum clutch size and a maximum clutch frequency only under favorable resource conditions.

Presumably, then, the total annual egg output of individuals or populations reflects prior environmental resource levels, and the maximum clutch size of an individual may not be realized in some situations because of resource limitations. This may partially explain the high variability in the relationship of clutch size and body size in every species examined. Also, reliable estimation of annual reproductive output in turtles is further confounded by variations in clutch frequency.

The impacts of environmental vagaries on individuals are exceedingly difficult to quantify. Dramatic variation can occur among individuals within a population in such growth-influential factors as thermoregulatory experiences (Gatten, 1974a) and acquisition of resources (Lagler, 1943; Moll, 1976a; Parmenter, 1980). However, the high variation in clutch size and interannual timing of egg laying within a single individual, and the variation in the proportion of females in a population laying eggs each year, support the ideas that extrinsic environmental factors govern annual reproductive output and that these influences vary among individual turtles within a population and also vary among populations. The influence of general habitat conditions on traits that directly or indirectly affect reproduction of individuals in populations has been identified (Gibbons, 1970b; Moll, 1977; Gibbons et al., 1979), but microhabitat conditions (e.g., tempera-

ture, diet arrays) presumably can be extremely influential, so that reproductive output is variable among the individuals within a population.

If resource availability and acquisition by the individual control clutch size and frequency, and if maximum body size of the female sets the upper limit on clutch size of eggs of a given size, then reproductive output within populations and within individuals would be expected to show high annual variability in environments that vary seasonally and annually in a stochastic manner. Such environmental variability will confound and mask patterns of reproduction, so that consistent formulas for the relationships between reproductive output and body size, environmental conditions, or other factors will continue to be difficult to identify and confirm. The amassing and analyzing of large, long-term data sets on natural populations are one means of addressing this problem. In addition, experimental approaches that manipulate thermal regimes, diet quality and quantity, or other environmentally crucial factors could contribute greatly to our understanding of these phenomena.

Acknowledgments

We appreciate comments by Jeff Lovich, Susan Novak, and Nat Frazer on the manuscript. As with several other chapters, numerous individuals assisted with the field efforts. Our appreciation is extended for this support. Research and manuscript preparation were made possible by contract DE-AC09-76SROO-819 between the University of Georgia and the U.S. Department of Energy and by National Science Foundation grant DEB-79-04758.

ARTHUR E. DUNHAM
Department of Biology
University of Pennsylvania
Philadelphia, Pennsylvania 19104

J. WHITFIELD GIBBONS
Savannah River Ecology Laboratory
Drawer E
Aiken, South Carolina 29802

10

Growth of the Slider Turtle

Abstract

Growth is one of the most pervasive of biological phenomena, affecting virtually all ecological and life historical characteristics of organisms. Methods of analyzing individual growth in turtles are reviewed, and Von Bertalanffy, logistic-by-length, and logistic-by-weight models for *T. scripta* populations from Ellenton Bay and Par Pond on the SRP are presented. There is significant sexual size dimorphism in all populations, with the asymptotic plastron length of females being larger than that of males. In addition, the absolute growth rate of females is higher than that of males in all populations, but growth rates of juveniles or adults do not appear to differ between the sexes. Finally, potential sources of variation in individual growth rates are discussed.

Introduction

Body size and growth rates of individuals are critically related to numerous evolutionary, ecological, and physiological features of animals. Among the reptiles, body size has been implicated as a factor to be considered with characteristics as diverse as clutch size (Tinkle, 1967; Tinkle et al., 1970; for review, see Dunham et al., 1988a), evaporative water loss (Foley and Spotila, 1978), rate of digestion (Gatten, 1974a), and interspecific competition (Harris, 1964; Rand, 1964; Trivers, 1972, 1976; Ruby, 1976; Shine, 1978). Growth rate, likewise, has been cited as being related to a number of variables, including age at maturity (Cagle, 1946) and food availability (Ballinger, 1977; Dunham, 1978). The identification of patterns and the development of explanations of various growth- and size-related phenomena in reptiles continue at both the theoretical and the empirical levels (Andrews, 1982; Dunham et al., 1988a). Our objective in this chapter is to examine selected growth and size phenomena that exist in reptiles in terms of their evolutionary and ecological significance by using long-term data bases on the slider turtle (*Trachemys scripta*). The findings complement those reported in previous publications of growth of *T. scripta* on the SRP (Gibbons et al., 1981).

Evaluation of Techniques for Determining Growth Rates of Reptiles

For our purposes, growth may be defined as a progressive, ontogenetic change in total body size of an individual. Although growth of the individual actually begins at the point of conception, we will restrict our discussions to post-hatching growth processes. Special forms of growth such as regeneration and allometric changes will not be considered at this time. Body size refers to the total animal and can be expressed in linear units (length, area, volume) or in terms of mass. The most appropriate unit of measurement is dictated by the biological question being asked and by the ease and accuracy with which the particular measurement can be made. Accurate assessment of age is also critical in establishing age-specific growth rates of individuals, although the determination of age is often difficult in studies of reptiles, as with most animals.

MEASUREMENTS OF SIZE

A major frustration in comparative studies of growth phenomena is the inconsistency resulting from investigators' use of different measurements on the same species or on different species within a group. For example, body size in turtles has been expressed in terms of plastron length (e.g., Cagle, 1950), straight-line carapace length (e.g., Tinkle, 1961), and curved carapace length (Hughes et al., 1967; Gaymer, 1968; Zug et al., 1986). Curved carapace lengths are commonly used on extremely large species of turtles such as sea turtles and island tortoises because gigantic calipers for taking straight-line measurements are less convenient than a flexible tape is. Additional variation in size measurements results from taking them in different planes (see Fig. 7.1) or from different definitions of the dimension. For example, some investigators take shell measurements along the midline (Pritchard, 1969). Others measure the greatest length of the structure, a measurement that is rarely parallel to the long axis (Lovich et al., 1985; Ernst and Lovich, 1986).

One consequence of the selection of a particular measurement to represent body size is that the measurement may be inappropriate in a biologically functional sense. In some instances, for example, a functionally related variable (e.g., volume) may be prohibitively difficult to measure, whereas another size variable, such as length or weight, may not be. In such cases it may prove worth-

while, although time-consuming, to establish the mathematical relationship between the variables used for measurement. Thus, the relationship between body size and a particular environmental feature or individual characteristic can be established by inference.

The relationships between plastron length, carapace length, and body mass for large sample sizes of turtles can be used to demonstrate certain points. As expected, plastron length and carapace length have a strict linear relationship with one another, whereas body mass increases as a semilogarithmic function of plastron length (Fig. 10.1). A clear example of how the measurement selected could influence a biological interpretation is that of using plastron length rather than carapace length as a measure of size in the mud turtle (*Kinosternon subrubrum*) when the sexes are being compared, because plastron length is sexually dimorphic (Gibbons, 1983a).

DETERMINATION OF AGE

A variety of techniques for determining age have been attempted with reptiles, most with limited success. Methods of aging reptiles have been critically reviewed by Gibbons (1976) and Dunham et al. (1988b) and will be reconsidered below in the context of their applicability to studies of growth rates of turtles and with the inclusion of recent findings.

MARK-RELEASE-RECAPTURE. In studies of individual growth in natural populations of reptiles, only the mark-release-recapture approach provides reliable data on the size of individuals of known age whose growth can be followed across successive time intervals. A few long-term field studies have relied on this technique to elucidate growth patterns. Notable examples include studies on lizards (Blair, 1960; Tinkle, 1967; Smith, 1977; Dunham, 1978, 1981; Schoener and Schoener, 1978; and Van Devender, 1978), snakes (Fitch, 1960; Prestt, 1971; Feaver, 1977), and turtles (Sexton, 1959a; Wilbur, 1975b; Gibbons, 1987). Such long-term projects are essential if the nature and extent of variation in the growth processes among and within natural populations of reptiles are to be adequately quantified. Determination of growth rates in captive individuals of known age is also possible but must be considered circumspectly because of the unnaturalness of the situation.

EXTERNAL ANNULI. Except for continued observation of individuals of known-age at initial capture, the most reliable approach for determining age and subsequently growth rate in populations of reptiles is by using "growth rings" of turtles (Sergeev, 1937). However, the rings must be documented as being annual in formation for the particular species and location. The annuli method was described, tested on known-age individuals of the slider tur-

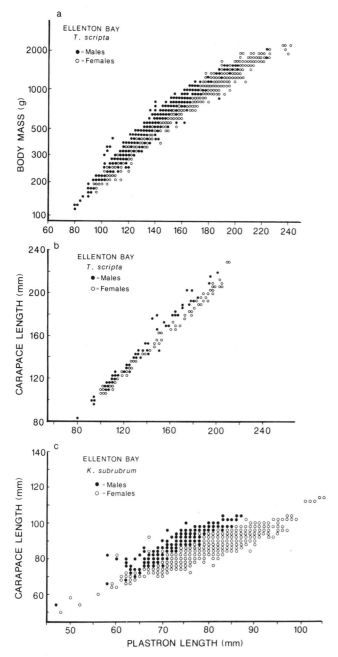

FIGURE 10.1. The relationships between different measurements of size in freshwater turtles. All turtle species would be expected to have a semilogarithmic relationship between plastron length and body mass (*a*). The relationship between plastron length and carapace length is the same for both sexes in some species (*b*) but not others (*c*).

tle in the field, and subsequently used extensively by Cagle (1946, 1950). The technique has been found reliable and used successfully with other species, such as the painted turtle, *Chrysemys picta* (Sexton, 1959a; Gibbons, 1968a; Ernst, 1971a); the ornate box turtle, *Terrapene ornata* (Legler, 1960a); and the Indian Ocean giant tortoise, *Geochelone gigantea* (Gaymer, 1968; Grubb, 1971). The

technique has proved unsatisfactory in studies of *Trachemys scripta* from Panama (Moll and Legler, 1971) and *Xerobates agassizii* (Woodbury and Hardy, 1948; Miller, 1955). Studies using external annuli to age individuals are reviewed by Dunham et al. (1988b) and by Galbraith and Brooks (1987a).

The method exploits the phenomenon that, in some species, an epithelial layer develops over each epidermal scute during a major period of growth. The epidermis that formed during the preceding period of minimal growth is thus sandwiched between the tissues of the major growth periods. The layer of deposited epithelium is thinner, and a "growth ring" indentation is thus produced. In temperate species, major indentations may occur during winter, thus indicating annual intervals. The distance between rings is directly related to the amount of growth for a given period. A thorough description of the process was given by Moll and Legler (1971), who found that more than one ring developed during a single year in a tropical population of *T. scripta*.

Growth rings are generally apparent and clear-cut in juveniles but are more closely spaced and less clear in older adults. Also, the rings of earlier years may gradually disappear as the turtle ages. Galbraith and Brooks (1987a) provided evidence that annuli counts in *Chelydra serpentina* are not completely reliable in older individuals. A useful extension of the aging technique was the demonstration by Sexton (1959a) that age estimates can be made for adult turtles on which some annuli are not visible (Wilbur, 1975b; Dunham et al., 1988b). The procedure consists of determining the mean and variance in annulus length for each known year class on a particular plastral plate. If one assumes that the length of the oldest visible annulus indicates, within certain confidence limits, the animal's age when it was formed, then age can be estimated for older animals in which early annuli are no longer apparent. Subsequent annuli can then be counted to determine the individual's present age. Although the technique has been used in several studies (e.g., Ernst 1971a), cautious interpretation of the rings as temporal indicators within a particular species or population must always precede the undertaking of new studies (Dunham et al., 1988a).

BONE RINGS

The growth rings appearing on the bones in various vertebrate groups have been reported as indicators of age. However, the skeletochronological technique has proved of limited use in the study of most reptiles (Dunham et al., 1988b; but also see Castanet and Cheylan, 1979; Zug et. al., 1986; Castanet, 1987). Bryuzgin (1939) asserted that the rings on the os transversum in a series of European snakes indicated annual cessation of growth (winter). Although the rings may have represented annuli that could identify the age of the individuals, Bryuzgin apparently did not use known-age specimens for verification. Therefore, there is no assurance that the number of rings was correlated with anything other than the size of individuals. Nonetheless, the technique was used by Petter-Rousseaux (1953) to denote individual age in the grass snake *Natrix natrix,* without a comparison of the number of rings and the age of known-age individuals. In another study of *N. natrix,* Bourliere (1954) furthered the idea that growth rings in snakes represent annuli. His data apparently documented only a relationship between body size and number of rings, because he extended the age-size correlation observed in known-age juvenile snakes (*N* = 6) to adults. Thus, he used an adult individual's size as a confirmation of its "age" (based on number of rings), without proving that a precise age-size correlation existed in mature individuals.

Peabody (1958) stated that "growth zones" observed on bones from a *Pituophis melanoleucus* were "excellent indicators of age," but no evidence was presented to show that a growth zone represented one year. Peabody (1961) also concluded in a general paper on ectothermic vertebrates that annual rings commonly occur on the bones of individuals living in temperate regions. In every instance, however, the supporting evidence for reptiles was not based on known-age specimens, and an appreciable amount of variation was often observed in the number of rings appearing on different bones from the same specimen. Castanet (1974) inferred that rings in the bones of *Vipera aspis* indicate age in individuals experiencing seasonal variation but noted that the technique had yet to be demonstrated experimentally on known-age animals.

Griffiths (1962) strongly contested the use of bone rings as reliable indicators of age in reptiles, presenting data on a series of known-age snakes. The rings on the ectopterygoid bone did not conform in number to the age of the individual and even varied in number on separate portions of the same bone. Tinkle (1962) likewise considered the number of growth rings in the surangular bone of western diamondback rattlesnakes (*Crotalus atrox*) to be unreliable indicators of age. Enlow (1969) discussed the osteological complications that can arise in trying to relate age to number of growth rings on the bones of reptiles.

Rings on the bones of painted turtles (*Chrysemys picta*) were presumed by Mattox (1935) to represent annual growth rings, but Suzuki (1963) considered bone rings to be of no use in determining the age of turtles because of "the continual remodeling" that occurs on and within the bones. A poor relationship was found between "bone annuli" and scute annuli in the alligator snapping turtle, *Macroclemys temminckii* (Dobie, 1971), and the common snapping turtle, *Chelydra serpentina* (Hammer, 1969). However, the skeletological technique has been considered to be of great value in determining the age of

tortoises (Castanet and Cheylan, 1979) and sea turtles (Zug et al., 1986).

Solid confirmation that the rings visible on snake or turtle bones are correlated with age in older individuals, rather than with size or cessations in growth due to causes other than winter dormancy, has not been demonstrated. This problem deserves thorough experimental investigation with the use of older, known-age individuals. Determination of the cause-and-effect relationships among age, environmental factors, and the development of bone rings would clearly enhance the study of growth rates of turtles and other long-lived reptiles.

SIZE CLASS COMPARISONS

In some instances, growth rates of individuals have been inferred by comparing size classes within a population. Juveniles of some long-lived, late-maturing reptiles can be separated into discrete size classes that are assumed to represent year classes. Such comparisons, although probably accurate in the initial juvenile years, become difficult to interpret as individuals approach maturity, because growth slows and size classes begin to overlap considerably. Other factors, such as multiple clutches and subsequent differences in the timing of hatching during a year or high variability in growth rate among individuals, can also confound the interpretation of such groupings because of overlap in size categories of different ages. To be used reliably, the age-specific variance in size should be established for the study population, and the technique should be avoided when the assignment of age based on size class is not unequivocal.

Estimation of age, and consequently growth rate, by comparison of juvenile size classes of long-lived reptiles has been done frequently with snakes (Fitch, 1965; Clark, 1970; Gibbons, 1972). These studies did not convincingly confirm a close relationship between size and age in the older individuals in the populations. The estimation of age and, hence, growth rate from size class data has potential for use on a population level, but its use must be based initially on animals of known age. The technique should be used only within the constraints imposed by variability in individual growth rates and the distinctness of different size classes.

Expression and Interpretation of Growth Rates and Body Size

Growth rates of individuals within a reptile population are expressible in a variety of ways ranging from elementary range and scatter diagrams to regression equations to complex growth models (Andrews, 1982). No single approach to the consideration of growth data is likely to be found universally appropriate. For example, the range diagrams used by Legler (1960a) were sufficient to document the phenomenon that juvenile *Terrapene ornata* grow more rapidly than adults, whereas a complex mathematical model allowed Wilbur (1975b) to construct growth curves on the basis of selected size and population variables for *Chrysemys picta*. The fitting of empirical growth data to growth models such as the Von Bertalanffy, Gompertz, logistic, and Richards equations (reviewed in Andrews, 1982) can also provide useful insight into the physiological or ecological factors governing or influencing growth patterns in a particular population.

Fabens (1965) and Schoener and Schoener (1978) derived equations for an animal's size at the end of a growth interval as a function of its size at the beginning of the interval and the duration of the interval. These were derived from the solutions to the differential equations for the Von Bertalanffy, logistic-by-length, and logistic-by-weight growth models. These are termed the interval equations for each model, and they can be used to fit each model to standard recapture data using nonlinear least-squares regression procedures (Dunham, 1978; Schoener and Schoener, 1978). The interval equation for each model has two free parameters—the asymptotic body length $(\hat{P})$ and the characteristic growth parameter $(\hat{r})$—which are identical to the parameters in the differential equations defining each model. The use of a nonlinear least-squares regression procedure allows several types of confidence intervals to be computed for each estimated parameter from the asymptotic standard deviations for each parameter estimate (Marquardt, 1964; Schoener and Schoener, 1978).

Recapture data on *Trachemys scripta* populations from Ellenton Bay, Par Pond, and Risher Pond on the SRP were used in estimating the free parameters of the Von Bertalanffy, logistic-by-length, and logistic-by-weight growth models. Significantly different growth rates have been reported for Ellenton Bay and Par Pond populations (Gibbons, 1970b; Gibbons et al., 1981). Plastron length was used as the linear measure of body size. Other potentially appropriate growth models, such as the Gompertz, were not examined at this time, because extensions of these models that allow analyses of recapture data are not yet available. Models were estimated for males and females of each population separately, and then the models were compared on the basis of goodness-of-fit to the recapture data. The estimated growth models are presented in Table 10.1.

For each recapture data set, the model with the smallest residual error mean square (REMS) was considered the best model for describing individual growth. Following Marquardt (1964), Dunham (1978), and Schoener and Schoener (1978), we computed 95% "support plane" confidence intervals about each parameter estimate. These are extremely conservative confidence intervals. In addition,

we computed standard deviations for each parameter estimate using Tukey's jackknife procedure (Moesteller and Tukey, 1977). In all comparisons, parameter estimates were considered significantly different $(p < .05)$ if the 95% confidence intervals derived from the jackknife estimates of the standard deviations of each parameter did not overlap. This is a conservative test.

In each case the Von Bertalanffy model had the lowest REMS, and this model was used in all comparisons. The change in plastron length (PL) per unit time as a function of mean PL over the growth interval in the Ellenton Bay population indicates that individual growth rates are highly variable, especially in young animals. Second, individual growth rates tend to decline with increasing PL, as is characteristic of reptiles. One biologically important point is that there is presently no evidence that either juvenile or adult growth rates differ between the sexes. Although the sexes begin to approach the asymptote at different times in each population, the two sexes grow at the same absolute rate before and after reaching the asymptote. An additional observation is that indeterminate growth occurs in *T. scripta;* growth continues in older, larger individuals, although at a low rate and in an inconsistent manner.

Young individuals are underrepresented in the recapture data. As was pointed out by Dunham (1978), model discrimination by the criterion of lowest REMS is questionable when all size classes are not well represented in the data set. Nonetheless, all three models yielded similar growth trajectories, and the hypothesis tests reported below, based on jackknifed confidence intervals, yielded identical results regardless of the model used. The logistic-by-weight model has usually been the model with the lowest REMS in studies of lizard growth (Dunham, 1978; Schoener and Schoener, 1978; Andrews, 1982). In those studies small individuals were well represented, and that may account for the differences in model performance. Recapture studies of turtle growth should endeavor to ensure that recaptures of small (young) are well represented.

Data on size distributions of known-age individuals and growth trajectories based on the Von Bertalanffy growth models are presented for each population in Figure 10.2. The data in these figures demonstrate that the sizes and, hence, growth rates of individuals of virtually every age are highly variable. This variation presumably reflects seasonal, annual, and individual variation in resource acquisition and allocation to growth. It is clear that these growth models tend to overestimate the size of individuals of intermediate ages. Two factors contribute to this overestimation.

First, as was discussed by Dunham (1978), these models are stationary, and growth trajectories derived from models such as those presented here ignore the effects of

Table 10.1. Comparison of two-parameter growth models fit to individual
recapture data from three *Trachemys scripta* populations

Model	N	P̂		r̂		REMS	R^2
Von Bertalanffy model							
Ellenton Bay							
Males	198	164.16	(12.06)	7.88E-04	(2.03E-04)	9.53	.93
		147.10	(23.04)	1.10E-03	(8.01E-04)		
Females	188	197.98	(6.88)	7.63E-04	(8.11E-05)	16.32	.99
		191.48	(25.16)	9.35E-04	(4.98E-04)		
Par Pond							
Males	75	199.18	(7.98)	9.50E-04	(1.64E-04)	15.27	.99
		191.46	(13.51)	1.46E-03	(5.86E-04)		
Females	47	263.36	(11.38)	8.99E-04	(1.40E-04)	11.14	.99
		269.93	(18.62)	6.97E-04	(2.29E-04)		
Risher Pond							
Males	56	161.22	(5.12)	8.01E-04	(7.31E-05)	5.75	.99
		155.50	(11.44)	8.00E-04	(1.70E-04)		
Females	77	178.59	(13.42)	7.83E-04	(1.68E-04)	43.45	.98
		181.78	(9.96)	7.62E-04	(1.10E-04)		
Logistic-by-length model							
Ellenton Bay							
Males	198	167.77	(4.18)	1.08E-03	(1.16E-04)	13.46	.92
		169.45	(4.57)	1.07E-03	(4.16E-04)		
Females	188	195.42	(3.41)	1.65E-03	(1.44E-04)	17.41	.98
		194.47	(9.80)	1.58E-03	(3.57E-04)		
Par Pond							
Males	75	200.06	(6.21)	1.37E-03	(2.15E-04)	17.09	.98
		204.34	(7.12)	1.00E-03	(4.30E-04)		
Females	47	247.95	(5.28)	1.87E-03	(1.97E-04)	10.76	.99
		261.37	(7.74)	1.39E-03	(3.61E-04)		
Risher Pond							
Males	56	164.92	(5.65)	1.33E-03	(2.25E-04)	15.96	.98
		161.37	(16.61)	2.05E-03	(1.04E-03)		
Females	77	185.33	(7.04)	1.77E-03	(4.44E-04)	49.92	.96
		177.52	(11.47)	1.39E-03	(7.80E-04)		
Logistic-by-weight model							
Ellenton Bay							
Males	198	172.84	(4.35)	1.26E-03	(1.56E-04)	15.33	.91
		171.35	(4.87)	1.42E-03	(4.41E-04)		
Females	188	196.65	(2.49)	2.43E-03	(2.18E-04)	17.86	.98
		193.77	(3.00)	1.69E-03	(5.75E-04)		
Par Pond							
Males	75	202.22	(5.59)	1.72E-03	(2.85E-04)	18.88	.98
		198.23	(4.47)	1.74E-03	(7.59E-04)		
Females	47	244.78	(4.06)	2.72E-03	(2.84E-04)	12.37	.98
		250.75	(6.04)	1.69E-03	(8.41E-04)		
Risher Pond							
Males	56	172.97	(8.49)	1.15E-03	(3.37E-04)	21.59	.97
		186.27	(20.68)	4.26E-04	(8.78E-04)		
Females	77	188.78	(8.14)	1.64E-03	(7.02E-04)	55.79	.96
		188.12	(8.81)	8.40E-04	(1.78E-03)		

Note: P̂ is the asymptotic plastron length (mm), r̂ is the characteristic growth parameter (Schoener and Schoener, 1978), and REMS is the residual error mean square. On the first line for each model are the parameter estimates and corresponding asymptotic 95% confidence intervals. On the second line are the jackknifed parameter estimates and 95% confidence intervals (Moesteller and Tukey, 1977). The 95% confidence interval half-widths about the parameter estimates are in parentheses. Models were fit using the Marquardt nonlinear least-squares algorithm (Dunham, 1978).

seasonal variation in growth rate. Individual growth rates of turtles are significantly lower during colder months in these populations (Gibbons, unpubl. data), and the magnitude of this effect is likely to vary among populations because of habitat differences that result in different feeding patterns (Schubauer and Parmenter, 1981). Inclusion of seasonal differences in growth rate would greatly improve the ability of these models to predict size as a function of age in these populations. However, such effects are

likely to be complex and population-specific. Growth models incorporating such effects do not currently exist (especially for recapture data) and are likely to be difficult to construct. Development of such models is beyond the scope of this chapter but would be a worthwhile objective in future research efforts on growth phenomena.

The second factor contributing to differences in observed and predicted growth rates is that all individuals captured between the ages of x and $x + 1$ are assumed to

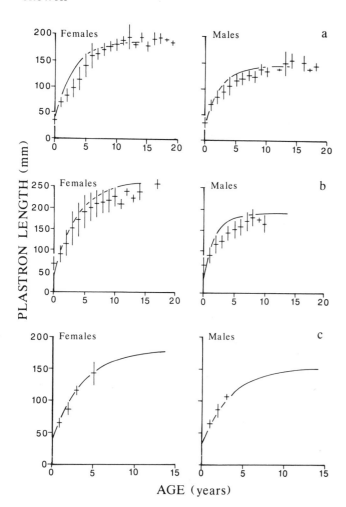

FIGURE 10.2. Von Bertalanffy growth trajectories (solid lines) and range diagrams based on known-age turtles from three populations of *Trachemys scripta* on the SRP (see Table 10.1). Vertical lines represent the mean ± one standard deviation of known-age individuals. *a*, Ellenton Bay; *b*, Par Reservoir; *c*, Risher Pond.

be exactly age *x* regardless of when they were captured during that interval. The use of more precise within-year ages of individuals would greatly improve the agreement between the size predicted, based on growth models such as those presented here, and the actual size observed in recaptured individuals of known age.

Consideration of the data in these figures and of the model parameters listed in Table 10.1 demonstrates that all three populations exhibit significant sexual size dimorphism in plastron length. In all three populations the asymptotic PL ($\hat{P}$) of females is significantly greater than that of males ($p < .05$). In contrast, the characteristic growth parameter ($\hat{r}$) does not differ significantly between males and females in any population. These results indicate that females attain a significantly larger asymptotic PL than males in all populations but that both sexes approach their respective asymptotes at the same rate ($\hat{r}$).

Therefore, the absolute growth rates of females must be significantly higher than those of males in all populations (Dunham, 1978), but the growth rates of juveniles of the two sexes do not vary. These results are unaltered by choice of growth model and are shown clearly in the distributions of PL of known-age individuals (Fig. 10.2).

Comparison of growth models and recapture data from different populations reveals that females and males from the Par Pond population reach a significantly larger asymptotic PL than do individuals of the same sex from either Risher Pond or Ellenton Bay. The characteristic growth parameter ($\hat{r}$) from the Von Bertalanffy model for a given sex does not vary significantly among these populations, indicating that individuals in these populations are approaching their respective asymptotic PLs at the same rates. Thus, individual *T. scripta* living in Par Pond exhibit significantly higher PLs and absolute growth rates than do individuals of the same sex living in Risher Pond or Ellenton Bay. These results are also unaltered by choice of growth model.

A variety of visual presentations of changes in size of individuals over time have been used in reptile studies. Histograms (Wilbur, 1975b) can provide a visual comparison of growth patterns but have the disadvantages that they do not permit any statistical comparison among age classes and cannot be used to establish a quantified growth curve. Range diagrams (Fig. 10.2), in contrast, are statistically more succinct and give a quantitative expression of the range of variability in size among the different age categories. Connecting the means gives an estimate of growth rates, whereas the variance estimates provide an indication of ontogenetic variation in growth and size.

Tabular presentations of growth data allow statistical comparisons to be made between age or size categories. In addition, they permit the use of quantitative data by other workers who may wish to reanalyze the findings. One limitation is that the categories selected by the original author may not be the most appropriate ones for consideration of an aspect of growth or size other than the one originally addressed. The inclusion of variance estimates can greatly enhance the statistical value of tabular data because of the high variability in growth rate that can occur among individuals in a population.

Factors Influencing Growth Processes and Size Attainment in Reptiles

A variety of known or suspected factors influence growth rate and the ultimate size attained by individuals within a species of reptiles. These can be dichotomized into environmental factors and factors intrinsic to the individual or population itself. For the latter, an important consideration is that the selective partitioning of the energy available to an individual will have a major influence on growth rate. The individual options and influential factors are considered in Chapters 3 and 8.

ENVIRONMENTAL FACTORS, INCLUDING FOOD AVAILABILITY AND QUALITY

Although growth rate comparisons are inherently complex because of natural variation among individuals, populations, and species, numerous studies have attempted to establish the impact of particular environmental features on individual growth rates. The combination of measurement technique, small samples, and choice of analyses, coupled with natural high variability in many instances, has resulted in an overzealous interpretation of the data in some studies. A critical assessment of these considerations must be made in each case where environmental factors are stated or suggested as being influential in the determination of individual growth rates.

In the comparison of individual growth rates in Par Pond and Ellenton Bay, earlier papers concluded that growth was more rapid in the former (Gibbons, 1970b; Gibbons et al., 1981). The present analyses confirm this relationship. The explanation originally given and subsequently supported in a variety of ways is that the faster growth rates in Par Pond were a consequence of elevated temperatures and enhanced diet quality. Graham (1971) indicated a possible relationship between diet quality and growth rate for *Pseudemys rubriventris,* in which the annual growth increment decreased steadily until the fourth year, when rapid growth was observed. The growth change may have been associated with a diet shift from herbivory to carnivory in the fourth year, although supporting data based on large sample sizes would provide more convincing evidence that this is a characteristic phenomenon in this species. Earlier studies with *T. scripta* and other emydid species documented a carnivorous diet and rapid growth in young turtles, with a shift to herbivory in adults (Marchand, 1942; Clark and Gibbons, 1969). Faster growth in different habitats was reported by Moll (1976a) for *Graptemys pseudogeographica* and by Thornhill (1982) for *T. scripta.*

Several desert reptiles have been reported to respond to environmental conditions by displaying variation in individual growth rates. Loss of weight by *Sauromalus obesus* in the Mojave Desert was attributed to environmental conditions that resulted in a poor condition of the plants available as food (Nagy, 1973). Although lengths were not given, the average weight of lizards in the fall was only 63% of that in the spring. Medica et al. (1975) measured growth rates of *Xerobates agassizii* in a southern Nevada desert region. Over a five-year period in which 22 individuals were captured 216 times, the average increase in length was about 9 mm per year, with considerable variation. The major source of variation was attributed to the

yearly differences in precipitation and subsequent vegetation cover, with the slowest-growth years being the driest. The season at which growth occurs is unquestionably important among reptiles, because lower temperatures lead to dormancy in most instances. Differences that occur during the growing season may be more difficult to identify but can be of major biological significance.

Early (July) hatchlings of *Anolis carolinensis* from Texas were reported to grow more rapidly on a day-to-day basis than late (August–September) hatchlings (Michael, 1972). The first 90 days of growth for the July animals may have been during a more environmentally optimal time than for the late-summer animals. Thus, under similar conditions, growth rates might have been the same for the two groups. Parker and Pianka (1975) found a strong positive correlation between length of the growing season and average body size of *Uta stansburiana* in northern U.S. locations. They suggested that critical periods of early growth are enhanced in localities with longer growing seasons so that larger body sizes can be attained. The correlation between growing season and body size was found to be negative in those populations considered to be southern; thus the early-growth explanation, at least as a function of length of growing season, is not as easily invoked. Although hatchlings of *Sceloporus woodi* appeared throughout the warm months and were separated into early summer and later summer-autumn groups, Jackson and Telford (1974) did not note a difference in growth rates between the two.

Cagle (1946) attributed differences in individual growth rates among populations of *Trachemys scripta* to differences in food abundance and temperature. Gibbons (1967b) provided evidence that similar differences among populations of *Chrysemys picta* were due to differences in food quality. As noted above, Medica et al. (1975) showed that individual growth rates in the desert tortoise (*Xerobates agassizii*) in Nevada were higher following winters of high precipitation, presumably in response to increased primary productivity. Legler (1960a) provided convincing evidence that growth rates of *Terrapene ornata* in Kansas were greater in years characterized by high precipitation and prey (grasshoppers) abundance.

Ballinger (1977) presented data suggesting that individual growth rates of *Urosaurus ornatus* from the Animas Mountains of southwestern New Mexico were lower in years characterized by reduced precipitation and food availability. Smith (1977) demonstrated that growth rates of striped plateau lizards (*Sceloporus virgatus*) and tree lizards (*Urosaurus ornatus*) from the Chiricahua Mountains of southeastern Arizona were significantly lower during the drought period than during more favorable periods. Dunham (1978, 1981) showed that individual canyon lizards (*Sceloporus merriami*) and *U. ornatus* from populations in the Chihuahuan Desert of southwest Texas exhibited greater foraging success and individual growth rates during periods of food scarcity. Licht (1974) demonstrated an increase in lean growth of *Anolis cristatellus* in response to experimental food supplementation in nature. Andrews (1976) and Schoener and Schoener (1978) demonstrated differences in individual growth rates among populations of *Anolis* consistent with the hypothesis that growth rates in these lizards are positively correlated with food abundance, although food abundance was not measured in either study.

Resolution of the influence of seasonal or annual environmental changes that affect diet opportunities of turtles must come from intensive field or experimental studies focusing on that question.

INJURY

Legler (1960a) stated that growth may temporarily cease in *Terrapene ornata* following injury, although data were not presented that show this to be the case. Tinkle and Ballinger (1972) demonstrated that in populations of *Sceloporus undulatus* and *Sceloporus scalaris,* growth rates were lower in individuals that were regenerating lost tails than in animals that had not lost tails. Although individual turtles have been documented to survive after severe physical injury (Cagle, 1945; Rose, 1969), extensive data on how growth rates are affected are unavailable.

COMPETITION

Any factor that reduces the availability of resources to individuals might be expected to result in lower individual growth rates. Therefore, all other things being equal, an increase in the intensity of interspecific or intraspecific competition for nutrients could be expected to reduce the growth rates of individuals exposed to the increase. Dunham (1980) has experimentally demonstrated the effect of interspecific competition on growth rates in *U. ornatus.* In an experiment in which all *S. merriami* were removed from plots containing both species, remaining *U. ornatus* of both sexes exhibited significantly greater size-specific growth rates than did *U. ornatus* from plots without such removals. This effect was detectable only during years of lowered precipitation and reduced food abundance. *Urosaurus ornatus* on the removal plots also exhibited significantly greater foraging success than on control plots during periods of food scarcity, suggesting that the removal of *S. merriami* effectively increased the resources available to *U. ornatus* on the removal plots during periods of food scarcity.

Similar experiments have not been conducted with *Trachemys scripta* or any other species of turtle, although such studies could be of value in establishing the impor-

tance of interspecific or, perhaps more significant, intraspecific competition in turtle populations.

GENETIC COMPOSITION

Ferguson and Brockman (1980) reared hatchlings of several species of iguanid lizards under identical laboratory conditions and observed significantly different population-specific growth rates. Although inconclusive, their results suggest genetic influences on growth rate. As the authors pointed out, eggs used in the analysis were collected from wild-caught females under different environmental conditions, and nongenetic maternal influence could not be ruled out. However, the authors concluded that a genetic difference was likely. Thus, a genetic factor is a potential explanation for growth rate differences among turtle populations, although habitat differences are presumably a major influence.

Growth-Related Phenomena and Considerations

SEXUAL DIMORPHISM

Numerous workers have stated or implied that in certain species of reptiles differences occur in the growth rate of one sex or the other or that sexual dimorphism in size occurs. Such phenomena deserve particular attention because they could indicate differential selection between the sexes or a significant difference in their ecology. The evolutionary bases for the derivation of sexual dimorphism in growth rate and body size seem of utmost importance (Trivers, 1976).

Because the size of an individual of age x is the integral of growth rate from birth to age x, sexual size dimorphism (SSD) can occur only when there are differences between the sexes in growth rate at some age(s) resulting in significant differences in the expected size of males and females of the same age at some time in the life history (Fig. 10.3). Thus, if SSD is to be unequivocally demonstrated, comparisons must be between males and females of the same age.

Comparisons of static size distributions of individuals of uncertain age cannot be used to demonstrate SSD. Because of factors such as different survivorships of males and females, the mean ages (and hence body sizes) in the samples being compared may differ, leading to the appearance of SSD in a population in which the sexes possess identical growth trajectories (Fig. 10.4). The reverse error is also possible. That is, the appearance of no SSD can result with a population in which the sexes actually have different rates of growth. This can happen if differential survivorship occurs in such a manner that the slower-growing sex outlives the faster-growing sex, so that

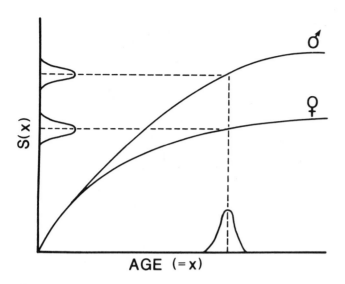

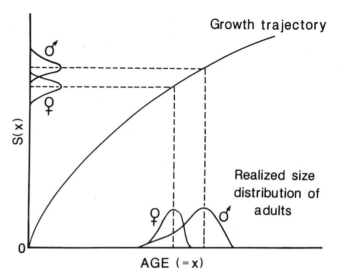

FIGURE 10.3.   Graph showing the existence of significant sexual size dimorphism (SSD). Note that size at age x ($S(x)$) is given by

$$S(x) = \int_{t=0}^{x} \frac{ds(t)}{dt}\, dt$$

and therefore the existence of significant SSD must imply the existence of differences in male and female growth rates at some stage in the life history.

FIGURE 10.4.   Graph showing the existence of apparent sexual dimorphism in body size in a population in which there is no difference between males and females in growth trajectory. This sampling error could be caused by a difference in the survivorship of males and females. The distributions of adult body size in the population are different, with adult males being significantly larger than adult females, but this is not a case of sexual size dimorphism, because the growth trajectories of the two sexes do not differ.

maximum adult sizes are similar but ages are dissimilar. A thorough review of sexual dimorphism in sliders and other species of turtles is given by Gibbons and Lovich (1990).

JUVENILE GROWTH RATES

Differential growth between the sexes has been reported for juveniles of some species of reptiles (e.g., Mosimann, 1958; Jolicoeur and Mosimann, 1960; Ernst, 1975, 1977; Trivers, 1976), whereas evidence of no difference has been given for others. Many studies have resulted in assertions that are seemingly unsupported by the available data or are results of possible misinterpretations. For a proper comparison of growth rates in a species in which sexual dimorphism in adult size occurs, a distinction must be made between pre- and postmaturity growth rates. This entails a determination of size at maturity in each sex and the subsequent careful consideration of specimens that are of a size at which one sex has attained maturity and the other has not.

Numerous examples are given in the literature of reptiles in which one sex reportedly has a more rapid juvenile growth rate than the other. Immature individuals of one sex of some snake species appear to grow more rapidly (e.g., Fukada, 1959, 1960; Dmi'el, 1967), but in some reports small sample sizes (i.e., number of recaptures) and/or high variability confounded a statistical or graphi-

cal presentation that would support the conclusion of differential growth between juveniles of the two sexes (Fitch and Glading, 1947; Woodbury, 1951; Carpenter, 1952; Fitch, 1960; Clark, 1970). In some instances the error may be caused by the inclusion of young adult specimens of the earlier-maturing sex in the juvenile sample (e.g., Mount, 1963; Pianka and Parker, 1972; Jackson and Telford, 1974; Parker and Pianka, 1975). This can result in a bias that lowers the upper end of the regression line for that sex and can be falsely interpreted as indicating that the other sex grows more rapidly as juveniles, although there is actually no consistent difference on a day-to-day basis. This type of error should be guarded against in species that show obvious sexual dimorphism in the mean or maximum adult body size, because this often indicates differences in size at maturity.

According to the growth models and recaptures of known-age individuals of *Trachemys scripta*, both sexes grow at similar rates as juveniles. However, the rapid advent of male maturity could conceivably confound interpretations in studies of some populations.

Conclusions

Several aspects of turtle growth remain to be adequately investigated. We lack suitable explanations for differences in individual growth trajectories within populations. For example, it may be that differences in individual growth trajectories in some cases are due to differences in resource availabilities. Heritable differences in resource allocation patterns may exist among individuals in a population, and such differences may account for some of the variability in individual growth rates. In no case can we currently partition variation in individual growth rates within populations into environmental or genetic components, or the interaction between them.

The same questions about the causes of growth rate variability among individuals remain unanswered when geographically distinct populations are compared. We generally do not know whether differences in individual growth trajectories for conspecific populations are due to habitat differences in resource availability, heritable differences between the populations in resource-processing physiology, or differential allocation of assimilated resources to growth. Also, interactions may occur between absolute resource availability and physiological (e.g., thermal) limitations on acquisition, processing, or assimilation rates. As a result, in two populations characterized by equivalent absolute per capita resource availabilities, individuals may still experience different levels of resource limitation. This can happen if they have different thermal characteristics because of the dependence of digestive processes and metabolic rates on temperature in ectotherms. Until questions relating to issues such as these are answered, our understanding of the ecology and evolution of turtle growth patterns will remain inadequate.

Acknowledgments

We appreciate the assistance of Judith L. Greene in the collection and reduction of data used in the analyses. Jeffrey E. Lovich provided constructive comments on the manuscript. Research and manuscript preparation were aided by contract DE-AC09-76SROO-819 between the U.S. Department of Energy and University of Georgia. We thank Pat Davis for typing the manuscript.

JOSEPH C. MITCHELL
Department of Biology
University of Richmond
Richmond, Virginia 23173

CHRISTOPHER A. PAGUE
Department of Biological Sciences
Old Dominion University
Norfolk, Virginia 23508

Current address:
Virginia Natural Heritage Program
203 Governor Street, Suite 402
Richmond, Virginia 23219

11

Body Size, Reproductive Variation, and Growth in the Slider Turtle at the Northeastern Edge of Its Range

Abstract

Variation in body size and relationships of clutch size and egg size to female body size were compared in two populations of *Trachemys scripta* in southeastern Virginia. Sliders from both populations consist of large females (200–255 mm in plastron length) and males (92–189 mm). Clutch size and total clutch mass do not differ between populations and are not related to body size. Length, width, and wet mass of eggs do not differ between populations but are positively and significantly related to parental body size. Some females in each population produce at least two clutches in a single season. Juvenile growth rate (ages 1 through 6) averages about 13 mm per year. Possible causes of large-bodied adults are presented. Problems encountered demonstrate that caution must be taken when constructing generalizations about cause and effect in turtle life histories based on a limited number of comparisons. Comparisons of growth and reproductive characteristics with South Carolina sliders show concordance in most aspects. Differences can be explained on the basis of sample composition.

Introduction

Much of what is known about the life histories of animals has been gained from comparative studies of populations in different parts of the species' range (e.g., Tinkle and Ballinger, 1972; Leggett and Carscadden, 1978; M. Murphy, 1983). We can provide insights into the causes and relationships of these phenomena by comparing the variation in life history attributes among widely separated populations once the regional variation is known. Our focus in this paper is to provide comparative data on selected life history attributes of the slider turtle so we can evaluate environmental effects on these traits.

The northeastern margin of the range of *Trachemys scripta* is in southeastern Virginia (Conant, 1975) in the area roughly corresponding with the 5° C isotherm (Gibbons, 1983a). Natural populations of *T. s. scripta* occupy freshwater habitats in rural and urban areas of the state from the Atlantic coast westward to about the Fall Line. This paper summarizes our current knowledge of the reproductive variation of two *T. s. scripta* populations at the northeastern edge of its range. Introgressive hybridization with the introduced *T. s. elegans* is apparently affecting the genetic structure of urban populations in southeastern Virginia (Mitchell and Pague, pers. obs.). However, there appears to be little influence of *T. s. elegans* on the populations chosen for study. We compare differences in body size, and relationships of reproductive characteristics to parental size, between a coastal barrier population and an interior population. These parameters, as well as growth rates from the barrier population, are compared with published information from elsewhere in *T. scripta*'s range.

Materials and Methods

The coastal barrier population we studied is located in Back Bay National Wildlife Refuge and adjacent False Cape State Park, Virginia Beach, Virginia. This area is bordered to the north by the community of Sandbridge and to the south by the Virginia–North Carolina state line on the Currituck Spit. This landmass separates the Back Bay estuary from the Atlantic Ocean. Sliders primarily occupy the freshwater impoundments and canals but also are occasionally seen in the mostly clear, variably brackish bay. The second population is located in the Virginia portion of the Great Dismal Swamp National Wildlife Refuge, Suffolk, Virginia, 53 km west of the Back Bay–False Cape population. Here sliders are found in the freshwater canals crisscrossing the forested refuge and occasionally in Lake Drummond. The water in Dismal Swamp is dark and acidic.

We studied the Back Bay–False Cape population from 1980 to 1983 and in 1986. The Dismal Swamp population was studied in 1985 and 1986. In Back Bay–False Cape we captured sliders with sardine-baited funnel traps (Iverson, 1979a), with fyke nets, and by hand. Traps were set in the canals and in the bay, but turtles were captured only in freshwater sites. Most turtles were individually marked by notching the margins of the carapace (Mitchell, 1982) and released at the capture site. In both study areas we captured ovigerous females while they were on land seeking nest sites or nesting. We measured carapace length (CL), plastron length (PL), and length of

all visible annuli on the right abdominal scute (to the nearest 0.1 mm). Body mass was recorded to the nearest gram with Pesola scales. Eggs were obtained by dissection of gravid females and from females that had just finished nesting. Each egg was measured (length and width to the nearest 0.1 mm) and weighed (to the nearest 0.1 g). Total clutch mass is the sum of the individual egg masses for each clutch. Individually numbered eggs were incubated in vermiculite (1:1 with water by weight) at 27° ± 3° C until hatching. Hatchlings were measured (CL, PL) and weighed (to the nearest 0.1 g), and many were released.

We determined growth rates for juveniles (unsexed) by counting clearly distinguishable annuli on the plastron. Assigning ages to individuals with this method is reliable only for the first few years of life because of the loss of annuli due to wear (Moll and Legler, 1971; Wilbur, 1975b). We were confident in our age assignments for most sliders through age 6 and for three specimens at ages 7 and 8.

Statistics follow Zar (1974) and were performed with SPSS^x programs (SPSS, 1986). Nonparametric statistics were used when assumptions of normality were not met. Statistical significance was established at $p \leq .05$ unless otherwise noted. Reported means are followed by ± one standard error.

Results

BODY SIZE

Mature females from both populations were similar in body size. Mean carapace length for Back Bay–False Cape ovigerous females (248.2 ± 11.5 mm, 232–272 mm, $N = 21$) did not differ significantly from mean carapace length of Dismal Swamp females (252.6 ± 12.7 mm, 226–273, $N = 23$; $t = -1.04$, $p = .304$). Average carapace length for both populations combined was 250.8 ± 12.2 mm ($N = 44$). Plastron lengths showed a similar relationship (Table 11.1, Back Bay–False Cape, 215–250 mm; Dismal Swamp, 204–254 mm) and were not significantly different ($t = -0.51$, $p = .613$).

Mature males at Back Bay–False Cape averaged 158.4 ± 30.6 mm CL (102–215 mm, $N = 20$) and 143.5 ± 27.8 mm PL (94–189 mm, $N = 20$). A single male from the Dismal Swamp site measured 161 mm CL and 147 mm PL.

REPRODUCTIVE VARIATION

Clutch size for southeastern Virginia sliders ranged from 6 to 15 but showed an insignificant relationship with female body size (Fig. 11.1, Table 11.2). There was no significant difference in clutch sizes between populations (Mann-Whitney U test, $U = 180.0$, $p = .144$). A Kruskal-Wallis test revealed a significant difference in clutch means among years (each yearly sample coded sepa-

Table 11.1. Body size and reproductive characteristics for *Trachemys scripta* from two southeastern Virginia populations

Sample	N	Plastron length	Clutch size	Egg length	Egg width	Egg wet mass	Clutch wet mass
Back Bay–False Cape							
1983	7	230.0	9.29	34.47	22.93	10.51	96.76
		4.7	0.60	0.50	0.53	0.54	6.04
1986	14	233.5	9.93	34.07	23.26	11.01	111.50
		3.3	0.67	0.43	0.25	0.41	7.83
Combined	21	232.2	9.71	34.20	23.14	10.84	106.59
		2.4	0.43	0.29	0.22	0.29	5.00
Dismal Swamp							
1985	13	238.0	9.54	34.82[a]	23.41[a]	10.97[a]	105.14[a]
		3.3	0.58	0.42	0.27	0.36	6.14
1986	10	229.3	12.30	33.74	23.18	10.43	127.20
		4.3	0.68	0.47	0.32	0.41	6.98
Combined	23	234.2	10.74	34.33[b]	23.20[b]	10.73[b]	115.17[b]
		2.7	0.52	0.33	0.20	0.27	5.07
All samples	44	233.3	10.25	34.27[c]	23.23[c]	10.78[c]	110.98[c]
		1.8	0.35	0.22	0.15	0.20	3.58

Note: Upper number is the mean, and lower number is one standard error. Sizes are in mm, and masses are in g.

[a] N = 12.
[b] N = 22.
[c] N = 43.

rately; $\chi^2 = 9.872$, df $= 3$, $p = .0197$). The 1986 Dismal Swamp sample contained a significantly larger mean clutch size (Table 11.1) than the other three yearly samples.

Each measure of egg size and egg wet mass (Table 11.1) exhibited positive and significant relationships with plastron length (Fig. 11.1, Table 11.2). The amount of variation (r^2) explained by plastron length ranged from 18% to 29%. Analysis of covariance with plastron length as the covariate revealed no significant differences between populations or among years for egg length ($p = .801, .422$), egg width ($p = .758, .736$), or egg wet mass ($p = .468, .835$). Egg length (EL) decreased significantly as clutch size (CS) increased ($\bar{x}_{EL} = 36.78 - 0.244$ [CS], $r^2 = .151$, $p = .0101$). However, the relationships with clutch size were insignificant for egg width (EW; $p = .293$) and egg wet mass ($p = .066$). Egg wet mass (EWM) was positively and significantly related to egg length ($\bar{x}_{EWM} = -15.811 + 0.7780$ [EL], $r^2 = .741, p < .001, N = 43$) and egg width ($\bar{x}_{EWM} = -16.612 + 1.1793$ [EW], $r^2 = .7866, p < .001, N = 43$).

Total clutch wet mass was insignificantly related to plastron length (Table 11.2). Analysis of variance indicated that clutch wet mass (Table 11.1) did not differ significantly between populations ($F_{1,41} = 1.415$, $p = .2411$) but did differ significantly among years ($F_{1,39} = 3.010$, $p = .0416$). Tukey's Honestly Significant Difference test indicated ($\alpha = .05$) that only the 1986 Dismal Swamp sample was significantly different from the other yearly samples.

Females from both populations were found to produce multiple clutches, as evidenced by the presence of two distinct sets of corpora lutea on the ovaries. In Back Bay–False Cape, 94% of 17 females caught 11–25 June produced multiple clutches. Of 11 Dismal Swamp females caught 5–7 June, 36% produced multiple clutches.

GROWTH

Hatchlings from eggs maintained in the laboratory averaged 29.2 ± 0.38 mm PL (26–33 mm, $N = 120$). Plastron lengths of two hatchlings (28.6 mm, 30.6 mm) caught in Back Bay–False Cape while still showing umbilical scars agree well with this size range. Mean PL of sliders caught during their first year in the population was 57.4 ± 1.78 mm (46–71 mm, $N = 16$). Annual growth from ages 1 through 6 (Fig. 11.2) averaged 13.1 ± 2.15 mm PL. The largest sliders in each of ages 3 through 6 were immature females. Males age 5 and older that had plastron lengths greater than 100 mm were mature. The 8-year-old female was immature.

Discussion

BODY SIZE

Variation in body size of adult *T. scripta* among populations has been demonstrated by Cagle (1950), Moll and Legler (1971), Gibbons et al. (1979), and Gibbons et al.

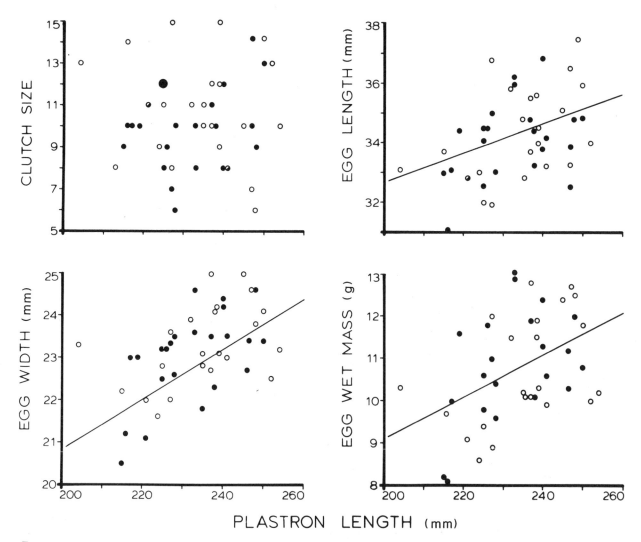

FIGURE 11.1. Relationships of clutch size, egg measurements, and egg wet mass with plastron length in *Trachemys scripta* from southeastern Virginia. Solid circles represent Back Bay–False Cape samples, and hollow circles represent samples from Dismal Swamp. The large circle represents two observations, and half-filled circles indicate identical measurements for both populations. Table 11.2 provides sample sizes and linear statistics for the regression lines.

(1982). In the eastern portion of its range, populations of large-bodied females have been associated with thermally influenced reservoirs (Gibbons, 1970b) and barrier islands (Gibbons et al., 1979). Thus, we had not expected to find large-bodied female *T. scripta* in both Back Bay–False Cape, which is a coastal barrier system, and Dismal

Swamp, an interior system. The range of body sizes for mature females in these two populations is most like that reported for Par Pond on the Savannah River Plant in South Carolina; it receives thermal effluent from a nuclear reactor (Gibbons, 1970b; Gibbons et al., 1979). The range of body sizes for mature males from the Back Bay–False

Table 11.2. Linear relationships of reproductive characteristics with female body size
(plastron length) in *Trachemys scripta* from southeastern Virginia

Characteristic	N	Intercept (SE)	Slope (SE)	r^2	p
Clutch size	44	8.605 (6.889)	0.0071 (.029)	.0014	.8122
Egg width	43	13.207 (2.617)	0.0429 (.012)	.2639	.0004
Egg length	43	22.935 (4.137)	0.0485 (.018)	.1550	.0090
Egg wet mass	43	-0.854 (3.624)	0.4977 (.016)	.2013	.0026
Clutch wet mass	43	-11.535 (71.647)	0.5241 (.306)	.0667	.0944

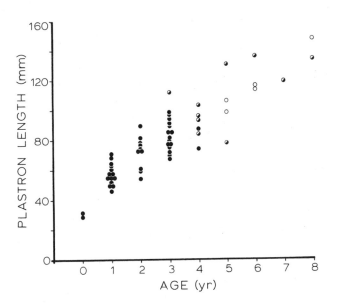

FIGURE 11.2.   Relationship of plastron length to age in *Trach-emys scripta* from the Back Bay–False Cape population in south-eastern Virginia. Open circles are males, half-shaded circles are females, and closed circles are unsexed individuals. Each age category indicates the year of growth.

Cape population is also most like that of the Par Pond population (Gibbons et al., 1979). If all freshwater ponds and impoundments in barrier ecosystems provide sliders with a source of high-protein food and if fish in the diet contribute to greater growth rates and body sizes (Par-menter, 1980), then the large sliders found in the Back Bay–False Cape barrier ecosystem are not unusual. Their somewhat smaller size range relative to sliders on South Carolina barrier islands is consistent with the prediction of Gibbons et al. (1979) that growth rates and body sizes "should diminish in a northerly direction due to progres-sively lower temperatures."

Why, however, are Dismal Swamp sliders equally as large as those in Back Bay–False Cape? There may be several possible explanations. The Dismal Swamp eco-system may be enriched by agricultural runoff, which may increase productivity and turtle food resources. However, such runoff contains pesticides, as well as nitrogen, and is limited to a small portion of the refuge (M. K. Garrett, pers. com.). First, sliders in Dismal Swamp occur in much lower densities than in Back Bay–False Cape (Mitchell and Pague, pers. obs.), so they may have similar amounts of energy available per individual. Second, our sample may be biased in favor of large females, although the refuge personnel assisted us in slider collection and re-ported none smaller. Another possibility is that Dismal Swamp sliders are simply older and thus larger. Third, we question whether there may be a genetic basis for faster growth rates and large body sizes in some populations. Could the sliders in Dismal Swamp have evolved from a

large-bodied lineage? Samples of large-bodied and small-bodied females in Congdon and Gibbons (1983) possessed different reproductive characteristics because of the varia-tion in body size. Although the sets of samples correspond well with environmental differences, it has not been proven that thermal enhancement and high-protein diet are the causes of large-bodied sliders. We have observed considerably less aquatic vegetation in Dismal Swamp than in Back Bay–False Cape and have found plant frag-ments in the feces of sliders from both areas. We do not know, however, if sliders in both populations eat similar amounts of protein. Comparative studies of growth re-lated to natural resource utilization, as well as com-parisons of the size structure of slider populations throughout southeastern North America, are needed to elucidate the causes of body size variation. In addition, experimental studies could provide insight into this question.

REPRODUCTIVE VARIATION

Until recently, descriptions of the relationships of re-productive characteristics to body size have been limited to clutch size and, for some, egg length (e.g., Moll and Legler, 1971; Iverson, 1977b). Because the suggestion that egg width may be closely related to the size of the female pelvic opening (Tucker et al., 1978), more-recent papers have examined the relationships of a variety of egg and clutch characteristics to body size (e.g., Congdon and Tinkle, 1982b; Congdon et al., 1983a; Mitchell, 1985a,b; Schwarzkopff and Brooks, 1986). Congdon and Gibbons (1985) demonstrated positive relationships of egg and clutch size within and among the 12 species studied, in-cluding *T. scripta*.

Clutch size has been shown to be positively related to body size in *T. scripta* by Gibbons (1970b), Moll and Legler (1971), Gibbons (1982), Gibbons et al. (1982), and Congdon and Gibbons (1983, 1985). Slider populations in Virginia more closely resemble sliders from Par Pond, South Carolina, in body size and clutch size than other populations studied by Gibbons and his co-workers. Al-though most of the papers noted above on South Carolina sliders combine large- and small-bodied population sam-ples, Gibbons et al. (1982) reported results for two popu-lations separately. The sample of large-bodied females from Par Pond exhibited a positive relationship of clutch size to plastron length, although only 12% of the variation was explained by the linear regression model. This con-trasts with the combined sample from southeastern Vir-ginia, which showed no significant relationship. Gibbons et al. (1982) suggested that their large sample size played a major role in demonstrating the subtle relationship.

Measurements of egg size (length and width) and egg wet mass were positively and significantly related to body size in both southeastern Virginia populations. Except for egg length, Congdon and Gibbons (1983) found similar results for a combined sample of large- and small-bodied *T. scripta* from South Carolina. In the Virginia populations there was a positive but insignificant relationship of total clutch wet mass with body size, even though egg size increased significantly with body size; a significant relationship was reported by Congdon and Gibbons (1983). Variation in egg number over the range of body sizes probably contributed to the insignificant relationship.

The applicability of optimal-egg-size theory (Smith and Fretwell, 1974; Brockleman, 1975) to freshwater turtles has been examined by Congdon and Tinkle (1982b), Congdon et al. (1983a), and Congdon and Gibbons (1985). They conclude that turtles appear to be exceptions to the prediction that variation in reproductive output should result from variation in egg number rather than in egg size. Our results for southeastern Virginia populations of *T. scripta* conform to the pattern being established for turtles. Our comparisons between Back Bay–False Cape and Dismal Swamp turtles suggest that reproductive investment in eggs and clutches is the same between these two populations, despite the differences in habitats described above.

GROWTH

Shapes of growth trajectories for those freshwater turtles exhibiting strong sexual size dimorphism (female larger), like *T. scripta* (Berry and Shine, 1980) tend to be similar. Growth is rapid early in life until maturity is reached, at which time growth slows but never completely stops (e.g., Wilbur, 1975b; Gibbons et al., 1981; Mitchell, 1982). Comparisons of the early growth curve for the Back Bay–False Cape population with the growth curves in Gibbons et al. (1981) suggest a trajectory that lies between those plotted for Par Pond and Ellenton Bay populations in South Carolina. Growth for juveniles between hatching and their first year in the population encompasses the entire range of variation shown in Gibbons et al. (1981) for this age group.

If growth trajectories for males and females continue to fall between those in Gibbons et al. (1981), then Back Bay–False Cape males should mature at 4 or 5 years of age, and females should mature at about age 8 but at sizes intermediate to those in Par Pond and Ellenton Bay. Our results suggest that the projection is correct for males. We had insufficient data to confirm age at maturity for females.

Our study of *Trachemys scripta* in Virginia leads to two conclusions. Studies of reproductive variation should be conducted over several years so that variation among yearly samples is taken into account. Our difficulty in ascertaining why Dismal Swamp sliders are as large-bodied as those in Back Bay–False Cape and those in Par Pond, South Carolina, suggests that we should be cautious about using only a few comparisons as the basis of generalizations about the causes of such traits. The question is, how many populations must be studied before we can make such generalizations?

Acknowledgments

We are grateful to Back Bay National Wildlife Refuge, Dismal Swamp National Wildlife Refuge, and the Virginia Division of Parks and Recreation for issuing permits to collect and study turtles. Numerous park and refuge personnel assisted in a variety of ways, even catching some turtles for us. We are grateful to Allen Hundley, Russ Landis, Bonnie Larson, Don Merkle, Wendy Mitchell, Ted Turner, and David Young for assistance in the field. Wendy Mitchell also helped measure turtle eggs. This study was supported by funds from the Nongame Wildlife and Endangered Species Program of the Virginia Commission of Game and Inland Fisheries. We thank Justin D. Congdon and Edward O. Moll for comments on the manuscript.

DON MOLL
Department of Biology
Southwest Missouri State University
Springfield, Missouri 65804

EDWARD O. MOLL
Zoology Department
Eastern Illinois University
Charleston, Illinois 61920

The Slider Turtle in the Neotropics: Adaptation of a Temperate Species to a Tropical Environment

Abstract

The slider turtle, *Pseudemys scripta*, is a polytypic species of North Temperate origin that has established itself widely in the American tropics. Flexible in habitat and dietary requirements, tropical sliders generally grow larger than temperate ones because of longer growing seasons and year-long productivity of warm tropical environments, but growth processes are similar. Tropical sliders have greater reproductive potentials, larger eggs, and longer nesting seasons than temperate sliders, but characteristics and timing of gonadal cycles are similar. Available reproductive data concerning Old World batagurines suggest that tropical sliders have not evolved reproductive strategies similar to their closest tropical aquatic and semiaquatic relatives. Available evidence suggests the likelihood that tropical races of *P. scripta* are Pleistocene immigrants into the tropics and that their successful establishment and rapid dispersal are more attributable to generalized habits than to specific adaptations to tropical environments.

Introduction

Pseudemys scripta is a polytypic species of temperate origin that ranges from southern Michigan in the United States, sporadically through the American tropics, and, if neo-temperate forms are conspecific (Carr, 1952), across the Tropic of Capricorn into temperate Argentina—the most extensive range of any nonmarine chelonian. The obvious success of this turtle in coping with the diverse array of environmental conditions encountered over such a vast range makes its ecology and biogeography of considerable interest.

The lowlands of the American tropics are commonly viewed as the stronghold of the specialist, with available niches filled to capacity by a multiplicity of species (Pritchard and Trebbau, 1984). Under such circumstances the chances for successful colonization by a generalized, temperate-adapted species would seem slight indeed. However, the late Cenozoic was a period of extensive, rapid, and repeated environmental and geological change in the Neotropics, when specialized, resident species may have been at a disadvantage—and particularly vulnerable because of the linkage of the continents via the Panamanian isthmus. Many northern vertebrate species, including *Pseudemys scripta*, successfully invaded and established themselves in the tropics at this time (e.g., see Simpson, 1950; Myers, 1966; Savage, 1966; Duellman, 1979; Pritchard and Trebbau, 1984). Slider turtles, in fact, probably dispersed into the Neotropics as recently as the Pleistocene (Savage, 1966). The objective of this chapter is to examine the ecology of this species in its modern tropical habitats and elucidate its successful strategy for survival as a component of the modern Neotropical fauna. This will entail comparing the ecology of Neotropical sliders with that of North Temperate slider populations that presumably possess the ancestral traits of the group, as well as with that of other emydids known to have had a long-term evolution in the tropics. These comparisons may lead to a better understanding of the degree to which a generalized ecology or specific adaptation to tropical environments explains a population's successful colonization of the American tropics.

Realization of these objectives is hampered by the dearth of studies and information concerning the ecology of *Pseudemys scripta* in the American tropics. The early naturalist-explorers of the Neotropics were mainly collectors, and the work resulting from their collections was largely taxonomic in nature. An exception is provided by the observations of Sumichrast in 1880 and 1882 (summarized in Smith and Smith, 1979) concerning the natural history of *P. s. grayi* in habitats on the Pacific slope of Mexico's Isthmus of Tehuantepec. Breder (1946) provided some ecological information concerning *P. scripta* in the Río Chucunaque drainage of Darien, Panama. The most extensive study of Neotropical slider turtles to date, and the foundation of the conclusions presented in this chapter, was conducted from March 1964 through July 1968 (including field studies conducted on the Río Chagres at Juan Mina, Panama Canal Zone, July 1965–August 1966) by Moll and Legler (1971). Other information concerning Mexican and Central American slider ecology is available in the work of Casas-Andreu (1967), Smith and Smith (1979), Alvarez del Toro (1982), and Vogt (see Chapter 13) for Mexico, and Drummond (1983) and D. Moll (1986) for Central America. The ecology of South American populations has received attention from Medem (1962, 1975) and Pritchard and Trebbau (1984).

Present Distribution in the Tropics

The slider turtle's distribution in the tropics is sporadic from the Tropic of Cancer southward through Mexico and Central America along the Gulf, Caribbean, and Pacific coasts (Moll and Legler, 1971; Smith and Smith, 1979). Sliders may be encountered wherever suitable habitat becomes available (see Habitat Requirements, below; for Mexican range maps, see Smith and Smith, 1979). *Pseudemys scripta nebulosa*, also technically a tropical slider at the southern tip of its range, inhabits pools in intermittent streams of Baja California. Subspecific designations for these populations are unclear in some cases and have been discussed in some detail by Moll and Legler (1971), Smith and Smith (1979), and Pritchard and Trebbau (1984). Legler (see Chapter 7) provides a more recent analysis. In tropical South America this species' distribution pattern is discontinuous with populations in Colombia, Venezuela, Brazil, and possibly Paraguay and Bolivia. South Temperate populations exist in Argentina and Uruguay, although some investigators consider these a separate species, *P. dorbigni*. Pritchard and Trebbau (1984) discuss their distribution, zoogeography, and taxonomy in detail.

Habitat Requirements of Tropical Sliders

Moll and Legler (1971) have described ideal habitat for tropical sliders as follows: (1) relatively large, permanent, slow-moving or lotic bodies of water with associated backwaters or small tributaries, (2) large amounts of aquatic vegetation, especially submergent, (3) periodic open or cleared areas in fringing forest (as opposed to solid forest), and (4) abundant basking sites. The lack of one or more of these requirements does not necessarily exclude *P. scripta* from a particular habitat, however, as their tolerance of variation is broad indeed. Tropical sliders may be encountered almost anywhere there is permanent water, and dense populations may exist in apparently barren habitats containing limited resources. Moll and Legler (1971) described one such population from a small muddy Panamanian pond where there was essentially no aquatic vegetation or basking sites and where mud was the primary food source. At the other extreme, sliders may live in brackish-water habitats such as mangrove swamps and estuaries, as observed by J. M. Legler and J. L. Christiansen in Mexico and by Legler in Honduras (Moll and Legler, 1971).

Unbroken rain forest seems to be one of the most difficult habitats for *P. scripta* to colonize, probably because of the difficulty in finding suitable (i.e., relatively open) nesting sites (Moll and Legler, 1971; Pritchard and Trebbau, 1984). Even so, a few rain-forest populations exist in Central America. Pritchard and Trebbau (1984) presented evidence that some of these populations may be using sea beaches as nesting sites in a fashion similar to that of the Asian beach-nesting emydid *Callagur borneoensis* (Dunson and Moll, 1980), but there is not yet enough information to determine the extent of this behavior in *P. scripta* or the degree of success in hatching or hatchling survival from such nests. If this behavior is truly a genetically fixed population characteristic, then it may be considered a real adaptation to a tropical habitat, because beach nesting is unknown in temperate populations. Alternatively, beach nesting may simply be another example of flexibility allowing *P. scripta* to cope with unfavorable habitats or environmental conditions.

Tropical *P. scripta* appear to benefit from certain types of habitat alteration. Moll and Legler (1971) considered the Río Chagres to be better habitat for sliders after dams slowed and widened the river than before they were built about 1910. Also, populations occurring in forested areas of Panama nested only in areas such as golf courses and abandoned citrus groves, whereas nesting and nests were never observed in dense forest. This is supported by the observation of Breder (1946) that Río Chucunaque populations nested only in areas devoid of vegetation cover. Open areas near aquatic habitats seem to be as close to an inflexible habitat requirement as any possessed by *P. scripta*.

Within a given habitat, juveniles and adults are segregated to some extent (Moll and Legler, 1971; D. Moll, 1986). Three main microhabitats were identified in Moll and Legler's study area in Panama. Hatchlings were generally restricted to the edge of floating mats of grass in lagoons and backwaters of the Río Chagres, larger juveniles were associated with open, lotic situations where thick mats of submergent vegetation were prevalent, and sexually mature adults were in fluviatile portions of the river, associated with mats of *Elodea*. *Pseudemys scripta* studied in a slow-moving stream in Belize by D. Moll (1986) displayed similar ontogenetic preferences.

With the exception of the possible beach-nesting behavior in some tropical sliders, there is essentially nothing in the literature to indicate any particularly unique adaptations in habitat usage in the tropics. The description of ideal tropical slider habitat by Moll and Legler (1971) could as easily characterize ideal temperate slider habitat as well (see Carr, 1952; Ernst and Barbour, 1972; Morreale and Gibbons, 1986). Furthermore, temperate sliders can exist and even thrive in such barren habitats as roadside ditches and stock ponds (Cagle, 1950), desert streams (Carr, 1952; Smith and Smith, 1979), and polluted rivers (Moll, 1977). Similar ontogenetic shifts in habitat usage are also known in temperate *P. scripta* populations (Moll, 1977; Hart, 1983). The generalized behavior and broad habitat tolerance of this species, without specific genetically fixed adaptations to local conditions, have probably been key factors in its successful exploitation of the tropics.

Size and Growth in Tropical Sliders

Mean and maximum sizes attained by sliders vary within and among populations, presumably depending upon both environmental and genetic factors. Usually, tropical and subtropical populations attain greater body size than those of temperate regions (Pritchard and Trebbau, 1984). Populations of particularly large individuals occur along the Caribbean drainage of Central America, with some females exceeding 400 mm in carapace length (Pritchard and Trebbau, 1984). D. Moll (pers. obs.) found 188 adult females in a northern Belize stream to have a mean plastron length of 292.2 mm (332 mm maximum) and 152 adult males to have a mean plastron length of 180.6 mm (301 mm maximum). Moll and Legler (1971) recorded the largest female in their Río Chagres study area at 352 mm carapace length (CL) and 345 mm plastron length (PL), and the largest male at 342 mm CL and 304 mm PL. Tropical South American subspecies do not seem to be as large. Pritchard and Trebbau (1984) measured 14 unsexed *P. s. chichiriviche* from a lake in Venezuela that ranged from 185 to 305 mm PL and 195 to 325 mm CL. The authors stated that this subspecies is larger than *P. s. callirostris*. Colombian females attaining 300 mm CL and males reaching 252 mm CL were reported by Medem (1975). Most females (190–240 mm CL) and males (150–200 mm CL) were smaller, however. Average adult size may have diminished because of overexploitation of adults for human consumption (Medem, 1975; Pritchard and Trebbau, 1984).

Growth cycles and possible factors influencing growth in Río Chagres sliders were studied by Moll and Legler (1971). Hatchlings begin to grow after reaching the water and beginning to eat. Growth is rapid in the years prior to sexual maturity, then slows markedly with age. Juvenile females and males grow at about the same rate until the third year, when most males approach sexual maturity and their growth slows markedly. Females continue to grow rapidly through their third and fourth years, but growth declines markedly by their fifth year as some reach maturity. Sexual maturity is attained by males around 125–135 mm PL in two to four years and by females around 240–260 mm PL in five to seven years. D. Moll (pers. obs.) found Belizean *P. scripta* males to mature at about 130 mm PL in three to four years, and females at 248 mm PL in six to seven years. Attainment of sexual maturity has a marked effect on growth rate and ultimate size in *P. scripta*, because males not only mature sooner but also remain smaller than females, on the average, throughout life. In the population studied by Moll and Legler (1971) only 1% of adult males exceeded 300 mm PL, whereas 32% of adult females were over that size. Only 18% of the males attained the minimum size at which females reached puberty (240 mm PL). Adult growth in both sexes was characteristically slow and irregular, with indications (from fusion of plastral scutes) that growth may begin to cease in females exceeding 300 mm PL. No evidence for growth cessation in males exists, and the largest male that Moll and Legler captured (304 mm PL) showed a narrow zone of new growth.

Even though air and water temperature, food supplies, and photoperiod were nearly constant throughout the year, Río Chagres sliders displayed cyclic growth (Moll and Legler, 1971). Some growth in juveniles occurred in all months but was slowest during the rainy season (August–November), increased in December, and was relatively rapid throughout the dry season and early wet season (January–July). Growth rings formed whenever growth slowed or stopped. Moll and Legler determined that this usually occurred during periods of heavy rain and flooding, when sliders probably became inactive and did not feed. Juvenile growth was directly correlated with amount of sunlight available on a daily basis. Most adults did not grow during periods of maximal reproductive activity, when energy may be diverted from shell growth to gametogenesis or searching for mates.

Although mean and maximum sizes attained in tropical slider populations are usually larger than those attained in temperate populations, overall patterns of growth are similar (Cagle, 1946, 1948a, 1950; Webb, 1961; Moll, 1977). Growth is very responsive to environmental phenomena such as water temperature and food supply (Cagle, 1946, 1948a, 1950; Webb, 1961; Gibbons, 1970b; Avalos, 1975; Moll, 1977), and growth rings are formed when growth temporarily ceases. Growth is cyclic in temperate populations (Cagle, 1950) even if activity is continuous, as in southern springs (Jackson, 1964). The obvious difference between temperate and tropical populations is that opportunities for growth cease entirely when winter's cold temperatures force temperate populations into hibernation, limiting the growing season to a relatively short period of the year for most populations.

Food Habits of Tropical Sliders

Tropical sliders are opportunistic feeders, normally eating a combination of plant and animal foods, the exact composition of which is largely dictated by size and sex of the turtles, and the food sources available in the particular habitat. Tropical sliders are capable of surviving almost anywhere by feeding on almost anything. In prime habitat, aquatic plants are an important component of the diet. In the Río Chagres, plants—especially waterweed (*Elodea* sp.) and grass (*Paspalum* sp.)—composed 93% of the total volume of food consumed by adults (Moll and Legler, 1971). Animal food was present in the gut contents of nearly half of the adults (49%), but it composed only of 7% of total volume. Animal prey consisted mainly of insects, carrion fish, and gastropods, the latter possibly ingested largely as a calcium supplement for gravid females.

Juveniles were more carnivorous than adults, but animal food still composed only 19% of their total food volume. D. Moll (1986) found that *P. scripta venusta* females in a heavily vegetated stream of northern Belize were omnivorous, ingesting large amounts of grass (*Paspalum peniculatum*), but animal food, mainly insects, made up nearly 31% of their food volume. Adult males were more insectivorous than females but still ate large amounts of plant material. Juveniles were almost entirely insectivorous. Moll and Legler (1971) found that *P. scripta* changed principal dietary components opportunistically, depending on availability. Flexibility is demonstrated by the presence of a dense population in a small muddy pond in which organic mud (or perhaps blue-green algae on mud) was the major dietary component, followed by roots and leaves from grasses on the pond margins and minute amounts of animal matter (Moll and Legler, 1971). Pritchard and Trebbau (1984) considered Venezuelan *P. scripta* to be equally flexible and opportunistic in diet, with one population (*P. s. callirostris*) known to prey on swimming waterfowl, and another population (*P. s. chichiriviche*) developing a macrocephalic condition often associated with molluscivory. Other dietary analyses and fragmentary data available concerning tropical populations confirm that *P. scripta* is opportunistic and omnivorous over its entire range (Moll and Legler, 1971). This flexibility helps to explain why sliders are successful over such a wide diversity of environments and habitats within their range.

Feeding habits of temperate *P. scripta* populations have been relatively well studied and can be described as essentially identical to those described above for tropical populations (see Cahn, 1937; Cagle, 1950; Carr, 1952; Webb, 1961; Ernst and Barbour, 1972; Moll, 1977). All populations are omnivorous, relying heavily on plant material but taking animal material whenever available. Some populations exist in barren and polluted habitats where little food other than that which is blown or washed into the water is available (Minyard, 1947; Cagle, 1950; Moll, 1977). Cagle (1944b) reported that *P. scripta* will forage for terrestrial vegetation on land, returning to water to swallow. Temperate juvenile *P. scripta* are characteristically more carnivorous than adults in most populations, and ontogenetic shifts in degree of carnivory (toward greater herbivory) occur (Clark and Gibbons, 1969; Hart, 1983).

Reproduction in Tropical Sliders

MATING BEHAVIOR

Moll and Legler (1971) observed attempts at copulation by sliders in August, September, and October in the Río Chagres and assumed that mating also occurred between January and June because of a progressive reduction in sperm levels in the epididymides and lipid levels in the interstitial cells of the testes during this period. The similarity of the timing of the male reproductive cycle in Panama to that of temperate males, which have spring and fall mating peaks (Cagle, 1950), also suggests that peaks of breeding activity may be similar. Medem (1975) reported that Colombian *P. s. callirostris* mate from September through December. Copulation usually occurs in quiet deep water (Moll and Legler, 1971; Medem, 1975) and takes only two to three minutes to complete (Medem, 1975). Available evidence indicates little or no elaborate precopulatory behavior in tropical sliders in comparison with temperate populations (Rosado, 1967; Moll and Legler, 1971; Medem, 1975).

REPRODUCTIVE CYCLE OF MALES

Moll and Legler (1971) found that testes are smallest and lightest from early January through May and are largest and heaviest from early July through December in Panamanian *P. scripta*. Epididymides enlarge later than the testes and remain enlarged well after testicular regression. In Panama, seasonal changes in size of testes are associated with the male's spermatogenic cycle. Spermatogenesis begins in May, when spermatogonia begin to proliferate in the seminiferous tubules, and Sertoli cells become less numerous. In June, spermatogonia predominate, primary spermatocytes are present, and in some males secondary spermatocytes, spermatids, and a few metamorphosed sperm are already present. Spermiogenesis is under way in July, and all spermatogenic and spermiogenic stages are well represented. Spermatogenesis continues from August through November, filling the lumina of most tubules with mature sperm. The spermatogenic cycle is completed about a month earlier in smaller males (below 190 mm PL) than in larger males, which may continue producing sperm until early December. The germinal epithelium is inactive from January through May (the Panamanian dry season). The epididymides begin receiving sperm in August, receiving peak amounts by January. Although some sperm are present all year, they reach their lowest level in the epididymides in June and July, possibly because of expenditure during the spring mating season. The spermatogenic cycle of male *P. scripta* in Panama does not differ appreciably in detail or timing from that of North Temperate *P. scripta* and other North Temperate chelonians that have been studied (see Moll, 1979, for a summary of male cycles and other references). Data concerning the reproductive characteristics of South Temperate populations are too sparse for meaningful comparisons.

REPRODUCTIVE CYCLE OF FEMALES

Moll and Legler (1971) divided the ovarian cycle of tropical sliders into four phases: (1) follicular enlargement, (2)

ovulation and intrauterine period, (3) oviposition, and (4) a period of quiescence, during which the ovaries are small and follicular development is minimal. Follicular enlargement begins in late August and September (the latter half of the rainy season), and follicles reach ovulatory size in late November and December in the Río Chagres population. Follicular development is continuous until late May, with large follicles ovulating while the next-largest class of follicles enlarge and become preovulatory. Follicular activity and ovarian weights are greatest from early January through March. In April and May the size and number of enlarging follicles and ovarian weights decrease markedly. Ovulatory-sized follicles disappear by late April. The ovaries are quiescent from June through July, when activity and weights are minimal. Ovarian cycles of *P. scripta* in Mexico and elsewhere in Central America are similar to those described above for the Panamanian population, but ovulation and oviposition probably begin and end later in more northern latitudes (Moll and Legler, 1971). The timing of the ovarian cycle of tropical sliders does not greatly differ from that observed in North Temperate emydids (see Moll, 1979, for a summary of cycles and other references). The most conspicuous difference lies in the constraints imposed by the shorter activity period of temperate species, resulting in greater crowding of the steps in the cycle (Moll and Legler, 1971).

REPRODUCTIVE CHARACTERISTICS OF TROPICAL POPULATIONS

The reproductive patterns of the tropical slider populations that have been investigated are remarkably similar (Table 12.1). Populations in Panama, Colombia, Venezuela, Mexico, Nicaragua, and Belize produce multiple (up to 6) clutches of 5 to 30 small (in relation to female body size), oblong, leathery-shelled eggs in flask-shaped cavities dug in relatively open sites during an extended spring nesting season. The eggs take between two and three months to hatch. The nesting seasons in most populations correspond with the dry seasons in their respective habitats, and the hatchlings tend to emerge with the onset of the rainy seasons. In Colombian *P. s. callirostris* and Venezuelan *P. s. chichiriviche* there is some possibility of a secondary nesting season in August (Medem, 1975; Pritchard and Trebbau, 1984). Although the data upon which these generalizations are based are limited for many tropical populations (and there are no data at all for many populations), they support the conclusions of the more extensive studies of Moll and Legler (1971) in Panama and of Medem (1975) in Colombia. These studies suggest a common reproductive strategy for extant slider populations across the Neotropics that is similar to that of temperate, presumably ancestral slider populations and is drastically different from that of many other tropical turtle species.

Table 12.1. Reproductive data concerning tropical sliders (*Pseudemys scripta*)

Location/subspecies	Reference	Eggs per clutch	Clutches per year	Egg characteristics (sizes in mm)	Nest characteristics	Incubation period (days)	Nesting season
Pacific coast of Isthmus of Tehuantepec, Mexico/ *grayi*	4	16-18	--	Oblong, oval, 16 × 45	--	--	Mar.
Atlantic drainage, Chiapas/ Mexico/*venusta*	5	12-20	--	Elongate, ≈25 × 40	Communal, flask-shaped, ≈200 mm deep	--	Jan.-Apr.
Pacific drainage, Chiapas/ *grayi*	5	10-20	--	--	On beaches of rivers and lakes	≈90	Feb.-Apr.
Atlantic drainage, Chiapas/ *venusta*	8	5-21	1-3	--	--	--	Feb.-May
Corozal district, Belize/ *venusta*	7	8-20	2-3	Oblong, leathery, flexible, ≈28.0 × 41.0	Flask-shaped cavity in fields	--	Feb.-May
Lake Nicaragua, Nicaragua/ subspecies unclear	2	$\bar{X}$ = 20 (15-25)	--	--	--	--	--
Río Chagres, Panama Canal Zone/subspecies unclear, possibly *venusta*	2	$\bar{X}$ = 17 (9-25)	1-6	Oblong, leathery, flexible, $\bar{X}$ = 42.2 × 28.8	Communal, sealed flask-shaped cavity	71-86	Dec.-May
Department of Chocó, Colombia/ subspecies unclear, possibly *venusta*	1	12-24	--	--	--	--	--
Northwestern Venezuela and northern Colombia/ *callirostris*	3,6	9-30	2-3	Oblong, soft-shelled, flexible, 21 × 27 to 26 × 41	Flask-shaped, maximum dimensions (mm) = 180 deep × 110 wide at entrance × 130 wide at base	69-92	Colombia: Dec.-Apr., perhaps a second season in Aug. Venezuela: Apr.-June principal season.
Northern Venezuela/ *chichiriviche*	6	11-28	--	--	--	--	Uncertain

References: 1, Medem, 1962; 2, Moll and Legler, 1971; 3, Medem, 1975; 4, Sumichrast, in Smith and Smith, 1979; 5, Alvarez del Toro, 1982; 6, Pritchard and Trebbau, 1984; 7, D. Moll, pers. obs.; 8, see Chapter 13.

Temperate and tropical slider populations would be characterized as possessing Pattern I reproductive strategies (Moll, 1979). This is a primitive pattern in which large, multiple clutches of relatively small, soft-shelled eggs are produced during a well-defined nesting season. Nesting occurs in well-defined areas, and nests are carefully constructed and sealed. Several other large freshwater and marine tropical genera have also evolved toward Pattern I strategies (e.g., *Batagur*, *Chelonia*, *Dermochelys*, *Podocnemis*, *Trionyx*). Alternately, many other tropical species that are smaller, aquatic and semiaquatic to terrestrial, and often morphologically specialized (e.g., *Cuora*, *Cyclemys*, *Kinosternon*, *Rhinoclemmys*) have evolved toward Pattern II reproductive strategies (Moll, 1979). Pattern II strategies entail the production of small clutches of relatively large, hard-shelled eggs, acyclic or year-round reproduction, solitary nesting with no special nest area, and nests poorly constructed or not even attempted (Moll, 1979). Although both strategies are successful, as evidenced by their recurrence in extant populations, Moll (1979) and Moll and Legler (1971) considered Pattern II as an advanced trait evolving in conjunction with trends toward smaller size and increasing specialization, and associated with long-term tropical residency. Two very old members of the Neotropical fauna (i.e., present by early to mid-Pliocene), *Kinosternon leucostomum* and *Rhinoclemmys funerea* (Savage, 1966), were studied in detail by Moll and Legler (1971) to provide comparisons with tropical *P. scripta* in Panama (Table 12.2). The oldest tropical resident of the three, *K. leucostomum*, whose genus is a member of the Middle American Element of Savage (1966), has the most extreme reproductive Pattern II, and the emydid *R. funerea*, whose genus, like *Pseudemys*, is a member of the Old Northern Element (Savage, 1966) but probably a much earlier tropical immigrant, has a reproductive pattern nearly as extreme toward Pattern II as *K. leucostomum*. Panamanian *P. scripta*, already considered a recent immigrant based upon biogeographic evidence

Table 12.2. Comparison of life history of *Pseudemys scripta elegans* in the United States and three species of turtles in Panama

Characteristic	*Pseudemys scripta elegans*, United States	*Pseudemys scripta*, Panama	*Rhinoclemmys funerea*, Panama	*Kinosternon leucostomum*, Panama
Size at sexual maturity (PL in mm)	90-100, male; 150-195, female	125-135, male; 240-260, female	≈200, male; ≈200, female	≈100, male; ≈80, female
Male gonadal cycle	Spermatogenesis in late spring and summer; spermiogenesis in fall; germinal epithelium quiescent in winter	Spermatogenesis begins in May and June; spermiogenesis July-Dec.; germinal epithelium quiescent Jan.-May	Cyclic; periods of gonadal quiescence short; spermatogenesis July-early May	Cyclic; periods of gonadal quiescence short; spermatogenesis and spermiogenesis in most months
Female gonadal cycle	Follicles begin enlarging autumn (Aug.?); ovulation late Apr.-late July	Follicles begin enlarging in lateAug. or Sept., mature in Dec.; ovulation late Dec.-May	Beginning of cycle unknown; ovulation at least Apr.-Aug.; most specimens from Aug. in postreproductive state	Continuous as a population; some individuals ovulating each month
Mean size of eggs (mm)	Leathery, flexible, oblong; $\bar{X} = 36.2 \times 21.6$ (Ill.), 37.7×22.6 (La.)	Leathery, flexible, oblong; $\bar{X} = 42.2 \times 28.8$	Hard, brittle shell; oblong; $\bar{X} = 68 \times 35$	Hard, brittle shell; oblong; $\bar{X} = 37.1 \times 19.4$
Mean size of hatchlings (mm)	32.8 PL, 34.2 CL; $N = 7$	35.2 PL, 36.5 CL; $N = 42$	58.5 PL, 64.0 CL; $N = 3$	25.6 PL, 32.7 CL; $N = 3$
Eggs per clutch	4-18, $\bar{X} = 9$ (Ill.); 2-19, $\bar{X} = 7$ (La.)	9-25, $\bar{X} = 17$	1-6, $\bar{X} = 3$	1-2; 1 more common
Clutches per season	1-3	1-6	1-4	Multiple
Nest	Communal; sealed flask-shaped cavity in ground	Communal; sealed flask-shaped cavity in ground	Solitary; probably no nest; eggs laid at surface and covered with leaf litter	Solitary; shallow nest, or eggs laid at surface and covered with leaf litter
Incubation period	67-79 days (24°-30° C)	71-86 days (20°-33° C)	98-104 days (≈20°-35° C)	126-148 days (20°-33° C)
Food habits	Opportunistic; omnivorous to vegetarian; feeds chiefly in water	Opportunistic; herbivorous when aquatic plants are plentiful; feeds only in water	Opportunistic; chiefly herbivorous; feeds equally well in and out of water	Opportunistic; omnivorous (snails, insects, aquatic plants); probably feeds only in water
Growth cycle	Cyclic; May-Oct. (Ill.); Apr.-mid-Nov. (La.)	Cyclic; greatest Jan.-Aug.; least Aug.-Dec.	Cyclic, but periods of growth unknown	Cyclic, but periods of growth unknown

Source: Modified from Moll and Legler, 1971.
Abbreviations: CL, carapace length; PL, plastron length.

discussed by Savage (1966), is further implicated in this regard by the great contrast between its reproductive pattern and that of the old tropical residents above, and by the great similarity of its pattern with that of its close temperate relatives, such as *P. s. elegans* (Table 12.2). Although ecological data concerning tropical *Terrapene* are too sparse for meaningful comparison, comparisons are possible between tropical slider populations and some Old World tropical species.

Other than the emydine genera *Pseudemys* and *Terrapene*, all members of the family Emydidae inhabiting the tropics belong to the subfamily Batagurinae. Considering that the greatest diversity of batagurines occurs in the Old World tropics of the oriental region, it is likely that the area has been both a major and an ancient center of evolution for the group. Most genera found in this region today are restricted to the tropics or at least the subtropics. Presumably then, life history traits shared by the majority

of this group, including the Neotropical representatives of the genus *Rhinoclemmys*, can logically be considered adaptations to a tropical environment.

In regard to reproduction, those batagurines for which we have knowledge (*Batagur, Callagur, Cuora amboinensis, Cyclemys dentata, Geoemyda silvatica, Kachuga, Melanochelys trijuga, Rhinoclemmys funerea,* and *Siebenrockiella*) appear to have seasonal sexual cycles correlated with rainy and dry seasons. However, some *Rhinoclemmys* may lay eggs throughout the year (see Medem, 1962; Pritchard and Trebbau, 1984). Perhaps the most distinctive feature of their reproduction is their tendency to produce exceptionally large, oblong eggs. Largest are the eggs of *Orlitia borneensis*, which average 79 mm × 43 mm and weigh around 100 g each. Another distinctive feature of the eggs of most batagurine species (particularly forest-dwelling forms) is their thick, brittle shell. This shell effectively makes these eggs independent of the hydric environment

Table 12.3. Mean reproductive specifications of selected batagurine emydids and temperate and tropical populations of the emydid *Pseudemys scripta*

Species	Locality	N	CL (mm)	Body mass (kg)	Clutch Size	Clutch Mass (g)	Egg length × width (mm)	EMI	RCM
Batagur baska	Malaysia	40	488	17.9	26	1,694	66 × 40	0.36	0.095
Callagur borneoensis	Malaysia	75	466	16.8	11	799	70 × 41	0.42	0.05
Cuora amboinensis	Malaysia	2	175	1.00	1	19.5	47 × 26	1.95	0.02
Cyclemys dentata	Malaysia	2	200	1.25	3	89.1	56 × 29	2.30	0.07
Heosemys spinosa	Malaysia	1	186	0.95	1	48.7	65 × 35	5.10	0.05
Kachuga dhongoka	India	2	420	7.27	23	809	57 × 36	0.52	0.11
K. kachuga	India	1	560	21.10	17	940	64 × 40	0.26	0.044
K. tentoria	India	8	225	1.56	6	126	49 × 27	1.38	0.08
Melanochelys trijuga	India	1	175	0.76	3	45	44 × 22	1.98	0.06
Orlitia borneensis	Malaysia	2	475	12.40	12	1,132	79 × 43	0.70	0.09
Rhinoclemmys punctularia	Panama	1	243	2.70	5	187	52 × 34	1.4	0.07
Siebenrockiella crasscollis	Malaysia	3	186	0.94	1.3	37	52 × 30	3.0	0.04
Pseudemys scripta	Central United States	16	225	1.20	12	116	36 × 22	0.95	0.11
	Panama	8	333	4.20	20	421	43 × 28	0.49	0.10

Abbreviations: CL, carapace length; EMI, egg mass index; RCM, relative clutch mass.

(M. Packard et al., 1982) and hence possibly adapted to the high moisture content of tropical forest soils. With desiccation-resistant eggs, at least some batagurines have been able to abandon the traditional behavior of digging nests in the root-ridden, often waterlogged soils of the tropical forest in favor of placing their clutches in leaf litter and other protected sites at the surface (e.g., certain *Rhinoclemmys*; see Medem, 1962, and Pritchard and Trebbau, 1984). Eggs with brittle shells are probably also adaptive in repelling attacks by the profusion of ants and microbes inhabiting moist tropical forests. In support of this hypothesis, it is significant that the only batagurines known to lack brittle-shelled eggs are riverine species (*Batagur, Callagur,* and *Kachuga*), which typically nest on exposed sandbanks.

Table 12.3 summarizes reproductive characteristics of a selection of Malaysian and Indian batagurines. Clutch size varies widely within the group, but 1 to 3 large eggs are common for the smaller species, whereas clutches exceeding 20 eggs are found only in a few large riverine forms such as *Batagur* and *Kachuga dhongoka*. Body size is not necessarily a good predictor of clutch size in batagurines, because certain large species such as *Orlitia, Callagur,* and *Kachuga kachuga* lay relatively small clutches.

Although a thorough examination of batagurine reproductive strategies is impossible because of a lack of ecological data on most species, a general comparison of the reproductive output of certain species is possible and provides some insight into how batagurines have adapted to the tropical environment. Two instructive statistics are egg mass index (EMI) and relative clutch mass (RCM). EMI and RCM respectively measure the size of the egg and the size of the clutch relative to the body size of the female turtle. EMI is the weight of the egg divided by the

weight of the spent female multiplied by 100. RCM, modified from the usage of Vitt and Price (1982), is the clutch mass divided by the body mass of the spent female.

Relative to their body size, small turtles put a proportionately greater investment into each egg than do large turtles. Consequently the EMI is negatively correlated with the size of the female. Figure 12.1 shows the regression of a logarithmic plot of the EMIs on carapace length for the 12 tropical and subtropical batagurine species listed in Table 12.3. The mean EMI for 16 sliders from the central United States (solid circle) and for 8 Panamanian sliders (open circle) are shown. This graph supports the idea that the temperate-adapted sliders put a much lower energy investment into individual eggs than do comparably sized batagurines (both slider plots fall below the 95% confidence limits of the regression line). Tropical sliders show no convergence toward the batagurine condition. In fact, a line drawn between the EMI plots of temperate and tropical populations parallels the batagurine line, suggesting that the EMI–body size relationship is the same in batagurines and emydines.

The RCM presents a more confusing picture. Small batagurines (less than 30 cm CL) have low RCMs (0.02 to 0.08). The larger species show a dichotomy, with *Batagur, Kachuga dhongoka,* and *Orlitia* having high RCMs (greater than 0.09), whereas *Callagur* and *Kachuga kachuga* have relatively low RCMs (0.05 or less). These large differences in RCM, at least between *Batagur* and *Callagur,* may be related to a higher degree of density-independent mortality in the former (E. Moll, 1986a). Despite rather large differences in the EMI, the temperate and tropical slider populations used for comparison do not differ significantly with respect to RCM (0.11 and 0.10). Relative to batagurines of comparable body size, the slider popula-

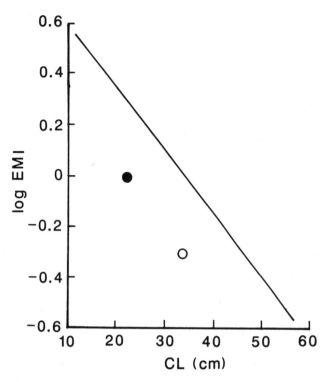

FIGURE 12.1.   Regression of egg mass index (EMI) on carapace length (CL) in 12 tropical and subtropical batagurine emydids. The solid circle represents the EMI of 16 sliders from central Illinois; the open circle, the EMI of 8 Panamanian sliders. The regression line is calculated by this formula: log EMI = 0.8506 − 0.02524(CL in cm).

tions have larger RCMs. From these data, one could conclude that *Pseudemys* expend less energy on individual eggs but put more into a clutch than do the batagurines. However, this conclusion is negated by other studies among sliders; for example, populations studied by Congdon and Gibbons (1985) in South Carolina have a mean RCM of only 0.05. The factors causing the aforementioned interspecific and intraspecific variability in the RCM are in obvious need of study. The RCM may be more useful in studying adaptation of species and populations to more-localized environmental conditions than as a generalized adaptation to the tropical environment.

Moll and Legler (1971) found that clutch size in Panamanian *P. scripta* was positively correlated with increasing body size (plastron length) of gravid females. Cagle (1950) reported a similar correlation in *P. s. elegans*, and Gibbons et al. (1982) and Congdon and Gibbons (1983, 1985) demonstrated a similar relationship in *P. s. scripta*. Emphasis on accumulating mensural data rather than weights in the study by Moll and Legler (1971) precludes detailed comparisons concerning some relationships between female body size and egg-clutch components discovered by Gibbons et al. (1982) and Congdon and Gibbons (1983, 1985) in temperate *P. s. scripta* (see comparisons of

RCM above, however). They found that in addition to clutch size and egg width, clutch wet mass and egg wet mass increased with female body mass and length. Congdon and Gibbons (1983, 1985) also determined that mean egg width in *P. s. scripta* is probably a better indicator of reproductive output than is egg length (used by Moll and Legler, 1971) in determining parental energy investment per egg as clutch sizes increase. Therefore, the observation by Moll and Legler (1971) that mean egg length decreases as clutch size increases may not indicate less parental investment per egg with increasing clutch size in tropical populations. Congdon and Gibbons (1985) found no direct evidence for a trade-off between egg size and clutch size in temperate *P. s. scripta* populations. Also, because no long-term studies of marked populations have been conducted in the tropics, other comparisons with temperate *P. scripta* concerning variation in annual clutch size or clutch frequency are not possible at this time.

The most apparent difference in the life histories of Neotropical sliders, as compared with temperate populations, lies in their increased reproductive potentials, which, as stated above, are directly related to larger body sizes attained in most tropical populations (see Tables 12.1 and 12.2; Cagle, 1950; Moll and Legler, 1971; Gibbons, 1982; Gibbons et al., 1982; Congdon and Gibbons, 1983, 1985). High reproductive potentials may be necessary for survival of Pattern I species in tropical habitats because of the intensity of predation on eggs and young (Moll and Legler, 1971; Medem, 1975; Drummond, 1983). Greater reproductive potentials and larger size are probably directly related to the extended annual activity period permitted by tropical climates. Feeding can continue throughout the year, and although growth rates, as discussed, are largely cyclic, some growth in individuals in the population may occur throughout the year (Moll and Legler, 1971). Another selective force favoring large size in some tropical populations may be predation by crocodilians, because crocodilians and sliders are sympatric over much of the latter's tropical range. Although reproduction is also cyclic, the benign climate allows a much longer nesting season than is possible in temperate zones (Moll and Legler, 1971), consequently allowing more clutches to be successfully oviposited in a given season. The increased reproductive potentials in tropical populations are approximated (to a lesser extent) in temperate populations of *P. scripta* from heated impoundments (Gibbons, 1970b; Thornhill, 1982), probably through a similar interrelationship of temperature, primary productivity, feeding, and growth phenomena.

These data suggest only differences in degree rather than drastic changes in the reproductive ecologies of slider tropical populations when compared with temperate populations. Even the characteristic of nesting during the dry season is not clearly a tropical adaptation, because North

Temperate populations would presumably ovulate and oviposit at the same time of year if the reproductive cycle were not interrupted by a period of hibernation in winter (Moll and Legler, 1971). The cycle of dry-season nesting and wet-season hatching (characteristic of many tropical reptiles) may be a fortuitous result of a temperature-induced temperate gonadal cycle preadapted to fit into it.

Conclusions

Moll and Legler (1971) concluded that the Neotropical slider is a tropical turtle by virtue of its distribution, not its ecology. It is morphologically and ecologically closer to North Temperate subspecies of *P. scripta* than it is to any tropical turtle. In the 18 years that have elapsed since that study was published, additional data on tropical slider populations from different locations have supported this conclusion.

Pseudemys presumably evolved into a generalist and an opportunist in the Holarctic region. These traits, which were so suited to the unpredictable temperate environment, also preadapted *P. scripta* for dispersal into the Neotropics during the subsequent environmental and geological turmoil of the Pleistocene. A plausible scenario is that the slider invaded and moved through the tropics to emerge in the South Temperate Zone during a period or periods of drought and lowering of sea level, which brought about recession of the rain forest and created corridors along the coasts. With no other large, diurnal, basking, predominantly aquatic emydids with which to contend, sliders flourished and spread in the new environment. With the return of pluvial conditions, however, the rain forest (perhaps with rain-forest-adapted turtles such as the pelomedusids) reinvaded much of its former range, thus fragmenting the sliders' range (e.g., eliminating it from the Amazon Basin). The success of another generalized tropical invader, *Homo sapiens*, may have prevented extirpation of sliders in some parts of the tropics by maintaining clearings in the reinvading forest.

Today, despite extreme differences in environment, the life history of tropical sliders is still similar to that of their temperate zone ancestors. The most significant differences in the ecologies of temperate and tropical slider populations are related to reproduction. In particular, the nesting season is longer, reproductive potential is greater, and eggs are larger in the tropical turtles. For the most part these differences can probably be attributed to direct environmental effects of the year-round warmth of the tropical climate, not to major genetic changes. Nesting seasons can begin earlier in the year and last longer than in temperate habitats. Tropical sliders feed and grow throughout the year, although rates may vary with the season. They may grow to larger size in this environment,

and egg size, clutch size, and perhaps number of clutches in turn are related to the body size of the female.

Batagurine emydids have evolved in the Old World tropics and today are largely confined to tropical and subtropical environments. The majority of these tend toward Pattern II reproduction, laying small clutches of exceptionally large eggs. Sliders, temperate and tropical, are typical of the majority of emydines, which lay moderate to large clutches of relatively small eggs (tending toward Pattern I reproduction). There is no indication that tropical sliders have been evolving in the direction taken by the batagurines, their closest aquatic and semiaquatic tropical relatives.

A final question to be explored concerns why tropical slider populations have not adapted appreciably to this new and radically different environment. Moll and Legler (1971) offered the explanation that lack of adaptation was due to the relatively recent arrival of the species into the tropics, suggesting that time had simply been insufficient for new adaptations to evolve. In light of recent evolutionary theory, however, it is conceivable that *Pseudemys scripta* will never change appreciably, no matter how long it remains in the tropics. The publication of the punctuated equilibrium concept by Eldredge and Gould (1972) has offered an alternative view of how organisms adapt to their environments. It is their thesis that species to a large extent maintain their adaptations for long periods without change. They contend that most changes in adaptation are associated with speciation events and that once adaptation is established, little change occurs thereafter.

Species are often viewed as being tied to particular habitats. Rather than adapting to new habitats as environmental conditions change, most species track (i.e., follow) their old habitat. Where new conditions prevail, open niches may be filled by speciation events or by species preadapted to these new conditions (a process called species selection; see Eldredge, 1985, for review). Generalist species such as the slider are best able to track favorable habitat conditions in changing environments. Because of their generalized nature, they can occupy a wider geographic range and will likely persist longer as species than specialist types will. This view, which has gained considerable credence since being proposed in 1972, predicts that we might expect the generalized slider turtle to have a promising future in the tropical environment. Furthermore, as man continues to alter the tropical environment through clearing of the forest, slider turtles may be among the few species to benefit.

Acknowledgments

We thank Peter C. H. Pritchard, Justin D. Congdon, and Jeff Lovich for their helpful comments on the manuscript.

13

RICHARD C. VOGT
Estación de Biología Tropical "Los Tuxtlas"
Instituto de Biología
Universidad Nacional Autónomo de México
Apartado Postal 94
San Andres Tuxtla, Veracruz, México

Reproductive Parameters of *Trachemys scripta venusta* in Southern Mexico

Abstract

The female reproductive cycle and other life history parameters of *Trachemys scripta venusta* were studied in southern Veracruz and Chiapas, Mexico, over a five-year period. Females are reproductively mature at a carapace length of 19.4 cm. Vitellogenesis begins in mid-September, coinciding with a decrease in temperature, and continues until ovulation in late January. The nesting season coincides with the dry season, late January through May, when one to four clutches of 5 to 22 ($\bar{x} = 12$) eggs are laid. Female body size is significantly correlated with clutch size. Both clutch size and egg size are larger than those found in northern populations but smaller than those in Panama. Incubation periods, hatchling sizes, adult sex ratios, and effect of incubation temperature on sex determination are also reported.

Introduction

Neotropical freshwater cryptodires are a diverse assemblage in southern Veracruz and Chiapas, Mexico. Although reproduction in *Trachemys scripta* has been well studied in temperate zone populations (Cagle, 1944c, 1950; Gibbons, 1970b; Gibbons et al., 1981, 1982; Congdon and Gibbons, 1983), little published information other than anecdotal accounts exists concerning the reproduction of any turtle species in the Neotropics, with the exception of the study by Moll and Legler (1971) in Panama. The purpose of this paper is to provide comparative data from a geographically intermediate population near the northern edge of the Neotropics.

Methods

This study was conducted from 1981 to 1986 in southern Veracruz and Chiapas, Mexico (lat. 18 N). Turtles were

162

collected from natural populations in Chiapas (the Río Lacantún and its tributaries in the Reserve of Montes Azules and Laguna de Catazaja) and in Veracruz (lagunas and rivers in or near the Estación de Biología Tropical "Los Tuxtlas" near Catemaco and from the Río Papaloapan and its tributaries near Lerdo de Tejada and Alvarado).

Turtles were collected by fyke nets or trammel nets (Vogt, 1980a) or obtained from local fishermen who used baited hoop traps. Females were palped for the presence of shelled eggs to determine reproductive conditions. The turtles were injected with oxytocin (Ewert and Legler, 1978) for collection of eggs and released where captured, held in the holding facilities of Los Tuxtlas, or euthanized with Nembutal for dissection. The gonads of all dissected turtles were fixed in neutral buffered 10% formalin and are in the collection at Los Tuxtlas. All data regarding incubation times are from experimental incubations of eggs in incubators ($\pm 0.5°$ C) or under ambient conditions. All eggs were incubated in vermiculite:water, at a 1:1 proportion by weight. Incubation times were calculated from laying date to pipping date (defined as when the first opening occurs in the eggshell). Hatchling sex was determined by gross inspection of dissected gonads under a dissecting microscope (Bull and Vogt, 1979). Egg weights and measurements were taken immediately after laying or dissection to avoid changes due to water absorption. Hatchlings were weighed and measured within four days after hatching, usually within 24 hours. Clutch sizes were based only on oviductal eggs; those obtained by oxytocin injection were not included, because of the potential error of underestimating clutch size (Congdon and Gibbons, 1985). The number of clutches per year was determined by oviductal eggs, corpora lutea, and enlarged follicles. Follicles were placed in four size classes (Moll and Legler, 1971): Class I, 6 mm or smaller; Class II, 7–13 mm; Class III, 14–20 mm; Class IV, 21 mm or larger.

Results

SIZE AT SEXUAL MATURITY

Those females for which clutch data are available measured 19.4–31.1 mm in carapace length ($\bar{x}$ = 23.6 mm, SD = 3.09, N = 31) and weighed 963–4,100 g ($\bar{x}$ = 1,813 mm, SD = 690.6, N = 31). Smaller females may be reproductively mature in some instances, but none were encountered in this study. No dissected female smaller than 19.4 cm in carapace length (N = 84) showed evidence of enlarged follicles or expanded oviducts.

OVARIAN CYCLE

Follicular enlargement begins in late September (N = 3), coinciding with the beginning of the period of highest

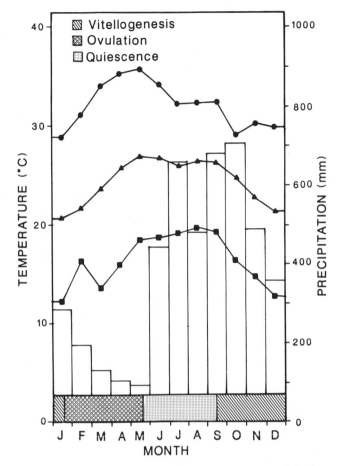

FIGURE 13.1.   Ovarian cycle and monthly mean precipitation (bars) and temperature (circles = mean daily highs, triangles = means, squares = lows). Temperature and precipitation data are from Los Tuxtlas at the Coyame meteorological station (means from 1953 to 1981).

rainfall and lower temperatures (Fig. 13.1). By mid-October (N = 6), individuals have developed Class II follicles and are beginning to produce Class III follicles. By January (N = 8), reproductive females have Class IV follicles and do not produce oviductal eggs until the cold rainy season ends and temperatures begin to rise. The earliest collection date of a female with oviductal eggs was 15 January in the Río Tsendales, Chiapas. During the period of 15 January to 15 February, only 20% of the females examined (N = 200) contained oviductal eggs. From 15 February to 1 March, 30% contained oviductal eggs. Females have been found with oviductal eggs until 23 May. Variation in the beginning of the dry season appears to influence the beginning of the nesting season from year to year as much as three weeks. The nesting season coincides with the dry season (February–May), when daytime temperatures reach 35° C. However, even in the dry season, monthly mean rainfall is at least 100 mm. The onset of the summer rainy season, with lower temperatures and more than 400 mm of monthly

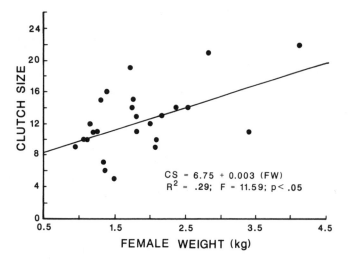

FIGURE 13.2. Relationship of clutch size (CS) with female weight (FW) in kg.

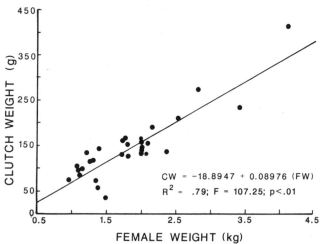

FIGURE 13.3. Relationship of clutch weight (CW) in g with female weight (FW) in kg.

precipitation, marks the end of the nesting season and the initiation of a quiescent period of four months. Vitellogenesis is apparently stimulated by the cooler temperatures in late September (Ganzhorn and Licht, 1983).

CLUTCH AND EGG SIZE

Because atretic follicles were found in three females collected in September and October, enlarged follicles were not used to estimate clutch size. However, a count of enlarged follicles, corpora lutea, and oviductal eggs was used to estimate the number of clutches per year at a maximum of four ($\bar{x} = 3.5$, range $= 2$–4, $N = 23$). Clutch size varied from 5 to 22 ($\bar{x} = 12.03$, SD $= 3.75$, $N = 31$). The number of eggs per clutch was significantly corre-

lated with both carapace length ($p < .05$, $r^2 = .15$) and female weight ($p < .05$, $r^2 = .29$, Fig. 13.2). Clutch mass varied from 33.7 to 417.0 g ($\bar{x} = 143.8$, SD $= 69.86$, $N = 31$). Both carapace length ($r^2 = .54$) and female weight ($r^2 = .79$, Fig. 13.3) were significantly correlated with clutch mass.

Eggs measured 2.80–4.88 cm ($\bar{x} = 3.81$, SD $= 0.33$) in length and 1.86–2.93 cm ($\bar{x} = 2.26$, SD $= 0.23$) in width ($N = 373$). Egg weight ranged from 6.4 to 22.7 g ($\bar{x} = 11.78$, SD $= 3.33$, $N = 373$). Egg size was not highly correlated with clutch size ($r^2 = .015$). Both carapace length and female weight were significantly positively correlated with egg length, width, and mass ($p < .01$, Figs. 13.4–13.6). Female weight in all cases, however, had a higher correlation than did carapace length or clutch size.

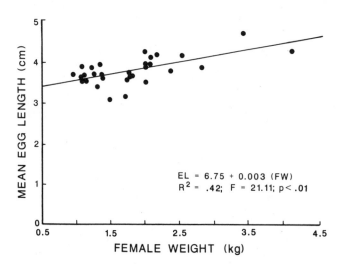

FIGURE 13.4. Relationship of mean egg length (EL) in cm with female weight (FW) in kg.

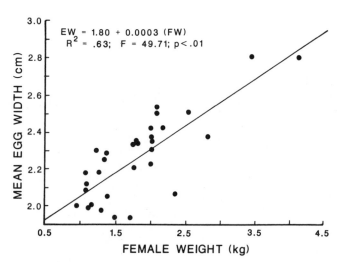

FIGURE 13.5. Relationship of mean egg width (EW) in cm with female weight (FW) in kg.

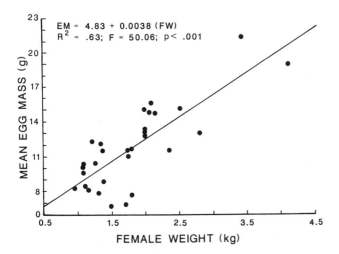

FIGURE 13.6.   Relationship of mean egg mass (EM) in g with female weight (FW) in g.

INCUBATION PERIODS AND HATCHLINGS

Natural nests were not monitored, but eggs incubated at ambient temperature (26°–28° C) hatched in 63 to 74 days. Eggs in the laboratory hatched after 42 to 74 days when incubated under the following temperatures: 27.5°–28.5° C (62–74 days); 28.5°–29.5° C (50–62 days); 29.5°–30.5° C (42–57 days). Only females were produced at temperatures above 29° C. At 28.5° C the sex ratio was 4.2 females:1 male, and at 27.5° C the sex ratio was 1:1 (Table 13.1). Hatchlings varied from 2.5 to 3.78 cm ($\bar{x}$ = 3.18, SD = 0.27, N = 154 from 18 clutches) in carapace length and weighed from 3.5 to 10.7 g ($\bar{x}$ = 7.24, SD = 1.68, N = 154 from 18 clutches).

ADULT SIZE AND SEX RATIO

From October 1984 through February 1986, 112 *Trachemys* were captured in unbaited fyke nets in 840 trap nights in the Río Lacantún and its tributaries. The adult sex ratio was highly skewed toward males (1.91 males:1 female). The 34 adult females weighed 1,100–5,050 g ($\bar{x}$ = 3,350, SD = 974.4), with a carapace length of 188–330 mm ($\bar{x}$ = 284, SD = 32.3) and a plastron length of 188–318 mm ($\bar{x}$ = 266, SD = 34.0). The 65 adult males weighed 900–4,400 g ($\bar{x}$ = 1,896, SD = 668.4), with a carapace length of 187–331 mm ($\bar{x}$ = 241, SD = 28.1) and a plastron length of 172–305 mm ($\bar{x}$ = 222, SD = 32.5). The 13 males that were considered subadults did not have greatly enlarged tails and ranged in weight from 300 to 900 g ($\bar{x}$ = 621, SD = 223.6), from 128 to 179 mm in carapace length ($\bar{x}$ = 162, SD = 20.2), and from 125 to 178 mm in plastron length ($\bar{x}$ = 153, SD = 16.2). No subadult females or hatchlings were seen or captured during the trapping periods.

Discussion

SIZE AT SEXUAL MATURITY

Gibbons (1982) and Thornhill (1982) have both shown that growth and size at sexual maturity in populations of sliders are directly affected by water temperatures. Tropical waters are presumably warmer than those in temperate zones, so it is not surprising to find that the mean size of reproductive females is larger in Mexico and Panama than in the temperate regions. Cagle (1950) found that reproductive females in Illinois ranged from 15 to 19.5 cm in plastron length. Mexican *Trachemys* began maturing at a larger size (around 19 cm) and females in the Panamanian study were even larger (24 cm) before maturity was reached (Moll and Legler, 1971). Although it has been stated that turtles need to reach a minimum size before becoming reproductive and that size rather than age determines when female turtles begin laying eggs (Cagle, 1950; Bury, 1979), the results of both field studies (Moll and Legler, 1971; Gibbons et al., 1982) and lab studies (Vogt, n.d.) support the opposing viewpoint, that age rather than size determines the onset of reproduction. This is apparent from the studies of thermally altered areas as well as the latitudinal variation within this species.

OVARIAN CYCLE

The ovarian cycle of Veracruz sliders varies little from that reported in northern or more southern latitudes; only

Table 13.1. Sex ratio of hatchlings produced in the laboratory under constant incubation temperatures

Locality	Temperature (° C)						
	27.5	28.0	28.5	29.0	29.5	30.0	30.6
Alabama	100 (21)			37 (16)		0 (17)	
Tennessee		92 (36)			30 (40)		5 (42)
Mexico	53 (34)		20 (45)	0 (44)			0 (41)

Source: Alabama and Tennessee data from Bull et al., 1982.

Note: Ratios are presented as percent male, with sample size in parentheses.

the dates corresponding to the local temperatures are slightly shifted (Fig. 13.1). Vitellogenesis begins at a later date than in the north, most likely because of higher temperatures, as found in *Chrysemys* (Ganzhorn and Licht, 1983) and coincides to what was reported for Panama (Moll and Legler, 1971). Ovulation is shifted three months earlier than in northern latitudes, where nesting does not begin until late April (Cagle, 1950). This coincides with the beginning of nesting in Panama, where the earliest nest found was on 13 January, even though nesting is presumed to occur one month earlier in Panama. Nesting in Veracruz begins in the dry season, as in Panama, with the majority of the females laying in March and April and fewer laying in January-February or May. An important factor, both in Mexico and in Panama, is that the dry season also coincides with a rise in temperature after a distinct cool period. It was demonstrated in *Chrysemys picta* (Ganzhorn and Licht, 1983) that high temperatures inhibit vitellogenesis. In addition, temperate zone species have been shown to need a cool period to induce ovulation (Vogt, 1980a). Wisconsin *Graptemys* brought directly from brumation in the Mississippi River in November and maintained under warm conditions in the laboratory failed to develop oviductal eggs and began reabsorbing the yolked follicles. However, individuals in the sample that were kept under cold conditions (5° C for six weeks) developed oviductal eggs after two weeks under temperatures of 28°–30° C. Thus, it is more likely that the lowering of temperatures in September stimulates vitellogenesis and that the even lower temperatures of December and January inhibit ovulation. Warmer temperatures in February and March stimulate ovulation, and the even warmer temperatures of April and May inhibit vitellogenesis, resulting in fewer clutches in Mexico (four), than in Panama (six). This is an increase, however, over temperate zone populations, where a maximum of three clutches is laid (Gibbons et al., 1982).

Although some populations show no relationship between body size and the incidence of multiple clutches (Gibbons et al., 1982), there seems to be a latitudinal variation coinciding with both an increase in the number of clutches and the mean size of females in southern populations (Table 13.2). This increase in body size may explain, in part, why Panamanian turtles lay up to six clutches annually, although Mexican turtles deposit only four clutches annually. The laying season is also longer in Mexico and Panama than in Illinois (Cagle, 1950) or South Carolina (Gibbons et al., 1982), allowing for the production of more nests. However, no evidence exists that individual turtles have an extended laying season. I would predict that the season of an individual turtle is shorter but the range of variation found is greater because of population and microhabitat differences.

Comparison of the female reproductive cycle of *Trachemys* with that of Neotropical endemic species (*Kinosternon*

Table 13.2. Clutch size variation in populations of *Trachemys scripta*

Locality	Mean	Range	N	Reference
Illinois	9.5	4-18	217	2
Tennessee	10.5	5-22	47	2
South Carolina	7.7	2-17	121	2
Oklahoma	8.8	1-12	6	2
Lousiana	7.2	4-11	188	2
Southern Mexico	12.03	5-22	31	3
Panama	17.4	9-25	38	1

References: 1, Moll and Legler, 1971; 2, Fitch, 1985; 3, this study.

acutum, K. leucostomum, Claudius angustatus, Staurotypus triporcatus, and *Dermatemys mawii*) suggests that *Trachemys* is "stranded" in its present reproductive cycle because of phylogenetic constraints. The other species are capable of vitellogenesis during the warm summer months, begin an extended egg-laying season with the onset of the cold rainy season, from September to November, and continue laying eggs until April or May (Vogt, n.d.).

CLUTCH AND EGG SIZE

Clutch size is a variable related to the size, age, and energetic state of the female, as well as the date of oviposition. Clutch size has been shown to be highly variable among populations within a single geographic area (Congdon and Gibbons, 1983) and among years. Because my samples are from various populations over a span of several years and taken from throughout the nesting season, they are not readily comparable with the studies of discrete populations. These data are, however, comparable with the means compiled by Fitch (1985) to show regional trends in clutch sizes (Table 13.2). It is interesting to note that the range of variation between Mexico and Tennessee is the same, but the mean clutch size is larger in Mexico. This does not follow the trend for smaller clutches as one moves farther south, as stated by Fitch (1985), especially considering that the mean clutch size in Panama is 17.4. Studies of a long-term nature need to be conducted on discrete populations in southern Mexico before conclusions can be made concerning trends in clutch size.

Clutch size in this study was positively correlated with two measures of body size: carapace length and female weight. Clutch mass, a better estimate of the amount of energy a female expends on a particular clutch, was significantly correlated with female weight ($r^2 = .79, p < .001$). Female weight was more important than plastron or carapace length in estimating clutch size. There was no significant difference in the variability of egg size (weight, length, or width) in relation to weight, carapace length, or plastron length of the female. Clutch size, however, was negatively correlated with variability of egg length ($r^2 =$

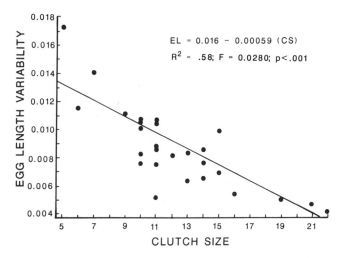

$$EL = 0.016 - 0.00059\,(CS)$$
$$R^2 = .58;\ F = 0.0280;\ p < .001$$

FIGURE 13.7.   Relationship of egg length variability (standard deviation divided by mean egg length) with clutch size (CS).

.58, $p < .001$, Fig. 13.7). An increase in clutch size resulted in a decrease in the variability of egg length. Within-clutch variability of both egg weight ($r^2 = .11$, $p < .001$) and width ($r^2 = .14$, $p < .05$) increased significantly with an increase in clutch size. This suggests that females are selecting for an optimum egg length and the independent variable of egg weight; how much energy a female devotes to a single egg is expressed by an increase in egg width. As has been shown in northern populations (Congdon and Gibbons, 1983, 1985), egg width and egg mass increase proportionally with the size of the female, but egg length does not (Figs. 13.4–13.6). Although the range of variation of egg size is great, there appears to be a trend to produce larger, heavier eggs in tropical localities as opposed to northern latitudes (Table 13.3). This trend could be emphasized by larger sample sizes from Neotropical populations.

INCUBATION

The incubation period was shorter than that reported for northern populations under controlled laboratory conditions (Ewert, 1985): 57–65 days at 29°–30° C for northern populations versus 50–62 days at 28.5°–29.5° C in this study, and a mean of 58 days at 30° C for northern populations versus 42–57 days at 29.5°–30.5° C in this study. One would expect to find shorter incubation periods in northern latitudes at the same temperature if there is a premium on leaving the egg at a faster rate. As was reported for several populations of *Chelydra* (Ewert, 1985), faster incubation rates in northern populations of *Trachemys* do not appear to be selected for. Perhaps because winter temperatures even in the northern edge of the range of this species are not sufficiently low to increase the mortality of unhatched embryos, there is no strong selective advantage for early hatching as in other species.

SEX DETERMINATION

One would predict that threshold temperatures for sex determination would be higher in the tropics or in the southern United States than in more northerly latitudes (Bull et al., 1982). Table 13.1 shows distinctly that the threshold temperature is 1° C lower in Neotropical Mexico than in the southern United States. Nesting sites appear similar in the areas studied. Along the Río Lacantún, slider nests have been found on sandbars 3 to 6 m from the water, both in shaded and open areas. Nests near Lerdo, Veracruz, are found on higher mounds of sand or clay at the edge of marshes, sites that are often overgrown by vegetation. In order to interpret the significance of these results, natural nests must be monitored by recording detailed temperature data. Only with such data can we begin discussing the selective advantage of a lower threshold temperature. It seems highly probable that the eggs of *Trachemys* in Veracruz and Chiapas are actually experiencing lower temperatures, making it advantageous to produce females at a lower temperature. Sex ratios of adults in Chiapas (this study) and Panama (Moll and Legler, 1971) were skewed 2 : 1 in favor of males. If in fact these data are not artifacts of sampling error, then they would suggest that there is an overabundance of males, and selection would favor those females that either placed their eggs in warmer sites or had a lower threshold temperature. Cagle (1950) found a 1 : 1 sex ratio in a sample of 825 adults from Illinois, suggesting that in northern popu-

Table 13.3.   Geographic variation in egg size of *Trachemys scripta*

Locality	Length (mm)	Width (mm)	Mass (g)	N	Reference
Illinois	36.2 (30.9-43.0)	21.6 (19.4-24.8)	9.71 (6-15.4)	221	1
South Carolina	36.39	22.17	19.52	489	3
Southern Mexico	38.1 (28.0-48.8)	22.6 (19.6-29.3)	11.78 (6.4-22.7)	373	4
Panama	42.2 (37.1-47.6)	28.2 (25.5-41.3)	20.66 (16.4-25.6)	87	2

Note: Mean and range (in parentheses) of measurements are shown.
References: 1, Cagle, 1944c; 2, Moll and Legler, 1971; 3, Congdon and Gibbons, 1985; 4, this study.

lations an equilibrium has been reached between threshold temperature and nest site selection.

Mean hatchling weight (7.24 g, range = 3.5–10.7 g) and mean carapace length (31.8 mm, range = 25.0–38.0 mm) were lower in this study than in both northern studies: 8.07 g (5.4–10.0 g) and 32.46 mm (28.4–34.2 mm) in the study by Cagle (1950) and 36.5 mm (28.4–40.2 mm) in the Panamanian study. All of the hatchlings measured in this study were from eggs incubated under constant temperatures in the laboratory, many of which were from high temperatures. Smaller turtles hatch out at higher incubation temperatures (Ewert, 1985), explaining the conflicting results of larger eggs in Mexico producing smaller hatchlings. The range of the carapace length is greater in Mexico than in either Panama or Illinois, reflecting again the effects of incubation temperature.

ADULT SIZE AND SEX RATIO

The limited amount of data on the population of *Trachemys scripta venusta* from the Río Lacantún suggests that the population is skewed toward adults. Predation of both adults and juveniles is high in the region, *Crocodylus moreletii* being one of the most abundant predators. About 25% of the adult *Staurotypus triporcatus* from this area have holes in the carapace from attempted crocodile predation. *Trachemys* lack these holes and are also much less abundant, suggesting that when crocodiles bite *Trachemys*, they are able to eat them. Juveniles of *Staurotypus*, a bottom dweller, are abundant in the population, suggesting that it is not nest predation that is removing the juvenile *Trachemys* from the population. Although the skewed sex ratio may represent sampling error, it is also important to note that of the 13 subadults captured, all were males. This suggests that males are being overproduced and that these sex ratios are in fact real. A more intensified effort to locate juveniles and subadults and to monitor nest temperatures and hatchling sex ratios is needed before any statements about the population biology of this species can be made in the Río Lacantún.

This chapter would not be complete without commenting that tropical Mexican sliders are very similar in every aspect of their biology to sliders in the southern United States and Panama. They do not seem to have changed in the least to adapt to life in the tropics and have not seemed to suffer for it. A slider is a slider is a slider.

Acknowledgments

This study would not have been possible without the assistance of numerous people in the field and laboratory. My sincere appreciation is given to my field assistants, who worked under the bites of *sancudos* and the biting words of El Maestro for paltry wages or the opportunity to learn more about turtles: Oscar Flores Villela, Mardocheo Palma Munoz, Chucho Ramirez Ramos, Paco D. Soberon, and Marcelo Paxtian Sinaca. My *lanchero* on the Río Lacantún, Augustin, was more of a biologist's caretaker than a *lanchero*. Funding for the Chiapas portion of this study was provided, in part, by the Secretaria de Desarrollo Urbano y Ecología through the guiding hands of Dr. Mario Ramos of the Instituto Nacional de Investigaciones sobre Recursos Bióticos and the assistance of Marco Lazcano. Some funding for other aspects of the study came from the Instituto de Biología de Universidad Nacional Autónomo de México. Miguel Martínez Ramos is thanked for helping me with data analysis. Finally, Rodolfo Dirzo, El Jefe de la Estación de Biología "Los Tuxtlas," is appreciated for giving me the freedom to study turtles unhindered and directing all of the support he could my way. Manuscript preparation was aided by Miriam Stapleton at the Savannah River Ecology Laboratory under contract DE-AC09-76SROO-819 between the U.S. Department of Energy and the University of Georgia's Institute of Ecology. Whit Gibbons, Rich A. Seigel, James L. Knight, and Justin D. Congdon are thanked for their help in narrowing the focus of the chapter and clarifying the prose.

Structure, Demography, and Interaction among Populations

J. WHITFIELD GIBBONS
Savannah River Ecology Laboratory
Drawer E
Aiken, South Carolina 29802

14

Sex Ratios and Their Significance among Turtle Populations

Abstract

Sex ratios of adults in natural populations of turtles have been reported to vary both within and among species. Long-term studies with the slider turtle (*Trachemys scripta*) indicate that sampling biases can result from a variety of causes, including season of capture, determination of maturity, and trapping method. Four demographic factors influence actual sex ratios within a population: (1) sex ratios of hatchlings, (2) differential mortality of the sexes, (3) differential emigration and immigration rates of the sexes, and (4) differences in age at maturity of the sexes. The last reason is considered to be the primary cause of biased adult sex ratios within many populations of turtles, although future studies should investigate the other possibilities.

Introduction

The sex ratio of a population is an important demographic measurement because of the potential influence that the relative proportion of the sexes can have on certain aspects of population dynamics (e.g., time spent searching for receptive mates, intrasexual competition, and annual egg productivity of a population). Both even and unbalanced secondary sex ratios have been reported for natural populations of turtles (Bury, 1979). Unbalanced sex ratios may occur naturally in some populations (Moll and Legler, 1971; Bury, 1979), but biased sampling has been suggested as being responsible for at least some of the reports of unbalanced sex ratios in the turtle literature (Ream and Ream, 1966; Gibbons, 1970c). The reports of skewed sex ratios among hatchling turtles in a variety of species following incubation at different temperatures (e.g., Pieau, 1974; Bull and Vogt, 1979; Bull, 1980; Morreale et al., 1982; Vogt and Bull, 1984) also give a potential explanation for varied adult sex ratios in natural populations. The purpose of this chapter is to discuss the

Table 14.1. Comparison of sex ratios (male:female) of freshwater turtles
captured at Ellenton Bay using two different collecting techniques

Species	Baited aquatic traps				Terrestrial drift fence			
	Males	Females	Sex ratio	X^2	Males	Females	Sex ratio	X^2
Slider turtle	556	282	1.97	**	592	556	1.06	NS
(*Trachemys scripta*)	314	153	2.05	**	296	206	1.44	**
Eastern mud turtle	289	158	1.83	**	1,067	1,631	0.65	**
(*Kinosternon subrubrum*)	138	70	1.97	**	298	271	1.10	NS
Chicken turtle	230	54	4.26	**	396	333	1.19	**
(*Deirochelys reticularia*)	110	25	4.40	**	128	67	1.91	**
Florida cooter	39	15	2.60	**	115	104	1.11	NS
(*Pseudemys floridana*)	10	3	3.33	NS	27	14	1.93	NS
Stinkpot	202	168	1.20	NS	106	156	0.68	**
(*Sternotherus odoratus*)	46	36	1.28	NS	24	24	1.00	NS
Snapping turtle	68	40	1.70	**	30	45	0.67	NS
(*Chelydra serpentina*)	16	6	2.67	NS	9	5	1.80	NS

Note: Only adult individuals are included. The top number for a species indicates all captures and recaptures from 1967 through 1987. The lower number is based on each individual as a single capture. Chi-square (X^2) tests corrected for continuity were used to compare the preceding sex ratio (observed) for each technique in each row with a 1:1 sex ratio (expected). Abbreviation: NS, $p \geq .05$.
** $p < .01$.

various causes of the observed sex ratios of adult turtles in natural populations and to determine the evolutionary significance of equal or unequal numbers of the sexes. I base interpretations of sex ratio estimates (and they must categorically be understood to be only estimates, unless every individual is accounted for) on examples from the literature and from field studies of the slider turtle (*Trachemys scripta*) and other freshwater species on the Savannah River Plant (SRP) in South Carolina.

Defining Sex Ratios

Although a sex ratio simply represents the relative proportion of males to females, a consideration in the discussion of sex ratios is the proper quantification of how a population is classified demographically in terms of various functional categories. For example, defining the sex ratio in a sample of newborn turtles whose sexes have been identified is straightforward, because all individuals are members of the same cohort. However, with species that show dramatic sexual size dimorphism, such as slider turtles, the sexes reach maturity at widely differing ages, so that some cohort comparisons will include immature females and mature males. Although the proportion of all mature and immature turtles of both sexes in a population can provide information on other demographic features, the functional sex ratio is based only on individuals that have reached maturity. Therefore, it is necessary to know the size and age at maturity of individuals within a particular population if functional adult sex ratios are to be established.

Factors Influencing Perceived and Actual Sex Ratios in Turtle Populations

The sex ratio perceived by an investigator is influenced by biases that result from sampling or interpretation as well as by the actual sex ratio resulting from changes that occur as a consequence of normal population processes. The potential effect of either of these processes and the interaction between them must be considered in any examination of adult sex ratios in natural populations.

SAMPLING BIASES AFFECTING PERCEIVED SEX RATIOS

The influence of sampling bias should be a primary consideration for any investigator in the determination of sex ratios in natural populations of turtles or most other animals. Different impressions of what the sex ratio is in a population can result from collecting technique, differences in behavior of the sexes, determination of age or size at maturity, or a combination of these factors. Several examples can emphasize this point. In thorough sampling efforts of populations of slider turtles on the SRP, the proportional number of captured adult males and adult females varied seasonally, annually, and as a result of collecting technique (Tables 14.1 and 14.2).

The methods by which turtles are collected can also severely influence the size classes or sexes that are captured. This is intuitive for many species of turtles (e.g., some *Graptemys*) in which the males are appreciably smaller than the females. Therefore, if an investigator uses traps with a mesh large enough for smaller turtles to es-

Table 14.2. Variability in perceived sex ratios (male:female) in South Carolina populations
of *Trachemys scripta* resulting from sampling bias as a function of season and year

Year	Winter (Dec.-Feb.)				Spring (Mar.-May)				Summer (June-Aug.)				Fall (Sept.-Nov.)				Total year			
	M	F	Ratio	X^2	M	F	Ratio	X^2	M	F	Ratio	X^2	M	F	Ratio	X^2	M	F	Ratio	X^2
Ellenton Bay																				
1967									50	18	2.78	**	59	21	2.81	**	100	35	2.86	**
1968					42	32	1.31	NS	21	4	5.25	**					70	37	1.89	**
1969																	12	3	4.00	*
1970																	17	6	2.83	*
1975					55	74	0.74	NS	29	26	1.12	NS					77	88	0.88	NS
1976					15	27	0.56	NS	32	16	2.00	*	31	21	1.48	NS	71	54	1.31	NS
1977					19	14	1.36	NS	30	16	1.88	NS	12	6	2.00	NS	60	30	2.00	**
1978	7	10	0.70	NS	94	54	1.74	**	34	34	1.00	NS	15	10	1.50	NS	118	85	1.39	*
1979					21	7	3.00	*	10	4	2.50	NS	14	3	4.67	*	41	19	2.16	**
1980					47	37	1.27	NS	20	23	0.87	NS	10	6	1.67	NS	62	50	1.24	NS
1981					129	96	1.34	*	64	26	2.46	**					185	120	1.54	**
1982	16	11	1.45	NS	16	11	1.45	NS	10	8	1.25	NS								
1986					17	18	0.94	NS	11	23	0.48	NS					27	36	0.75	NS
All years	54	37	1.46	NS	393	270	1.46	**	273	160	1.71	**	147	67	2.19	**	511	294	1.74	**
Par Pond																				
1968					5	8	0.63	NS					12	5	2.40	NS	20	14	1.43	NS
1969																	5	3	1.67	NS
1970																	7	4	1.75	NS
1975																				
1976									10	9	1.11	NS					12	9	1.33	NS
1977					6	14	0.43	NS	57	20	2.85	**	39	7	5.57	**	92	33	2.79	**
1978	40	2	20.00	**	48	28	1.71	*	40	24	1.67	NS					126	53	2.38	**
1979					11	7	1.57	NS					9	1	9.00	*	27	7	3.86	**
1980					10	8	1.25	NS	1	3	0.33	NS					19	14	1.36	NS
1981																				
1982	69	17	4.06	**	89	41	2.17	**	4	1	4.00	NS	15	6	2.50	NS	164	63	2.60	**
1983					25	15	1.67	NS	31	11	2.82	**					59	25	2.36	**
1984									27	17	1.59	NS					28	20	1.40	NS
1985													6	5	1.20	NS	7	16	0.44	NS
1986													18	5	3.60	*	23	11	2.09	NS
All years	143	27	5.30	**	200	139	1.44	**	201	106	1.90	**	121	54	2.24	**	526	256	2.05	**
Lost Lake System																				
1967													37	32	1.16	NS	37	34	1.09	NS
1968	15	12	1.25	NS	17	16	1.06	NS	6	11	0.55	NS					34	31	1.10	NS
1969	5	7	0.71	NS					1	12	0.08	**					12	19	0.63	NS
1970									3	8	0.38	NS					3	8	0.38	NS
1975																				
1976													9	5	1.80	NS	10	8	1.25	NS
1977									14	13	1.08	NS					14	16	0.88	NS
1978																				
1979													22	1	22.00	**	22	5	4.40	**
1980					50	37	1.35	NS	30	27	1.11	NS	47	19	2.47	**	114	69	1.65	**
1981	24	10	2.40	*	44	24	1.83	*									67	34	1.97	**
1982					10	5	2.00	NS					110	24	4.58	**	119	29	4.10	**
1983	68	13	5.23	**	141	45	3.13	**	29	22	1.32	NS	15	7	2.14	NS	235	84	2.80	**
1984					40	15	2.67	**	27	13	2.08	*					67	33	2.03	**
1985					7	8	0.88	NS	59	34	1.74	*	41	18	2.28	**	101	55	1.84	**
1986					24	7	3.43	**					60	16	3.75	**	89	31	2.87	**
All years	112	49	2.29	**	301	147	2.05	**	164	158	1.04	NS	315	121	2.60	**	556	290	1.92	**
Risher Pond																				
1968									16	23	0.70	NS					16	23	0.70	NS
1969									3	9	0.33	NS	9	8	1.13	NS	12	15	0.80	NS
1970					18	24	0.75	NS	12	9	1.33	NS					21	30	0.70	NS
1975																				
1976													10	17	0.59	NS	11	17	0.65	NS
1977					10	10	1.00	NS									10	10	1.00	NS
1978					9	11	0.82	NS					10	10	1.00	NS	12	14	0.86	NS
1979													5	7	0.71	NS	6	7	0.86	NS
1980													11	11	1.00	NS	11	11	1.00	NS
1981													7	7	1.00	NS	9	11	0.82	NS
1982									11	7	1.57	NS					11	7	1.57	NS
1983					4	6	0.67	NS									4	6	0.67	NS
1984					8	10	0.80	NS	7	12	0.58	NS					17	16	1.06	NS
All years					38	45	0.84	NS	43	43	1.00	NS	28	31	0.90	NS	59	54	1.09	NS

Note: Samples are based on original captures of adult individuals in a particular season or year (winter samples include December of the preceding year) when 10 or more adult individuals were captured. Chi-square (X^2) tests corrected for continuity were used to compare the sex ratio (observed) within each season and year with a 1:1 sex ratio (expected). Abbreviation: NS, $p \geq .05$.

*$p < .05$.

**$p < .01$.

cape, an obvious bias will occur. The converse, using a trap entrance too small for large females, could result in the differential capture of smaller individuals. However, some collecting techniques have a more subtle bias and require quantitative documentation of differential captures (e.g., see Ream and Ream, 1966).

A technique-by-technique evaluation of differential capture of adult turtles would offer little guidance other than that some collecting techniques can have a dramatic or minor effect on the proportional capture of either sex. This evaluation can best be made by the investigator in the context of the particular study species and collecting situation. A comparison of sex ratios of the turtle species captured at Ellenton Bay by baited aquatic traps and terrestrial drift fences is instructive (Table 14.1). The results demonstrate that even a long-term sampling effort can be strongly biased with regard to the probability of capture of an individual on the basis of its sex and could greatly influence the perceived sex ratio in some instances. For example, the numbers for individuals of Eastern mud turtles (*Kinosternon subrubrum*) captured in aquatic traps give the impression that the sex ratio is significantly unbalanced toward males, whereas the numbers captured terrestrially suggest that the sex ratio is not significantly different from 1:1. An earlier study that considered all adults captured by any means in the Ellenton Bay population revealed a significant, male-biased sex ratio (1.34, 268 males : 200 females; Gibbons, 1983a), as does the total of all captures through 1987 (1.31, 405 males : 308 females; this study).

The propensity of adult females to travel terrestrially during nesting results in a higher proportion of females in the samples collected with drift fences. In contrast, male *K. subrubrum* apparently are more likely to enter aquatic traps, perhaps because of a greater tendency to wander in search of females, and they therefore have a greater opportunity to encounter a trap. The result is that aquatic trapping apparently underestimates females, whereas with terrestrial trapping the opposite is true, so that the actual adult sex ratio lies somewhere in between. The sex ratio of aquatically trapped individuals of *T. scripta* is 2.05, and that of terrestrially captured individuals is 1.44 (Table 14.1), whereas the ratio based on all slider turtles at Ellenton Bay is intermediate at 1.74 (Table 14.3). This same phenomenon—aquatic traps' being more selective for males and terrestrial traps' being biased toward females—appears to be true for each of the six species at Ellenton Bay (Table 14.1). Comparisons with other types of aquatic traps or with other means of capturing turtles would also undoubtedly reveal a sex ratio bias and should be considered in establishing the perceived sex ratios.

The seasonal behavioral differences between the sexes can also have a direct effect on sex ratio perception (Table 14.2) and can interact differentially with collecting method. For example, more females of most species are captured on land during late spring and early summer than in other seasons because of nesting activities. The greater capture of males in some seasons (e.g., *T. scripta* during the fall at most sites, Table 14.2) is presumably a reflection of the reported greater mating activity of males (Morreale et al., 1984; Parker, 1984; Gibbons, 1986).

Aside from the identifiable effects of collecting method and season, numerous less obvious factors presumably operate independently and interactively to result in the sex ratio perceived by the investigator. The annual variability in the sex ratio determined for four SRP populations of slider turtles (Table 14.2) demonstrates that even large sample sizes can result in dramatically different estimates of adult sex ratios in a turtle population during different years. For example, during the seven years at Ellenton Bay in which the number of adults captured was greater than 100, the sex ratio was highly significant ($p <$ .01) in favor of males in three years, significant ($p < .05$) in one year, and not statistically significantly different from 1:1 in three years. Clearly, a single year's estimate should be considered circumspectly. This should not be taken as a discouragement to those of us interested in the demography of turtle populations but is intended as a word of caution in the interpretation of data.

DETERMINATION OF MATURITY OF INDIVIDUALS

Aside from the biases in sex ratio estimates resulting from sampling techniques and probabilities, an error can be

Table 14.3. Influence of perceived size of each sex at maturity on adult sex ratio (male:female) in two South Carolina populations of *Trachemys scripta*

Females	Males					
	80	90	100	110	120	130
Ellenton Bay						
140	1.47	1.46	1.38	1.24	0.99	0.72
150	1.62	1.61	1.53	1.37	1.09	0.79
160	1.85	1.83	1.74	1.56	1.24	0.90
170	2.23	2.21	2.10	1.88	1.50	1.09
180	3.25	3.22	3.06	2.74	2.19	1.58
190	5.27	5.22	4.96	4.45	3.54	2.56
200	9.87	9.78	9.29	8.33	6.64	4.80
Par Pond						
160	1.59	1.59	1.57	1.54	1.45	1.31
170	1.66	1.66	1.64	1.61	1.51	1.37
180	1.76	1.76	1.74	1.71	1.60	1.45
190	1.91	1.91	1.88	1.85	1.74	1.57
200	2.09	2.08	2.05	2.02	1.89	1.71
210	2.41	2.40	2.37	2.33	2.19	1.98
220	2.70	2.69	2.66	2.61	2.45	2.22

Note: Column and row headings indicate plastron length in mm. Numbers in table indicate sex ratios based on numbers of turtles of each sex captured in each population at the indicated size categories. The actual sex ratio of each population based on known sizes at maturity of each sex is underlined. The mean size at maturity for males in both populations is 100 mm. Females in Ellenton Bay mature at about 160 mm; those at Par Pond mature at 200 mm. Sample sizes at the sizes at maturity: Ellenton Bay, 511 males, 294 females; Par Pond, 526 males, 256 females.

made because of the improper determination of maturity in one or both sexes. This type of mistake has been inherent in many population studies with turtles (Gibbons, 1970c) and other animals, resulting in inaccurate adult sex ratio estimates. Estimates of size and age at maturity have been made for the populations at Ellenton Bay and Par Pond (Gibbons et al., 1981), so the potential impact of errors on the accurate determination of the mean size and age at maturity can be observed for SRP slider turtles (Table 14.3). Thus, if the Ellenton Bay size at maturity for females were used with the Par Pond sample, the adult sex ratio would be calculated as 1.57 rather than 2.05. Conversely, the Ellenton Bay sex ratio, using the Par Pond size of maturity for females, would be 9.29 rather than 1.74.

The problem of differential growth rates and subsequent differences in ages or sizes at maturity among different populations of the same species within a region (Gibbons et al., 1981) confounds designation of size at sexual maturity. Studies must be tempered with the knowledge that misjudgment of size at maturity, and of its interpopulational variability, can be a major influence on the determination of sex ratio estimates.

BIOLOGICAL FACTORS AFFECTING ACTUAL SEX RATIOS

Wilson (1975) cites three factors as normally determining the functional sex ratio in a population of animals, and they are applicable to turtles: (1) the sex ratio of hatchlings, (2) the differential mortality of the sexes, and (3) the difference in ages at maturity of the sexes. A fourth factor that could potentially affect the sex ratio is differential emigration or immigration of the sexes in the study population. Each of these can be considered on the basis of what is known about turtle populations and in terms of how sex ratios are likely to be influenced.

HATCHLING SEX RATIOS. Pieau (1974) first suggested that the sex of some turtles may be influenced by the temperature at which the eggs are incubated. A plethora of publications (Bull and Vogt, 1979; Morreale et al., 1982; Vogt and Bull, 1982; and many others) has demonstrated that many species of freshwater, terrestrial, and marine turtles lay eggs that develop as females at high incubation temperatures and as males at low ones. The reported pivotal temperatures vary but are generally within the range of 26°–29° C. The determination of sex has been based categorically on histological or gross examination of the reproductive organs in the hatchlings. To my knowledge, no one has conducted a controlled experiment to document that the juveniles actually develop into adults in the ratios predicted from the incubation temperatures. That is, I am not aware of any experiment in which eggs incubated at different temperatures were apportioned into two sets: (1) those dissected to determine sex ratios by histological dissection of hatchlings, and (2)

those hatched and raised to maturity, or at least to a point at which maturity is obvious in males, in order to determine if the sex ratio is consistent with what would be expected. This is a definitive experiment that deserves investigation. The use of laparoscopy would even permit such a study to be conducted on the same individuals that were sexed as hatchlings.

In species in which the primary sex ratio is a consequence of nest incubation temperatures, more of one sex could enter a population and ultimately affect the sex ratio of adults. This has not yet been conclusively documented to be a factor in determining the functional sex ratio of any natural population of turtles. However, Vogt (1980a) discovered unusually high proportions of females in *Graptemys ouachitensis* in Wisconsin. Although a sampling bias may have existed from his trapping heavily in the areas where females were likely to nest (Vogt, 1980a), he also attributed the sex ratio imbalance to the fact that females in his study area nest on open river beaches, which would result in higher temperatures and thus the production of mostly females (Vogt and Bull, 1984; Vogt, pers. com.). Limpus et al. (1983) reported a situation for loggerhead sea turtles (*Caretta caretta*) nesting on the Great Barrier Reef in which human interference of nesting beaches may have reduced the proportion of beach that normally produced females, thus potentially altering the hatchling sex ratio. The potential certainly exists, and other investigators should consider hatchling sex ratios as a possible influence on adult sex ratios.

DIFFERENTIAL MORTALITY OF THE SEXES. Once hatchlings enter a turtle population, any factor that results in differential survivorship of the sexes can affect the functional sex ratio. I see no reason to expect that juvenile turtles should show differential mortality on the basis of sex. Until the advent of maturity, when secondary sex characteristics and behavioral differences appear, natural selection would presumably operate equally on both sexes. However, at this time, no unequivocal evidence has been presented in the literature to demonstrate that one sex of juvenile turtles has a probability of mortality that is higher than, lower than, or equal to the other's.

Differential mortality of the sexes as adults, or in sexually size-dimorphic species in which one sex may be an adult while the other is a juvenile, may be an important factor. However, documentation of the actual or potential effects of differential mortality on sex ratio, and whether the patterns are consistent or vary interpopulationally, has not been reported for any species of turtle. Hurly (1987) reported a male-biased adult sex ratio in a red squirrel (*Tamiasciurus hudsonicus*) population in Ontario, Canada, and stated that it was the first example of differential mortality of the sexes in the species.

Numerous reports have been made of females that died during nesting excursions as a consequence of terrestrial

Table 14.4. Adult sex ratios (male:female) and the effect of maturation rate on
sex ratio in South Carolina populations of *Trachemys scripta*

Location	All adults				All above 100 mm		
	Males	Females	Ratio	X^2	Females	Ratio	X^2
Pond B	185	78	2.37	**	131	1.41	**
Capers Island	14	45	0.31	**	45	0.31	**
Kiawah Island	19	17	1.12	NS	19	1.00	NS
Ellenton Bay	511	294	1.74	**	505	1.01	NS
Par Pond	526	256	2.05	**	406	1.30	**
Risher Pond	59	54	1.09	NS	77	0.77	NS
McElmurray's Pond	280	123	2.28	**	155	1.81	**
Cecil's Pond	82	33	2.48	**	47	1.74	**
Lost Lake System	556	290	1.92	**	380	1.46	**

Note: Turtles were captured from 1967 to 1986. Adults include all individuals above the mean size of maturity: males ≥ 100 mm plastron length, females ≥ 160 mm, for all populations except Par Pond (females ≥ 200 mm) and Capers Island and Kiawah Island (minimum sizes at maturity not determined). Because of the long-term study of some populations, some ratios include (1) individuals captured as many as 19 years apart from each other and (2) individuals that were immature at first capture but reached maturity during the study. A chi-square (X^2) test corrected for continuity was used to determine level of significance. Abbreviation: NS, $p ≥ .05$.
** $p < .01$.

predators (e.g., Shealy, 1976; Seigel, 1980b; Congdon, pers. com.), a differential mortality phenomenon that would result in shifts in the adult sex ratio. Differential mortality is presumably responsible for the sex ratio of the slider turtle population on Capers Island, South Carolina (Table 14.4), where the predominance of females is believed to be a consequence of heavy predation by alligators (Gibbons et al., 1979). Of the adults, smaller males are presumably more susceptible to large alligators in the relatively vegetation-free habitat and have been disproportionately eliminated from the population. This population had no juvenile recruitment from 1978 to 1986, and only large individuals of either sex remain.

Other examples of how differential size or behavior (e.g., overland mating quests by males) could result in one sex's being more vulnerable at certain times or in certain habitats can be envisioned. At this point, however, we need documentation of how differential mortality of the sexes affects sex ratios and whether the phenomenon is characteristic for the species or only peculiar to particular situations.

DIFFERENTIAL EMIGRATION AND IMMIGRATION OF THE SEXES. Male turtles of some species are more likely to travel greater distances and more often between populations than are female turtles (Gibbons, 1986; also see Chapter 16). Because of this difference in overland movement of the sexes, local populations of some freshwater turtles may be dynamic in the proportion of the sexes. The influence of emigration and immigration should affect only local populations, with a presumed balance being achieved over time among the local populations within a region. Thus, whereas populations in a region may differ in sex ratios at one season or during one year, the ratios

may be counterbalanced at other times because of emigration and immigration. This could explain much of the seasonal and annual variation observed in the four populations of *T. scripta* in South Carolina (Table 14.2). Investigators should be aware that the habitat they define as being occupied by a population may be interactive with noncontiguous habitats, so sampling errors result over short periods or during certain seasons or even different years. Thus, the actual sex ratio in a local population at a given time may not be representative of the functional sex ratio with regard to potential genetic exchange. This is a problem in many demographic studies in which the boundaries of the population cannot be precisely defined.

INFLUENCE OF MATURATION RATE. The single most important influence on actual sex ratios that has been documented in some turtle populations is the differential rate of maturity of the sexes that is characteristic of some species. Male slider turtles generally mature several years earlier than females (see Chapter 9.). Therefore, if no other factors are involved that result either in differential ratios at hatching or in differential mortality rates of the sexes, slider turtle populations experiencing juvenile recruitment will have more adult males than adult females (Table 14.4). The importance of this fact can be seen by comparing the sex ratios based only on mature females with the sex ratios that also include immature females above the male size at maturity, so that cohorts are compared (Table 14.4). The sex ratio more closely approaches 1.0 for some South Carolina populations by including these immature females. However, the resultant ratio is still significantly different from 1:1 in most cases, suggesting that other factors besides maturation rate may be involved in determining sex ratios in these populations.

Variation in Adult Sex Ratios among Sliders and Other Turtles

The discovery of consistent variation in a biological trait can give insight into its dynamics and the mechanisms that influence it. However, no strong geographical trend in sex ratio bias is evident in the few species of turtles, including slider turtles, for which several estimates are available (Table 14.5). Sufficient population records exist for too few turtle species to justify a categorical statement of whether sex ratios vary in any consistent pattern. One might speculate that if any trend were to be revealed, it would be that there are more males in cooler climates because of temperature-dependent sex determination, although local habitat variation or nest site selection could have an influence on natural nests that would override climatic trends (Morreale et al., 1982; Vogt and Bull, 1984). Also, one might conclude that if one sex had a fitness advantage over the other, natural selection at the histological level would operate to equalize the sex ratios.

Based on the estimates for slider turtles (*Trachemys scripta*), stinkpots (*Sternotherus odoratus*), eastern mud turtles (*Kinosternon subrubrum*), and chicken turtles (*Deirochelys reticularia*) in South Carolina (Table 14.5), sex ratio variability among populations within a region can be as great as that among regions. In fact, the variation within South Carolina populations of these species encompasses the range of ratios observed for them in most other regions. This suggests that geographical trends may be difficult to document if they are subtle and occur in species with high variability among regional populations. Before further speculation is made on this issue, thorough sampling must be done to determine the range of variability among regional populations as well as among different geographic regions.

The presentation of sex ratios in Table 14.5 does not reveal any clear phylogenetic trend at the family level. In fact, most species for which several samples are available vary from male-biased to female-biased sex ratios. However, many of the sex ratios given, including some of those from South Carolina, are based on small samples and on samples that are biased because of time and method of collections. Thus, adequate comparisons are difficult to make. At this time, I do not consider that any categorical statement can be made regarding any expectation that sex ratios are a trait tied to phylogenetic relationship per se. Differential sizes of the sexes at maturity are the only mechanism that can be considered a species trait that clearly affects adult sex ratios directly in some species of turtles, although differential mortality, emigration and immigration, or sexes at birth may influence the outcome in local populations.

Some of the ratios in Table 14.5 are aberrant from those expected mathematically, based on the sizes at which maturity is reached by the sexes. Using *T. scripta* as an exam-

ple, natural populations would be expected to have a significantly higher proportion of adult males, unless one or more of the other three factors are involved in altering the numbers of the sexes. In the 17 samples of *T. scripta*, 9 have more males than females ($p < .01$), 6 have sex ratios not significantly different from 1:1, and the remaining 2 have more females ($p < .01$). Of the South Carolina populations, the higher numbers of adult females are possibly explained by differential mortality of the sexes (Capers Island) and inadequate sampling (Kiawah Island). No apparent explanation can be given for the similar numbers of each sex at Risher Pond. The sample of Cahn (1937) was too small to make a valid assessment, but the large samples of Cagle (1942, 1950) and D. Moll (pers. com.) cannot be challenged in this way, suggesting either that an undetected sampling bias was involved or, perhaps more likely, that a true female-biased sex ratio occurred for some reason in these populations. Likewise, no obvious explanation is available for the higher female abundance reported by Webb (1961). The sample of Viosca (1933) was obviously a biased one, being composed of purchased animals from various populations, and should not be considered in an assessment of sex ratios for the species.

So when the 3 questionable *T. scripta* samples are eliminated (Kiawah Island; Cahn, 1937; Viosca, 1933), 9 have significantly more males, 2 have significantly more females, and 3 are not significantly different from 1:1. Therefore, 9 of 14 of the samples result in adult sex ratios that would be expected based on the differential sizes at which maturity is attained, and even they vary appreciably in the degree of the proportion of males. The variability that is apparent in the seemingly straightforward measure of sex ratios of a relatively well-studied species, whether as a result of sampling biases or natural occurrences, indicates that the interpretation of the causes of adult sex ratio in turtle populations is not a simple process and involves a complex of considerations.

Model for Natural or Sexual Selection of Sex Ratios

Data from several thoroughly assessed populations of *T. scripta* from South Carolina indicate that sex ratios in this species are weighted heavily toward males, although exceptions do exist (Capers Island). This is in contrast to the tendency for biased sex ratios of most animal species to be a consequence of greater female numbers, because of higher mortality of males (Trivers, 1972). The primary explanation for the high proportion of males observed in the South Carolina populations of slider turtles (Table 14.4) is differential maturation rates of the sexes. Male *T. scripta* reach maturity as a function of their body size after approximately 2 to 5 years of age, depending upon juvenile growth rates (Gibbons et al., 1981). Thus, fast-growing males from Par Pond reach maturity at a plastron

Table 14.5. Adult sex ratios of turtle species from published studies of natural populations

Taxon	Location	Males	Females	Sex ratio	X^2	Reference
Chelidae						
Phrynops dahli	Colombia	13	19	0.68	NS	20
Platemys platycephala	South America	28	50	0.56	*	78
Cheloniidae						
Chelonia mydas	Aldabra	83	54	1.54	*	33
	Miskito Cay	132	337	0.39	**	14
	Indian Ocean	112	178	0.63	**	29
	Oman	128	114	1.12	NS	69
	Mexico	144	862	0.17	**	19
	Nicaragua	68	99	0.69	*	56
Lepidochelys olivacea	India	15	39	0.38	**	68
Chelydridae						
Chelydra serpentina	South Dakota	37	291	0.13	**	26
	SRP, S.C.	55	21	2.62	**	83
	Michigan	74	77	0.96	NS	6
		87	79	1.10	NS	76
	Quebec	27	28	0.96	NS	16
	Tennessee	14	8	1.75	NS	44
Macroclemys temminckii	Louisiana	25	33	0.76	NS	31
Emydidae						
Batagur baska	Malaysia	83	64	1.30	NS	54
Chinemys reevesii	Asia	119	110	1.08	NS	70
Chrysemys picta	Illinois	14	14	1.00	NS	10
		28	39	0.72	NS	4
		17	14	1.21	NS	10
		39	3	13.00	**	10
		55	45	1.22	**	39
	Louisiana, Arkansas	21	37	0.57	*	39
	Michigan	51	51	1.00	NS	10
		265	215	1.23	NS	24
		849	481	1.77	**	83
		875	325	2.69	**	76
		242	184	1.32	**	15
	New Mexico	55	54	1.02	NS	38
	New York	42	29	1.45	NS	43
		62	28	2.21	*	5
	Ontario	129	179	0.72	**	75
	Pennsylvania	374	375	1.00	NS	32
	Saskatchewan	64	61	1.05	NS	63
	Wisconsin	32	28	1.14	NS	38
		32	23	1.39	NS	39
		270	209	1.29	NS	21
	Tennessee	17	19	0.89	NS	39
Clemmys guttata	Indiana	17	15	1.13	NS	37
	Pennsylvania	61	79	0.77	NS	45
	Ohio	21	42	0.50	*	79
C. insculpta	Michigan	86	105	0.82	NS	50
	New Jersey	311	464	0.67	**	50
C. marmorata	California	246	210	1.17	NS	36
C. muhlenbergii	United States	22	29	0.76	NS	11
		82	75	1.09	NS	80
Deirochelys reticularia	Ellenton Bay, S.C.	265	95	2.79	**	83
	Lost Lake, S.C.	19	17	1.12	NS	83
	Risher Pond, S.C.	22	11	2.00	NS	83
Emydoidea blandingii	Massachusetts	41	33	1.24	NS	49
	Michigan	49	173	0.28	**	76
		14	55	0.25	**	28
Graptemys barbouri	Florida	180	131	1.37	**	41
G. geographica	Quebec	132	79	1.67	*	53
	Wisconsin	45	15	3.00	**	55
G. nigrinoda	Alabama	39	10	3.90	**	57
G. ouachitensis	Louisiana	48	85	0.56	*	71
	Wisconsin	68	265	0.26	**	55
G. pseudogeographica	Upper Missouri River	36	36	1.00	NS	25
	Wisconsin	68	109	0.62	**	55
G. pulchra	Southeastern United States	49	53	0.92	NS	81
Malaclemys terrapin	Kiawah Island, S.C.	138	84	1.64	**	83
Mauremys caspica caspica	Europe	56	44	1.27	NS	52
M. c. rivulata	Europe	30	21	1.43	NS	52
M. leprosa	Europe, Africa	44	38	1.16	NS	52
Pseudemys concinna	Florida	66	57	1.16	NS	30
P. floridana	Ellenton Bay, S.C.	59	45	1.31	NS	83
Rhinoclemmys diademata	Venezuela	11	30	0.37	**	67

Table 14.5 -- *Continued*

Taxon	Location	Males	Females	Sex ratio	X^2	Reference
Terrapene carolina	Indiana	15	24	0.63	NS	37
	Maryland	107	122	0.88	NS	9
	Missouri	384	314	1.22	NS	42
T. coahuila	Mexico	70	94	0.74	NS	40
Trachemys scripta	Louisiana	123	102	1.21	NS	2
	South Carolina	(See Table 14.4)				
	Mississippi	115	77	1.49	**	66
	Illinois	403	441	0.91	NS	8
		396	576	0.69	**	4
		5	9	0.56	NS	3
	Oklahoma	46	13	3.54	**	18
	Panama	137	71	1.93	**	35
	Belize	152	188	0.81	NS	82
Kinosternidae						
Kinosternon flavescens	Oklahoma	23	20	1.15	NS	22
	Oliver National Wildlife Refuge, Okla.	64	88	0.73	NS	27
	Donita's Pond, Okla.	20	13	1.54	NS	27
K. f. arizonense	Arizona	7	22	0.32	**	64
	Arizona, Mexico	8	15	0.53	NS	51
K. f. flavescens	Nebraska	18	18	1.00	NS	64
	United States, Mexico	311	263	1.18	*	64
		158	137	1.15	NS	51
K. f. spooneri	Illinois, Iowa, Missouri	60	58	1.03	NS	64
K. integrum	Mexico	28	33	0.85	NS	13
K. sonoriense	Tule Stream, Ariz.	99	90	1.10	NS	46
K. subrubrum	Oklahoma	21	20	1.05	NS	22
	Cowan Creek, Okla.	47	71	0.66	*	27
	Tishomingo, Okla.	16	24	0.67	NS	27
	Lake Texoma, Okla.	16	28	0.57	NS	27
	Berry's Pond, Okla.	23	35	0.66	NS	27
	Ellenton Bay, S.C.	268	200	1.34	**	62
	SRP, S.C.	82	81	1.01	NS	62
	Ellenton Bay, S.C.	405	308	1.31	**	83
	Risher Pond, S.C.	27	40	0.68	NS	83
	Rainbow Bay, S.C.	79	76	1.04	NS	83
Sternotherus carinatus	Oklahoma	22	36	0.61	NS	27
		17	15	1.13	NS	22
S. depressus	Alabama	224	92	2.43	**	77
S. minor	United States	310	341	0.91	NS	47
S. odoratus	United States	80	97	0.82	NS	17
		43	46	0.93	NS	17
		40	42	0.95	NS	17
		29	36	0.81	NS	17
		65	83	0.78	NS	17
		51	35	1.46	NS	17
	Jacob, Ill.	33	16	2.06	*	4
	Elkville, Ill.	18	57	0.32	**	4
	Oklahoma	18	18	1.00	NS	22
		118	115	1.03	NS	27
	Michigan	36	32	1.13	NS	83
	Whitmore Lake, Mich.	77	178	0.43	**	1
	Indiana	11	19	0.58	NS	37
	Ellenton Bay, S.C.	94	80	1.18	NS	83
	Lost Lake, S.C.	37	29	1.28	NS	83
	Risher Pond, S.C.	27	25	1.08	NS	83
	Par Pond, S.C.	44	17	2.59	**	83
	Steel Creek, S.C.	32	28	1.14	NS	83
Pelomedusidae						
Podocnemis vogli	Venezuela	27	61	0.44	**	67
Testudinidae						
Chersina angulata	South Africa	109	76	1.43	*	65
Geochelone gigantea	Aldabra	30	31	0.97	NS	34
	Anse Mais, Aldabra	51	94	0.54	**	23
	Takamaka, Aldabra	80	73	1.10	NS	23
Testudo graeca	Turkey, Greece	48	23	2.09	*	58
T. hermanni	France	166	168	0.99	NS	72
	Greece	121	114	1.06	NS	73
Xerobates agassizii	Mexico	69	57	1.21	NS	59
	Utah	65	50	1.30	NS	7
X. berlandieri	Hargill, Tex.	31	8	3.88	**	60
	Yturria Ranch, Tex.	36	32	1.13	NS	60

Table 14.5 -- *Continued next page*

Table 14.5 -- *Continued*

Taxon	Location	Males	Females	Sex ratio	X^2	Reference
	Loma Tio Alejos, Tex.	75	36	2.08	**	61
	Laguna Atascosa, Tex.	67	39	1.72	**	74
Trionychidae						
Trionyx muticus	Kansas	1,148	168	6.83	**	48
T. spiniferus	Minnesota	73	98	0.74	NS	12
	Illinois	24	17	1.41	NS	4

Note: Sex ratios are based on best estimates from tables, figures, text, or personal communication with the author. Abbreviation: NS, $p \geq .05$.

References: 1, Risley, 1933; 2, Viosca, 1933; 3, Cahn, 1937; 4, Cagle, 1942; 5, Raney and Lachner, 1942; 6, Lagler and Applegate, 1943; 7, Woodbury and Hardy, 1948; 8, Cagle, 1950; 9, Stickel, 1950; 10, Cagle, 1954; 11, Barton and Price, 1955; 12, Breckenridge, 1955; 13, Mosimann, 1956; 14, Carr and Giovannoli, 1957; 15, Sexton, 1959b; 16, Mosimann and Bider, 1960; 17, Tinkle, 1961; 18, Webb, 1961; 19, Caldwell, 1962a; 20, Medem, 1966; 21, Ream and Ream, 1966; 22, Mahmoud, 1967; 23, Gaymer, 1968; 24, Gibbons, 1968b; 25, Timken, 1968; 26, Hammer, 1969; 27, Mahmoud, 1969; 28, Gibbons, 1970c; 29, Hirth and Carr, 1970; 30, Jackson, 1970; 31, Dobie, 1971; 32, Ernst, 1971c; 33, Frazier, 1971; 34, Grubb, 1971; 35, Moll and Legler, 1971; 36, Bury, 1972; 37, Minton, 1972; 38, Christiansen and Moll, 1973; 39, Moll, 1973; 40, Brown, 1974; 41, Sanderson, 1974; 42, Schwartz and Schwartz, 1974; 43, Bayless, 1975; 44, Froese and Burghardt, 1975; 45, Ernst, 1976; 46, Hulse, 1976; 47, Iverson, 1977a; 48, Plummer, 1977; 49, Graham and Doyle, 1979; 50, Harding and Bloomer, 1979; 51, Iverson, 1979c; 52, Busack and Ernst, 1980; 53, Gordon and MacCulloch, 1980; 54, Moll, 1980; 55, Vogt, 1980a; 56, Mortimer, 1981; 57, Lahanas, 1982; 58, Lambert, 1982; 59, Osorio and Bury, 1982; 60, Rose and Judd, 1982; 61, Auffenberg and Weaver, 1969, in Rose and Judd, 1982; 62, Gibbons, 1983a; 63, MacCulloch and Secoy, 1983a; 64, Berry and Berry, 1984; 65, Branch, 1984; 66, Parker, 1984; 67, Pritchard and Trebbau, 1984; 68, Silas et al., 1980, in Pritchard and Trebbau, 1984; 69, Ross, 1984; 70, Lovich et al., 1985; 71, Shively and Jackson, 1985; 72, Stubbs and Swingland, 1985; 73, Stubbs et al., 1985; 74, Bury and Smith, 1986; 75, Balcombe and Licht, 1987; 76, Congdon, pers. com.; 77, K. Dodd, pers. com.; 78, Ernst and Lovich, pers. com.; 79, Lovich, pers. com.; 80, Lovich and Ernst, pers. com.; 81, Lovich and McCoy, pers. com.; 82, D. Moll, pers, com.; 83, this study.

*$p < .05$.

**$p < .01$.

length of about 100 mm, similar to males from Ellenton Bay, which grow more slowly. Females in these two populations reach maturity at approximate ages of 6 to 8 years, not as a function of size. Thus, Par Pond females are greater than 200 mm in length at maturity, and those at Ellenton Bay are usually at least 160 mm. Consequently, a portion of the males of the population will have matured at least one to two years and as many as five to six years before females in the same cohorts. Therefore, the adult sex ratio is strongly influenced by the differential maturation rates of the sexes.

The impact of biased hatchling sex ratios, extreme differential mortality, or differential emigration and immigration of the sexes is more difficult to assess and has not been documented for the SRP populations at this time. Males commonly mature one to several years before females in many turtle species; hence, a higher frequency of males would be expected unless other factors override the effect. The hatchling sex ratio should not be expected to be 1:1 in any particular year, or even over long-term intervals, in *T. scripta* or other species of turtles with temperature-dependent sex determination. However, establishing the influence of hatchling sex ratios will be difficult in natural populations and is yet to be documented.

Survivorship curves of adult male and female *T. scripta* have not been shown to differ appreciably on the SRP (see Chapter 15); therefore, differential mortality patterns do not satisfactorily explain the observed sex ratio im-

balance. In fact, the numbers of males and females in age classes above that at which males reach maturity in the large Ellenton Bay population are effectively equal (Table 14.4), suggesting that mortality of the sexes within each cohort is similar in this population, with an assumption of 1:1 hatchling sex ratios. Differential survivorship of adults of both sexes is almost certain to occur in populations of many species simply because of differences in behavior patterns. Predator selection of adult females during nesting has been documented (e.g., Seigel, 1980b). Predation on males because they are smaller has been inferred in the Capers Island population of *T. scripta*. Because of the variability and unpredictability of environments, no universal rule would seem to apply as to which sex might be favored. Differential mortality of the sexes would be a population-specific phenomenon. This could be an explanation for why not all of the South Carolina populations had a 1:1 sex ratio after adjustment for the differing ages at maturity (Table 14.4), although the available data do not support or refute this contention.

Finally, the effects of differential emigration and immigration on sex ratio must be considered, although data available at this time shed only a dim light on the subject. Adult male turtles have a propensity for moving more often and for longer distances than females (Morreale et al., 1984; Parker, 1984; Gibbons, 1986; also see Chapter 16), resulting in females that are relatively sedentary within a habitat and males that have a high rate of exchange among areas. This can confound sex ratio estimates, depending on when and for how long sampling was done. For example, long-term sampling efforts in a single, localized area could result in a higher proportion of males in the overall region being sampled because of the higher turnover of males as they moved among habitats. Short-term sampling efforts would be biased by whether more males had departed the study area than had arrived at the particular time of the census.

The variation in estimated sex ratios for *T. scripta* during different seasons and years at Ellenton Bay is partially a function of this phenomenon (Table 14.2), because of the movement of individuals between Ellenton Bay and surrounding aquatic habitats suitable for slider turtles. A final bias that should also be considered is that resulting from the size of the study area. Clearly, the effects of emigration and immigration are reduced as more and more populated areas are encompassed in the sampling program.

Imbalanced sex ratios favoring males should be expected in adults of *T. scripta* or other species in which males mature first. Furthermore, an expected ratio can be predicted based on mean ages at maturity. Aside from the obvious possibilities of sampling biases, an alteration in this ratio would be a consequence of biased hatchling sex ratios, differential mortality, or emigration and immigration. None of the biological variables discussed, except differential sizes of the sexes at maturity, would appear to be a species trait, because all can vary as a function of conditions specific to each particular population.

Future Studies with Sex Ratios

Sex ratios in a population will continue to be an important demographic parameter to determine. Because of numerous sampling biases that can influence the investigator's perception of the sex ratio, it is essential that actual sex ratios in turtle populations be established with as much certainty as possible through thorough sampling programs. The casual reporting of sex ratios based on small, seasonal, or otherwise potentially biased samples will not further our understanding of the significance of sex ratios in turtle populations.

Because the observed sex ratio at any time is dependent on only four factors (sex ratios of hatchlings that ultimately make up the adult population, differential mortality rates of the sexes, differential emigration and immigration rates of adults of both sexes, and differential ages of maturity of the sexes), certain predictions can be made about what should be expected within a population. In sexually size-dimorphic species, the sex ratio will normally be imbalanced in the direction of a higher proportion of the earlier-maturing sex. This is based on the premise that in sexually size-dimorphic species, the smaller sex will mature at a significantly younger age than

the larger. For example, male-biased sex ratios should be particularly apparent in genera such as *Graptemys* and *Trionyx,* in which females attain dramatically larger sizes than males. When this is not the case, the first suspicion should be directed toward sampling bias, although natural factors may ultimately be determined as the cause. In turtle populations of species in which males and females are approximately the same size, the sex ratio will not be imbalanced by the maturity factor.

Actual sex ratios would differ from the condition expected from maturation rates as a result of aberrant hatchling sex ratios or because of sex-specific rates of mortality or emigration and immigration. Observation of a sex ratio that differs from that predicted for a population on the basis of maturation rates should first entail an examination of mortality rates of the two sexes and a search for evidence that they are indeed different. It is unlikely that any difference would be observed in the juvenile stages of the two sexes, because male and female turtles are presumably similar ecologically and physiologically until maturity is reached. Therefore, evidence of differential mortality of the adults should be sought. If the population interacts with others in the region, consideration should be given to whether the sexes vary in their emigration or immigration rates.

If equal mortality rates between adults of the two sexes are demonstrated in a population in which the sex ratio is different from that predicted from the maturation rates, and if emigration and immigration effects are ruled out, then differential mortality of juveniles or an unequal sex ratio among hatchlings is the only possible explanation. All of these considerations must be tempered with an awareness of how sampling methods influence the numbers of each sex captured and whether an investigator can distinguish between actual ratios and perceived ones that are strongly biased.

My prediction is that no documentation is forthcoming that reveals a significant difference in mortality between the two sexes during the juvenile stage. The shift in adult sex ratio because of a difference in sex ratio of the hatchlings from previous years could be a possible explanation in some situations (e.g., Vogt and Bull, 1984; Congdon, pers. com.) and should be looked for in natural populations. It is conceivable, for example, that unusually cool temperatures during the first part of the summer in successive years could result in an excess of male turtles in the populations of a region and could be ultimately reflected in the adult sex ratio in populations in that region. Unusually warm summers could, of course, result in an excess of females. Should this explanation seem like the appropriate one to use because of the observation of an aberrant sex ratio, a test would be to examine more than one population in the same region. If climatic temperatures are responsible, other regional populations having similar nest characteristics with regard to shading, hydric conditions, soil type, and so forth should also show the same phenomenon.

My recommendation to investigators determining sex ratios in natural populations is to consider every possible bias in the estimate of the actual, functional, adult sex ratio before the ratios are reported in the literature as meaningful. The reporting of sex ratios that are based on small samples or that have a high possibility of having been influenced by various sampling biases should be avoided. Such information is counterinstructive to anyone attempting to attribute significance in some synthetic or conceptual manner to sex ratios in natural populations. A special caution is urged in regard to determinations of age and size at maturity of individuals of each sex in particular populations. An error in establishing maturation times can strongly influence perceived sex ratios. A careful examination of age structure and age-specific ratios should be a primary target in turtle population studies where sex ratio is an element of interest.

The sex ratio has been demonstrated to be a species attribute of turtles only with respect to the influence of differential maturation rates. That is, in species in which males ordinarily mature earlier than females, a male-biased sex ratio should be expected and could be considered a characteristic of the species. The other potential demographic influences have not been documented to follow characteristic trends in any species of turtle to date. However, such trends may indeed exist and should be sought.

In a consideration of the application of evolutionary concepts to turtle sex ratios, a theory that emerges as a paradox in the slider turtle, as well as other species in which males mature at significantly younger ages than females, is the one first proposed by Fisher (1930) that the female should produce more of the sex that is the least costly and in shortest supply. Because the sex of a turtle egg of many species is apparently not determined until after egg laying, natural selection cannot operate on this trait unless female turtles select nest sites on the basis of anticipated sex-determining temperatures and with a proper assessment of which sex would be more successful in the population. Convincing evidence that such behavior and insight occurs in female turtles has not been demonstrated.

Acknowledgments

I thank Judith L. Greene for assistance in analysis of the South Carolina data. Justin Congdon offered numerous helpful suggestions and provided data on turtles from the University of Michigan's E. S. George Reserve. Stephen J. Morreale contributed ideas and provided assistance in data collection. Jim Knight assisted in the literature review. Jeff Lovich contributed greatly in gathering reference material and reviewing the manuscript. My thanks to Bruce Bury, Joe Schubauer, and Susan Novak for critical comments on the manuscript. I appreciate the assistance of Pat Davis in typing the manuscript. Research was supported by contract DE-AC09-76SROO-819 between the U.S. Department of Energy and the University of Georgia and by National Science Foundation grant DEB-79-04758.

Life Tables of a Slider Turtle Population

NAT B. FRAZER
Department of Biology
Mercer University
Macon, Georgia 31207

J. WHITFIELD GIBBONS
JUDITH L. GREENE
Savannah River Ecology Laboratory
Drawer E
Aiken, South Carolina 29802

Abstract

A complete life table is constructed for the slider turtle, *Trachemys scripta*, based on the population at Ellenton Bay, South Carolina. Survival from the time eggs are laid until hatchlings enter the water the following spring averages 10.5%. Annual survivorship of 1-, 2-, and 3-year-olds ranges from 53.9% to 82.9%. Annual survivorship of turtles more than 4 years old averages 84.4% for males and 81.4% for females. Annual per capita fecundity of females is estimated as 1.28 female eggs, taking into account a 1:1 sex ratio of eggs and the mean proportion of adult females that are reproductively active in any given year (37%). Various assumptions that must be taken into account are discussed. The population is declining at a rate of 15% per year if both death and emigration are combined to calculate ℓ_x. The net reproductive rate (R_0) is 0.137, with a realized intrinsic rate of increase (r) of -0.1675. Also presented are alternative life tables representing best- and worst-case scenarios that depict highs and lows of annual variation in survivorship and fecundity estimates.

Introduction

Life tables provide a digestible summary of vast amounts of information on survivorship, fecundity, and age at maturity for a particular population. Given certain assumptions about the stability of the age distribution of the population, the information in a life table may also provide insight into population dynamics and life history evolution.

Elegant mathematical models of population dynamics, and detailed methods for describing populations in terms of age-specific survivorship and fecundity, were developed by the middle of the present century (e.g., Lotka, 1922; Fisher, 1930; Leslie, 1945, 1948; Deevey, 1947). Since 1950, ecologists have examined the mathematical consequences of incorporating various life histories into population models in an attempt to provide a unifying theory of life history evolution (e.g., Cole, 1954; Lewontin, 1965; Hamilton, 1966; MacArthur and Wilson, 1967; Gadgil and Bossert, 1970; Pianka, 1970, 1972; Mertz, 1971; Hirshfield and Tinkle, 1975; Schaffer and Rosenzweig, 1977; Caswell, 1983; for reviews, see Stearns, 1976, 1977, 1980).

Lack (1966, 1968) and Tinkle (1969) pioneered efforts to assess life history theory for vertebrate populations with extensive evidence from field studies of birds and lizards, respectively. More than a decade ago, Wilbur (1975a) pointed out that the study of life history tactics suffered from a dearth of information on long-lived, iteroparous organisms. Turtles are among the longest-lived of all vertebrates (see review by Gibbons, 1987), and many species exhibit iteroparity both within and among years (see review by Moll, 1979). Turtles are conspicuously absent from a recent review comparing life history traits among reptiles (Stearns, 1984), primarily because, until recently, too few published studies provided easy access to values for all of the following traits in one reference: average length of adult females, age at maturity, clutch size, and number of clutches per year.

Wilbur and Morin (1988) attempted to provide an assessment of life history evolution in turtles based on an extensive review of published information on body size, age at maturity, clutch size, egg size, clutch number, and female cycle (i.e., "the number of years between bouts of reproduction") across taxonomic groups, latitude, habitats, and diets. Their comparisons among populations and among species were based almost exclusively on egg volume, clutch size, and clutch frequency, which are not the only determinants of life history evolution or even of reproductive effort (Hirshfield and Tinkle, 1975).

Although Wilbur and Morin (1988) discussed general trends related to female body size and habitat, it is not yet possible to assess the finer aspects of trade-offs between survival and reproduction in life history evolution within the order Testudines, because of the paucity of complete life tables. For example, information is available on clutch sizes, female body sizes, and clutch frequencies for local or geographically distinct populations of several species (e.g., Chelonia mydas, Sternotherus odoratus, and Chrysemys picta, in Wilbur and Morin, 1988), but we do not know how their population dynamics differ or whether individuals from populations with a relatively smaller annual reproductive output have higher annual survival rates that allow for additional deferred reproduction, as predicted by theories of life history evolution (e.g., Hirshfield and Tinkle, 1975; Schaffer and Rosenzweig, 1977). Few field studies on turtles provide estimates of survival rates for all

age classes or include an assessment of reproductive output that takes into account the female cycle of interseasonal reproductive frequency, both of which are necessary for constructing realistic life tables and assessing differences in life history evolution.

Complete life tables have been provided for only one population of freshwater turtles, Chrysemys picta (Wilbur, 1975a; Tinkle et al., 1981), and for three marine species, Lepidochelys olivacea (Márquez M. et al., 1982b), L. kempi (Márquez M. et al., 1982a), and Caretta caretta (Frazer, 1983a; Crouse et al., 1987). It is noteworthy that most life tables thus far constructed for turtles have been based upon studies that did not have the life table as a goal when they began (i.e., they were a posteriori analyses). It is clear that further advances in elucidating and interpreting the life history evolution of turtles await the compilation of additional life tables (Wilbur and Morin, 1988). In this chapter, we provide the first complete life table analysis for Trachemys scripta.

Methods

Before beginning to assess the characteristics needed to compile a life table for a given population, the ecologist must decide upon a definition of the population to be studied. This is not so easy with freshwater turtles as it might seem, because of the high rate of exchange of individuals among aquatic habitats in a region (Chapter 16). A discussion of what constitutes a population of turtles and the limitations of the population concept is given in Chapter 1. For the purposes of these analyses, the Ellenton Bay population is considered to be the slider turtles inhabiting the Carolina bay itself or the satellite bodies of water within 2 km for which Ellenton Bay is the focal habitat.

The attributes necessary for compiling a life table for turtles are (1) mean age at maturity; (2) realized per capita fecundity for females, incorporating clutch size clutch frequency (intraseasonal) and adjusted for interseasonal reproductive frequency (i.e., fecundity estimates must be adjusted on the basis of the "female reproductive cycle," sensu Wilbur and Morin, 1988, or the mean proportion of adult females that are not reproductively active each year); and (3) survivorship of all age (or stage) classes from egg through adulthood.

AGE AT MATURITY

Obtaining estimates of mean age at maturity is important in life history studies because the realized rate of population increase (or decrease) is especially sensitive to changes in age at maturity (Lewontin, 1965; Gadgil and Bossert, 1970). Although many turtle ecologists might agree that "sexual maturity is related to obtaining a certain size rather than a certain age" (Bury, 1979), things probably are much more complex in reality because of interactions between size and age that are not well understood.

Gibbons et al. (1981) compared growth and maturity of *T. scripta* in natural (Ellenton Bay) and thermally enhanced (Par Pond) environments. They found that female *T. scripta* in the two ponds matured at about the same age, but those living on a more protein-rich diet in the warmer Par Pond matured at a larger average size than did those in Ellenton Bay. On the other hand, males matured at about the same size but at different ages (i.e., earlier in Par Pond than in Ellenton Bay). In contrast, Thornhill (1982) found that female *Trachemys scripta elegans* living in a thermally enhanced pond matured faster and at a larger average size than those living in control lakes.

Attempts to determine *the* age or size at maturity, even within a given turtle population, will continue to be met with frustration. Even though the mean size of adult female *Chelonia mydas* may differ in geographically separated populations, Carr and Goodman (1970) suggested that individual females mature at different sizes and that growth slows markedly once maturity has been achieved. Thus, an individual that matures at a small size may remain relatively small all her life (Carr and Goodman, 1970). We suspect that the same is true for many other species; hence, maturity is neither strictly size- nor age-dependent.

According to dissections, measurement of external secondary sexual characteristics such as claw length, and x rays of Ellenton Bay *T. scripta* of known age (see Chapter 9), most females are mature by the time they are 6 to 8 years old. The great majority of females less than 159 mm in plastron length are immature. The majority of males are mature by the time they reach age 4 at an average body size of 100 mm. For the purposes of the life table analysis, we assume that females mature at age 7 and males mature at age 4.

FECUNDITY

A first approximation of mean annual fecundity was derived by multiplying mean clutch size by mean annual clutch frequency. Clutch sizes were determined by x rays (Gibbons and Greene, 1979) for 95 clutches, yielding a mean clutch size of 6.25 eggs (SD = 1.79, range = 5–15) for females leaving Ellenton Bay. Mean clutch size does not vary significantly among years for *T. scripta* (Gibbons, 1982; Gibbons et al., 1982); therefore, we consider 6.25 to be an adequate estimate of mean clutch size.

Some *T. scripta* may lay more than one clutch in a reproductive season (Gibbons, 1982; Gibbons et al., 1982). Therefore, mean fecundity of those turtles nesting in a particular season is somewhat greater than mean clutch size. We recorded the number of females laying one and two clutches each year and estimated mean clutch fre-

Table 15.1. Clutch frequencies for *Trachemys scripta* at Ellenton Bay

Year	Number laying single clutches	Number laying two clutches
1976	2	0
1977	9	0
1978	20	2
1980	22	5
1981	14	1
1986	3	0
1987	12	1
Total	82	9

Note: Average clutch frequency = [(82 × 1) + (9 × 2)]/(82 + 9) = 1.10.

quency for each year as the total number of clutches divided by the total number of females that laid those clutches (Table 15.1). Multiplying mean clutch size (6.25) by mean annual clutch frequency (1.10) gave 6.88 as the mean annual fecundity of reproductively active females in the population. Because this portion of the life table analysis pertains only to females, we then multiplied the fecundity estimate by 0.50 (assuming a 1:1 sex ratio of eggs), resulting in an estimate of 3.44. However, further adjustments were necessary in order to estimate per capita mean annual fecundity for the whole female population.

Like other turtle species (e.g., *Chelonia mydas*, Carr and Carr, 1970; *Caretta caretta*, Hughes, 1976; *Deirochelys reticularia*, Gibbons and Greene, 1978; *Gopherus polyphemus*, Auffenberg and Iverson, 1979, and Landers et al., 1980; *Chrysemys picta*, Tinkle et al., 1981; *Emydoidea blandingii*, Congdon et al., 1983b; *Chelydra serpentina*, Congdon et al., 1987), some adult female *T. scripta* apparently may lay no eggs in a given year (Gibbons, 1982). Age-specific fecundity, m_x, is conventionally recorded as the mean number of eggs laid per female of age *x* (Mertz, 1970). Therefore, the estimate of mean annual fecundity (6.88 eggs) calculated above was adjusted to account for the substantial proportion of adult females alive in Ellenton Bay that were not known to be reproductively active in any given year. This was accomplished by multiplying 6.88 by the mean proportion of females known to be reproductively active. The mean proportion of reproductively active females was determined as follows.

For each year the drift fence was patrolled, we divided adult females into four categories (Table 15.2). The first category (A) consisted of females that were known to have eggs in a given year, because they were palpated or x-rayed. We also included any females that both left and returned to the bay during the reproductive season (April–July). We assumed that any female that had eggs was reproductively active and that any female both leaving and returning to the bay during the reproductive season was doing so to reproduce.

The second category (B) consisted of any additional

Table 15.2. Numbers of adult females known to be in Ellenton Bay
each year that complete drift fence was up

Year	A	B	C	D
1975	39	28	29	4
1976	8	11	36	6
1977	11	4	37	7
1978	25	8	34	3
1980	32	8	24	2
1981	12	76	28	2
1982	3	2	11	0
1986	5	9	26	0
1987	13	1	12	1

Abbreviations: A, adult females that were palpated or x-rayed with eggs or that exited and reentered during nesting season; B, additional adult females that exited during nesting season; C, additional adult females known to be alive in Ellenton Bay during sampling period; D, additional females known to be alive in Ellenton Bay and suspected to be adults that year, based on growth curve and size at next capture or previous capture.

Table 15.3. Estimated percentages of adult females present in
Ellenton Bay that were reproductively active in a given year

Year	Low	High
1975	39.00	67.00
1976	13.11	31.15
1977	18.64	25.42
1978	35.71	47.14
1980	48.48	60.61
1981	10.17	74.58
1982	18.75	31.25
1986	12.50	35.00
1987	48.15	51.85
Mean	27.17	47.11
SD	15.62	17.60

Note: Percentages are based on information in Table 15.2. For each year the low estimate = $A/(A + B + C + D) \times 100$, and the high estimate = $(A + B)/(A + B + C + D) \times 100$.

adult females that left the bay between April and July but did not return during that time. These females were considered to be potentially reproductively active. Some of them may have nested inside the fence and subsequently fallen into a bucket (i.e., turtles captured in buckets on the inside of the drift fence are considered to be leaving the bay).

The third category (C) included adult females that were known to be alive in Ellenton Bay in a given year. This category included four subgroups of turtles:

1. Adult females that were captured in the bay or caught entering the bay at the drift fence immediately before the reproductive season and that did not leave the bay were assumed to have been in the bay during the reproductive season.
2. Adult females that were caught in the bay immediately after the reproductive season were assumed to have been in the bay during the reproductive season.
3. Adult females that were caught inside the bay were included in category C for previous years if the drift fence had been up continuously over the period and if they were known to have been adults in those earlier years because they had been caught previously as adults (i.e., with plastron lengths greater than 159 mm).
4. Adult females that were caught in the bay were included in category C for subsequent years if the drift fence had been up continuously and if they were known to be alive in the intervening year(s) because they had been caught again at a later date.

In short, category C included all known adult females not included in categories A or B but known to have been alive in the bay in a given year.

The last category (D) contained any additional females known to be alive in the bay and estimated to have been adults in a given year based on the growth curve (Fig. 15.1) and their known size at some previous or subsequent capture. That is, any female known to have been in the bay and estimated to have had a plastron length greater than 159 mm was assumed to have been an adult female capable of reproduction.

The information in Table 15.2 was used to obtain high and low estimates of the proportion of adult females that were reproductively active in the population each year (Table 15.3). The results indicate that an average of 27.17% (mean low estimate) to 47.11% (mean high estimate) of the adult females present in Ellenton Bay are reproductively active in any given year. To adjust mean annual fecundity of nesting females to reflect the substantial proportion of females not reproducing, we multiplied 3.44 by 0.3714, the average of our mean high and low estimates of the proportion of females that reproduce in any given year (Table 15.3). This resulted in an estimate of mean annual fecundity of 1.28 female eggs per adult female.

Our estimate of mean annual fecundity (1.28 female eggs per adult female) may appear somewhat low to many readers, given that clutch size for *T. scripta* in Ellenton Bay ranges from 5 to 15 eggs and that some females may lay more than one clutch in a particular season. However, mean clutch size and intraseasonal clutch frequency are only two of the three major attributes necessary to estimate average female fecundity. The other is interseasonal reproductive frequency. In the event that individual females do not reproduce at all in a given season, realized per capita fecundity will be greatly reduced.

The vast majority of field studies on turtle reproductive ecology report only mean clutch size, although many studies also provide estimates of interseasonal clutch frequency or internesting intervals (see Moll, 1979, for review; Lovich et al., 1983). With the exception of studies on sea turtles (e.g., Carr and Carr, 1970; Hughes, 1976; Richardson et al., 1978), earlier accounts of female turtles that failed to reproduce on an annual basis were likely to be interpreted as evidence of senility (e.g., Cagle, 1944c; Gibbons, 1969). In recent years, carefully conducted long-term studies are providing further evidence to indicate that the failure or inability to reproduce annually is not a rare phenomenon among female turtles.

C. Limpus (pers. com.) has monitored adult female *Caretta caretta* at their feeding grounds in Australia by means of laparoscopy and suggests that periods as long as 10 years may elapse between reproductive episodes for some individuals. After 17 years of intensive tagging, Richardson and Richardson (1982) estimated that, on average, 56% of adult female *C. caretta* did not nest in any given year on the coast of Georgia. A similar pattern was earlier suggested for *Chelonia mydas* at Tortuguero, Costa Rica (Carr et al., 1978).

Nor is the attribute apparently limited only to sea turtles and *T. scripta*. Gibbons and Greene (1978) reported nonannual reproduction in *Deirochelys reticularia*. Findings by Landers et al. (1980) for *Gopherus polyphemus* and by Dobie (1971) for *Macroclemys temminckii* suggest that these species display the same characteristic. Tinkle et al. (1981) found that 30% to 50% of the adult female *Chrysemys picta* on the E. S. George Reserve in Michigan did not reproduce every year. Christens and Bider (1986) reported that only 40% to 80% of the adult female *C. picta marginata* in southwestern Quebec from 7 to 11 years old reproduced each year, whereas all females greater than 11 years old were reproductively active each year. Schwartzkopf and Brooks (1986) found that only 43% to 73% of adult female *C. picta* nest each year in Ontario.

In further work on the E. S. George Reserve, Congdon et al. (1983b) reported that only 23% to 48% of adult female *Emydoidea blandingii* may reproduce in a given year. Only 60% of the adult females believed to be in a population of *Chelydra serpentina* on the reserve were reproductively active each year, based on nest counts and sightings of nesting females (Congdon et al., 1987).

Previous reports of senescence or senility in female turtles may have been based on observations of adult females that simply were not reproductively active in the season in which they were examined. Cagle (1944c) reported "senile ovaries" in *Pseudemys scripta elegans* but did not define the term. Legler (1960a) reported seeing "seemingly inactive ovaries" in some older female *Terrapene ornata*. Gibbons (1969) suggested that the absence of enlarged follicles in *Deirochelys reticularia* might have indicated senility or a reduced reproductive potential in older individuals. However, he also suggested that *D. reticularia* might simply have a biennial reproductive cycle. More detailed study is needed to determine whether turtles do in fact exhibit senescence in terms of their reproductive capabilities. At present we know of no conclusive evidence that

they do nor any reason why a long-lived species without parental care should be expected to. We believe that nonannual reproduction is a normal occurrence, perhaps resulting from resource availability and energy acquisition, and we assume that *Trachemys scripta* continues reproducing (although not necessarily every season) through its adult lifetime.

Congdon et al. (1987) pointed out that it is difficult, if not impossible, to prove that an animal does not do something (e.g., reproduce) in the field. We agree and stress that it is imperative to determine the number (or proportion) of females that are reproductively active each year when assessing fecundity; otherwise, fecundity will likely continue to be grossly overestimated. Long-term studies must seek to provide estimates of the mean and variance in the annual proportions of females reproducing, to tie those characteristics to current theories of life history evolution, and to assess the role of environmental variables, if any, in determining whether an individual reproduces in any particular year.

It is difficult to establish a relationship between environmental quality and reproductive output, as measured by turtle clutch sizes and intraseasonal clutch frequencies (Gibbons et al., 1982). Perhaps the major effect of environmental quality does not influence these two attributes but acts to determine interseasonal reproductive frequency. That is, a good year may be a year in which a larger proportion of adult females is able to reproduce, rather than a year in which more individuals lay two clutches or larger clutches. However, because turtles may integrate energy acquisition over two or more years before reproducing, it will be difficult to identify the key environmental variables that would allow us to develop models predicting the timing and quantity of reproductive output. Such efforts represent one of the future challenges in the study of reproductive variability of all turtle species. An even greater challenge is to devise some means of determining the relative contributions of genotype and environment to observed reproductive variability. These challenges can be met only with continued improvement of long-term research.

SURVIVORSHIP

In attempting to assess survivorship, we looked at three life stages separately. First, we assessed survival from the time eggs were laid until the hatchlings entered Ellenton Bay (ages 0 to 1), based on egg counts and hatchlings captured at the drift fence. Next, we estimated survivorship for larger juveniles and adults (ages ≥ 4 years), based on recapture of live animals and recovery of shells of dead animals. Finally, we addressed the more difficult assessment of survival of young turtles between ages 1 and 4, turtles that are rarely seen and hence are difficult to study.

In the absence of available data, estimates of survivorship for this last group were fraught with assumptions.

SURVIVAL OF EGG TO HATCHLING. Survivorship during the first year of life (i.e., age 0 to 1) was assessed from the time eggs were laid to the time hatchlings entered Ellenton Bay. The number of eggs laid outside the drift fence was estimated for each year in which all females were x-rayed for egg counts (Gibbons and Greene, 1979) as they left the bay. The total number of eggs counted in x rays became the estimate of eggs leaving the bay for a given year. The number of hatchlings resulting from those eggs was estimated as the total number of hatchlings entering the bay the subsequent spring after overwintering in the nests (Gibbons and Nelson, 1978). Rarely, hatchlings are discovered entering the bay during the fall, presumably without overwintering in the nest. Any fall hatchlings were assumed to have resulted from eggs laid that same year.

Assessing the number of eggs leaving the bay and the number of hatchlings entering the bay the following year necessitated our using data only from certain years, because of the requirement that the drift fence be up both during the year in which eggs were counted as they left the bay and during the following spring in which hatchlings were counted as they entered the bay. Survivorship between the time eggs were laid and the time hatchlings entered the bay averaged 10.5% for the five years for which data were available (Table 15.4). Our estimate of survival rates for *T. scripta* from egg deposition to the time that hatchlings enter Ellenton Bay (10.5%) is unquestionably subject to error. Any factors that result in inaccurate estimates of the number of eggs leaving or the number of hatchlings entering Ellenton Bay will skew the survivorship estimate for that year (Table 15.4).

Because Ellenton Bay fluctuates in size within and among years, some females occasionally lay nests inside the drift fence (Table 15.5). Any hatchlings that leave such nests to enter the water presumably would not be caught in pitfall traps outside the drift fence. Nests laid

Table 15.4. Survivorship from egg to hatchling stage of *Trachemys scripta* at Ellenton Bay

Year	Eggs out	Hatchlings in	% survival
1977	51	14	27.5
1978	154	10	6.5
1980	157	15	9.6
1981	103	1	1.0
1986	25	2	8.0
Mean	98.0	8.4	10.5
SD	59.5	6.6	10.0

Note: Eggs out are based on x-ray photography of gravid females leaving the bay. Hatchlings in include hatchlings found at the drift fence in the fall of the same year and the spring of the next year.

Table 15.5. *Trachemys scripta* nests or nesting females discovered inside the drift fence at Ellenton Bay

Date	Turtle ID	Nearest bucket number
Known to be *T. scripta*		
24 May 1975	ABHO	34
9 June 1975	Unknown	4
9 May 1980	KMV	214
30 May 1980	BCMO	2
5 June 1980	YZCLP	56
22 June 1980	LWX	208
10 May 1986	Unknown	154
11 May 1986	Unknown	90
19 May 1987	BMOQ	92
28 May 1987	Unknown	98
29 May 1987	BCJZ	78
Destroyed nests thought to be *T. scripta*'s		
16 August 1986	Unknown	224
6 June 1987	Unknown	134
27 June 1987	Unknown	122
7 August 1987	Unknown	82
Not recorded	Unknown	174
Not recorded	Unknown	190

Note: For information on turtle IDs and bucket numbers, see Chapter 2.

inside the fence would not lead to substantially inaccurate determination of survival rates unless (1) the number of such nests was large relative to the number of nests laid outside the fence and/or (2) the percentage of hatchlings successfully entering Ellenton Bay from nests laid inside the fence was greatly different from that of hatchlings originating from nests laid outside the fence. It is not possible to determine whether these conditions are met at Ellenton Bay using data currently available. At Ellenton Bay the area inside the fence that is deemed suitable for nesting is minimal, and most areas are observed on a daily basis during drift fence checks. Personnel presently patrol the drift fence at Ellenton Bay at least once daily (twice during the nesting season; see Chapter 2) and occasionally find some evidence of new or destroyed nests inside the fence (Table 15.5). Although nests laid inside the fence are subject to predation in spring and summer months, quantification of nest and hatching success is lacking because of the requirement of finding every nest. Accurate determination of the number of nests laid inside the fence and subsequent nest or hatching success would necessitate that field workers patrol the terrestrial area inside the drift fence at approximately hourly intervals continually throughout the nesting season and periodically during the remainder of the year. Although this may seem an insurmountable task, such labor-intensive methods are presently used at the E. S. George Reserve in Michigan (Congdon, pers. com.), where the most accurate determinations of freshwater turtle nesting biology are being made. However, our assumption is that nesting by females inside the fence is a minor consideration in the present analyses.

Emigration and immigration of hatchlings are, by necessity, lumped with mortality and survivorship in our estimation procedure. The estimates of hatchling survivorship can be negatively biased if hatchlings emerging from Ellenton Bay eggs laid outside the drift fence migrate to aquatic habitats other than Ellenton Bay. This could happen, for example, if a female left Ellenton Bay and nested near another body of water. Although the female might return to Ellenton Bay after nesting, hatchlings later emerging from the nest might enter the nearer aquatic environment. Quantifying such behavior, if it exists, would necessitate continual monitoring of Ellenton Bay nests laid outside the drift fence and following hatchlings as they emerged in order to determine their destinations and, thus, the proportion of a cohort that enters Ellenton Bay. The question of what proportion of the hatchlings in a population actually are recruited into their mother's habitat deserves investigation in itself. It can be speculated that the habitat suitable for adults is not necessarily the most suitable for juveniles (e.g., see Moll and Legler, 1971), so natural selection might favor females that are discretionary in nesting with regard to the environment that will be encountered by their hatchlings. Ellenton Bay is presumed to be a suitable hatchling and juvenile habitat in most years and is surrounded by suitable nesting areas. Thus, we assume that most hatchlings of Ellenton Bay females make their initial entry into the aquatic environment at Ellenton Bay.

Our calculated values for hatchling survivorship can be overestimates in the more likely event that hatchlings from nests laid by females resident in other aquatic habitats move into Ellenton Bay after emerging from their nests. Although this is a possibility, Ellenton Bay represents the largest concentration of *T. scripta* within several kilometers in most years, so numbers of migrant nesting females from other populations are likely to be small.

Turtle ecologists know that eggs and hatchling turtles are vulnerable to predators and abiotic factors (e.g., Cagle, 1950; Auffenberg and Iverson, 1979; Bury, 1979; Bustard, 1979; Ehrenfeld, 1979; Ewert, 1979). Wilbur (1975a) suggested that the resulting high mortality was a primary cause for the evolution of multiple-broodedness (and hence longevity). Several authors have attempted to quantify survival rates for nests, eggs, and hatchlings. Most studies concentrate on determining nest success (e.g., the proportion of nests that are undisturbed or produce at least some hatchlings) or hatching success (e.g., the total number of hatchlings produced divided by the total number of eggs laid).

Ernst (1971c) reported a 34% hatching success for *Chrysemys picta* eggs left in situ in Pennsylvania. Wilbur (1975a) estimated that survivorship from the time eggs were laid until hatchlings entered the water was .18 for *C. picta* on the E. S. George Reserve in Michigan. Tinkle et al. (1981) later reported first-year survival rates to be

much higher (.67) in the same population. Christens and Bider (1987) found that only 24% of 185 *C. picta marginata* eggs deposited in southwestern Quebec resulted in hatchlings.

Other freshwater species have similar survival rates while in the nest. Wilhoft et al. (1979) reported that up to 100% of snapping turtle nests (*Chelydra serpentina*) may be destroyed by predators in New Jersey in some years. Congdon et al. (1987) recorded annual rates of 30% to 100% for predation on *Chelydra* nests in Michigan over a seven-year period. Ernst (1976) reported a 58% hatching success for *Clemmys guttata* in Pennsylvania. Congdon et al. (1983b) found that over a six-year period only 22% of *Emydoidea blandingii* nests produced at least some hatchlings and that emerging hatchlings represented only 18% of the eggs laid in their study area in Michigan. Ernst (1986) reported a 15.6% nest success for *Sternotherus odoratus* in Pennsylvania, with an overall hatching success of 15.4%.

Terrestrial turtles also suffer high mortality at early stages. Landers et al. (1980) reported that 89% of gopher tortoise nests were destroyed, mostly by mammalian predators. Diemer (1986) reviewed studies indicating predation rates of 74% to 100% on eggs and of 41% to 70% on hatchlings of gopher tortoises (*Gopherus polyphemus*). Fowler de Neira and Roe (1984) indicated that natural emergence success of *Geochelone elephantopus vandenburghi* eggs on Volcán Alcedo, Galápagos Islands, was 65% during the 1979–80 nesting season.

A review of the sea turtle literature by Hirth (1980) indicated that hatching success typically ranges from 60% to 85%. However, these figures almost certainly represent undisturbed nests. More-detailed studies suggest that hatching success may be much lower. For example, Fowler (1979) reported a hatching success of 83% for undisturbed *Chelonia mydas* nests at Tortuguero, Costa Rica. However, only 43% of the nests in her study area were in the undisturbed category; predators destroyed 39.7%, and other nests were destroyed by human poachers (6.6%), beach erosion (5.7%), and other problems (Fowler, 1979). Other marine species have similar records of destruction when disturbed nests are considered. Hopkins et al. (1978) reported that a combination of biotic and abiotic factors may cause hatching success of *Caretta caretta* nests in South Carolina to fall well below 10% in some years. Eckert (1987) reported that beach erosion alone may destroy 45% to 60% of all *Dermochelys coriacea* nests laid on Sandy Point, St. Croix.

The majority of turtle nesting studies indicate a clear pattern of low egg and hatchling survivorship in a wide variety of turtle species. However, most of the studies cited above are not strictly comparable to our estimate for survivorship during the first year of life. Studies that report only nest success or hatching success may lead to overestimation of the true proportion of eggs that result in hatchlings entering the population. For example, the fact that only 50% of the nests are depredated in a given population does not mean that 100% of eggs in all remaining nests will hatch. On the other hand, the fact that undisturbed nests have hatching rates of 85% does not mean that 85% of all eggs laid that year will become hatchlings. Furthermore, not all hatchlings will emerge from every nest (Fowler, 1979). Even after emergence, hatchlings may face further problems before they enter the habitat in which they will live. Ehrenfeld (1979) believed that the hatchlings of freshwater and marine species are particularly vulnerable to predation as they move from terrestrial to aquatic habitats (also see Chapter 16). Any death of hatchlings during this period will result in even lower survival rates during the first year of life. Although our estimate of 10.5% survival may seem lower than many others reported above, it must be kept in mind that our estimate encompasses the entire period from the time eggs were laid until just before the point that hatchlings entered the aquatic environment. Thus, losses due to nest failure, hatching success rates lower than 100%, death while overwintering in the nest, and mortality as the hatchlings move overland are all incorporated into our estimate. Estimates that cover only some portion of this period are expected to be somewhat higher than ours, all else being equal.

The determination of simple nest success or hatching success is certainly of ecological interest and should continue to be a part of any nesting study. Such work will help to pinpoint the critical timing of factors that influence survival and life history evolution. What is more important from the standpoint of demographic studies, however, is the overall determination of the proportion of eggs that become recruited into the population as hatchlings or yearlings.

It is difficult to compare findings from one study with those from another if terminology is confusing and methods are not clearly reported. In future studies, care must be taken to clarify what has been accomplished. Perhaps what is needed is some agreement on methodology for calculating and reporting hatching success, such as that provided in the *Manual of Sea Turtle Research and Conservation Techniques* (Pritchard et al., 1983).

SURVIVAL BEYOND AGE 4.   Survival rates for *T. scripta* more than 4 years old were assessed in two ways. One method used the remains (shells) of dead turtles to determine an age-at-death curve (Wilbur, 1975a). The other was based on compiling the records of live turtles to determine their ages at last observation (Tanner, 1978). For each method, survivorships of males and females were assessed separately.

Survival rates based on collection of dead shells.   Each winter, when water levels are low, SREL herpetologists conduct a shell roundup at Ellenton Bay and other study sites to

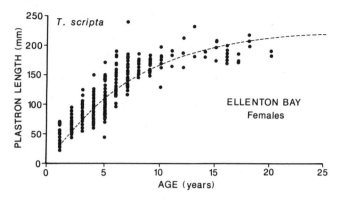

FIGURE 15.1.   Growth curve for known-age female *T. scripta* from Ellenton Bay. $Y = 234.0(1 - e^{-.128X})$; $N = 586$; $R^2 = 0.90$.

collect any remains of dead turtles in the area. We assumed that complete shells represented turtles that had died in the year they were discovered, based on shell-disintegration experiments that demonstrated a high disarticulation rate over only a few months. When marked shells were found, it often was possible to determine the age of the individual turtle at death if data were available from previous records of the animal's capture. For shells that were not marked and for individuals for which no age data were available, we measured the plastron length and used growth curves to estimate age (Figs. 15.1 and 15.2). This resulted in a sample of 77 female and 39 male shells for which ages could be estimated (Tables 15.6 and 15.7). In the case of males there was no difference in the cumulative numbers of 4- and 5-year-olds in our sample. Therefore, for males we assessed survivorship only from age 5 onward.

Cumulative frequencies for each age class were converted to reflect survivorship for a theoretical cohort of 1,000 for each sex (Tables 15.6 and 15.7). Linear regression was conducted on the logarithm (base 10) of the number of

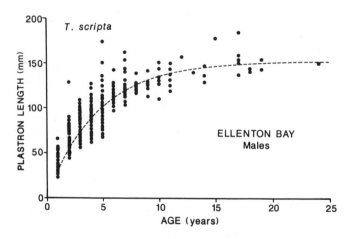

FIGURE 15.2.   Growth curve for known-age male *T. scripta* from Ellenton Bay. $Y = 151.4(1 - e^{-.218X})$; $N = 528$; $R^2 = 0.87$.

Table 15.6. Female shells recovered at Ellenton Bay

Age	Number of shells	Cumulative frequency	Scaled to 1,000
4	1	77	1,000
5	4	76	987
6	3	72	935
7	1	69	896
8	4	68	883
9	8	64	831
10	9	56	727
11	2	47	610
12	4	45	584
13	11	41	532
14	7	30	390
15	3	23	299
16	3	20	260
17	9	17	221
18	2	8	104
19	3	6	78
20	2	3	39
21	0	1	13
22	0	1	13
23	0	1	13
24	0	1	13
25	0	1	13
26	0	1	13
27	0	1	13
28	0	1	13
29	0	1	13
30	0	1	13
31	1	1	13

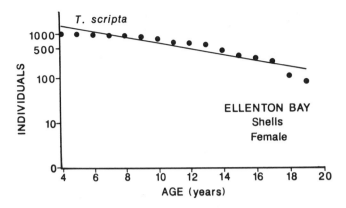

FIGURE 15.3. Linear regression of annual survivorship of an imaginary cohort of 1,000 four-year-old females, based on recovered shells of dead female *T. scripta* at Ellenton Bay. $Y = 3.451 - .0683X$; $p < .0001$; $r^2 = .86$.

the survival curve (i.e., overestimation based on a few old shells in the relatively small samples would be avoided).

The slopes of the regression lines were $-.0683$ for females and $-.0707$ for males (Table 15.8, Figs. 15.3 and 15.4), and both slopes were significantly different from zero (t test on each regression coefficient; $p < .0001$ in both cases). Therefore, the estimates of annual survivorship were $10^{-.0683}$, or .854, for females and $10^{-.0707}$, or .850, for males.

Actual survivorship of Ellenton Bay *T. scripta* is probably even higher than our estimated values. The procedure of assigning estimated ages to shells with growth curves based on plastron lengths (Figs. 15.1 and 15.2) likely results in an underestimation of age at death and hence leads to an underestimation of survivorship. For example, ages were known for 17 of the female shells, with an average age of 13.1 years (SD = 5.72). Had we assigned these individuals' ages based on the growth curve, their average estimated age would have been 9.1 years (SD = 2.59; 12

individuals in an age-frequency distribution to determine the average annual survivorship, assuming that survival rates were constant across these age classes. We limited the regression procedure to those age classes for which the original cumulative frequencies numbered at least five individuals (Tables 15.6 and 15.7), so that individual turtles that survived for long periods would not unduly skew

Table 15.7. Male shells recovered at Ellenton Bay

Age	Number of shells	Cumulative frequency	Scaled to 1,000
5	1	39	1,000
6	8	38	974
7	5	30	769
8	6	25	641
9	4	19	487
10	3	15	385
11	1	12	308
12	1	11	282
13	1	10	256
14	1	9	231
15	1	8	205
16	1	7	179
17	2	6	154
18	0	4	103
19	1	4	103
20	0	3	77
21	2	3	77
22	0	1	26
23	0	1	26
24	1	1	26

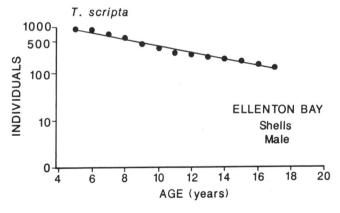

FIGURE 15.4. Linear regression of annual survivorship of an imaginary cohort of 1,000 five-year-old males, based on recovered shells of dead male *T. scripta* at Ellenton Bay. $Y = 3.349 - .0707X$; $p < .0001$; $r^2 = .98$.

Table 15.8. Slopes (b), 95% confidence limits of slopes (CL), survivorship estimates (S), and approximate 95% confidence limits on survivorship estimates (CLS) for *Trachemys scripta* from Ellenton Bay

Turtles	b	CL	S (10^b)	CLS $(10^{b + CL}, 10^{b \cdot CL})$	r^2
Females					
Shells	-.0683	±.0155	.854	.825, .886	.86
Live	-.111	±.00656	.774	.763, .786	.99
Males					
Shells	-.0707	±.00742	.850	.835, .864	.98
Live	-.0766	±.00660	.838	.826, .851	.98

underestimated, 2 overestimated, 2 equal). The same is true for the male growth curve. The 5 males for which exact ages were known averaged 7.6 years old (SD = 1.82). Their average age as assigned by the growth curve would have been 7.0 years old (SD = 1.00; 3 underestimated, 1 overestimated, 1 equal). One possible explanation for this discrepancy is that measurements on shells of long-dead turtles are slightly below those on live individuals because of the flaking off of epidermal laminae.

Another reason for the underestimation of ages with the growth curve is that we disregarded any fractional portion of a turtle's estimated age. For example, if the growth curve provided an estimated age of 8.7 years old, we assigned the turtle an age of 8 instead of rounding up to 9. That is, we assumed that it was still in its 8th year of life and had not yet become a 9-year-old.

A third reason that ages were underestimated more frequently than overestimated is that any shells with plastral measurements larger than the asymptotes of the growth curves (i.e., 234.0 > mm for females or 151.4 > mm for males) could not be assigned an age (i.e., the curve is undefined for sizes larger than the asymptotes). Hence, very large shells did not bias age estimates upward; instead of becoming estimates for very old turtles, they were omitted because the growth curve could not be used to assign an age to them. Thus, available evidence indicates that, if anything, the growth curves result in underestimates for the ages of shells in our analysis, leading to a conservative estimate of survivorship.

Survival rates based on capture of live turtles. The capture of live *T. scripta* in aquatic traps and in pitfall traps at the drift fence allows us to compile survival records for individual turtles of known age. This was done for survivors of female and male annual cohorts, beginning with age 4 as the base of each cohort.

Records of subsequent survival were compiled for all turtles known to have reached at least age 4 (Tables 15.9 and 15.10). Cohorts after 1979 were not used for the following reasons:

1. Adult females are more likely to be caught than immature ones. To increase the likelihood that individ-

uals would be seen, we first restricted the analysis to only those cohorts that could have matured by 1987, when the analysis was carried out. This eliminated the 1985–87 cohorts of 4-year-olds from the analysis.

2. Because adult females are most easily caught when they leave Ellenton Bay to nest, and because the proportion of females reproducing in any given year may be quite low (see Table 15.3), we further restricted the analysis to those cohorts that had been mature for at least five years as of 1987, to give adult females a greater chance of being seen if they were alive. This eliminated the 1980–84 cohorts of 4-year-olds from the analysis.

3. Although most males are mature by age 4, we restricted the analysis of male survivorship just as we did that of the females to ensure that survival of the two sexes was compared over the same years.

4. Just as we did with the analysis of shell remains, we stopped our survivorship records when fewer than five individuals remained in a given age class (see horizontal lines in Tables 15.9 and 15.10).

Once the data were truncated as described above, we estimated annual survival rates as follows. Each column in Tables 15.9 and 15.10 represented a cohort of 4-year-olds, with the numbers indicating how many individuals survived to each subsequent age. Row totals represented the total numbers of individuals surviving to each age beyond 4 years for all cohorts taken together as a composite. The survival rate from each age class to the next (S_i, where $i = 4, 5, 6, \ldots 13$ for females and $4, 5, 6, \ldots 17$ for males) was estimated by dividing the total number of individuals known to be alive at age $i + 1$ by the number of individuals alive at age i (Tanner, 1978). For example, the estimated survival rate of females from age 5 to age 6 (i.e., S_5) was estimated as $27 \div 34$, or .794 (Table 15.9). Once annual survivorship estimates were available for each age (Table 15.11), they were used to provide a survivorship curve for an imaginary cohort of 1,000 four-year-olds for each sex.

The S_i values were used to determine survivorship from age 4 to each subsequent age as follows, where L_i is survivorship from age 4 to age i:

$$L_i = \prod_{j = 4}^{i - 1} S_j$$

That is, L_i was calculated as the product of all the S values from S_4 to $S_{i - 1}$. For example, the calculation of survivorship from age 4 to age 7 for males was as follows (see Table 15.11):

$$L_7 = S_4 \times S_5 \times S_6 = .793 \times .978 \times .889 = .689$$

In other words, total survivorship from age 4 to any subse-

Table 15.9. Cumulative frequencies for survivorship records of cohorts of
4-year-old female *Trachemys scripta* from Ellenton Bay

Age	Cohort								Total
	1967	1968	1969	1975	1976	1977	1978	1979	
4	13	3	3	1	6	10	7	5	48
5	4	2	3	0	6	8	6	5	34
6	2	2	3	0	4	6	5	5	27
7	2	2	3	0	3	6	5	0	21
8	2	2	3	0	3	6	0	0	16
9	2	2	3	0	3	2	0	0	12
10	2	2	3	0	1	1	0	0	9
11	2	2	2	0	0	1	0	0	7
12	2	1	2	0	0	1	0	0	6
13	1	1	2	0	0	1	0	X	5
14	0	1	2	0	0	1	X	X	4
15	0	1	2	0	0	X	X	X	3
16	0	1	2	0	X	X	X	X	3
17	0	1	0	X	X	X	X	X	1

Note: X indicates that a given cohort could not possibly have survived to the age indicated as of 1987. Average annual survival rates were estimated only to age 13 (horizontal line); see text for further details.

quent age i is simply the product of all the annual survivorships from one age to the next for all ages, that is, from age 4 to age $i - 1$.

The resulting L_i values (Table 15.11) were multiplied by 1,000 to represent numbers of surviving individuals from a theoretical cohort of 1,000 four-year-olds. The logarithms (base 10) of the numbers of individuals in the resulting age-frequency distribution were then fit by linear regression, with the assumption that survival rates were constant for age classes beyond age 4 (Table 15.8, Figs. 15.5 and 15.6).

The results of the linear regression indicate that annual survivorship of females is $10^{-.111}$, or .774 (Table 15.8, Fig. 15.5), and survivorship of males is $10^{-.0766}$, or .838 (Table 15.8, Fig. 15.6). As with the analysis of shell data, our methodology for assessing survival rates for live turtles likely results in an underestimation of survival. This underestimation has two primary causes. First, we do not

Table 15.10. Cumulative frequencies for survivorship records of cohorts of
4-year-old male *Trachemys scripta* from Ellenton Bay

Age	Cohort									Total
	1967	1968	1969	1970	1975	1976	1977	1978	1979	
4	11	4	2	1	4	7	7	19	3	58
5	6	4	2	1	4	5	7	14	3	46
6	6	4	2	1	4	5	7	13	3	45
7	6	4	2	1	4	3	7	12	1	40
8	6	4	2	1	2	3	7	1	0	26
9	6	4	2	1	1	3	3	1	0	21
10	6	4	2	1	1	1	2	1	0	18
11	6	4	2	0	0	0	1	1	0	14
12	6	4	2	0	0	0	1	1	0	14
13	5	4	2	0	0	0	1	0	X	12
14	4	4	1	0	0	0	1	X	X	10
15	3	3	1	0	0	0	X	X	X	7
16	2	3	1	0	0	X	X	X	X	6
17	2	3	1	0	X	X	X	X	X	6
18	2	0	1	0	X	X	X	X	X	3
19	2	0	1	0	X	X	X	X	X	3
20	2	0	1	0	X	X	X	X	X	3
21	2	0	1	0	X	X	X	X	X	3
22	2	0	1	X	X	X	X	X	X	3
23	2	0	X	X	X	X	X	X	X	2
24	2	X	X	X	X	X	X	X	X	2

Note: X indicates that a given cohort could not possibly have survived to the age indicated as of 1987. Average annual survival rates were estimated only to age 17 (horizontal line); see text for further details.

Table 15.11. Survivorship of *Trachemys scripta* from age 4 onward

Age	Females		Males	
	S_i	L_i	S_i	L_i
4	.708	1.000	.793	1.000
5	.794	.708	.978	.793
6	.778	.562	.889	.776
7	.762	.437	.650	.689
8	.750	.333	.808	.448
9	.750	.250	.857	.362
10	.778	.187	.778	.310
11	.857	.146	1.000	.241
12	.833	.125	.857	.241
13	--	.104	.833	.207
14	--	--	.778[a]	.172
15	--	--	.857	.134
16	--	--	1.000	.115
17	--	--	--	.115

Note: Figures are based on data contained in Tables 15.9 and 15.10. S_i = survivorship from age i to age $i + 1$ or the number in age class $i + 1$ ÷ number in age class i; $L_i = \prod\limits_{j=4}^{i-1} S_j$ = survivorship from age 4 to age i.

[a]We used 7 ÷ 9, or .778, to calculate S_{14} instead of 7 ÷ 10, or .700, because the 14-year-old male from the 1977 cohort could not possibly have survived to become a 15-year-old by 1987 (see Table 15.10); therefore, he was omitted from the analysis at this point (Tanner, 1978).

distinguish between emigration and mortality. Therefore, emigration is coupled with mortality because turtles are not seen again. Some of the turtles from the cohorts we used migrated from Ellenton Bay (but did not necessarily die) during the two massive droughts in 1981 and 1986 (see Chapter 16). Second, turtles are assumed to have died (or emigrated) immediately after the last time they were captured. However, some likely lived another year or two in Ellenton Bay before dying or emigrating. In that event, survivorship would be slightly higher than we have estimated.

Comparison with other studies. Averaging our results from

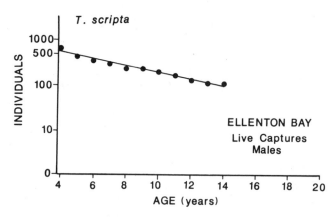

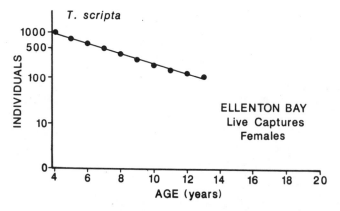

FIGURE 15.5. Linear regression of annual survivorship of an imaginary cohort of 1,000 four-year-olds, based on records of live female *T. scripta* captured at Ellenton Bay. $Y = 3.413 - .111X$; $p < .0001$; $r^2 = .99$.

FIGURE 15.6. Linear regression of annual survivorship of an imaginary cohort of 1,000 four-year-olds, based on records of live male *T. scripta* captured at Ellenton Bay. $Y = 3.296 - .0766X$; $p < .0001$; $r^2 = .98$.

the two methods described above gives annual survival estimates of .814 for females and .844 for males greater than 4 years old. Given the potential inaccuracies inherent in our methodologies, we do not have any basis to support the contention that survival rates of males and females are significantly different.

These results, which are similar to those reported in other studies of turtle survivorship, indicate that adults and larger juveniles of *T. scripta* exhibit relatively high annual survival. Wilbur (1975a) estimated instantaneous mortality rates of .15 for male and .18 for female *Chrysemys picta* in a Michigan population that was declining because the marsh habitat was drying as succession proceeded. This indicates an annual survival rate of $e^{-.15}$, or .86, for males and $e^{-.18}$, or .84, for females. However, Wilbur (1975a) also estimated that annual survival rates for adults were falling from around .83 to .76 over the long-term study. Tinkle et al. (1981) later estimated annual survivorship of female *C. picta* in the same population to be .76. The Ellenton Bay habitat has been increasingly drier in recent years (Chapter 2), with concomitant emigration of turtles from the area (see Chapter 16). Thus, our survival rates probably reflect the deterioration of habitat, just as those of Wilbur (1975a) do.

Other investigators have recorded higher survival rates in what may be more stable habitats. Mitchell (1988) estimated annual survival rates of .94 to .96 for adult *Chrysemys picta* and .84 to .86 for all age classes of *Sternotherus odoratus* in Virginia. Galbraith and Brooks (1987b) found that annual survivorship of adult female snapping turtles (*Chelydra serpentina*) was between .93 and .97 in Ontario. Williams and Parker (1987) reported annual mortality rates of only 6% to 7% in adult *Terrapene carolina* in Indiana; thus, survival rates were between .93 and .94. Our calculations based on data presented by Stickel (1978) indicate that annual survivorship rates for her box turtles (*Terrapene carolina*) in Maryland were between .85 and .94, assuming the rate is constant across all age classes. Turner et al. (1984) reported annual mortality rates of 4.4% to 18.4% for adult desert tortoises (*Xerobates agassizi*) in California (i.e., survival rates of .816 to .956). Swingland and Lessells (1979) estimated that annual mortality rates for adult *Geochelone gigantea* on the Aldabra Atoll range from 2% in inland habitats to 16% in coastal areas; hence, annual survival rates are between .84 and .98.

Estimates of survivorship for sea turtles typically fall somewhat below those of freshwater and terrestrial species. This is probably because almost all populations of sea turtles are exploited either intentionally or incidental to other directed fisheries. Based on instantaneous death rates (d) estimated by Bjorndal (1980) for 14 cohorts of adult female *Chelonia mydas* at Tortuguero, Costa Rica, we calculated annual survival rates (e^{-d}) of .58 to .75. Caribbean green turtle populations continue to be harvested by local fishermen, which may help to explain the relatively low annual survival rates for green turtles (Bjorndal, 1980). Márquez M. and Doi (1973) reported an annual survival rate of .81 for *Chelonia* in the Gulf of California. Later, Márquez M. et al. (1982a) estimated annual survival rates for adult *Chelonia mydas agassizi* to be .171, based on tag returns, but indicated that the estimate may not have been reliable, because of the small number of tagged individuals. Márquez M. et al. (1982b) estimated annual survival rates of .482 for tagged *Lepidochelys olivacea* in Pacific Mexico. The low survival rate of *L. olivacea* is probably due to the heavy exploitation of the population for leather (Woody, 1986).

Frazer (1983b) estimated annual survival rates for adult female loggerheads (*Caretta caretta*) to be .81. Frazer (1987) also provided preliminary estimates of .70 per year for large (50 cm) juvenile *C. caretta*. The rates for both adult and juvenile *Caretta* probably reflect natural mortality combined with mortality caused by incidental capture in shrimp trawl nets (Hillestad et al., 1982). Márquez M. et al. (1982b) estimated annual survival rates of .43 of *Lepidochelys kempi*, a species that is also subject to mortality in shrimp trawl nets (Hildebrand, 1982).

The pattern that emerges from all of these studies is clear, although hardly surprising to most turtle ecologists. In the absence of severe habitat deterioration or human exploitation, most turtle species apparently have the potential for extremely high levels of annual survival among adults. This is consistent with a life history that incorporates iteroparity as a means of compensating for the high mortality rates of eggs and young juveniles (Wilbur, 1975a). Annual survival rates of greater than 90% are probably not unusual for unexploited turtle populations inhabiting relatively stable habitats.

SURVIVORSHIP FROM AGES 1 TO 4.   In attempting to assess survivorship of *T. scripta* between ages 1 and 4, we assumed that there are no differences between the sexes,

because we are not able to determine the sex of juvenile turtles in these age classes by external examination (see Chapter 2).

Once young turtles enter the water, they usually are not seen as often as are adults. Although adults may be captured at the drift fence as males move overland and as females make nesting excursions, hatchlings are less likely to make terrestrial trips after their initial journey from the nest site to the aquatic habitat (see Chapter 16). Young turtles are also less likely to be captured in aquatic traps than are adult males and females (see Chapter 2). Therefore, assessing survivorship of young turtles is difficult.

Some authors have assumed that once freshwater turtles reach the aquatic habitat, survival rates remain fairly constant (Wilbur, 1975a; Tinkle et al., 1981; Gibbons and Semlitsch, 1982). If this assumption is valid, then annual survival rates for *T. scripta* between ages 1 and 4 should be in the range of the estimates obtained for adults (see Survival beyond Age 4, above). Under this assumption, we averaged the four estimates we obtained for survivorship of adult male and female *T. scripta*, resulting in an estimate of .829.

It may be, however, that young turtles are subject to more excessive mortality than are adults. For example, Frazer (1983b, 1987) obtained lower estimates of annual survival rates (.70) for wild juvenile loggerhead turtles (*Caretta caretta*) than for adult females (.81) in the same waters. However, it is unclear whether the differences were the result of differential mortality or of the methods used to assess survivorship for the two groups. Juvenile *T. scripta*, particularly yearlings, might possibly have lower survival rates than adults because of their smaller size and hence increased susceptibility to predators (see Sources of Mortality, below).

Survival of young turtles can be estimated from recapture of marked individuals. However, such estimates may be inaccurate because turtles are rarely seen at younger ages. Records of 125 *T. scripta* marked at Ellenton Bay as 1-year olds (Table 15.12) indicated that 4 were recaptured at age 2 and not seen subsequently, 4 others were recaptured at age 3 and never again seen, and 23 others were recaptured at age 4 or older. Thus, 24.8% were known to have survived at least to age 2. Similarly, only 21.6% were known to have survived to age 3, and 18.4%

Table 15.12. Records of 125 hatchling *Trachemys scripta* marked at Ellenton Bay

Age	Number known alive	Survival rate to next age	Cumulative survival from age 1 to present age
1	125	31/125 = .248	1.000
2	31	27/31 = .871	.248
3	27	23/27 = .852	.216
4	23	--	.184

were known to have survived to age 4. However, these figures represent absolute minimum estimates.

For example, the 23 individuals later caught at age 4 or older, the 4 individuals captured at age 3, and the 4 captured at age 2 were combined to estimate the number of turtles known to be alive at age 2 (23 + 4 + 4 = 31). However, this almost certainly results in an underestimate of actual survival to age 2. There were undoubtedly other turtles that died at ages 2, 3, 4, or later without ever being seen again in the meantime, because young turtles are rarely caught between age 1 and adulthood.

Similarly, the apparently high annual survival (Table 15.12) between age 2 (31 known turtles) and age 3 (27 known survivors) is probably an artifact, because turtles are not commonly seen at age 2. The great majority of 2-year-olds (denominator) and 3-year-olds (numerator) were counted only because they were seen at age 4 or older. Thus, 23 of the turtles in both numerator and denominator were known to be alive both at age 2 and at age 3. An additional 4 turtles in both numerator and denominator were known to be alive at age 2 and at age 3 because they were seen at age 3. Only the 4 turtles caught at age 2 that were not seen again at age 3 or later contribute to mortality estimates between ages 2 and 3. This probably underestimates mortality, because few turtles are caught at age 2 even if they are alive. Similar arguments apply to the apparent high survival between ages 3 and 4.

Thus, following records of hatchlings between ages 1 and 4 provides estimates in which survival is probably underestimated between ages 1 and 2 and then overestimated from age 2 to age 4 because turtles are rarely caught between ages 1 and 4 even if they are alive. The few that are seen make survival estimates appear low at first. The few survivors that are caught at one age but then not at the subsequent age make it appear as though survival is high, because the majority of individuals known to be alive in the two age classes were determined from the same later sighting.

To some extent, the same arguments can be applied to our estimates of adult survival rates, above. However, the error is probably greater for young turtles because they are less likely to be seen than are older turtles. Because older turtles are more likely to be seen alive at the drift fence as they leave the water and because they are caught in aquatic traps more frequently than the younger ones are, they are more likely to be seen at any given age if they are alive.

We suspect that survival of yearlings may be somewhat lower than that of adults and that the apparent low survival rate calculated between age 1 and age 2 is an artifact. Similarly, for reasons given above, we believe that it is unlikely that the survival rates of 2- and 3-year-olds are higher than those of adults. For the purposes of the life table analysis below, we assume that survival of 1-year-

olds is probably between the estimate calculated above (.248) and the average of the four estimates (.829) we obtained for adults (see Table 15.8). For lack of a better estimate, we take the mean of the two (i.e., [.248 + .829] ÷ 2 = .539). For the estimate of annual survival of 2- and 3-year-olds, we follow the lead of other investigators (Wilbur, 1975a; Tinkle et al., 1981) and assume that it is the same as the average rate for adults (.829). It is clear that more work needs to be done to assess survivorship of young turtles in the wild.

SOURCES OF MORTALITY.   The predator with the most impact on freshwater turtles in the eastern United States is probably the raccoon (*Procyon lotor*). The turtles and turtle nests destroyed by raccoons are legion and have been observed and reported numerous times by turtle biologists (e.g., Cagle, 1950; Seigel, 1980b; Talbert et al., 1980). The tendency of *T. scripta* hatchlings to overwinter in the nest (Cagle, 1944a; Gibbons and Nelson, 1978) may increase the mortality due to terrestrial predators in some instances. Raccoons also readily kill hatchlings and even adult slider turtles and are probably the major source of predation on individuals in terrestrial or shallow-water environments.

The small size of hatchling *T. scripta* may make them more susceptible than adults to predators such as alligators (*Alligator mississippiensis*), largemouth bass (*Micropterus salmoides*), and bowfin (*Amia calva*). Studies are presently under way at SREL to assess the vulnerability of *T. scripta* hatchlings as food for largemouth bass and alligators. Preliminary results indicate that even small alligators will accept hatchlings as food, although bass tend to reject them. Thus, we have no direct evidence that largemouth bass eat hatchlings, despite their apparent capability to do so. However, a student recently brought us two *T. scripta* hatchlings reportedly taken from the stomach of a largemouth bass he caught while fishing. None of these predators is of concern at Ellenton Bay because they are absent (alligators were last present in 1968).

Foxes and skunks (Congdon, pers. com.), kingsnakes (*Lampropeltis getulus;* Knight and Loraine, 1986), crows (Cagle, 1950), and coatis (*Nasua narica;* Drummond, 1983) have been reported to eat *T. scripta* eggs, and numerous other vertebrates have been implicated in the mortality of turtle eggs or small turtles, particularly when they are encountered terrestrially. Even vegetation (Lazell and Auger, 1981) and fly larvae (Vogt, 1981) have been reported to destroy turtle eggs. Cottonmouths (*Agkistrodon piscivorus*) and snapping turtles (*Chelydra serpentina*) presumably eat small turtles in aquatic habitats.

Life Tables for the Slider Turtle

The information presented above can be used to provide a standard life table for *T. scripta* in Ellenton Bay in terms of

ℓ_x, defined as age-specific survival from age 0 to age x, and m_x, defined as age-specific fecundity, or the average number of eggs laid per individual female at age x. Having determined estimates for the annual survival rates (S_x) for each age, ℓ_x is simply the product of the annual survival rates of all ages from age 0 to age $x - 1$. That is,

$$\ell_x = \prod_{y=0}^{x-1} S_y$$

The life table was restricted to females because we have no information concerning the fecundity of males.

The resulting life table (Table 15.13) is based on the following assumptions and estimations:

1. $S_0 = .105$. Mean survival from the time eggs are laid until hatchlings enter the water at age 1 is 10.5% (Table 15.4).
2. $S_1 = .539$. Survival from age 1 to age 2 is 53.9% (see Survival from Ages 1 to 4, above).
3. $S_2 = S_3 = .829$. Annual survival rates for 2- and 3-year-olds is the average of that estimated for adult males and females, or 82.9% (see Survival from Ages 1 to 4, above, and Table 15.8).
4. $S_x = .814$ for females of all ages $x \geq 4$ (Table 15.8).
5. Mean per capita annual fecundity (1.28 females eggs per female per year) does not change substantially as the turtles age.
6. Females mature at age 7.

The resulting ℓ_x values were used to draw a survivorship curve for a theoretical cohort of 1,000 turtles (Fig. 15.7, solid line; also see Table 15.14).

The life table and survivorship curve present no surprises. Most of the mortality is associated with early life stages (egg and first year). Once hatchlings enter the water and become established, the turtles enjoy fairly low mortality. The net reproductive rate $(R_0 = \Sigma \ell_x m_x = .137)$ indicates that females are not replacing themselves in the population (Ricklefs, 1979). The realized intrinsic rate of increase $(r = -.1675)$ was obtained by analytically solving this equation (Ricklefs, 1979):

$$1 = \Sigma \ell_x m_x e^{-rx}$$

with the assumption of a stable age distribution. The results indicate that the population size is changing by a factor of .85, or e^r, each year. In other words, the estimate of r indicates that the population is declining by some 15% each year. Note, however, that our estimations of ℓ_x combine death and emigration.

We know that the size of the *T. scripta* population in Ellenton Bay has been declining over the past two decades. Many turtles emigrate from the bay during drought years (see Chapter 16), and only a few of those that left

Table 15.13. Life table for *Trachemys scripta* in Ellenton Bay

Age	l_x	m_x
0	1.000	0.00
1	.105	0.00
2	.0566	0.00
3	.0469	0.00
4	.0389	0.00
5	.0317	0.00
6	.0258	0.00
7	.0210	1.28
8	.0171	1.28
9	.0139	1.28
10	.0113	1.28
11	.00921	1.28
12	.00750	1.28
13	.00610	1.28
14	.00497	1.28
15	.00404	1.28
16	.00329	1.28
17	.00268	1.28
18	.00218	1.28
19	.00178	1.28
20	.00145	1.28
21	.00118	1.28
22	<.00100	--

Note: Figures are based on mean estimates for survivorship and fecundity. See text for further details. $R_0 = 0.137$; $r = -0.1675$.

during the 1981 drought had returned before the 1986 drought set in.

A series of population estimates based on a modified Lincoln Index (Table 15.15) was used to estimate the rate of population decline. Although the estimates showed great fluctuations, linear regression of the $\log_{10}$ frequencies in Table 15.15 indicated a slope of $-.03583$ ($r^2 = .375$; $F_{1,6} = 3.596$; $.10 < p < .25$). These results indicate that from 1975 to 1982 the population decreased at a mean

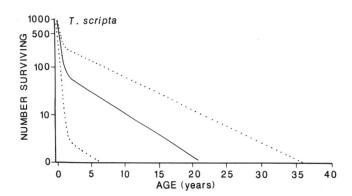

FIGURE 15.7. Survivorship curves for *T. scripta* in Ellenton Bay. Each line represents a theoretical cohort of 1,000 individuals. The solid line represents survivorship based on mean estimates (see Table 15.13 and text for further details). The upper dotted line represents a best-case scenario, based on upper estimated values; the lower dotted line represents a worst-case scenario, based on lower estimated values (see Table 15.14 and text for further details).

Table 15.14. Alternative life tables for *Trachemys scripta* in Ellenton Bay based on high and low estimates of survivorship and fecundity

	High[a]		Low[b]	
Age	l_x	m_x	l_x	m_x
0	1.000	0.00	1.000	0.00
1	.275	0.00	.0100	0.00
2	.228	0.00	.00248	0.00
3	.189	0.00	.00185	0.00
4	.158	0.00	.00137	0.00
5	.134	0.00	.00102	0.00
6	.114	0.00	<.00100	--
7	.0976	1.62		
8	.0833	1.62		
9	.0712	1.62		
10	.0608	1.62		
11	.0519	1.62		
12	.0443	1.62		
13	.0379	1.62		
14	.0323	1.62		
15	.0276	1.62		
16	.0236	1.62		
17	.0201	1.62		
18	.0172	1.62		
19	.0147	1.62		
20	.0125	1.62		
21	.0107	1.62		
22	.00915	1.62		
23	.00781	1.62		
24	.00667	1.62		
25	.00570	1.62		
26	.00486	1.62		
27	.00415	1.62		
28	.00355	1.62		
29	.00303	1.62		
30	.00259	1.62		
31	.00221	1.62		
32	.00189	1.62		
33	.00161	1.62		
34	.00138	1.62		
35	.00118	1.62		
36	.00100	1.62		
37 +	<.00100	--		

Note: See text for further details.
[a]$R_0 = 1.060$.
[b]$R_0 = 0$.

Table 15.15. Estimates of population size of *Trachemys scripta* in Ellenton Bay, using a modified Lincoln Index

Year	Estimated population size
1975	1,150
1976	611
1977	918
1978	763
1979	428
1980	698
1981	729
1982	460

from year to year, it is doubtful that the population ever reaches a stable age distribution. However, the estimate of a rate of decline of 8% per year based on linear regression of the estimates of population sizes is also subject to error. In actuality the decline of the population probably is not constant over time (i.e., is not linear on a logarithmic scale as estimated by regression) but instead occurs in spurts, as droughts force individuals to emigrate. Because droughts have been more frequent in recent years, we expect that the rate of decline has accelerated (see Chapter 16). In any case, our population of *T. scripta* in Ellenton Bay is declining, and the decline is probably due to the stresses imposed by the drying of the environment, just as it was with the *Chrysemys picta* population of Wilbur (1975a).

Our life table (Table 15.13) and survivorship curve (Fig. 15.7, solid line) for *T. scripta* indicate that fewer than 1 in 1,000 individuals will survive to age 22, primarily because of the low survivorship during the first year of life. If an average of only 10.5% of the eggs survive to become hatchlings entering the bay (Tables 15.4 and 15.13), then few turtles will survive into their second decade, irrespective of high adult survival rates. This is an indication of one way in which a static life table can be misleading. What is missing is an indication of the variability of life history parameters (Wilbur and Morin, 1988).

The l_x value of age 1 (i.e., .105, Table 15.13) is an average estimated over several years (Table 15.4). For those years in which eggs and hatchlings experience relatively little mortality, a greater percentage would enter the aquatic environment, and adults would then have a greater chance of attaining higher ages. For example, 27.5% of eggs laid in 1977 resulted in hatchlings that entered the water. Having made it past a critical stage in their life history, these turtles might then have an increased chance of living into their third decade.

To examine the range of possible values afforded *T. scripta* in the Ellenton Bay environment, we constructed two alternative life tables (Table 15.14; Fig. 15.7, dotted lines), representing high and low estimates for each parameter. These may be interpreted as best-case and worst-case scenarios based on the data we have available.

rate of about 8% per year (i.e., $10^{-.03583} = .92$). Note, however, that in more recent years the population has probably decreased at an even greater rate. For example, many turtles that emigrated in the drought of 1981 had not yet returned before many others emigrated during the drought of 1986. There can be little doubt that the Ellenton Bay population of *T. scripta* has been declining in recent years.

The estimate of the rate of population decline of 15% per year obtained from the life table analysis may represent an overestimate. On the one hand, survival rates probably represent underestimates, as was discussed above. On the other hand, the assumption of a stable age distribution necessary for estimating r by analytical solution of Lotka's equation ($1 = \Sigma \ell_x m_x e^{-rx}$) is probably invalid. Given that hatchling survival varies considerably

Given the variability, particularly in terms of egg and hatchling survivorship, some annual cohorts will have an advantage for survival, whereas others will be at a great disadvantage.

The best-case scenario (Table 15.14, high) was based on the following assumptions and estimations:

1. $S_0 = .275$. Survival from the time eggs are laid until hatchlings enter the water at age 1 is 27.5%, the estimate for 1977 (Table 15.4).
2. $S_1 = S_2 = S_3 = .829$. Annual survival rates for young turtles in the aquatic environment are similar to those for adults (Wilbur, 1975a; Tinkle et al., 1981). More specifically, annual survival rates for 1-, 2-, and 3-year-olds are the average of those estimated for adult males and females, or 82.9% (see Survival from Ages 1 to 4, above, and Table 15.8).
3. $S_x = .854$ for females of all ages $x \geq 4$ (see upper estimate for females in Table 15.8).
4. Fecundity does not change substantially as the turtles age. Average clutch frequency is 1.10 clutches, and mean clutch size is 6.25. The mean proportion of females nesting in a given year is 47.11%, the upper estimate in Table 15.3. We assume a 1:1 ratio of male eggs to female eggs. Therefore, the mean number of female eggs laid per female per year is calculated as follows: $1.10 \times 6.25 \times .4711 \times 0.5 = 1.62$.
5. Females mature at age 7.

If, in addition to increased survival rates, the adults in such a population were lucky enough to live during years of increased resources, so that a larger percentage of females could reproduce in a given season, the mean fecundity might be higher than in the average-case scenario depicted in Table 15.13. In this best-case scenario, $R_0 = 1.06$, and the population is able to sustain itself (Table 15.14, high). Some turtles might survive well into their third decade (Table 15.14, high; and Fig. 15.7, upper dotted line), Indeed, we have found individual females more than 25 years old, indicating that the average-case scenario tends to underestimate survivorship for at least some turtles.

In reality the conditions outlined in Table 15.14 (high) probably are met occasionally, primarily because of increased survivorship of hatchlings in some years. (Note that annual adult survival, .854, is not much higher than for the average scenario, .814.) If selected cohorts enjoyed increased hatchling survival rates as indicated in Table 15.4, the population might not be declining as rapidly as predicted by the average-case scenario depicted in Table 15.13.

On the other hand, some annual cohorts are apparently doomed by heavy mortality on eggs or hatchlings, resulting in first-year survival rates of only 1% (Table 15.4, 1981). We also estimated a worst-case scenario, using low estimates for each parameter. The resulting life table (Table 15.14, low; Fig. 15.7, lower dotted line) is based on the following assumptions and estimations:

1. $S_0 = .010$. Mean survival from the time eggs are laid until hatchlings enter the water at age 1 is 1%, the estimate for 1981 (Table 15.4).
2. $S_1 = .248$. Survival from age 1 to age 2 is 24.8% (see Survival from Ages 1 to 4, above, and Table 15.12).
3. $S_2 = S_3 = .774$. Annual survival rates for 2- and 3-year-olds are the same as the low estimate for adult females, or 77.4% (see low estimate in Table 15.8).
4. $S_x = .774$ for females of all ages $x \geq 4$ (see low estimate in Table 15.8).
5. Fecundity does not change substantially as the turtles age. Average clutch frequency is 1.10 clutches, and mean clutch size is 6.25. The mean proportion of females nesting in a given year is 27.17%, the lower estimate in Table 15.3. We assume a 1:1 ratio of male eggs to female eggs. Therefore, the mean number of female eggs laid per female per year is calculated as follows: $1.10 \times 6.25 \times .2717 \times 0.5 = .93$.
6. Females mature at age 7.

Such cohorts may be destined to add nothing to the next generation because the distinct possibility exists that none of the few remaining individuals will survive to adulthood. Even if annual adult survivorship is higher (say, .854) than depicted in this worst-case scenario (.774), few individuals, if any, would survive to adulthood, given the 99% mortality of eggs and hatchlings. In actuality there may be some years in which none of the eggs or hatchlings survive to enter the water; if so, then there are even worse cases than our worst-case scenario.

One thing is clear from all three scenarios presented above. Although turtles are touted as being among the longest-lived vertebrates (Gibbons, 1987), most individuals die during their first or second year of life. The great majority of turtles probably do not live even long enough to emerge from their nests (see Ernst, 1971c, 1986; Wilbur, 1975a; Hopkins et al., 1978; Landers et al., 1980; Congdon et al., 1983b; Diemer, 1986; Christens and Bider, 1987; Eckert, 1987). In fact, most probably fall prey to mammalian predators before pipping the egg or even before the embryo is large enough to be easily discernible as a turtle. The few individual turtles fortunate enough to live long enough to attract the notice of naturalists interested in longevity represent only a minuscule fraction of all the individuals in the order.

Suggestions for Further Study

It is interesting to note that all of the turtle populations for which life table analyses are available are populations that are declining. For freshwater species, the decline is due to drying of the aquatic habitat (Wilbur, 1975a; Tinkle et al., 1981; this study). For sea turtles, the decline is presumably due to human interference (Márquez M. et al., 1982a,b; Frazer, 1983a; Crouse et al., 1987). It will be illuminating to have life tables prepared for relatively stable or for increasing, perhaps colonizing, populations of turtles.

There is also a need for long-term studies that will provide life table analysis of the same species in different localities or for different species in the same habitat. The comparisons provided by such studies are necessary for further interpretation of the life history evolution of turtles (Wilbur and Morin, 1988).

Turtle population ecologists should strive to develop a terminology and a methodology that will allow easy comparison of results of future studies on egg, hatchling, and nest survivorship. If comparisons are to be made, we must be certain of what is being compared. When one investigator presents results on nest success and another presents results on hatchling success, readers may not be able to compare the results, especially for cases in which neither author defines the terms used.

In future studies of reproductive output, attention must be paid to all three of the ways in which the number of eggs per female may vary—clutch size, intraseasonal clutch frequency, and interseasonal clutch frequency (or "female cycle" sensu Wilbur and Morin, 1988). The average number of eggs in a clutch is certainly important, as is the average number of clutches a female lays in a season in which she is reproductively active. However, equally important is the number (or proportion) of seasons during her adult life that she is reproductively active. Information on clutch size and intraseasonal clutch frequency is still needed for individual populations. However, such information will be of little value in studies of life history

evolution unless we also learn how per capita interseasonal clutch frequency is influenced by the proportion of females that fail to reproduce in any given season, for particular populations or species.

Future studies of any aspect of turtle demography must also encompass sufficient years or seasons that variability of any measured characteristics can be assessed. An understanding of such variability is fundamental to understanding how life histories evolved (Wilbur and Morin, 1988). Finally, we must attempt to link observed variability among populations to genetic analysis (see Chapter 6 and Scribner et al., 1984a, 1986) in order to determine whether there is evidence that any such characteristics are heritable.

All of these needs point to the necessity of continuing existing long-term population studies and beginning others. Because adult female turtles may integrate energy acquisition over several years before reproducing, it will be difficult to identify the key environmental variables that would allow us to develop models predicting the timing and quantity of reproductive output for any given population. Attempts to follow individual turtles over several years in order to determine the causes of fluctuations in their interseasonal reproductive intervals represent one of the challenges in our studies of reproductive variability. An even greater challenge is to devise some means of determining the relative contributions of genotype and environment to observed reproductive variability. These challenges can be answered only with the continuation of long-term studies of turtles.

Acknowledgments

Research and manuscript preparation were made possible by contract DE-AC09-76SROO-819 between the University of Georgia and the U.S. Department of Energy and by National Science Foundation grant DEB-79-04758.

J. WHITFIELD GIBBONS
JUDITH L. GREENE
JUSTIN D. CONGDON
Savannah River Ecology Laboratory
Drawer E
Aiken, South Carolina 29802

16

Temporal and Spatial Movement Patterns of Sliders and Other Turtles

Abstract

Movement by turtles can be considered spatially in terms of whether it is intrapopulational or extrapopulational. Intrapopulation movements are primarily for purposes related to feeding, reproducing, basking, and hiding. Extrapopulational movements are primarily for purposes of migrating between seasonally variable habitats, abandoning unsuitable habitats, nesting by females, and mate searching by males. The daily and seasonal timing of movement varies among species in response to environmental, physiological, and demographic conditions. Data on slider turtles (*Trachemys scripta*) and other freshwater species in South Carolina indicate that movement by many individual turtles is highly directional and consistent among years, although environmental variability influences timing and direction. Suggestions for future research are given, based on findings with slider turtles and previous reports in the literature.

Introduction

Movements within and among animal populations are critical to a variety of life history and ecological processes. Identifying the temporal and spatial patterns of movement by individuals of a population is prerequisite to understanding the ecological and evolutionary reasons for dispersal, migration, or intrahabitat movements by individuals of a species. The purpose of this chapter is to consider movement phenomena of turtles in the context of the slider turtle (*Trachemys scripta*) and other species of freshwater turtles collected over a 20-year period on the Savannah River Plant (SRP) in South Carolina (Gibbons, 1987). Although the material presented is mostly descriptive, the information should answer certain questions about movement phenomena in turtle populations, serve as the foundation for future questions, and lead to experimental approaches to answer those questions.

Table 16.1. General factors potentially influencing movements
of turtles in a population

Environmental	Demographic
Daily temperature patterns	Population density
Seasonal temperature patterns	Sex ratio
Weather events	Age structure
Habitat type and condition	Size structure

Maturity and physiological state
    Sex
    Body size
    Recent experience

Movement by individuals in a turtle population can be categorized spatially in terms of whether it is intrapopulational or extrapopulational and temporally in terms of whether it occurs on a daily, seasonal, or sporadic basis. Movement by an individual may be in response to or as a consequence of local environmental situations and events; demographic features that characterize the population, such as sex ratio and size and age structure; or the reproductive or other physiological conditions of individuals in the populations (Table 16.1). A discussion of what constitutes a freshwater turtle population is given in Chapter 1, and it is apparent that no definition of a turtle population is totally satisfactory for all circumstances and considerations. For the lentic-habitat species occurring on the SRP, a population generally is considered to be the individuals of a species inhabiting an identifiable aquatic habitat. Therefore, for the purposes of discussion in this chapter, terrestrial departure from a circumscribed aquatic habitat or any long-distance movement of more than 0.5 km is defined as extrapopulational. This definition will in some instances encompass terrestrial movements (such as some nesting excursions) in which the individual actually returns to the same aquatic habitat.

A premise in this chapter is that the movements of animals are not random but are directed in terms of leaving or reaching a particular location or are driven by some other motive. Thus, a painted turtle may move directly and unerringly toward a favorite basking log or to a particular feeding site to which it has been on other occasions. Or a male slider turtle may wander away from an aquatic habitat in what is seemingly a trip without a plan, though he has a primary motive: to find a receptive female for mating. His movements, therefore, are those that have the highest probability of achieving this goal. Thus, movement by turtles is assumed to have some probability of benefit to the individual and is balanced by negative feedback of various sorts. Some obvious potential costs of movement by an individual turtle are an increased risk of predation and possibly exposure to desiccation or thermal extremes that may confront overland travelers. In addition, all movement requires an expenditure of energy and therefore an energy cost.

One approach to examining movement patterns by turtles is to quantify distances and directions moved and time spent moving, within the framework of spatial categories (intrapopulational and extrapopulational), temporal categories (daily, seasonal, and sporadic), and particular purposes (Table 16.2). If these patterns can then be coupled with an assessment of risks (costs) and benefits and a consideration of how natural selection operates on movement patterns, we will be closer to understanding the significance of why turtles move and to predicting when and where their movement is most likely to happen. Our objective in this chapter is to quantify the movement of freshwater turtles in as many of the defined categories as possible and to discuss the ecological and evolutionary significance of the findings.

Intrapopulational movements are made by turtles for

Table 16.2. Categories of movement by individual turtles and factors that must be
assessed when considering movement phenomena

Category	Purpose	Primary benefits potentially gained by moving
Intrapopulational (short-range)	Feeding	Growth; lipid storage
	Basking	Increased mobility due to body temperature increase; reduction of external parasites; enhanced digestion
	Courtship and mating (adults only)	Reproductive success
	Hiding, dormancy	Escape from predators or environmental extremes
Extrapopulational (long-range)	Seasonal	
	Seeking food resources	Growth; lipid storage
	Nesting (adult females)	Direct increase in fitness
	Mate seeking (adult males)	Direct increase in fitness
	Migration (hibernation; estivation)	Survival
	Travel from nest by juveniles	Initiation of growth
	Departure from unsuitable habitat	Survival

Note: Movement for each purpose needs to be placed in the contexts of daily and seasonal timing.

four obvious purposes: (1) feeding, (2) reproduction (mate seeking, courtship, and nesting), (3) basking, and (4) seeking favorable sites in which to hide or remain dormant for extended periods (Table 16.2). Additional reasons also exist, but these are the four most apparent ones.

Extrapopulational movement, as defined above, can be categorized either as seasonal and generally predictable activity or as abandonment of a habitat that has become unsuitable. Seasonal movements of freshwater turtles can be attributed to (1) overland movement by hatchlings from nest to aquatic habitat, (2) searching for resource features of a habitat that vary seasonally in their availability or importance to individuals in the population, (3) departure to or return from overwintering sites, (4) searching by adult males for receptive females during circumscribed mating periods, and (5) nesting by females. A consequence of long-range movement by turtles is increased genetic exchange among populations (Scribner et al., 1986; also see Chapter 6), but this cannot be considered as a reason for movement without more-elaborate theoretical arguments than are warranted in this presentation.

Risks and Benefits of Movement

Movement patterns among turtle species can theoretically be quantified in terms of probable risks (costs) and benefits, assuming that taking risks associated with some aquatic or overland movement has a probability of positive returns that are greater than the probability of negative consequences. For example, the traveling by some freshwater turtles, at some risk of predation, of long, seemingly unnecessary distances from water to lay eggs is presumably warranted in terms of natural selection, because proper choice of a nesting site results in a higher fitness probability. Such risks can be carried to extreme, of course, and a point can be reached at which the probable risk of predation outweighs the probability of a fitness gain from finding a proper nest site.

This type of risk-benefit relationship is presumably balanced by natural selection within a population, with some individuals overextending themselves in the risk category while others err on the conservative side of risk taking and do not fare as well with the potential benefits. Naturally, local environmental circumstances can shift the balance in one direction or another. For example, the female turtles on an island with no terrestrial predators should be less constrained in nest-seeking behavior, and the highest fitness probabilities would lie with individuals that would be extreme risk takers on the mainland.

The primary risks in various categories of movement (Table 16.2) are those that can result in death of the individual through increased exposure to predators, thermal extremes, and desiccation. Among freshwater species the latter two risks would be mainly restricted to ter-

restrial activities. Each of these risks is presumably dependent on body size within a species and should be assessed in these terms. Also, sex and stage of maturity should be considered significant factors in the level of risk because behaviors may differ among individuals in the different categories.

In addition to the more dramatic risks of predation and environmental extremes are the low-level risks associated with expenditure of energy. Any movement requires energy. Thus, by moving from one location to another, the organism risks using more energy than is warranted by the ultimate benefits.

Quantitative data for comparing risk and benefit probabilities for various categories of movement by turtles are not available, to our knowledge, from any study. In fact, only limited quantitative information is available from this study and a few other studies of the temporal and spatial aspects of movement in the intrapopulational and extrapopulational categories that have been identified (Tables 16.1 and 16.2). Turtle biologists should (1) further refine the movement categories in which risks and fitness benefits can be quantified, (2) continue to determine the extent of the movement within and among populations, and (3) strive for the ultimate goal of assessing the significance of the movement patterns in terms of relative risks and benefits.

Spatial Activity

The long-term SRP studies with large numbers of captures in a variety of habitats in a region provide an opportunity to quantify phenomena that occur on an infrequent as well as a regular basis. Although some emphasis has been placed on movement patterns of turtles within habitats on the SRP (see Chapter 18), extrapopulational movement has received the greatest attention. The exchange of individual turtles among aquatically disconnected habitats that are distant from one another (see Chapter 2) has been repeatedly confirmed through the recapture of individuals that have moved.

Intrapopulational (Short-range) Movement

Many ecologists, including turtle biologists, have focused on establishing some form of home-range quantification for their study species. The approaches, biases, qualifying considerations, and even the definitions associated with home-range determinations seem endless and are beyond the scope of this book. A discussion of some approaches for considering home range is given in Chapter 18.

Home-range calculations and point-to-point movements reported by turtle biologists suggest that some species use relatively large amounts of habitat, whereas others are much more restricted in their movement patterns (e.g., Ernst, 1968a,b; Hammer, 1969; Mahmoud, 1969;

Ernst, 1970c; Moll and Legler, 1971; Bury, 1972; Brown, 1974). In general, larger species move longer distances than smaller species do, and adults are more likely to move farther than juveniles. A caution must be observed not to overinterpret findings as characterizing a species, because of the inherent biases associated with the particular time and place that a study was done, especially if the study was conducted over a short period that did not incorporate a variety of annually variable environmental situations.

Although intrahabitat movement patterns are a significant area for research, our studies on the slider turtle and other freshwater species in South Carolina can contribute little to the quantification of short-range movements within populations because we did not focus on intrapopulational movement and have few meaningful measurements. However, such research will be necessary to provide a foundation for developing quantitative models of movement patterns and intrapopulational risk-benefit assessments (Tables 16.1 and 16.2). The questions to be asked can be stated as follows:

1. What is the total amount of intrapopulational movement, and what is the level of variability in movement among individuals and among populations of a species?
2. What are the timing and the amount of movement that is directed toward achieving particular goals?
3. How are the risk probabilities and energy costs of intrapopulational movement balanced against the potential benefits of particular movement patterns?

Acquiring answers to these questions can lead to understanding why turtles expend energy and risk predation in intrapopulational movement and how the extent of such movements is controlled by natural selection. Of course, one potential answer for some, perhaps most, situations is that the risks associated with intrapopulational movement are trivial and that the emphasis should be placed on the benefits gained by such movements. Nonetheless, the question of why turtles move about within a population is a valid inquiry, and the questions listed above must be answered if a level of predictability of the phenomenon is to be achieved.

Extrapopulational (Long-range) Movement

Long-range movements associated with nesting by females, mate-seeking behavior by males, or other seasonal behaviors are predictable activities that occur annually. Thus, observations or experiments can potentially be planned to quantify these in a population. Information on forced migration from an unsuitable habitat is more difficult to acquire because of its unpredictability. Although a

population may respond to adverse conditions, the opportunity for the investigator to observe the phenomenon may not arise. Nonetheless, each of these categories of long-range movement deserves attention in a consideration of turtle populations and has been addressed to some degree by the studies on the SRP. Because of the large data base and the high variation in timing, distance, and direction of movement among individuals, it is most expedient to address extrapopulational movement by examining selected segments of the data.

RECAPTURES IN OTHER LOCATIONS

Records of individuals that were originally captured at one site and subsequently recaptured at another confirm that interpopulational exchange has occurred. Another approach, use of the terrestrial drift fence and pitfall traps, can provide circumstantial evidence of extrapopulational movement by individuals, assuming that those captured at the fence have intentionally departed from the aquatic habitat and are thus leaving the population. The limitation of the technique is that the ultimate destination of an individual is not known, so the potential distance traveled is not determined. However, the timing and other features of extrapopulational movement can be established for turtle species with this technique.

Besides mark-recapture and the drift fence technique, an unusual situation exists on the SRP for documenting the propensity of turtles to move extrapopulationally. A population of T. scripta and a few individuals of other species inhabited a radioactively contaminated area (A-Area Seepage Basins) for many years (Gibbons and Congdon, 1986). Until 1983 the basin area was unfenced, and turtles had free overland access to other bodies of water in the Lost Lake System. Because the A-Area Seepage Basins were the only ones of this type in the vicinity, the next closest seepage basin being 8 km away from Lost Lake, any turtle captured in the Lost Lake System and detected as radioactive was assumed to have been an inhabitant of the A-Area Seepage Basins at one time. A portion of the long-range movement data (Fig. 16.1) is based on such captures.

Slider turtles were by far the most commonly recaptured species on the SRP at sites different from the one of original capture. Of the 4,768 individuals from Ellenton Bay, Par Pond, and the Lost Lake System that had been marked during these studies, 244 were verified to have made extrapopulational moves to other habitats, ranging from 0.2 to 9 km away from their original capture sites. The minimum distances traveled, based on the shortest straight-line measurements between habitats, are consistently higher for males than for females (Fig. 16.1), even when the male-biased sex ratios in this species (see Chapter 14) are taken into account. Few recaptures of juveniles have been made at other sites, suggesting that successful

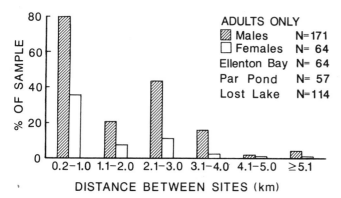

FIGURE 16.1.   Distances of long-range movement (more than 200 m) by adult *T. scripta* on the SRP, based on recapture of individuals in habitats other than the one of original capture. Ellenton Bay and Lost Lake exchanges were primarily between habitats not connected by waterways, so the majority of travel was overland. All measurements are given as straight-line, minimum distances. Most of the exchanges in Par Pond could have been achieved by aquatic travel for longer distances along shorelines. Radioactive turtles captured in Lost Lake sites were assumed to have been in the A-Area Seepage Basins at some earlier time (see text).

extrapopulational movements are more common for adults (Fig. 16.2).

Evidence that movements by turtles from one habitat to another are not dead-end trips is given by the ultimate recapture of individuals in their habitat of original capture following intermediate recapture at another site. Individual *T. scripta* that traveled extrapopulationally and then returned to the site of original capture included individuals from Par Pond ($N = 3$), Ellenton Bay ($N = 17$), and the Lost Lake System ($N = 6$). Whether such movements represent typical annual migration patterns between habitats by certain individuals or whether they are responses of individuals to alternating unsuitable habitat situations is unknown at this time. Determination of the regularity of such occurrences and the proportion of the population of a species that alternates between habitats would be extremely useful in the interpretation of movement patterns.

In addition to revealing long-distance movement, the turtles from the A-Area Seepage Basins provided a second measure of comparative vagility of the sexes. The body burden of radioactivity of an individual inhabiting the basins indicates the period of time it has been there. An individual that had departed the habitat would not continue to have an uptake of radioisotopes, and the primary gamma-emitting isotopes (cesium-137, strontium-90) have a finite biological half-time of only a few months (Scott et al., 1986). Therefore, an individual that had left the basin and returned or that had entered from another habitat would have a lower body burden than a longer-term resident. Based on this idea, we measured the level of

radioactivity of turtles of both sexes that were captured in the basins (Fig. 16.3). The conclusion is that females are more sedentary, as is indicated by their significantly higher body burdens of radioactive cesium and strontium. This is converse evidence that males are more likely to move among habitats, thus spending less time at any specific location.

DRIFT FENCES WITH PITFALL TRAPS

A total of 8,412 captures and recaptures of six common species of turtles was made at drift fences in three separate locations (Ellenton Bay, Risher Pond, and Rainbow Bay) on the SRP. Additional captures were made at several other study sites where sampling was for less than two years or where turtles were a minor part of the herpetofauna, but the three sites named above provided the primary data on extrapopulational movement based on drift fence data.

During certain years Ellenton Bay provided the opportunity to examine whether particular size classes were more likely to move extrapopulationally when overland movement was optional rather than forced by drying of the aquatic habitat. Although individuals smaller than 10 cm in plastron length constituted an appreciable portion of the population, few of them left Ellenton Bay during the four-year period (1975–78) during which the bay was encircled by the drift fence and water levels remained high. Males began leaving the aquatic habitat upon reaching the size of sexual maturity ($\approx$100 mm plastron length). A high proportion of individuals in each size category that exited from the bay did not return within a year. Immature females in the size category of 12 to 15 cm began departing from the bay with increasing frequency, relative to those in smaller size classes. However, the greatest numbers of exiting females were adults (Fig. 16.4). One conclusion from these data and from Figure 16.2 is that larger turtles are more likely to leave the aquatic habitat than smaller individuals are. Another is that size per se, independent of reproductive condition, is an important component of extrapopulational movement, because immature females 12 to 15 cm in length moved frequently. Nonetheless, the advent of maturity in both sexes is the strongest correlate with a propensity to travel. A general comparison among species indicates that adults of each of the six species of turtles inhabiting Ellenton Bay are more likely to make overland excursions than are juveniles.

These data are circumstantial evidence of extrapopulational mobility by individual *T. scripta*, although the final destination is known for few. The terrestrial behavior of *Kinosternon subrubrum* indicates that this semiaquatic species makes excursions away from the aquatic habitat for a purpose (hibernation) besides travel to other aquatic sites, although a few individuals have been known to relo-

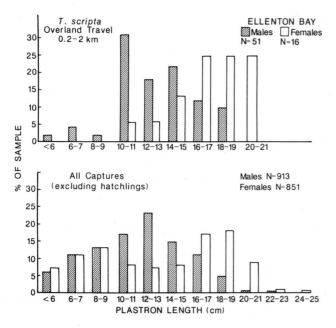

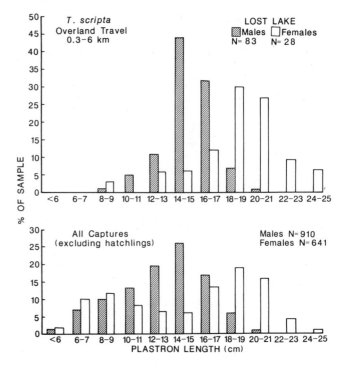

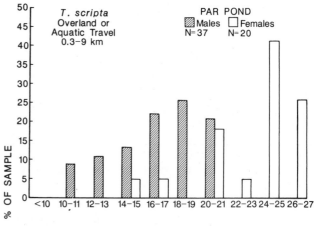

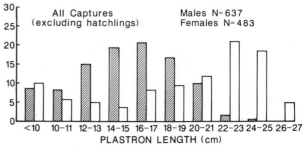

FIGURE 16.2 (ABOVE AND RIGHT). Sizes of *T. scripta* exhibiting travel between aquatic habitats, based on recapture in a habitat other than the one of original capture (see Fig. 16.1). Plastron lengths are the minimum sizes at which individuals were known to have traveled. Bottom graphs for each habitat represent total numbers of individuals captured in each size-sex category in the same study population, based on sizes of individuals at last capture. The overland travel at Ellenton Bay includes drought years in which most individuals left (Gibbons et al., 1983).

cate in other habitats (Gibbons, 1986). Little evidence is available to indicate the extent to which other species will burrow at the soil and litter surface upon leaving an aquatic area, but we are aware of a few instances of such behavior in *T. scripta* and *Deirochelys reticularia*. Therefore, the evidence that major segments of a population depart the aquatic area must be viewed cautiously in terms of the purpose or destination. Movement identified by drift fences is extrapopulational, as defined earlier, but movement to another aquatic site is not a requisite feature.

Based on the drift fence data and the evidence from recaptures of individuals at sites other than their original one, it is apparent that overland movement occurs among sliders and other turtles generally considered to be aquatic. A variety of explanations can be given for terrestrial movement by aquatic species, assuming that overland travel is a risky business for a turtle and must have some potential benefit to the individual that outweighs the risks. One explanation relates to sex and reproductive purpose.

NESTING FEMALES

Movements to nesting sites may be classed as intrapopulational in that the females, in many instances where

data are available, generally return to the aquatic habitat from which they came, although the return trip may not be immediate. It should be noted that a major segment of the Ellenton Bay adult females leaving the aquatic habitat did not return the same year (Fig. 16.4). Many of these departures were known to be nesting excursions, because

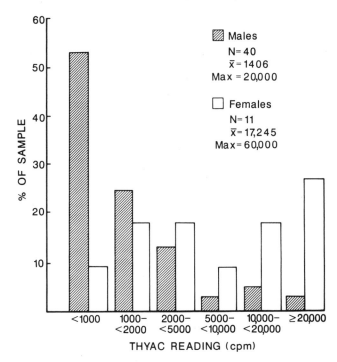

FIGURE 16.3. Levels of radioactivity, primarily from cesium-137 and strontium-90, as determined by Thyac readings of the carapace of 51 *T. scripta* inhabiting the A-Area Seepage Basins on the SRP. All individuals from the basins had readings above background—normally less than 100 counts per minute (CPM)—for the region.

the females were carrying fully shelled eggs. Because of the freshwater turtle biologist's bent for thinking of the population as being centered around a particular aquatic habitat where most of the individuals stay most of the time, we have arbitrarily assigned such movements as a special case in the extrapopulational category.

Many species of turtles are known to make long-distance movements to find suitable nesting sites. Cagle (1950) observed slider turtles (*T. scripta*) in Louisiana traveling more than 1.6 km overland to nest. Moll and Legler (1971) observed nesting females of this species in Panama up to 400 m from the nearest water. Plummer and Shirer (1975) reported female softshell turtles (*Trionyx muticus*) moving 2 to 6 km down a river to nest. Female snapping turtles (*Chelydra serpentina*) in Canada traveled more than 5 km to a particular nesting site, and the same general area was chosen by the same females each year (Obbard and Brooks, 1980). For their small size, even nesting *K. subrubrum* travel relatively long distances, based on their capture at the Ellenton Bay drift fence more than 50 m from the water's edge. Burger and Montevecchi (1975) found that diamondback terrapins (*Malaclemys terrapin*) selected nest sites in high dune areas approximately 150 m from the closest water. Truly marine species move the longest distances. The records for marine turtles that may travel hundreds of kilometers

from feeding areas to nesting beaches are widely recognized (Carr, 1965).

The most detailed report on travel by nesting freshwater turtles has been by Congdon et al. (1983b) for the Blanding's turtle (*Emydoidea blandingii*). Studies on the E. S. George Reserve in southern Michigan revealed that a few females with eggs travel more than 1 km overland, presumably in search of a favorable nesting site. Fidelity to general nesting areas was observed from year to year, but females did not necessarily return to the same area each nesting season. However, particular care about where their eggs were laid was displayed by females in each instance. Females of both *E. blandingii* and *C. serpentina* (Congdon et al., 1987) characteristically returned to their original aquatic habitats after nesting.

Identifying nesting activity by terrestrial species as extrapopulational is more difficult because of the uncertainty in many cases of what constitutes the normal activity area of a population. Species in the genus *Gopherus* are apparently able in most instances to find suitable nesting sites without making unusually long treks. Although gopher tortoises (*G. polyphemus*) have been reported to nest several meters away from their burrows (Iverson, 1980; Landers et al., 1980), Landers et al. (1980) reported that 85% of 110 nesting sites in Georgia were in the vicinity of burrows, some being within the burrow mound. The Bolson tortoise (*G. flavomarginatus*) may also lay its eggs in or near its burrow (Morafka, 1982). Berlandier's tortoise (*G. berlandieri*) does not build a conventional burrow but has not been reported to travel long distances for nesting (Auffenberg and Weaver, 1969; Rose and Judd, 1982). Ernst and Barbour (1972) stated that eggs of the desert tortoise (*G. agassizii*) are "occasionally laid in the mouths of burrows." Most desert tortoises apparently nest inside burrows (F. B. Turner and Kristin H. Berry, pers. com.). Long-distance movements by females for nesting could occur, because the burrows used by an individual in a colony may be far apart, but we would not construe this to be extrapopulational.

The studies on SRP turtles add little to an understanding of the factors influencing the distance traveled by nesting females. However, the information from the drift fence and pitfall traps at Ellenton Bay provides evidence of the level of directional fidelity of nesting females in terms of their departure from the aquatic habitat. It should be noted that few females were followed to their chosen nesting sites, and the drift fence data indicate only the general direction of movement several meters from the water's edge. However, the variability among individuals of a population in their choice of direction for nesting (Fig. 16.5) was much greater than the consistency shown by individuals in their choice of direction in different years (Tables 16.3 and 16.4). Thus, the directions taken by nesting females (*N* = 420) of six species at Ellenton Bay were not equally distributed around the perimeter (*p* <

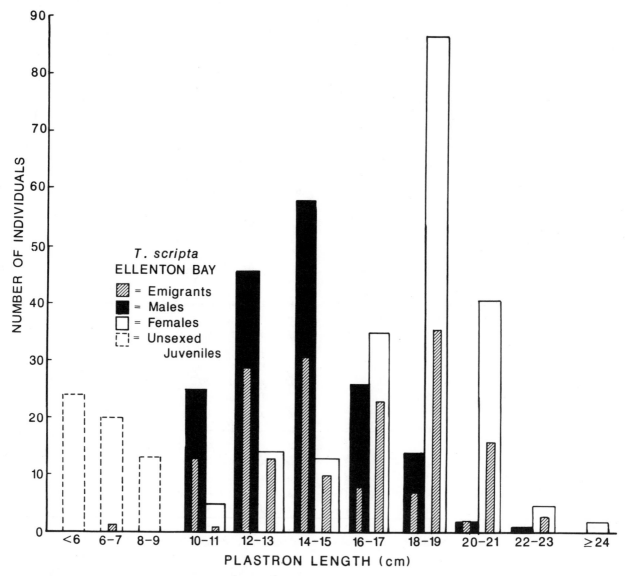

FIGURE 16.4.   Extrapopulational movement by *T. scripta,* based on captures of individuals at drift fences during nondrought years at Ellenton Bay (1 January 1975–31 December 1978). The external bars represent the cumulative number of each sex and size class known to be present in the habitat during the annual sampling periods. The nested bars represent the numbers of each sex and size class that were captured exiting the aquatic habitat and that did not return during the year of departure. An individual turtle may be included more than once, because the purpose is to compare what proportion of a size class exited in a year with the number available. Hatchlings were not included in the juvenile samples.

.01, $X^2 = 37.03$, $df = 4$), nor were the directions chosen by females within any of the species (Fig. 16.5). Nonetheless, the choice of nesting direction by an individual on a subsequent trip was most likely to be in the same direction as its previous trip (Tables 16.3 and 16.4).

The explanation for these particular observations is that the terrestrial habitat surrounding Ellenton Bay is relatively homogeneous, so a nesting female turtle can depart from the aquatic habitat in any of several directions without a preconception that some directions are unsatisfactory for nesting. Once a female has nested safely, it would not be surprising to find that she tends to

travel toward the same area to seek a suitable nesting site in the following year. The risks associated with terrestrial travel can be great, and a nesting individual would be expected to follow a known route that resulted in her own survival and a satisfactory nest on a previous occasion, rather than to wander randomly during each nesting bout.

Although the consistency of females in their direction of departure was high, variability in the direction of departure was observed among some females at the Ellenton Bay drift fence and may be a consequence of several factors directly associated with nesting biology. For example,

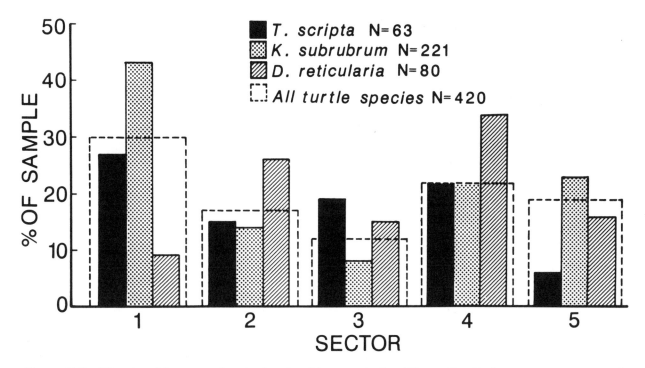

FIGURE 16.5. Direction of departure of nesting females of three species from Ellenton Bay. Each sector represents approximately 250 m of drift fence with pitfall traps (see Fig. 2.4) that completely encircled the aquatic habitat. Hence, sectors 1 and 5 are adjacent. Only females known to be carrying eggs, based on x rays, palpation, or eventual nesting activity, were used in the analysis. In addition to including the samples of *T. scripta*, *K. subrubrum*, and *D. reticularia*, the total sample includes *S. odoratus* (*N* = 28), *P. floridana* (*N* = 22), and *C. serpentina* (*N* = 6).

a female may have chosen a marginal site because of particular circumstances of physiology, environmental conditions, and timing. In the following year, the same female may choose to exit the aquatic habitat in a different direction in search of a more favorable nesting site. Another possible cause of a female's changing her direction of departure from the aquatic habitat is that although she left in a particular direction on the previous nesting excursion, she wandered extensively before finding a nesting

location, and then returned to the aquatic habitat from a different direction. Therefore, on her next departure for nesting purposes she might leave in the direction of the previous nesting site. The extensive efforts to track nesting female freshwater turtles on the University of Michigan's E. S. George Reserve should be a major source of enlightenment about this critical yet poorly understood phase in a turtle's ecology (Congdon et al., 1983b, 1987).

DEPARTURE FROM AN UNSUITABLE HABITAT

Animal populations are commonly confronted with conditions that are less than satisfactory. When conditions become untenable because of environmental extremes, individuals take compensatory measures that may not influence others in the population. Two general adaptations are apparent among species that have evolved in habitats that can sporadically become unsuitable for continued inhabitation. One approach is to remain in the habitat in a quiescent state. The other is to leave in search of a better situation. Freshwater turtles have evolved both strategies.

Cagle (1944b) observed extrapopulational movement by *Chrysemys picta* and *T. scripta* in response to the drying of a lake, and Hamilton (1944) recounted a migration of *G. berlandieri* that were assumed to be leaving a flooded habitat. Parker (1984) reported that *T. scripta* emigrated

Table 16.3. Consistency of direction of departure by nesting females of three species of freshwater turtles captured in different years

| Species | Relationship between sectors of first and second captures | | |
	Same	Adjacent	Opposite pair
Trachemys scripta	6	4	2
Kinosternon subrubrum	34	7	4
Deirochelys reticularia	4	6	3
Total	44	17	9

Note: The sector of the second nesting event of an individual nesting in a subsequent year was compared with the sector of the first event. Thus, each individual is represented only once. Multiple nesting events are indicated in Table 16.5, and those individuals are not included here. Sectors and methods of identifying nesting females are explained in Figure 16.5. Sectors 1 and 5 are adjacent.

Table 16.4. Sectors from which Ellenton Bay egg-carrying females
departed in three or more years from 1976 to 1987

Species	Number of individuals	Individuals nesting in same sector for three or more consecutive years	Individuals nesting in same or adjacent sector for three or more consecutive years
Trachemys scripta	3	0	2
Kinosternon subrubrum	21	16	20
Deirochelys reticularia	9	2	7

Note: If an individual nested more than once in a particular year, the sector of the first nesting excursion for that year was used. Sectors 1 and 5 are adjacent. Sectors and methods of identifying nesting females are explained in Fig. 16.5.

from a farm pond where an algicide was used that eliminated their primary food source. Gibbons et al. (1983) documented an emigration by a large segment of the populations of *T. scripta* and *P. floridana* from Ellenton Bay in the direction of the nearest body of water during an extreme drought. *Kinosternon subrubrum* and *D. reticularia* did not leave Ellenton Bay during the same drought, nor did *Chelydra serpentina* leave the drying lake observed by Cagle (1944b). Cahn (1937) concluded that a large number of *Chrysemys picta* died because they failed to leave a drying lake in Illinois, in contrast to those observed by Cagle (1944b).

Ellenton Bay data permit examination of the survival aptitude of freshwater turtles confronted with conditions in which their habitat became untenable for an aquatic existence. Ellenton Bay dried completely or almost so during the summers of 1968, 1981, and 1985 (see Chapter 2), but during the intervening years, turtles were active in the aquatic habitat. One or more individuals of each of the six species lived through each of the major droughts. Some individuals of *T. scripta* ($N = 5$) and *K. subrubrum* ($N = 7$) lived successfully through all three droughts (Table 16.5). These observations indicate that both extrapopulational movement (*T. scripta*) and quiescence (*K. subrubrum*), two entirely different strategies, can be effective for some individual turtles.

To understand further how some species of turtles respond to unfavorable habitat changes, we conducted an experiment in which Risher Pond was fenced and then drained, and the response of turtles occupying the pond was observed. The pond was completely enclosed by a drift fence with pitfall traps from January 1969 to January 1971. The fence was reestablished in January 1984. All movements by turtles into or out of the aquatic area were monitored in each of these years. In the summer of 1984 the pond was drained.

In the five months before the pond was drained, only 79 turtles, including nesting females, had left the habitat. During the few days that the water level was lowered (15–22 July 1984), 120 turtles emigrated (Table 16.6). *Kinosternon subrubrum* and *Chelydra serpentina* did not leave in

response to the draining, although both were present in the pond. As was noted above, *C. serpentina* have been reported to bury themselves in the mud under such conditions (Cagle, 1944b), and *K. subrubrum* did not emigrate from Ellenton Bay in greater than usual numbers during a drought (Gibbons et al., 1983). In contrast to our earlier observations at Ellenton Bay, *D. reticularia* responded to the abrupt drop in water level by emigrating. Perhaps the rate of drying of an aquatic habitat can be highly influential in determining the response of some species to falling water levels.

EXTRAPOPULATIONAL MOVEMENT OF MALES

Some long-distance movements reported for adult turtles are apparently unrelated to nesting or seasonal environmental changes. The explanation for many of these observations may lie in the tendency of adult males of a polygynous species to move extensively in search of mating opportunities with receptive females (Gibbons, 1986). The highest reproductive success should be achieved by male turtles that encounter and mate with the most females, even though adult males that engage in long-distance travel would undergo greater risks and incur higher energy costs associated with movements than turtles that remain in a habitat. Adult female turtles would be expected to have less potential fitness gain from multiple mating encounters than would males. Presumably a single mating is sufficient to fertilize a clutch of eggs, but in addition female turtles are capable of storing sperm and producing fertile eggs for up to four years after mating (see Chapter 9). This would further lessen any tendency for females to take unnecessary risks in search of mating encounters. Males, therefore, would be expected to be more active than females or immature males, moving longer distances and more often in search of mates. The extent of the mating season has not been carefully defined for most species of turtles but is a critical factor in this phenomenon.

The period of greatest sexual activity of *T. scripta* is presumed to be from fall to spring (approximately late

Table 16.5. Number of individuals of six freshwater turtle species that survived major droughts and total drying of the aquatic habitat at Ellenton Bay

Table 16.5 -- *Continued*

Species	Sex	Number captured before drought year			Number recaptured		
		1967-68	1969-81	1982-85	After 1968	After 1981	After 1985
Trachemys	M	150			38	1	4
scripta	F	150			52	1	1
	J	115			11	0	0
	M		417			33	29
	F		412			22	48
	J		329			6	1
	M			62			8
	F			45			4
	J			27			1
Kinosternon	M	73			19	3	3
subrubrum	F	96			26	1	4
	J	12			0	0	0
	M		298			25	43
	F		219			10	49
	J		89			4	0
	M			80			11
	F			55			5
	J			24			1
Deirochelys	M	73			13	0	0
reticularia	F	38			7	0	0
	J	15			2	0	0
	M		134			16	5
	F		85			3	2
	J		222			1	1
	M			23			1
	F			9			0
	J			8			0

Species	Sex	Number captured before drought year			Number recaptured		
		1967-68	1969-81	1982-85	After 1968	After 1981	After 1985
Sternotherus	M	27			0	1	0
odoratus	F	24			4	0	0
	J	1			0	0	0
	M		78			1	0
	F		67			1	0
	J		22			1	0
	M			9			0
	F			2			0
	J			4			0
Pseudemys	M	5			3	0	0
floridana	F	8			4	0	0
	J	9			0	0	0
	M		54			2	2
	F		60			2	4
	J		70			0	0
	M			2			0
	F			4			0
	J			3			1
Chelydra	--a	3			2	0	0
serpentina	M	3			1	0	0
	F	0			--	--	--
	J	3			0	0	0
	M		23			2	1
	F		9			2	2
	J		76			1	1
	M			7			0
	F			3			1
	J			7			0

Note: Recaptures in the after-1981 and after-1985 categories are not included in earlier categories. Abbreviations: M, adult males; F, adult females; J, juveniles.
aUnsexed adults.

Table 16.6. Emigration of aquatic turtles in response to draining of Risher Pond in 1984

Species	Jan. 1969-Jan. 1971				1 Jan.-15 July 1984				15-22 July 1984 (draining of pond)			
	M	F	J	Total	M	F	J	Total	M	F	J	Total
T. scripta	7	16	8	31	2	12	3	17	4	6	15	25
K. subrubrum	32	29	7	68	1	10	3	14	3	--	4	7
D. reticularia	9	10	11	30	1	10	3	14	4	3	20	27
S. odoratus	3	10	1	14	7	9	1	17	--	9	11	23
P. floridana	1	3	5	9	2	12	3	17	18	--	20	38
C. serpentina	3	6	2	11	--	--	--	--	--	--	--	--
Total	55	74	34	163	13	53	13	79	32	18	70	120

Note: Numbers indicate turtles leaving the lake, as measured by captures at a drift fence during different times. Abbreviations: M, males; F, females; J, juveniles.

September to early April) in South Carolina, although actual observations of courtship and copulation are rare (see Chapter 9). Slider turtles will apparently mate during the winter if temperatures are warm enough for activity. Springtime mating is assumed for *K. subrubrum*, but fall breeding may also occur, as in *Sternotherus odoratus* (McPherson and Marion, 1981a). The reproductive pattern of *D. reticularia* seems at variance with all other U.S. species. Female chicken turtles lay eggs from September to March (Gibbons and Greene, 1978), the exact period when other species do not lay eggs.

Few investigators have considered the differential behavior patterns of the sexes within turtle populations. Adult female *Chrysemys picta* were found to move significantly greater distances in the Sherriff's Marsh population in Michigan than were adult males (Gibbons, 1968d), presumably because the large and continuous aquatic habitat resulted in females' traveling long distances to find suitable nesting sites and then returning to the nearest aquatic area, not necessarily the area from which they had departed. In *T. scripta* populations adult males have been reported as characteristically making most of the lengthy overland excursions and being active during a greater portion of the year than are females (Morreale et al., 1984; Parker, 1984; Gibbons, 1986). Among terrestrial turtles, Rose and Judd (1982) noted larger home ranges for males than for females in *G. berlandieri* populations. All of the transient box turtles (*Terrapene carolina*) that made long-distance movements exceeding the distances normally moved by other members of the population were males (Kiester et al., 1982). Male *Clemmys marmorata* in a population studied by Bury (1972) had significantly larger home ranges than did females.

In comparing extrapopulational movement patterns of the sexes, several spatial and temporal measurements permit quantification of different movement patterns and provide means of testing the hypothesis that adult males move more frequently and greater distances during the mating period than females and juveniles, presumably to increase mating probabilities. As is indicated in Figure 16.1, male *T. scripta* on the SRP moved farther than females, based on recaptures at different sites. Turtles from the A-Area Seepage Basins give additional confirmation of differential movement by the sexes, with females apparently being more sedentary (Fig. 16.3).

During nondrought years, adults of both sexes of *T. scripta* made more extrapopulational moves than did juveniles, although a few immature females above 120 mm in plastron length were registered leaving the aquatic habitat (Fig. 16.4). Of 172 adult males (cumulative over four years) present and potentially capable of leaving Ellenton Bay, 95 (55%) exited during a year and did not return; of 168 adult females, 76 (45%) failed to return (Fig. 16.4). Most of the exits from aquatic areas by female *T. scripta* are during the spring (Table 16.7). The

Table 16.7. Seasonal extrapopulational movement by adults of five species of freshwater turtles at Ellenton Bay

Species	Season	Out		In	
		Male	Female	Male	Female
T. scripta	Winter	7	5	3	8
	Spring	154	191	70	85
	Summer	50	41	56	68
	Fall	165	4	7	8
K. subrubrum	Winter	7	1	25	10
	Spring	54	178	128	203
	Summer	39	112	40	137
	Fall	122	84	13	14
D. reticularia	Winter	4	20	1	9
	Spring	67	85	47	78
	Summer	24	25	32	16
	Fall	31	32	4	11
S. odoratus	Winter	0	0	0	1
	Spring	8	51	3	27
	Summer	19	8	16	120
	Fall	6	0	4	2
P. floridana	Winter	1	0	1	0
	Spring	22	16	4	7
	Summer	11	28	5	31
	Fall	4	0	4	2

Note: Records are based on captures in all nondrought years. Those reported as exiting were individuals that did not return to the aquatic habitat during the year. Those entering were first captures of the year. Entering hatchlings and other juveniles are excluded.

majority of the females are leaving to nest, although whether their failure to return is primarily a consequence of predation or emigration to another site is unresolved. Therefore, many of the departures by females may have been made with the intention of returning after nesting, whereas the departures by males were presumably for the purpose of reaching another habitat. The high incidence of springtime exiting and entering of aquatic habitats by both sexes, especially males (Table 16.7), may represent overland movement from other aquatic sites.

With the exception of data on nesting females, these observations of terrestrial activity do not confirm the purpose of the extrapopulational movement. The departure of immature females suggests that a search for more favorable habitat may be involved. Eighty-nine percent (24 of 27) of the immature females with plastron lengths ranging from 120 to 159 mm, and only 62% (64 of 104) of the adult males in those size classes, were last captured exiting Ellenton Bay in one or more of four years (Fig. 16.4), indicating that other factors may be involved in the departures of individuals from the aquatic habitat.

Temporal Activity

The objective in determining when turtles move is to relate movement to predictable changes that occur on a daily and seasonal basis, intrinsic factors such as hunger and state of maturity, and unpredictable environmental factors such as flooding and drought. The responses of individuals in populations to particular conditions are undoubtedly a consequence of the interaction of all three factors. Some of these have been discussed in earlier sections. Diel and seasonal activity patterns are discussed below.

DIEL ACTIVITY PATTERNS

The slider turtle contains a diurnal activity pattern throughout its geographic range, as far as is known. The studies on the SRP can contribute little to the knowledge of diel activity patterns of the slider or other species of turtles, beyond the categorical statement that freshwater turtles on the SRP do not travel overland during darkness, nor do they appear to be active aquatically at night. SREL personnel have spent hundreds of hours collecting reptiles and amphibians on highways at all hours of the day and night and during all seasons. No turtle has ever been collected on a highway during darkness, although large numbers have been collected crossing roads during the daytime. Nighttime observations of slider turtles in the water have not revealed them to be active at night except in response to disturbance by a collector. Those seen at night are normally underwater on the surface of the mud or buried beneath the substrate, but some species are active nocturnally in the water. Some sea turtles characteristically nest at night (Carr, 1952; Ernst and Barbour, 1972), and individuals of some freshwater species have been reported to nest at night on some occasions, although other individuals of the same species nest during the day (Congdon et al., 1983b, 1987).

SEASONAL ACTIVITY PATTERNS

Spring is the period of greatest terrestrial activity for both sexes of most species observed on the SRP. We have little information on how aquatic intrapopulational movement varies seasonally, but we assume that the high level of travel across the land-water interface indicates an overall level of activity. The adult activity patterns of certain species are revealed in an examination of observed terrestrial activity (Table 16.7). For example, K. subrubrum shows high activity in summer and fall, indicating the departure of individuals to hibernation areas, and a high entry into the aquatic habitat as they return in the spring. The observations of D. reticularia reveal the fall and winter nesting of females. Male emigration activity is higher in the fall than in the summer and perhaps indicates a fall breeding period. Clearly, additional studies must be conducted to quantify and understand these activity cycles.

HIBERNATION AND ESTIVATION

Many species of turtles migrate significant distances in response to seasonal changes to hibernate and estivate. We use the traditional and straightforward definitions that hibernation is dormancy during winter, and estivation is dormancy during summer or drought. All turtles in cold temperate zones hibernate. Estivation appears to be a common, though less predictable or perhaps less well-documented, phenomenon in areas with seasons that are hot and dry.

Hibernation is essential for turtles living in regions where winter temperatures approach or fall below freezing. Freshwater turtles that live in larger bodies of water are buffered from thermal extremes by the water itself, and many simply retreat into the mud or under the bank to wait out the colder periods. Many species in South Carolina that remain in aquatic areas become active on sunny days if their body temperatures can be raised sufficiently by aquatic or aerial basking. The risks to survival during winter from inaction are obviously of sufficient magnitude that they outweigh the risks encountered in overland or aquatic travel by freshwater species to hibernation sites. Thus, extrapopulation migration to and from hibernation sites is a common occurrence in many species of turtles.

Netting (1936) concluded that spotted turtles (Clemmys guttata) traveled in the spring from an upland hibernation site to a low-lying area. Painted turtles (Chrysemys picta) on the E. S. George Reserve left shallow marsh areas and retreated to deeper hibernation ponds during fall (Sexton, 1959b). After winter they returned to the shallow, vegetated areas. Adult mud turtles (K. subrubrum) on the SRP leave aquatic habitats during fall to overwinter on land, sometimes more than 1 km from water (Bennett et al., 1970).

Seasonal movements to avoid cold temperatures occur among sea turtles, which migrate toward tropical waters during winter. For example, leatherback sea turtles (Dermochelys coriacea) have a wide oceanic distribution in which individuals observed at high latitudes during warmer months of the year presumably return to equatorial waters during winter (Pritchard and Trebbau, 1984). Among terrestrial species, Gopherus agassizii have been reported to move to hibernaculum sites (Woodbury and Hardy, 1948), although the locations were apparently not far from their summer feeding areas.

Long-range seasonal movement patterns by freshwater turtles have been observed by means of the Ellenton Bay drift fence and pitfall traps. These observations have revealed only one species in the region (K. subrubrum) to display extrapopulational migration for hibernation consistently (Bennett et al., 1970). Although large numbers of T. scripta and Pseudemys floridana departed from Ellenton Bay during a period of extreme drought (Gibbons et al.,

Table 16.8. Seasonal entry of hatchling freshwater turtles to aquatic habitats

Species	Month											Total
	J	F	M	A	M	J	J	A	S	O	N	Total
T. scripta		2	110	46	8	7		4	3	1		181
K. subrubrum		29	358	118	15	7	3					530
D. reticularia			143	114	3	3		2	6			271
S. odoratus			6	2	1	5	1	2	6		1	24
P. floridana			33	51	9	9	1			1		104
C. serpentina	1		1	1	2	1			6			12
Total	1	31	651	332	38	32	5	8	21	2	1	1,122

Note: Figures are based on pitfall trap captures on the SRP from 1968 through 1987. No hatchlings were captured during December of any year.

1983), this is not an annual occurrence with these species, whereas *K. subrubrum* characteristically leaves in late summer or fall and returns when spring arrives (Table 16.7).

Observations of *T. scripta* in Ellenton Bay during wet years when winter water levels have been high indicate that this species will remain in the aquatic habitat for hibernation. This is also true at Risher Pond, Par Pond, and Pond B, where turtles have been captured in the water during December, January, and February (Par Pond, $N = 166$; Pond B, $N = 92$; Risher Pond, $N = 9$; Ellenton Bay, $N = 58$). It is possible that *T. scripta* in some situations may move to particular areas for hibernation, as observed in *Chrysemys picta* by Sexton (1959b). However, no evidence has been presented to suggest that *T. scripta* does anything other than respond individually to the onset of cold by finding a safe retreat in the area of normal activity.

MOVEMENT TO AREAS WITH DIFFERING RESOURCES

Aside from activities associated with hibernation or other responses to winter conditions, many animals move long distances seasonally in response to changing food resources or other nutrient requirements. It is conceivable that some turtles may make determined travels beyond the limits of the normal population habitat to acquire a predictable resource in another area. Desert tortoises are known to travel to specific sites to eat soil, presumably to acquire required nutrients that are not in sufficient quantity in their normal diet (Kristin Berry, pers. com.). Some individual tortoises may have to travel long distances outside their usual activity area to achieve this objective, but they would have to have made such a trip already without any assurance of finding the resource, because they could not have known of it initially.

Certain circumstances could lead to a generalized searching behavior in a population. For example, an Al-

dabra tortoise exposed to ultimately lethal conditions of overheating would be expected to set out in search of shade (Swingland and Lessells, 1979). Once a satisfactory spot is found, it may be used on a regular basis thereafter, even if it is a long distance from normal feeding areas.

Although seasonal diet shifts probably occur in several species of turtles, and some sea turtles make significant migrations from nesting beaches to feeding areas (Carr and Coleman, 1974; Mortimer, 1981), we are aware of only one observation in which major segments of a population of freshwater turtles actually make annual, long-distance movements during the normal activity period to capitalize on a particular food resource. Moll and Legler (1971) observed seasonal shifts in the activity area of tropical *T. scripta* in response to rainfall patterns, presumably because of the predictable availability of resources. An initial prediction for the unusual situation at Par Pond, the large reservoir receiving thermal effluent on the SRP, was that slider turtles would follow the thermal gradient and move from the colder regions of the lake to the warm end during winter, where feeding could occur almost year-round. Such a concentration phenomenon has been observed in American alligators (Murphy and Brisbin, 1974) and largemouth bass (Gibbons et al., 1978a) but was not documented to occur in turtles (Schubauer, 1981a).

If predetermined habitat shifts by turtle populations are discovered, they will most likely occur in aquatic species occupying large bodies of water, such as rivers, where detectable gradients exist that would provide cues to all individuals in the population about available resources in another area. It is unlikely that annual migrations would develop among the many species that occupy temporary aquatic habitats and that rely on extensive overland travel. Under most circumstances, movement to capitalize on food resources that vary seasonally in different areas is most likely to be a consequence of individual experience and chance, not a population phenomenon.

MOVEMENT OF HATCHLINGS FROM NEST TO WATER

The initial movement by all species of aquatic turtles is the overland trip from the nest to the water, the entry into the population. The hatchling movement per se need not be discussed in terms of benefit to the individual, for indeed the trip is one of necessity. However, the seasonal timing of nest departure varies among species, and whether hatchlings leave the nest soon after hatching or overwinter in the nest (Gibbons and Nelson, 1978) has presumably been influenced by natural selection on the basis of the risks and benefits of the timing.

The turtles belonging to five of the six species that inhabit Ellenton Bay generally lay eggs in the late spring (*Deirochelys reticularia* nest in fall, winter, or early spring; see Chapter 9), and the hatchlings enter the water about a year later (Table 16.8). However, high variability in the seasonal timing occurs in every species, and at least a small proportion of most species apparently emerge soon after hatching, without overwintering. For most species of turtles the risks associated with immediate emergence seem to outweigh those of a delayed emergence, which may double the amount of time in the nest. A careful look at how risks vary among species, years, and habitats would be instructive in addressing the question of why turtles emerge from the nest when they do, and such risks should become a focus of studies on hatchling emergence phenomena.

Acknowledgments

Much of the research reported was supported by contract DE-AC09-76SROO-819 between the U.S. Department of Energy and the University of Georgia and by National Science Foundation contract DEB-79-04758. Sue Novak and Joseph P. Schubauer provided critical comments on the manuscript. Jeff Lovich contributed greatly in critically reviewing the manuscript, augmenting the literature base, and commenting editorially on the manuscript. We appreciate the assistance of Malinda Doherty, Jan Hinton, and Pat Davis with the manuscript preparation.

WILLIAM S. PARKER
Division of Science and Mathematics
Mississippi University for Women
Columbus, Mississippi 39701

17

Colonization of a Newly Constructed Farm Pond in Mississippi by Slider Turtles and Comparisons with Established Populations

Abstract

Colonization by slider turtles (*Pseudemys scripta*) of a 0.3-hectare farm pond newly constructed in 1980 in Clay County, Mississippi, was recorded over five years. Population size peaked after three years at 26 individuals, then declined slightly in the next two years. Most colonists were immature animals, and population structure was strongly biased toward immatures. Turnover of individuals between years was higher in adults than in immatures and higher than in established ponds, but two individuals were present for four consecutive years. Juvenile growth rate was half that in established ponds during the pond's third year but increased to nearly comparable levels by its fifth year. Population and biomass densities remained below those of nearby established ponds.

Introduction

Freshwater turtles may move long distances overland to reach other bodies of water with better food supplies, lower population densities, or better mating opportunities (Gibbons, 1986). In the slider turtle (*Pseudemys scripta*), types of aquatic or terrestrial habitats separating local populations are less important than distance in the extent of genetic divergence between such semi-isolated populations (Scribner et al., 1986). Adult male sliders move more frequently and over greater distances than other age or sex groups (Morreale et al., 1984; Parker, 1984).

With these dispersal attributes in mind, I studied a 0.3-hectare pond constructed in 1980 in Clay County, Mis-

Table 17.1. Summary of captures and population estimates of slider turtles
in a newly constructed pond and an established pond

Year	Number of sampling days/Month(s)	Individuals captured	Individuals newly marked	% new	Number of recaptures	Total captures	Population estimate
New Clay County pond							
1981	6/July	1	1	100.0	1	2	1
1982	10/Aug.	12	12	100.0	14	26	13
1983	8/July	26	20	76.9	39	65	26
1984	14/July	22	8	36.4	23	45	23
1985	17/July	14	2	14.3	14	28	20
Established Lowndes County pond (pond 1)							
1975	45/May-July	132	132	100.0	47	179	220
1976	38/May-Aug.	226	142	62.8	134	360	340
1977	33/May-Aug.	254	91	35.8	281	535	305
1978	28/May-Aug.	195	41	21.0	133	328	240
1979	29/May-July	194	51	26.3	217	411	205

Note: The new pond was constructed in 1980 in Clay County, Mississippi. Population sizes (number of turtles in pond) were estimated by the Schnabel Method (Overton, 1971).

sissippi, to observe its colonization by slider turtles (*P. scripta*). I also compared population structure, turnover rate, and biomass and population densities of this new pond with those for populations in established ponds nearby.

Materials and Methods

STUDY AREAS

The primary study area was a 0.3-hectare rectangular pond about 3 km south of West Point, Clay County, Mississippi. This pond (herein called new pond) was constructed by excavation in autumn 1980 and allowed to fill with rainwater to a depth of about 1 m. A drainage pipe eliminated overflow from excessive rain. I sampled its turtle populations each year from 1981 to 1985 (Table 17.1).

Sources of immigrating turtles were located on an aerial photograph; the nearest permanent bodies of water were 1.8 km or more away, although a seasonally flowing ditch channel was about 85 m away. The pond was located on a rural, residential corner lot, with a lawn mowed regularly up to the water's edge. Immigrating turtles would have to cross wide expanses of cultivated fields and a heavily traveled two-lane highway to the east; a moderately traveled country road and residential areas immediately to the north; open lawn, patches of woodland, cultivated fields, and other residential areas to the west and south. At my request, the owner of the pond kindly refrained from using any chemicals such as fertilizers, herbicides, or algicides in the pond during the five years of study. He did, however, introduce fingerling catfish in 1982, which were large enough by 1984 to swallow juvenile turtles. The

pond was also colonized by sunfish (*Lepomis* sp.) in 1983, and these were caught in large numbers in turtle traps in 1984 and 1985. There was little obvious rooted aquatic vegetation or algal mats in the pond during any year of study. A small grove of trees near the east edge of the pond shaded it early in the day, but later the entire pond was completely insolated. There were no basking sites other than the shoreline.

For comparison, data were used from earlier studies of turtle populations at two nearby sites from 1975 to 1982: four farm ponds (ponds 1–4) and a stream about 17.6 km west of Columbus, Lowndes County (Parker, 1984), and a fifth farm pond (pond 5) about 7 km west of Columbus. Ponds 1–4 were 14 km south-southeast, and pond 5 was 16 km east-southeast of the new pond. The numbering of ponds follows Parker (1984), and additional pond size and depth characteristics are in Table 17.4, below. Pond 1 was treated with large amounts of algicides and herbicides and possibly fertilized starting in 1977. I was unable to secure information about these activities from the owner. Pond 2 was not treated with chemicals; algal growth was extensive; the surrounding land was mostly open woodland and old fields in early stages of succession. Pond 2 was sampled briefly in 1976 and more extensively from 1980 to 1982. Ponds 3 and 4 were surrounded by open pasture, and their margins were heavily disturbed by cattle; algal growth was extensive. Pond 5 was bordered by patches of woodland and open fields in early successional stages; there was no chemical treatment; algal growth was extensive. Ponds 3, 4, and 5 were sampled in only one year (1981 or 1982). The stream was a tributary of Tibbee Creek, with steep mudbanks up to about 8 m, extensive seasonal flooding, and dense vegetation along its banks. The stream was briefly sampled in 1980 and 1981.

TRAPPING AND MARKING

A combination of wire-mesh funnel traps baited with fish parts or canned fish-flavored cat food and unbaited basking traps with hinged planks was used. Traps were checked and rebaited daily at the new pond. Trap-days (number of traps × number of trapping days) averaged 278/year (8 years) in pond 1, 60/year (3 years) in pond 2, 44/year (1 year) in pond 3, 45/year (1 year) in pond 4, 80/year (1 year) in pond 5, and 42/year (5 years) in the new pond. Captures per trap-day averaged 1.1 in pond 1 (mean for 8 annual values), 1.0 in pond 2 (3 years), 2.1 in pond 3, 1.5 in pond 4, 1.2 in pond 5, and 0.8 in the new pond (5 years).

Turtles were permanently marked by notching marginal scutes with a pocket saw. Each turtle was measured to the nearest millimeter for plastron length (PL) using vernier calipers for small turtles up to 125 mm PL and a meter stick for larger turtles. Turtles were weighed to the nearest 25 g in a plastic bucket suspended from an Ohaus spring balance. Processing was done on the shore nearest a trap, and turtles were released into the water immediately after processing. See Parker (1984) for further details.

TERMINOLOGY AND DATA INTERPRETATION

The term "juvenile" here refers to sexually immature individuals below 100 mm PL whose sex could not be determined. The term "immature" refers to all immature individuals, adding in immature females 101–159 mm PL. Sexual maturity for females was arbitrarily assigned as 160 mm PL, based on the literature and dissections of 18 females between 145 and 185 mm PL during the reproductive season. Those newly captured after the second year of study (starting in 1977) were assumed to be colonists in pond 1. In the new pond unmarked individuals were obviously colonists the first four years, because the pond was not in existence previously, recapture rates were high, and population estimates were identical to the number of individuals captured in 1983.

As an inverse indicator of annual population turnover, I used the proportion of an age group known or assumed to be in a pond more than one year. This is considered justified because the trapping effort was prolonged over eight years in pond 1, using both baited and unbaited traps to minimize sex or age bias in trapping, and allowed several subsequent years to capture individuals that may have been missed one year. In the new pond I was clearly capturing virtually all the individuals in the pond through 1983, and in 1985 I added an unbaited basking trap (not previously used) to capture individuals that may have ceased responding to baited traps. I also made daily head counts of turtles visible in the new pond; these declined in 1984 and 1985, as did the population estimates.

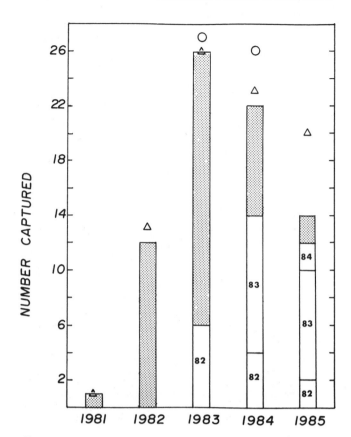

FIGURE 17.1. Captures and population estimates (using the Schnabel Method) for slider turtles captured during five years after construction of a farm pond in 1980. Histograms = actual number captured each year; open circles = number known alive based on subsequent years' captures; triangles = population estimates; stippling = newly marked individuals; numerals in histograms = year that cohort was first marked.

Results

COLONIZATION OF THE NEW POND

POPULATION SIZE AND COLONIZATION RATE. Sampling characteristics of colonization are given and compared with corresponding data for five years at an established pond in Table 17.1. All or most of the turtles in the new pond were captured several times each year, so population estimates were probably close to actual population size. After 1981 the proportion of unmarked, new turtles in the new pond followed a pattern of decline similar to that observed in the established pond.

Population size increased rapidly to a peak in 1983, then leveled off and declined slightly in 1984 and 1985 as numbers of colonists dropped off (Fig. 17.1). Population estimates were at or slightly above the number of turtles actually captured each year. Five turtles apparently remaining in the pond were not captured in one year, and assuming their presence back through 1983 or 1984 gave population sizes above the estimates based on recapture rates. Colonizing cohorts from 1982 through 1984 were each gradually reduced in subsequent years, most severely in the 1984 cohort (Fig. 17.1).

POPULATION STRUCTURE OF COLONISTS.   Most turtles captured in the new pond were juveniles or immatures (Fig. 17.2). Colonists were scattered across several size-age groups, but a majority of the population was composed of one cohort of juveniles in the 61–80 mm PL size range, which arrived in 1983 and which made up an easily discernible group in 1984 and 1985 as well. Males in this group marked as juveniles in 1983 were attaining sexual maturity, as indicated by secondary sexual characteristics, by 1985. Adults, especially larger adult females, were poorly represented in all years.

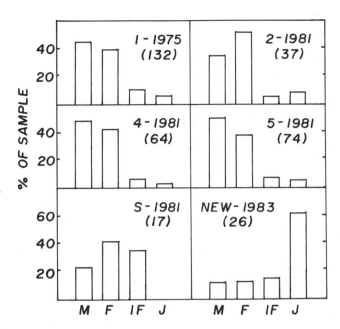

FIGURE 17.3.   Comparative population structure in four ponds (1, 2, 4, 5) and a stream (S) in Lowndes County, Mississippi, and a new pond in Clay County, Mississippi, for the years indicated. Pond numbering follows Parker (1984). Numbers in parentheses are total number of individuals captured. Juveniles (J) < 90 mm PL; immature females (IF) = 90–159 mm PL. Mature males (M) and mature females (F) are also shown.

COMPARISONS WITH ESTABLISHED POPULATIONS

POPULATION STRUCTURE.   Ratios of mature to immature individuals were similar in four established ponds whose populations had 84.1% to 90.6% adults and 9.4% to 15.9% immatures (Fig. 17.3). A small sample from a stream population contained only 64.7% mature turtles. The new pond was substantially different, with a reverse age structure of 23.0% matures and 76.9% immatures in 1983.

POPULATION TURNOVER.   The proportion of turtles in a cohort remaining in a pond for two or more years was used as an inverse indicator of turnover rate. Turnover by this measure was higher in the new pond than in the established pond in all three years of measurement (Table 17.2). When considered by age and sex groups, turnover was virtually identical among juveniles in the two pond types but higher for all other age or sex groups from the new pond. Among adults, turnover was nearly complete; only 2 of 12 were present in more than one year. In pond 1 the highest turnover and recapture rates occurred among adult males (42% of 1,136 total captures were recaptures); the lowest occurred among adult females (33% of 632 total captures were recaptures).

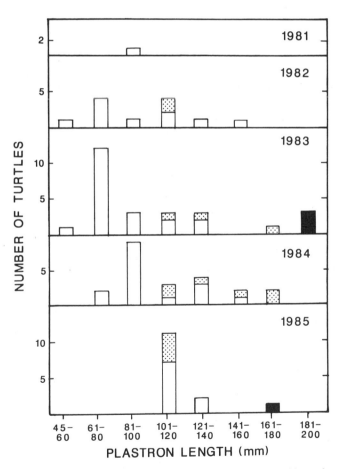

FIGURE 17.2.   Plastron lengths of slider turtles captured in each of five years of colonization of the new pond. Unshaded areas = immature turtles, shaded = adult females, stippled = adult males.

Table 17.2. Colonizing slider turtles present more than one year at
a newly constructed pond and an established pond

	New pond		Established pond	
Age group	N (Year)	Proportion present more than one year	N (Year)	Proportion present more than one year
--	12 (1982)	.58	131 (1975)	.81
--	20 (1983)	.65	138 (1976)	.85
--	8 (1984)	.20	88 (1977)	.67
Juveniles (plastron length < 90 mm)	21	.76	198	.78
Immature females	8	.50	59	.80
Maturing males (matured during study)	7	.71	65	.92
Mature females	3	0.0	97	.72
Mature males	9	.22	170	.58

Note: Year and age group indicate when turtles were first marked. The new pond was constructed in 1980 in Clay County, Mississippi. The established pond was pond 1, studied in Lowndes County for eight years (Parker, 1984). Data exclude turtles that drowned in traps in the established pond.

JUVENILE GROWTH RATES. Sample sizes for growth records were unavoidably small during the first years of colonization of the new pond, but differences from established ponds were still apparent (Table 17.3). Growth rates by age interval and sex were generally lower among juveniles from the new pond than among juveniles from the established pond, but significantly so (t test, $p < .01$) only among juvenile females in the 1-to-2-year-old class.

Table 17.3. Comparative growth rates in individuals first captured as juveniles in an established farm pond and a newly constructed pond

	Growth rate by age interval or year interval		
Sex and pond	1-2 years old	2-3 years old	3-4 years old
Juvenile males			
Established pond	21.65 (26) (12-37)	16.9 (38) (6-33)	10.2 (24) (2-17)
New pond	9.0 (1)	20.1 (2) (14-26.2)	--
Juvenile females			
Established pond	22.96* (26) (14-42)	23.4 (26) (12-35)	20.2 (18) (7-34)
New pond	11.3* (3) (9.2-14.5)	18.7 (6) (14.3-28.6)	19.8 (5) (14.0-28.7)
	1982-83	1983-84	1984-85
Sexes and ages combined by year for new pond	11.2 (3) (9.0-14.5)	16.6 (8) (14.0-26.2)	21.2 (6) (14.0-28.7)

Note: Growth rates are expressed in mm of plastron length (PL) per year. Means are followed by sample sizes and extremes in parentheses. Groups were compared by t tests or F tests; significant differences were found only with t tests. Individuals were sexed on the basis of later captures at sizes greater than 100 mm PL. The new pond was constructed in 1980 and was studied from 1981 to 1985; the established pond (pond 1) was studied from 1975 to 1982.

*$p < .01$ (t test).

Combining the three age groups by years of capture showed almost a doubling of juvenile growth rate as the pond aged from its third to its fifth year, despite an increase in the average age of the individuals involved. However, these differences were not significant (F test).

POPULATION AND BIOMASS DENSITIES. Density figures for three established ponds and the new pond in four years are given in Table 17.4, where population estimates for pond 1 and the new pond were based on data in Table 17.1. As was expected on the basis of previous results, both population and biomass densities of turtles in the new pond were well below those in established ponds. The average weight of individual turtles in the new pond was less than half that in established ponds, resulting in biomass densities that were generally less than one-fifth the density in established ponds. The average weight of individual turtles in the new pond increased between 1982 and 1983 but leveled off and declined slightly in 1984 and 1985.

Discussion

CAUSES AND RESULTS OF DISPERSAL

Colonization of a newly created habitat, such as described here for slider turtles, may be dependent upon numerous factors affecting dispersal of neonates from hatching sites and older individuals from suitable aquatic habitats. Dispersal in animals found in patchy habitats may be caused by reproductive motivations (searching for nest sites by females, searching for mates by males), variations in hab-

Table 17.4. Comparative population and live-weight biomass densities
of slider turtles in a variety of pond habitats

Pond	Year	Area (ha)	Maximum depth (m)	Population estimate	Population density (turtles/ha)	Individual mean weight (g)	Biomass (kg/ha)
Established ponds							
Pond 1	1975	0.9	2-3	225	250	--	--
	1976	0.9	2-3	300[a]	333	648.5 (156)	215.9
	1978	1.3	3	261	201	683.6 (176)	137.4
	1981	2.8	3-4	215	77	672.5 (119)	51.8
Pond 2	1980	0.2[b]	2-3	37	185	697.3 (28)	129.0
Pond 5	1981	0.9	2-3	162	180	912.4 (73)	164.2
New pond	1982	0.3	1	13	43	255.0 (9)	10.9
	1983	0.3	1	26	87	305.2 (25)	26.6
	1984	0.3	1	23	77	305.6 (22)	23.5
	1985	0.3	1	20	67	285.0 (13)	19.1

Note: Sample sizes are given in parentheses following mean weight. Population estimates are based on the data in Table 17.1.

[a]Estimate adjusted below that given in Table 17.1, to the number known alive based on subsequent years' captures.

[b]Area at summer low point, not taking area of entering stream into account.

itat quality or resultant nutritional status, overcrowding, low social status, or inherent factors (Horn, 1983; Swingland, 1983; Gibbons, 1986). Such multiple causes of dispersal may be typical in many vertebrates (Dobson and Jones, 1985). Successful dispersal may depend on the distance to other adequate habitat and its quality (in terms of food, shelter, mates, etc.) and may result in increased nesting or mating success, more rapid growth if nutrition is improved, occupation of more open and less crowded habitat, and acquisition of higher social status. For the entire population these results may increase overall population densities and decrease inbreeding through genetic homogenization of local populations (Horn, 1983).

The capability of slider turtles for long dispersal movements (greater than 4 km) was documented by Morreale et al. (1984), so my results of successful, rather rapid colonization of open habitat 1.8 km from the nearest source populations are not surprising. In fact, the questions addressed here have more to do with the retention of individuals that have located a new habitat than with the search for and location of new habitat. Because I was able to sample for only a few weeks a year, any short-term flux of individuals was not detectable. Instead, my captures mostly represent individuals that became established in the new pond. Below, I discuss my results as specifically related to the causes and results of dispersal identified above.

MALE SEARCH FOR MATES. Adult male slider turtles move longer distances and in greater numbers than do adult females, which are more philopatric (Morreale et al., 1984; Parker, 1984). Presumably these movements maximize male reproductive success, although this is yet to be demonstrated. Larger, dominant males drive small-

er, subordinate males away from mature females (Cagle, 1950; Lardie, 1983) and may be the only breeders in captivity (Rundquist, 1985), although females still control culmination of mating (Berry, 1984). Only three adult females were captured in the new pond (Fig. 17.2), and none of them was present more than one year (Table 17.2). Among nine males first captured as adults, only two (104–133 mm PL) were captured more than one year, and all five of the largest males (148–173 mm PL) were captured in only one year. The largest males probably do not remain where there are few or no adult females. However, it is less clear why any mature males or males reaching maturity in the new pond would remain longer. Lower turnover in maturing males than in adult males was also noted in the established population (Table 17.2). Risks to smaller males during dispersal movements may be too great even if there is a high likelihood of remaining subordinate to larger males in large ponds or encountering no adult females in small ponds.

NUTRITION AND GROWTH. Growth rates in freshwater turtles may be positively affected by high-protein diets (Gibbons, 1967b; Parmenter, 1980) and/or elevated water temperatures (Christy et al., 1974) and may be negatively affected by increased salinities (Novak and Morreale, 1985). Carnivorous habits extend into the second year of life in *P. scripta* (Clark and Gibbons, 1969) and may continue when high-protein food sources such as fish carrion are present (Parmenter, 1980).

Productivity of farm ponds may vary widely; biomasses of consumer organisms frequently increase with increasing primary production (Arruda, 1979). My results of (1) a reduced growth rate among turtles during their first two years in the new pond relative to those in an established pond (Table 17.3), and (2) an increase in growth rate as the new pond aged, both presumably reflect a correlation between growth rates and food availability or quality, although the prey organisms and pond productivity were not measured.

A few turtles at the new pond were clearly undernourished relative to similar-aged individuals in established ponds. Slower growth early in life could have affected health and survivorship and perhaps delayed sexual maturity. It is not clear why some turtles would stay under such conditions, but growth rates (and presumably food supply) increased to near normal levels as the pond aged and primary production apparently increased. Chemical removal of much of the food supply in an established pond seemed to increase the dispersal rate (Parker, 1984). Perhaps the threshold for nutritionally induced dispersal movements varies among individuals.

POPULATION STRUCTURE AND TURNOVER. Proportions of immature turtles were generally lower in my larger samples (9.4% to 15.9%, Fig. 17.3) than in populations sampled by Cagle (1942, 1950) in the United States and Moll and Legler (1971) in Panama (27% to 37%, excluding small samples below 60 individuals). Populations in newer, smaller, and/or shallower ponds may have much higher proportions of immatures. Cagle (1942) sampled a 0.025-hectare stock pond in Illinois two years after its construction; 13 of 63 turtles in the pond were *P. scripta*. Among those 13, 76.9% (10) were immatures, a figure similar to my result in the new pond (83.3%) at the same age.

Colonization rate was also almost identical between the two studies two years after pond construction (13 in Illinois, 12 in Mississippi), although Cagle's pond was much smaller and had 53 turtles of other species, whereas my new pond was larger and had only 9 turtles of one other species (*Kinosternon subrubrum*). Cagle's pond was "distant" from colonization sources, but the distance was not given.

BIOMASS AND POPULATION DENSITIES. My biomass and population densities for *P. scripta* in Table 17.4 all fall well within figures for other populations of this species in a

literature summary by Iverson (1982) and in a more localized interhabitat comparison by Congdon et al. (1986). The new pond I studied was expectedly at the lower end of this range; as it ages more, perhaps it will approach the higher figures found at pond 2, an older pond of similar size but greater depth (Table 17.4). Decreasing densities in pond 1 were more from pond expansion by beaver damming than from a decrease in population size. The densities I recorded in established ponds were mostly toward the high end of the range for this species, perhaps partially as a result of lower numbers of sympatric populations of other turtle species. Only small numbers of one or two other species (*Chelydra serpentina* and *K. subrubrum*) occurred in any of my study areas.

FUTURE WORK

Closely controlled farm pond systems are potentially ideal for developing an understanding of dispersal dynamics in freshwater turtles such as *P. scripta*. Ponds newly constructed in good habitat could be standardized for size, depth, and distance from sources of colonization. A relatively rapid colonization such as reported here could lead to stabilized populations in only a few years. Manipulations of populations could include varying available food and observing its effect on dispersal and reproduction. Population densities could be artificially increased or decreased. Social status (dominance) in both sexes could be determined through behavioral observations, and its role in dispersal could be identified. A series of such field experiments would enhance our understanding of the mechanisms by which such freshwater turtles have achieved their conspicuous success at frequently high population and biomass densities.

Acknowledgments

This work was supported by Faculty Summer Research Grants from Mississippi University for Women. I especially thank Scott Allen for access to his property. My wife, Beth, generously provided moral support and statistical advice.

JOSEPH P. SCHUBAUER
Institute of Ecology and Department of Zoology
University of Georgia
Athens, Georgia 30602

Current address:
Marine Sciences Research Center
State University of New York at Stony Brook
Stony Brook, New York 11794

J. WHITFIELD GIBBONS
Savannah River Ecology Laboratory
Drawer E
Aiken, South Carolina 29802

JAMES R. SPOTILA
Department of Biology
State University College
1300 Elmwood Avenue
Buffalo, New York 14222

Current address:
Department of Bioscience and Biotechnology
Drexel University
Philadelphia, Pennsylvania 19104

18

Home Range and Movement Patterns of Slider Turtles Inhabiting Par Pond

Abstract

The home range and individual movement patterns of slider turtles (*Trachemys scripta*) inhabiting a thermally altered reservoir were determined using mark-recapture and radio-telemetry over a 16-month period. Home range areas of turtles inhabiting a thermally altered site and a site with normal water temperatures were not significantly different, nor were the activity patterns of the turtles different between sites except for those of males in the fall. Turtles did not inhabit the warmest areas, nor did they shuttle in and out of the thermal plume, even in the coldest months. Telemetric estimates of home range areas for both sexes were significantly larger, and presumably more accurate, than estimates based on mark-recapture records. Telemetry revealed that the total and aquatic home range areas for males (104 ha and 27 ha, respectively) were significantly larger than those for females (37 ha and 15 ha).

Introduction

Studies in Par Pond have documented how thermal effluents influence the ecology and behavior of fish (Gibbons et al., 1978a) and other aquatic vertebrates, such as alligators (Murphy and Brisbin, 1974), but few studies have addressed how the behavior of aquatic turtles might be affected by thermal effluents (Schubauer, 1981a; Thornhill, 1982). In addition, few behavioral studies of aquatic turtles have been conducted in large reservoirs or lakes, though several have been done in riverine habitats (Wickham, 1922; Mahmoud, 1969; Moll and Legler, 1971; Bury, 1972; Florence, 1975; Plummer and Shirer, 1975; Moll, 1980), bogs and wetlands (Hammer, 1969; Obbard and Brooks, 1981b), and small lakes and ponds (Mahmoud, 1969; Ernst, 1970, 1971c; Moll and Legler, 1971; also see Ernst and Barbour, 1972). Webb (1961) provided information on the movements of aquatic turtles in a large reservoir, but the report was limited to approximate distances moved between points of capture and release for four marked *T. scripta*. Although the slider turtle is one of the most studied aquatic turtles, little quantitative information is available regarding aquatic home range areas, particularly in large bodies of water. Finally, although studies concerned with quantifying the movements and home ranges of aquatic turtles have classically used one or a combination of three main methods (telemetry, mark-recapture, and visual observations), few, if any, have addressed how the results obtained from these different techniques compare with one another.

Our objectives were (1) to examine the home range and movements of a population of slider turtles inhabiting Par Pond, a large thermally altered reservoir, and (2) to determine if estimates provided by two common techniques (mark-recapture and telemetry) were comparable.

Study Site

The study was conducted at Par Pond (Fig. 18.1; Gibbons and Sharitz, 1981; also see Chapter 2). When the reactor is operating, heated water is introduced by a subsurface pipe at a point in the Hot Arm called the Boil (Fig. 18.2). As a consequence, temperatures near the Boil are maintained, on average, about 10° C above ambient (Schubauer, 1981a) during periods of reactor operation. Temperatures near the Boil may reach 40° C in the summer and 30° C in the winter (Schubauer, 1981a), but temperatures in most of the reservoir, because of its large size and its morphology, are not dramatically affected (for a more detailed discussion of these points, see Lewis, 1974a,b; Vigerstad and Kiser, 1977; Hazen, 1978; Schubauer, 1981a), although they are 3° to 5° C higher than those of farm ponds in the region (Schubauer and Parmenter, 1981).

Much of the open littoral zone of the lake is lined with cattails (*Typha latifolia* and *T. domingensis*) and a thick mat of submerged macrophytes, including *Myriophyllum spicatum*. Most of the open-water areas of the shallow bays are covered with spatterdock (*Nuphar luteum*), American lotus (*Nelumbo lutea*), and water lilies (*Nymphaea odorata*). During this study, floating vegetation was sparse or absent in the warmest areas of the Hot Arm.

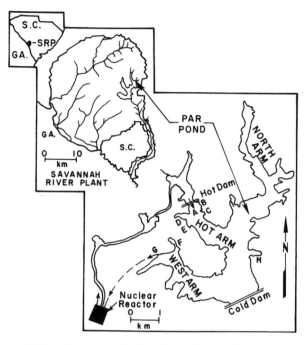

FIGURE 18.1.   Study areas in Par Pond. The study focused on the areas marked A through G in the Hot Arm and the West Arm. A = the point at which thermal effluents enter the reservoir.

Methods

MARK-RECAPTURE

Trachemys scripta activity, abundance, and distribution were monitored in areas of the Hot Arm and the West Arm (Fig. 18.2). We trapped in all seasons from April 1977 to June 1978 (8,848 total trap-days), using traps constructed of chicken wire or hardware cloth as well as funnel net traps. Traps were baited with largemouth bass (*Micropterus salmoides*) obtained from Par Pond or with canned sardines. At the end of each trapping period the traps were removed from the water to minimize habituating turtles to traps and to avoid unintentional containment of animals in traps for long periods. Traps were not set in areas more than 6 m deep. Deeper areas were sampled with trotlines, dip nets, and visual sightings.

Captured turtles were returned to the laboratory, permanently marked with an individual code, sexed, measured for plastron length and mass, and aged. With the exception of the marking procedure, recaptured individuals were similarly treated. All turtles were released at the exact point of capture. Trap locations and captures were marked on scaled aerial maps.

TELEMETRY

Thirty-three adult *T. scripta* (19 males and 14 females) were studied with telemetry, following the techniques de-

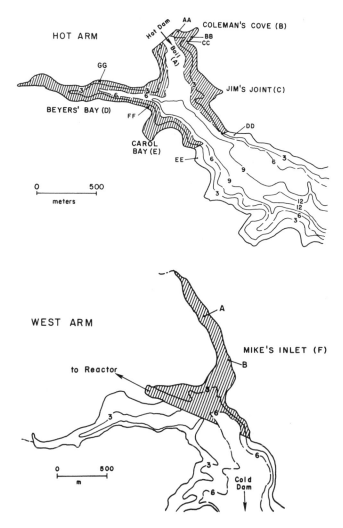

FIGURE 18.2. Enlarged hydrobathymetric maps of the Hot Arm and West Arm study sites in Par Pond. Depth isopleths are marked in meters. The hatch marks depict trapping areas less than or equal to 6 m in depth.

scribed by Schubauer (1981a,b). Twenty-one of these animals (9 males and 12 females) were used to estimate home range areas and movements (Fig. 18.3). Generally, the position of individuals was determined to within 5 m on an average of once a week, from 7 a.m. to 9 p.m., throughout the study. In addition, the movements of 7 individuals (4 males and 3 females) were examined at 4-hour intervals over a 24-hour period in the summer to assess diel activity patterns. Locations of animals were recorded with the date and time of the observation on a scaled map. Mud or thick vegetation did not prevent relocation of transmitters (Schubauer, 1981a,b).

Buoyancy control and movements of turtles were not noticeably affected by the transmitters. Transmitters typically amounted to less than 10% (maximum 12%) of an individual's body mass. Transmitters did not differentially affect a turtle's chances of being trapped, nor was any

mortality attributed to transmitter attachment (Schubauer, 1981b).

MOVEMENT PATTERNS AND HOME RANGE ESTIMATES

Many methods have been used to quantify the home ranges of animals, including turtles (for reviews of a number of these methods, see Bury, 1979, and Schubauer, 1981b). The most commonly used methods for aquatic turtles include the convex polygon method of Jennrich and Turner (1969), the minimum polygon index of Mohr (1947) and Mohr and Stumpf (1966), a modified minimum polygon index (Harvey and Barbour, 1965; Ernst, 1970), a linear representation (Moll and Legler, 1971; Bury, 1972), and the recapture radius method (Hayne, 1949; Dice and Clark, 1953). Each technique has inherent advantages and disadvantages. To simplify calculation and comparison and to meet all of the different study objectives simultaneously, we chose to express our results using the convex polygon method (Jennrich and Turner, 1969). Home ranges were determined by recording successive location points ($N \geq 3$) of each turtle on a scaled map, using either mark-recapture or telemetry.

We defined the total home range of *T. scripta* as the total area used in the normal activities of an individual turtle,

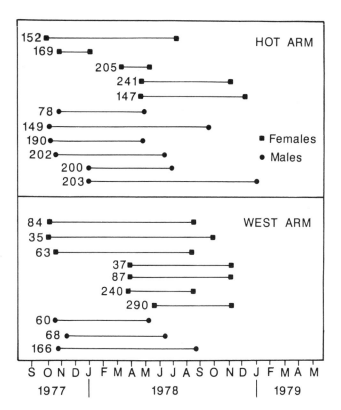

FIGURE 18.3. Tracking length records for 21 of the original 33 turtles used for telemetric home-range analyses in this study. Lengths are based on original battery-transmitter packages without replacement.

including land areas traversed (i.e., for nesting or other activities) but excluding emigration movements to other bodies of water. Animals that emigrated to other nearby aquatic areas or never established a home range were considered transient individuals and were eliminated from this analysis. Although this definition of total home range included land area and eliminated transient individuals from the analysis, we believe that it is valid, for the following reasons: (1) Other authors have noted that adult *T. scripta* migrate out of areas of suitable habitat in great numbers only in cases of extreme drought (Cagle, 1944b; Gibbons et al., 1983), and (2) *T. scripta* are known to move onto land for reasons other than emigration, specifically for feeding and egg laying (Cagle, 1944b). We defined *T. scripta*'s aquatic home range as a subset of its total home range that excluded the terrestrial portions of the total home range. We considered this second measure of home range to be a modified form of the convex polygon, to the extent that any water-land boundaries followed the contour of the shoreline. Home range length was defined as the longest straight-line distance between any two points delineating the home range boundaries.

Home range areas were electronically digitized and analyzed using a Tektronics 4051 microcomputer. Vernier calipers were used to measure distances between locations. Parametric methods were considered appropriate for significance testing after movement data were normalized using a logarithmic transformation (Scheffe, 1959; Kirk, 1968). Differences in movements and home ranges between sexes, areas, and seasons were determined using single-classification analysis of variance, or ANOVA (Sokal and Rohlf, 1969). Null hypotheses were rejected at the .05 level of significance. Differences between means were revealed using the Student-Newman-Keuls (SNK) procedure (Sokal and Rolhf, 1969).

Results and Discussion

HOME RANGE AREAS

The home range areas estimated from telemetry data for *T. scripta* in Par Pond are among the largest reported for a freshwater turtle (Table 18.1). Our maximum estimate for males of nearly 104 ha is almost 30 times greater than the estimate using sonic telemetry for nine *T. scripta* (eight females and one male) in a Panamanian river (Moll and Legler, 1971). Florence (1975), using radiotelemetry with four adult female *T. scripta* in the Tennessee River, reported a home range of 0.66 ha.

Methodology may be partially responsible for these differences. The estimates of Moll and Legler and of Florence were calculated using the linear representation method and were based primarily on females and on relatively small sample sizes. In addition, telemetric observa-

tions in the other studies lasted from 30 to 70 days, with most of Florence's observations being made in May and June and Moll and Legler's observations being scattered throughout the year. Our measurements were based on observation periods of 55 to 321 days in all seasons and on both sexes. Thus, longer observation periods, more observations on males, and larger sample sizes may all have contributed to the larger estimates of home range size in our study.

Although methodological differences may have partially contributed to the observed differences among studies, both the size and the type of aquatic habitats in which the studies were conducted may also have played an important role. For example, our mark-recapture estimate of female home ranges is approximately five times larger than the telemetric estimate of Florence (1975) and is similar to the sonic transmitter estimate of Moll and Legler (1971). According to the limited evidence available in the literature (Table 18.1), it appears that turtles living in larger bodies of water have larger home ranges. Obbard and Brooks (1981b) reported a maximum home range of 3.44 ha for snapping turtles (*Chelydra serpentina*) in some Ontario bog lakes, and Mendonca (1983) estimated a home range of 288 ha for green sea turtles in a Florida lagoon. Finally, Moll and Legler (1971) reported a home range of 3.58 ha for *T. scripta* in a river in Panama. However, this does not necessarily imply that a given species in a small aquatic area will have a smaller home range than one in a large aquatic habitat if overland travel is a major component of the species' home range.

Looking at metabolic considerations, McNab (1963) reasoned that an increase in animal body size (= mass) should also result in larger animal home range sizes. Neither Moll and Legler (1971), studying *T. scripta* in Panama, nor Obbard and Brooks (1981b), studying *C. serpentina* in Canada, found a relationship between home range size and body size. Although Mendonca (1983) found that the overall home range size of juvenile green turtles was positively correlated with increasing body mass, she also noted that centers of activity were not. In the present telemetric study, we found that home range size was significantly and positively related to the body mass of adult female slider turtles, but we did not observe a similar relationship for males. Thus, the relative importance of turtle body size in determining home range size cannot be assessed from available data. Although home range length tended to increase with increasing home range area in our study, home range lengths and areas do not appear to be predictably related in general (Table 18.1), so an increase or a decrease in one measure of home range does not always result in an increase or a decrease in the other measure.

None of the turtles examined with telemetry or mark-recapture ever established a home range within 500 m of the Boil in the Hot Arm. Furthermore, no significant dif-

Table 18.1. Examples of home range areas and lengths for various species of aquatic turtles

Species	Locality	Habitat	N and sex	Home range Area (ha)	Length (m)	Methods	Reference
Trachemys scripta	Panama	River	8F,1M	3.58	287	TEL,A	4
		Lagoon	24J	0.42	61	MR,B	4
			10H	0.004	34	MR,A	4
	Tennessee	River	4F	0.66	274	TEL,A	7
	South Carolina	Lake	4F	3.29	133	MR,C	10
			7F	14.96		TEL,D	10
			7F	36.53	401	TEL,C	10
			16M	6.74	200	MR,C	10
			9M	39.75		TEL,D	10
			9M	103.53	731	TEL,C	10
Clemmys marmorata	California	Stream	19M	0.97	976	MR,A	5
			23F	0.25	248	MR,A	5
			18J	0.36	363	MR,A	5
C. guttata	Pennsylvania	Pond	6M	0.53		MR,B	3
			5F	0.53		MR,B	3
Terrapene coahuila	Mexico	Marsh	33F,21M	0.05	13	MR,E	6
Chelydra serpentina	Pennsylvania	Pond	9	1.84	74	MR,E	1
	Canada	Lake	1F,4M	1.54		MR,B	8
			4F,6M	3.44		TEL,B	8
Sternotherus odoratus	Oklahoma	Creek	39M	0.02	67	MR,C	2
			37F	0.05	44	MR,C	2
Kinosternon subrubrum	Oklahoma	Creek	79M	0.05	52	MR,C	2
			115F	0.05	62	MR,C	2
K. flavescens	Oklahoma	Creek	4M	0.10	198	MR,C	2
Chelonia mydas	Eastern Florida	Lagoon	9J	288		TEL,B	9

Note: Studies not expressing home range on an areal basis are excluded. Sample size refers to home range areas and not necessarily home range lengths. Abbreviations: M, male; F, female; J, juvenile; H, hatchling; TEL, telemetry; MR, mark-recapture in some form (includes visual observations and any form of live capture); A, linear representation; B, minimum polygon; C, convex polygon; D, modified convex polygon; E, radius.
References: 1, Ernst, 1968b; 2, Mahmoud, 1969; 3, Ernst, 1970; 4, Moll and Legler, 1971; 5, Bury, 1972; 6, Brown, 1974; 7, Florence, 1975; 8, Obbard and Brooks, 1981; 9, Mendonca, 1983; 10, this study.

ferences in home range area were noted between West Arm and Hot Arm males or between West Arm and Hot Arm females using either method; as a consequence, these data were combined for further analysis. Data from both mark-recapture and telemetry revealed that most of the daily activities of the turtles tended to be centered in shallow (less than 6 m deep) vegetation-covered coves in the lake (see Fig. 18.4 for representative home ranges). Some movement across areas with open, deep water or overland to other bodies of water did occur but was not common. Transplant studies (Schubauer, 1981b) indicated that movement by *T. scripta* from one arm of Par Pond to another also was uncommon. Only 1 of 267 animals marked in this study moved from one arm of the lake to another. No movement was detected at night.

Home range areas determined by telemetry were significantly larger than those determined by mark-recapture (Table 18.2). Telemetry indicated that male turtles had significantly larger total and aquatic home range areas

than females. Although mark-recapture determined that the total and aquatic home range areas of males were larger than those of females, these differences were not significant (Table 18.2). The aquatic home ranges of male and female slider turtles monitored by telemetry were significantly smaller than their total home range areas. Land constituted approximately 60% of the area of the total home ranges of the animals studied with telemetry, whereas land constituted little of the total home range areas of mark-recapture females (0%) and males (13.9%; Table 18.2). Home range areas determined by mark-recapture were less than one-fourth the size of those determined by telemetry. The lengths of total home range areas of males and females were significantly larger when determined by telemetry than by mark-recapture (Table 18.3). The longest home ranges were those of males monitored by telemetry (average length of 731 m). Telemetry determined that the average home range length for females was 401 m, whereas mark-recapture determined that length

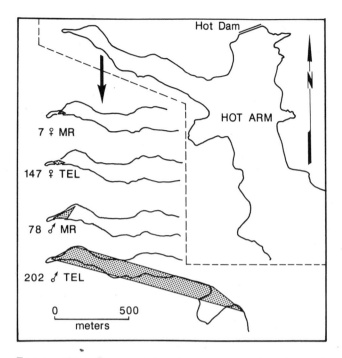

FIGURE 18.4. Representative home ranges of males and females, determined by mark-recapture (MR) and telemetry (TEL). Areas outlined are total home range areas. The shaded subset of each total home range that excludes the land area and is contiguous with the shoreline defines each aquatic home range area.

to be 133 m. Males had significantly longer home ranges than females, according to either method (Table 18.3). However, even the smallest telemetric estimate of home range length for females was significantly larger than the largest mark-recapture estimate for either sex (Table 18.3).

Examination of records of individuals that were simultaneously monitored by both methods (Table 18.4) substantiated that the differences observed using these methods were real and not an artifact of sampling bias. In every instance, home range areas described by telemetry were larger than those described by mark-recapture. When the home ranges determined by the two methods were compared after the same number of relocations, thus truncating the records of animals monitored by telemetry, the home range areas determined by telemetry still exceeded those determined by mark-recapture in all but one case (Table 18.5). This relationship was true even though the observation period was always greater for mark-recapture estimates. Likewise, if the observation periods of the telemetric estimates of these animals were truncated as closely as possible to match the observation periods of the mark-recapture estimates and the home range areas compared, the estimates using telemetry were always greater.

The home range sizes of females monitored by telemetry appeared to be influenced by body mass. A significant positive correlation was found between total home range size and body mass of females (Fig. 18.5). Total home range size was also correlated with body mass for females monitored by mark-recapture ($r = .76$) but was not significant ($F = 3.486$; df = 1, 3). No relationship between total

Table 18.2. Total and aquatic home range areas for *Trachemys scripta* inhabiting Par Pond, determined by mark-recapture and telemetry

Study group[a]	N	THR (ha)[b,c]		AHR (ha)[b,d]		Land area (% of total)	Area[f] THR	AHR
Males								
MR	16	6.74	(1.61)	5.80	(1.13)	13.9	6.5	14.6
TEL	9	103.53	(26.76)[e]	39.75	(6.10)[e]	61.6		
Females								
MR	4	3.29	(0.55)	3.29	(0.55)	0	9.0	22.0
TEL	7	36.53	(5.73)[e]	14.96	(3.51)[e]	59.0		

Note: See text for computation methods. One standard error is given in parentheses to the right of each mean. Data were logarithmically transformed before testing for statistical significance. Abbreviations: AHR, aquatic home range area; MR, mark-recapture; TEL, telemetry; THR, total home range area.

[a]Female estimates are based only on animals monitored in the West Arm of the lake. Only one MR record was available for Hot Arm females because of low capture rates. No significant differences were found between estimates for males studied in different arms of the lake (Schubauer, 1981a), so those groups were combined.

[b]Significant differences between estimates for MR males and females could not be detected; however, significant differences among all other values within this column were detected.

[c]One-way ANOVA: $F = 28.181$; df = 3, 32; $p < .05$, followed by Student-Newman-Keuls procedure (SNK).

[d]One-way ANOVA: $F = 39.315$; df = 3, 32; $p < .05$, followed by SNK.

[e]THR is significantly different from AHR (one-way ANOVA: $F = 6.61$; df = 1, 16; $p < .05$; and $F = 11.2$; df = 1, 12; $p < .05$, followed by SNK).

[f]Area is (MR area/TEL area) × 100, or the percentage of the TEL home range area that consists of the MR home range area.

Table 18.3. Comparison of total home range length of *Trachemys scripta* inhabiting Par Pond, determined by telemetry and mark-recapture

Study group	N	Mean length of total home range (m)	
Males			
MR	36	200	(26)
TEL	11	731	(130)
Females			
MR	12	133	(35)
TEL	12	401	(80)

Note: One standard error is given in parentheses to the right of each mean. Data were logarithmically transformed. All groups were significantly different from one another (one-way ANOVA: $F = 13.585$; df = 3, 67; $p < .05$, followed by Student-Newman-Keuls procedure). Abbreviations: MR, mark-recapture; TEL, telemetry.

home range size and body mass for males was detected with mark-recapture or telemetry.

Total home range measurements for male turtles were influenced by the length of time the animals were observed. A significant positive relationship was detected between total home range size and the length of time observed for male turtles monitored by both methods (Fig. 18.6). No such relationship was detected for females by telemetry ($r = .187$; $F = 0.361$; df = 1, 10) or mark-recapture ($r = -.249$; $F = 0.198$; df = 1, 3).

The sampling effort that was needed to define the home ranges was examined by plotting the percentage of the estimated home range size against the number of observations for each animal (Fig. 18.7). Most male turtles monitored by telemetry reached 100% of their total estimated

Table 18.5. Influence of sampling period and frequency on home range estimates determined by telemetry and mark-recapture

Turtle ID and sex	Method	Total home range Area (ha)	% determined by MR[a]	Days observed	Times located
78M	MR	3.27	--	94	3
	TEL1	1.14	286.8	32	3
	TEL2	10.70	30.5	101	10
149M	MR	2.38	--	188	4
	TEL1	2.42	98.3	13	4
	TEL2	15.95	14.9	183	10
166M	MR	3.93	--	34	3
	TEL1	11.08	35.5	24	3
	TEL2	44.74	8.8	33	4
35F	MR	4.36	--	188	4
	TEL1	4.80	90.8	23	4
	TEL2	30.44	14.3	179	14
37F	MR	2.70	--	319	5
	TEL1	10.14	26.6	2	35
	TEL2	18.76	14.4	205	8
63F	MR	4.05	--	188	4
	TEL1	32.74	12.4	16	4
	TEL2	45.20	9.0	172	16

Abbreviations: MR, mark-recapture; TEL1, telemetry, with number of relocations equal to maximum number of recaptures using MR for that individual; TEL2, telemetry, with observation period matched as closely as possible to total MR observation period.
[a][(MR area/TEL1 area) × 100] or [(MR area/TEL2 area) × 100].

Table 18.4. Comparison of home range areas of individuals simultaneously monitored by mark-recapture and telemetry

N and sex	Method	Home range (ha) Total	Aquatic	Area[a] Total	Aquatic	Days observed	Times located
78M	MR	3.27	3.27	7.8	10.8	94	3
	TEL	41.84	30.04			182	21
49M	MR	2.38	2.38	1.9	4.6	188	4
	TEL	124.31	51.55			253	22
166M	MR	3.93	3.52	2.2	7.7	34	3
	TEL	74.20	45.79			321	24
35F	MR	4.36	4.36	11.1	18.6	188	4
	TEL	39.04	23.51			297	20
37F	MR	2.70	2.70	14.4	25.7	319	5
	TEL	18.76	10.49			205	9
63F	MR	4.05	4.05	9.0	13.2	188	4
	TEL	45.20	30.59			238	20

Abbreviations: MR, mark-recapture; TEL, telemetry.
[a]Area is (MR area/TEL area) × 100.

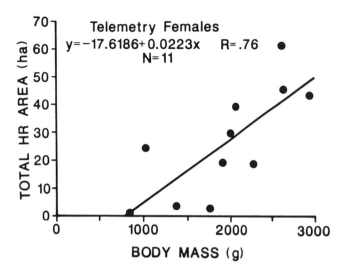

FIGURE 18.5. Relationship between body size and total home range area for females monitored by telemetry. HR = home range.

home range sizes after 15 to 20 observations; however, this relationship was highly variable. In contrast, the total home ranges of females monitored by telemetry could be described more easily. Most reached 100% of their final home range size within 15 observations and with much less variability than males. No such analysis was possible for animals monitored by mark-recapture, because most were captured fewer than 3 times (Schubauer, 1981b).

HOME RANGE DIFFERENCES BETWEEN MALES AND FEMALES

Male home range areas and lengths measured with telemetry in this study were significantly larger than those of females (Table 18.2). Most of the home ranges of male *T. scripta* overlapped with home ranges of other males and females inhabiting the same arm of the lake. The limited results available in the literature for other species of freshwater turtles are conflicting. Bury (1972) reported that home range areas and lengths of male *Clemmys marmorata* were larger than those of females, but there was no difference between the home ranges of male and female *Clemmys guttata* (Ernst, 1970) and *Chelydra serpentina* (Obbard and Brooks, 1981b). Mahmoud (1969) reported that the home ranges of *Kinosternon subrubrum* and *Sternotherus odoratus* males were smaller than those of females, but that those of *K. flavescens* males and females were equal. The relationship of home ranges of males and females may be species-specific, and additional studies will be necessary to resolve it.

THERMAL EFFECTS

That the turtles in this study did not incorporate any of the warmer areas within their home ranges is puzzling,

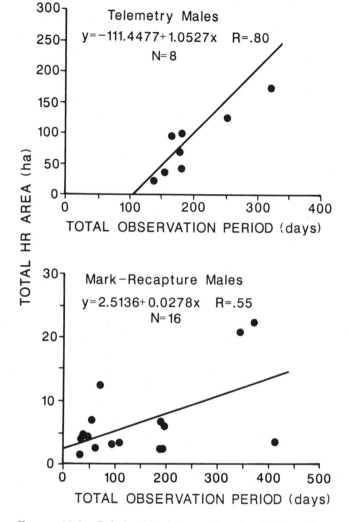

FIGURE 18.6. Relationship between length of observation period and total home range area for males monitored by both methods. HR = home range.

because water temperatures in these areas usually did not approach their critical thermal maximum (40° C; Hutchison et al., 1966) and moderated temperatures in these areas in the winter months. However, there is at least one plausible explanation for this response.

At the time the study was performed, water lilies, spatterdock, and American lotus were conspicuously less abundant within approximately 500 m of the Boil than in the surrounding area and in the West Arm site. It appears that *T. scripta* may avoid colonizing these areas because of the lack of this vegetative structure. Sexton (1959a) reported that *Chrysemys picta* avoided open water. In addition he noted that they were attracted to areas with plants that produced a surface mat attached to the bottom by long stems. He also demonstrated a relationship between habitat preferences of hatchling snapping turtles and the physical structure of vegetation (Sexton, 1958). Similarly, based on the results of our study and transplant studies

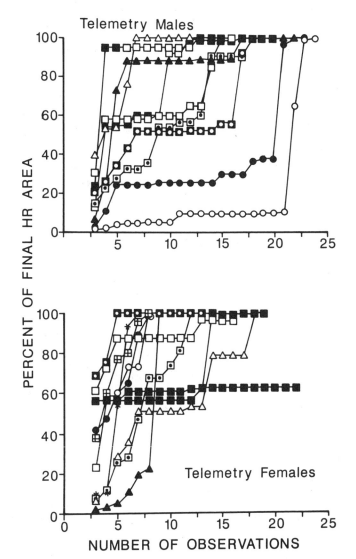

FIGURE 18.7. Relationship between number of observations and estimated home range size for *T. scripta* males ($N = 9$) and females ($N = 11$) monitored by telemetry in Par Pond.

tina (Table 18.1) and found that the telemetric estimate of home range was more than twice as large as the mark-recapture estimate, but the difference was not statistically significant, according to a *t* test. However, if the original data reported in Obbard (1977) are normalized using a logarithmic transformation, the resulting two estimates are significantly different ($t = 2.293$, df $= 13$, $p < .05$).

The results mentioned above are not surprising, considering the biases and sampling problems associated with common capture methods. Because bait is generally used to lure the animals into traps, capture success and thus data acquisition can be influenced or interrupted by seasonal cessation of feeding due to low body temperatures (Ernst, 1972, 1976; Bury, 1979) or shifts in diet (Mahmoud, 1968a; Schubauer and Parmenter, 1981). Furthermore, baited traps may distort movements and home ranges by revealing only the movements of hungry turtles or by luring animals to areas occupied by the traps. In this way, trap density (too many or too few) or placement could distort or misrepresent home ranges and most likely miss long, unexpected movements out of the study areas.

Although visual sightings avoid many of the biases mentioned for trapping, and examples of their successful use exist in the literature (Moll and Legler, 1971; Plummer and Shirer, 1975), they are generally limited to use in small areas and for monitoring relatively short movements. Also, visual sightings are inherently severely limited by objects that can obscure them, such as aquatic vegetation or terrain.

Ideally, telemetry should provide a much less biased estimate of the movements and home ranges of aquatic turtles. However, even this technique can produce biases. For instance, both sexes and a range of body sizes should be well represented in the group monitored telemetrically, and the telemetric package should not alter or interfere in any way with the normal movements or behavior of the animals. In fact, in some situations (as with hatchling turtles) telemetry may be of limited usefulness, and trapping, some other form of mark-recapture, or visual observations may provide the only means of assessing movements.

The two major types of transmitters used to study animal movements are radio transmitters and sonic transmitters. Many factors must be considered in choosing the correct type of transmitter for a particular application. The signal produced by radio transmitters is highly attenuated by water of high conductivity (including salt water), and thick aquatic vegetation will produce similar results with sonic transmitters. Furthermore, noise produced by turbulent waters such as river rapids may also prevent relocation and signal reception from sonic transmitters. Our experience with both types of transmitters (Schubauer, 1981a,b; Spotila et al., 1984) has convinced us that radio transmitters are better suited for use with freshwater turtles.

reported by Schubauer (1981a), it appears that *T. scripta* in Par Pond select areas in the lake with a particular habitat structure rather than areas that simply offer higher water temperatures. This is probably because the selected areas offer either better refugia or a higher-quality diet (Parmenter, 1980; Schubauer, 1981a). Whether the higher water temperatures prevented the growth of particular aquatic plants close to the Boil is unclear.

MARK-RECAPTURE VERSUS TELEMETRY

Telemetry provided significantly larger estimates of home range area than did mark-recapture, even though the effort exerted with the latter method was greater. Obbard and Brooks (1981b) compared telemetric and mark-recapture estimates of home range area for *Chelydra serpen-*

The power requirements of the transmitter (i.e., the size and mass of the battery) and the packaging materials themselves generally set the lower limit on the size of animal that can be monitored telemetrically. Situations that require increasing the transmitter signal strength (related to transmitter range), lengthening the transmitter life, or increasing the durability or waterproofing of the package usually necessitate increasing the size and mass of the transmitter package.

Summary and Conclusion

It appears that introduction of heated effluents into the Hot Arm of Par Pond indirectly excludes turtles from using areas close to the Boil by affecting the availability of suitable habitat. No other major effects of the effluents on the behavior of *T. scripta* were noted.

The mark-recapture method can severely underestimate home range areas of aquatic turtles, especially estimates for aquatic turtles inhabiting large habitats such as Par Pond. We suspect that up to a point, as available aquatic habitat size decreases (with other factors being equal), home range areas estimated by mark-recapture and telemetry should converge. Thus, for most species of aquatic turtles inhabiting relatively small (less than 50 ha) aquatic habitats, the mark-recapture method may be sufficient for assessing home ranges, assuming that capture biases are not severe and that terrestrial movements are not a major component of the species' home range.

Telemetry provides a number of experimental advantages over mark-recapture, exclusive of the expected distortions due to capture-method biases. Most important, telemetry provides more experimental control over design features such as sample size and sampling time and rate. Once the animals are tagged, these features are under the control of the observer, not the experimental subject. Additionally, long movements and unusual behavior are less likely to be missed. Other important advantages of telemetry are that it allows observation of both terrestrial and aquatic movements and is by far more cost-effective in terms of time and effort. Although telemetry is an excellent tool to study the short-term ecological studies of turtles (particularly movements), it is not sufficient by itself to gather long-term information that is collected on an intermittent basis. In most instances, using a combination of mark-recapture and telemetry methods will prove to be the best course of action.

Acknowledgments

We thank numerous colleagues at SREL who provided assistance during the course of this study. We particularly thank J. Coleman for her help in drafting a number of the illustrations used in this chapter and S. Smith and E. Standora for help in developing the transmitter used in the study. This research was supported by research grants from the U.S. Department of Energy to SREL (E-381-1-819) and SUNY College at Buffalo (E-11-1-2502), student research grants from the Society for the Sigma Xi and the Faculty of Natural and Social Sciences (SUNYCAB), and travel grants from Oak Ridge Associated Universities.

JEFFREY E. LOVICH
Savannah River Ecology Laboratory
Drawer E
Aiken, South Carolina 29802

CLARENCE J. McCOY
Carnegie Museum of Natural History
4400 Forbes Avenue
Pittsburgh, Pennsylvania 15213

WILLIAM R. GARSTKA
Department of Biological Sciences
University of Alabama
Huntsville, Alabama 35899

19

The Development and Significance of Melanism in the Slider Turtle

Abstract

Male slider turtles (*Trachemys scripta*) undergo dramatic melanic changes as they become larger and older. This transformation occurs well past the size at which most attain sexual maturity. However, the process is not strictly size-dependent. The mean body size of melanistic males varies concordantly among populations in the same region as a function of growth rate. Additionally, data do not necessarily support an age-related explanation for the phenomenon, except as predicted under population-specific growth rates. The advent of melanism is coincident with population-specific female size at maturity and with maximal development of male foreclaw length, a secondary sexual characteristic. Melanistic individuals generally form a small portion of a given population but typically predominate within larger size classes. Physiological, histological, and hormonal differences between melanistic and nonmelanistic males are demonstrated. Behavioral differences also exist and may be due to intersexual or intrasexual selection.

Introduction

The phenomenon of melanism is well known in adult male slider turtles (*Trachemys scripta;* Table 19.1). In most populations that have been studied, sexually mature males undergo dramatic melanic changes involving the shell and, later, the soft parts of the body. In spite of the familiarity of this dramatic condition, little is known regarding its onset, development, and possible significance. For example, although a large proportion of adult males in a given population may become melanistic, others do not. In addition, various studies have reported a tendency toward the melanic condition in female *T. scripta* (Viosca, 1933; Conant, 1951; Legler, 1960b; Webb, 1961; McCoy, 1968; Moll and Legler, 1971; Lardie, 1983). Thus, from available data it is not clear if the phenomenon is related to size, age, or even sex. To confuse the issue further, several closely related species do not appear to exhibit melanism, for reasons that are as yet unknown. Although there are many unanswered questions with regard to melanism in turtles, our objectives in this chapter are (1) to review what is known about the occurrence and development of melanism in turtles, (2) to suggest and test possible mechanisms of sexually dichromatic melanization in *T. scripta* that might be applicable to other turtles, and (3) to provide an understanding of the adaptive significance of melanism in *T. scripta*.

In this review we compare melanistic with nonmelanistic, but sexually mature, males and report the results of experiments performed to test hypotheses generated by our comparisons. All of these hypotheses have concerned possible hormonal mechanisms that could explain the melanization process. In the case of *T. scripta*, a hypothesis of hormonal control would have to explain the permanence, the sexual dichromatism, and the timing (not coincident with gonadal maturation) of melanic change.

Melanism and Turtle Taxonomy

The existence of melanistic forms of some species has been responsible for numerous errors of classification. For example, although melanism is well known in adult male *Chinemys reevesii* (Sachsse, 1975; Lovich et al., 1985), such individuals were previously considered to be separate species: *Damonia* (= *Chinemys*) *unicolor* (Gray, 1873). Similar problems, exacerbated by dramatic sexual size dimorphism, plagued taxonomists working with turtles of the genus *Trachemys* for more than 100 years. Early naturalists recognized melanistic and nonmelanistic forms of West Indian *Trachemys* as different species, even though each "species" was represented in collections as mostly males or mostly females (DeSola and Greenhall, 1932; C⸱ant and DeSola, 1934). Recognition of melanistic males as *Pseudemys* (= *Trachemys*) *rugosa* persisted from the original description of Shaw (1802) until Barbour and Carr (1940) revealed the true condition. According to Carr (1952), Cuban provincials also recognized male and female *T. decussata* as different turtles. Danforth (1925) reported that Puerto Rican natives considered the green (nonmelanistic) and black (melanistic) individuals of *Pseudemys palustris* (= *T. stejnegeri stejnegeri*) to be distinct species, although he found "intergrades" between the two.

A similar situation existed with *T. scripta*, whereby a melanistic obviously male-only form was described by

Table 19.1. References to melanism in selected populations of *Trachemys scripta*

Location	Subspecies	Reference	Comment
Alabama	*scripta*	16	--
Illinois	*elegans*	2,4	--
		9	Both sexes
Indiana	*elegans*	15	--
Louisiana	*elegans*	1	--
North America	--	5,7,14,17	--
		21	Both sexes
Mexico	*taylori*	8	Both sexes
	Refer to text	18	Refer to text
Ohio	*elegans*	6	Both sexes
Oklahoma	*elegans*	10,12	--
		20	Both sexes
Panama	"Panamanian"	13	Both sexes
South Carolina	*scripta*	22	--
Texas	*gaigeae*	3	--
	elegans	20	Both sexes
Virginia, North Carolina, South Carolina	--	19	--
West Virginia	*elegans*	11	--

References: 1, Viosca, 1933; 2, Cahn, 1937; 3, Hartweg, 1939; 4, Cagle, 1948b; 5, Cagle, 1950; 6, Conant, 1951; 7, Carr, 1952; 8, Legler, 1960b; 9, Smith, 1961; 10, Webb, 1961; 11, Adler, 1968a; 12, McCoy, 1968; 13, Moll and Legler, 1971; 14, Ernst and Barbour, 1972; 15, Minton, 1972; 16, Mount, 1975; 17, Pritchard, 1979; 18, Smith and Smith, 1979; 19, Martof et al., 1980; 20, Lardie, 1983; 21, Ward, 1984; 22, this study.

Holbrook (1836) as *Emys troostii* and the nonmelanistic form was described as *P. elegans* (Wied, 1839). Viosca (1933) concluded that the *troostii* form was based on melanistic males, but herpetologists were slow to accept the new proposal (Carr, 1952). The situation was further complicated by temporary retention of the name *P. troostii* (as a senior synonym) for turtles currently recognized as *T. scripta*. Moreover, subsequent revisions at the subspecies level resulted in use of the trinomen *Trachemys scripta troostii* for one of the geographic races of *T. scripta* (see Chapter 4). Far more detailed accounts of the taxonomic turmoil resulting from the failure of early herpetologists to recognize the true nature of ontogenetic melanization in *T. scripta* are found in Viosca (1933), Cahn (1937), Barbour and Carr (1940), and Carr (1952).

More recently described variants such as *Chelonia mydas carrinegra* (Caldwell, 1962b) and *Platemys platycephala melanonota* (Ernst, 1983) are subspecies of otherwise nonmelanistic species and are characterized by unusual development of dark pigmentation. In *P. p. melanonota* the melanic condition is well established even in juveniles (Carl Ernst, pers. com.). The Mexican trionychid *Trionyx ater* (Webb and Legler, 1960) is a derivative of *T. spiniferus* distinguished mainly by the early onset and complete development of melanic coloration in both sexes. A thorough understanding of the incidence and development of melanism is crucial in assessing the validity of taxa based on this character.

Table 19.2. References to melanism in selected turtle species

Taxon	Location	Reference	Comment
Emydidae			
Batagur baska	Malaysia	23	Seasonal in males
Chinemys reevesii	Asia	27	Both sexes, plastral melanism
		1,3,13,16	--
Chrysemys picta	North America	14	--
		26	Females
	Minnesota	15	Both sexes, reticulate melanism
	North Dakota	11	Reticulate melanism
	Canada	22	Reticulate melanism
		24	Both sexes, reticulate melanism
Clemmys guttata	United States	14	--
C. muhlenbergii	United States	18	--
Graptemys ouachitensis	Wisconsin	20	Both sexes
Hieremys annandalii	Southeast Asia	21	--
Malaclemys terrapin	Louisiana	7	--
Notochelys platynota	Thailand	12	--
Pseudemys concinna mobilensis	United States	4	--
P. dorbigni[a]	South America	9,10	--
P. floridana	United States	8	--
P. nelsoni	United States	14	Both sexes
		8	--
P. rubriventris	United States	8,21,26	--
		14	"Old individuals"
Rhinoclemmys funerea	Central America	19	--
Sacalia bealei	Asia	16	--
Trachemys decorata	Hispaniola	4	Melanism not as marked as in other West Indian forms
		25	--
T. decussata	Cuba	2,4,21,28	--
	Cayman Islands	6	--
T. scripta	See Table 19.1	See Table 19.1	See Table 19.1
T. stejnegeri	Central Antilles	4	--
T. s. vicina	Hispaniola	25	Both sexes
T. terrapen felis	Bahamas	4	--
T. t. terrapen	Jamaica	4,5	--
Kinosternidae			
Kinosternon sonoriense	Arizona	17	--

Note: Scientific names for West Indian *Trachemys* and subspecific designations for *T. scripta* follow Iverson (1986).

References: 1, Gray, 1873; 2, DeSola and Greenhall, 1932; 3, Liu and Hu, 1939-40; 4, Barbour and Carr, 1940; 5, Lynn and Grant, 1940; 6, Grant, 1940; 7, Cagle, 1952; 8, Carr, 1952; 9, Freiberg, 1967a; 10, Freiberg, 1969; 11, Smith et al., 1969; 12, Taylor, 1970; 13, Mao, 1971; 14, Ernst and Barbour, 1972; 15, Ernst and Ernst, 1973; 16, Sachsse, 1975; 17, Hulse, 1976; 18, Holub and Bloomer, 1977; 19, Ernst, 1978; 20, Vogt, 1978; 21, Pritchard, 1979; 22, MacCulloch, 1981; 23, Moll et al., 1981; 24, Schueler, 1983; 25, Seidel and Inchaustegui Miranda, 1984; 26, Ward, 1984; 27, Lovich et al., 1985; 28, Sampedro et al., 1985.

[a]Considered to be a subspecies of *T. scripta* by Iverson (1986) and Pritchard (1979).

Patterns of Melanization in Turtles

Several levels of melanic expression occur in turtles (Table 19.2). We recognize four basic types: permanent melanism, seasonal melanism, senile reticulate melanism, and ontogenetic melanism. Although the first three types occur principally in species other than *T. scripta* and its allies, we will present a brief review of each before proceeding to a detailed description of the process in *T. scripta*.

The type that we refer to as permanent melanism occurs in those species that are black throughout life, or at least as adults, including *Emys, Emydoidea, Clemmys guttata,*

Mauremys, Cuora, Melanochelys, Annamemys, Chinemys, Geoclemys, Heosemys, Siebenrockiella, and some *Rhinoclemmys* (Ernst, 1982). Although lighter pigments may form various patterns on some of them, the above species are primarily black. Another example of this type of melanism apparently occurs in the eastern Pacific populations of *Chelonia mydas.* Hirth and Carr (1970) discussed the distribution of the "black turtle," a race of *C. mydas* characterized by heavy black pigmentation (see above). However, it is not known whether this condition is a polymorphism or a true taxonomic novelty, as suggested by Bocourt (1868) and Caldwell (1962b), because "black

Table 19.3. Size and proportion of melanistic individuals in selected populations of *Trachemys scripta*

| Location | Plastron length (mm) | | | N | | MEL/NON | Sex | Reference |
| | At maturity | At attainment of melanism | | | | | | |
		Minimum	Mean	MEL	NON			
Illinois	--	152	177	7	--	--	M	2
	90-100	126	--	10	55	0.18	M	3
Louisiana	--	140[a]	165[a]	35	88	0.28	M	1
Oklahoma	≈ 100	145	--	--	--	--	M	6
	≈ 166	147	--	--	--	--	F	6
	≈ 100	150	--	--	--	--	M	5
Tennessee, Illinois	90-100[b]	130[b]	--	--	--	--	M	4
Texas	90-100[b]	100[b]	--	--	--	--	M	4
Texas, Oklahoma	--	--	--	1	81	0.01	M	7

Note: Numbers are based on best estimates from figures, tables, or text. Abbreviations: MEL, melanistic; NON, nonmelanistic.

References: 1, Viosca, 1933; 2, Cahn, 1937; 3, Cagle, 1948b; 4, Cagle, 1950; 5, Webb, 1961; 6, McCoy, 1968; 7, Lardie, 1983.

[a]Carapace length (mm), rather than plastron length.

[b]Size variable not specified.

turtles" and normally pigmented forms are sympatric in parts of Polynesia as well as Guatemala (Pritchard, 1971).

The second level of melanic expression, seasonal melanism, has been most thoroughly studied in *Batagur baska*. In this species, males develop black head and shell pigmentation during the breeding season (Moll, 1980; Moll et al., 1981). A reversal of this phenomenon has been reported in the closely related *Callagur borneoensis*, whereby some males become lighter during the breeding season because of a loss of epidermal melanosomes (Moll et al., 1981). Although seasonal dichromatism has been reported in other turtle species, such as *Kachuga kachuga* (E. Moll, 1986b), *Geochelone travancorica* (Auffenberg, 1964), and *Heosemys silvatica* (Groombridge et al., 1983; but also see Moll et al., 1986), these are the only examples of seasonal melanism that we are aware of in turtles. The complex mechanics and histology of these transmutations are discussed in detail by Moll et al. (1981).

Reticulate melanism results from dendritic deposition of melanin in epidermal scutes that is usually superimposed on a relatively unchanged underlying pattern. This phenomenon has been reported in several northern populations of *Chrysemys picta* (Table 19.2) and is illustrated in Agassiz (1857: plate 27) and Babcock (1919: plate 24) for male *Pseudemys rubriventris*. Other possible examples of this phenomenon have been discussed by Schueler (1983). The process is not progressive and may affect only the oldest individuals in *C. picta* (MacCulloch, 1981); hence the term "senile reticulate melanism." Once the pattern is established, it presumably remains essentially unchanged for the life of the turtle. Whether this type of melanism affects males and females alike is unclear.

The fourth and perhaps most familiar type of melanism is the one we refer to as ontogenetic melanism. In this case

the development of the melanic condition is progressive, generally occurs in males, and is associated with age or body size. This type of melanization is best known in some populations of *T. scripta* and its allies (Tables 19.1–19.3) and is discussed below.

Other patterns of melanic change, not included in the four primary types noted above, have been reported in turtles. Species such as *Rheodytes leukops* (Legler and Cann, 1980) and *Gopherus berlandieri* (Auffenberg and Weaver, 1969) appear to become lighter with age, a reversal of the usual trend. This change is dramatic in male *R. leukops* and appears to result from a progressive loss of melanin accompanied by subsequent replacement with brighter pigments (Legler and Cann, 1980). Some large male *Trachemys terrapen* are reported to "assume an overall white color," and the plastral pigmentation of large female *Trachemys scripta cataspila* may fade out completely (Pritchard, 1979). Ontogenetic patterns of melanic plastral pigment reorganization have been reported in juvenile Hawaiian *Chelonia mydas* (Balazs, 1986). In this case, hatchlings possess a white plastron that becomes diffused with black pigment at a length of about 6 to 8 cm. From this point on the pigment fades, usually disappearing completely by 13 cm; formation and deposition of pigment are dependent entirely on size and not age. Another example of pattern reorganization apparently occurs in *Trionyx spiniferus*. In this species the carapace pattern of adult females may be obscured by blotches of dark pigment (Webb, 1962).

Finally, no discussion of melanism would be complete without reference to such classic examples as "industrial melanism" in moths (Kettlewell, 1965; Wickler, 1968; Askew et al., 1971), other forms of reptilian melanic proliferation or reduction associated with background matching (for review, see Porter, 1972), and the existence of melanomorphic forms in some other groups of vertebrates, including felids (Searle, 1968), fishes (Regan, 1961; Angus, 1983), and snakes (e.g., *Sistrurus catenatus*— Conant, 1951; *Crotalus horridus* and *Heterodon platyrhinos*— Conant, 1975). With the possible exception of background matching in *Chelodina longicollis* (Woolley, 1957), these forms of melanic expression have not been reported in turtles. Woolley (1957) demonstrated that *C. longicollis* melanophores contracted when live specimens were maintained over a white background and expanded when maintained over a black background. The transmutation from one state to the other required approximately 30 days. Intraperitoneal injections of melanophore-expanding pituitary hormone caused melanophore expansion in pale specimens.

Ontogenetic Melanization in *Trachemys scripta*

Ontogenetic melanization in *Trachemys scripta* has been described as a process of pattern reorganization not necessarily accompanied by an overall increase in pigmentation (McCoy, 1968). In an Oklahoma population of *T. scripta* the melanization process involves shifting of melanic pigments, in a regular sequence, between areas of the shell and the skin (McCoy, 1968). Melanic changes in the subadult pattern appear first on the plastral scutes, with subsequent involvement of the scutes of the carapace and the skin of the legs, tail, head, and neck. The first evidence of melanization is the deposition of a smudgy black spot in the center of each plastral scute, overlying and obscuring the juvenile ocellate spot (Carr, 1952). These black spots, especially those on the posterior pairs of scutes, gradually enlarge to form a continuous or almost continuous ring of black pigment around the plastron. The plastron retains a yellow center and yellow edges, and there is no melanin deposition along the scute sutures at this stage. The spots of the posterior scutes usually join, but the spots on the anterior scutes remain discrete (McCoy, 1968: Fig. 1A). As the melanization process continues, the melanin in the large, smudgy, and coalescent plastral spots is withdrawn and redeposited at other points on the plastron. In both males and females, foci of melanin redeposition occur at the junctions of the pectoral-abdominal and abdominal-femoral sutures with the central suture. Secondary foci develop where the more anterior and posterior cross-sutures intersect the central suture. Pigment transfer continues until the suture areas are broadly smudged with black, and the original central laminal spots are reduced, perhaps even light-centered (Fig. 19.1). In the population studied, the progress of ontogenetic melanization was approximately the same in males and females to this stage, but beyond this point males and females followed different patterns. In females the central plastral melanin deposits enlarge and expand

in all directions and eventually wash the entire plastron with black pigment, virtually obscuring all markings. Concurrently with the development of a general blackening of the plastron from the central area, large black smudges reappear near the positions of the original central laminal spots. Remnants of the original spots may be seen as faint ringlike edgings around these new spots. The black smudges in the centers of the scutes remain visible until finally obscured by the overwash of melanin. Webb (1961) reported that the plastrons of large females from Lake Texoma, Oklahoma, were 80% blackened by melanic pigments.

Adult females retain the bright carapace pattern of juveniles virtually throughout life. In the population studied, the carapace pattern of some very old females was slightly obscured by a thin overwash of melanin. The striped pattern of the skin of the head, neck, legs, and tail remains unaffected by melanization in adult females. It is important to note that although slight melanic changes can be demonstrated in females of the *scripta* subgroup (sensu Weaver and Rose, 1967), these changes are only superficially similar to those typical of males. In fact, of the more than 9,000 *T. scripta* that have been collected on the Savannah River Plant in South Carolina during the past 20 years, none of the females were melanistic.

In males the transfer of pigment to the plastral sutures at the expense of the spots continues until the spots are completely lost or are only ring-shaped, and the pigment is concentrated along the sutures. The centers of the scutes are yellow or slightly vermiculated with melanin, but both the juvenile ocelli and the melanic smudges that replaced them are lost (McCoy, 1968: Fig. 1D).

At an early stage the bright juvenile pattern of the carapace scutes in males is obscured by general deposition of melanin over the carapace. Subsequently, there is a progressive depigmentation of the carapace scutes, with the melanin moving to and concentrating along the sutures. Ultimately, the sutures of the carapace scutes are narrowly and vividly outlined in black, and the centers of the scutes are greenish yellow and without dark markings. This is the classic *"troostii"* or *"rugosa"* phase that confounded early naturalists.

A further and final stage in the melanization of adult males involves complete obliteration of the striped pattern of the head, neck, legs, and tail and replacement with a gradually darkening. black-mottled melanic pattern on an olive ground color (Fig. 19.2). Carr (1952) reported that a further stage involves a secondary wash of black pigment over the plastron, obscuring the pattern of melanin along the sutures.

Evidence of melanic change in male *T. scripta* from Alabama consists of (1) an obscuring of the yellow and black rosette or swirl pattern on the carapace, (2) a similar obscuring on the skin of neck, limbs, and tail accompanied by a breakup of the juvenile and female head stripe pat-

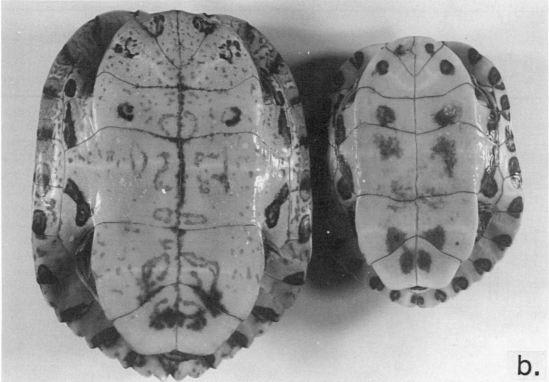

FIGURE 19.1.   Color pattern of melanistic (left) and nonmelanistic (right) male *Trachemys scripta* collected in northern Alabama. Turtles were collected monthly by drag seine, trap, or trammel net from drainage canals in the White Springs Unit, Harris-Sweetwater dewatering area, Wheeler National Wildlife Refuge, Limestone County, Alabama. *a*, carapace color pattern; *b*, plastron color pattern. Note the concentration of black color along the scute margins and the disappearance of pattern from the scute centers in both views of melanistic specimens.

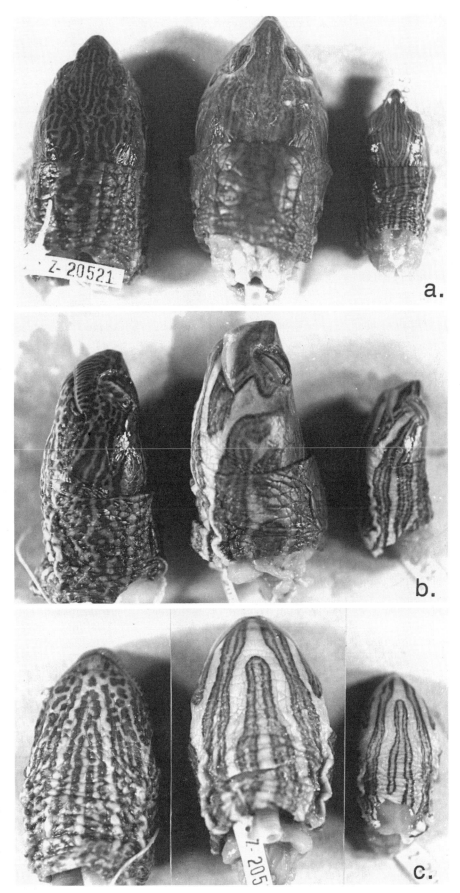

FIGURE 19.2. Comparison of the head color pattern of a melanistic male (left), a female (center), and a nonmelanistic male (right) from northern Alabama. *a*, dorsal view; *b*, lateral view; *c*, ventral view. Note the breakup of the striping pattern in the melanistic male to short wavy lines and dots.

tern into series of dots, and (3) the appearance of dark pigmentation at the scute margins of both carapace and plastron (Figs. 19.1 and 19.2). Few males in the Alabama population attained a uniformly black carapace, but all males in that population with a plastron length greater than 160 mm exhibited clear evidence of changes in color pattern. However, in other populations adult males may retain the juvenile pattern throughout life (Cahn, 1937; Barbour and Carr, 1940). Because overall darkening does not always occur, the condition in male slider turtles may not be strictly melanism. However, we will continue to use the term because of its precedence in describing this phenomenon. The preceding description of the melanization process is based on the assumption that less melanic patterns undergo a transition to more-melanic patterns. To the best of our knowledge, no one has ever studied the process over time with known individuals in a controlled experiment.

Quantifying Melanism

A major problem with reviewing the phenomenon of melanism in slider turtles is that a quantitative method for measuring the degree of melanization has not been employed or even suggested. Thus, a condition defined as partially melanistic by one researcher may be considered fully melanistic by others. The situation is complicated by differential involvement of the shell and soft parts in the melanization process. A partial solution would be to measure qualitatively the degree or pattern of melanization exhibited by a given structure such as the plastron. In *Chinemys reevesii,* for example, several plastral patterns appear to form a continuum toward complete melanism (Lovich et al., 1985; also see Table 19.4); however, involvement of the soft parts is difficult to predict from the level of plastral melanism observed. A shortcoming of this approach is the loss of information regarding the concomitant involvement of other anatomical units.

Another technique is to use a photo coordinate grid overlay (Forestry Suppliers, stock no. 45026). This is a clear acetate sheet printed with a dot matrix that can be placed over photographs or photocopies of a turtle's carapace or plastron. By counting the numbers of grid points that are superimposed on light and dark areas, an estimate of the percentage of area that is black can be calculated. Flat surfaces such as the plastron can be analyzed directly without the use of photocopies. The relative area of the carapace that was black was measured in a sample of nonmelanistic males ($N = 14$; 100–158 mm plastron length, or PL), melanistic males ($N = 23$; 154–197 mm PL), and females ($N = 14$; 108–212 mm PL) from northern Alabama using the grid overlay technique (Terrell and Garstka, 1984). The extent of carapace

Table 19.4. Relationship between size and plastral melanism in *Chinemys reevesii*

Amount of pigmentation	Mean plastron length (mm)			
	Male	Female	Juveniles	Total sample
Light	62.5 (10)	83.9 (5)	46.7 (1)	68.2 (16)
Intermediate	77.2 (49)	94.5 (46)	45.2 (13)	80.7 (108)
Dark	75.4 (27)	107.6 (48)	43.8 (10)	89.9 (85)
Melanistic	107.1 (30)	144.7 (7)	-- --	114.2 (37)

Source: Lovich and Ernst, pers. com.

Note: Sample size is given in parentheses after each mean. Pigmentation categories follow Lovich et al. (1985). There is a significant difference in plastron lengths between pigmentation categories (ANOVA, juveniles excluded; $F = 9.45$, $p < .0001$, df = 3, 218).

darkening differed significantly between groups: Nonmelanistic male carapaces were 30% ($\pm 3.8\%$) black, melanistic males were 58% ($\pm 3.2\%$) black, and females were 37% ($\pm 4.1\%$) black ($F = 17.35$, df = 2/48, $p < .001$). However, there was considerable overlap between nonmelanistic and melanistic males: Nonmelanistic carapace black ranged to 68% (132 mm PL), and melanistic carapace black was as low as 36% (162 mm PL). Although some very large females may exhibit a darkened carapace (to 74% black in a 212 mm PL female), none of the more than 300 females examined in the northern Alabama population showed evidence of color pattern reorganization on the carapace scute margins or of neck skin stripe reorganization characteristic of the male morphological color change. Thus, even this preliminary quantitative approach may not be sufficient to indicate color pattern changes.

A more precise approach would involve the use of a digitizer to scan turtle shells or photographs. This technique evaluates and quantifies the degree of lightness or darkness in small areas (pixels) of the image, thus greatly increasing resolution of minute pigment differences. An overall value reflecting the degree of melanization can be obtained and easily compared with other values. This technique is presently being evaluated for detailed analysis and quantification of melanic changes in *T. scripta* (Lovich, unpub. data).

We also investigated the microscopic structure of the skin of melanistic and nonmelanistic male *T. scripta*. This comparison of sections of the neck skin of 21 nonmelanistic and 34 melanistic males revealed that the melanophores in the dark stripes of nonmelanistic males were principally dermal and that the melanophores of melanistic males were principally epidermal (Fig. 19.3). Cytocrine deposition by the epidermal melanophores is clearly indicated. Furthermore, the expansions of the nonmelanistic dermal and of the melanistic epidermal melanophores were noticeably different from each other.

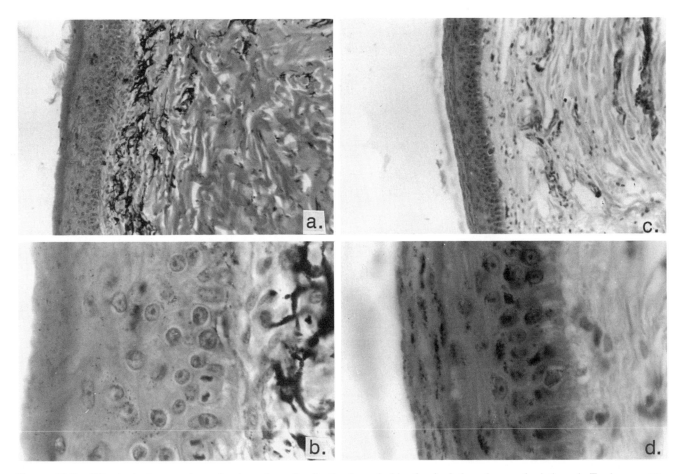

FIGURE 19.3.   Histological comparison of melanophore distribution in neck skin of melanistic and nonmelanistic male *Trachemys scripta*. Tissues were fixed in 10% neutral buffered formalin, dehydrated in a graded ethanol series, embedded in paraffin, sectioned at 7 μm, and stained with hematoxylin and eosin. *a*, nonmelanistic male section showing principally dermal distribution of melanophores; *b*, higher-magnification view of the same tissue section as in *a*; *c*, melanistic male section showing principally epidermal distribution of melanophores with cytocrine deposition; *d*, higher-magnification view of the same tissue section as in *c*.

Geographic Variation

The melanization process described for male *T. scripta* appears to vary among subspecies, although there is some disagreement among authors. For example, of the 17 currently recognized races (Iverson, 1986), some, such as *T. s. ornata,* show only slight levels of melanism (Smith and Smith, 1979), and *T. s. venusta* does not normally exhibit melanism (Pritchard, 1979). In contrast, Smith and Smith (1979) report melanism in both male and female *T. s. venusta*. This condition, bisexual melanism, is unusual in the complex and is shared with *T. s. yaquia, T. s. grayi,* and *T. s. taylori* (Legler, 1960b; Smith and Smith, 1979). If any trend exists, it may be that melanism is more characteristic of North Temperate races of *T. scripta* than races in Mesoamerica (see Chapter 7).

Variation within subspecies has also been suggested.

Cahn (1937) reported that melanistic *T. scripta elegans* were more common in southern Illinois than in the northern portion of the state. Others have suggested that the size at full attainment of melanism varies geographically in this race (Cagle, 1950; McCoy, 1968). In contrast, the closely related and widely distributed *Chrysemys picta* appears to develop reticulate melanism only at the northern limit of its range (Table 19.2). Latitudinal clines in pigmentation have been reported in the tortoises *Gopherus flavomarginatus* (Morafka and McCoy, 1988) and *G. polyphemus* (Landers et al., 1982).

Seidel (1988) reviewed the occurrence and progress of melanization in West Indian species of *Trachemys*. The phenomenon is poorly developed in *T. terrapen* and nearly absent in *T. decorata*. The pattern of pigment reorganization in *T. stejnegeri* is similar to that of *T. scripta*. In *T. decussata* the process results in a vermiculate or speckled

Table 19.5. Plastron length (mm) statistics for melanistic and nonmelanistic male *Trachemys scripta* from selected South Carolina populations

Pond	Pigmentation	N	Mean	SE	Minimum	Maximum	MEL/NON
Cecil's Pond	MEL	17	166	2.9	145	189	0.23
	NON	75	133	2.0	105	178	
Capers Island	MEL	10	200	4.8	177	226	2.50
	NON	4	155	16.4	108	178	
Steel Creek	MEL	30	180	3.6	126	206	0.23
	NON	130	151	2.4	100	209	
McElmurray's	MEL	30	163	2.4	136	194	0.73
Pond	NON	41	154	2.2	113	177	
Par Pond	MEL	167	190	1.3	146	226	0.41
	NON	406	153	1.3	100	243	
Ellenton Bay	MEL	135	168	1.6	104	223	0.27
	NON	493	133	0.9	100	207	
Lost Lake System	MEL	145	164	1.3	116	207	0.34
	NON	429	140	1.0	100	210	
Risher Pond	MEL	16	174	5.5	122	203	0.33
	NON	48	131	3.0	103	191	

Note: Data for animals with multiple captures are based on last capture. Only sexually mature males (plastron length > 100 mm) were used in the analysis. Abbreviations: MEL, melanistic; NON, nonmelanistic.

pattern on the carapace or plastron. These differences in the degree and progression of melanic involvement are perhaps not surprising, given the paraphyletic nature of West Indian *Trachemys* (Seidel, 1988).

Variation in Size, Age, and Relative Abundance

Information presented and reviewed thus far suggests that ontogenetic melanism, typified by *T. scripta*, is associated with large body size or advanced age. This tentative conclusion has not always been supported in the literature. Barbour and Carr (1940) suggested that the onset of melanism in *Trachemys* was not size- or age-dependent but rarely occurred in males smaller than 150 mm, and Hulse (1976) found no correlation between size and ventral melanism in *Kinosternon sonoriense*. In contrast, the development of juvenile plastral melanism in *Chelonia mydas* is entirely dependent on size and not age (Balazs, 1986). Lovich et al. (1985) observed that larger and presumably older *Chinemys reevesii* exhibited increased levels of plastral melanism (also see Table 19.4). Cagle (1948b) reported that all male *T. scripta* greater than 170 mm in an Illinois population were melanistic. Minimum sizes of *T. scripta* at attainment of full melanism were compiled by McCoy (1968) for various populations and ranged from 100 to 152 mm (Table 19.3). These contradictory data illustrate the state of uncertainty regarding the onset of melanism.

Detailed analysis of eight South Carolina populations of *T. scripta* with different growth rates allows insight into the timing and variation of melanic change within a small

geographic area (Table 19.5). Sexually mature non-melanistic males range from 100 to 243 mm in plastron length, and melanistic males from 104 to 226 mm PL. This extensive overlap is a reflection of at least two factors. First, our data do not discriminate between the various levels of melanism. Thus, a turtle showing only very early signs of melanic development is still classified as melanistic. Second, although a substantial portion of the adult male population may be melanistic, some individuals apparently retain the juvenile pattern throughout life or develop melanism much later than others. The mean size of melanistic males from all populations is 175 mm PL. Melanistic males from fast-growth populations on Capers Island (Gibbons et al., 1979) and in Par Pond (Gibbons et al., 1981) have a mean size of 191 mm PL, whereas those in slow-growth populations (Gibbons et al., 1981) have a mean of 167 mm PL. Based on a cumulative frequency distribution of body size, 80% of the melanistic males in the Ellenton Bay population attain their condition by 170 mm PL. In Par Pond a similar percentage attain their condition by 190 mm PL. The mean body size of non-melanistic males in all populations is less than the values reported above. The mean body sizes of melanistic males are all larger than 100 mm PL; the approximate size at which maturity is reached in all populations (Gibbons et al., 1981; Table 19.3). In northern Alabama all males larger than about 150 mm PL exhibit at least some of the characteristics of melanism. These wide-ranging values among populations suggest that melanic development in *T. scripta* is not strictly size-dependent.

Limited data on the actual age of melanistic males in the slow-growth populations of Lost Lake and Ellenton Bay suggest a mean of 14.8 years (range = 7–24, N = 12). In Par Pond, melanistic males have a mean age of 8.8 years (range = 5–18, N = 20). Nonmelanistic males in slow-growth populations have a mean age of 5.7 years (range = 4–24, N = 293). The dramatic difference in the mean timing of melanic development between slow-growth populations and Par Pond populations suggests that the phenomenon is not age-dependent either. The onset of melanism also appears to be dissociated with the age at which males attain sexual maturity. Males in Ellenton Bay reach sexual maturity in 4 to 5 years, whereas those in Par Pond may mature in only 3 to 4 years (Gibbons et al., 1981). The difference between sexual maturity and the mean age of melanistic males in Ellenton Bay is about 10 years. The difference in Par Pond is about 4 years.

Sexual maturity in male *Trachemys* of the *scripta* subgroup is evidenced by androgen-dependent foreclaw and tail elongation (Evans, 1946, 1951, 1952; Cagle, 1948a). The elongated foreclaws are used during courtship behavior (Cagle, 1950). In our sample of 131 male *T. scripta* collected in Alabama during the recrudescent period, melanistic males (N = 45, claw length/carapace length = 10.1 ± 0.17) differed from nonmelanistic males (N = 86, claw length/carapace length = 11.9 ± 0.16; t = 6.99, df = 129, p < .001). Three of 32 nonmelanistic males under 120 mm PL had foreclaws longer than 16 mm, as did 20 of 51 nonmelanistic males between 121 and 160 mm PL; 30 of 45 melanistic males had foreclaws longer than 16 mm. Furthermore, the largest absolute claw lengths measured in each group were 18.9 mm (175 mm PL) in a melanistic male and 17.7 mm (125 mm PL) in a nonmelanistic male. These results suggest that foreclaws may increase in length very slowly, if at all, after males become melanistic. Plots of claw length versus plastron length for Ellenton Bay and Par Pond *T. scripta* again demonstrate that melanism occurs at different body sizes in populations with different growth rates (Fig. 19.4). Two other associations can be seen. First, the advent of melanism is coincident with population-specific female size at maturity. This unusual relationship is also reflected in the mean plastron lengths of melanistic males given in Table 19.5. In Ellenton Bay and all other slow-growth populations, females mature at about 160 mm, and in Par Pond and Capers Island populations, females mature at about 200 mm (Gibbons et al., 1981). The mean body sizes of melanistic males closely match these respective values. Second, as suggested by data from the Alabama population, melanism is coincident with maximal claw length. The association between androgen-dependent claw length and melanism provides circumstantial support for a hormonal mechanism of melanization of *T. scripta*.

Overall, melanistic males are rarely more abundant

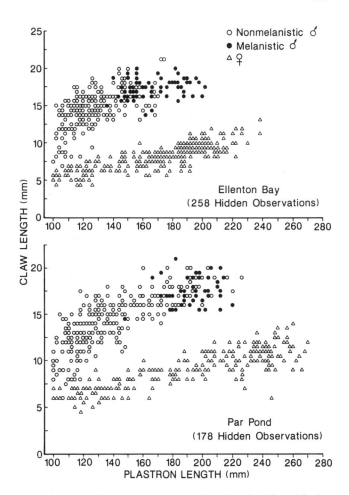

FIGURE 19.4.   Relationship between foreclaw length and body size in two South Carolina populations of *Trachemys scripta*. Several outliers (questionable data points) were removed.

than nonmelanistic adult males in a given population (Tables 19.3 and 19.5). However, melanistic males may predominate in larger size classes (Fig. 19.5). Ratios of melanistic to nonmelanistic sexually mature males in Tables 19.3 and 19.5 range from 0.01 to 2.50 with a mean of 0.50. The value reported for Capers Island is unusual and can be explained as a result of size-specific predation. Smaller turtles in this relatively vegetation-free habitat are presumably preyed upon by alligators and eliminated disproportionately (Gibbons et al., 1979). This has resulted in a population composed primarily of very large turtles. In the case of males, this includes mainly large melanistic specimens; hence the inverse ratio observed. Deleting this unusual value gives an overall mean value of 0.30. The proportion of melanistic versus nonmelanistic males varies significantly among the populations shown in Table 19.5 (contingency table analysis: including Capers Island, χ^2 = 42.2, p < .001; excluding Capers Island, χ^2 = 27.1; p < .001). These differences may be due to sampling error, differential mortality, or differential

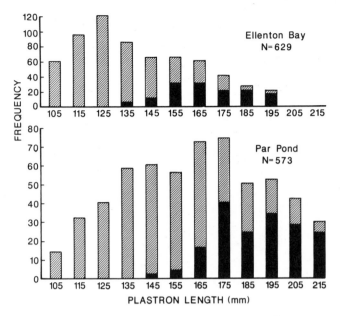

FIGURE 19.5. Size frequency distributions for sexually mature melanistic (dark bars) and nonmelanistic (shaded) male *Trachemys scripta* from two populations in South Carolina. Data are for multiple-capture animals and are based on last capture. Midpoints of each interval are shown.

interpopulation movement patterns in the two male color morphs.

Physiological Basis of Melanization in Male *Trachemys scripta*

There are basically two types of melanization seen in vertebrate animals: (1) physiological color change, an acute phenomenon of rapid darkening (or lightening) typically studied in amphibians or lizards, and (2) morphological color change, a permanent or long-term darkening that occurs with age, season, or some other variable (Bagnara and Hadley, 1974). It is the latter type that concerns us here, specifically the causes and consequences of darkening in older adult, mostly male, emydid turtles.

Hormonal Basis of Melanization in Vertebrates

Previous study of the controlling mechanisms of melanization has concentrated on several hormone systems known to affect the cellular processes involved in darkening. Specifically, these hormone systems may affect the proliferation of melanin-containing pigment cells (melanophores), the dispersal of melanin pigment granules within the melanophores, and the donation of melanin granules by melanophores onto keratinized cells within the skin by cytocrine deposition (Baden et al., 1966; Bagnara et al., 1968; Chavin, 1969; Bagnara and Hadley, 1974). Furthermore, hormonal control of melanization may be complex, with hormones acting sepa-

rately, synergistically, or antagonistically. In addition, melanization is affected by the distribution and dispersal of pigment cells, processes that are known but are little understood.

Hormonal studies of color change in reptiles have concentrated on the physiological color change seen in *Anolis* lizards (Goldman and Hadley, 1969; Bagnara and Hadley, 1974); there is comparatively little in the literature on the physiology of reptilian morphological color change. Hormones recognized to be involved in the regulation of morphological color change include the following (for general reviews, see Bagnara and Hadley, 1974, and Norris, 1980): (1) pituitary gonadotropins—seasonal breeding colors in birds (Ralph, 1969), melanization in African weaver finches (Segal, 1957), beak demelanization in Lal Munia (Thapliyal and Tewary, 1961); (2) pituitary hormones other than gonadotropins—melanocyte-stimulating hormone, MSH, induces melanocyte dispersion, and hence darkening, as well as coat color deposition in mice (Bagnara and Hadley, 1974), and corticotropin, ACTH, exerts a similar darkening effect (Norris, 1980); (3) pineal melatonin—blanches melanophores in a variety of vertebrates (Bagnara and Hadley, 1974) and reverses the gonadotropic effects on plumage in Lal Munia (Gupta et al., 1987); (4) steroid hormones—estrogens induce the female color in brown leghorn chickens (Trinkhaus, 1948), androgens promote the black portions of male coloration in fence lizards (Kimball and Erpino, 1971), androgens induce the dark bill of the male house sparrow (Witschi and Woods, 1936; Witschi, 1961), and progesterone (or ovarian androgen) induces the characteristic colors in gravid or recently ovulated iguanid lizards (reviewed in Cooper, 1984); (5) thyroid hormones—thyroxine (T4) and triiodothyronine (T3) have been implicated in a variety of skin functions, including developmental processes, especially in salamanders (Bagnara and Hadley, 1974; Norris, 1980), and molting in both birds (Payne, 1972) and squamate reptiles (Chiu et al., 1983; Maderson, 1984); thyroidectomy results in bill lightening in the house sparrow, but testosterone, even at very high doses, is unable to darken the bills of thyroidectomized birds (Lal and Thapliyal, 1982); T4 can inhibit gonadal recrudescence and LH-dependent breeding plumage in Lal Munia (Thapliyal and Gupta, 1984).

Although each of the above hormone systems may act independently, there is evidence of considerable interaction among them. For example, thyroid hormones can affect levels of corticosteroids (Holmes and Phillips, 1976). In chickens, corticosteroids and ACTH deactivate thyroid hormones, depressing plasma levels of T4 and T3 (Decuypere et al., 1982). Both thyroid hormones and corticosteroids may affect food intake as well as nutrient storage and mobilization. In chickens, fasting may result in reduced rhythmicity of plasma thyroid hormones, and even the sight of food can depress corticosteroid levels in chickens (Sharp and Klandorff, 1985). Furthermore, levels of corticosteroids, androgens, and other hormones of direct importance in regulating coloration can be profoundly affected by social factors (Leshner, 1978; Norris, 1980). Thus, hormone interactions may cause nutritional and metabolic factors, social organization, and sexual and agonistic behaviors to have profound effects on morphological coloration.

Therefore, in examining possible mechanisms of the morphological color change in male *Trachemys scripta*, we investigated differences between nonmelanistic and melanistic males in (1) the timing and extent of gametogenesis, (2) pineal morphology, and (3) measures of energetics. Any differences in these variables might reflect underlying differences in (1) gonadotropins or sex steroids, (2) melatonin, and (3) thyroid hormones, corticotropin, or corticosteroids.

Comparison of Melanistic and Nonmelanistic Male *Trachemys scripta*

TIMING AND EXTENT OF GAMETOGENESIS

In northern Alabama, *T. scripta* appears to be exclusively a spring breeder (Gross, 1986), but in other areas this species may breed in both spring and fall (Cagle, 1950; Moll and Legler, 1971; Lovich, pers. obs.). In most seasonally breeding vertebrates in temperate regions, gametogenesis in both sexes precedes breeding, so mating occurs when ova and spermatozoa are mature (van Tienhoven, 1983; Crews, 1984). However, in many reptiles, as well as in an assortment of other vertebrates, gametogenesis in one or both sexes occurs at a time other than the time of breeding (Volsoe, 1944; Crews, 1984; Silva et al., 1984). This dissociated condition (Crews, 1984) occurs in male but not female *T. scripta* in northern Alabama (Gross, 1986). In this population, spermatogenesis occurs in the summer and early fall, and vitellogenesis is not complete until spring. Thus, a study of the gametogenic function in male *T. scripta* requires an analysis of both spermatogenesis and sperm storage.

Spermatogenesis in seasonally breeding vertebrates can be described on the gross anatomic level by changes in testicular size, and at the microscopic level by changes in the size of the seminiferous tubules, in the extent of spermiogenesis (the maturation of spermatozoa from spermatids), and in the movement of spermatozoa from the testes. Testicular mass in monthly samples of male *T. scripta* in northern Alabama differed over the year (melanistic, $F = 8.32$, df = 9/40, $p < .001$; nonmelanistic, $F = 5.43$, df = 10/67, $p < .001$) and was greatest during summer and fall (Fig. 19.6). Testes of melanistic males were largest during August, whereas testes of nonmelanis-

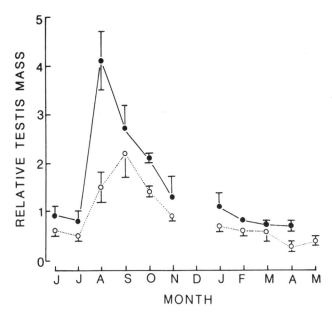

FIGURE 19.6.   Monthly variation in relative testis mass of nonmelanistic (open circles, dotted lines) and melanistic (solid circles, solid lines) male *Trachemys scripta* collected in northern Alabama. Relative testis mass was calculated by dividing the wet mass (g) of both freshly dissected testes by the plastron length (mm) and multiplying by 100. The numbers of individuals examined, by month and color phase (nonmelanistic, then melanistic), are as follows: Jan. = 4, 3; Feb. = 9, 1; Mar. = 5, 3; Apr. = 5, 6; May = 4, 0; June = 13, 10; July = 14, 8; Aug. = 11, 7; Sept. = 7, 6; Oct. = 5, 10; Nov. = 8, 2; Dec. = 0, 0. Means ± SE are shown. Data are from Gross (1986) and Garstka et al. (pers. obs.).

tic males were largest during September, and melanistic testis mass exceeded nonmelanistic during August and September ($t = 3.08$, df = 29, $p < .005$). Seminiferous tubule diameter in the testes differed also in the same monthly samples (melanistic, $F = 7.08$, df = 8/33, $p < .001$; nonmelanistic, $F = 5.47$, df = 9/36, $p < .001$; Fig. 19.7). Seminiferous tubules of both melanistic and nonmelanistic males were largest in the September sample, but were not significantly different in size ($t = 2.02$, df = 8, $.10 > p > .05$). Both nonmelanistic and melanistic males exhibited transforming spermatozoa in the seminiferous tubules beginning in July and lasting, at a much reduced level, through February (Fig. 19.8).

To determine if there was an effect of gonadal hormones on scute melanization, we made use of an observation of Gross (1986). He castrated male *T. scripta* in his studies of sperm storage and activation and noted that shell tissue sometimes regenerated to fill the holes in the carapace made during castration. These holes were normally capped with the removed shell piece and sealed with epoxy putty (Lawson and Garstka, 1985; Gross, 1986). In some animals the old shell did not heal but was replaced entirely by new shell from below. Thus, a short-term system was

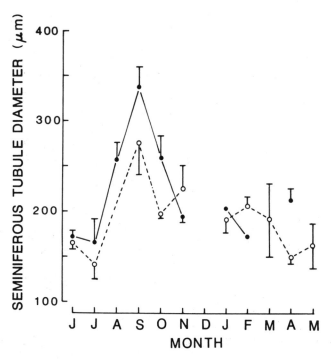

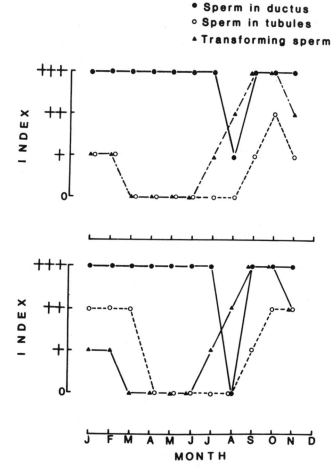

FIGURE 19.7.   Monthly variation in seminiferous tubule diameter of nonmelanistic (open circles, dotted lines) and melanistic (solid circles, solid lines) male *Trachemys scripta* in northern Alabama. Tissues were fixed in Zenker's fluid, dehydrated in a graded ethanol series, embedded in paraffin, sectioned at 8 μm, and stained with hematoxylin and eosin. Seminiferous tubule diameter was measured with an ocular micrometer; three tubules per section and two sections per male were measured. Group means were calculated from individual turtle means. Group means ± SE are shown. The numbers of males examined, by month and color phase (nonmelanistic, then melanistic), are as follows: Jan. = 4, 1; Feb. = 8, 1; Mar. = 3, 0; Apr. = 5, 5; May = 2, 0; June = 2, 3; July = 9, 8; Aug. = 0, 7; Sept. = 4, 6; Oct. = 1, 9; Nov. = 8, 2; Dec. = 0, 0. Data are from Gross (1986) and Garstka et al. (pers. obs.).

FIGURE 19.8.   Monthly pattern of gametogenesis in nonmelanistic (above) and melanistic (below) male *Trachemys scripta* collected in northern Alabama. Tissues were fixed in Zenker's fluid, dehydrated in a graded ethanol series, embedded in paraffin, sectioned at 8 μm, and stained with hematoxylin and eosin. The numbers of spermatozoa free in the seminiferous tubules and in the ductus deferentia were scored in each of three sections for each male as 0 = none observed, + = 1–100, + + = 101–500, and + + + > 500. A similar numerical scale was used to estimate the number of spermatozoa transforming within the seminiferous tubules. The numbers of testes examined, by month and color phase (nonmelanistic, then melanistic), are as follows: Jan. = 4, 2; Feb. = 9, 1; Mar. = 4, 3; Apr. = 5, 6; May = 2, 2; June = 2, 3; July = 10, 8; Aug. = 6, 7; Sept. = 4, 6; Oct. = 4, 9; Nov. = 8, 2; Dec. = 0, 0. Median scores of each group are shown. Data are from Gross (1986) and Garstka et al. (pers. obs.).

available to examine the effect of castration on carapace coloration. Several such surgeries were performed, but few turtles refilled the holes with shell, and fewer lived long enough to establish a color pattern. However, castrated males seemed to replace the shell with its original pattern: melanistic with black shell, nonmelanistic with striped shell.

PINEAL MORPHOLOGY

To determine if the pineal glands of nonmelanistic and melanistic male *T. scripta* differed, pineal glands were dissected from 29 males collected during the period of gonadal recrudescence between August and November (Lawson and Garstka, unpubl. data). Measurements of pineal mass were normalized to body size by dividing pineal mass (mg) by plastron length (cm). Relative pineal mass

did not differ between nonmelanistic (0.212 ± 0.027, $N = 15$) and melanistic (0.178 ± 0.025, $N = 14$) males ($t = 0.90$, df = 29, $p > .35$). Histological analysis of 7 μm paraffin sections stained with hematoxylin and eosin revealed no obvious morphological difference between the two groups of males.

To determine if there was an effect of the pineal on carapace color pattern, a pilot experiment in which 18 males were surgically manipulated was performed (Law-

Table 19.6. Monthly variation in energy use and availability in male *Trachemys scripta* collected from Limestone County, Alabama, as measured by circulating levels of nutrients

Month	Total serum protein (g/100 ml)		Total serum lipid (mg/100 ml)		Serum glucose (mg/100 ml)	
	NON	MEL	NON	MEL	NON	MEL
Jan.	--	--	232 ± 91 (5)	--	--	169 ± 42 (2)
Feb.	2.5 ± 0.3 (9)	2.4 (1)	206 ± 72 (9)	--	135 ± 141 (8)	44 (1)
Mar.	2.4 ± 0.5 (5)	2.1 ± 0.4 (3)	153 ± 88 (5)	--	119 ± 72 (5)	247 ± 200 (3)
Apr.	2.8 ± 1.3 (5)	2.7 ± 0.3 (6)	139 ± 92 (5)	--	252 ± 42 (5)	175 ± 49 (6)
May	2.4 ± 0.2 (4)	--	83 ± 49 (4)	--	56 ± 70 (4)	--
June	4.9 ± 0.4 (10)	4.3 ± 0.3 (10)	448 ± 275 (10)	524 ± 298 (4)	200 ± 74 (9)	259 ± 17 (5)
July	3.3 ± 0.2 (12)	4.2 ± 0.2 (8)	237 ± 228 (12)	344 ± 212 (8)	112 ± 17 (12)	200 ± 20 (8)
Aug.	3.6 ± 0.3 (10)	4.0 ± 0.3 (7)	155 ± 80 (10)	416 ± 105 (7)	71 ± 21 (10)	48 ± 27 (7)
Sept.	3.6 ± 0.5 (4)	3.2 ± 0.3 (5)	300 ± 46 (4)	297 ± 69 (6)	35 ± 25 (4)	73 ± 29 (6)
Oct.	3.0 ± 0.6 (5)	3.8 ± 0.2 (9)	275 ± 62 (5)	324 ± 41 (9)	107 ± 50 (5)	169 ± 59 (9)
Nov.	3.5 ± 0.3 (8)	2.9 ± 0.3 (2)	294 ± 30 (8)	184 ± 7 (2)	138 ± 80 (8)	169 ± 42 (2)

Sources: Terrell and Garstka, 1984; Gross, 1986; Garstka et al., pers. obs.

Note: Serum protein was measured by the biuret reaction, serum glucose by the *o*-toluidine reaction, and total serum lipid by the sulfuric acid-vanillin reaction (all methods in Tietz, 1982). Turtles were killed by decapitation immediately after capture. Blood was collected, allowed to clot on ice and at 5° C overnight, and centrifuged, and the serum was stored at -20° C until tested. Means ± SE are shown, with sample size in parentheses. No turtles were collected in December. Abbreviations: MEL, melanistic; NON, nonmelanistic.

son and Garstka, unpubl. data). Seven males were pinealectomized and castrated, two were pinealectomized and sham-castrated, five were castrated and sham-pinealectomized, and four were simply castrated. Biopsies were removed from the healing wounds in the shell of the animals, which died between 9 and 67 days following surgery. However, only three animals survived more than 30 days, and of them only one was pinealectomized. It was a melanistic male (169 mm PL) that died 67 days after surgery, and it showed definite linear arrays of melanophores in the regenerating shell. Details of the role that the pineal complex plays in vertebrate color change are reviewed by Ralph et al. (1979).

ENERGETICS

Seasonal cycling of nutritionally important molecules and of the size of metabolically important organs has been reported in many reptile species (Dessauer, 1955; Hutton and Goodnight, 1957; Masat and Musacchia, 1965; Emerson, 1967; Telford, 1970; Aleksiuk and Stewart, 1971; Brisbin, 1972; Goldberg, 1972; Derickson, 1976; Garstka et al., 1983; Silva et al., 1984; and others). We sought first to make comparisons of the cycling of serum protein, serum lipid, and serum glucose, especially during critical breeding and recrudescent periods. Because we had already seen differences in gametogenic function between melanistic and nonmelanistic males, we hypothesized that energetics might be more pronounced during reproductively important periods. Monthly samples of nonmelanistic and melanistic males were analyzed (Table 19.6). Although serum protein of both nonmelanistic ($F = 3.11$, df = 9/62, $p < .005$) and melanistic ($F = 6.17$, df = 8/42, $p < .001$) males varied over the year, there was no

difference between the color phases during either the April breeding period or the July–September period of testicular recrudescence. Serum lipid of nonmelanistics ($F = 3.44$, df = 10/64, $p < .005$) varied over the year, but comparisons with melanistics were complicated by the lack of spring samples for melanistics. Serum glucose of both nonmelanistics ($F = 4.12$, df = 9/50, $p < .001$) and melanistics ($F = 7.13$, df = 8/31, $p < .001$) varied over the year, and April breeding samples differed significantly between melanistic and nonmelanistic males ($t = 2.56$, df = 8, $p < .005$).

Turtles do not have the gonad-associated fat bodies of lepidosaurian reptiles. Fat bodies of lepidosaurians have been shown to vary in size inversely with the gonads and to provide an important nutrient store for gonadal recrudescence (Derickson, 1976; Crews, 1979; but see Congdon and Tinkle, 1982b; Long, 1985). However, because the liver is so important in nutrient cycling, and because its size and function have been shown to vary seasonally in reptiles (Dessauer, 1955; Emerson, 1967; Aleksiuk and Stewart, 1971; Goldberg, 1972), we examined monthly liver samples of male *T. scripta* for evidence of seasonal fluctuations. Relative liver mass (Fig. 19.9) varied among the sampled months in both nonmelanistic ($F = 5.20$, df = 9/70, $p < .001$) and melanistic ($F = 3.62$, df = 9/40, $p < .005$) males. Although no difference was detected between nonmelanistic and melanistic males during recrudescence, relative liver mass did differ between male groups during the April breeding season ($t = 2.85$, df = 9, $p < .02$).

Total liver protein, lipid, and glycogen were measured in monthly samples of nonmelanistic and melanistic males (Table 19.7). Neither significant variation among monthly samples nor male group differences were detected in liver protein results. Total liver lipid of non-

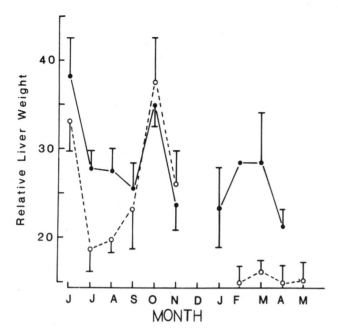

FIGURE 19.9. Monthly variation in relative liver mass in non-melanistic (open circles, dotted lines) and melanistic (solid circles, solid lines) male *Trachemys scripta* collected in northern Alabama. Relative liver mass was calculated by dividing the wet mass (g) of freshly dissected liver by the plastron length (mm). Monthly means ± SE are shown. The numbers of males examined, by month and color phase (nonmelanistic, then melanistic), are as follows: Jan. = 0, 3; Feb. = 5, 1; Mar. = 9, 3; Apr. = 5, 6; May = 5, 0; June = 14, 5; July = 11, 8; Aug. = 1, 7; Sept. = 7, 6; Oct. = 5, 10; Nov. = 8, 2; Dec. = 0, 0.

melanistic males did not differ among monthly samples, but in monthly samples of melanistic males it did ($F = 6.24$, df = 8/38, $p < .001$). No differences in liver lipid between nonmelanistic and melanistic males were detected during either recrudescence or breeding. Liver glycogen varied among monthly samples of nonmelanistic ($F = 3.18$, df = 10/62, $p < .005$) but not melanistic males. Liver glycogen further differed between male groups during the April breeding season ($t = 3.83$, df = 9, $p < .005$).

Cholesterol was also measured. Cholesterol may provide additional insight into lipid cycling because of its connection with circulating lipoprotein and because it serves as the precursor for the biosynthesis of steroid hormones. Serum cholesterol was expressed as a fraction of total serum lipid (mg cholesterol per 100 ml divided by mg total lipid per 100 ml; Fig. 19.10). The fraction of total lipid as cholesterol differed between nonmelanistic and melanistic males during the recrudescence period ($t = 3.61$, df = 55, $p < .001$). Testicular cholesterol (Fig. 19.11) also differed between the male groups during recrudescence ($t = 12.39$, df = 68, $p < .001$), but it was the melanistics that had significantly higher testicular cholesterol, although the nonmelanistics had significantly higher serum cholesterol. Melanistic males also exhibited testicular cholesterol levels higher than nonmelanistics during the April breeding period ($t = 2.36$, df = 8, $p < .05$).

Hypothesis of the Control of Melanism in Male *Trachemys scripta*

There are consistent differences relating seasonal energetics and reproduction in melanistic and nonmelanistic male *T. scripta* sampled from northern Alabama. During

Table 19.7. Monthly variation in metabolic stores and turnover as measured by total protein, total lipid, and glycogen concentrations in the liver of male *Trachemys scripta* collected in northern Alabama

Month	Total protein (g/100 g)				Total lipid (mg/100 g)				Glycogen (μmole/g)			
	NON		MEL		NON		MEL		NON		MEL	
Jan.	0.06 ± 0.03	(5)	0.60 ± 0.08	(3)	244 ± 194	(5)	314 ± 90	(3)	1.02 ± 0.22	(5)	0.11 ± 0.17	(3)
Feb.	0.90 ± 0.11	(9)	--		405 ± 290	(9)	--		1.20 ± 0.50	(9)	--	
Mar.	--		0.90 ± 0.12	(3)	334 ± 406	(5)	218 ± 40	(3)	0.80 ± 0.30	(5)	0.06 ± 0.04	(2)
Apr.	--		0.70	(1)	633 ± 717	(5)	151 ± 59	(5)	0.38 ± 0.20	(5)	0.03 ± 0.01	(6)
May	--		--		271 ± 225	(2)	--		0.93 ± 0.40	(3)	--	
June	0.90 ± 0.11	(9)	0.90 ± 0.13	(5)	533 ± 412	(9)	600 ± 216	(4)	0.59 ± 0.25	(9)	0.20 ± 0.07	(5)
July	0.60 ± 0.11	(10)	0.40 ± 0.03	(8)	238 ± 82	(10)	188 ± 94	(8)	0.86 ± 0.48	(10)	0.44 ± 0.32	(8)
Aug.	0.50 ± 0.07	(10)	0.40 ± 0.06	(7)	357 ± 351	(10)	244 ± 140	(7)	0.66 ± 0.23	(10)	0.30 ± 0.07	(7)
Sept.	0.50 ± 0.02	(4)	0.40 ± 0.04	(6)	171 ± 119	(3)	435 ± 168	(6)	1.18 ± 0.57	(4)	0.06 ± 0.12	(6)
Oct.	0.30 ± 0.09	(5)	0.60 ± 0.10	(9)	592 ± 297	(5)	442 ± 209	(9)	1.08 ± 0.41	(4)	0.04 ± 0.07	(9)
Nov.	0.80 ± 0.14	(8)	0.70	(1)	521 ± 359	(8)	686 ± 182	(2)	1.18 ± 0.06	(8)	0.05 ± 0.07	(2)

Sources: Gross, 1986; Garstka et al., pers. obs.

Note: Turtles were killed by decapitation and exsanguinated, and the liver and other organs were removed. Liver mass was recorded; 3 g of liver tissue was homogenized with 12 ml reptilian Ringer's saline and centrifuged; and 5 ml of the supernatant was reserved for analysis at -20° C. Supernatant total protein was measured by the biuret reaction, and total lipid by the sulfuric acid-vanillin reaction (Tietz, 1982). Glycogen was ethanol-precipitated from a KOH digest and then hydrolyzed to glucose, which was measured colorimetrically with phenol-sulfuric acid (Montgomery, 1957). Means ± SE are shown, with sample size in parentheses. No turtles were collected in December. Abbreviations: MEL, melanistic; NON, nonmelanistic.

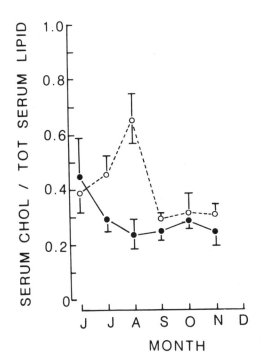

FIGURE 19.10. Monthly variation in serum cholesterol as a fraction of total serum lipid in nonmelanistic (open circles, dotted line) and melanistic (solid circles, solid line) male *Trachemys scripta* collected in northern Alabama. Serum cholesterol was measured by the ferric chloride reaction after isopropanol extraction, and total serum lipid by the sulfuric acid–vanillin reaction (methods in Tietz, 1982). Means ± SE are shown. The numbers of males examined, by month and color phase (nonmelanistic, then melanistic), are as follows: Jan. = 4, 0; Feb. = 9, 0; Mar. = 5, 3; Apr. = 5, 6; May = 4, 3; June = 11, 11; July = 12, 8; Aug. = 10, 7; Sept. = 4, 6; Oct. = 5, 9; Nov. = 8, 2; Dec. = 0, 0. Abbreviations: CHOL, cholesterol; TOT, total.

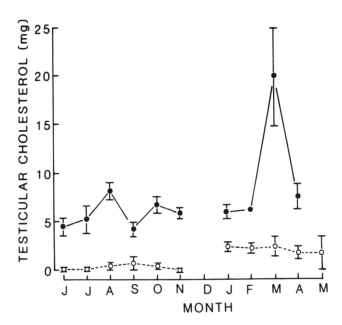

FIGURE 19.11. Monthly variation in testicular cholesterol in nonmelanistic (open circles, dotted lines) and melanistic (solid circles, solid lines) male *Trachemys scripta* collected in northern Alabama. Cholesterol was measured by the ferric chloride reaction (Tietz, 1982) in 1:5 wt./vol. testes homogenates in reptilian Ringer's saline and is expressed as mg/testes. Means ± SE are shown. The numbers of testes examined, by month and by color phase (nonmelanistic, then melanistic), are as follows: Jan. = 5, 3; Feb. = 9, 1; Mar. = 5, 3; Apr. = 5, 6; May = 4, 0; June = 13, 11; July = 12, 8; Aug. = 10, 7; Sept. = 4, 6; Oct. = 5, 9; Nov. = 8, 2; Dec. = 0, 0.

the breeding period melanistic males exhibited significantly lower levels of serum glucose, liver lipid, and liver glycogen than nonmelanistic males. However, melanistic males had significantly greater liver mass during that period. These findings suggest that melanistic males may have higher energy-use rates than nonmelanistic males during the breeding period. Melanistic males further exhibited higher (albeit not significantly) cloacal body temperature than nonmelanistic males during the breeding period.

It is tempting to connect higher rates of energy devoted to reproduction with the fact that testicular size during recrudescence is greater in melanistic than nonmelanistic males. However, measured parameters of energy storage and mobilization do not differ between melanistic and nonmelanistic males during the recrudescent period. It is only in measures of cholesterol that melanistic and nonmelanistic males differ during testicular recrudescence; melanistic males have lower circulating and higher testicular cholesterol than nonmelanistics.

Because of the importance of cholesterol as a biosynthetic precursor for steroid hormones, and because of the differences found between melanistic and nonmelanistic males in both serum and testicular cholesterol, we investigated aspects of steroid hormone metabolism in both male groups. We expected to find differences in the metabolism of androgens, perhaps with increased conversion to estrogens (Callard et al., 1977; vanTienhoven, 1983) in melanistic males. Conversion of the androgen testosterone to the estrogen estradiol occurs in neural and other tissue, and the estradiol is thought to be the behaviorally active hormone, inducing male sexual behavior (Callard et al., 1977; Leshner, 1978).

We approached the problem of androgen determinations in melanistic and nonmelanistic *T. scripta* with some hesitation. Like male *T. scripta*, garter snakes (*Thamnophis*) also exhibit dissociated gametogenesis, and previous extensive study of hormones and behavior in *Thamnophis sirtalis* showed no evidence that testosterone could induce male courtship behavior, no correlation of circulating testosterone and sexual behavior, and indeed no necessity for the presence of the gonads (Crews, 1984; Crews et al., 1984). Our interest here with male *T. scripta* was in hormone metabolism, however.

Little is known directly about steroid metabolism in reptiles (Eik-Nes, 1969; Sandor, 1969; vanTienhoven, 1983). However, we do know that (1) turtles possess aromatase enzymes to convert androgens to estrogens (Callard et al., 1977), (2) androgen levels in the blood are generally highest when testis size is greatest (Hews and Kime, 1978; Courty and Dufaure, 1980; Crews et al., 1984; Silva et al., 1984; and others), (3) androgen levels may be elevated during the breeding season even though the breeding season may be dissociated from testicular recrudescence (Kuchling et al., 1981), and (4) although the basic pattern of steroid biosynthetic pathways seems to be consistent throughout the vertebrates, there is varia-tion among reptilian taxa in the importance of certain paths, and the paths may vary seasonally (Bourne and Seamark, 1978; Bourne, 1981; Bourne and Licht, 1985; Bourne et al., 1985).

We used gas-liquid chromatography to fractionate androgen and estrogen extracts of blood serum, liver, and testes collected from nonmelanistic and melanistic male *T. scripta* during early spring emergence from hibernation, April breeding, and fall testicular recrudescence (Garstka et al., unpubl; Table 19.8). This is the first report of such a comprehensive examination of steroid metabolism in any reptile. Several results are striking: (1) Testosterone was detected in only a few samples of testis

Table 19.8. Steroid hormones identified in blood sera, testes homogenates, and liver homogenates of male *Trachemys scripta* collected in northern Alabama

Hormone	Emergence		Breeding		Recrudescence	
	NON	MEL	NON	MEL	NON	MEL
Androgen precursors in testes						
Pregnenolone	--	--	--	--	DET	DET
Progesterone	DET	DET	DET	DET	DET	DET
17-OH-pregnenolone	--	--	--	--	--	DET
17-OH-progesterone	DET	DET	DET	DET	DET	DET
20-OH-progesterone	--	--	--	DET	--	--
Androgens in testes						
Dehydroepiandrosterone	DET	DET	DET	DET	DET	DET
Androstenedione	DET	DET	DET	DET	DET	DET
Testosterone	DET	--	--	--	DET	--
Epitestosterone	--	--	--	--	--	--
Dihydrotestosterone	DET	--	DET	--	--	--
Androgens in blood serum						
Dehydroepiandrosterone	DET	DET	DET	DET	DET	DET
Androstenedione	DET	--	DET	DET	DET	--
Testosterone	DET	--	--	--	--	--
Epitestosterone	--	DET	--	DET	--	--
Dihydrotestosterone	--	--	--	--	--	--
Androgen metabolites in testes						
Androsterone	DET	--	DET	--	DET	--
Etiocholanolone	DET	DET	DET	DET	DET	DET
Epiandrosterone	--	--	--	--	DET	--
Estrone	DET	DET	DET	DET	DET	DET
17-β-Estradiol	--	--	--	--	--	--
Estriol	--	--	DET	--	--	--
Androgen metabolites in liver						
Etiocholanolone	DET	DET	DET	DET	DET	DET
Androsterone	DET	--	DET	--	DET	--
Epiandrosterone	DET	--	--	--	DET	--
Dihydrotestosterone	--	--	--	--	DET	DET

Note: Samples were pooled to obtain sufficient data for analysis; "emergence" refers to pooled samples collected from January through March during emergence from hibernation, "breeding" refers to pooled samples collected during the April breeding period, and "recrudescence" refers to pooled samples collected from August through October during annual testicular recrudescence. Replicate pools were made: 4 nonmelanistic emergence pools, 2 nonmelanistic breeding pools, 5 nonmelanistic recrudescence pools, 1 melanistic emergence pool, 2 melanistic breeding pools, and 5 melanistic recrudescence pools. Each pool was of the corresponding samples from the same three males. For example, pool SM3 (melanistic breeding) was of the sera of males 20686, 20688, and 20689, their liver homogenate pool was LM3, and their testes homogenate pool was GM3. Tabulated results indicate that the hormone in question was detected in at least one pool (DET) or was not detected in any pool (--). Steroids were analyzed by gas-liquid chromatography as their trimethylsilyl ether derivatives on a 30-meter fused silica capillary column using a 160°-240° C temperature profile elution. Steroids were identified based on their retention time relative to the retention time of cholestane, a nonbiological steroid used as an internal standard. Although quantification is possible with this method, quantitative data are not reported because the specimens were pooled. Abbreviations: MEL, melanistic; NON, nonmelanistic.

and blood serum, (2) 20-OH-progesterone, an important progesterone metabolite in the lizard *Tiliqua rugosa* (Bourne and Seamark, 1978; Bourne, 1981), was rare in male *T. scripta*, (3) dehydroepiandrosterone (DHEA) and androstenedione, which are androgenic precursors of testosterone, were identified in almost all serum and testis samples, unlike findings for lacertid lizards (Hews and Kime, 1978; Courty and Dufaure, 1980), (4) androsterone, a metabolite (inactive?) of testosterone, was present in all nonmelanistic testis and liver samples but was not detected in any melanistic samples, (5) epitestosterone, an alpha stereoisomer of testosterone reported in the lizard *Tiliqua rugosa* (Bourne et al., 1985), was detected in melanistic but not nonmelanistic serum samples, and (6) although estradiol was not detected in any sample, the estrogen estrone, which is the aromatization product of androstenedione (Sandor, 1969; van-

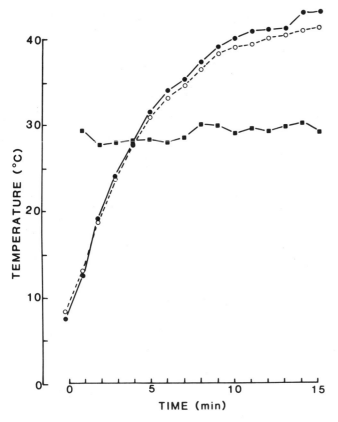

FIGURE 19.12. Rate of warming of size-matched nonmelanistic (open circles with dotted line) and melanistic (solid circles with solid line) male *Trachemys scripta*. Size-matched pairs of *T. scripta* males were placed in crushed ice and monitored by means of a cloacal Yellow Springs Instruments thermistor probe until equilibration at between 5° and 10° C. Both were set in adjacent small arenas and the cloacal temperatures were recorded. Environmental temperatures during the experiments were recorded (squares). In this typical example, no difference between the melanistic and nonmelanistic size-matched males is seen in rate of warming. Data are from Terrell and Garstka (1984).

Tienhoven, 1983), was detected in all groups of testis samples.

These results clearly indicate differences in steroid metabolism between nonmelanistic and melanistic male *T. scripta*. Furthermore, they suggest that in male *T. scripta* the biosynthetic conversion of androstenedione to testosterone to estradiol, found to be the most important pathway in other vertebrates (vanTienhoven, 1983), may be supplanted by one of the following alternate pathways: (1) androstenedione to epitestosterone, (2) androstenedione to androsterone via androstanedione intermediate, or (3) aromatization of androstenedione to estrone. This situation could result from suppressing the activity of 17-β-hydroxysteroid dehydrogenase, which catalyzes the conversions of androstenedione to testosterone and estrone to estradiol, and from regulating other enzymes differently between nonmelanistic and melanistic males.

Ultimately, the question is whether these differences in steroid metabolism account for the differences in color pattern between nonmelanistic and melanistic male *T. scripta*. Because the change from nonmelanistic to melanistic apparently involves a suppression of dermal melanocytes and enhancement of epidermal melanocytes (Fig. 19.3), and because steroid hormones characteristically interact with epidermal rather than dermal melanophores, we suggest that steroid differences might indeed account for the color pattern differences between melanistic and nonmelanistic male *T. scripta*. However, castrated males regenerate their shell color pattern without change, and shell regeneration in a pinealectomized melanistic male exhibited linear arrays of melanophores. Clearly, more experiments studying the effects of various treatments on shell color-pattern regeneration as well as more study of steroid biosynthesis must be done. In addition, the behavioral and energetic effects of the steroids identified in male *T. scripta* need clarification.

Adaptive Significance of Male Melanism in *Trachemys scripta*

Thus far we have discussed the occurrence and ontogeny of melanization in male *T. scripta* and have suggested a possible hormonal mechanism for the phenomenon. Yet this question remains: What are the possible adaptive functions of this dramatic color change?

Boyer (1965) tested the hypothesis that melanistic male *T. scripta*, being black, would thermoregulate more efficiently than nonmelanistic males. He found no difference in the rates of heating in his experiments. In another experiment, Terrell and Garstka (1984) obtained similar results with 11 size-matched pairs of males (Fig. 19.12). In each case, nonmelanistic-melanistic pairs reached ambient air temperature within one minute of each other. In contrast, Bustard (1970) suggested that the black carapacial coloration of hatchling *Chelonia mydas* plays an important role in elevating body temperature while the turtle floats at the surface. However, his results were based on experiments using whitewashed turtles as a treatment group, a most unlikely extreme in nature. Boyer (1965) interpreted his findings as being consistent with the idea that visible (to humans) wavelengths have little to do with overall light absorption. As a further test, we measured cloacal temperatures of a sample of 7 melanistic and 17 nonmelanistic males during the April breeding period (females collected on the same date showed sperm in cloacal lavages). No difference was observed (water temperature = $16.7°–17.8°$ C by depth, melanistic temperature = $17.2°$ C $± 0.15°$, nonmelanistic temperature = $16.8°$ C $± 0.11°$, $t = 1.61$, df = 22, $0.2 > p > .1$).

Thermoregulatory efficiency might also be affected by the shape of the absorbing surface. The ratio of carapace height to carapace width was calculated for a sample of 12 nonmelanistic (82–159 mm PL) and 8 melanistic (141–197 mm PL) male T. scripta. No difference was found (nonmelanistic = $0.34 ± 0.009$, melanistic = $0.36 ± 0.007$, $t = 1.59$, df = 18, $0.2 > p > .1$).

The possible role of color in reptilian thermoregulation has been suggested many times (Parker, 1935; Cole, 1943; Hutchison and Larimer, 1960; Norris, 1967; Bustard, 1970; Hamilton, 1973). Whether or not a dark-colored turtle will heat faster or stay warmer than a lighter-colored turtle depends on the complex interaction of the absorption of solar radiation, metabolic heat gain, reradiation of heat in the thermal portion of the electromagnetic spectrum, convective cooling, evaporative cooling, and conduction. In the case of T. scripta, we would not expect a melanistic individual to heat more rapidly than a normally pigmented turtle of the same size, because there is little difference in their solar absorptivities. Normal T. scripta vary in absorptivity from .86 to .90 (see Chapter 22), whereas a melanistic individual would probably have an absorptivity of about .95 to .97. Thus, there would be only a slight difference in their rate of heat gain from basking in the sun, and their rate of heat loss would be the same. This would result in at most a very small difference in body temperature. Even on a cold, clear day with little wind the effect of this color difference on body temperature would be minimal.

Boyer (1965) effectively laid to rest hypothetical functions related to thermoregulation in turtles, at least insofar as melanism's increasing the rates of warming. Ernst (1982) and Cloudsley-Thompson et al. (1985) noted the prevalence of melanism among tropical turtles and suggested that the opposite might be true: Black shells might aid radiant heat loss. Ernst (1982) further suggested that cloacal temperatures might be an inappropriate measure of any energetic significance of melanism and that increased activity during the cooler periods of the year and decreased basking time might be alternative effects to

measure. Landers et al. (1982) noted a reverse latitudinal cline in coloration of Gopherus polyphemus (darker in the north) and suggested thermal adaptation as an explanation. A thermoregulatory function has also been suggested for the reticulate melanism observed in Chrysemys picta (Schueler, 1983). We have shown energetic differences between melanistic and nonmelanistic male T. scripta, but from our data it is impossible to determine if one is cause and the other consequence or if both are effects of an underlying, possibly steroidal cause.

A second possible function of melanism is protection from radiation (McGinness and Proctor, 1973). Melanin dissipates as heat the energy absorbed from light over a wide spectral range from far ultraviolet through infrared, as well as energy absorbed from free radicals. It seems unlikely that light would penetrate a turtle shell, yet by holding a turtle carapace to a light as if candling an egg it is easy to demonstrate that it does. In addition, more light is visible in areas lacking melanin pigmentation. Bodenheimer et al. (1953) found that even ultraviolet radiation below 300 nm passed through some animal tissue. In an extensive study of light transmission through reptile skin (mostly of desert lizards), Porter (1967) clearly showed that although ultraviolet radiation could penetrate lizard tissue, the black peritoneum of most desert species blocked those wavelengths. In Cnemidophorus and Eumeces, which lack the black peritoneum, skin melanophores functioned similarly. Cloudsley-Thompson et al. (1985) attributed darker coloration of equatorial tortoises to protection from shortwave radiation.

If protection is the function of melanism in larger male T. scripta, why not in small males and females? What is being protected? Male T. scripta exhibit dissociated gametogenesis, with sperm being stored within the body cavity from fall through the following April. Dissociated gametogenesis and sperm storage have also been reported in the closely related, and possibly conspecific (Pritchard, 1979; Iverson, 1986), Pseudemys dorbigni (Silva et al., 1984). Fall and early spring are the times of the year in which increased basking by T. scripta is observed (Boyer, 1965; Garstka and Terrell, pers. obs.). Therefore, melanism might be a gamete protection device. This hypothesis is further substantiated by the fact that the organ of sperm storage, the ductus deferens, is heavily melanized (Fig. 19.13). Porter (1967) reported that diurnal snakes possess the black peritoneum only posteriorly, and Neill (1974) reported the highest incidence of black body linings in snakes that are diurnal and arboreal. Snake gonads and snake sperm storage areas are posterior (Camazine et al., 1981). If gamete protection under conditions of long-term storage in the male is a function of melanism, what about the smaller yet sexually mature males?

Another possible function of melanism is communica-

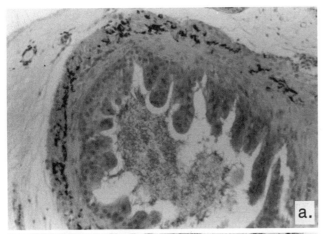
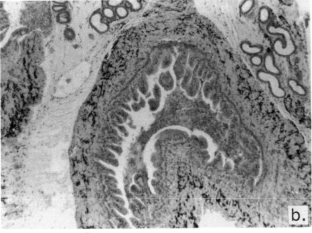

FIGURE 19.13.   Photomicrographs showing the ductus deferens of *Trachemys scripta* from Alabama. *a*, nonmelanistic individual; *b*, melanistic individual.

tion. Although Madison (1977) has suggested that chemical cues are probably the primary mode of communication in turtles, he admits that visual cues cannot be excluded. The importance of color and pattern in turtles during behavioral interactions has already been suggested (Bury and Wolfheim, 1973; Schueler, 1983; Lovich, 1988). If visual communication is important, then perhaps it is the dark forelimbs and the distinctive pattern of wavy lines and dots on the head and neck that are important, because those features would be visible to a female during the foreclaw titillation phase of courtship (Cagle, 1950). But what would be communicated? Perhaps male mating ability, an effect of steroid hormones? Sexual selection by females could possibly be expected under this scenario and may ultimately be responsible for the origin, maintenance, and enhancement of the polymorphism. Alternatively, the development of melanism may facilitate species recognition by prospective mates (Moll et al., 1981). This would be particularly important in areas where *T. scripta* is sympatric with other similarly

patterned emydids (those with head and forelimb stripes) such as *Pseudemys floridana*, *P. nelsoni*, *P. rubriventris*, *Chrysemys picta*, and *Deirochelys reticularia*. It is of interest to note that melanism is apparently infrequent in tropical populations of *T. scripta* where similarly patterned emydids are rare or absent (Moll and Legler, 1971; also see Chapter 7). Sexual dichromatism may also allow males to recognize the sex of conspecifics. This has been demonstrated for the lizard *Sceloporus undulatus* by Cooper and Burns (1987).

The idea that melanism might form an important social cue indicating maturity or social status is not without precedent. The ornithological literature in particular is replete with examples. For instance, Harris's sparrows show tremendous variability in winter plumage related to social status (Rohwer, 1975). In this case, blacker birds are "studlier" (sensu Rohwer, 1975); that is, they are socially dominant, presumably physiologically different, and possibly endowed with greater sexual prowess. Other examples of the importance of plumage polymorphisms in avian social systems are discussed by Rohwer (1975), Lawton and Guindon (1981), Rohwer and Ewald (1981), Lawton and Lawton (1985, 1986), and Whitfield (1987). Whether melanism functions as a "badge signaling" device (Rohwer and Ewald, 1981) in possible *T. scripta* dominance hierarchies (Lardie, 1983) remains to be demonstrated.

Not surprisingly, behavioral differences have been observed between melanistic and nonmelanistic turtles. The first report of unusual behavior in melanistic male *T. scripta* was given by Cahn (1937), who noted, "The nonmelanistic 'elegans' is a rather quiet, inoffensive, peaceful species, not given especially to snapping or pugnacious qualities in either sex; the melanistic 'troosti', on the other hand, frequently exhibits decided pugnacity." Aggressive interactions among melanistic male *T. scripta* were also reported by Lardie (1983). He observed that groups of turtles occupying pools in a stream habitat usually had one melanistic male that exhibited territorial behavior toward other males whenever they were present. Under laboratory conditions, melanistic males were predictably aggressive to conspecific and heterospecific turtles of about the same size and color. A possible dominance hierarchy existed, and melanistic males dominated over other males during courtship behavior. This latter observation requires further investigation. Kramer (1986) reported that aggressive interactions between *Pseudemys nelsoni* were initiated primarily by large melanistic males.

Differences in the behavior of melanistic and nonmelanistic male mosquitofish (*Gambusia affinis*) have also been reported (Martin, 1977, 1986). Martin (1977) observed that at high laboratory densities, melanistic males were highly aggressive to nonmelanistic males and exhibited a clear dominance advantage during behavioral interactions. Sexual activity was also elevated in melanistic males at these high densities. However, in 120 separate trials, females responded equally to both morphs when given a choice (Martin, 1986).

A possible explanation for why melanism is primarily a male-only phenomenon in *T. scripta* may be associated with differential terrestrial activity between the sexes. Adult males may make extensive overland movements between aquatic habitats, presumably in search of mating opportunities (Morreale et al., 1984; Parker, 1984). It is likely that the bright pattern of stripes characteristic of young males is overly conspicuous to potential terrestrial predators. Thus, melanistic males may be more cryptic. Given that melanism generally occurs in larger males, we would expect them to move more frequently than smaller males, if this hypothesis is correct. Data reported in Chapter 16 appear to support this contention.

Conclusions

Although the phenomenon of ontogenetic melanism in *T. scripta* is complex, certain trends and mechanisms are now apparent. First, although the onset of this condition was previously thought to be size-specific, data from populations with different growth rates clearly indicate that the beginnings of melanic change vary concordantly. In Par Pond, for example, males characteristically exhibit signs of melanism at a plastron length of 190 mm, whereas males in Ellenton Bay and all other slow-growth populations achieve the same condition at approximately 160 mm PL. In addition, melanism appears to become evident in Par Pond males at an earlier age and sooner after sexual maturity than in Ellenton Bay males. Collectively, these data on body size and age suggest that the onset of melanism in *T. scripta* is related to population-specific growth rates. Populations in environments favoring rapid growth appear to become melanistic at an earlier age and larger body size than populations in slow-growth conditions.

However, because size and age are confounded, these results do not necessarily rule out the possibility of an age-specific mechanism. Of particular interest is that for all populations we examined, the onset of melanism is coincident with population-specific female size at maturity. Whether this association is an artifact of age-related melanism or of some complex feedback mechanism associated with dominance hierarchies (Lardie, 1983) or reproductive behavior is a question that should be asked in future investigations. It is also of interest that the advent of melanism is coincident with maximum claw length development. Because claw elongation has been demonstrated to be androgen-dependent, it is possible that the two processes are interlinked, thus strengthening the argument for a hormonal basis of melanization, as indicated in our analyses. Alternatively, melanism may simply be a non-adaptive by-product of the hormonal processes responsible for claw elongation.

Acknowledgments

Special thanks are due to the many people who assisted during this study. Judy Greene labored tirelessly at the computer to provide data on melanism from turtle populations on the Savannah River Plant. K. W. Wasmund, M. Gross, C. W. Terrell, G. O. Lawson, and S. Tunstill provided technical assistance to William R. Garstka, and Tom Atkeson, refuge manager, provided access to Wheeler Wildlife Refuge in Alabama. Laboratory space and technical support were provided by the Savannah River Ecology Laboratory, the University of Alabama in Huntsville (UAH) Research Administration, and the UAH Biological Sciences Department. Jim Spotila provided enlightening discussion on the topic of thermoregulation and color. Research and manuscript preparation were supported by contract DE-AC09-76SROO-819 between the U.S. Department of Energy and the University of Georgia's Savannah River Ecology Laboratory.

Bioenergetics

ROBERT R. PARMENTER
Department of Biology
Utah State University
Logan, Utah 84322

Current address:
Department of Biology
University of New Mexico
Albuquerque, New Mexico 87131

HAROLD W. AVERY
Department of Biology
University of California, Los Angeles
Los Angeles, California 90024-1606

20

The Feeding Ecology of the Slider Turtle

Abstract

Slider turtles (*Trachemys scripta*) are widely foraging opportunistic omnivores, consuming a diversity of aquatic vegetation, invertebrates, and, to a lesser extent, vertebrate food matter. Although their food preference is generally for animal matter, changes in feeding habits toward herbivory are observed in response to changes in proximate environmental factors (e.g., seasonal changes in food availability), as well as to ontogenetic changes and associated constraints (e.g., increased body size). Ambient temperature has a profound influence on the behavioral timing and duration of foraging, as well as on the physiological rates associated with digestion. Population studies of free-living slider turtles inhabiting comparatively warmer aquatic environments show relatively higher growth rates and/or higher reproductive output compared with those of turtles that inhabit cooler aquatic environments. Data from controlled nutritional studies indicate that associated increases in trophic productivity of food items in warmer environments may also enhance the net productivity of slider turtle populations. Dietary protein content is probably a major factor in food selection, especially among juveniles.

Introduction

The slider turtle (*Trachemys scripta*), long known for its opportunistic feeding habit, has been the subject of numerous ecological studies concerning its foraging behavior, prey selection, and digestive physiology. Research has focused on the influence of environmental factors (e.g., spatial and temporal differences in temperature regimes and food availability) on diets, growth rates, and digestive processes. Results of these studies not only have expanded our knowledge of reptilian feeding ecology but also have provided insights into ecosystem changes due to anthropogenic perturbations.

The purpose of this chapter is to review in detail the literature to date on the feeding ecology of sliders and to identify areas of relevant future research. Of necessity, this report will concentrate on *Trachemys scripta*. For general surveys of turtle feeding behavior and reptilian digestion, the reader is referred to the excellent reviews by Mahmoud and Klicka (1979) and Skoczylas (1978).

Diet Analysis Techniques

The basic data for virtually all studies on slider feeding ecology are derived from diet analyses. The examination of ingested food items can provide data on the kinds, the amounts, and ultimately the nutritional quality of food resources. Historically, assessments of slider diets have been accomplished using dissection procedures, wherein the stomachs and intestines of killed turtles are opened and examined for food items. Such dietary analyses are generally performed in concert with other studies dealing with anatomical descriptions, systematic evaluations, and reproductive capacities. Although dissection produces a complete sample of the entire digestive tract, it has the disadvantage of permitting only a single sample per turtle. Because of immense variability in diets among individuals, age classes, populations, and seasons, large numbers of turtles must be killed to characterize the diet adequately. In view of the modern ecologist's concern for wildlife conservation, techniques that result in large-scale destruction of study populations are becoming increasingly undesirable. Fortunately, alternative methods are available.

One such technique, using live captive specimens, involves laboratory feeding trials, in which the researcher offers a variety of foods to the turtles and records which items are consumed. This method yields food preference data and general diet information, although application of such data to wild populations depends largely on the researcher's ability to select a menu representative of the actual food items available in the field.

Another method of diet determination involves the analysis of feces obtained from live, recently captured specimens. Microscopic inspection of the feces can yield a reasonable species list of food items. This type of analysis has the advantages of being nondestructive to the turtle and allowing multiple samples to be taken from the same individuals over long periods of time. Unfortunately, it is exceedingly difficult to reconstruct the original meal quantitatively (including numbers, volumes, or masses of each food item) from the postdigestive remnants found in the feces. Soft-bodied insects, fruit, and meat leave little residual material, and counts of insects or seeds (reassembled from small fragments) may contain considerable sample errors.

Stomach flushing techniques (Fig. 20.1) can be used to obtain recently ingested food items (for details, see Legler, 1977; Parmenter, 1980). This method, when properly applied, has proved effective in extracting nearly all of the food items from a turtle's stomach while inflicting no permanent injury on the turtle. Food items can be readily sorted, identified, and measured. Stomach flushing allows multiple samples to be taken from individual turtles over their lifetimes and can be integrated with other nondestructive techniques for studying turtle natural history, such as radiotelemetry for movement patterns (Schubauer, 1981b; Standora, 1982) and x-ray photography of egg production (Gibbons and Greene, 1979).

The Slider's Diet

DIET COMPOSITION

The slider turtle is an opportunistic omnivore, consuming a wide variety of invertebrates, vertebrates, and vegetation (Table 20.1). Plant materials in the diet include both blue-green and green algae, as well as leaves, stems, roots, fruits, and seeds of vascular plants. Larger invertebrates are taken deliberately (flushed from or plucked off both submerged and emergent vegetation), and smaller invertebrates may be inadvertently consumed along with aquatic plants. Small fish, tadpoles, and frogs can be actively pursued and captured, although larger vertebrate food items in the diet usually result from feeding on carrion. A notable exception is given in an account by Pritchard and Trebbau (1984), in which they report that in Venezuela the Colombian slider (*T. scripta callirostris*) captures waterfowl by biting the birds' legs and pulling them underwater to drown. Although the vast majority of reported food items are aquatic organisms, some terrestrial insects and plants can be observed in the diet on occasion. These prey items presumably represent allochthonous inputs to the aquatic environment. Sliders are known to venture considerable distances on land (e.g., Bennett et al., 1970; Gibbons, 1970d), but there are few data to suggest that they regularly forage away from water, although Cagle (1944b) observed individuals moving onto land to eat terrestrial vegetation.

SEASONAL CHANGES IN DIET

Seasonal shifts in slider diet composition have been illustrated in a South Carolina population of *T. s. scripta* (Parmenter, 1980; Schubauer and Parmenter, 1981; see Table 20.1). The summer diet includes vegetation and a sub-

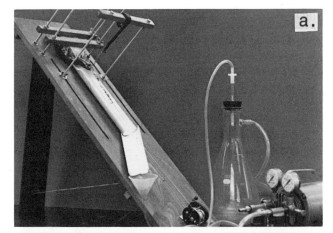

FIGURE 20.1. Turtle stomach flushing apparatus and procedure. *a*, turtle is secured in restraining braces, mouth held open by cables and fishhooks; hooks are attached to bony parts of mandible and maxilla to avoid injury to soft tissues. *b*, a flexible plastic tube connected to a running water faucet is slowly inserted down the esophagus into the stomach; food items from the stomach are flushed out of the turtle and carried down the plastic gutter into a funnel. *c*, food items are collected in a screen placed in the funnel; excess water is pulled through by a vacuum pump and collected in the sidearm flask shown in *a*.

stantial quantity and variety of animal prey. In contrast, the winter diet is composed entirely of aquatic vegetation. A similar shift from summer omnivory to winter herbivory has been observed in kinosternids (Mahmoud, 1968a). Seasonal diet changes of sliders can be partially attributed to changes in prey availability; abundance of animal prey, especially insects, decreases during winter (perhaps more so in northern regions). However, reduced prey availability does not entirely explain the observed diet shifts. Drastic declines in trapping success using fish or meat baits of otherwise omnivorous turtles (Cagle, 1950; Ernst, 1972) suggest that foraging activity or hunger levels may also be reduced. If so, consumption of easily acquired aquatic vegetation may be sufficient to meet lower energy demands.

BODY SIZE AND DIET SHIFTS

As sliders increase in body size from juveniles to adults, the diet composition changes from a fairly balanced mix of plant and animal matter to one dominated by vegetation (Fig. 20.2; Marchand, 1942; Clark and Gibbons, 1969; Moll and Legler, 1971; Hart, 1983).

Because the demand for amino acids is probably greater for faster-growing juvenile turtles than for slower-growing adults (Wood, 1974), such a dietary shift could be predicted. Energetic constraints may also partially explain why adult turtles stop feeding predominantly on animal prey. Small turtles, having less mass, use less total energy than large adults in pursuit of an animal prey item. Hence, for the same prey item, the juvenile may achieve a greater energy gain than an adult. In addition, the size of the meal is proportionally larger for the juvenile (with respect to the slider's body mass), which further enhances the energetic benefit-cost ratio of the prey encounter.

Alternatively, nonrandom distributions of animal prey in the environment may contribute to the observed diet shifts. For example, adult sliders may avoid shallow-water habitats, normally teeming with invertebrate prey, because of maneuverability constraints (Hart, 1983). Such a scenario of microhabitat exclusion could conceivably produce diet composition differences among age classes without invoking energetic models. In any case, the perhaps fortuitous outcome of juvenile carnivory is an increase in the diet of proteins and essential nutrients, particularly calcium (Clark and Gibbons, 1969), which results in faster growth and carapace development for the young slider. Similar omnivore-to-herbivore diet shifts can be observed in *Graptemys pseudogeographica* (Moll, 1976b), *Emydura krefftii* (Georges, 1982), and *Mauremys caspica* (Sidis and Gasith, 1985), whereas the reverse situation is found in *Chrysemys rubriventris* (Graham, 1971). In this latter case, juveniles (3 years old and younger) were predominantly herbivorous; but in their fourth year, they achieved sufficient body size to prey successfully on

Table 20.1. Food items of *Trachemys scripta*

Subspecies	Reference	Study location	Study period	N	Food items			
					Vegetation	Invertebrates	Vertebrates	Miscellaneous

T. s. scripta	10	South Carolina	July-Aug.	65	Algae (unspecified)
					Bacopa caroliniana
					Brasenia schreberi
					Grass (unspecified)
					Najas guadalupensis
					Nymphaea odorata
					  (seeds and leaves)
					Potamogeton sp.
					Sagittaria sp.
					Utricularia sp.
						Gastropoda: Physidae
						Insecta:
						  Coleoptera
						  Diptera
						  Hemiptera
						  Hymenoptera
						    (*Bombus*)
						  Odonata:
						    Anisoptera
						    Zygoptera
						  Orthoptera:
						    Locustidae
							Pisces
							Unknown claws
							Unknown bones
								Turtle scutes
								Pebbles, sand
								Wood

	11		Dec.-Feb.	17	*Bacopa caroliniana* *Potamogeton* sp. *Sagittaria* sp. *Utricularia* sp.			

	2	Florida	Oct., Feb.	2	Algae (unspecified)
					Ceratophyllum sp.
					Lemna sp.
					Najas sp.
						Gastropoda (crayfish
						  and shrimp)
						Insecta:
						  Odonata:
						    Anisoptera
						    Zygoptera
								Turtle scute

T. s. troostii	3	Louisiana	Oct.-June	104	Algae:
					  Cladophora sp.
					  Oscillatoria sp.
					  Spirogyra sp.
					Celtis occidentalis
					Ceratophyllum demersum
					Cornus asperifolia
					Persicaria sp.
					Piaropus crassipes
						Amphipoda
						Arachnida
						Decapoda (crayfish)
						Insecta:
						  Coleoptera
						  Diptera
						  Ephemeroptera
						  Hemiptera
						  Homoptera
						  Hymenoptera
						  Lepidoptera
						  Odonata
						  Orthoptera
						Isopoda
						Isopoda
							Amphibia
							  (frog eggs)
							Reptilia:
							  Nerodia
							  rhombifera
							Unknown bone
								Detritus
								Paper
								Watermelon
								  rind

	2	Tennessee	June-July	22	Algae: *Spirogyra* sp.
					Azolla caroliniana
					Cabomba sp.
					Caltha natans
					Ceratophyllum sp.
					Lemna sp.
					Spirodela sp.
					Wolffia sp.
					Seeds (unspecified)
						Amphipoda
						Decapoda (crayfish
						  and shrimp)
						Insecta:
						  Diptera
						  Odonata:
						    Zygoptera
						  Trichoptera
								Detritus

	1	Illinois	--	--	Aquatic vegetation
					  (unspecified)
						Decapoda (crayfish)
						Insecta (aquatic)
						Mollusca
							Pisces
							Amphibia
							  (tadpoles)	

T. s. elegans	8	Louisiana	Feb.-Dec.	88	Algae (unspecified)
					Ceratophyllum sp.
					Egeria sp.
					Eichhornia sp.
					Lemna sp.
					Limnobium sp.
					Najas sp.
					Nyssa sp.
					Potamogeton sp.
					Spirodela sp.
					Taxodium sp.
					Wolffia sp.
						Amphipoda
						Bryozoa
						Cladocera
						Decapoda (crayfish)
						Gastropoda
						Insecta:
						  Coleoptera
						  Diptera
						  Hemiptera
						  Homoptera
						  Hymenoptera
						  Odonata
						  Orthoptera
						Isopoda
						Ostracoda
						Pelecypoda
							Pisces	Wood

Table 20.1 -- *Continued*

Subspecies	Reference	Study location	Study period	N	Food items			
					Vegetation	Invertebrates	Vertebrates	Miscellaneous
	8	Illinois	Mar.-Oct.	26	*Myriophyllum* sp.	Porifera: Spongillidae Decapoda Insecta: Diptera Pelecypoda		
	5	Oklahoma	June-July	3	*Lippia incisa*			Fishhook
T. s. gaigeae	4	Mexico, Texas	June	--	Aquatic vegetation (unspecified)			
T. s. taylori	4	Mexico	Sept.	--	Vegetation (unspecified)			
T. s. grayi	10	Mexico	--	--	Vegetation (unspecified) *Ficus* sp. (fruit)	Insecta (aquatic)		
T. s. ssp.	6	Mexico, British Honduras, Honduras, Nicaragua, Costa Rica, Panama	--	78	Vegetation (unspecified, mostly grasses) Fruits, seeds (*Ficus* sp. and palm nuts)	Decapoda (crayfish) Insecta Mollusca	Vertebrates (unspecified)	
T. s. ssp.	6	Panama	Aug.-Aug.	58	Algae: *Oscillatoria* sp. *Elodea* sp. *Najas* sp. *Paspalum* sp.	Gastropoda Insecta: Blattodea Coleoptera Odonata Orthoptera Pelecypoda	Pisces	Mud
T. s. callirostris	12	Venezuela	--	--			Aves (waterfowl)	
T. s. chichiriviche	12	Venezuela	--	--	Grass (unspecified)	Decapoda (crayfish)	Pisces	

References: 1, Cahn, 1937; 2, Marchand, 1942; 3, Minyard, 1947; 4, Legler, 1960b; 5, Webb, 1961; 6, Moll and Legler, 1971; 7, Avalos, 1975; 8, Hart, 1979; 9, Smith and Smith, 1979; 10, Parmenter, 1980; 11, Schubauer and Parmenter, 1981; 12, Pritchard and Trebbau, 1984.

crayfish. A concomitant acceleration of growth was observed following the diet shift (Graham, 1971).

Foraging Behavior

GENERAL FORAGING

Slider turtles tend to forage during the day, patrolling areas of shallow water (less than 1–3 m deep), particularly in the vicinity of aquatic vegetation (if present). The shallow, littoral environment not only harbors the greatest quantities of potential food items but also possesses sufficient sunlight for sliders to identify and target their prey. Large expanses of deep, open water are generally rapidly traversed or avoided altogether. Adult and juvenile sliders further partition the foraging microhabitat, in that juveniles frequent quieter, shallower waters than adults do (Moll and Legler, 1971; Hart, 1983). Hatchling juveniles commence foraging almost immediately after

emerging from the eggs. Cagle (1946) reported that *T. s. elegans* hatchlings in Illinois had stomachs and intestines packed with food even though they still possessed unused yolk masses.

Sliders spend a considerable portion of their activity time in foraging. Moll and Legler (1971) observed three juvenile sliders that allocated a mean of 6.8 hours (range = 4 to 8.5 hours) of an 11-hour day to foraging activity. Submergence times during foraging ranged from 20 seconds to 5 minutes for juveniles, and 5 to 6 minutes for adults (Moll and Legler, 1971).

During foraging, the slider swims slowly beneath the water's surface, periodically poking its head into clumps of aquatic vegetation in an apparent effort to flush out hidden invertebrates. Sliders, especially juveniles, are attracted to prey movements and will pursue small fish, tadpoles, and frogs (much in the manner of painted turtles, *Chrysemys picta;* see Sexton, 1959b). However, such pursuits are abandoned if the prey is obviously faster than the turtle. Once captured, small prey items are swallowed

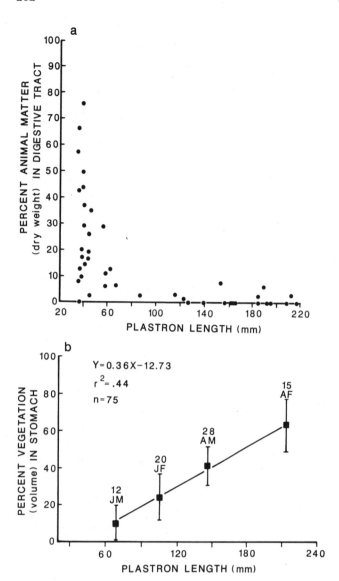

FIGURE 20.2. The relationship between diet and body size in *Trachemys scripta*, showing the diet shift from juvenile carnivory to adult herbivory. *a*, data for *T. s. scripta* from the Savannah River Plant, South Carolina; from Clark and Gibbons (1969) with permission. *b*, data for *T. s. elegans* from Lafourche Parish, Louisiana; group means (±2 SE) of plant volumes are presented for juvenile males (JM), juvenile females (JF), adult males (AM), and adult females (AF) at the mean plastron length of each group; from Hart (1983) with permission.

mouth, the water is forced out through the nostrils and between the jaws. The remaining food particles are then swallowed. The entire system functions as a crude filtration process. Neustophagia in turtles was first reported in *Podocnemis unifilis* and *Chrysemys picta* (Belkin and Gans, 1968), which were induced to feed on finely powdered foods in outdoor pond enclosures. Subsequently, this feeding strategy was reported for natural populations of *T. s. scripta* and *Chrysemys floridana peninsularis* feeding on duckweed (Lemnaceae) in a dystrophic pond in Florida (Auth, 1975). It seems probable that sliders can use this technique extensively, especially populations feeding mainly on free-floating algae and duckweed.

A potential, but as yet unobserved, slider feeding behavior is geophagy, the deliberate consumption of stones or pebbles. Such objects in reptilian stomachs may assist in mechanical grinding of larger food items, thereby promoting faster and more efficient digestion. Geophagy has been reported in *Terrapene ornata* (Skorepa, 1966), *Testudo hermanni*, *Gopherus agassizii* (Sokol, 1971), and a variety of other reptiles. Analyses to date of slider stomach contents have produced little evidence of geophagy; Parmenter (1980) noted pebbles in the stomach contents in only 2 of 65 sliders from South Carolina. No other reports on slider diet mention stones or pebbles (see Miscellaneous in Table 20.1). Hence, geophagy in sliders, if it exists at all, appears to be extremely rare.

PREY DETECTION

There is little doubt that visual detection of food items, particularly moving prey, is of paramount importance to the foraging success of the slider turtle. In *Pseudemys nelsoni* even the visual perception of other feeding turtles provides sufficient stimulus to elicit feeding behavior and increase food ingestion (Bjorndal, 1986). Olfaction also plays a role in prey detection, though its importance relative to vision is as yet unknown (Burghardt, 1970; Manton, 1979). Although turtles possess a well-developed olfactory structure in the central nervous system (Goldby and Gamble, 1957; Scott, 1979), the range and sensitivity of their olfactory organs have yet to be rigorously tested. Sliders are capable of detecting odors underwater (Cagle, 1950; Boycott and Guillery, 1962), as are kinosternids (Mahmoud, 1968a) and *Podocnemis unifilis* (Belkin and Gans, 1968). However, preliminary comparative tests suggest that sliders may be less responsive to olfactory cues than other freshwater turtle species are (e.g., *Chelydra serpentina*, *Kinosternon subrubrum*, *Deirochelys reticularia*, *Pseudemys floridana*, and *Sternotherus odoratus*—Cagle, 1950). Nevertheless, free-ranging sliders do respond to odors from fish-meat baits placed in perforated containers (Parmenter, 1980), indicating that location of carrion can be facilitated by olfactory cues.

intact, but larger prey (including plants and vertebrate carrion) are ripped into smaller pieces by the slider's powerful jaws and muscular, clawed forelegs.

Another aspect of foraging behavior, although scarcely reported for sliders, is neustophagia (Belkin and Gans, 1968), a foraging maneuver similar to that of a baleen whale. The turtle ingests tiny particles of food floating on the water's surface (neuston) by skimming the surface with its lower jaw (mouth agape), collecting water and food particles in the pharynx. When the turtle closes its

PREY SELECTION

As with any opportunistic omnivore, the selection of food items by the slider turtle is greatly influenced by local availability of prey, with the result that the most common plants and invertebrates in the environment make up the bulk of the diet (Cahn, 1937; Minyard, 1947; Avalos, 1975; Parmenter, 1980). Although most field studies of adult turtle diets show that vegetation makes up the majority of the diet (see Table 20.1), results of laboratory feeding experiments indicate that sliders actually prefer fish meat and insects to aquatic vegetation (Parmenter, 1980). These results are supported by the successful use of fish meat as turtle bait in a variety of field studies. Presumably, the prevalence of vegetation in adult slider diets reflects both the greater abundance and ease of acquisition of edible plants relative to animal prey.

Food preferences in turtles appear to be established early in the turtle's life. Laboratory studies on hatchling sliders (*T. s. elegans*—Mahmoud and Lavenda, 1969) and snapping turtles (*Chelydra serpentina*—Burghardt and Hess, 1966, and Burghardt, 1967) suggest that food preferences are greatly influenced by early feeding experiences, preferences can change with increased exposure to a wider variety of foods, and there may be innate (genetically determined) preferences for some food types.

Temperature Effects on Feeding and Digestion

The importance of environmental temperature regimes on the slider's feeding ecology cannot be overstated. Temperature influences not only foraging behavior but also virtually every physiological aspect of digestion. Seasonal changes in temperature directly affect overall foraging activity levels and diet composition (as discussed above), and daily temperature cycles control short-term behavior and digestive physiology.

Basking behavior facilitates the deviation of a turtle's body temperature away from the ambient air or water temperature, allowing the turtle to select a more potentially optimal body temperature (Boyer, 1965; Spotila et al., 1984; Schwarzkopf and Brooks, 1985; also see Chapter 22). Laboratory studies have indicated that sliders spend more time basking after ingesting food. Moll and Legler (1971) found that *T. scripta* juveniles basked significantly longer within a 48-hour period after ingesting food than when not fed for 48 hours. Gatten (1974) showed that *T. s. elegans* increases its selected body temperature from 24.5° to 29.1° C after ingesting a meal, an increase that could easily be accomplished by basking on a clear day in the wild (Auth, 1975; Standora, 1982). Hammond et al. (1988) found that fed *T. scripta* basked significantly longer than unfed sliders in spring and early summer months, but basking duration did not differ between fed and unfed groups in fall and winter months.

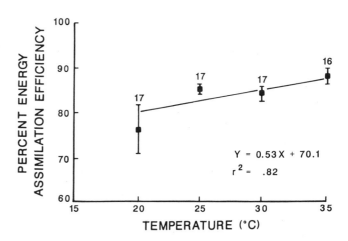

FIGURE 20.3. The effect of temperature on energy assimilation efficiency in laboratory specimens of *Chrysemys picta*, a close relative of the slider turtle. Squares are means, vertical lines are ± 2 SE, and numbers are sample sizes. From Kepenis and McManus (1974) with permission.

Various physiological aspects of turtle digestion exhibit temperature-mediated responses that could be regulated by basking behavior. For example, higher body temperatures induce greater gastric acid and enzyme secretion (Kenyon, 1925; Chesley, 1934; Anderson and Wilbur, 1948; Wright et al., 1957), faster stomach evacuation times (Fox and Musacchia, 1959), and higher intestinal motility rates (Studier et al., 1977). Protein digestion, sugar absorption, and energy assimilation proceed at faster rates with warmer body temperatures (Riddle, 1909; Fox and Musacchia, 1959; Fox, 1961; Avery, 1987). Assimilation efficiency also exhibits a modest increase at warmer temperatures (Fig. 20.3; Kepenis and McManus, 1974). As a result, the total digestive turnover time (ingestion to defecation) becomes shorter at higher temperatures (Fig. 20.4; Parmenter, 1981). These studies support the hypothesis of Cagle (1950) that basking may be an important behavior that allows sliders to optimally regulate the physiological processes of digestion through the control of body temperature.

The rate of food intake in the slider is also a function of body temperature (Fig. 20.5), with maximal ingestion occurring at 29° C (Parmenter, 1980). A similar relationship exists in the painted turtle (*Chrysemys picta*—Kepenis and McManus, 1974). Basking could enhance the ingestion rate of food, because body temperatures of postbasking sliders reentering the water remain elevated over the water temperature for several minutes (Spray and May, 1972; Schubauer and Parmenter, 1981) to a few hours (Moll and Legler, 1971).

Given the above considerations, we can hypothesize that the ultimate effect of elevated turtle body temperature would be a faster growth rate and earlier attainment of sexual maturity (assuming an adequate food supply). In support of this, Porter and Tracy (1983) demonstrated

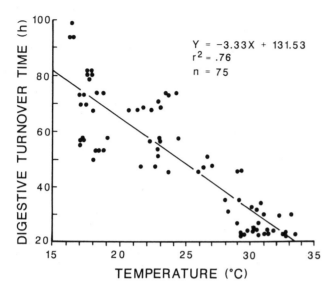

FIGURE 20.4. The effect of temperature on the digestive turnover time in laboratory specimens of *Chrysemys picta*. Turnover time is the residence time of a food item in the turtle from ingestion to defecation. From Parmenter (1981) with permission.

that growth and the attainment of sexual maturity in desert iguanas (*Dipsosaurus dorsalis*) are significantly accelerated in thermally favorable microenvironments in the laboratory; desert iguanas sexually matured in about seven months instead of the four to seven years required in nature, presumably at the same body size. However, definitive laboratory studies addressing the magnitude of temperature effects on slider growth rates and age at sexual maturity are presently lacking.

Diet Quality and Environmental Effects on Slider Growth

NUTRITIONAL REQUIREMENTS

In addition to temperature, the quality and quantity of available food in the slider's environment can have a profound effect on growth rate and maturation time. Unfortunately, age-specific feeding behavior and nutritional requirements of turtles are among the least-known aspects of their feeding ecology. The quantities and nutritional qualities of ingested foods are critical components of ecological energy budgets and growth models (Porter and Tracy, 1983), yet these data are often lacking in such studies (e.g., Glidewell, 1984). Requisite parameters for such models include prey caloric values; proportions of carbohydrates, fats, and proteins; and concentrations of essential dietary components, that is, vitamins, mineral salts, and specific amino and fatty acids that cannot be biosynthesized. The determination of the feeding rates and nutritional quality of food consumed by wild slider populations, combined with an understanding of the

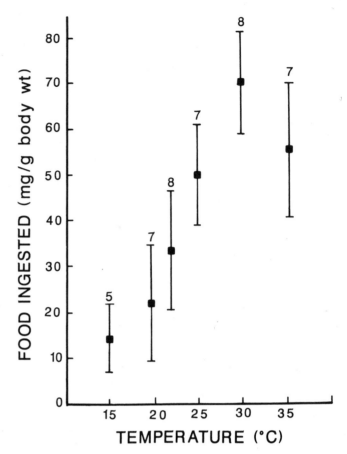

FIGURE 20.5. The effect of temperature on ingestion in laboratory specimens of the slider turtle *Trachemys scripta scripta*. Points are means, vertical lines are ± 2 SE, and numbers are sample sizes. From Parmenter (1980) with permission.

effects of environmental fluctuation and perturbation on these values, is therefore essential for the development of energy budgets and growth models.

The first dietary study on turtle growth rates was conducted by Pearse et al. (1925). Diets containing a mix of protein, carbohydrates, vitamins, and essential nutrients promoted faster turtle growth than "pure" diets consisting of a single food type. Recent work by Avery (1987) has demonstrated that the protein content of the slider's diet dramatically influences its growth rate, with high-protein foods promoting rapid increases in both turtle body size and mass (Fig. 20.6). In addition, sliders that were fed on foods containing only 10% crude protein exhibited a curling of the posterior plastron, thereby reducing their overall shell size (Fig. 20.6*b*; Avery, 1987).

From Figure 20.6 it is clear that slider turtles require more than 10% crude protein in their diet in order to grow properly. Boyd (1970) found that the mean crude protein content of aquatic plants from Par Pond, South Carolina, was 13.1% ± 1.3%, a concentration similar to that of the lowest-protein diet fed to turtles in Avery's study. Fish carrion is the other predominant food source available to

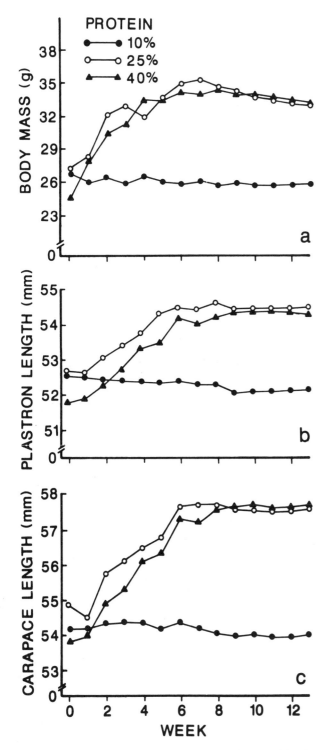

FIGURE 20.6.   Growth-related changes in body mass (a), plastron length (b), and carapace length (c) of captive juvenile sliders (*T. scripta*) raised on ad libitum rations of variable protein diets. Ration energy content and other nutrient concentrations were equal for all treatment groups. Sliders given diets of 25% and 40% protein exhibited significantly faster growth than sliders fed a diet of 10% protein (one-way ANOVA and Tukey test for treatment differences, $p < .0001$, $N = 20$ sliders per group; Avery, 1987).

Par Pond juvenile sliders and has a crude protein concentration of about 20%, which is comparable to that of the 25% crude protein diet in Figure 20.6. Data from this study indicate that carnivory, or omnivory with a significant amount of fish or other dietary protein, may be essential to maintain the high juvenile growth rates exhibited by free-living juvenile sliders. These growth data therefore provide nutritional reasons for the marked carnivory observed in the first year of slider growth (Clark and Gibbons, 1969) and support the hypothesis that varying dietary protein availability accounts for differences in growth rates of sliders from different populations in the same geographic area (Gibbons, 1970b; Parmenter, 1980).

Data on other nutrient requirements of sliders are currently unavailable; however, nutritionally essential amino acids have been identified for the green turtle *Chelonia mydas* (Wood, 1974), and quantitative requirements for each amino acid have been determined for optimal weight gain in juveniles (F. Wood and Wood, 1977; J. Wood and Wood, 1977). Some of the amino acids essential for juvenile green turtle growth are found in only limited quantities in plants (J. Wood and Wood, 1977). As a result, green turtle growth rates and reproductive output decrease because of the nutrient limitation in their diets (Bjorndal, 1985). If juvenile sliders have similar qualitative and quantitative amino acid requirements, high amounts of animal protein in the diet should facilitate rapid growth. Hence, juvenile carnivory would be advantageous for attaining larger body size and earlier sexual maturity.

Although dietary nutritional requirements for sliders are as yet undetermined, some insight into the importance of diet quality on slider health and growth can be obtained from accounts of reptile nutritional disorders reported in the veterinary medicine literature (e.g., Frye, 1973; Jackson and Cooper, 1981). We now know that reptiles, like other vertebrates, are susceptible to various maladies resulting from nutritional deficiencies or excesses. For example, dietary protein deficiencies lead to body emaciation and muscle atrophy, and insufficient quantities of vitamins A and B_1 cause degradation of a variety of body tissues. Scurvy (caused by a vitamin C deficiency) appears to be rare in reptiles. However, rickets (caused by a vitamin D deficiency) has been reported in reptiles, as have goiters (from iodine deficiency) and steatitis (from vitamin E deficiency). Calcium deficiencies are particularly well documented in sliders. A dietary imbalance in the calcium-phosphorus ratio, which normally should remain between 1:1 and 1.5:1, causes osteodystrophy in turtles and results in shell and bone deformations (Frye, 1973). Similarly, excess concentrations of some dietary nutrients cause debilitating diseases in reptiles, such as an excess of vitamin D, which results in anorexia and lameness (Jackson and Cooper, 1981). In summary, it is clear that diet nutritional quality can have a major influence on the growth and physical health of the slider turtle; however, we emphasize that the extent of nutritional disorders in natural populations of slider turtles is currently unknown.

ENVIRONMENTAL EFFECTS ON DIET AND GROWTH

Correlations between growth rates in wild turtles and diet quality (or estimates of environmental food abundance) show that highly productive habitats tend to produce larger turtles with accelerated growth rates. Exceptionally rapid growth rates have been observed in turtle populations inhabiting environments characterized by naturally high organic levels (Moll, 1976b) or artificially altered environments, such as chemically polluted rivers (Gibbons, 1967b; Knight and Gibbons, 1968) and thermally altered reservoirs (Gibbons, 1970b; Christy et al., 1974; Avalos, 1975; Thornhill, 1982).

Turtles inhabiting thermally altered habitats may experience an interaction effect between temperature and diet, in that thermal loading of the environment may (1) promote greater productivity at all trophic levels, thereby increasing the quantity and quality of available food resources, (2) extend the turtle growing season into early spring and late autumn (for high-latitude populations), and/or (3) raise turtle body temperatures, influencing behavior, metabolic rates, and digestive processes. For example, sliders exhibiting high growth rates from Par Pond, South Carolina (a highly productive nuclear reactor cooling reservoir), ingest twice as much protein (fish carrion and insects) in their diet as slower-growing sliders from a farm pond and a Carolina Bay (Parmenter, 1980). Water temperatures differ somewhat (4° to 6° C) among these habitats, and although reservoir turtles in this study were not captured in the thermally altered areas, temperature effects on this population may have influenced their feeding behavior. Winter activity and feeding occur in the Par Pond population (Schubauer and Parmenter, 1981) but are not observed in other nearby populations. In contrast, slider populations from both a reactor cooling reservoir (Lake Baldwin, Illinois) and two natural lakes have similar diets, yet individuals in the reservoir population exhibit a faster growth rate (Avalos, 1975; Thornhill, 1982). In this case, temperature differences alone among habitats (4° to 8° C) may allow increased foraging by reservoir turtles and/or cause a longer growing season.

In addition to populations in artificially heated environments, there are examples of slider populations that inhabit naturally warm, shallow-water habitats, rich in high-protein food resources, and also show high growth rates and large body size. Sliders living in shallow roadside ditches in Illinois consume massive quantities of insects (Cagle, 1946), and sliders in pools on the Atlantic coast barrier islands feast on an inexhaustible supply of euryhaline fishes (Gibbons et al., 1979).

The synergistic effect of diet quality and temperature on slider feeding ecology has been examined recently in laboratory experiments. Avery (1987) measured consumption rates, digestion rates, and digestive efficiencies in captive sliders at four temperatures (15°, 22°, 28°, and 34° C) while using three diet qualities (10%, 25%, and 40% ration protein content). Not only did Avery find that sliders displayed greater consumption rates, digestion rates, and digestive efficiencies at warmer temperatures, but he also discovered a significant interaction effect of temperature and diet quality on digestion rates and digestive efficiencies. He demonstrated that sliders feeding on high-protein rations exhibit a disproportionately greater temperature response in their digestion rate than sliders feeding on low-protein rations. Such a physiological synergism would undoubtedly contribute to the observed growth rates and large body sizes recorded in slider populations from highly productive, warm-water habitats.

Thus, environmental temperature and trophic productivity are fundamentally important environmental factors influencing the feeding ecology of *T. scripta*. Further studies are needed to determine the interactive effects of temperature, food abundance, and food quality on feeding rates, digestive physiology, growth, and development of sliders under natural thermal conditions, with natural food types from different habitats, and with different age classes. Determining the essential nutritional requirements for slider growth and development and assessing the naturally ingested food types for the availability of these nutrients (e.g., essential amino acids, calcium) would greatly enhance our understanding of differential growth exhibited among and within wild slider populations.

Acknowledgments

Research and manuscript preparation were made possible by contract DE-AC09-76SROO-819 between the University of Georgia and the U.S. Department of Energy and by National Science Foundation grant DEB-79-04758.

THOMAS G. HINTON
DAVID E. SCOTT
Savannah River Ecology Laboratory
Drawer E
Aiken, South Carolina 29802

21

Radioecological Techniques for Herpetology, with an Emphasis on Freshwater Turtles

Abstract

Radioisotopes, in concert with other techniques, can address important ecological research questions. In this chapter we review the literature regarding the historic uses of radionuclides in herpetology, with an emphasis on freshwater turtles. Two of the classic techniques—the estimation of field metabolic rates using doubly labeled water and the determination of feeding rates of free-ranging animals using ^{22}Na—have had limited success on freshwater turtles; we describe why and suggest possible alternatives. The chapter also contains sections on (1) a comparison of fallout radionuclide concentrations found in turtles to those found in other organisms; (2) the relative radiosensitivity of turtles; (3) the use of radioactive tags in studies concerned with population dynamics; (4) energetics, feeding-rate estimations, and metabolic research, including the uptake and elimination rate of specific isotopes; (5) kinship determinations using radionuclides; (6) the use of radioisotopes to determine the functional aspects of ecosystems; and (7) miscellaneous topics, including the use of radioactive tags for rate-of-passage measurements in the gastrointestinal tract. An appendix presents a short description of radionuclide kinetics. Overall, this chapter provides an introduction to the field of radioecology and, specifically, acquaints the reader with the utility of radioisotopes in herpetological research.

Introduction

Over the past 40 years the use of radionuclide techniques in the biological and physical sciences has increased dramatically (Schultz and Whicker, 1982). A discipline called radioecology has developed that (1) uses radioisotopes as tracers to study biological or ecological processes, (2) determines the accumulation and movement rates of radioisotopes in the environment, and (3) studies the effects of radiation on organisms, populations, communities, and ecosystems. In the study of ecosystems these techniques have led to advances in the understanding and measurement of primary productivity, food-web dynamics, nutrient cycling, and various abiotic processes (e.g., water flux, sediment movement). Population ecology has been enhanced by the development of radioactive tracer techniques that allow important parameters such as home range size and age-specific dispersal to be estimated. At the level of the individual, radiological techniques have allowed numerous physiological and behavioral questions to be addressed.

In this chapter we review the literature regarding historic uses of radionuclides in the study of freshwater turtles, particularly the yellow-bellied slider, *Trachemys scripta scripta*. We also describe the primary radiological techniques and summarize how they may be used in the study of turtle populations. It is interesting that certain radiological techniques, which have been used successfully in the study of terrestrial organisms, have not worked for aquatic turtles; we describe why and suggest viable alternatives. In general, there is a paucity in reptilian, particularly turtle, radiological research relative to the volume of work conducted on mammals and fish. Consequently, we examine radiological studies of other ectotherms and homeotherms to depict the potential use of a given technique on turtles. We also compare turtles with other organisms with respect to sensitivity to radiation and the uptake and elimination of radionuclides. The lack of data limited comparisons and forced us to concentrate on two widely studied radionuclides in mammalian species: cesium-137 and strontium-90. Strontium, a chemical analogue of calcium, accumulates mainly in bone, whereas cesium, because of its similarity to potassium, resides primarily in muscle. Both nuclides are relatively mobile within the environment and have been the subject of substantial research because of their worldwide distribution as a result of fallout from aboveground nuclear testing and inadvertent releases from nuclear production facilities.

Radioecological research usually deals with one of four classes of radioactive materials. The first is the naturally occurring primordial nuclides and their daughter products, such as the decay chains of uranium-238 and thorium-232, each of which contains radioactive isotopes of many different elements. The parent nuclides have half-lives on the order of 10^9 years and are found at low levels in soils. The disequilibrium of the parent nuclides with their daughter products often allows their use in determining the age of biological materials and studying geochemical cycles (Ivanovich and Harmon, 1982). If nuclide migration within a "system" (as defined by the researcher and representing a single organ, an organism, a community, or an ecosystem) has not occurred for a time that is long,

relative to the half-life of the parent nuclide, then the activities (the transformation rate of radioactive elements) of all the daughter nuclides should be equal to the activity of the parent (i.e., secular equilibrium). However, chemical and physical processes in most environments cause differential migrations of elements, resulting in breaks in the radioactive decay chains. Under these circumstances, a member of the series is separated from its parent and subsequently decays at a rate determined by its own half-life. The activity of the parent nuclides is no longer equal to the activities of the daughters (i.e., disequilibrium), and relationships correlated to chronology may then be developed.

The second broad area of radioecological research is centered around irradiation of organisms or communities with high-energy gamma sources. This technique has been used to determine the dose required to cause various kinds of damage to individuals and to determine effects on populations and communities. Results have been summarized for plant communities by Whicker and Fraley (1974) and for animal populations by Turner (1975).

The third area involves administering radioactive tracers to organisms to determine percent assimilation and the subsequent elimination rate of the tracer or to determine transfer rates between system compartments (Whicker and Schultz, 1982). The behavior and movement of stable elements can also be determined through the use of radioactive tracers. Such techniques document not only the movement of materials but, more important, the rate of movement; thus one can examine the functional aspects of a system. Transfer rates between system compartments can then be used in environmental-transport or bioaccumulation models to understand and predict fundamental processes. The use of this technique with regard to turtles will be described in detail later in this chapter. It is important to realize that with the sensitivity of today's instruments, the quantity of a tracer necessary for measurement is often incredibly small (typically less than 10^{-15} g, with a level of radioactivity comparable to that found in the household smoke alarm).

The fourth class of radionuclides used in radioecological studies is those present in elevated levels as a result of anthropogenic releases from nuclear production facilities, reactors, weapons testing, mining and milling, waste disposal, and so on. One can often make positive use of these circumstances in ecological research. For example, in the preface of *Forevermore: Nuclear Waste in America*, Barlett and Steele (1985) described a scenario in which "the turtles that creep along the banks of the Savannah River near Aiken, South Carolina, are radioactive." Although this is a sensational statement, it is true that some turtles in the area (but probably very few, if any, in the Savannah River) contain elevated levels of radionuclides as a result of the operations of the Savannah River Plant (SRP), a nuclear fuels production facility located near Aiken. Populations of these contaminated turtles have been the subject of substantial research, advancing our knowledge of turtle ecology with respect to long-distance terrestrial movement (Morreale et al., 1984), seasonal changes in field metabolic rates (Scott et al., 1986), and radionuclide kinetics (Peters, 1986). Many of the data presented in this chapter were generated from studying these populations.

Use of Radioisotopes in Turtle Research

We categorize our discussion of the radioecological studies of turtles into eight sections that include a compilation of radionuclide concentrations in turtles and other organisms, a discussion of the radiosensitivity of these organisms, and various topics for which radiological techniques provide a useful research tool. These include terrestrial movement in turtles, metabolic studies, feeding rates in free-ranging animals, kinship studies, ecosystem analysis, and miscellaneous topics.

Before a discussion of the various radionuclide techniques can be meaningful, some background knowledge of kinetics is essential (details are presented in Appendix 21.1). In the present context, "kinetics" refers to the transfer of radionuclides into, within, and out of a system. Radionuclide kinetics depend upon numerous extrinsic and intrinsic factors. Extrinsic factors include the type of radionuclide, geochemical characteristics of the environment, and temperature. Important intrinsic parameters are body size, age, sex, metabolic rate, and physical condition (Reichle et al., 1970). Processes whereby an organism can accumulate radionuclides are, therefore, affected by properties of the radionuclide, the organism, and the ecosystem (Whicker, 1983).

RADIONUCLIDE CONCENTRATIONS

Radiological assessment and general understanding require determining the concentrations of isotopes within organisms. This information can give us insights into (1) the relative accumulation of isotopes by comparing radionuclide concentrations among organisms, (2) the behavior of radionuclides within a system, (3) potential food-chain transport, and (4) dose estimates to the organisms from the internally deposited nuclides. Comparisons among organisms are seldom straightforward, because it is often not known if the reported values represent equilibrium conditions. This is particularly true for ^{90}Sr, which may take a long time to reach equilibrium in calcareous tissues. It has been shown that radionuclide concentrations can be affected by season (Scott et al., 1986), age (McClellan et al., 1962; Della Rosa et al., 1965), temperature (Nakahara et al., 1977; Storr et al., 1982), body surface area and/or mass (Richmond, 1958; Stara et al., 1971), chemical nutrient content in the environment (Agnedal, 1967; Whicker et al., 1972), and metabolic rate

(Reichle et al., 1970). Concentrations of fission products in the biota from fallout also vary with year and geographical location (Whicker and Schultz, 1982).

Holcomb et al. (1971) were the first to report levels of radioactivity in the exoskeletons of turtles. They examined ^{90}Sr concentrations from nuclear fallout in the shells of eight species ($N = 102$) from six southeastern states. Individuals varied in ^{90}Sr concentrations from 0 to 10.4 Bq/g bone ash. (A Becquerel, or Bq, is the International System of Units measurement of radioactivity equal to one disintegration per second.[1]) Holcomb noted a tendency for specimens from Florida ($N = 7$) to differ from specimens of other regions in ^{90}Sr concentrations. Jackson et al. (1974) also analyzed ^{90}Sr levels in turtles from the Southeast ($N = 73$) and found geographic differences in concentrations. Consistently low concentrations were found in Florida species taken from a fast-flowing spring habitat of limestone origin. The authors attributed this to the possible removal of ^{90}Sr fallout by ion exchange and the quick transport of direct fallout away from the area by the rapid flow of water. With the exception of the limestone spring habitat, aquatic turtle species exhibited reasonably uniform concentrations.

Species differences in radionuclide concentrations can be related to differences in diet. Hanson (1967) has shown that caribou generally contain higher levels of ^{90}Sr than other ungulates because of the caribou's consumption of lichens. Lichens absorb radionuclides from air and precipitation with remarkable efficiency and thus contain radionuclide concentrations higher than most other vegetation. There is some evidence that the gopher tortoise (*Gopherus polyphemus*) accumulates higher concentrations of ^{90}Sr than other species of turtles. This is shown in Figure 21.1, a graph of the pooled data sets of Holcomb et al. (1971) and Jackson et al. (1974) along with ^{90}Sr concentration data for other organisms. The mean ^{90}Sr concentration in the ashed shell of *Gopherus* is higher than in other turtles. Jackson et al. (1974) attributed this difference to the herbivorous diet of *Gopherus*, in that ^{90}Sr levels are generally higher in vegetation than in upper trophic levels, thus possibly explaining why the ^{90}Sr concentrations are lower in the carnivorous and omnivorous turtles.

Fallout concentration levels of ^{90}Sr in turtles are similar to those found in other organisms (Fig. 21.1). The exoskeleton of a "shelled mammal," the nine-banded armadillo (*Dasypus novemcinctus*), contained 0.4 to 4.6 Bq/g bone ash of ^{90}Sr (Jackson et al., 1972). Strontium levels in an ectotherm (trout) from mountain lakes in Colorado

---

[1]The traditional, comparable unit of radioactivity is the picocurie (pCi), and 1 Bq = 27 pCi. For comparison, Bennett (1971) estimated the average daily dietary intake of ^{90}Sr for humans in New York as 0.43 Bq. Strontium-90 concentrations in New York City tap water reached a peak of 0.08 Bq/l in 1963 (Eisenbud, 1973). The Department of Energy allows deer hunters to take home animals harvested on federal property if Cs body burdens are less than 3.7 Bq/g (Brisbin, pers. comm.).

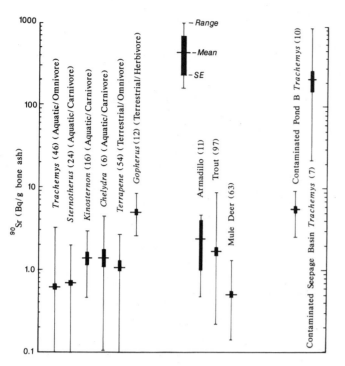

FIGURE 21.1.   Fallout ^{90}Sr concentrations (Bq/g bone ash) in turtles (from the pooled data sets of Holcomb et al., 1971, and Jackson et al., 1974), other organisms (armadillo, Jackson et al., 1972; trout, Whicker et al., 1972; mule deer, Whicker et al., 1967), and turtles from contaminated environments (Towns, 1987). Sample sizes are given in parentheses.

ranged from 0.2 to 8.8 Bq/g bone ash (Whicker et al., 1972), and the range found in Colorado deer was 0.1 to 1.3 Bq/g (Whicker et al., 1967).

Under conditions where the level of radioactivity is increased, turtles, like other organisms, assimilate higher concentrations of radioisotopes. Towns (1987) measured the Sr and Cs levels in *Trachemys* inhabiting a contaminated cooling reservoir (Pond B) on the Savannah River Plant. Strontium-90 concentrations ranged from 2.7 to 9.2 Bq/g bone ash with a mean of 5.6, three times the mean concentration found in turtles contaminated by fallout ^{90}Sr (Jackson et al., 1974). Mean ^{137}Cs concentrations were 0.9 Bq/g whole-body wet weight in the animals from Pond B (Towns, 1987).

Isolated contaminated seepage basins on the SRP have radioactivity levels considerably above the level of Pond B. Seven *Trachemys* from one such basin had mean ^{90}Sr concentrations of 230 Bq/g bone ash, with a range of 20 to 930 (Fig. 21.1; Towns, 1987). Mean ^{137}Cs concentrations were 5.7 Bq/g whole-body wet weight. To our knowledge, the highest measured ^{90}Sr concentration in a turtle was in a 482 g female *T. scripta* captured in a contaminated seepage basin. Its radioactivity levels were above the quantitative limits of a Geiger-Müller counter (80,000 counts per minute). Subsequent analysis of the animal by the Du Pont company's Savannah River Laboratory re-

vealed ^{90}Sr levels of approximately 1,850 Bq/g bone ash. Analysis of ^{137}Cs in muscle tissue yielded 63 Bq/g wet weight (Garrett, 1986). For comparison, the maximum ^{137}Cs concentration from waterfowl collected on a radioactive leaching pond at the Idaho National Engineering Laboratory was 150 Bq/g flesh wet weight (Halford et al., 1981). Obviously, turtles are not unique in their ability to concentrate high levels of radiation. The point is that as the level of radionuclide exposure increases, so do the radionuclide concentrations in the biota. Not knowing the various levels of radiation exposure in the above discussion makes comparisons difficult. It appears from Figure 21.1 that under normal conditions turtles do not accumulate unusual concentrations (Bq/g) of radionuclides when compared with other organisms. However, the high proportion of bone tissue in turtles ($\approx$42% of their total mass; Towns, 1987) will result in turtles' having a greater ^{90}Sr total body burden (Bq) than unshelled animals of similar mass have. A more direct comparison is afforded by the examination of radionuclide concentrations in the biota from a single location and through the use of concentration ratios. Both concepts are explored further in the section Ecosystem Analysis, below.

RADIOSENSITIVITY

In an attempt to determine the sensitivity of organisms to radiation, many researchers have established the "median lethal dose" by irradiating organisms and determining the dose at which 50% of them die within a specified time frame (e.g., 30 days in most mammalian studies, designated as $LD_{50[30]}$). Lethal dose experiments with reptiles and amphibians are generally carried out for a longer period to achieve 50% mortality ($LD_{50[90]}$ or $LD_{50[120]}$) because of a longer latency period (the time before which radiation effects are manifested). When animals survive for prolonged periods following irradiation, a median lethal dose based on 30 days gives falsely high LD_{50} values (Sparrow et al., 1970; Willis and Lappenbush, 1975).

Differences in latency periods can be due to temperature. Cooler temperatures lengthen the mean survival time in exposed amphibians (Patt and Swift, 1948; Allen et al., 1951; O'Brien and Gojmerac, 1956) and hibernating ground squirrels (Barr and Musacchia, 1972). Other factors such as reduced radiation exposure, long mitotic cycle times, and slower rates of cell renewal are likely to lengthen the latency period (Patt and Quastler, 1963). Differences in laboratory versus field conditions and in the feeding regime of test animals also make LD_{50} comparisons difficult. General trends do exist, however, and Whicker and Schultz (1982) have provided a relative ranking of radiosensitivities in various taxa (Fig. 21.2). Within taxa, the lower end of the range includes the most sensitive species and life stages, and the upper end generally represents adults of the most resistant species.

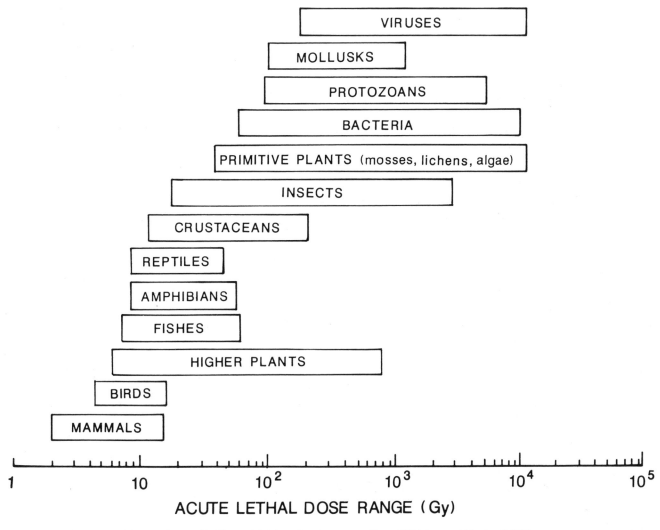

FIGURE 21.2.   Radiosensitivities of various taxa. From Whicker and Shultz (1982).

Generally, reptiles are less sensitive to radiation than mammals are; however, caution should be applied when comparing individual species, because of the problems mentioned above. Comparative radiosensitivity, according to Sparrow et al. (1970), should be based on the lowest exposure required to reach a given end point without regard to the length of the postirradiation period. LD_{50} values should be determined only after enough time has elapsed that most or all of the radiation-induced deaths have occurred. We have compiled the LD_{50} values for turtles and representative values for other taxa (Table 21.1). Unfortunately, it is not possible to tell if the recommendations of Sparrow et al. (1970) were followed by the original researchers. It is particularly questionable on those groups of animals that were followed for only 30 days (lizards, ducks, and rodents). If radiation-induced deaths were still occurring after 30 days, then the reported LD_{50} is too high. With these limitations in mind, the data from Table 21.1 suggest that if the herpetofauna were ranked according to radiosensitivity, turtles would

probably occupy an upper position (i.e., they are more resistant).

An alternative approach in comparing the radiosensitivity of organisms is related to characteristics of the cell nucleus. The relationship of radiosensitivity of plants to nuclear volume, chromosomal volume, and DNA content is well documented (Sparrow, 1962; Sparrow and Sparrow, 1965). Increased sensitivity is related to a large nucleus volume, a large interphase chromosome volume, and a large amount of DNA per chromosome (Kaplan and Moses, 1964; Sparrow et al., 1967; Sparrow et al., 1968). The radiosensitivities of various amphibian species, which are known to have the greatest range of nuclear size of any vertebrate class, have been compared by Conger and Clinton (1973). Their results were similar to those found for plants: There is a positive correlation between nuclear volume and radiosensitivity.

Using this concept to examine the radiosensitivity of turtles was not productive. The DNA content per cell in turtles is similar to that found in a wide variety of other

Table 21.1. LD$_{50}$ values for various taxa

Organism	LD$_{50}$ (Sv)	Postirradiation period (d)	Reference
Turtles			
Box turtle	10–15	--	3
	10.3	120 (adult)	10
Chelydra	<8	120 (juvenile)	10
Chrysemys	<10	120 (juvenile)	10
Terrapene	8.5	120	4
Lizards			
Sceloporus	15	--	8
Uta	10–12	30	5
	17–22	30	6
Snakes			
Elaphe, Coluber	3–4	90	4,10
Frogs			
Hyla	11.2	50	12
Rana	7	730	2
	7.2	730	9
	7.8	150	12
Fish			
Goldfish	8	--	1
Salamanders			
Desmognathus	5.3	70	9
Necturus	0.8	200	9
	<2	180	12
Notophthalmus	4.7	150	12
Ducks			
Blue-winged teal	7.2	30	7
Green-winged teal	4.8	30	7
Shoveler	8.9	30	7
Rodents			
Citellus	12.6	30	11
Ochotona	3.8–5.6	30	11
Peromyscus	9.2–11.5	30	11
Rattus	9.5–13.3	30	11
Humans	3–6	30	13

References: 1, Ellinger, 1940; 2, Stearner, 1950; 3, Altland et al., 1951; 4, Cosgrove, 1965; 5, Dana and Tinkle, 1965; 6, Turner et al., 1967; 7, Tester et al., 1968; 8, Willis and McCourry, 1968; 9, Sparrow et al., 1970; 10, Cosgrove, 1971; 11, Sacher and Staffeldt, 1971; 12, Conger and Clinton, 1973; 13, Whicker and Schultz, 1982.

organisms (Shapiro, 1968). Given this overlap, it is not possible to predict the relative radiosensitivity of turtles based on their nuclear volume. However, based on this very limited data base (Fig. 21.2; Table 21.1; Shapiro, 1968), turtles do not appear to differ substantially from other reptiles, amphibians, or fish in sensitivity to radiation. If a larger data base were available, we suspect that turtles would be found to be less sensitive to external radiation than most of the other herpetofauna, if for no other reason than that the carapace provides an approximate 20% shielding (Cosgrove, 1971).

TERRESTRIAL MOVEMENT

Numerous studies concerned with population dynamics have used radioactive tagging techniques to determine home range size and dispersal distances (reviewed in Schultz and Whicker, 1982). Pendleton (1956) described the advantages of marking animals with radionuclides as (1) the animal is generally unaware of the presence of the

isotope; (2) isotopes are generally easy to apply to large numbers of animals; (3) the radioactive tag becomes part of the animal, with little danger of the identifying device's being lost; and (4) accurate observation can often be made without interference by the observer. Ferner (1979) also discussed radioactive tagging in his review of marking techniques for reptiles and amphibians. Radiotags are especially useful with burrowing animals, and because of the uniqueness of this technique, we have included a brief review of the findings. Karlstrom (1957) used radioactive cobalt (^{60}Co) wire as a tag to recover toads (*Bufo canorus*) in the field. Breckenridge and Tester (1961) documented the subsurface vertical migration of *Bufo hemiophrys* during hibernation by using radioactive tantalum (^{182}Ta) tags. Both radionuclides are high-energy gamma emitters that can be easily detected in the field with a Geiger-Müller counter or scintillometer. Breckenridge and Tester (1961) could detect an animal on the surface at a distance of 6 m, and an animal under 0.5 m of water was detected 1.5 m away.

Several studies have used ^{182}Ta tags to examine terrestrial movement of salamanders (Madison and Shoop, 1970; Shoop and Doty, 1972; Shoop, 1974; Semlitsch, 1981a; Semlitsch, 1983). Semlitsch (1981b) stated that the effect of the radioactive tag itself on the mole salamander (*Ambystoma talpoideum*) was not a problem for short-term studies (i.e., less than a month). He did, however, document discoloration of the skin area adjacent to 1.5 MBq ^{182}Ta tags 40 days after implantation. At 50–80 days, the skin around the tag ulcerated. By the end of 100 days, 83% of the salamanders had lost their tags. Both Ashton (1975), who also worked with salamanders, and Hirth et al. (1969), who tracked the dispersal of three snake species from a hibernaculum in Utah, reported tag loss due to ulceration. Neither Barbour et al. (1969) nor Madison and Shoop (1970) reported problems in their use of ^{60}Co tags (1.7 MBq) on *Desmognathus fuscus* and ^{182}Ta tags (0.7–1.8 MBq) on *Plethodon jordani*. Several studies on lizard species have successfully used similar tagging techniques (O'Brien et al., 1965; Fitch and von Achen, 1977).

Terrestrial activity of aquatic turtles was monitored by Bennett et al. (1970) using tantalum pins. The pins were easily attached in holes drilled in the carapace of three species (*Kinosternon subrubrum, Trachemys scripta,* and *Deirochelys reticularia*). Twenty-seven *K. subrubrum* were radioactively tagged, of which 20 were recaptured. Individuals generally moved short distances (m/day) and then burrowed below the litter (2–11 cm deep) but occasionally moved 10 m/day. Movement ceased in December. The technique revealed that *K. subrubrum* adults normally overwinter on land away from their aquatic habitat. Fewer *T. scripta* and *D. reticularia* were tagged, but in general these two species were found not to move as far from the site as *K. subrubrum.* Ward et al. (1976) used Bennett's technique to determine seasonal habits of the spotted turtle (*Clemmys guttata*). At the start of the study, turtles were detected at distances as great as 10 m. The technique permitted Ward to locate estivating turtles burrowed under moist, loosely matted vegetation.

Morreale et al. (1984) measured radioisotope levels in previously contaminated *T. scripta* to examine the differences in long-range movements between males and females. Contaminated radioactive sediments and food items are present in some catchment basins on the SRP. Turtles inhabiting these basins incorporate varying levels of radioisotopes into their tissues. Before 1982, individuals could migrate from unfenced, contaminated sites to nearby natural aquatic sites. Thus, turtles with abnormally large radioactivity levels found in uncontaminated sites could be assumed to represent a relocation. This observation, coupled with 16 years of mark-recapture data, allowed Morreale et al. (1984) to assess sexual differences in movement. More males moved among bodies of water than females, and males moved greater distances. Fourteen of 15 radioactive turtles emigrating from catchment basins were males. In addition, females captured within the basins exhibited higher levels of radioactivity than males, possibly an indication of their tendency to be more sedentary. These results were interpreted as evidence for differences in the sexual strategy of males and females.

Generally, more information on field movements of organisms can be gained with radiotransmitter technology than with radioactive tagging. Current transmitter techniques often allow the researcher to obtain data on parameters such as body temperature and heart rate, as well as location of the organism. In current studies of turtle movements within and among populations, it is doubtful that radioisotope tracking techniques would be superior to conventional radiotransmitter methods. The exception to this may be in the study of hatchling dispersal from the nest cavity or in the study of small species such as *K. subrubrum*. Radiotransmitters are, in general, too large to be used on such animals, whereas some form of radioactive tag might be useful.

METABOLIC STUDIES

Perhaps the greatest potential use of radioisotopes in turtle research is in energetics and metabolic studies. Such techniques may prove profitable in two areas of interest: (1) the determination of field metabolic rates and (2) the metabolic study of specific elements from which rate constants among system compartments can be determined. The prospects for both areas are outlined below.

FIELD METABOLIC RATES. Water containing stable and/or radioactive tracers has been used to measure water, energy, and material fluxes in many species of animals (Lifson and McClintock, 1966; Nagy, 1975). Water flux through

an animal can be estimated with deuterium (^{2}H) or tritium (^{3}H). Tritium is easier to measure and is used in most studies. The ^{3}H is injected into the animal and allowed to equilibrate with the body water of the animal (which takes one to four hours, depending on the organism's size). Blood samples are then periodically taken from the free-ranging animal. The ^{3}H will decline through time because of water loss due to evaporation and excreta as well as the simultaneous dilution of the ^{3}H by metabolic water production and the intake of food and liquids (Nagy, 1982). The rate of decrease in the specific activity of ^{3}H is an estimate of the water flux. The ^{3}H is analyzed with a liquid scintillation counter after microdistilling the blood samples (Wood et al., 1975). Nagy and Costa (1980) believed that the tritiated water method can give estimates of water flux within $\pm 10\%$ of actual rates.

By introducing water labeled with heavy oxygen (^{18}O), in addition to ^{3}H or ^{2}H, one can estimate CO_2 production (i.e., metabolic rate). The doubly labeled water (^{3}H$_2$^{18}O) is injected into the animal and allowed to equilibrate with the oxygen of CO_2 in the blood because of the action of carbonic anhydrase (Lifson et al., 1949). The specific activity of ^{18}O in the body water declines faster than that of the ^{3}H because ^{18}O is being lost in CO_2 as well as in H_2O (Lifson and McClintock, 1966). Therefore, the difference in the rate loss of ^{18}O and that of ^{3}H is an estimate of the CO_2 production. Oxygen-18 content of the distilled blood samples is determined by proton activation, transforming ^{18}O into a gamma-emitting isotope of fluorine (Wood et al., 1975). Mass spectrometry can also be used to analyze the ^{18}O (Boyer et al., 1961), but the method is more difficult than the proton activation technique (Congdon et al., 1978).

The doubly labeled water method has been compared with other techniques and, according to Nagy (1987), has an accuracy comparable to the tritiated water method ($\pm 8\%$). Once the method is validated for the taxon of interest (Congdon et al., 1978), it affords an extremely powerful means of determining the energy metabolism of animals in their natural environment (Mullen, 1973). This technique has been used in several field studies of lizards (Nagy and Shoemaker, 1975; Bennett and Nagy, 1977; Congdon, 1977; Congdon et al., 1979; Congdon and Tinkle, 1982a; Green et al., 1986) and birds and mammals (reviewed by Nagy, 1987).

The technique has proved to be of little use in metabolic studies of aquatic turtles, however, because of their extremely rapid water flux. Preliminary studies of water flux in *Chrysemys picta* and *Trachemys scripta* revealed that turtles may turn over half their body water each day (Congdon, pers. com.). The concentration of doubly labeled water, therefore, is quickly reduced to levels below the detection limits of standard instrumentation. Until the technique or the instrumentation is further refined, the effective use of labeled water may be limited to nonaquatic species.

As an alternative to the doubly labeled water technique, elimination rates of radioisotopes may be used as a relative index of metabolic activity. Odum (1961) suggested this as a method to compare laboratory and field metabolic rates in arthropod populations. It has since been used with varying success in studies of field metabolic rates in small mammals (Orr, 1967; Baker and Dunaway, 1969; Pulliam et al., 1969; Chew, 1971). In general there appears to be a relationship, on a gross level, between energy use and elimination rates of some tracer substances. Pulliam et al. (1969) found significant correlations ($r^2 > .92$) between the biological half-time of ^{65}Zn in mice maintained at three different temperatures and the metabolic rates as estimated by respirometers and metabolic cages (Table 21.2). Biological half-times were significantly different ($p < .01$) between temperature groups but not between individuals within any one group.

A strong positive relationship between standard metabolic rate and temperature is well documented for ectotherms (Bennett and Dawson, 1976). The same relationship is true for the elimination rate of certain radioisotopes and temperature. A temperature drop from 15° to 5° C slowed the elimination of ^{137}Cs by a factor of 2 to 3 in freshwater fish (Kevern et al., 1964, in Hasanen et al., 1967; Hasanen et al., 1967). Hakonson et al. (1975) observed the biological half-time of Cs to increase in trout from about 100 days in summer to 850 days in winter. Gallegos and Whicker (1971) also correlated radiocesium elimination in trout with temperature. Similar relationships have been documented in marine organisms (O'Hara, 1968; Nakahara et al., 1977) and the freshwater clam (Storr et al., 1982).

As was shown in Table 21.2, Pulliam et al. (1969) obtained excellent relationships between temperature and ^{65}Zn elimination in the laboratory. However, when they looked at ^{65}Zn elimination in mice kept within outdoor enclosures, the predicted biological half-time based on the animal's mean field temperature was 12.0 days, whereas the actual measured half-time was 4.8 days. Obviously, temperature does not explain all of the variance in radionuclide elimination or metabolic rate, especially under field conditions. Elimination rates of radioisotopes have been shown to be related to food intake (Staton et al., 1974) as well as to ingestion rates of stable isotopes and analogous elements (Marey et al., 1967; Whicker, 1983). Staton et al. (1974) examined ^{137}Cs elimination in 32 captive snakes collected from contaminated habitats on the SRP. Elimination rates were positively correlated with caloric intake and exhibited a negative exponential relationship with body mass. Scott et al. (1986) found that the elimination of ^{90}Sr and ^{137}Cs in *T. scripta* varied according to season but was not governed solely by temperature. Free-ranging turtles that had previously incorporated ^{90}Sr and ^{137}Cs from contaminated sites were enclosed in an 18 × 20 m uncontaminated, outdoor, experimental

Table 21.2. Biological half-time of ^{65}Zn ($t_{1/2}$) and metabolic rate as estimated by respirometer (Δ_1) and metabolic cages(Δ_2) for *Mus musculus* at three temperatures

Temperature (° C)	N	$t_{1/2}$ (d)	Δ_1 (kcal/g/d)	Δ_2 (kcal/g/d)
5	10	5.9 ± 0.7	0.39 ± 0.04	1.07 ± 0.06
10	10	6.4 ± 0.9	0.32 ± 0.01	0.94 ± 0.05
20	10	9.9 ± 0.5	0.22 ± 0.01	0.55 ± 0.05

Source: Pulliam et al., 1969.
Note: Means and standard deviation are given.

pond with a maximal depth of 3 m, fed weekly ad libitum, and analyzed for radioactivity at two-month intervals. As expected, elimination rates were very low during winter periods, when activity was minimal and little, if any, feeding occurred (Fig. 21.3). Elimination rates increased dramatically during the spring period (April–June) but significantly decreased by a factor of 4 during the summer months, despite warmer water temperatures. The authors speculated that the higher spring elimination rates (and associated high metabolic rates) were probably related to reproductive behavior.

The elimination rate of radioisotopes, therefore, is probably a better estimator of field metabolic rates (FMR) than of basal or standard metabolic rates. Nagy (1987) stated that FMR includes "the costs of basal metabolism, thermoregulation, locomotion, feeding, predator avoidance, alertness, posture, digestion and food detoxification, reproduction and growth, and other expenses that ultimately appear as heat, as well as any savings resulting from hypothermia." All these parameters could conceivably affect the elimination of certain radioisotopes.

The usefulness in estimating an animal's metabolic rate varies with individual isotopes. Reichle and Van Hook (1970) termed tracers "biologically indeterminate" if their turnover at steady state proceeded at a rate proportional to the whole-body metabolism of the animal. The similarity between whole-body metabolism and tracer metabolism may be based on the relationship of both to body mass. Equilibrium amounts of a tracer in similarly exposed individuals from the same population are often related to body mass by the equation

$$Q_e = \gamma(W_i)^\beta$$

where Q_e is the equilibrium amount of the tracer, W_i is the body mass of individual i, and γ and β are fitted parameters (Eberhardt, 1969; Boyden, 1974; Fagerström, 1977). The metabolic allometric equation (Kleiber, 1975) is very similar:

$$M_i = a(W_i)^b$$

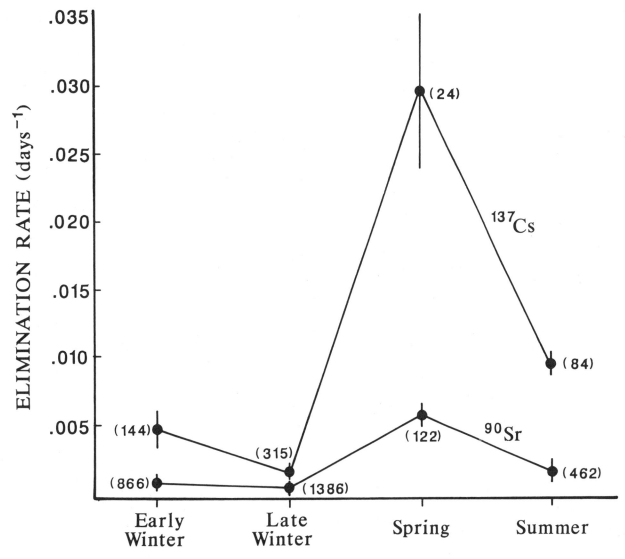

FIGURE 21.3. Seasonal differences in the elimination of ^{137}Cs and ^{90}Sr in *T. scripta* ($\bar{x} \pm 1$ SE). Numbers in parentheses represent the respective long-term biological half-times in days. Adapted from Scott et al. (1986).

where M_i is some measure of steady-state energy flux, and a and b are fitted parameters. Fagerström (1977) derived equations to test whether a given tracer is biologically indeterminate and thus a feasible tracer of energy flow in ecological systems. He stated that, within a population of animals, the biological half-time, body burden, and whole-body concentration of an indeterminate tracer should be proportional to body weight raised to $(1 - b)$, 1, and 0, respectively, where b is the exponent relating body weight to standard metabolic rate. The value for b can be determined experimentally, or the commonly accepted value of 0.8 for b can be used (Hemmingsen, 1950). If the relationships between body mass and the tracer parameters (biological half-time, body burden, and whole-body concentration) do not hold, it could be that (1) the system is not in equilibrium with respect to energy and/or

the tracer, or (2) the turnover rate of the tracer is governed by the activity of a specific enzyme or organ rather than by whole-body metabolism (Fagerström, 1977). Cesium-137 and ^{65}Zn have successfully been used in the past as realistic estimators of metabolic rate (Reichle et al., 1970) and may be particularly suited for situations where the doubly labeled water technique is inappropriate. However, we caution that at this time the relationship of metabolic rate to radionuclide elimination rate needs more rigorous experimental testing.

Stara et al. (1971) examined the metabolism of radionuclides in mammals and found a relationship between ^{137}Cs long-term elimination and body mass. A plot of this relationship revealed that ruminants eliminate ^{137}Cs more quickly than similar-sized nonruminants. Reichle et al. (1970) found that when the logarithm of cesium biolog-

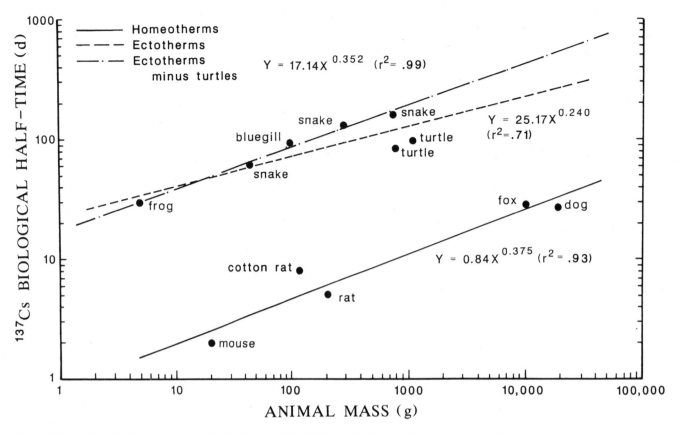

FIGURE 21.4.   Relation between animal body size and ^{137}Cs biological half-time. Regressions given for homeotherms, ectotherms, and ectotherms minus turtles. Data are from Kitchings et al. (1976) and Table 21.3.

ical half-times is plotted as a function of the logarithm of animal mass, various groups of organisms fall into discrete patterns. Regressions yielded the general formula

$$\hat{y} = AX^b$$

where $\hat{y}$ is an estimate of the ^{137}Cs biological half-time, A is the y-intercept of the regression line, X is the mass of the animal in grams, and b represents the slope of the regression line. The ^{137}Cs biological half-times for invertebrates (other than insects) and cold-blooded vertebrates were regressed together against body weight to yield

$$\hat{y} = 38.02X^{0.139}$$

Insects and warm-blooded vertebrates fell along a common regression line:

$$\hat{y} = 3.46X^{0.206}$$

Because the invertebrates have a large influence in the above regressions, we have compared the mass/(Cs half-time) relationships for vertebrate homeotherms and ectotherms separately (Fig. 21.4). The mammalian data come from Kitchings et al. (1976), who reviewed the literature

and listed the masses of various animals with their respective cesium elimination rates. The ectotherm data come from portions of Table 21.3 (i.e., data sets where both ^{137}Cs half-times and animal masses were reported by the original authors). The snake data reported by Staton et al. (1974) were averaged for animals <100 g, 100–500 g, and >500 g. The cesium half-times reported by Kolehmainen (1972) for the bluegill were normalized to 25° C using a Q_{10} of 2 (i.e., a 10° C increase in temperature doubles the elimination rate). Significant regressions were obtained for both groups (mammals, $p < .01$, $r^2 = .93$; ectotherms, $p < .01$, $r^2 = .71$). Analysis of covariance was used to test for differences between the two regressions and revealed significant differences between the intercepts ($p < .01$) but not between the slopes ($p = .17$). As suggested by Beauchamp and Olson (1973), one-half of the error mean square was added to the logarithm-transformed intercept estimate before converting the regression equations to their untransformed values. This corrects for possible bias obtained from using the antilogarithms and results in the following allometric equations (Fig. 21.4):

$$\hat{y} = 0.84X^{0.375} \text{ for mammals}$$

$$\hat{y} = 25.17X^{0.240} \text{ for ectotherms} \qquad (21.1)$$

Life History and Ecology of the Slider Turtle

Table 21.3. Long-term biological half-times ($t_{1/2}$) of ^{137}Cs in various organisms

Organism	$t_{1/2}$ (d)	Comment	Reference
Invertebrate			
Oyster	70-90	--	9
Fish			
Bluegill	187	--	7
Perch	175-200	15° C[a]	2
Carp	174	12.5° C	1
	98	20° C	1
Trout	25-80	15° C[a]	2
	74	5° C	4
	69	12.7° C	4
	49	18.3° C	4
Reptiles and amphibians			
Snakes	24-430, $\bar{X} = 131$	Five species	8
Trachemys scripta	315	Winter	12
	24	Spring	12
	84	Summer	12
	64	Yearly average	12
	96	Summer	11
Hyla	30	Captive, unfed	10
Mammals			
Mice	6	Oral dose	6
Rats	13	Oral dose	6
Dog	43	IV dose	6
Mule deer	14	^{134}Cs	3
Reindeer	6-19	--[b]	5
Monkey	40	IV dose	6
Man	60-160	IV dose	6

References: 1, Kevern et al., 1964, in Hasanen et al., 1967; 2, Hasanen et al., 1967; 3, Hakonson and Whicker, 1969; 4, Gallegos and Whicker, 1971; 5, Holleman et al., 1971; 6 Stara et al., 1971; 7, Kolehmainen, 1972; 8, Staton et al., 1974; 9, Cranmore and Harrison, 1975; 10, Dapson and Kaplan, 1975; 11, Peters, 1986; 12, Scott et al., 1986.

[a]Older fish had longer Cs $t_{1/2}$.

[b]Cs $t_{1/2}$ varied with potassium intake.

Equation 21.1 overpredicts the mean ^{137}Cs half-time in turtles, as determined by Peters (1986) and Scott et al. (1986), by about 40%, although the prediction is still within their 95% confidence interval. This could be due to the low predictive power of the regression ($r^2 = .71$) or may reflect the presence of the turtle's shell and its effect on the reduced flesh mass to total mass ratio when compared with that of other organisms. The shell has previously been considered metabolically inert (Benedict, 1932; Hughes et al., 1971). Inclusion of such inert material, which constitutes ≈40% of adult *T. scripta*'s mass (Towns, 1987), could lead to an overestimation of the cesium biological half-times. However, reducing the turtles' total mass by 40% and then estimating the ^{137}Cs half-time according to equation 21.1 do not totally compensate the initial overprediction. Bennett and Dawson (1976) did not find significant differences in the resting metabolic rates (RMR) among lizards, snakes, and turtles. This suggested that either the shell is not metabolically inert or the metabolic rate of the other tissues in turtles is high enough to compensate for the inert characteristics of the shell. Bennett and Dawson (1976) suggested that the former explanation is more plausible. Towns (1987) found

that 23% of *Trachemys*'s total ^{137}Cs body burden is in the shell and bones ($N = 14$), indicating that the shell is at least partially labile to potassium-analogous elements.

It is obvious from Figure 21.4 that the two turtle data points are below those for the other ectotherms and influence the regression line. If the turtle data are eliminated from the analysis, the r^2 value increases from .71 to .99, and the probability value decreases from .018 to .001 (Fig. 21.4). This change also increases the similarity between the slopes of the ectotherm and homeotherm regression lines (p values increase from .17 to .78). The ectotherm regression equation, minus turtles, becomes

$$\hat{y} = 17.14X^{0.352} \qquad (21.2)$$

It is interesting that the slopes of the homeotherm and ectotherm regressions are equal. This disagrees with what has been reported in the literature. Our data set, however, contains the widest range of ectothermic vertebrate taxa analyzed. Reichle et al. (1970) regressions included fish (perch, trout, bluegill, and carp), invertebrates, and one amphibian. Admittedly, our sample size is small, and more data are needed.

It is evident from Figure 21.4 that the biological half-time of ^{137}Cs in ectotherms is greater than in similar-sized homeotherms. A 250-gram ectotherm would retain ^{137}Cs between 14 and 17 times longer than a similar-sized homeotherm (depending on whether equation 21.1 or 21.2 is used, and assuming the ectotherm is in a 25° C environment). This compares to Nagy's (1987) finding that the FMR of iguanid lizards is about 17 times lower than the FMR of similar-sized mammals.

Radioisotopes such as ^{137}Cs may be useful relative indexes of metabolic rates but have not been adequately studied or validated to the extent and usefulness of the doubly labeled water methodology. This area needs more research. The comment of Odum and Golley (1963), who discussed the use of radionuclides as estimators of metabolic rates, is still pertinent: "The approach, even if difficult, is well worth investigation because the stakes are very high. At the present time we can see no other way to measure metabolic rate in completely free-living populations. Even approximate guesses are better than wild guesses. Until we are able to estimate these energy transformations we cannot hope to understand, much less manage intelligently, the ecosystems in which man, himself, is an integral part."

METABOLISM (UPTAKE AND ELIMINATION) OF SPECIFIC RADIOISOTOPES. To examine accurately the consequences of radioactivity in the environment, it is necessary to understand the transport and bioaccumulation of radioisotopes within systems. The complex properties of individual radionuclides, organisms, and the fundamental processes of ecosystems can lead to a wide spectrum of scenarios ranging from negligible impacts to potentially high doses to humans and other organisms (Whicker, 1983). The data are not complete; much is yet to be learned with respect to the kinetics of radioisotopes, particularly within the herpetofauna (see Appendix 21.1 for details on radionuclide kinetics). Important factors such as percent assimilation and biological half-time, which are well documented in mammals, have only recently been examined in the turtle. In this section, we review the radionuclide kinetic studies conducted on turtles.

Scott et al. (1986), whose work was discussed briefly in the previous section, were the first to examine the kinetics of ^{137}Cs and ^{90}Sr in turtles. Seasonal biological half-times ranged from 24 to 315 days for ^{137}Cs and from 122 to 1,386 days for ^{90}Sr. The yearly average biological half-times for Cs and Sr were 64 and 364 days, respectively. Analysis of covariance indicated no significant effect of either body mass or sex of the animal on elimination of the isotopes. However, there were significant seasonal differences in the elimination of both isotopes, as well as significant differences between isotopes (Fig. 21.3). Cesium elimination demonstrated a greater seasonal response than did Sr elimination, which the authors attributed to the different target tissues of the two isotopes. Approximately 77% of the ^{137}Cs is found in the soft tissues of *T. scripta*, and 99% of the ^{90}Sr resides in the shell and bones (Towns, 1987). The turnover rate of ^{137}Cs in soft tissues is likely to respond more dramatically to changes in overall metabolic rate than is that of ^{90}Sr in the calcareous tissues.

Because Scott et al. (1986) used previously contaminated *T. scripta* in their research, the assimilation efficiency of ingested isotopes could not be determined. Percent assimilation is an important parameter that is often more sensitive to the sex, size, and age of an animal than is long-term retention (Coughtrey and Thorne, 1983). The assimilation fraction can be determined by orally administering a known quantity of a radioisotope to an animal and performing whole-body analysis through time as described in Appendix 21.1. The methods of administering radioisotopes to organisms include (1) intramuscular, intraperitoneal, and intravenous injections, (2) external absorption, (3) subcutaneous insertion of radioactive pellets or wires, (4) gavage, in which solutions are introduced directly into the stomach, and (5) voluntary intake via labeled food or water. The best method of administration depends upon the individual research goals, because the method can affect the results of the experiment. Creger et al. (1967) demonstrated that the means of administration significantly affected ^{89}Sr excretion rates in chickens. Similar results were obtained by Behne and Gessner (1987) for ^{137}Cs excretion in rats. Bhattacharyya et al. (1985) showed that substantial amounts of plutonium, cadmium, and lead, which were supplied in drinking water to mice, adsorbed onto the teeth before the isotopes could be assimilated in the gastrointestinal tract. This biased the

Table 21.4. Gastrointestinal absorption of strontium in adult animals

Species	% absorption	Reference
Goat	5	4
Pig	9	5
Sheep	15	2
Rat	15	1
	28	6
Dog	19	7
Man	19	3
Trachemys scripta	40-60	8

References: 1, Hamilton, 1947; 2, Jones and Mackie, 1959; 3, Spencer et al., 1960; 4, Comar et al., 1961; 5, Hogue et al., 1961; 6, Marcus and Lengemann, 1962; 7, Della Rosa et al., 1965; 8, Hinton and Whicker, 1985.

calculated percent assimilation. Other potential problems include leaching of the isotope from labeled food of aquatic organisms, determining the exact quantity of isotope ingested, obtaining unrealistic values because of animal stress, and possible regurgitation of the tracer when gavage is used. Hinton and S. A. Ibrahim (unpubl. data) believe that a gavage method gives the most realistic assimilation estimates, and they developed a technique for administering tracers to turtles that eliminates many of the problems mentioned above.

Hinton and Whicker (1985) examined the kinetics of ^{226}Ra and ^{85}Sr in *T. scripta* maintained in the laboratory at temperatures of 18° and 28° C. They found that turtles assimilate a higher percentage of strontium than do endothermic organisms (Table 21.4). This may indicate unusual calcium metabolism in turtles (because Sr and Ra are chemical analogues of Ca, and the turtle has such a large percentage of calcareous tissues relative to its total mass) or may be related to their ectothermic nature. The influence of temperature on assimilation of radionuclides in ectothermic animals has not been adequately researched. Hinton and Whicker (1985) also found that after 200 days, the rate constant for Sr elimination (at both temperatures) was not significantly different from zero, indicating extremely long biological half-times (1,500–6,000 days). This was also true for the radium elimination from the turtles kept at 18° C. The animals maintained at 28° C had a significantly greater radium elimination rate (0.0049 ± 0.002), which corresponded to a biological half-time of 141 days. The unusually long half-times might be explained by the laboratory conditions (the animals were kept in 3×0.8 m fiberglass holding tanks that were 0.8 m deep), which restricted activity. No differences in elimination were detected between the sexes or among age classes. Because of the large variation among individual turtles, the Sr elimination rates reported by Hinton and Whicker (1985) were not statistically different from those reported by Scott et al. (1986).

Peters (1986) examined the elimination of ^{137}Cs in

T. scripta under both laboratory and field conditions. The laboratory turtles were kept in water-filled 14-liter plastic dishpans within an environmental chamber set at 28° C ± 2°. The field turtles were kept in the same outdoor ponds used by Scott et al. (1986). There were no differences in loss rates between the laboratory and field groups, nor were elimination rates affected by the sex of the turtle. The 95% confidence interval (CI) for the biological half-time was 69 to 194 days, with a mean of 96 days. This compares well with the summer elimination data (84 days) of Scott et al. (1986). Peters (1986) also found a positive correlation between loss rate and initial body weight. Other investigators have found significant negative relationships between body size and elimination rates in both endotherms and ectotherms (Reichle et al., 1970; Stara et al., 1971).

In an organism under chronic exposure, the radionuclide concentration within the organism may reach equilibrium conditions with the environment (i.e., the contaminant enters and leaves the organism at the same rate). Peters (1986) developed a 95% CI of 213 to 643 days as the time required for his turtles to reach equilibrium, assuming a chronic exposure to ^{137}Cs. This time frame is longer than the active period of most ectotherms. Thus, the typical buildup curve for radionuclide accumulation under chronic input (i.e., exponential increase) may not be applicable to ectotherms. Instead, a stepped function, in which intermittent periods of little uptake or even loss correspond to the organism's reduced seasonal metabolic rate, may be more realistic (Peters, 1986). A number of steps could occur before the ectotherm reaches its true equilibrium. Depending on the organism's behavior, physiology, and environment and the characteristics of the particular isotope, such a stepped function could result in either an increase or a decrease in the organism's ultimate radionuclide body burden.

Shellabarger et al. (1956) presented data on the metabolism of radioiodine by *Pseudemys* and *Terrapene*. Thyroid function was directly related to environmental temperature, as has been noted in other studies of ectotherms (Barrington and Matty, 1954, and Gorbman and Berg, 1955, both cited in Shellabarger et al., 1956). The opposite relationship exists in homeotherms (Shellabarger et al., 1956). No differences in ^{131}I metabolism were found between *Pseudemys* and *Terrapene*. However, both species exhibited greater assimilation and retention of ^{131}I under dry conditions. Shellabarger et al. (1956) attributed this to recirculation of iodine by the cloaca.

In summary, turtles (and ectotherms in general) exhibit longer half-times for ^{137}Cs than homeotherms (Table 21.3 and Fig. 21.4), although the same trend is not apparent for ^{90}Sr (Table 21.5). Differences between isotopes are related to the metabolic activity of the different organs in which the isotopes are deposited. The metabolism of calcareous tissue, where Sr is bound, is lower than

Table 21.5. Long-term biological half-time ($t_{1/2}$) of ^{90}Sr in various organisms

Organism	$t_{1/2}$ (d)	Comment	Reference
Fish			
Atlantic croaker	138	--	3
Reptiles and amphibians			
Trachemys scripta	1,386	Winter	8
	122	Spring	8
	462	Summer	8
	364	Yearly average	8
	1,500–6,000	Lab conditions	7
Newt	79	20° C	4
	131	10° C	4
Bird			
Chicken	141	Pullets	6
Mammals			
Rat	533	Chronic intake	6
Pig	277	--	6
Beagle	848–2,251	Chronic intake	1
Mule deer	190	^{85}Sr	5
Man	750	Chronic intake	2

References: 1, Goldman and Della Rosa, 1967; 2, Rundo, 1967; 3, Baptist et al., 1970; 4, Willis and Lappenbush, 1975; 5, Schreckhise and Whicker, 1976; 6, Coughtrey and Thorne, 1983; 7, Hinton and Whicker, 1985; 8, Scott et al., 1986.

that of muscle tissue, the major site of deposition for Cs. Similarly, the differences between organism groups are also likely related to metabolic differences; that is, the metabolic rates of ectotherms are lower than those of homeotherms. That Sr and Cs elimination rates do not parallel each other when ectotherms and homeotherms are compared reinforces the concepts presented in the discussion of field metabolic rates. Cesium-137 behaves more like an indeterminate tracer and thus could possibly be used as an estimator of field metabolic rate, whereas Sr elimination is governed by processes within a specific organ (bone).

FEEDING RATES

Estimation of food consumption in free-ranging aquatic turtles is hampered by many of the same difficulties as the determination of field metabolic rates. Techniques suitable in the laboratory may be unsuitable for use in a field study. Parmenter (1981) estimated the digestive turnover rates for five species of freshwater turtles in the laboratory but was unable to quantify total food consumption in field animals (Parmenter, 1980). Estimates of food intake for lizards have been made by relating food intake to output of fecal waste in laboratory animals and then measuring the fecal output of field-captured animals (Avery, 1971; Avery, 1978). The relationship between food intake and fecal output has been established for *T. scripta* (H. Avery, pers. com.) but has not been used to estimate dietary intake in the field. The technique requires the removal of an animal from the field for several days at a time and consequently may cause abnormal behavior and unrealistic estimates of intake (Gallagher et al., 1983). Doubly labeled water is sometimes used to estimate food consumption (Minnich and Shoemaker, 1970), but as was discussed above, the technique has had limited success in the study of aquatic turtles. Mullen (1973) cautions that the doubly labeled water technique may be of little use in estimating food intake in the field because the diverse diet of most organisms prohibits a knowledge of the dry diet yield of metabolic CO_2.

Several recent studies have used the turnover of ^{22}Na to measure food intake in free-ranging animals (Green and Dunsmore, 1978; Williams and Ridpath, 1982; Gallagher et al., 1983; Green et al., 1986). Stable Na turnover can be estimated by measuring the elimination rate of ^{22}Na (Buscarlet, 1974), which is dependent on the amount of stable Na in the diet (Fairbanks and Burch, 1968). However, reliable estimates of food intake can be obtained only if the Na content of the diet is known and if the major source of Na is dietary. Dunson, who used radioisotopic methods to examine sodium flux, found that active uptake of Na from the water column occurs in at least two species of freshwater turtles (Dunson, 1964; Dunson and Weymouth, 1965; Dunson, 1966; Dunson, 1969). In *T. scripta* the cloacal region (cloacal bursae and cloaca) accounts for 48% to 68% of the sodium influx rate (Dunson, 1967). It is therefore unlikely that ^{22}Na turnover can be used to estimate food consumption in aquatic turtles.

The study of turtles inhabiting radioactively contaminated habitats may provide the best estimates of food intake in the field. Consumption rates can be determined by using the relationship between intake and elimination of a radionuclide when the concentration of the radionuclide in the animal is in equilibrium with its food source. The technique was first suggested by Davis and Foster (1958) and has since been used for numerous species (insects, Crossley, 1963; carp, Kevern, 1966; reindeer, Holleman et al., 1971; bluegill, Kolehmainen, 1972; trout, Hakonson et al., 1975). In its simplest form the technique uses the following model, which is also discussed in Appendix 21.1:

where R_{in} is the intake rate of the isotope (Bq/time), k is the loss rate constant (time^{-1}), and q is the total body burden (Bq).

The change in q over time (dq/dt) can be written as

$$\frac{dq}{dt} = R_{in} - kq$$

By integrating this equation and evaluating at time = 0,

$$q_t = \frac{R_{(in)}}{k}(1 - e^{-kt}) + q_0 e^{-kt} \quad (21.3)$$

where q_0 is the radionuclide content of the organism at $t = 0$, and q_t is the radionuclide content at any time t.

The intake of a radionuclide can also be written as

$$R_{in} = RCa \quad (21.4)$$

where R_{in} is the intake rate, R is the rate of food consumption (g/day), C is the concentration of radionuclide in food (Bq/g), and a is the assimilation fraction (i.e., percentage of the ingested contaminant actually incorporated into the body).

If we substitute equation 21.3 into equation 21.4 and rearrange terms, we can determine the rate of food consumption (R) in g/day:

$$R = \frac{(q_t - q_0 e^{-kt})k}{aC(1 - e^{-kt})}$$

Estimates of k, q_t, q_0, a, and C are required to solve for food intake rates and are obtained through techniques described in Appendix 21.1. A knowledge of radionuclide kinetics (uptake and retention) within the animal and the radionuclide concentrations of the food sources is therefore necessary. Cadwell and Schreckhise (1976) used a convolution integral to determine the consumption rate of ^{32}P-labeled blue grama grass by grasshoppers. Their technique does not require that the concentration of radionuclide in the animal be in equilibrium with its food source. Successive calculations of the consumption rates were made at various points in time as the body burden changed because of continued feeding on labeled forage. Radionuclide-contaminated environments represent ideal situations where food consumption rates could be determined for free-ranging aquatic turtles.

KINSHIP DETERMINATION

Field attempts to identify the young of a particular female of any organism are extremely difficult and time-consuming. In one long-term study of turtle populations at the E. S. George Reserve in Michigan, more than 1,500 man-hours are spent each nesting season in an attempt to associate individual females with their nests and subsequently with their hatchlings (Congdon et al., 1983b, 1987). Radioisotopes could conceivably reduce the labor necessary to acquire the same information and are potentially less disruptive. Radionuclides have been used in small-mammal populations to determine matrilineal kinship (Wolff and Holleman, 1978; Tamarin et al., 1983). Labeling captured females with a mixture of several gamma-emitting radioisotopes (each of which has a characteristic emission spectrum) allows subsequent identification of trapped offspring. The technique works well in small mammals because there is transfer of nuclides across the placenta or through milk to the young. It is unknown at this time whether there is sufficient material transfer from a reproductive female turtle to her follicles and embryos. However, our preliminary data indicate that Sr and Ca radioisotopes are transferred from females to their embryos. If feasible, the technique, in conjunction with the drift-fence capture of hatchlings, would allow identification of hatchling-mother relationships. It could also prove useful in the identification of individual nest predators.

ECOSYSTEM ANALYSIS

Functional ecology (i.e., energy flow, nutrient cycles, and biological regulation) has lagged behind descriptive ecology. Functional ecology hinges on measuring the rate of change per unit of time, that is, measuring the degree of energy flow, not just the standing crop (Odum, 1962). Radiotracers have greatly extended our ability to analyze the functional aspects of ecosystems by providing a means of detecting actual movements of materials and of estimating cycling or turnover rates within the systems.

Such analysis can often give insights to an organism's particular niche within an ecosystem. Pendleton and Grundmann (1954) were among the first to use radioactive tags on an ecosystem level by examining an insect-predator complex and plant pollinator relationships. Odum and Kuenzler (1963) used ^{32}P to determine arthropod trophic-level positions and predator-prey interactions in an old-field ecosystem. They labeled three dominant species of plants and then examined the subsequent amounts and distribution of tracer in arthropod populations. By plotting the concentration of tracer per unit of biomass against time, graphic separations of certain trophic and habitat groups became evident. In addition to isolating specific sections of a food web, the authors were able to determine the energy source being used by specific heterotrophic populations. Similarly, Crossley (1963) used ^{137}Cs to examine insect-plant relationships, and Coleman and McGinnis (1970) used ^{65}Zn to describe the fungus-arthropod food chain quantitatively.

Gallegos et al. (1970) documented a somewhat unexpected non-food-web intake pathway of Cs in rainbow trout. They determined that the major source of ^{137}Cs for a population of trout living in a high mountain lake was not through food items but by ingestion of bottom sediments. Evidence for this phenomenon included the following: (1) The major food items of the trout did not contain enough ^{137}Cs to account for the observed levels in the fish, (2) surface sediment and detritus were sufficiently high in ^{137}Cs that less than 0.1 g would need to be ingested daily to account for the observed levels in the trout, and (3) sediment and detritus were observed in the intestinal

Table 21.6. Concentration ratios (CR) for Pond B components

Component	^{137}Cs	^{90}Sr
Filtered water	1.0 (0.76 Bq/l)	1.0 (0.14 Bq/l)
Sediment (0-3 cm)	1.6×10^4	6.0×10^2
Aquatic macrophytes	2.4×10^3	6.4×10^2
Benthic macroinvertebrates		
Insect nymphs and larvae	8.0×10^2	5.2×10
Gastropods (snails)	1.2×10^2	5.4×10^3
Fish (five species)	6.4×10^3	4.6×10^3
Turtles (Trachemys)	1.3×10^3	1.0×10^4
Waterfowl (coots)	2.5×10^3	--
Frog (Rana)[a]	4.8×10^2	--
Snake (Natrix)[b]	1.0×10^4	--

Source: Whicker et al., 1984.

Note: CR = (Bq/kg organism wet weight)/(Bq/l filtered water).

[a]S. G. McDowell and R. U. Fischer, unpubl. data.

[b]T. G. Hinton and H. Zippler, unpubl. data.

tracts of the fish. It is interesting that in 1970 the levels of ^{137}Cs in the trout dropped to one-third the levels in 1969. Gallegos et al. (1970) attributed this to a significant reduction in the trout's primary food source, Gammarus, with a subsequent shift to Daphnia. Daphnia occur nearer the surface in open water and do not evade predation by swimming toward the sediment or vegetation as do Gammarus. This change in diet and subsequent feeding behavior of the trout probably reduced their intake of sediment and detritus.

Other research using radiotracers to analyze the functional aspects of ecosystems includes work by Richardson and Marshall (1986), who used ^{32}P to quantify the inflow, storage, and export of phosphorus in peat land, and Whicker et al. (1984), who are examining the dynamics of radioisotopes within the previously mentioned Pond B, a contaminated warm monomictic lake on the SRP. Whicker et al. (1984) have preliminary data on ^{137}Cs and ^{90}Sr concentrations within various compartments of Pond B (i.e., sediments, water column, macrophytes, benthos, fish, turtles, and waterfowl). Because the data are from a single system, many of the problems associated with comparing data from different sources (as discussed in the section Radionuclide Concentrations, above) are eliminated.

We have presented the data of Whicker et al. (1984) in Table 21.6, in the form of concentration ratios (CR). The CR for aquatic organisms is defined as

$$CR = \frac{Bq/kg \text{ organism (wet mass)}}{Bq/l \text{ water (filtered)}}$$

Concentration ratios are useful in making comparisons among organisms as they normalize for variations in the radionuclide concentration of the water. Concentration ratios indicate the propensity for a radioisotope to concentrate within specific organisms.

Several important points can be gleaned from Table 21.6. First, there are fundamental differences in how Cs and Sr are distributed in the system. When compared with the concentration in the water, Cs levels are four orders of magnitude greater in the sediments and three orders of magnitude higher in the macrophytes. Strontium-90 concentrations, however, are the same in the sediments and macrophytes and are only two orders of magnitude greater than the water. Recall that ^{137}Cs mimics potassium, and ^{90}Sr behaves like calcium. This is evident in the benthic macroinvertebrates. The ^{137}Cs CR in snails and insect nymphs are about the same, but the ^{90}Sr CR for the snails is three orders of magnitude greater than that of the insects, probably because of the greater quantity of calcareous tissues in snails. The same analogy can be extended to the turtle, which has the highest ^{90}Sr CR but has a ^{137}Cs CR comparable to that of fish and waterfowl. In the section Radionuclide Concentrations, above, we stated that ^{90}Sr concentrations (Bq/g bone ash) in turtles do not differ greatly from those of other organisms. However, if animals are compared on a whole-body basis (as we have presented the CR), then the turtle's propensity to accumulate ^{90}Sr is evident.

Whicker (1984) stated that high concentration ratios are generally associated singly or in combination with low availability of nutrient element analogues, longevity of biological tissues, high assimilation of the radionuclide, and long retention time of the radionuclide. If we look at some of the biological characteristics of *Trachemys*, it becomes apparent that it is quite possible for them to have high CR values: (1) They have a long life span of 20 to 30 years (Gibbons and Semlitsch, 1982), which gives them sufficient opportunity to accumulate radionuclides; (2) they have a high percentage of slowly developing bone tissues, which with chronic input could achieve high concentrations of long-lived calcium-analogous radionuclides (i.e., ^{226}Ra, ^{90}Sr); and (3) indications exist that their assimilation of radionuclides is high, and retention times are long, particularly for isotopes that are nutrient analogues of calcium (Tables 21.4 and 21.5). These observations demonstrate the importance of how an organism's biological properties can affect its accumulation of radionuclides.

It is also interesting that a trophic-level effect is suggested from the cesium CR in Table 21.6; insects, snails, and frogs are on one order, followed by turtles, waterfowl, and fish on the second order, and the totally carnivorous brown water snake (*Nerodia taxispilota*) resides on top. Cesium is unique among radionuclides in that increased concentrations often occur in the upper trophic levels. A ninefold increase in ^{137}Cs in the plant→mule deer→cougar food chain was documented by Pendleton et al. (1965). An approximately twofold increase at each link in the lichen→caribou→wolf chain was reported by Hanson (1967), and an increase by a factor of three has

been shown in humans over that of their food (McNeill and Trojan, 1960). Although cesium concentrations in aquatic food chains generally do not increase as dramatically as has been documented in terrestrial systems (Reichle et al., 1970), Whicker et al. (1972) documented a trophic relationship of 3.3 for a predator-prey association in freshwater trout. It will be interesting to see if the trend in the Pond B system continues as more data are collected.

In this section we have tried to show how radionuclide techniques and measurements can be useful in understanding ecosystems. The next logical step is the construction of mathematical models that can be used to simulate biological processes. (Some fundamental radionuclide modeling concepts are discussed in Appendix 21.1.) For an excellent example of a radionuclide model, see Whicker and Kirchner (1987). They have developed a dynamic simulation model of the transport of radionuclides from fallout through the agricultural food chain to man. Such models are useful for predicting the dynamics of radioisotopes within ecosystems. In doing so, they can further our knowledge on the transport and cycling of stable isotopes as well as on the biology and interactions of individual organisms. The role of aquatic turtles in ecosystem function has not been thoroughly examined and deserves consideration for future research. Reichle et al. (1970) stated, "It is not that we lack sophisticated mathematical techniques to develop predictive models of ecosystem processes, but rather that we have neither sufficiently detailed nor widely representative radioecological data with which to work." This is particularly true with respect to the herpetofauna.

MISCELLANEOUS STUDIES

Numerous physiological studies use radioisotopes but, for the most part, are beyond the scope of this chapter. In a review of physiological methods in studying reptiles, McDonald (1976) discussed techniques that use radiotags ^{51}Cr, ^{59}Fe, and ^{131}I for the determination of blood or plasma volumes. As was mentioned previously, ^{22}Na has been used to identify the sites of active transport of Na in freshwater turtles (Dunson, 1969). Schwartz and Flamenbaum (1976) used radioisotopes of Na and Cl to identify heavy metal–induced alteration of sodium transport in *Trachemys scripta* urinary bladders. They found that heavy-metal salts inhibit the active transport of sodium without altering passive ion fluxes. In a study of intestinal epithelial proliferation in *Chrysemys picta*, Wurth and Musacchia (1964) used tritiated thymidine to examine temperature effects on epithelial mitosis and cell replacement. Total cell replacement was estimated to be eight weeks in turtles maintained at 20° to 24° C. The above studies indicate the potential usefulness of radioisotope techniques when ion transport mechanisms and cellular physiology are of primary interest.

Radioactive tags have also been successfully used in rate-of-passage measurements in the gastrointestinal tract. Absolute measurements of passage rates require markers that do not separate from the labeled fraction and are easily recovered. Solid markers such as powdered Brazil nuts, rubber pieces, glass beads, and plastics have been used in the past (Kotb and Luckey, 1972), but with questionable results, for it is not known whether they move with the fraction they are intended to label (Uden et al., 1980). Dyes used to stain feed are generally appreciably absorbed from the gut and thus bias the results (Kotb and Luckey, 1972). Uden et al. (1980) reviewed many of the historic methods of marking digesta and found that ^{51}Cr applied to prepared plant fibers proved to be successful. The preparation of both solid and liquid Cr markers is described by Uden et al. (1980).

Two other radionuclide techniques deserve mention: autoradiography and neutron activation. If a radioactive substance is placed on a photographic film, the ionizing radiation will expose the film and produce an image when the film is developed. The technique is valuable in determining the distribution of a radiotracer within a sample. Isotopes that emit soft beta particles (e.g., ^{45}Ca, ^{14}C) work best. Schultz and Whicker (1982) reviewed applications of autoradiography (see also Gude, 1968; Baserga and Malamud, 1969; Rogers, 1973). We did not find any reference to the use of this technique in the chelonian literature. However, one appropriate use would be in determining the movement of calcium within the carapace.

Neutron activation is a powerful technique that uses stable elements placed in a neutron field (beam), which then transforms the stable nuclide into a radioisotope. Hakonson et al. (1975) examined the kinetics of cesium within a public lake in Colorado by spiking the lake with stable cesium (^{133}Cs). Subsequent samples from the lake were neutron-activated, transformed into radioactive ^{134}Cs, and then measured by gamma spectrometry. The technique allowed the study of cesium kinetics in a situation in which the addition of radioactive cesium was not desirable. The technique, however, requires access to a neutron beam (i.e., a nuclear reactor or a Pu-Be source), thus complicating the research methodology.

Conclusions

The use of radioisotopic techniques in the study of freshwater turtles has tremendous potential. When compared with the volume of work on mammals, the paucity of turtle research involving radionuclides is obvious. Despite the lack of data, general trends do exist:

1. Turtles are similar to other organisms in their concentration of fallout ^{90}Sr and ^{137}Cs, when compared on the basis of concentration (activity per gram of ashed bone).

2. Turtles have the capacity to accumulate large total-body burdens of radionuclides because of their
   a. long life span;
   b. high percentage of slowly developing bone and shell tissue, which with chronic input could achieve high concentrations of long-lived bone-seeking isotopes;
   c. tendency to assimilate a high percentage of ingested radioisotopes;
   d. ectothermic nature, which has implications for longer radionuclide retention times and for seasonal shifts in elimination.

3. Although the data are scant, turtles do not seem to be unusually sensitive or resistant to radiation when compared with amphibians and fish.

4. Turtles, especially hatchlings, are good candidates for radiotagging experiments to study movement. The hard carapace should eliminate some of the problems encountered with radiotags placed on salamanders and lizards.

5. Because of the rapid turnover of body water and absorption of Na via the cloacal region in aquatic turtles, doubly labeled water and ^{22}Na techniques used to determine field metabolic and feeding rates in other taxa have had limited success in the study of aquatic turtles. Elimination rates of other radioisotopes may offer viable alternatives in determining field metabolic and feeding rates.

6. The use of radioisotopes to determine kinship relationships seems to be a likely, yet presently unexplored technique.

7. The lack of data on environmental transport and bioaccumulation of radioisotopes is probably greater for the herpetofauna than for any other group of vertebrates. The knowledge gained from radionuclide transport can contribute to our understanding of fundamental processes and help us better define the function of freshwater turtles within ecosystems.

Obviously, radionuclide techniques are not a panacea. Many questions are best addressed using other methods. The disadvantages of radioisotopic work include state and federal licensing requirements. Approval by these agencies often hinges on the applicant's knowledge of radioisotopes and their safe use. The use of radioisotopes by the untrained is a hazardous situation at best; there is potential for personal harm, contamination of equipment and laboratories, and the accumulation of meaningless data due to poorly calibrated equipment. However, the quantities of radionuclides needed for today's tracer experiments are often incredibly small, less than what many people wore on their wrist when radium was commonly used in luminescent watches. With proper planning, the use of radioisotopes constitutes an extremely powerful tool that, in concert with other techniques, can help answer important questions in freshwater turtle research.

Acknowledgments

We would like to thank J. D. Congdon, J. W. Gibbons, J. H. K. Pechmann, J. E. Pinder III, P. J. West, and F. W. Whicker for their stimulating thoughts and helpful comments on early versions of this chapter. The use of our colleagues' unpublished data is greatly appreciated. J. Coleman prepared the figures. Keyboard artistry and editing were done by J. Hinton and K. Knight, respectively. Preparation of the manuscript was funded by U.S. Department of Energy contract DE-AC09-76SROO-819 through the University of Georgia's Institute of Ecology.

APPENDIX 21.1.   Radionuclide kinetics

The movement of radionuclides through a system is often depicted with box-and-arrow diagrams. The system is generally composed of one or more compartments, represented by boxes, and associated radionuclide transport processes, depicted as arrows. The compartments are system components that have uniform and distinguishable transport kinetics (Atkins, 1969). An open, two-compartment system with interchange might be represented as follows:

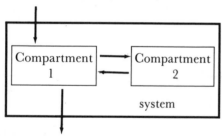

Examples of various transport processes include aerial deposition, resuspension, sorption, desorption, ingestion, excretion, molting, secretion, and decomposition (Whicker and Schultz, 1982). Each transport process in a first-order system has an associated rate constant. The determination of the various rate constants is the cornerstone of radionuclide kinetics. Rate constants allow one to explore the dynamics of the system by determining rates of flow among compartments. These rates govern compartmental increases and decreases in radionuclide burdens over time. Odum (1962) compared the power of isotopes in ecological research to the power of the microscope in biology. The microscope allows the examination of structure, whereas isotopes, through the determination of rate constants, allow the examination of function.

The amount of radionuclide within a compartment is generally symbolized by q, and the primary factors that determine q are the rates of input to the compartment (R_{in}) and output from it (R_{out}; Whicker and Schultz,

1982). Radionuclide loss from a compartment generally obeys first-order processes where loss rate is proportional to compartment inventory. Thus:

$$R_{out} = -kq$$

where k is the rate constant with units of time^{-1}. Schematically, this is represented as:

The change in radionuclide inventory (q) in the above system with respect to time would be

$$\frac{dq}{dt} = R_{in} - kq$$

All radioisotopes have an associated physical half-life, $t_{1/2}$, which represents the time required for half of the original material to decay. Radioisotopes decay exponentially according to

$$q = q_0 e^{-kt}$$

where q is activity at time t, q_0 is the initial activity, and k is the rate constant. The rate constant (k) is related to the physical half-life of the isotope by

$$t_{\frac{1}{2}} = \frac{\ln 2}{k}$$

Isotopes also have a biological half-time within compartments that represents the time required for half of the material to be lost by means other than physical decay (e.g., excretion, transport, etc.). The rate constants of all mechanisms that reduce an isotopic inventory within a compartment can be combined into the effective rate constant (k_{eff}). For instance:

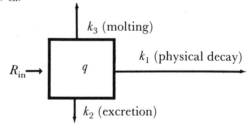

could be reduced to

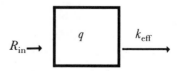

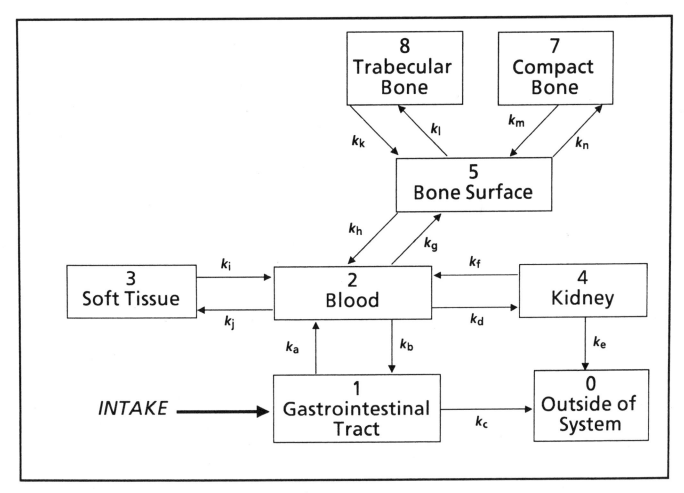

FIGURE 21.5.   Model of the possible distribution and movement of strontium in a turtle (adapted from Schreckhise, 1974). Each letter designates a particular pathway.

where $k_{\text{eff}} = k_1 + k_2 + k_3$. The effective half-life then becomes

$$t_{\frac{1}{2}\text{eff}} = \frac{\ln 2}{k_{\text{eff}}}$$

If modeling the movement of radionuclides within a system is of interest, it soon becomes apparent that isolating and quantifying each individual rate process is a difficult task. Consider the movement of radionuclides within a single organism. For example, the anatomical and physiological kinetics of strontium in the turtle could be illustrated as in Figure 21.5. The accurate determination of each rate constant in such a complex system would require numerous experiments and a rather complicated mathematical model. Often the more useful models are those that are sufficiently realistic to answer specific questions or to help understand a particular process, yet are still computationally manageable (Whicker and Schultz, 1982). Two questions often asked in radioecology research are (1) how much of the ingested contaminant is

actually incorporated into the body (percent assimilation), and (2) how long does the assimilated contaminant subsequently stay in the body (the biological half-time or elimination rate)? Answers to these questions can be estimated, without knowing every individual rate constant in Figure 21.5, by orally administering a known quantity of tracer to the turtle and examining its subsequent elimination. This is accomplished by performing a series of whole-body radiation measurements on the live animal over time. A graph of the elimination of ^{85}Sr in a representative individual *T. scripta* following an acute dose is presented in Figure 21.6. The data can be fit to a two-component elimination model by nonlinear regression techniques (SAS Institute, 1982), in which the fraction of the ingested dose remaining in the turtle (i.e., the amount of ^{85}Sr, or q_t) at any time t is expressed mathematically as

$$q_t = A_1 e^{-\lambda_1 t} + A_2 e^{-\lambda_2 t} \qquad (21.5)$$

The short component (in relation to time) is generally an estimate of that portion of the initial amount of tracer

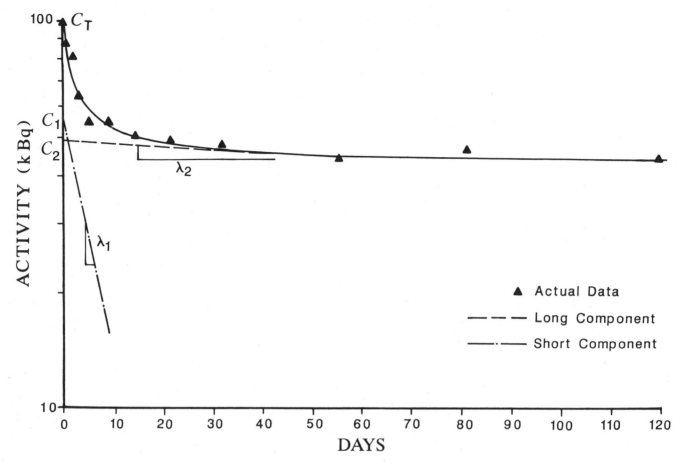

FIGURE 21.6.   Elimination of ^{85}Sr from *T. scripta* following an acute oral administration. Elimination rates for the respective components are estimated from λ_1 and λ_2. C_1 and C_2 are y-intercepts; C_T is the initial amount of tracer administered. Percent assimilation is estimated as C_2/C_T.

that is rapidly excreted by gut clearance. The fractional amount (A_1) is determined by dividing the y-intercept of the short component (C_1 in Fig. 21.6) by the initial amount of tracer administered (C_T in Fig. 21.6). The rate constant for gut clearance is the slope of the line for the short component (λ_1; in this example, 0.018/day). The long component of the curve represents material actually incorporated into body tissues. The y-intercept of the long component (C_2) divided by C_T is an estimate of the percent assimilation (A_2). The slope of the long component (λ_2) estimates the rate at which the assimilated tracer is subsequently eliminated from the body. A_2 and λ_2 are the values most often compared in the radioecology literature and are the parameters that can answer the two questions presented earlier. In the above example the turtle lost 52% of the ^{85}Sr through initial gut excretion of nonassimilated material with a half-time of 3.8 days (ln $2/\lambda_1$). It assimilated 48% of the ingested ^{85}Sr with a long-term biological half-time in excess of 1,000 days, resulting in this equation:

$$q_t = 0.52e^{-0.018t} + 0.48e^{-0.0006t}$$

Obviously, this simplified model is not a true physiological representation of the animal. However, the simpler model allows one to estimate the parameters A_2 and λ_2 (i.e., percent assimilation and rate of elimination), processes that are vital to the understanding of isotope kinetics within the animal.

Remember that transport models are generally quantitatively simple representations of real, complex systems (Whicker and Schultz, 1982). In equation 21.5 we have followed the notation of Whicker and Schultz (1982) by using the symbol λ as an estimate of the true rate constant (k). The λ values, although having the same dimensional units as k values (t^{-1}), are derived parameters that are not necessarily equal to the real rate constants of a system (Whicker and Schultz, 1982), the real rate constants being the k's in Figure 21.5. In the above example the simplified two-component elimination model could be depicted as

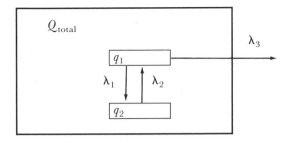

Q_{total} is the quantity of ^{85}Sr determined by whole-body counting of the turtle at various times and corresponds to q_t in equation 21.5. Compartment q_1 is a simplification of the first four compartments in Figure 21.5 (gastrointestinal tract, blood, soft tissue, and kidney), with compartment 1 (gastrointestinal tract) of primary importance. Compartment q_2 is a simplification of the bone compartments, where most of the Sr resides. The k values in Figure 21.5 are related to the estimated rate constants λ_1, λ_2, and λ_3. The differential equations for the quantity of tracer in each compartment are

$$\frac{dq_1}{dt} = q_2\lambda_2 - q_1(\lambda_1 + \lambda_3) \qquad (21.6)$$

$$\frac{dq_2}{dt} = q_1\lambda_1 - q_2\lambda_2 \qquad (21.7)$$

The numerical values for the parameters in equations 21.6 and 21.7 can be estimated efficiently by a computerized curve-fitting routine that adjusts the parameters to the best fit of the data (Whicker and Schultz, 1982). If required for a specific question, further experimentation and more detailed modeling could be used to refine our conceptual and mathematical representation of the system. More thorough and detailed presentations of radionuclide kinetics can be found in Atkins (1969), Wagner (1979), and Whicker and Schultz (1982).

JAMES R. SPOTILA
Department of Biology
State University College
1300 Elmwood Avenue
Buffalo, New York 14222
and
Savannah River Ecology Laboratory
Drawer E
Aiken, South Carolina 29802

Current address:
Department of Bioscience and Biotechnology
Drexel University
Philadelphia, Pennsylvania 19104

ROBERT E. FOLEY
New York Department of Environmental Conservation
Hale Creek Field Station
Gloversville, New York 12078

EDWARD A. STANDORA
Department of Biology
State University College
1300 Elmwood Avenue
Buffalo, New York 14222

Thermoregulation and Climate Space of the Slider Turtle

Abstract

Trachemys scripta has a selected temperature of 28°–29° C, and its greatest capacity for activity is between 25° and 30° C. Temperature tolerance ranges from 2° to 44.5° C, although the critical thermal maximum is 41.0°–41.7° C. In general, freshwater turtles are 7 to 25 times more tolerant to anoxia than are other reptiles; however, mechanisms of winter survival of *T. scripta* remain to be determined. The climate space indicates that in full sun this turtle can withstand 32° C in wind of 400 cm/sec and 19° C in still air. Under a clear night sky it can survive a low of 9° C in still air and 3° C at 400 cm/sec. It can live in water between 1° and 40° C. The climate space predicts the opportunistic behavioral thermoregulatory response reported for *T. scripta* in Par Pond.

Introduction

The pond slider turtle (*Trachemys scripta*) is an aquatic turtle inhabiting ponds, lakes, and slow-moving bodies of water that have abundant aquatic vegetation, basking sites, and occasional cleared areas nearby for nesting (Morreale and Gibbons, 1986). On the Savannah River Plant (SRP) in South Carolina, *T. scripta* inhabit a variety of habitats ranging from Carolina bays to the Par Pond Reservoir system (Gibbons, 1970b). They live primarily in water throughout their lives, emerging onto land to lay their eggs and to migrate to other bodies of water (Morreale et al., 1984; Gibbons, 1970d, 1986). Like other turtles, they have the ability to regulate their body temperature by means of physiology and behavior within the constraints imposed on them by biophysical interactions with the physical environment (Spotila et al., 1984).

For the past several years researchers in our laboratory have been studying the thermal ecology of *T. scripta*, especially related to the environment of the SRP. The thermal biology of reptiles has been reviewed by Avery (1982), Bartholomew (1982), and Huey (1982), and thermoregulation of turtles has been discussed by Hutchison (1979). Recently we (Spotila and Standora, 1985b) discussed the effect of body size on the thermal energetics of turtles. In this chapter we review our past studies and those of others on the thermoregulation of *T. scripta* and discuss the role of heat energy exchange in determining the constraints of the physical environment on the thermoregulation of this turtle. A climate space diagram is developed for *T. scripta*, and the behavioral thermoregulation of this species in Par Pond is discussed in terms of the limits imposed by its biophysical ecology.

Physiological Thermoregulation

Several studies have shown that turtles can exert some control over body temperature (T_b) by physiological mechanisms. Webb and Johnson (1972) confirmed that considerable physiological control of head temperature is exhibited by *Chelodina longicollis* heated radiantly. Spray and May (1972) reported that *T. scripta* and *Chrysemys picta* heated faster than they cooled and that the heating rates of dead turtles were the same as cooling rates of live turtles. Lucey (1974) suggested that changes in heating and cooling rates of *T. scripta* may be due to changes in heart rate and blood flow to the skin and carapace. He found that, initially, the head heats faster than the body. When head temperature reaches 30° C, the body heating rate becomes greater and is associated with a change in heart rate. Hutton et al. (1960) and Jackson (1971) demonstrated that changes in ventilation, heart rate, and oxygen consumption of *T. scripta* were proportional to changes in body temperature. Weathers and White (1971) stated that peripheral vascular responses to heating and cooling in *Pseudemys floridana* appear to represent a means of changing functional insulation and may contribute to the thermoregulatory capacities of this turtle. Thus, these turtles have considerable physiological control over their T_b.

The integument of *T. scripta*, like that of other reptiles, is not specialized to retain internally generated heat but rather has an important effect in modifying heat flow to

and from the environment (Cena et al., 1986). The conductivity of reptile skin lies between 392 and 502 mW/m·K (Gates, 1980; Drane, 1981). Because most substrates have a greater conductivity than animal tissue, the rate-limiting step in conduction is usually within the skin (Spotila et al., 1972; Monteith, 1973; Tracy, 1976). Changes in blood flow can greatly affect heat loss or gain (Morgareidge and White, 1969; Grigg and Alchin, 1976; Smith et al., 1978) because blood shunted to the skin rapidly transfers heat between the body core and surface. Under this circumstance, heat transfer between the surface and the environment then becomes the limiting step in warming or cooling the turtle.

Blood flow to the skin of the turtles *T. scripta* and *Chelydra serpentina*, crocodilians, and several lizards appears to be controlled by a reflex response such that warm skin is perfused with more blood than is cold skin. Flows are similar during heating, cooling, and steady-state body temperatures at the same skin temperature in the alligator *Alligator mississippiensis* (Weinheimer et al., 1982). In the Australian lizard (*Tiliqua scincoides*), this local effect of heat on skin perfusion appears to act through changes in the arterioles and venules of the inner surface component of the superficial dermis (Drane and Webb, 1980). We expect that the same is true for turtles. In *Trachemys scripta*, changes in blood flow should affect heat loss and gain from the soft skin of the legs and neck and, to a lesser extent, the heat transfer through the skin on the shell. This may explain the commonly observed behavior of basking turtles in which they extend their head and limbs during basking. Heat loss from the green turtle (*Chelonia mydas*) also occurs through the soft tissues of the neck and the proximal area of the flippers (Heath and McGinnis, 1980). Thus, local changes in blood flow to the skin would tend to increase the rate of heat absorption when the skin warmed during basking and would tend to decrease the rate of heat loss when the skin cooled upon the turtle's reentry into the water. This involuntary mechanism should maximize the time *T. scripta* spends at physiologically and behaviorally optimal temperatures.

Metabolism

In addition to the physiological changes that affect T_b and heat transfer in *T. scripta*, the turtle generates some heat through metabolism. The standard metabolic rate (SMR) of *T. scripta* increases with body temperature (T_b) according to the equation

$$\log \text{SMR} = -2.8780 + 0.0458(T_b) \qquad (22.1)$$

where SMR is measured as oxygen consumption in cm³ O_2/g·h at standard temperature and pressure, dry air (Fig. 22.1). Active metabolic rate (AMR) in *T. scripta* that are stimulated to activity increases with increasing T_b

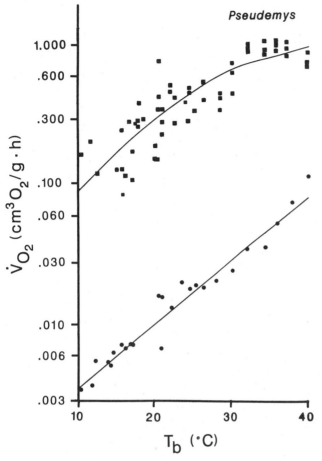

FIGURE 22.1. Standard and active metabolic rates ($\dot{V}_{O_2}$) in *T. scripta*. Each circle is the mean of approximately 10 hours of measurement of standard metabolic rate of an individual at a given temperature; squares represent individual determinations of active metabolic rate. Regression lines were constructed on the basis of equations 22.1 and 22.2. From Gatten (1974b) with permission.

from 10° to 32° C, remains constant from 32° to 38° C, and decreases slightly at 40° C. This is described as

$$\log AMR = -1.7541 + 0.0754(T_b) \\ - 0.00078(T_b)^2 \qquad (22.2)$$

The aerobic metabolic scope (AMR − SMR) for activity is 1.75 times greater in *T. scripta* than in the more sluggish box turtle (*Terrapene ornata*) at 30° C (Gatten, 1974b). Heart rate also increases with T_b in both resting and active slider turtles and is described as

$$\log SHR = 0.4557 + 0.0286(T_b)$$

where SHR is standard heart rate (beats/min), and as

$$\log AHR = 0.5461 + 0.0624(T_b) - 0.00067(T_b)^2$$

where AHR is active heart rate (beats/min). Heart rate increases in activity by a factor of 3.3 at 25° C and by a factor of 2.3 at 10° and 40° C (Gatten, 1974b). An increase in heart rate is not sufficient to provide the increased oxygen needed for aerobic metabolism during warming and exercise. The increase in oxygen pulse must be provided by an increase in stroke volume or arterial-venous oxygen difference. The relative contribution of these mechanisms is unknown (Gatten, 1974c), but unpublished data on *Chelydra serpentina* indicate that it probably changes with temperature (Gatten, pers. com.). These data and those for metabolism suggest that the capacity for activity in *T. scripta* is greatest at T_b between 25° and 30° C and is reduced at lower and higher temperatures.

Temperature Tolerance

Trachemys scripta can tolerate temperatures between 2° C (Schubauer and Parmenter, 1981) and 40° C. Boyer (1965) and Moll and Legler (1971) reported lethal temperatures (LT) of 44.4° to 44.5° C for *T. scripta* in rapid-heating experiments. However, their turtles were showing signs of severe heat stress at temperatures below 40° C. The LT_{50} is probably no higher than 40° C. The critical thermal maximum (CTM) is 41.0° to 41.7° C for turtles from Georgia and Oklahoma (Hutchison et al., 1966). Values for related turtles range from 39.4° C for *Pseudemys rubriventris* to 40.4° C for *P. nelsoni*, 40.8° C for *P. floridana*, and 41.8° C for *P. concinna*. *Chrysemys picta* from Rhode Island and Minnesota have a CTM of 40.9° C, whereas those from Michigan have a CTM of 42.2° C, and the same species from Nova Scotia, Wisconsin, and Louisiana have intermediate values. In general, the semiaquatic emydid turtles have intermediate tolerances to high temperatures ($\bar{x} = 41.6°$ C), the more aquatic Chelydridae (*Chelydra*, $\bar{x} = 39.4°$ C) and Trionychidae ($\bar{x} = 40.0°$ C) have low CTMs, and the terrestrial Testudinidae (*Gopherus* and *Testudo*) have high CTMs ($\bar{x} = 43.3°$ C; Hutchison et al., 1966). Body size and age do not affect the CTM of *Chelydra serpentina* (Williamson et al., 1989). There are differences in CTM with body size in *Chrysemys picta* (Hutchison et al., 1966), but it is not clear if this is due to differences between juveniles and adults or due to head-body temperature differences related to heating rates (Webb and Witten, 1973). Additional research is needed on the molecular adaptations to temperature in turtles that may be reflected in ontogenetic changes in thermal tolerance (Prosser, 1986).

Selected Temperature

The mean selected temperature of *T. scripta* is 28°–29° C as measured in the laboratory and field. Gatten (1974a) reported that recently fed *T. scripta* tested in a laboratory temperature gradient had a mean body temperature of

29.1° C, with a range of 19°–39° C and with 50% of the observations ranging between 26° and 32° C. The mean selected temperature of nonfed *T. scripta* was 24.6° C. Turtles provided with artificial basking sites in the laboratory had a mean T_b of 30.6° C, with a range of 27.2° to 38.0° C (Boyer, 1965). Cagle (1946) found this species active in the field at a T_b of 10°–37° C, with a "preferred activity temperature range" of 18°–30° C. In Panama, actively feeding *T. scripta* had a T_b of 26.0°–34.4° C ($\bar{x}$ = 29.1° C), and basking turtles had a T_b of 29.0°–34.0° C ($\bar{x}$ = 31.9° C; Moll and Legler, 1971).

Using multichannel telemetry, Standora (1982) found that free-ranging *T. scripta* in a pond on the SRP had deep body temperatures, throughout the year, from 4.6° to 38.2° C, with a selected (preferred) temperature in summer of 28° C. These turtles had a diel cycle in T_b, with mean daily excursions of 4.2° to 10.4° C, depending on the season. Body temperatures peaked during the afternoon and were lowest at night. The highest temperature recorded was 40.0° C for the carapace surface. During winter the most frequently recorded deep body temperature class (± 1° C) was 6° C. This changed to 26° C in spring, 28° C in summer, and 14° C in autumn. Thus, there appears to be a seasonal shift in T_b accepted for activity by this species. Standora observed turtles swimming and initiating basking at T_b below 6° C during winter. Likewise, Schubauer and Parmenter (1981) reported that *T. scripta* move sluggishly in Par Pond at water temperatures between 5° and 11° C and bask out of the water at air temperatures as low as 2° C. These seasonal differences are probably related to differences in nutritional status (Hammond et al., 1988), ambient temperature, photoperiod (Graham and Hutchison, 1979), age, and reproductive condition.

Winter Survival

Aquatic turtles overwinter at the bottom of a lake or river and may be buried in mud. The use of the term "hibernation" to describe the behavioral and physiological events accompanying winter dormancy in reptiles has been questioned by Mayhew (1965), Whittow (1973), and Hutchison (1979). However, Gatten (1987) stated that winter-dormant reptiles undergo profound physiological changes parallel to those in winter-dormant mammals and agreed with Gregory (1982) that the term "hibernation" is clearly applicable to reptiles.

During hibernation, anaerobic metabolism is very important because oxygen may be limited in the bottom mud. Freshwater turtles are well adapted to anoxia. They can survive several hours in a nitrogen atmosphere and can survive days of forced submergence (Belkin, 1963; Ultsch et al., 1984). Diving turtles exhibit bradycardia and redistribution of cardiac output (White and Ross, 1966). They are 7 to 25 times more tolerant to anoxia than

are lizards, snakes, crocodilians, and marine turtles. Their ability to survive hypoxia is due primarily to their capacity to rely on glycolysis and endure the buildup of lactate (Millen et al., 1964; Robin et al., 1964; Jackson, 1968; Seymour, 1982; Gatten, 1985, 1987).

When the soft-shelled turtle (*Trionyx spiniferus*), musk turtle (*Sternotherus odoratus*), *Chelydra serpentina*, and *Chrysemys picta* were forcibly submerged at 10° C under anoxic conditions, lactate concentrations rose and blood pH and HCO_3^- levels fell continuously in all species (Ultsch et al., 1984). Survival times were 2.6 days for *Trionyx*, 5.2 days for *Sternotherus*, 8.5 days for *Chelydra*, and 17.0 days for *Chrysemys*. In another experiment *Chrysemys picta* accumulated up to 3,000 μg per gram of total body lactate in two weeks when forcibly submerged at 5° C, without becoming comatose (Gatten, 1981). *Chrysemys picta* resting in air or freely diving at 5° C have low lactate levels ($\bar{x}$ = 870 μg/g). They build up high lactate levels (5,580 μg/g) while overwintering but can survive at 0° to 8° C in the field at least 67 days without breathing. At 3° C they can survive anoxia under water for up to 168 days (Ultsch and Jackson, 1982a,b). Thus, at low temperatures their metabolic rate is reduced enough to permit survival in ice-covered northern ponds by anaerobic metabolism without a buildup of lethal levels of lactate.

Trachemys scripta may have a similar capacity for anaerobic metabolism under cold conditions. However, in many parts of their geographic range they are not restricted to the bottom mud for the entire winter. In Par Pond and other aquatic habitats on the SRP, *T. scripta* spend much of their time on the bottom but occasionally swim through the water column and even bask out of water on clear sunny days (Schubauer and Parmenter, 1981; Standora, 1982; Spotila et al., 1984). During these periods body temperatures rise to as high as 28.1° C ($\bar{x}$ = 10.8° C; Standora, 1982), and the turtles can eliminate CO_2, take up O_2, and reduce the levels of lactate in their tissues and blood. These periods of aquatic and aerial activity may be crucial in allowing *T. scripta* to survive long periods of submergence during winter in the southern part of their range. Sexton (1959b) and Gibbons (1967a) reported that *C. picta* were active under ice in Michigan lakes in December and February. These turtles probably used aquatic gas exchange to supply the oxygen needed to sustain their activity metabolism during these periods when aerial exchange was generally unavailable.

Climate Space

Like all other animals, *T. scripta* obeys the laws of physics and is intimately connected to the physical environment by heat energy exchange as described by the laws of thermodynamics (Gates, 1962). Heat energy exchange determines the turtle's body temperature and thus affects biochemical, physiological, and behavioral processes.

The transfer of heat energy occurs by a variety of physical processes (Kreith, 1973). In the case of a turtle under water, the predominant modes of energy exchange are convection and conduction (see Erskine and Spotila, 1977, for application of underwater heat transfer to biological systems). In the aerial environment, a turtle encounters a more complex energy exchange because of additional modes of heat transfer. When turtles emerge into the atmosphere, they are subjected to evaporative water loss, to the effects of wind, to conduction, and to thermal loading from direct, scattered, and diffuse solar radiation and from thermal radiation from the atmosphere and its surroundings. Detailed descriptions of animal heat-energy budgets have been given by Birkebak (1966) and Porter and Gates (1969) and used or modified by Heller and Gates (1971), Spotila et al. (1972, 1973), Porter et al. (1973), Tracy (1976), Porter and James (1979), Bakken (1981), Scott et al. (1982), and Christian et al. (1983) among others. Gates (1980) described biophysical ecology in detail, and Tracy (1982) reviewed the application of biophysical modeling to reptiles. We discussed heat and food energy budgets of ectothermic vertebrates (Spotila and Standora, 1985a) and environmental constraints on the thermal energetics of sea turtles (Spotila and Standora, 1985b). Derivation of a climate space diagram for *T. scripta* now allows us to consider the role of heat energy exchange in the thermoregulation of this turtle.

The turtle-environment energy interaction can be defined by use of an energy budget equation that accounts for each mode of heat transfer between the turtle and its environment. As a good first approximation, we can assume that the turtle is in a steady-state energy balance with the environment. *Trachemys scripta* are small and have a relatively low capacity for heat storage, so that they are very close to heat energy equilibrium with the environment. In steady state, net energy flow between the turtle and its environment is zero, so that

$$\text{energy}_{\text{in}} = \text{energy}_{\text{out}}$$

The animal receives energy in the form of solar and thermal radiation from the environment and heat from metabolic activity. Energy leaves the animal in the form of thermal radiation to the environment, convection to the atmosphere, evaporation, and conduction to the substrate. These factors are combined into an energy budget equation:

$$Q_{\text{abs}} + M = \epsilon\sigma(T_{\text{r}} + 273)^4 + h_{\text{c}}(T_{\text{r}} - T_{\text{a}}) + E_{\text{t}} + C \tag{22.3}$$

where Q_{abs} is the radiation absorbed (W/m²), M is the heat produced by metabolism (W/m²), ϵ is the surface emissivity of the animal (1.0), σ is the Stefan-Boltzmann constant (5.673×10^{-8} W/m²·K⁴), T_{r} is the radiant sur-

face temperature (° C), h_{c} is the convective heat transfer coefficient (W/m².° C), T_{a} is the air temperature (° C), E_{t} is the total evaporative water loss (W/m²), and C is the conduction (W/m²). Radiant surface temperature (T_{r}) is a function of T_{b}, the thickness and quality of the animal's insulation, and the net heat production inside the turtle. This relationship is expressed as

$$T_{\text{r}} = T_{\text{b}} - \frac{d_{\text{s}}}{k_{\text{s}}}(M - E_{\text{r}}) \tag{22.4}$$

where d_{s} is the thickness of the shell (cm), k_{s} is the conductivity of bone (W/m·° C), and E_{r} is the respiratory evaporative water loss (W/m²). Insulation is dependent upon the average thickness and conductivity of the bony shell covering the turtle's body. We used the value for conductivity of bone (0.5004 W/m·° C) computed from Chato (1969). Bentley and Schmidt-Nielsen (1966) reported that 22% of *T. scripta*'s evaporative water loss is from the respiratory surfaces; thus, $E_{\text{r}} = 0.22E_{\text{t}}$.

Substituting equation 22.4 into 22.3, we have

$$Q_{\text{abs}} + M = [T_{\text{b}} - \frac{d_{\text{s}}}{k_{\text{s}}}(M - E_{\text{r}}) + 273]^4$$
$$+ h_{\text{c}}[T_{\text{b}} - \frac{d_{\text{s}}}{k_{\text{s}}}(M - E_{\text{r}}) - T_{\text{a}}] + E_{\text{t}} + C \tag{22.5}$$

This equation defines the heat energy balance between a turtle and its environment. We determined shell thickness, evaporative water loss, and convection coefficients in the laboratory and used these data to solve the energy budget equation 22.5 and to formulate a climate space for *T. scripta*.

We measured shell thickness (d_{s}) at a series of points on plastrons of fresh-killed turtles using a Helios vernier caliper (± 0.05 mm). Average plastron thickness (y, in mm) was related to plastron length (x, in mm) as described by the regression equation

$$y = 0.072x - 2.98$$

We also measured the percentage of the plastron surface area in contact with the substrate and found that it was minimal. Only 4% to 8% of the total surface area of a turtle is in contact with the substrate when the turtle is basking or resting on land or on a log out of the water. Because rates of heat exchange by conduction would be minimal, we have not included conduction in this first-order approximation.

We (Foley and Spotila, 1978) determined evaporative water loss (EWL) for a range of sizes of *T. scripta* at 15°, 25°, and 35° C and wind speeds of 10, 100, and 400 cm/sec. Rates of water loss increased as wind speed and air temperature increased but were inversely propor-

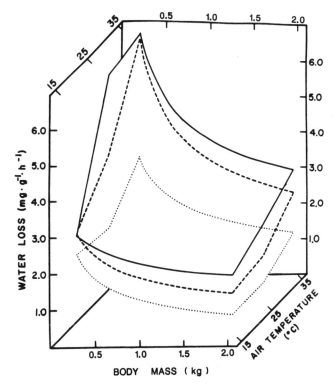

FIGURE 22.2. Three-dimensional plot of evaporative water loss from *Trachemys scripta* as a function of body mass, air temperature, and wind speed. The plane outlined with dotted lines is water loss in still air (10 cm/sec), the plane outlined with dashed lines is water loss at 100 cm/sec, and the plane outlined with solid lines is water loss at 400 cm/sec. The multiple regression equation to define evaporative water loss as a function of air temperature, wind speed, and body size is given by Foley and Spotila (1978). Used with permission.

tional to body size (Fig. 22.2). An increase in wind speed from 10 to 100 cm/sec caused a large initial decrease in boundary layer thickness and a large increase in EWL. A further increase in wind speed up to 400 cm/sec had a relatively smaller effect on EWL because much of the boundary layer was already removed at 100 cm/sec. We used regression equations to compute water loss rates for various sizes of turtles at different air temperatures and wind speeds.

Data from cooling curve experiments were used to calculate convection coefficients according to Wathen et al. (1971). Six turtles (12.2–25.6 cm in length) served as subjects for the construction of aluminum castings. A negative cast of each turtle was prepared using an alginate fast-setting dental molding compound. The live animal was removed unharmed, and hot wax was poured into the mold to produce a replica of the turtle. The wax turtle was placed in a cylindrical metal collet and imbedded in gray investment plaster. The wax mold was melted from within the plaster-filled collet, which was then dried and cured at 482° C for 15 to 20 hours. Molten aluminum was poured

into the plaster mold before it cooled, to produce a solid aluminum replica of the original turtle. This technique provided aluminum castings that were accurate representations of the size, shape, and surface characteristics of each turtle.

Each aluminum turtle was provided with three 38-gauge copper-constantan thermocouples, secured with epoxy cement. One was implanted at the center of mass through a 0.84-millimeter drilled hole; one was attached at the surface of the anterior edge of the carapace; and the third was attached at the posterior edge of the carapace. Casting temperatures were monitored throughout the course of experimentation by a Kaye multipoint recorder. The casting was heated in an oven to above 65° C and placed perpendicular to wind flow in the center of a wind tunnel (test section of 122 × 122 × 180 cm) on a polystyrene pad (61 × 56 × 2.5 cm). The time-temperature responses of the casting were measured between 65° C and equilibrium. Temperatures of the polystyrene, air stream, walls, and ceiling of the wind tunnel were continuously monitored throughout each cooling period. Castings were cooled to equilibrium with air temperature. This procedure was repeated for the six castings at three different wind speeds (10, 100, and 400 cm/sec). Details of these experiments were provided by Foley (1976). As wind speed increased, h_c increased. There was a clear effect of body size at a wind speed of 400 cm/sec, but at 100 cm/sec and 10 cm/sec there were no significant differences in h_c between different-sized turtles. A larger range of body sizes does result in differences in h_c (Spotila and Standora, 1985b). Convection coefficients were used to solve equation 22.5.

Several climate spaces were constructed for different sizes of *T. scripta*. Unlike those for alligators (Spotila et al., 1972), these climate spaces were almost identical in size and shape. Therefore, a typical climate space is presented for a turtle weighing 1,000 g (Fig. 22.3). Standard metabolic rates were taken from Gatten (1974b), and heat loss due to respiratory evaporative water loss (E_r) was calculated according to Bentley and Schmidt-Nielsen (1966), using our total evaporative water loss measurements. Evaporative water loss was multiplied by 2.430 × 10^6 J·K/g (latent heat of vaporization of water) to convert it to heat loss.

The boundaries of the climate space are fixed in part by the interaction of the turtle's physical properties (size, shape, absorptivity to solar radiation) and those of its environment (Fig. 22.3). The line marked "full sun" represents the radiation absorbed by a turtle at different air temperatures on a cloudless day when body orientation provides maximum exposure to direct sunlight. This sets the right side of the climate space. Absorptivity to solar radiation (a) was determined by measuring the reflectances of the carapace of a preserved *T. scripta* with a Beckman DK-2A spectroreflectometer in the laboratory

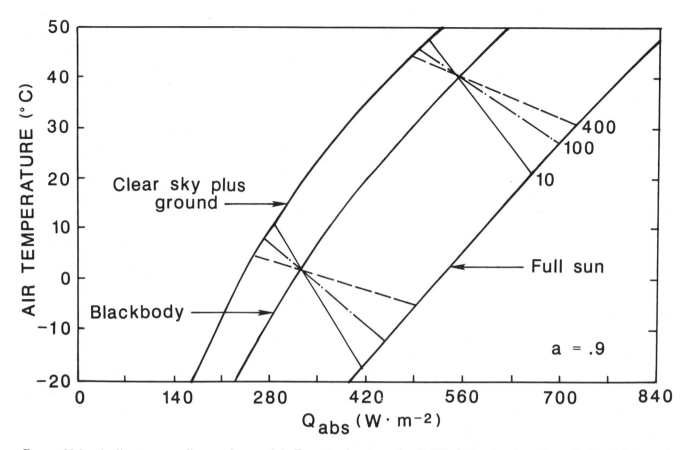

FIGURE 22.3.   A climate space diagram for an adult *T. scripta* of average size (1,000 g) showing the effects of solar and thermal radiation, air temperature, and wind speed under steady-state conditions. The solid, dashed, and dot-dashed lines in each set were calculated for wind speeds of 10, 100, and 400 cm/sec, respectively. Upper limits were calculated from equation 22.5 at a body temperature of 40° C, using corresponding values of metabolism = 0.0899 ml O_2/g·h, and heat loss from evaporative water loss = 19.54 W/m². Lower limits were drawn according to the same procedures at a body temperature of 1° C; metabolism = 0.0012 ml O_2/g·h, and heat loss from evaporative water loss = 14.65 W/m².

of W. P. Porter (University of Wisconsin—Madison). The average reflectances ($\bar{r}$) of various portions of the carapace were computed by integrating the reflectance spectrum over the normal solar spectrum with the computer program SOLRAD (McCullough and Porter, 1971). The absorptivity was calculated as $a = 1 - \hat{r}$. Light-colored areas of the carapace with yellow streaks had an a of .81; darker areas had an a of .86 to .89. Because the preserved animal appeared to be lighter in color than living *T. scripta* from the SRP, we assumed that a was .9 for these calculations. The absorptivity of the turtle's surface to long-wave radiation was assumed to be 1.0 (Gates, 1980).

The line labeled "clear sky plus ground" represents radiation absorbed by the turtle at night from the sky, the atmosphere, and the substrate. This sets the boundary for the left side of the climate space. The "blackbody" line is a reference line indicating the amount of energy received by a turtle in a blackbody cavity where energy flux is equal from all sides (e.g., an underground burrow). This also represents a turtle when it is under water. In water, heat

transfer occurs by conduction-convection because thermal radiation does not penetrate water. Solar radiation may add heat to a turtle that is at or just below the surface, but in general a turtle submerged more than a few centimeters below the surface will be in a unithermal environment where heat transfer is rapid.

The upper boundary was determined by solving equation 22.5 for Q_{abs}, using a body temperature of 40° C (a temperature causing extreme behavioral and physiological stress and assumed to be the LT_{50} value), corresponding metabolic rate and evaporative water loss, and the convection coefficient for a given wind speed. Substrate temperature was assumed to be equal to air temperature. This procedure was repeated for several air temperatures, and the upper lines were plotted as air temperature versus Q_{abs}. Lower lines were computed for a body temperature of 1° C following the above procedures. Upper and lower boundaries were determined for wind speeds of 10, 100, and 400 cm/sec.

From the climate space (Fig. 22.3), we can determine various limitations that are imposed on the turtle by the environment. A turtle must restrict its activities to those microclimates contained within its climate space. It can exceed these limits for short periods of time, depending upon its heat storage capacity. However, it cannot exceed these limits for extended periods without altering its energy equilibrium and risking death. In full sunlight, a turtle can withstand higher air temperatures (32° C) when subjected to wind speeds of 400 cm/sec than it can in still air (19° C). Still air reduces the rate of convective and evaporative heat loss, so these factors cannot compensate for the high radiation load absorbed. Convective heat loss is reduced at 10 cm/sec because a thick boundary layer of air surrounds and insulates the turtle (Foley and Spotila, 1978; Spotila and Standora, 1985b). Increasing wind speed decreases the boundary layer thickness and allows more heat transfer by convection and evaporation. Thus, the animal can withstand higher air temperatures in full sunlight because an increase in wind speed couples the animal more closely to environmental temperatures and reduces the effect of solar heating. A turtle can withstand ambient temperatures equal to its upper lethal temperature when sheltered in a blackbody cavity. At night, air temperatures as high as 48° C can be tolerated in still air under a clear sky; however, these are conditions that never occur in this turtle's habitat.

Under clear sky and ground conditions, the turtle loses large amounts of heat via thermal radiation; therefore, survival at cold night temperatures (in the lower left portion of the climate space) is dependent upon air temperature and wind speed. When exposed to a clear night sky, a turtle cannot survive an air temperature less than 9° C in still air or less than 3° C at a wind speed of 400 cm/sec. In still air, a turtle receives less heat via convection, thus reducing its ability to tolerate cold conditions while radiating heat away to the cold sky. Convective heat transfer to the turtle increases with wind speed, and the animal can survive colder temperatures because it is more effectively coupled to air temperature and less to the radiative environment. During cold weather, a blackbody cavity or water provides a tolerable habitat to temperatures as low as 1° C.

On cold sunny days, the turtle can survive at lower air temperatures than on cold nights because it is receiving large amounts of solar radiation. In still air, the turtle loses less of the heat gained from the sun by convection than at high wind speed and can survive at lower air temperatures. Higher wind speeds remove heat and shift the lower survival temperature upward because heat gained from the sun is lost to the wind.

From this type of energy budget analysis, Foley (1976) predicted interactions between this species of turtle and its environment. Periods that are energetically stressful to *T. scripta* in a terrestrial environment include the hot summer months, cold winter months, and portions of the spring and fall when changeable weather conditions pro-

duce large and potentially lethal temperature fluctuations. From late fall to early spring, throughout most of its range in the United States, *T. scripta* must spend most of its time in protective cavities or in water (a blackbody substitute), where microclimate variations are minimal and potentially stressful environmental conditions can be avoided. In water, this turtle could be active throughout the year.

Basking, a commonly observed behavior in *T. scripta* and related species, can be predicted using energy budget analysis. Turtles may bask under conditions that are found outside the climate space; however, they must return to a less adverse environment within the climate space to prevent overheating. Duration of excursions beyond the climate space is limited by the heat storage capacity of these turtles. During spring and fall, turtles can bask for long periods of time because they have a lower body temperature at initiation of basking, and solar radiation is at relatively low intensities. When temperatures and radiation levels are higher in summer, the time spent basking by turtles is reduced. Cold conditions during the winter greatly restrict basking except on calm sunny days. Under these conditions a turtle could bask out of the water and gain a considerable thermal advantage. For example, a turtle's body temperature could reach 20° C if it basked in full sun, with still air, at an air temperature of 0° C.

Based on our data and those in the literature, the daily basking pattern for *T. scripta* can be predicted as follows: Cool environmental conditions during early spring should influence the turtle to bask in a unimodal activity pattern during the middle of the day. Water and body temperatures are low, but air temperatures and solar radiation during the middle of the day should stimulate basking. If weather conditions are favorable, basking may continue for long periods of time because Q_{abs} during this time of year would not increase the turtle's body temperature to lethal levels. As the seasons progress, air temperature and solar radiation intensity increase and influence the turtle to bask predominantly in a bimodal activity pattern. Morning and late afternoon or evening become the most favorable portions of the day for the turtle to emerge from the water. Basking around solar noon during the summer would cause the turtle to exceed the limits of its climate space; therefore, this should seldom occur. When fall conditions prevail, turtles should return to a unimodal pattern of basking.

Behavioral Response to Biophysical Constraints of the Par Pond Environment

We tested the predictions of the climate space model in a series of experiments on *T. scripta* in Par Pond and Dick's Pond, a 0.8-hectare abandoned farm pond on the SRP. Crawford et al. (1983) measured the operative environmental temperatures (T_e) for basking *T. scripta* at these two locations. Operative environmental temperature has been developed as a thermal index of microclimate and is defined as the temperature of an inanimate object of zero heat capacity with the same size, shape, and radiative properties as the animal exposed to the same microclimate. It represents the temperature along the blackbody line of the climate space that corresponds to the point the turtle occupies on the full-sun line when basking, assuming wind speed is the same. T_e can be calculated following equation 12 of Bakken (1976) as modified by Crawford et al. (1983). We measured T_e with hollow copper replicas of *T. scripta* painted with flat black paint with $a = .9 - .95$ and $\epsilon = 1.0$.

Operative environmental temperature was a good predictor of basking behavior of *T. scripta*. In general, turtles did not bask until T_e reached or exceeded their selected temperature of 28° C (Fig. 22.4). More than 98% of the turtles basking did so at T_e greater than or equal to 28° C. This was not an artifact of the analysis, because we often measured T_e of less than 28° C and only a few turtles basked at low T_e. This suggests that basking is not a random behavior but is primarily thermoregulatory. Operative environmental temperature was positively related to shortwave and total solar radiation as well as to air and substrate temperature. Regression equations that define these relationships were provided by Crawford et al. (1983). Schwarzkopf and Brooks (1985) used the equations to compute T_e for *Chrysemys picta* in Algonquin Park, Ontario, Canada, and found that *C. picta* basked most often in the morning when T_e was close to the selected T_b for this species (21.4° C). They also calculated T_e for *Chelydra serpentina*, using data from Obbard and Brooks (1979, 1981b) and found that the peak in basking activity for this species occurred with T_e at 28° C, which was close to the selected temperature (28.1° C) measured by Schuett and Gatten (1980). Movement of the sun through the day results in spatial variation in T_e's available to the turtles and influences their location and basking behavior (Crawford et al., 1983). At midday on a sunny summer day at Dick's Pond, *T. scripta* in deep water would experience a T_e of 24° C, while a turtle basking on a log near the center of the pond would experience a temperature of 45° C (Fig. 22.5). In the morning when the sun was low on the horizon, a turtle basking near the southwest shore would experience a T_e of 40° C, and a turtle along the northeast shore would experience a T_e of 26° C. Turtles in Dick's Pond and Par Pond responded to these types of differences and chose basking sites with T_e's of 28° C and higher, changing basking sites as the day progressed. Auth (1975) noted similar shifts in the location of basking turtles in a Florida pond. Thus, measurements of T_e of basking turtles are consistent with our predictions from the climate space of *T. scripta* and indicate that basking is a thermoregulatory behavior.

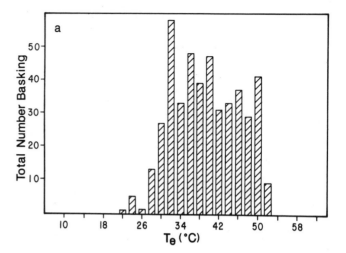

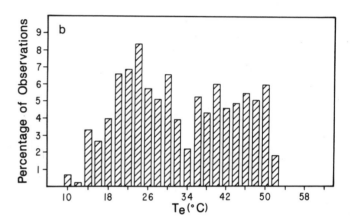

FIGURE 22.4. *a*, histogram of the total number of turtles (*T. scripta*) observed basking at Dick's Pond in 1979 and 1980, and their associated operative environmental temperatures (T_e, grouped by 2° C intervals). *b*, histogram of the frequencies of observed operative environmental temperatures (T_e) measured for hollow copper models of turtles at Dick's Pond on the SRP in 1979 and 1980 (temperatures are grouped by 2° C intervals). From Crawford et al. (1983) with permission.

Trachemys scripta in Par Pond used an opportunistic strategy of thermoregulation (Spotila et al., 1984) consistent with the constraints of their climate space. No *T. scripta* resided at the point of thermal discharge. Turtles in heated areas basked aquatically. Body temperatures telemetered from unrestrained individuals were within the selected temperature range. In the normothermic portions of the reservoir, turtles underwent atmospheric basking on sunny days throughout the year. In summer, basking during the day showed a bimodal curve (Fig. 22.6). On hot days, no turtles basked. In spring and fall, basking intensity showed a unimodal pattern. Schubauer and Parmenter (1981) reported turtles in normothermic areas of Par Pond basking on sunny, calm days at air temperatures as low as 2° C. These data support the

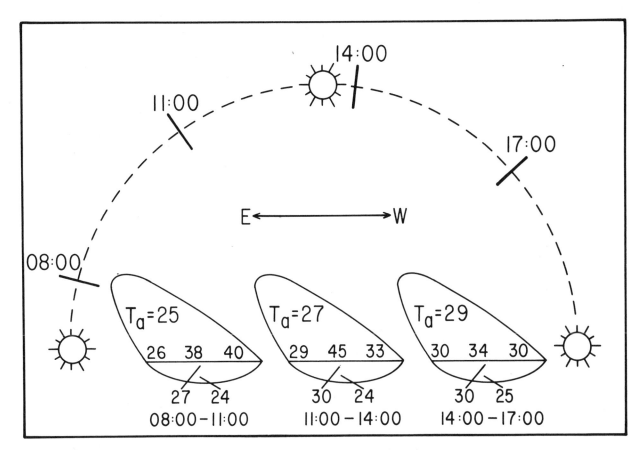

FIGURE 22.5. Operative environmental temperature (T_e) of *T. scripta* as affected by locations on Dick's Pond at different times on a sunny day in July and August. Temperatures on the maps of the pond are average T_e's for data collected every 30 minutes for the three-hour period indicated below the map. The dashed line indicates the path of the sun; intersecting solid lines represent the position of the sun at particular times. Each temperature indicates T_e for a different location on, in, or near the pond. In the cross-sectional diagram of the pond for 0800–1100 EDT, 26° C is T_e for a turtle basking on the northeast shore; 38° C is T_e for a turtle on a log or basking platform in the center of the pond; 40° C is T_e for a turtle basking on the southwest shore; 27° C is T_e for a turtle aquatically basking in the center of the pond; and 24° C is T_e for a turtle on the bottom. T_a is air temperature. The other cross sections of the pond present average T_e's for the periods 1100–1400 and 1400–1700. From Crawford et al. (1983) with permission.

predictions presented above and by Foley (1976). Data from other studies are also consistent with these predictions (Cagle, 1944b, 1950; Moll and Legler, 1971; Auth, 1975; Bury et al., 1979). These are discussed by Spotila et al. (1984). More recent data for *C. picta* (Schwarzkopf and Brooks, 1985) indicate that this species also displays unimodal basking patterns on cool days and bimodal basking patterns on warmer days in Algonquin Park.

Thus, *T. scripta* in Par Pond have adjusted to the thermoregulatory constraints imposed on them by this environment. They remain within their climate space and change their behavior as predicted from our heat energy budget analysis. Turtles in other locations respond with similar behavioral thermoregulatory strategies when exposed to similar microclimates. This should be reflected in various aspects of their life histories, including foraging strategies, growth, age and size at maturity, and re-

productive effort. The mechanistic relationships between these aspects of their ecological (heat and food) energetics remain to be determined.

Acknowledgments

We thank all the many colleagues at the State University of New York College at Buffalo and Savannah River Ecology Laboratory who have helped during various phases of this research. We especially appreciate the interest and enthusiasm of J. W. Gibbons, I. L. Brisbin, M. H. Smith, J. D. Congdon, R. I. Nestor, M. Vargo, J. L. Greene, K. K. Patterson, P. Johns, F. Stone, J. W. Coker, and S. Smith at SREL. At Buffalo, invaluable assistance was provided by K. Crawford, D. Erskine, F. Paladino, K. Terpin, J. P. Schubauer, R. D. Semlitsch, E. Berman, R. Koons, C. Scott, C. Ross-Block, C. Privatera,

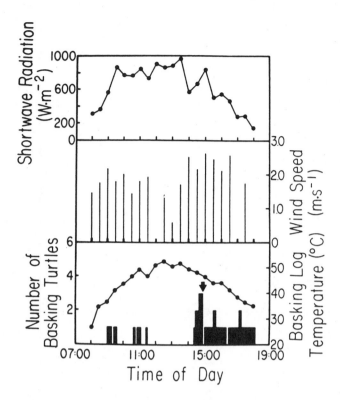

W. Schefler, R. Kubb, O. Rustgi, P. Dodson, J. Penalosa, P. Caron, L. Standora, and M. Jackson. This research was supported by DOE contracts to the State University of New York College at Buffalo (E-11-1-2502) and the University of Georgia (E-381-1-819), student research fellowships from the Savannah River Ecology Laboratory to J. P. Schubauer and R. D. Semlitsch, and travel grants from Oak Ridge Associated Universities to K. Crawford, J. P. Schubauer, R. D. Semlitsch, and the authors.

FIGURE 22.6.   Basking activity of *Trachemys scripta* and microclimatic conditions for a sunny July day at Susan's Swamp on Par Pond. Shortwave radiation (300–3,000 nm) shows depressions due to periodic cloud cover. Wind speeds are means for 15-minute periods. Basking log temperature is represented by a solid line connecting circles. Lower histogram indicates numbers of turtles basking. Arrow shows a disturbance that caused turtles to enter the water. Data are for 14 July 1976. From Spotila et al. (1984) with permission.

GERALD W. ESCH
DAVID J. MARCOGLIESE
TIMOTHY M. GOATER
KYM C. JACOBSON
Department of Biology
Wake Forest University
Winston-Salem, North Carolina 27109

Aspects of the Evolution and Ecology of Helminth Parasites in Turtles: A Review

Abstract

This chapter presents a review of the evolution and ecology of the helminth parasites of turtles, with primary emphasis on the slider (*Trachemys scripta*). Turtle parasites have probably undergone little adaptive radiation since turtles appeared in the Triassic. Species of nematodes and trematodes are well represented in turtles, but cestodes and acanthocephalans are not. Several studies have shown that seasonality, habitat stability, and ontogenetic shifts in diet are significant factors in influencing parasite populations in *T. scripta*. A comparative approach reveals that turtle feeding patterns are critical in affecting species diversity of helminth communities. The question of whether competition is an important structuring mechanism in the parasite communities in turtles is addressed. Recent results indicate that competitive interactions are minimal among four acanthocephalan congeners of *T. scripta*, because the four are both linearly and circumferentially sympatric in the host intestine. Future research should be directed at parasite infrapopulation dynamics and parasite biogeography in relation to turtle dispersal patterns. Such an approach would be valuable in addressing rapidly emerging concepts of parasite ecology as well as providing a useful source of information regarding the evolution and ecology of turtles.

Introduction

Parasitism, broadly defined, is a symbiotic relationship whereby one member of the association (the parasite) lives at the expense of the other (the host). More than 50% of the world's described organisms are parasitic in nature, and virtually every plant and animal species is, to some extent, parasitized during its life history (Price, 1980). Clearly, the success of the parasitic lifestyle is remarkable. Yet, surprisingly, only relatively recently have ecological and evolutionary concepts emerged for this diverse and highly successful group of organisms.

This review deals with the evolution and ecology of helminth parasites (Trematoda, Cestoda, Acanthocephala, and Nematoda) of turtles, with special emphasis on those of the slider turtle (*Trachemys scripta*). Investigators typically overlook the potential of using helminths as biological indicators of ecological relationships between hosts in terms of trophic interactions, migratory movements, foraging behaviors, and phylogenetic relationships. Many helminths have complex life cycles and, thus, commonly exploit food-web interactions, particularly predator-prey relationships, to effect transmission. Furthermore, because parasites have coevolved with their hosts, they are potential tools for understanding the evolutionary history of host species. These attributes present unique and valuable opportunities for developing additional insights into the ecology and evolution of the hosts that they infect.

We divide our review on the helminth parasites of turtles into two broad categories. The first emphasizes the systematics, taxonomy, and phylogenetic relationships between helminth parasites and their chelonian hosts. It focuses on reviewing the types of helminths infecting turtles, offering explanations for why some helminth taxa are depauperate, although others are well represented.

The second section of the review is concerned with the potential use of helminth parasites as indicators of turtle biology. First, we review the major theoretical concepts in parasite ecology, providing a framework for the remaining discussion. Second, we review certain critical features of slider turtle ecology and how factors such as host diet, age, temporal and spatial parameters, and seasonality influence the slider's parasite population dynamics. Third, helminth species diversities in a variety of turtles spanning aquatic to terrestrial habitats are examined within the context of several recent ecological concepts developed by Holmes and Price (1986) and Kennedy et al. (1986). Fourth, we examine what is probably the most contentious topic in community ecology, that is, the extent to which biotic interactions are important in structuring communities. In addressing this question, we illustrate the powerful comparative approach used in investigating patterns of helminth co-occurrence and structure within enteric helminth communities.

Finally, we conclude with prospects for future research employing turtles and their helminth parasites as study systems. We hope that the approach used in this review will entice further investigators to recognize the potential for using helminth parasites to assess evolutionary and ecological questions relating to their vertebrate hosts.

Evolutionary Considerations

The range of helminth parasite taxa infecting turtles is wide, extending from the primitive aspidogastrean trem-

atodes to the highly specialized acanthocephalans. Previously, it was believed that helminths evolved more slowly than their hosts. More recently, however, Price (1980) reasoned that certain properties of parasite populations, such as short generation times, large populations relative to the host, and isolated subpopulations of parasites, have led to high evolutionary capabilities. Therefore, parasites have been able to track evolutionary changes in their hosts and adapt to changing conditions quickly. Brooks (1979) suggested that the evolutionary history of a parasite taxon reflects the evolutionary history of the host. For example, he proposed that the digenean trematodes of crocodilians have coevolved with their hosts. Furthermore, the radiation of species of *Glypthelmins* (Trematoda) and proteocephalid cestodes has paralleled that of some anuran and salamander families (Brooks, 1977, 1978). Indeed, if the evolutionary history of a host is indicated by its parasite fauna, stability in a host lineage after a burst of adaptive radiation should be reflected by the parasites of that host (Baker, 1984). Chelonians appeared on the evolutionary scene early in the Triassic, 225 million years ago. These Mesozoic taxa differ little from their present-day counterparts (Martof et al., 1980). As a consequence, turtle parasites have undergone little adaptive radiation since the appearance of turtles in geologic history, certainly less radiation than parasites within the other major vertebrate taxa.

If one examines the geographic distribution of 21 families of nematodes that presumably evolved in reptiles and amphibians (Baker, 1984), 9 of 12 families found in turtles are cosmopolitan, and 1 other is found in at least six of the world's seven geographic regions (as defined by Baker, 1984; Table 23.1). If a cosmopolitan distribution indicates an older evolutionary age in a group, then it is suggested that there has been little opportunity for geographic isolation and subsequent adaptive radiation among turtle parasites.

On the other hand, certain components of the turtle parasite fauna do not reflect the evolutionary history of the host. That is, certain parasites have been acquired

Table 23.1. Geographic regions inhabited by families of nematodes that presumably evolved in amphibians and reptiles and in chelonians

Number of regions	Number of families	
	Amphibians and reptiles	Chelonians
0	--	9
1	1	0
2	2	1
3	3	1
4	1	0
5	0	0
6	1	1
7 (= cosmopolitan)	13	9

Note: Regions are from Baker (1984).

from other vertebrates by the so-called host-capture phenomenon, a common occurrence in the evolutionary history of the nematodes of vertebrates (Chabaud, 1981). However, Holmes and Price (1980) cautioned that these captured species, because of their subsequent speciation, will be difficult to distinguish from parasites that have had a long evolutionary association with their hosts. They noted that there are many generalist parasites with excellent potential for colonization and that these parasites will reflect the ecological, not the phylogenetic, history of the host. Baker (1984) asserted that captured parasites can be distinguished from heirloom parasites (whose ancestors were harbored by the host's ancestors) when the latter groups have a narrow host range and thus can be assumed to have evolved with their hosts. In contrast, captured parasites have a higher proportion of related genera and species in nonrelated host taxa.

An excellent review of the capture phenomenon is provided by Baker (1984) for nematodes parasitic in amphibians and reptiles. There are approximately 1,040 nematode species in amphibian and reptilian hosts. Of these, 146, or approximately 14%, are primarily parasites of chelonians. A relatively small number of nematode taxa (8 genera consisting of 22 species) are presumed to have originally evolved in invertebrates, fish, birds, or mammals (Table 23.2). As Baker et al. (1987) stated, "The presence of isolated monobasic genera in hosts such as salamanders and freshwater turtles represents individual parasite captures by these hosts in an aquatic habitat." These genera represent species from widely separated and geographically isolated localities, as well as those with a variety of life cycle patterns. Baker (1984) suggested that either they have been only recently acquired or they represent relatively long associations that have been unsuccessful in evolving further among their acquired host groups, presumably because of the stability of chelonian evolutionary history. With only 22 of 146 nematode species having been captured, the majority evolved directly with their hosts and represent long-term, coevolutionary partners. The latter group includes species of oxyuridans, ascaridans, spruridans, and strongylidans. Most of the nematode families possess a widespread distribution with little opportunity for speciation beyond the initial adaptive radiation that occurred during the Triassic. The great reptilian adaptive radiation at that time allowed for parallel radiation among reptilian parasites, with little phylogenetic splitting having occurred since.

It is feasible that other parasitic helminth taxa may have been captured as well. Digenetic trematodes show a high degree of specificity for their molluscan intermediate hosts. This indicates a long-standing evolutionary relationship between the Mollusca and Digenea and suggests the trematodes were primarily parasites of mollusks, with other intermediate and definitive hosts having been acquired during their subsequent evolutionary history.

Table 23.2. Nematode parasites of chelonians that presumably evolved in invertebrates, fish, birds, or mammals

Parasite	Number of genera in turtles	Number of species in turtles	Total number of genera
Ascaridia			
Seuratoidea			
Cucullanidae			
Cucullaninae	2	5	4
Ascaridoidea			
Anisakidae			
Anisakinae	1	1	6
Spirurida			
Camallanoidea			
Camallanidae			
Camallaninae	2	13	5
Dracunculoidea			
Dracunculidae	1	1	2
Physalopteroidea			
Physalopteridae			
Proleptinae	1	1	4
Filarioidea			
Onchocercidae			
Splendidofilariinae	1	1	16

Source: Condensed from Baker, 1984.

Thus, they have been amenable to capture by other taxa, including turtles. Cestodes, on the other hand, are suspected of having evolved initially in vertebrates, leading to increased host specificity for their definitive hosts. Generally, acanthocephalans are relatively host-specific, which implies a long coevolutionary history between them and their definitive hosts.

Turtles span a range of aquatic to terrestrial habitats and vary widely in their life histories and ecology. We believe that the relative paucity of acanthocephalan and cestode species in turtles is not related to habitat, behavior, or dietary preferences of the turtle hosts. The basis for this assertion rests with the knowledge that other vertebrate taxa are, generally, richly endowed with a wide mix of these helminth taxa, with chelonians being the exception (see Table 23.3). A taxonomic synopsis of chelonian parasites lends partial support to this notion. Approximately 70 families and 400 genera of digenetic trematodes infect vertebrates (Schell, 1980). Of this number, at least 21 families and 72 genera of trematodes are associated with chelonians; 11 families and 37 genera of nematodes are associated with chelonians (Ernst and Ernst, 1977). Yamaguti (1963) lists 37 families and 108 genera of acanthocephalans in vertebrates. Among turtles, however, there are only 1 family, 2 genera, and 8 species of acanthocephalans. Of the 58 families of Cestoda infecting vertebrates, only 1 is known to infect turtles (Ernst and Ernst, 1977).

A phylogenetic approach, based on the assumption that parasites characterize a host in much the same way as its morphological, cytological, and biochemical traits do, was used to examine the nature of phylogenetic relation-

Table 23.3. Checklist of the helminth parasites of *Trachemys scripta*

Trematoda	Cestoda
Monogenea	1. *Proteocephalus testudo*
1. *Neopolystoma domatilae*[a]	Acanthocephala
2. *N. orbiculare*	1. *Leptorhynchoides* sp.
3. *Polystomoidella hassalli*	2. *Neoechinorhynchus chelonos*
4. *P. oblongum*	3. *N. chrysemydis*
5. *Polystomoides coronatum*	4. *N. constrictus*[a]
Digenea	5. *N. emydis*
1. *Allassostoma magnum*	6. *N. emyditoides*
2. *Cephalogonimus vesicaudus*	7. *N. magnapapillatus*
3. *Dictyangium chelydrae*	8. *N. pseudemydis*
4. *Heronimus chelydrae*[a]	9. *N. stunkardi*[a]
5. *H. mollis*	Nematoda
6. *Macrovestibulum kepneri*	1. *Aplectana* sp.
7. *M. obtusicaudum*	2. *Camallanus microcephallus*
8. *Pneumatophilus variabilis*	3. *C. trispinosus*
9. *Protenes angustus*	4. *Chelonidracunculus* sp.
10. *Schizamphistomoides*	5. *Cissophyllus penitus*
tabascensis[a]	6. *Cucullanus cirratus*
11. *Spirorchis artericola*	7. *Gnathostoma procyonus*
12. *S. blandingioides*	8. *Icosiella quadrituberculata*
13. *S. elegans*	9. *Oxyuroides* sp.
14. *S. pseudemydae*	10. *Spironoura* sp.
15. *S. scripta*	11. *S. affinis*
16. *Telorchis corti*	12. *S. chelydrae*
17. *T. diminutus*[a]	13. *S. concinnae*
18. *T. medius*[a]	14. *S. gracilis*
19. *T. nematoides*	15. *S. procera*
20. *T. robustus*	16. *Spiroxys constrictus*
21. *T. singularis*	17. *S. contortus*
22. *Unicaecum dissimile*	
23. *U. ruszkowskii*	

Source: Ernst and Ernst, 1977.
[a]These parasites have been added to the checklist since Ernst and Ernst (1977).

ships among three emydid turtle genera—*Chrysemys, Pseudemys* (= *Trachemys*), and *Graptemys* (Ernst and Ernst, 1980). As outlined above, the degree of parasite host specificity can be used to demonstrate kinship of related species and is, therefore, appropriate for establishing phylogenetic affinities between hosts. After compiling a complete parasite checklist for host species within the three genera, Ernst and Ernst (1980) used the Index of Similarity developed by Sorensen (1948) for expressing generic relationships of the helminth faunas of the turtles. They concluded that similarity indexes of the helminth faunas in North American species of *Chrysemys, Pseudemys* (= *Trachemys*), and *Graptemys* show these to be separate turtle genera. They also indicated that species of *Trachemys* are not congeneric with *Chrysemys picta,* as has been previously suggested by other investigators (Zug, 1966; Weaver and Rose, 1967). Ernst and Ernst (1980) further concluded that species of *Graptemys* seem to be more closely allied taxonomically to *Trachemys* than to *Chrysemys picta.* Recently, Seidel and Smith (1986) recognized *Chrysemys* and *Trachemys* as distinct genera, based on morphological, biochemical, and paleontological evidence.

Although Brooks (1981) criticized some of the conclusions of Ernst and Ernst (1980), he recognized the value of comparing parasite faunas to solve problems of phylogenetic relationships between hosts. A more rigorous

analysis of the phylogenetic relationships of all parasite taxa in chelonians, coupled with further investigations of captured versus heirloom parasites, will be extremely productive in elucidating turtle evolutionary histories.

Ecological Considerations

Dogiel (1962) indicated that ecological parasitology is concerned with the study of the relationship between a parasite fauna treated as a unit on the one hand, and the changes in the environmental and physiological conditions of the host on the other. This description recognizes an essential feature of parasitism in that it emphasizes a relationship between two species populations. It remained for Crofton (1971) to delineate the elements of this relationship clearly and, moreover, to formulate a quantitative approach to understanding these elements. Crofton indicated that parasites are physiologically dependent on their hosts, are capable of killing heavily infected hosts, and have a higher reproductive potential than their hosts and that transmission dynamics of the parasite produce a contagious frequency distribution within the host population. In effect, a few hosts will carry most of the parasites and, thereby, limit potential negative effects to a few individuals within the host population.

At the population level, the quantitative concepts of Crofton (1971) were refined by Esch et al. (1975). They recognized that there are fundamental differences between the population dynamics of free-living organisms and helminth parasites. They defined a population as a group of organisms of the same species occupying a given space, but they stated that such a definition was inappropriate for most helminth parasites. The dilemma is clear when one asks whether parasites of a given species within a single host constitute a population or whether all members of a given parasite species within an ecosystem should be considered a population. They went on to point out that a population of free-living organisms increases in number through birth and/or immigration, whereas the number of helminth parasites within an individual host can usually increase only through immigration (recruitment). To provide an orderly means of assessing the dynamics of parasite population biology, Esch et al. introduced the concepts of the infrapopulation and the suprapopulation. They defined the former as all of the parasites of the same species within a given host. A suprapopulation was defined to include all the members of a given parasite species, in all stages of development, within an ecosystem. More recently, Riggs et al. (1987) introduced another term, "metapopulation," to describe all of the infrapopulations sampled from a given host species within an ecosystem. Given the complexity of parasite life cycles and the intricacy of host-parasite interactions, the concepts just outlined provide a systematic approach for the study of parasite populations at all levels.

In general, ecological theory as applied to communities has been developed through studies on free-living animals, with little attention given to specialist organisms such as parasites. P. Price (1980, 1984) accurately emphasized that specialists, such as parasites, are fundamentally different from more generalized free-living organisms and that, as a consequence, the organization of specialist communities may be fundamentally different from that of generalist communities.

Despite these apparent differences between specialist and generalist communities, Holmes and Price (1986) argued that helminth parasite communities have certain attributes that should permit them to contribute to several basic concepts in community ecology. First, helminth communities have discrete and unambiguous boundaries; that is, they occur within a host. Second, individual helminth communities from different hosts can be treated as replicates. Therefore, studies of comparative parasite community structure are powerful, because the host can be replicated through time and space much more readily than habitats for free-living organisms. Hosts with equivalent morphological structures (i.e., intestine, kidney, lung, etc.) are capable of supporting similar parasite communities in terms of parasite diversity and abundance. When they do not harbor similar parasite faunas, then the ecological and evolutionary mechanisms creating deficiencies in some hosts and not in others can be inferred. Third, an important factor known to influence the structure and dynamics of many free-living communities is predation. In parasite communities, predation does not occur, which means that this variable need not be considered in the analysis of parasite community structure and dynamics.

Holmes and Price (1986) developed a set of theoretical considerations suggesting that helminth infracommunities (parasite assemblages within individual hosts) span a continuum ranging from isolationist to interactive. Isolationist communities arise when the colonization abilities of parasites within the infracommunities are limited in scope. In isolationist infracommunities, biotic interactions such as competition are limited, and species diversity is low. On the other hand, interactive infracommunities occur when the colonization abilities of the parasites are high. Generally, interactive infracommunities have greater species diversity and tend to have higher parasite densities than isolationist infracommunities do. Within interactive infracommunities, there is more opportunity for biotic interaction, such as competition.

Holmes and Price (1986) recognized two other levels of hierarchial community organization among parasitic helminths (also see Root, 1973, who originally developed and discussed these concepts). The first is the component community, which includes all of the parasite infracommunities within a host species population. The second is the compound community, which consists of all of the helminth infracommunities within a community of host species.

Throughout the world, turtles comprise a large component of the vertebrate fauna of many freshwater habitats (Congdon et al., 1986), yet few investigators have studied the parasites of these long-lived vertebrates from the standpoint of their ecology. However, there is enough information available to make certain generalizations and predictions regarding the factors influencing turtle parasite populations and communities.

HOST AGE AND DIET

Many helminths colonize turtles through accidental ingestion or active predation of intermediate hosts. Consequently, helminth parasites reveal certain features of turtle ecology. Age and diet are inextricably linked in the recruitment of helminth parasites by turtles. The basis for this generalization rests with the knowledge that in many turtle species, juveniles are obligate carnivores, but adults are primarily herbivorous (Marchand, in Carr, 1952; Clark and Gibbons, 1969).

The relationship between age and diet in turtles is confirmed by an analysis of parasite recruitment patterns in two closely related species, *Trachemys scripta* and *Chrysemys picta*. Esch and Gibbons (1967) reported a relationship between nematode densities and host age in a population of *C. picta* in hypereutrophic Wintergreen Lake in southwestern lower Michigan. Mean densities of the nematodes increased through the turtles' first 4 years and then declined as the turtles aged beyond 5 years. This pattern also held for trematodes in the same host population. All species of nematodes and trematodes in the Wintergreen Lake fauna are transmitted via invertebrate intermediate hosts, mostly arthropods, which indicates a change in host diet as the turtles age beyond 4 years.

Except for two species of trematodes in *T. scripta* collected from a variety of habitats on the Savannah River Plant (SRP) in South Carolina, significant correlations were observed between densities of enteric helminths and host plastron length, weight, and length of intestine (Esch et al., 1979a). However, parasite densities tended to increase in *T. scripta* beyond 4 years of age. This observation was especially pronounced for infrapopulations of acanthocephalans (*Neoechinorhynchus* spp.). The explanation offered by Esch et al. (1979a) was that as *T. scripta* become older and larger, their diet consists of greater quantities of aquatic vegetation. The intermediate hosts for *Neoechinorhynchus* spp. are several species of ostracods, which are important components of the epifauna associated with the vegetation on which the turtles feed. It should be emphasized that the increase in densities of *Neoechinorhynchus* spp. is not a consequence of parasite accumulation over time, because these helminths are short-lived, being turned over and recruited on an annual basis.

SEASON

Seasonal changes in parasite infrapopulation densities in turtles are known to occur, but they also appear to be influenced by latitude. Esch and Gibbons (1967) reported that densities of nematodes in the Wintergreen Lake *C. picta* population appeared to increase progressively through all seasons during the turtles' first 3 years of life. Afterwards, densities were always lower in winter but increased in summer. The data for trematodes in *C. picta* are less obvious, but the same trend is apparent. In South Carolina, however, the nematode *Camallanus trispinosus* (also present in Michigan *C. picta*) overwintered in hibernating *T. scripta;* this was followed by losses in mid- to late summer. *Spironoura chelydrae,* also a nematode, appeared to decline during the period of hibernation and was then rapidly recruited in early spring (Esch et al., 1979a).

The pattern of seasonal change for *Neoechinorhynchus* spp. appears to be more complicated than that for nematodes in *T. scripta* (Esch et al., 1979a). At least two waves of infection (in May and July) were observed. From February to May, larger worms became more abundant. In May, densities and prevalence of larger worms sharply declined, and there was an equal increase in small individuals. Another cohort of smaller worms appeared in July. Esch et al. (1979a) also observed that the greatest mortality of acanthocephalans either shortly preceded or occurred simultaneously with parasite recruitment.

Dubinina (1949) indicated that young nematodes of *Testudo horsefieldii* continued to mature at a slow rate during hibernation, but older ones died early during the period. It is apparent from her work and that of Esch and Gibbons (1967) and Esch et al. (1979a) that hibernation does not always lead to parasite mortality and that seasonal change in parasite density in many cases appears to be a species-specific phenomenon. The seasonal change is probably linked to the seasonal dynamics of potential intermediate hosts, to changes in host feeding patterns, or to other factors such as the host's immune responsiveness, which in some poikilotherms can be influenced greatly by temperature extremes, both high and low (Esch et al., 1975).

HABITAT

The nature and quality of the habitat may greatly affect infrapopulation densities as well as the structure and dynamics of parasite infracommunities in turtles. This generalization is well illustrated by comparing the trematode and acanthocephalan faunas in Wintergreen Lake *C. picta* (Esch and Gibbons, 1967) with those of *T. scripta* from the SRP (Esch et al., 1979a,b). Eight species of enteric trematodes infect *C. picta* in Michigan. Only two, possibly three, species occur in *T. scripta* from South Carolina.

Trematodes dominate the overall parasite fauna in numbers of species in Michigan. In South Carolina the helminth fauna is dominated numerically by acanthocephalans. Because all trematodes require mollusks as their first intermediate hosts, the best explanation for these differences is related to the richness of the Michigan molluscan fauna, which is low in species diversity in South Carolina (Esch and Gibbons, 1967). This is probably a consequence of the relatively high pH and high calcium content of Michigan waters versus the comparatively lower pH and low calcium levels in South Carolina waters. Differences in the acanthocephalan faunas in Wintergreen Lake and the SRP are striking. Rather than being due to physiographic characteristics associated with the two areas in question, the differences are probably due to the absence of appropriate intermediate hosts in Wintergreen Lake. This assertion is based on an anecdotal observation (by Esch) of *Neoechinorhynchus* sp. in a box turtle captured in close proximity to the Wintergreen Lake shoreline. Certainly the opportunity for establishing *Neoechinorhynchus* in Wintergreen Lake exists.

Although only a single habitat was sampled in the Michigan study, a series of habitats was sampled on the SRP (Esch et al., 1979a,b). These habitats included sites that were currently receiving thermal effluent from several nuclear production reactors or that had received it and were in postthermal recovery and sites that had never been affected by thermal perturbation. Also included were streams, small farm ponds, a river swamp, and a large reservoir. In general, the results of comparing parasite infracommunity diversity in turtles from a wide range of habitats on the SRP indicate that parasite heterogeneity among the habitats is also wide. Parasite diversity appeared to be related to habitat stability. For example, the river swamp habitat had the most diverse helminth fauna; a small cooling pond that received large volumes of thermal effluent had the least diversity. The highest infracommunity diversity and species numbers were in turtles from stable habitats, whereas the lowest diversity and species numbers were from turtles in habitats subjected to perturbation or to the vagaries of natural environmental change such as irregular rainfall. These findings, according to Esch et al. (1979b), tend to support the time-stability hypothesis of Sanders (1968), which suggested that low species diversity may be a function of either severe or unpredictable environmental conditions.

Slobodkin (1967) suggested that the response of an individual organism to noncatastrophic perturbation will be an increase or a decrease in survival probability, a change in fecundity, or both. Any of these sorts of change would lead to alterations in the population biology of the organisms in question. According to Esch et al. (1975), environmental perturbations that produce ecosystem stress will inevitably lead to modification in host-parasite interactions, which in turn may lead to local extinction of hosts, parasites, or both. The studies by Eure and Esch (1974), Eure (1976), and Esch et al. (1979a,b) tend to support this prediction regarding the nature of change in host-parasite interactions within stressed or otherwise unpredictable habitats.

PATTERNS IN HELMINTH COMMUNITIES

As Holmes and Price (1986) pointed out, the challenge is to determine the factors that lead to a given position on the isolationist-interactive continuum. Recently, Kennedy et al. (1986) identified several factors that lead to establishment of isolationist or interactive helminth infracommunities, by comparing helminth infracommunities from piscine and avian hosts. They concluded that at least five factors were important in creating potentially interactive infracommunities: high host vagility, endothermy and complex alimentary canal, a broad host diet, selective feeding by the host on prey serving as intermediate hosts for a wide variety of helminths, and exposure to direct-life-cycle helminths. It is valuable to examine the extent to which turtle helminth systems fit these generalizations. Although diversity indexes are not available for individual turtle helminth infracommunities, we can make predictions based on presence-absence data from parasite survey data of selected turtles (Ernst and Ernst, 1977) of varying ecologies to test these concepts at the component level. The concepts at this level of helminth community organization focus on the factors that determine the helminth species richness in a host species (Holmes and Price, 1986).

Kennedy et al. (1986) reasoned that hosts with complex enteric systems would offer greater opportunity for helminth colonization and species diversity than hosts with simpler gut physiology. Reptiles are intermediate between amphibians and birds in terms of their gut complexity, being the first vertebrates in which true colic ceca are found (Weichert, 1970). Thus, based on this feature, we would predict that turtles would lie on an intermediate position on the isolationist-interactive continuum.

Intestinal complexity is related to endothermy. Birds and mammals, in maintaining endothermy, have greater metabolic demands than do fish and amphibians. As a consequence of their more vigorous feeding regimes, endotherms are more likely to be exposed to a greater variety of helminths than are ectotherms. Although reptiles generally cannot generate their own body heat, basking is an important thermoregulatory behavior, especially among turtles, in which atmospheric basking causes a rise in body temperature (Boyer, 1965; Crawford et al., 1983). This phenomenon would have important implications for the parasite fauna of turtles. Increased body temperatures would result in increased feeding, exposing turtles to a greater

variety of helminths transmitted as a consequence of host feeding patterns. We would predict that behaviorally thermoregulating hosts would be positioned at an intermediate location on the isolationist-interactive continuum.

Host vagility (movement through varied habitat types) plays an important role in influencing helminth species richness in hosts. The available data indicate that many chelonians are quite vagile. The most spectacular cases are those of many marine turtles, the females of which migrate hundreds of miles from their feeding grounds to nest (Carr, 1965). Freshwater turtles are also vagile. Indeed, the different reproductive strategies of the two sexes in several species of turtles are primary factors influencing differential activity and movement of turtles (e.g., Morreale et al., 1984). Long-range movements of nesting females as well as mate-seeking behaviors of male turtles have been described (for a review, see Gibbons, 1986). For example, males of *T. scripta* move extensively over long distances in search of mating opportunities (Morreale et al., 1984). We predict that such vagility would expose turtles to a wide range of potential intermediate hosts as well as to encysted stages of parasites on vegetation and species with direct life cycles.

As we have mentioned throughout our discussion, host feeding patterns are a critical factor affecting species richness of helminth infracommunities. Turtles with a broad host diet would be expected to harbor more speciose helminth faunas than turtles that are dietary specialists. For example, more parasite species have been described from semiaquatic emydid turtles (e.g., *Chrysemys*, *Trachemys*) than from turtles that are more terrestrial (e.g., *Kinosternon*, *Gopherus*, *Terrapene*). Helminth faunas of terrestrial turtles are dominated by nematodes, many of which have direct life cycles. Kinosternid and testudinid turtles are less likely to be exposed to parasites whose life cycles rely upon host feeding habits for transmission. Emydid turtles, being omnivorous, are exposed to significantly more parasites. For example, the rich acanthocephalan fauna transmitted as a function of herbivory in *T. scripta* (Esch et al., 1979a) is a result of accidental ingestion of ostracods, which are intermediate hosts and are associated with the vegetation on which *T. scripta* feeds. This supports the fourth prediction of Kennedy et al. (1986), which suggests that feeding on prey that serve as intermediate hosts for a variety of helminths would enhance species diversity. In turtles, dietary and habitat shifts are associated with host size (e.g., Hart, 1983). Because helminth colonization is largely a function of turtle feeding patterns, knowledge of the life cycles of the parasites present provides valuable information for the turtle ecologist wishing to understand the nature of such shifts.

Because of evolutionary factors and certain characteristics discussed above, turtle helminth communities should show diversity values intermediate between those of fish and birds. Moreover, based on the above characteristics, some turtle species should harbor abundant populations of certain helminths. These features should be reflected in an intermediate position on the isolationist-interactive continuum proposed by Holmes and Price (1986). Our predictions are supported by diversity analysis and helminth abundance data of individual infracommunities of *T. scripta* (Esch and Gibbons, 1967; Esch et al., 1979a; Jacobson, 1987). Application of the Brillouin's diversity index to individual infracommunities of *T. scripta* revealed that they are, indeed, intermediate between the fish and avian infracommunities studied by Kennedy et al. (1986).

It is at the infracommunity level that any direct interactions between parasites must take place, and it is at this level that evidence for interactions must be examined (Bush and Holmes, 1986). The significance of biotic interactions in helminth communities depends on characteristics of the component community discussed above. That is, interactions between helminth species should be common only if parasites exist at high intensities within the host. Clearly, this is feasible for some turtle species. We examine the potential for helminth interactions by comparing two turtle species that support abundant populations of enteric congeneric parasites.

A study of the infracommunity structure of enteric helminths in *T. scripta* has recently been completed (Jacobson, 1987). The procedure of Bush and Holmes (1986) was used to examine the nature of helminth organization within the intestine. It involves removing the intestine and freezing it instantly in dry ice and ethanol to prevent postmortem migration of helminths. The intestines can then be stored until examination, upon which they are measured and cut into 20 equal sections. Each section is then examined for parasites, and their location is expressed as a percentage of the intestinal length. In some turtles the precise location of a parasite was determined relative to others of the same and different species.

A large component (four species) of the helminth fauna of *T. scripta* consists of acanthocephalans of the genus *Neoechinorhynchus*. These are largely responsible for the diversity values mentioned above. Preliminary evidence reveals that these acanthocephalan species are sympatric in both their linear and their circumferential distributions. That is, it appears that the presence of one acanthocephalan species has little or no effect upon the location of another species. The noted patterns of co-occurrence suggest that competitive interactions are not important in structuring the infracommunities of *T. scripta*.

In marked contrast to the above study is the investigation of Schad (1963), who studied the infracommunity structure of the nematode fauna of the European tortoise *Testudo graeca*. An important feature of this host's fauna is that it consists of 10 congeneric species of the nematode *Tachygonetria*, all residing in the colon. Schad's initial ob-

servations indicated a significant overlap in the linear distribution of the 10 species, suggesting that they were capable of sharing the spatial resources within the colon. However, when he examined their radial distributions, he found the linear overlapping to be of little consequence. Using colons that had been quickly frozen at −147° C in liquid air, he was able to establish that several species showed a strong preference for the paramucosal lumen, whereas others were scattered in the lumen away from the mucosal area. Then, based on an analysis of the oral morphology and food habits of two species of overlapping nematodes, Schad was able to determine that one was an indiscriminant feeder on lumen contents, whereas the other fed exclusively on bacteria. He also observed striking dissimilarities in the oral morphology of other species combinations having similar distribution patterns and concluded that they probably also differed in food preferences. It is possible that this community was structured by historical competitive interactions with the development of resource partitioning among the nematodes.

Prospects for Future Study

Future investigations of the biology and ecology of turtle parasites should fall into three separate and distinct categories. The first is to use turtle parasites for developing a better understanding of the biogeographical distribution of American turtles belonging to the family Emydidae. As was noted earlier, a unique aspect of many host-parasite relationships is the phenomenon of strict host specificity, and such specificity generally implies a long association between host and parasite. More important, it means that certain parasite species within an infracommunity can be used as tags, or markers, and, as such, may be useful in assessing the radiation of the host species. For example, Barus and Moravec (1967) were able to identify seven species of helminth parasites from *Trachemys decussata* on the island of Cuba. Of these, five had been previously described by Harwood (1932) from emydid turtles in Texas. The same five were also identical to species recovered by Rausch (1947) from emydid turtles in Ohio, close to the northernmost geographic limits of these hosts. Because turtles of the genus *Trachemys* are scattered over many of the Caribbean islands and on the Western Hemisphere mainland down to South America, it would be possible to use their parasite faunas to study the biogeographical radiation of turtles from the southern United States into the northwestern, north central, and eastern United States as well as down into Central and South America. Such studies would also permit evaluation of the nature and extent of parasite exchange or transfer among closely related, or even distantly related, species of turtles, fish, and amphibians. A broad biogeographic approach such as that adopted by Price and Clancy (1983), when applied to turtles, would be of great interest in interpreting patterns and processes important in the structure and dynamics of helminth communities. Finally, it is conceivable that the study of emydid turtles in isolated areas of Central and South America, as well as on various Caribbean islands, might allow for the determination of the rate of evolutionary change that has occurred within infracommunities of relict host populations.

A second area for potential study is the infrapopulation dynamics of parasites in turtles from a range of habitats. Esch et al. (1979a,b) have clearly shown that parasite infrapopulation dynamics vary according to habitat stability. The precise mechanisms affecting this variability are, however, unclear. An understanding of these mechanisms would be useful in obtaining comparative informa-

tion relative to parasite population biology among hosts of different taxa in aquatic ecosystems.

Finally, we feel confident that additional knowledge regarding the basic biology of turtle parasites will contribute to a better understanding of the biology and ecology of the turtles themselves. Furthermore, such information will be useful in comparing similar phenomena among various freshwater vertebrate taxa, ranging from fish to amphibians and other turtles.

Acknowledgments

Research and manuscript preparation were made possible by contract DE-AC09-76SROO-819 between the University of Georgia and the U.S. Department of Energy and by National Science Foundation grant DEB-79-04758.

Significance of
Long-term Research on
Long-lived Species
of Turtles

24

J. WHITFIELD GIBBONS
Savannah River Ecology Laboratory
Drawer E
Aiken, South Carolina 29802

Recommendations for Future Research on Freshwater Turtles: What Are the Questions?

Introduction

This book's presentation of a variety of research projects on a diversity of topics sets the stage for major advancement in our understanding of turtles as significant components of freshwater, terrestrial, and marine environments in many temperate and tropical regions of the world. Admittedly, the presentation has been something of a collage pieced together from the fragments of turtle ecology for which we had information. The complete mural must await the addition of new findings to fill the many gaps in our knowledge. Some findings will emerge in time as a matter of the continued routine of conducting life history and ecological research on different species and populations. A thoughtful emphasis on particular issues and special problems and hypotheses will serve this effort. The application of available but minimally used techniques such as laparoscopy, radiotelemetry, and mitochondrial DNA analysis to address pertinent questions will help complete the ecological and evolutionary picture of turtles as an order. The development and more effective use of techniques to study aging could be a tremendous boost to the general knowledge of all facets of aging phenomena in long-lived species. Because of the potential longevity of individual turtles, long-term field studies will continue to be of value, and precise data on age and size at maturity, clutch frequency, and survivorship patterns of populations of different species will aid greatly in the integration of turtle studies with life history theory.

In this chapter I will discuss what I consider to be some of the more important and answerable questions regarding the life history, ecology, and evolution of turtles from the perspective of the material presented in this book, with some suggestions on how we might proceed.

Value of Long-Term Studies

Despite the need for constructing hypotheses and using field and laboratory techniques that are underutilized by turtle biologists, I consider long-term field investigations to be one of the most powerful approaches to understanding certain ecological and evolutionary phenomena. A distinction between most long-term research projects and short-term studies is that the latter often have a single hypothesis that is being tested or a specific question that is being asked. Long-term studies are different in that the investigator probably did not begin the research with the intent of extending it beyond a few years at most. Therefore, a study that has lasted for many years can often provide the empirical evidence needed to address certain biological issues, although the study was not designed initially with such issues in mind.

During the course of two decades of research on freshwater turtles, I believe that we have acquired information about these animals that would have been difficult to attain in only a few years of study, no matter how intensively we had done it. Some of the findings are applicable to animals in general, some more appropriately to reptiles alone, and many of them strictly to an understanding of the biology of turtles in general or to a particular species. Nonetheless, the information is valuable because of its revelation of certain attributes about animal populations that might not have been perceived in a short-term study.

The studies of turtles have revealed information useful in addressing a variety of issues empirically that have heretofore been approached primarily theoretically or speculatively. Among the issues are those related to reproduction as a function of age, indeterminate growth of reptiles, and sex ratios of vertebrates.

A great deal of emphasis has been placed on the importance of long-term studies in ecology. The LTER (Long-Term Ecological Research) program of the National Science Foundation is in itself a statement of the effort and investment that individuals and organizations are willing to make to assure that long-term research can proceed unhindered in certain habitats. Although the studies on freshwater turtles in South Carolina have not yet outlived some of the individuals in the populations, the research does provide insight into what can be learned only from long-term study. The following discussion of selected life history and ecological phenomena pertaining to turtles indicates some of the directions that might be taken. Many of the interpretations would have been inaccurate or absent if a short-term study had been relied upon, but they lead to questions that can be answered only through additional research.

Recommendations for Future Research

Numerous questions about the life history, ecology, and evolution of turtles might be worth pursuing. The infor-mation presented in the previous chapters has identified certain areas where research emphasis might be placed that would contribute to a general understanding of the ecology and evolution of turtles and, in many instances, would appeal even to population ecologists or evolutionary biologists. An attempt to consider all of the relevant and worthwhile questions would be an open-ended exercise with a high prospect for diminishing returns. Therefore, I will identify selected questions that have been revealed in this book as problems and that I believe are pertinent and appropriate for consideration now. This in no way implies that other areas or different approaches might not also result in fruitful research.

SYSTEMATICS, TAXONOMY, AND GENETICS

Clearly, anyone who thinks that the determination of phylogenetic relationships among genera and species is important would agree that the systematics of a group deserves attention. From the perspective of an ecologist, it would appear that one of the primary hindrances to our resolution of relationships within the *Trachemys scripta* complex is the inadequacy of samples from populations of this geographically wide-ranging group of animals, particularly from the West Indies and American tropics. The efforts of John Legler and other investigators to acquire samples from a wide variety of habitats and localities are admirable. The acquisition of additional samples for morphological measurements from a continuum of localities through a broad sampling program seems essential for clarifying many aspects of the systematics. The problem of intrapopulational variability can be resolved by sampling in several localities in a region, but perhaps more important for our understanding of distribution patterns is the need for samples along a geographical gradient from northern Mexico to South America, as well as in the West Indies.

One issue that can be examined with slider turtles is the importance of natural physiographic barriers to the diminishment or complete elimination of genetic exchange between particular populations. Turtle populations also appear to be ideal for addressing the question of whether certain individuals have a genetic propensity for emigration from a population. Besides determining if certain individuals are so inclined, by establishing their genetic makeup electrophoretically we can also ask whether such individuals are more likely to have a higher or lower level of fitness.

REPRODUCTIVE PATTERNS

One area of investigation that seems important is the determination of relationships among egg size, clutch size, and clutch frequency of female turtles. Each of these characteristics has a direct bearing on reproductive success and fitness of an individual, with a change in one characteristic potentially having a direct effect on others. An initial matter that must now be resolved is what factors influence the balance among these characteristics.

Clutch frequency is unquestionably a population statistic whose understanding can be greatly enhanced through extended annual observations. This has already been fully demonstrated for certain species of sea turtles in which multiple nesting by an individual occurs within years but individuals characteristically do not nest in consecutive years (Carr and Carr, 1970; Frazer, 1986). The frequency of nesting within a population and by individuals has also been observed to vary among freshwater species (Gibbons et al., 1982). Presumably, reproductive output is a function of environmental conditions of one or more preceding years and therefore would be expected to vary annually in many instances. Measurements of this variability intra-populationally and intra-individually with a long-lived iteroparous species can be refined through long-term study. Such frequency has been noted as a key area for investigation in turtle studies for the development of life tables or other presentations that depend upon a valid measurement of reproductive output (Gibbons, 1983a). Although fairly good estimates can now be made for a few turtle populations, none of them, including those on the SRP, has incorporated the full range of variability that would be expected in turtle populations over time.

GROWTH AND SIZE PHENOMENA

Two things seem apparent to me that have been discovered about growth phenomena in turtles as a consequence of long-term study. One of them concerns the issue of whether indeterminate growth is actually a phenomenon in the reptile world. Because growth rate slows considerably when turtles or other reptiles become adults, the experimental error of size measurements, particularly in smaller species, can lead to a fuzzy interpretation of whether an individual has grown slightly or has been slightly mismeasured. Also, techniques to measure aging, such as the use of annuli, are generally not reliable at the older ages and larger sizes that are of concern regarding indeterminate growth. Our studies with slider turtles have categorically demonstrated that adult animals, even several years after maturity, may continue to grow, although growth is not consistent across years. In fact, growth in some years is apparently zero. The data for mud turtles (*Kinosternon subrubrum*) suggest that not all species of turtles continue to grow as adults. Mud turtles apparently increase in size for a few years after maturity is reached but then do not continue to grow. A related issue is the differential growth rates of older adults of the two sexes. This matter has been addressed effectively for slider turtles but would not have been so in a short-term study because of the need for older, known-age individuals. Em-

pirical information concerning adult growth patterns is lacking for most species of turtles and should become a focus of investigation by researchers having access to populations of marked turtles.

POPULATION DENSITY

The population density of a habitat is a function of the number of animals and the size of the habitat they use. The latter becomes a matter of definition and can greatly affect density estimates. The studies at Ellenton Bay demonstrate categorically that the population density of slider turtles would have been judged to be as much as one order of magnitude different, depending upon which sets of years were used in the analysis, because of local environmental events. For example, if samples had been taken in the mid-1960s or late 1970s, the population size would have been extremely high relative to that of the early 1970s or mid-1980s, when numbers were low because of the departure of a major portion of the population following droughts. However, at certain times during each of these periods, the actual water level (i.e., the habitat apparently available for use) was similar, so the estimated population density would have been extremely miscalculated. A long-term study gives the investigator the advantage of knowing how local habitat conditions that could influence a population have varied, and this should become an area of interest in considerations of biomass standing crop and productivity of turtle populations. Turtles are clearly an important and dynamic component of many freshwater wetlands, and research should be conducted that quantifies their influence.

SEX RATIOS

A primary feature regarding the interpretation of population sex ratios that has been revealed by long-term study is that sampling bias can be the predominant factor influencing annual sex ratio estimates. Therefore, a longer-term sampling program would result in greater accuracy and interpretations by reducing or at least identifying the variability. Also, in one instance, actual sex ratios of a population (Capers Island) have apparently changed over time naturally, because of the differential mortality of the sexes. Clearly, conclusions from a 1-year study and a 10-year one about sex ratios in this population could vary. It is apparent that short-term sampling programs, especially those restricted to a particular season or to a particular habitat that might be used differently by the sexes, could result in strong biases. These types of errors are less likely during long-term sampling periods, which can result in more-thorough sampling over space and time.

The most interesting question to be investigated about sex ratios in natural turtle populations is whether differential mortality of the sexes or differential recruitment of hatchlings occurs because of nest temperatures. It is clear that if recruitment and survivorship rates are approximately equal in a population, then the expected sex ratio will be known from the age at which the two sexes reach maturity. A strong emphasis must be placed on the proper determination of when and at what size maturity is reached. The full influence of emigration and immigration phenomena is also merely a sampling problem of properly defining what constitutes the population being studied. Once both the age and size at maturity and the emigration and immigration rates have been determined for a population, the differential mortality and recruitment rates on adult sex ratios can be studied.

An initial general question is whether differential mortality and recruitment influences are characteristic of a species, vary geographically in a consistent pattern, or are population-specific because of local environmental conditions. My prediction, based on the evidence available, is that differences in adult sex ratios will be found to vary among regional populations and will not be identified as a species trait, except as determined by possible species-specific sizes at which maturity is reached. Emphasis should also be placed on testing the least-expensive-sex concept of Fisher (1930), but the null hypothesis—that sex ratios are a transitory phenomenon, merely reflecting certain features of population dynamics and having little evolutionary significance per se—should also be considered a possibility.

SURVIVORSHIP AND LONGEVITY

Long-term research with slider turtles and other species has provided unprecedented opportunities to examine the phenomenon of longevity in long-lived species. An earlier presentation of survivorship of the slider turtle from the Ellenton Bay population on the SRP revealed that individuals of this species live longer in natural populations than those of several other vertebrate species for which data were available (Gibbons and Semlitsch, 1982; Gibbons, 1987). However, a bias in the construction of survivorship curves exists because it is much easier to gather data for a short-lived species than for one that may outlive the funding for the study if not the investigators themselves. This is especially true of vertebrate species for which the determination of age in older individuals is difficult or impossible without long-term mark-recapture studies.

Turtles as a group may represent the ultimate achievement in reproductive longevity among the vertebrates. They do not appear to be encumbered by senility or the expenditure of parental care as are the mammals and birds, nor do they have, as adults, the continual threat of predation from as wide an array of predators as most amphibians and fishes do. Some of the sharks, crocodilians, and larger snakes and lizards may also fit this

category, but survivorship information in natural populations of these species is sparse.

Observations of the extraordinarily high mortality of turtle eggs have been reported for many species for many years. Thus, it could probably have been safely concluded, even on the basis of short-term studies, that most turtles (if an egg is counted as a turtle) do not reach an age of 1 year. At the other extreme, most statements about the extensive longevity of turtles have been based primarily on anecdotal observations of particular individuals in captivity or occasionally in the field. A few extensive field studies actually speculated maximum longevity of slider turtles being as much as 75 years (Cagle, 1950) and 30 years (Moll and Legler, 1971). Documentation of the actual survivorship patterns in specific natural populations in South Carolina has been accomplished through continued long-term observation of the individuals. It is conceivable that the age structure in a population of long-lived animals could be determined in some other manner, such as through skeletochronology (Zug et al., 1986). However, to date, long-term mark-recapture programs have proved to hold the highest assurance of making such determinations. According to our studies on the SRP, slider turtles reach a maximum age of about 25 years, or perhaps a little older if everything goes just right for the individual year after year. It is important to note that our findings for slider turtles on the SRP do not discount the estimates given by Cagle (1950) and Moll and Legler (1971), because survivorship patterns are undoubtedly dictated in part by local environmental conditions. Documentation can be accomplished only by the continued recapture of known-age individuals; thus the generality of our findings must await the presentation of data from other populations.

Longevity records, whether based on field observations or on captive specimens, indicate the exceptional individuals and tell us only what survivorship potentials are, not what the patterns and probabilities of individual survivorship actually are. Perhaps as meaningful as the confirmation that some individuals live a long time in natural populations is the quantification that most individuals live for much shorter periods and that the probability of mortality is high and relatively constant. I see no way that this can be determined in a short-term study with present techniques, because older, known-age individuals will be absent in the study sample. Thus, some of the most meaningful contributions in the area of age-related phenomena of turtles will come from the continuation of long-term mark-recapture studies by investigators who have access to such populations.

DELAYED EMERGENCE FROM THE NEST

Delayed emergence from the nest and overwintering by hatchling turtles are assumed to be a trait that is genetically controlled to some degree and upon which natural selection operates; hence, variation in the timing of emergence might be expected among different populations with consistently different environmental regimes. The test for establishing if this is true involves the determinations that, first, some species indeed vary among populations in the timing of emergence and, second, the hatchlings are genetically programmed to behave differently. For example, painted turtles and slider turtles characteristically overwinter, but most of the records of this behavior have been of populations around temporary aquatic habitats in which fall emergence would entail considerable risk. Natural habitats need to be identified that have large populations of these turtles and a historically high probability of abundant resources during late summer and fall and/or a high risk of nest destruction during winter. These conditions might exist in the floodplains of some large rivers or large lakes in warm temperate regions where winter flooding of nesting sites would be expected but the assurance of a heavily vegetated, productive aquatic environment in the fall would also be expected. If early emergence can be demonstrated in such a situation, then reciprocal transplantation of eggs between such a location and one where overwintering is the norm could determine if differential behavior of the hatchlings occurs under similar environmental conditions. Laboratory incubation experiments could also be performed to differentiate between emergence behaviors from the two locations. Experiments could also test whether individuals that do not delay emergence actually derive a growth advantage, the only clear benefit for early departure from the safety of the nest prior to winter. The determination that emergence varies among populations would support the hypothesis that the timing of hatchling emergence is a genetically controlled risk-benefit proposition on which natural selection operates. This finding would also demonstrate that what would ordinarily be considered a species trait can actually be influenced by local environmental conditions and presumably on a relatively short-term basis. Perhaps Reelfoot Lake in Tennessee would be a possible habitat for testing these ideas, because a large proportion of the hatchling slider turtles there do not overwinter relative to those in other areas, such as Ellenton Bay in South Carolina (Cagle, 1944a; Gibbons and Nelson, 1978).

MOVEMENT PATTERNS

Freshwater turtles occupying natural lentic habitats on the southeastern Coastal Plain have presumably been confronted with environmental conditions that can vary immensely among years. The data presented from the SRP reinforce both the consistency and the high variability in movement patterns in turtles, particularly terrestrial movement by primarily aquatic species as demonstrated by drift fences and pitfall traps. The discontinuities in our understanding of what turtles are doing and why they are doing it are immense, and the only consolation, in one respect, is that the SRP data have revealed the breadth of our lack of knowledge. The variability in what species, populations, and even individuals do in regard to what we have referred to as extrapopulational movement is extreme to the point of being almost annoying. A number of hypotheses can now be identified that deserve testing, and more-effective approaches to addressing the questions are also apparent.

The drift fence with pitfall traps is unquestionably a key approach for determining the timing of terrestrial movement patterns of aquatic species in circumscribed habitats. Certain spatial aspects can be studied in this manner also, particularly directionality of movement. Mark-recapture programs that are extensive enough to register movement by individuals among aquatic habitats will continue to be a valuable method of identifying differential movement patterns among sex and size categories.

One approach that has not been used extensively at SREL but can contribute in the study of movement patterns of turtles is continuous monitoring. Telemetry, radioactive tags, the string technique (Breder, 1927), and personal observation have all been used successfully in the study of terrestrial activity of turtles. Telemetry and personal observation are extremely time-consuming but can be highly revealing about certain aspects of when and where turtles go. With the development of minute radio-transmitters with long-range transmission and extended battery life, coupled with continuous-monitoring stations, we can look forward during the next few years to the resolution of many questions regarding activity patterns of turtles.

The following questions are some that I consider to be most apparent and answerable with appropriate use of mark-recapture programs, terrestrial drift fences with pitfall traps, and continuous tracking. Male turtles are assumed to take greater risks by more frequent movement and greater overland travel than females. The ideal study would quantitatively compare temporal and spatial activity and movement of the sexes in a population, determine energetics costs and predatory or other risks associated with the movement, and assess a level of fitness for different levels of movement and activity. For example, do males that move more often and greater distances actually use a significant amount of energy and have a higher probability of mortality, and do they offset these risks by higher numbers of successful matings, as would be predicted?

Overland travel apparently increases as a function of size in both sexes with an abrupt increase in terrestrial activity at the point at which maturity is reached. The predictions are that turtles can acquire benefits by moving to other aquatic habitats and that larger body size reduces the hazard of overland travel, so a larger turtle is more likely to take the risks than is a smaller individual. Detailed studies to address this issue would be worthwhile.

BIOENERGETICS

The relationship between the life history of a turtle and its bioenergetics is perhaps one of the most promising areas for hybridizing physiology, population ecology, and community ecology. An individual's welfare is governed by the availability and potential acquisition of energy resources in the environment for growth, maintenance, and reproduction. How these resources are apportioned within an individual and among individuals in a population is the foundation for understanding many of the ecological and evolutionary phenomena inherent in an animal species. Numerous questions have been posed in Chapters 8, 20, 22, and others regarding the acquisition and distribution of resources by individuals.

MELANISM

The topic of melanism in turtles is of more interest for *Trachemys scripta* than for many other species because of the characteristic darkening of scutes and skin in adult *T. scripta* males but not females. The topic has been reviewed thoroughly in Chapter 19, and the potential is great for examining this phenomenon. A primary consideration must be given to the development of a scheme for quantifying melanism in an individual, as this is undoubtedly one of the reasons that relationships between age, size, and interpopulational variation are so poorly understood. The use of black-and-white photography or high-quality copying machines should greatly facilitate the development of quantitative measurement. Once this has been established, the necessary and obvious relationship of melanism to such key variables as age, size, geographic location, and a host of hormonal and enzymatic conditions can then be addressed to satisfaction. One hypothesis that should not be dismissed is that melanism in adult male *T. scripta* has no particular adaptive significance but is only a nonadaptive by-product of male hormonal activity and occurs at a time in the animal's life when subtle differences in color patterns are insignificant.

GEOGRAPHIC VARIATION

One of the most abused topics in the consideration of ecology and life history of turtles as well as many other groups of animals is putative geographic variation in life history traits. There are numerous examples in which a sample from a single population in one region is used as the evidence that samples from another, faraway region differ significantly. Yet, samples still have not been taken from other populations in the region, especially those from different habitat types, to confirm that the measurements are indeed characteristic for the geographic region and not just for the particular population. I have been guilty of this (Gibbons, 1970a), as have a host of other turtle biologists. I used one population of *Sternotherus odoratus* from Florida as evidence that southern populations of this species have smaller clutch sizes than those from northern regions, as was proposed by Tinkle (1961). This is not to say that the phenomenon is not real, and in this case it probably is. However, the examination of a life history trait in a single population in essence constitutes a single observation when geographic comparisons are being made, no matter how big the sample size is from that population.

An example of how variable life history traits (e.g., clutch size) can be within a single geographic region has been amply demonstrated for *Chrysemys picta* (Gibbons and Tinkle, 1969) and *T. scripta* (Gibbons et al., 1982). I urge that the search for geographic variation in traits be tempered with an acute awareness that habitat can influence many traits as much as climatic differences due to geographic location can. This is not at all to imply that I think that geographic variation does not occur and is not evolutionarily based, but only that the empirical evidence to support this variability is often lacking.

ENVIRONMENTAL VARIABILITY

It is not surprising that certain age-related phenomena such as survivorship patterns and growth rates of adults can be examined more effectively and accurately with studies that extend over a longer period, because both are related to ages of older individuals. But environmental changes can also occur that are undetectable over short periods of time and yet are critical to a turtle population. These include unpredictable climatic changes that are extreme and influence animal populations in a region. Of course, even a study of 20 years has a low probability of encountering the 100-year flood, freeze, or drought, but the opportunities to observe the environmental variability with which a species is confronted increase with study length. So the length a study must be in order to reveal the environmental vagaries with which a species must contend with over evolutionary time becomes a probability exercise. Obviously, then, the longer the study, the better. A 40-year study is twice as likely as a 20-year one to identify some features that are critical to the evolution and ecology of a species but occur only at infrequent intervals. The 20 years' worth of turtle research on the SRP has identified some of the extreme environmental variability that turtle populations have faced and endured. Perhaps SRP studies in the next 20 years will reveal more, as will other studies that have been conducted in a specific habitat for long periods of time.

GENERAL VARIABILITY IN TRAITS

To me, perhaps the most instructive generality that has been a consequence of the length of study is the variability and inconsistency in certain traits. The variability within species, populations, or individuals is not unexpected, because variability in biological traits is an inherent property. However, large sample sizes coupled with a breadth of spatial and temporal samples have revealed an unexpectedly high variability at each level that could create uneasiness in those who enjoy simplistic models with high predictability and assurance that the species, population, or individual will behave consistently. Limited spatial and temporal samples can often give a perception of orderliness and consistency that is shattered with more-extensive observation. A prime example is growth rate of the slider turtle. The comparison of Par Pond and Ellenton Bay populations shows that a typical growth rate does not exist for the species, even in a single geographical area. Examination within populations gives evidence that the variation among individuals is also high, partly because of annual environmental variability as well as differential microhabitat opportunities of individuals. Tracking the growth pattern of an individual likewise reveals that growth rate in one year is independent of that in others, even when size, age, and state of maturity are taken into account.

The same is true of reproductive characters. Although the general trend of clutch size increasing as a function of increasing body size is true for all species examined, the variation is high, with larger individuals spanning the range in clutch size variability found in any population. Clutch frequency is also highly variable among individuals, years, and locations.

As was stated above, variability is the norm in natural systems. What has been revealed to me with the South Carolina studies is how extensive this variability can be at every level from the individual to the species so that the orderly trends we would like to see in the data are absent in many instances. To me, this variability bespeaks an evolutionary history in which populations have been confronted with variable and unpredictable environmental conditions. One consideration is that freshwater turtles, especially those that are tied to both land and water, such as slider turtles, have a greater repertoire of genetic response and plasticity because they must contend with the vagaries of both environments. I would predict, therefore, that the variability in life history traits of species, such as *T. scripta*, that have natural history requirements that place them in a responsive mode to both aquatic and terrestrial changes would be greater than of species that are almost exclusively terrestrial, such as *Gopherus*, or aquatic, such as sea turtles.

Epilogue

This book has a lot of information about turtles, particularly slider turtles. But the question that might be asked at the end is, Why are there so many unanswered questions about freshwater turtles? Certainly, one of my primary disappointments is that we do not have more data on certain aspects of their ecology. A problem was that when data were being collected, no one knew that certain findings would ultimately be important. This is, of course, the criticism of descriptive biology. That is, what is described is what was observed, and the application to theory or scientific predictions is after the fact, by accident rather than by design. Nonetheless, we can rest assured that by identifying the gaps in our knowledge about life history and natural history, the way is paved for future investigators who would do more and better than we have done.

Acknowledgments

Manuscript preparation was made possible by contract DE-AC09-76SROO-819 between the University of Georgia and the U.S. Department of Energy and by National Science Foundation grant DEB-79-04758.

Bibliography

References are cited in this order: References with a single author are followed by all references by that author plus a second author, arranged alphabetically; references with three or more authors, cited in the text as [Author] et al. [date], are listed by first author and then by date; references with the same combination of authors are listed chronologically under a single authorship line. Italic numbers following each entry refer to the chapters citing that reference.

A

Ackerman, R. A.
  1977. The respiratory gas exchange of sea turtle nests (*Chelonia, Caretta*). *Respiration Physiology* 31:19–38.

Ackerman, R. A., and H. D. Prange
  1972. Oxygen diffusion across a sea turtle (*Chelonia mydas*) egg shell. *Comparative Biochemistry and Physiology* 43A:905–909. *8*

Ackerman, R. A., R. Dmi'el, and A. Ar
  1985a. Energy and water vapor exchange by parchment-shelled reptile eggs. *Physiological Zoology* 58:129–137. *8*

Ackerman, R. A., R. C. Seagrave, R. Dmi'el, and A. Ar
  1985b. Water and heat exchange between parchment-shelled reptile eggs and their surroundings. *Copeia* 1985:703–711. *8*

Adler, K.
  1968a. *Pseudemys scripta* in West Virginia: Archeological and modern records. *Journal of Herpetology* 2:117–120. *19*
  1968b. Synonymy of the Pliocene turtles *Pseudemys hilli* Cope and *Chrysemys limnodytes* Galbreath. *Journal of Herpetology* 1:32–38. *5*

Agassiz, L.
  1857. *Contributions to the natural history of the United States of America.* 1st monograph, vol. 2, 451–643, plates 1–27. Little, Brown and Co., Boston. *1, 4, 8, 19*

Agnedal, P. O.
  1967. Calcium and strontium in Swedish waters and fish and accumulation of ^{90}Sr. In *Radioecological concentration processes*, edited by B. Aberg and F. P. Hungate, 879–896. Pergamon Press, New York. *8, 21*

Aleksiuk, M., and K. W. Stewart
  1971. Seasonal changes in the body composition of the garter snake (*Thamnophis sirtalis parietalis*) at northern latitudes. *Ecology* 52:485–490. *19*

Al-Hassan, L. A., C. J. Webb, M. Giama, and P. J. Miller
1987.   Phosphoglucose isomerase polymorphism in the common goby, *Pomatoschistus microps* (Kroyer) (Teleostei: Gobiidae), around the British Isles. *Journal of Fish Biology* 30:281–298. *6*

Allen, B. M., O. A. Schjeide, and L. B. Hochwald
1951.   The influence of temperature upon the destruction of hematopoietic cells of tadpoles by x-irradiation. *Journal of Cellular and Comparative Physiology* 38:69–82. *21*

Allendorf, F. W.
1983.   Isolation, gene flow, and genetic differentiation among populations. In *Genetics and conservation: A reference for managing wild animal and plant populations*, edited by C. M. Schoenwald-Cox, S. Chambers, B. MacBryde, and W. Thomas, 51–65. Benjamin/Cummings Publ. Co., London. *6*

Allison, A., and A. E. Greer
1986.   Eggshells with pustulate surface structures: Basis for a new genus of New Guinea skinks (Lacertilia: Scincidae). *Journal of Herpetology* 20:116–119. *8*

Alonso Biosca, M. E., O. Cruz Rui, V. Berovides Alvares, and G. Espinosa Lopez
1985.   Diferención de tres poblaciones de la jicotea (*Pseudemys decussata*), sobre la base del patrón de proteinas totales de musculo. *Academia de Ciencias de Cuba Serie Biologia* 14:91–97. *5*

Altland, P. B., B. Highman, and B. Wood
1951.   Some effects of x-irradiation on turtles. *Journal of Experimental Zoology* 118:1–14. *2, 21*

Alvarez del Toro, M.
1982.   Los reptiles de Chiapas, Mexico. Instituto Zoológico del Estado, Tuxtla Gutiérrez, Chiapas, Mexico. *12*

Amadon, D.
1959.   The significance of sexual differences in size among birds. *Proceedings of the American Philosophical Society* 103:531–536.

Anderson, N. G., and K. M. Wilbur
1948.   Gastric carbonic anhydrase and acid secretion in turtles. *Journal of Cellular and Comparative Physiology* 31:293–302. *20*

Andrews, R. M.
1976.   Growth rate in island and mainland anoline lizards. *Copeia* 1976:477–482. *10*
1982.   Patterns of growth in reptiles. In Vol. 13 of *Biology of the Reptilia*, edited by C. Gans and F. H. Pough, 273–320. Academic Press, London. *3, 10*

Andrews, R. M., and O. J. Sexton
1981.   Water relations of the eggs of *Anolis auratus* and *Anolis limifrons*. *Ecology* 62:556–562. *8*

Angus, R. A.
1983.   Genetic analysis of melanistic spotting in sailfin mollies. *Journal of Heredity* 74:81–84. *19*

Arellano, A. R. V.
1951.   Research on the continental Neogene of Mexico. *American Journal of Science* 249:604–616. *7*

Armstrong, R. A., and M. E. Gilpin
1977.   Evolution in a time-varying environment. *Science* 195:591–592. *3*

Arnold, S. J.
1983.   Sexual selection: The interface of theory and empiri-

cism. In *Mate choice*, edited by P. Bateson, 67–107. Cambridge University Press, Cambridge.

Arruda, J. A.
1979.   A consideration of trophic dynamics in some tallgrass prairie farm ponds. *American Midland Naturalist* 102:254–262. *17*

Ashe, V. M., D. Chiszar, and H. M. Smith
1975.   Behavior of aquatic and terrestrial turtles on a visual cliff. *Chelonia* 2:3–7.

Ashton, R. E., Jr.
1975.   A study of movement, home range, and winter behavior of *Desmognathus fuscus* (Rafinesque). *Journal of Herpetology* 9:85–91. *21*

Askew, R. R., L. M. Cook, and J. A. Bishop
1971.   Atmospheric pollution and melanic moths in Manchester and its environs. *Journal of Applied Ecology* 71:247–256. *19*

Asplund, K. K.
1974.   Body size and habitat utilization in whiptail lizards (*Cnemidophorus*). *Copeia* 1974:695–703.

Atkins, G. L.
1969.   *Multicompartment models for biological systems*. Methuen and Co., London. *21*

Auffenberg, W.
1958.   Fossil turtles of the genus *Terrapene* in Florida. *Bulletin of the Florida State Museum Biological Sciences* 3:53–92. *5*
1964.   A first record of breeding colour changes in a tortoise. *Journal of Bombay Natural History Society* 61:191–192. *19*
1977.   Display behavior in tortoises. *American Zoologist* 17:241–250.

Auffenberg, W., and J. B. Iverson
1979.   Demography of terrestrial turtles. In *Turtles: Perspectives and research*, edited by M. Harless and H. Morlock, 541–569. John Wiley and Sons, New York. *3, 15*

Auffenberg, W., and W. G. Weaver, Jr.
1969.   *Gopherus berlandieri* in southeastern Texas. *Bulletin of the Florida State Museum Biological Sciences* 13:141–203. *16, 19*

Auth, D. L.
1975.   Behavioral ecology of basking in the yellow-bellied turtle, *Chrysemys scripta scripta* (Schoepff). *Bulletin of the Florida State Museum Biological Sciences* 20:1–45. *2, 20, 22*

Avalos, D.
1975.   The growth of the red-ear turtle *Pseudemys scripta elegans* in a thermal lake in southwestern Illinois. Master's thesis. Eastern Illinois University. *12, 20*

Avery, H. W.
1987.   Roles of diet protein and temperature in the nutritional energetics of juvenile slider turtles, *Trachemys scripta*. Master's thesis. State University of New York College at Buffalo. *20*

Avery, R. A.
1971.   Estimates of food consumption by the lizard *Lacertina vivipara* Jacquin. *Journal of Animal Ecology* 40:351–356. *21*
1978.   Activity patterns, thermoregulation, and food consumption in two sympatric lizard species (*Podarcis muralis* and *P. sicula*) from central Italy. *Journal of Animal Ecology* 47:143–158. *21*
1982.   Field studies of body temperatures and thermoregula-

tion. In Vol. 12 of *Biology of the Reptilia*, edited by C. Gans and F. H. Pough, 93–166. Academic Press, New York. *22*

Avise, J. C., and M. H. Smith
1974. Biochemical genetics of sunfish, I: Geographic variation and subspecific intergradation in the bluegill, *Lepomis macrochirus. Evolution* 28:42–56. *6*

B

Babcock, H. L.
1919. The turtles of New England. *Memoirs of the Boston Society of Natural History* 8:327–431, plates 17–32. *19*

Baden, H. P., G. Szabo, and J. Cohen
1966. Cutaneous melanocyte system of the indigo snake, *Drymarchon corais. Nature* 211:1095. *19*

Bagnara, J. T., and M. E. Hadley
1974. *Chromatophores and color change: The comparative physiology of animal pigmentation.* Prentice-Hall, Englewood Cliffs, N.J. *19*

Bagnara, J. T., J. D. Taylor, and M. E. Hadley
1968. The dermal chromatophore unit. *Journal of Cell Biology* 38:67–79. *19*

Baird, T., and S. E. Solomon
1979. Calcite and aragonite in the eggshell of *Chelonia mydas* L. *Journal of Experimental Marine Biology and Ecology* 36:295–303. *8*

Baker, C. E., and P. B. Dunaway
1969. Retention of cesium-134 as an index to metabolism in the cotton rat (*Sigmodon hispidus*). *Health Physics* 16:227–230. *21*

Baker, M. R.
1984. Nematode parasitism in amphibians and reptiles. *Canadian Journal of Zoology* 62:747–757. *23*

Baker, M. R., T. M. Goater, and G. W. Esch
1987. Descriptions of three nematode parasites of salamanders (Plethodontidae: Desmognathinae) from the southeastern United States. *Proceedings of the Helminthological Society of Washington* 54:15–23. *23*

Bakken, G. S.
1976. A heat transfer analysis of animals: Unifying concepts and the application of metabolism chamber data to field ecology. *Journal of Theoretical Biology* 60:337–384. *22*
1981. How many equivalent blackbody temperatures are there? *Journal of Thermal Biology* 6:59–60. *22*

Balazs, G. H.
1986. Ontogenetic changes in the plastron pigmentation of hatchling Hawaiian green turtles. *Journal of Herpetology* 20:280–282. *19*

Balcombe, J. P., and L. E. Licht
1987. Some aspects of the ecology of the midland painted turtle, *Chrysemys picta marginata*, in Wye Marsh, Ontario. *Canadian Field Naturalist* 101:98–100. *14*

Ballinger, R. E.
1973. Comparative demography of two viviparous iguanid lizards (*Sceloporus jarrovi* and *Sceloporus poinsetti*). *Ecology* 54:269–283.
1977. Reproductive strategies: Food availability as a source of proximal variation in a lizard. *Ecology* 58:628–635. *10*

1983. On the nature of life history variation in lizards. In *Lizard ecology: Studies of a model organism*, edited by R. B. Huey, E. R. Pianka, and T. W. Schoener, 241–260. Harvard University Press, Cambridge. *3*

Baptist, J. P., D. E. Hoss, and C. W. Lewis
1970. Retention of ^{51}Cr, ^{59}Fe, ^{60}Co, ^{65}Zn, ^{85}Sr, ^{95}Nb, ^{141}In, and ^{131}I by the Atlantic croaker (*Micropogon undulatus*). *Health Physics* 18:141–148. *21*

Barbour, R. W., J. W. Hardin, J. P. Schafer, and M. J. Harvey
1969. Home range, movements, and activity of the dusky salamander, *Desmognathus fuscus. Copeia* 1969:293–297. *21*

Barbour, T., and A. F. Carr, Jr.
1940. Antillean terrapins. *Memoirs of the Museum of Comparative Zoology at Harvard College* 54:381–415. *19*

Barlett, D. L., and J. B. Steele
1985. *Forevermore: Nuclear waste in America.* W. W. Norton and Co., New York. *21*

Barney, R. L.
1922. Further notes on the natural history and artificial propagation of the diamond-back terrapin. *Bulletin of the United States Bureau of Fisheries* 38:91–111. *3, 9*

Barr, R. E., and Y. J. Musacchia
1972. Postirradiation hibernation and radiation response of ground squirrels: Telemetry surveillance. *Radiation Research* 51:631. *21*

Bartholomew, G. A.
1982. Physiological control of body temperature. In Vol. 12 of *Biology of the Reptilia*, edited by C. Gans and F. H. Pough, 167–211. Academic Press, New York. *22*

Barton, A. J., and J. W. Price, Sr.
1955. Our knowledge of the bogturtle, *Clemmys muhlenbergi*, surveyed and augmented. *Copeia* 1955:159–165. *14*

Barus, V., and F. Moravec
1967. A survey of helminths from the Cuban turtle—*Pseudemys decussata* Gray (Emydidae). *Vestnik Ceskoslovenske Spolecnosti Zoologicke* 31:313–324. *23*

Barwick, R. E.
1982. The growth and ecology of the gecko *Hoplodactylus duvauceli* at the Brothers Islands. In *New Zealand Herpetology*, edited by D. G. Newman, 377–391. New Zealand Wildlife Service, Wellington. *3*

Baserga, R., and D. Malamud
1969. *Autoradiography: Techniques and applications.* Harper and Row, New York. *21*

Bayless, L. E.
1975. Population parameters for *Chrysemys picta* in a New York pond. *American Midland Naturalist* 93:168–176. *14*

Beauchamp, J. J., and J. S. Olson
1973. Corrections for bias in regression estimates after logarithmic transformation. *Ecology* 54:1403–1407. *21*

Behne, D., and H. Gessner
1987. Effects of dietary K on the absorption and excretion of radiocesium in the rat. *Health Physics* 53:331–332. *21*

Belkin, D. A.
1963. Anoxia: Tolerance in reptiles. *Science* 139:492–493. *22*

Belkin, D. A., and C. Gans
1968. An unusual chelonian feeding niche. *Ecology* 49:768–769. *20*

Bell, G.
1977. The life of the smooth newt (*Triturus vulgaris*) after metamorphosis. *Ecological Monographs* 47:279–299. *3*

Benedict, F. G.
1932. *The physiology of large reptiles.* Carnegie Institution of Washington Publication no. 425. Washington, D.C. *21*

Bennett, A. F., and W. R. Dawson
1976. Metabolism. In Vol. 5 of *Biology of the Reptilia*, edited by C. Gans and W. R. Dawson, 127–223. Academic Press, London. *21*

Bennett, A. F., and K. A. Nagy
1977. Energy expenditure in free-ranging lizards. *Ecology* 58:697–700. *21*

Bennett, B. G.
1971. Strontium-90 in the diet. U.S. Atomic Energy Commission Report no. HASL-242. Washington, D.C. *21*

Bennett, D. H.
1972. Notes on the terrestrial wintering of mud turtles (*Kinosternon subrubrum*). *Herpetologica* 28:245–247. *2*

Bennett, D. H., and R. W. McFarlane
1983. *The fishes of the Savannah River Plant: National Environmental Research Park.* U.S. Department of Energy, Savannah River National Environmental Research Park, Aiken, S.C. *2*

Bennett, D. H., J. W. Gibbons, and J. C. Franson
1970. Terrestrial activity in aquatic turtles. *Ecology* 51:738–740. *2, 16, 20, 21*

Bennett, S. H., J. Glanville, and J. W. Gibbons
1980. Terrestrial activity, abundance, and diversity of amphibians in differently managed forest types. *American Midland Naturalist* 103:412–416. *2*

Bentley, P. J., and K. Schmidt-Nielsen
1966. Cutaneous water loss in reptiles. *Science* 151:1547–1549. *22*

Berry, J. F.
1975. The population effects of ecological sympatry on musk turtles in northern Florida. *Copeia* 1975:692–701. *1*

1978. Variation and systematics in the *Kinosternon scorpioides* and *Kinosternon leucostomum* complexes (Reptilia: Testudines: Kinosternidae) of Mexico and Central America. Ph.D. dissertation. University of Utah. *7*

1984. New information on the evolution of sexual size dimorphism in turtles [abstract]. Joint Meeting of the American Society of Ichthyologists and Herpetologists, the Herpetologists' League, and Society for the Study of Amphibians and Reptiles, Norman, Okla. *17*

Berry, J. F., and C. M. Berry
1984. A re-analysis of geographic variation and systematics in the yellow mud turtle, *Kinosternon flavescens* (Agassiz). *Annals of Carnegie Museum* 53:185–206. *14*

Berry, J. F., and R. Shine
1980. Sexual size dimorphism and sexual selection in turtles (order Testudines). *Oecologia* (Berlin) 44:185–191. *11*

Bhattacharyya, M. H., R. P. Larsen, H. C. Furr, D. P. Peterson, R. D. Oldham, E. S. Moretti, and M. I. Spaletto
1985. Adsorption of Pu, Pb, and Cd to mouth surfaces during oral administration to mice. *Health Physics* 48:207–213. *21*

Bickham, J., and R. J. Baker
1976a. Chromosome homology and evolution of emydid turtles. *Chromosoma* 54:201–219. *5*

1976b. Karyotypes of some neotropical turtles. *Copeia* 1976:703–708. *5*

Bidder, G. P.
1932. Senescence. *British Medical Journal* 2:583–585. *3*

Birkebak, R. C.
1966. Heat transfer in biological systems. In Vol. 2 of *The International Review of General and Experimental Zoology*, edited by W. J. L. Felts and R. J. Harrison, 268–344. Academic Press, New York. *22*

Bishop, S. C.
1947. *Handbook of salamanders.* Comstock Publ. Co., Ithaca, N.Y. *2*

Bjorndal, K. A.
1980. Demography of the breeding population of the green turtle, *Chelonia mydas*, at Tortuguero, Costa Rica. *Copeia* 1980:525–530. *15*

1985. Nutritional ecology of sea turtles. *Copeia* 1985:736–751. *20*

1986. Effect of solitary vs. group feeding on intake in *Pseudemys nelsoni*. *Copeia* 1986:234–235. *20*

Bjorndal, K. A., ed.
1982. *Biology and conservation of sea turtles.* Smithsonian Institution Press, Washington, D.C.

Blair, W. F.
1960. *The rusty lizard: A population study.* University of Texas Press, Austin. *10*

1976. Some aspects of the biology of the ornate box turtle, *Terrapene ornata*. *Southwestern Naturalist* 21:89–104. *3*

Blake, S. F.
1922. Sexual differences in coloration in the spotted turtle, *Clemmys guttata*. *Proceedings of the United States National Museum* 59:463–469.

Bleakney, J. S.
1963. Notes on the distribution and life histories of turtles in Nova Scotia. *Canadian Field Naturalist* 77:67–76. *8*

Bocourt, M-F.
1868. Description de quelques chéloniens nouveaux appartenant a la faune Mexicaine. *Annales des Sciences Naturelles, Zoologie et Biologie Animale* (Paris), ser. 5, vol. 10, 121–122. *4, 7, 19*

Bodenheimer, F. S., A. Halperin, and E. Swirski
1953. Experiments on light transmission through some animal integuments. *Bulletin of the Research Council of Israel* 2:436–438. *19*

Bogert, C. M.
1961. Los reptiles de Chiapas [review]. *Copeia* 1961:506–507. *7*

Bonhomme, F. S., S. Salvidio, A. LeBeau, and G. Pasteur
1987. Comparaison génétique des tortues vertes (*Chelonia mydas*) des oceans Atlantique, Indien, et Pacifique: Une illustration apparente de la théorie mullerienne classique de la structure génétique des populations? *Genetica* 74:89–94. *6*

Boulenger, G. A.
1889. *Catalogue of the chelonians, rhynchocephalians, and crocodiles in the British Museum (Natural History).* Taylor and Francis, London. *1, 4*

Bourliere, F.
  1954. The role of comparative physiology in studies of aging. In *Problems of aging*, edited by N. W. Schock, 126–296. Josiah Macy Foundation, New York. *10*

Bourne, A. R.
  1981. Blood metabolites of injected [^{14}C]progesterone in the lizard *Tiliqua rugosa*. *Comparative Biochemistry and Physiology* 70B:661–664. *19*

Bourne, A. R., and P. Licht
  1985. Steroid biosynthesis in turtle testes. *Comparative Biochemistry and Physiology* 81B:793–796. *19*

Bourne, A. R., and P. F. Seamark
  1978. Seasonal variation in steroid biosynthesis by the testis of the lizard *Tiliqua rugosa*. *Comparative Biochemistry and Physiology* 59B:363–367. *19*

Bourne, A. R., J. L. Taylor, and T. G. Watson
  1985. Identification of epitestosterone in the plasma and testis of the lizard *Tiliqua rugosa*. *General and Comparative Endocrinology* 58:394–401. *19*

Boycott, B. B., and R. W. Guillery
  1962. Olfactory and visual learning in the red-eared terrapin, *Pseudemys scripta elegans* (Wied). *Journal of Experimental Biology* 39:567–577. *20*

Boyd, C. E.
  1970. Amino acid, protein, and calorie content of vascular aquatic macrophytes. *Ecology* 51:902–906. *20*

Boyden, C. R.
  1974. Trace element content and body size in molluscs. *Nature* 251:311–314. *21*

Boyer, D. R.
  1965. Ecology of the basking habit in turtles. *Ecology* 46:99–118. *19, 20, 22*

Boyer, P. D., D. J. Graves, C. H. Suelter, and M. E. Dempsey
  1961. Simple procedure for conversion of oxygen of orthophosphate or water to carbon dioxide for oxygen-18 determination. *Analytical Chemistry* 33:1906–1909. *21*

Bramble, D. M.
  1974. Emydid shell kinesis: Biomechanics and evolution. *Copeia* 1974:707–727. *4, 5*

Branch, W. R.
  1984. Preliminary observations on the ecology of the angulate tortoise (*Chersina angulata*) in the Eastern Cape Province, South Africa. *Amphibia-Reptilia* 5:43–55. *14*

Brand, D. D.
  1937. *The natural landscape of northwestern Chihuahua*. University of New Mexico Bulletin, Geological Series, vol. 5, no. 2; whole no. 316. University of New Mexico Press, Albuquerque. *7*

Breckenridge, W. J.
  1955. Observations on the life history of the soft-shelled turtle *Trionyx ferox*, with especial reference to growth. *Copeia* 1955:5–9. *14*

Breckenridge, W. J., and J. R. Tester
  1961. Growth, local movements, and hibernation of the Manitoba toad, *Bufo hemiophrys*. *Ecology* 42:637–646. *21*

Breder, C. M., Jr.
  1946. Amphibians and reptiles of the Rio Chucunaque drainage, Darien, Panama, with notes on their life histories and habits. *Bulletin of the American Museum of Natural History* 86:375–436. *12*

Breder, R. B.
  1927. Turtle trailing: A new technique for studying the life habits of certain Testudinata. *Zoologica* 9:231–243. *2, 24*

Breitenbach, G. L., J. D. Congdon, and R. C. van Loben Sels
  1984. Winter temperatures of *Chrysemys picta* nests in Michigan: Effects on hatchling survival. *Herpetologica* 40:76–81. *8*

Briese, L. A., and M. H. Smith
  1974. Seasonal abundance and movement of nine species of small mammals. *Journal of Mammalogy* 55:615–629. *2*

Brisbin, I. L., Jr.
  1972. Seasonal variations in the live weights and major body components of captive box turtles. *Herpetologica* 28:70–75. *19*

Brockelman, W. Y.
  1975. Competition, the fitness of offspring, and optimal clutch size. *American Naturalist* 109:677–699. *8, 11*

Brooks, D. R.
  1977. Evolutionary history of some plagiorchioid trematodes of anurans. *Systematic Zoology* 26:277–289. *23*
  1978. Systematic status of proteocephalid cestodes of North American reptiles and amphibians. *Proceedings of the Helminthological Society of Washington* 45:1–28. *23*
  1979. Testing hypotheses of evolutionary relationships among parasites: The digeneans of crocodilians. *American Zoologist* 19:1225–1238. *23*
  1981. Raw similarity measures of shared parasites: An empirical tool for determining host phylogenetic relationships? *Systematic Zoology* 30:203–207. *23*

Brown, K. L.
  1981. An analysis of species diversity along a temporal gradient of loblolly pine stands in South Carolina. Master's thesis. Texas Christian University. *2*
  1985. Demographic and genetic characteristics of dispersal in the mosquitofish, *Gambusia affinis* (Pisces: Poeciliidae). *Copeia* 1985:597–612. *6*

Brown, W. S.
  1971. Morphometrics of *Terrapene coahuila* (Chelonia, Emydidae), with comments on its evolutionary status. *Southwestern Naturalist* 16:171–184.
  1974. Ecology of the aquatic box turtle, *Terrapene coahuila* (Chelonia, Emydidae), in northern Mexico. *Bulletin of the Florida State Museum Biological Sciences* 19:1–67. *14, 16, 18*

Bryant, E. H.
  1971. Life history consequences of natural selection: Cole's result. *American Naturalist* 105:75–76. *3*

Bryuzgin, V. L.
  1939. A procedure for investigating age and growth in Reptilia. *Comptes Rendus (Doklady) de l'Académie des Sciences de l'URSS* 23:403–405. *10*

Bueker, E. D.
  1961. Paper electrophoretic patterns of human serum proteins compared with those of lower forms. *Proceedings of the Society for Experimental Biology and Medicine* 106:373–377. *5*

Bull, J. J.
  1980. Sex determination in reptiles. *Quarterly Review of Biology* 55:3–21. *8, 14*

1983.   *Evolution of sex determining mechanisms.* Benjamin/
        Cummings, Menlo Park, Calif. *8*

Bull, J. J., and R. Shine
1979.   Iteroparous animals that skip opportunities for repro-
        duction. *American Naturalist* 114:296–303. *3*

Bull, J. J., and R. C. Vogt
1979.   Temperature-dependent sex determination in turtles.
        Science 206:1186–1188. *13, 14*
1981.   Temperature-sensitive periods of sex determination in
        emydid turtles. *Journal of Experimental Zoology* 218:435–
        440. *8*

Bull, J. J., R. C. Vogt, and C. J. McCoy
1982.   Sex determining temperatures in turtles: A geographic
        comparison. *Evolution* 36:326–332. *13*

Burchfield, P. M., C. S. Doucette, and T. F. Beimler
1980.   Captive management of the radiated tortoise *Geochelone
        radiata* at Gladys Porter Zoo, Brownsville. *International
        Zoo Yearbook* 20:1–6.

Burger, J.
1977.   Determinants of hatching success in diamondback ter-
        rapin, *Malaclemys terrapin. American Midland Naturalist*
        97:444–464. *8*

Burger, J., and W. A. Montevecchi
1975.   Nest site selection in the terrapin *Malaclemys terrapin.*
        Copeia 1975:113–119. *16*

Burghardt, G. M.
1967.   The primacy effect of the first feeding experience in the
        snapping turtle. *Psychonomic Science Section on Animal and
        Physiological Psychology* 7:382–384. *20*
1970.   Chemical perception in reptiles. In Vol 1. of *Com-
        munication by chemical signals*, edited by J. W. Johnston,
        D. G. Moulton, and A. Turk, 241–308. Appleton-
        Century-Crofts, New York. *20*

Burghardt, G. M., and E. H. Hess
1966.   Food imprinting in the snapping turtle, *Chelydra serpen-
        tina. Science* 151:108–109. *20*

Bury, R. B.
1972.   Habits and home range of the Pacific pond turtle, *Clem-
        mys marmorata*, in a stream community. Ph.D. disserta-
        tion. University of California, Berkeley. *14, 16, 18*
1979.   Population ecology of freshwater turtles. In *Turtles: Per-
        spectives and research*, edited by M. Harless and H. Mor-
        lock, 571–602. John Wiley and Sons, NY. *3, 5, 13–15,
        18*

Bury, R. B., and E. L. Smith
1986.   Aspects of the ecology and management of the tortoise
        Gopherus berlandieri at Laguna Atascosa, Texas. *South-
        western Naturalist* 31:387–394. *14*

Bury, R. B., and J. H. Wolfheim
1973.   Aggression in free-living pond turtles (*Clemmys mar-
        morata*). *BioScience* 23:659–662. *19*

Bury, R. B., J. H. Wolfheim, and R. A. Luckenbach
1979.   Agonistic behavior in free-living painted turtles
        (*Chrysemys picta bellii*). *Biology of Behavior* 1979:227–
        239. *22*

Busack, S. D., and C. H. Ernst
1980.   Variation in Mediterranean populations of *Mauremys*
        Gray 1869 (Reptilia, Testudines, Emydidae). *Annals of
        Carnegie Museum* 49:251–264. *14*

Buscarlet, L. A.
1974.   The use of sodium-22 for determining the food intake of
        the migratory locust. *Oikos* 25:204–208. *21*

Bush, A. O., and J. C. Holmes
1986.   Intestinal helminths of lesser scaup ducks: An interac-
        tive community. *Canadian Journal of Zoology* 64:142–
        152. *23*

Bustard, H. R.
1970.   The adaptive significance of coloration in hatchling
        green sea turtles. *Herpetologica* 26:224–227. *19*
1971.   Temperature and water tolerances of incubating croc-
        odile eggs. *British Journal of Herpetology* 4:198–200. *8*
1979.   Population dynamics of sea turtles. In *Turtles: Perspec-
        tives and research*, edited by M. Harless and H. Morlock,
        523–540. John Wiley and Sons, New York. *15*

Bustard, H. R., and P. Greenham
1968.   Physical and chemical factors affecting hatching in the
        green sea turtle, *Chelonia mydas* (L.). *Ecology* 49:269–
        276. *8*

C

Cabana, G., A. Frewin, R. H. Peters, and L. Randall
1982.   The effect of sexual size dimorphism on variations in
        reproductive effort of birds and mammals. *American
        Naturalist* 120:17–25.

Cadwell, L. L., and R. G. Schreckhise
1976.   Determination of varying consumption rates from ra-
        diotracer data. In *Radioecology and energy resources*, edited
        by C. E. Cushing, Jr., 123–125. Dowden, Hutchinson
        and Ross, Stroudsburg, Pa. *21*

Cagle, F. R.
1937.   Egg laying habits of the slider turtle (*Pseudemys troostii*),
        the painted turtle (*Chrysemys picta*), and the musk turtle
        (*Sternotherus odoratus*). *Journal of the Tennessee Academy of
        Science* 12:87–95. *8*
1939.   A system for marking turtles for future identification.
        Copeia 1939:170–173. *2*
1942.   Turtle populations in southern Illinois. *Copeia*
        1942:155–162. *14, 17*
1944a. Activity and winter changes of hatchling *Pseudemys.*
        Copeia 1944:105–109. *15, 24*
1944b. *Home range, homing behavior, and migration in turtles.* Mis-
        cellaneous Publications of the Museum of Zoology,
        University of Michigan, no. 61. *1, 12, 16, 18, 20, 22*
1944c. Sexual maturity in the female of the turtle *Pseudemys
        scripta elegans. Copeia* 1944:149–152. *3, 9, 13, 15*
1944d. A technique for obtaining turtle eggs for study. *Copeia*
        1944:60.
1945.   Recovery from serious injury in the painted turtle.
        Copeia 1945:45. *10*
1946.   The growth of the slider turtle, *Pseudemys scripta elegans.*
        American Midland Naturalist 36:685–729. *3, 10, 12, 22*
1948a. The growth of turtles in Lake Glendale, Illinois. *Copeia*
        1948:197–203. *12, 19*
1948b. Sexual maturity in the male turtle, *Pseudemys scripta
        troostii. Copeia* 1948:108–111. *9, 19*
1950.   The life history of the slider turtle, *Pseudemys scripta
        troostii* (Holbrook). *Ecological Monographs* 20:31–54. *1,
        3, 8–17, 19, 20, 22, 24*

1952. A Louisiana terrapin population (*Malaclemys*). *Copeia* 1952:74–76.

1953. An outline for the study of a reptile life history. *Tulane Studies in Zoology* 1:31–52.

1954. Observations on the life cycles of painted turtles (genus *Chrysemys*). *American Midland Naturalist* 52:225–235. *1, 9, 14*

Cagle, F. R., and A. H. Chaney
1950. Turtle populations in Louisiana. *American Midland Naturalist* 43:383–388. *5*

Cahn, A. R.
1937. *The turtles of Illinois*. Illinois Biological Monographs, vol. 35. *12, 14, 16, 19, 20*

Caldwell, D. K.
1959. The loggerhead turtles of Cape Romain, South Carolina. *Bulletin of the Florida State Museum* 4:319–348. *8*

1962a. *Carapace length–body weight relationship and size and sex ratio of the northeastern Pacific green sea turtle*, Chelonia mydas carrinegra. Contributions in Science (Los Angeles), vol. 62. *14*

1962b. *Sea turtles in Baja Californian waters (with special reference to those of the Gulf of California), and the description of a new subspecies of northeastern Pacific green turtle*. Contributions in Science (Los Angeles), vol. 61. *19*

Caldwell, J. P.
1987. Demography and life history of two species of chorus frogs (Anura: Hylidae) in South Carolina. *Copeia* 1987:114–127. *2*

Callard, G. V., Z. Petro, and K. J. Ryan
1977. Identification of aromatase in the reptilian brain. *Endocrinology* 100:1214–1218. *19*

Camazine B., W. Garstka, and D. Crews
1981. Techniques for gonadectomizing snakes (*Thamnophis*). *Copeia* 1981:884–886. *19*

Cantrall, I. J.
1943. *The ecology of the Orthoptera and Dermaptera of the E. S. George Reserve, Michigan*. Miscellaneous Publications of the Museum of Zoology, University of Michigan, no. 54.

Capinera, J. L.
1979. Qualitative variation in plants and insects: Effect of propagule size on ecological plasticity. *American Naturalist* 114:350–361. *8*

Carpenter, C. C.
1952. Growth and maturity of the three species of *Thamnophis* in Michigan. *Copeia* 1952:237–243. *10*

1955. Sounding turtles: A field locating technique. *Herpetologica* 11:120. *2*

1960. Reproduction in Oklahoma *Sceloporus* and *Cnemidophorus*. *Herpetologica* 16:175–182. *8*

Carr, A.
1942. A new *Pseudemys* from Sonora, Mexico. *American Museum Novitates* 1181:1–4. *7*

1952. *Handbook of turtles: The turtles of the United States, Canada, and Baja California*. Comstock Publishing Associates, Ithaca, N.Y. *1, 2, 4, 7–9, 12, 16, 19, 23*

1965. The navigation of the green turtle. *Scientific American* 212:78–86. *16, 23*

Carr, A., and M. H. Carr
1970. Modulated reproductive periodicity in *Chelonia*. *Ecology* 51:335–337. *9, 15, 24*

Carr, A., and P. J. Coleman
1974. Seafloor spreading theory and the odyssey of the green turtle. *Nature* 249:128–130. *16*

Carr, A., and L. Giovannoli
1957. The ecology and migrations of sea turtles, 2: Results of field work in Costa Rica, 1957. *American Museum Novitates* 1835:1–32. *14*

Carr, A., and D. Goodman
1970. Ecologic implications of size and growth in *Chelonia*. *Copeia* 1970:783–786. *15*

Carr, A., H. Hirth, and L. Ogren
1966. The ecology and migrations of sea turtles, 6: The hawksbill turtle in the Caribbean Sea. *American Museum Novitates* 2248:1–29.

Carr, A., M. Carr, and A. Meylan
1978. The ecology and migration of sea turtles, 7: The west Caribbean green turtle colony. *Bulletin of the American Museum of Natural History* 162:1–46. *15*

Carroll, R. L.
1969. Origin of reptiles. In Vol. 1 of *Biology of the Reptilia*, edited by C. Gans, A. d'A. Bellairs, and T. S. Parsons, 1–44. Academic Press, New York. *8*

Casas-Andreu, G.
1967. Contribución al conocimiento de las tortugas dulceaquícolas de Mexico. Master's thesis. University of Wisconsin—Madison. *12*

Case, T. J.
1976. Body size differences between populations of the chuckwalla, *Sauromalus obesus*. *Ecology* 57:313–323.

1978. On the evolution and adaptive significance of postnatal growth rates in the terrestrial vertebrates. *Quarterly Review of Biology* 53:243–282.

Castanet, J.
1974. Etude histologique des marques squelettiques de croissance chez *Vipera aspis* (L.) (Ophidia, Viperidae). *Zoologica Scripta* 3:137–151. *10*

1987. La squelettochronologie chez les reptiles, III: Application. *Annales des Sciences Naturelles, Zoologie et Biologie Animale* (Paris) 8:157–172. *10*

Castanet, J., and M. Cheylan
1979. Les marques de croissance des os et écailles comme indicateur de l'âge chez *Testudo hermanni* et *Testudo graeca* (Reptilia, Chelonia, Testudinidae). *Canadian Journal of Zoology* 57:1649–1665. *10*

Castaño M., O. V., and M. Lugo-R.
1981. Estudio comparativo del comportamiento de dos especies de morrocoy: *Geochelone carbonaria* y *Geochelone denticulata* y aspectos comparables de su morfología esterna. *Cespedesia* 10:55–122.

Caswell, H.
1983. Phenotypic plasticity in life-history traits: Demographic effects and evolutionary consequences. *American Zoologist* 23:35–46. *3, 8, 15*

Caudle, A. L.
1984. Effects of nest humidity and egg size on hatching suc-

cess and growth of embryonic freshwater chelonians. Master's thesis. University of Georgia. *8*

Cena, K., J. A. Clark, and J. R. Spotila
1986.   Thermoregulation. In *Vertebrates*, vol. 2 of *Biology of the integument*, edited by J. Bereiter-Hahn, A. G. Matoltsy, and K. S. Richards, 517–534. Springer-Verlag, New York. *22*

Chabaud, A. G.
1981.   Host range and evolution of nematode parasites of vertebrates. *Parasitology* 82:169–170. *23*

Chaney, A., and C. L. Smith
1950.   Methods for collecting map turtles. *Copeia* 1950:323–324. *2*

Charlesworth, B.
1980.   Evolution in age-structured populations. Cambridge University Press, Cambridge. *3*

Charnov, E. L., and W. M. Schaffer
1973.   Life history consequences of natural selection: Cole's result revisited. *American Naturalist* 107:791–793. *3*

Chato, J. C.
1969.   Heat transfer in bioengineering. In *Advanced heat transfer*, edited by B. T. Chao, 395–414. University of Illinois Press, Urbana. *22*

Chavin, W.
1969.   Fundamental aspects of morphological melanin color changes in vertebrate skin. *American Zoologist* 9:505–520. *19*

Chesley, L. C.
1934.   The influence of temperature upon the amylases of cold- and warm-blooded animals. *Biological Bulletin* (Woods Hole) 66:330–338. *20*

Chesser, R. K., and M. H. Smith
1987.   Relationship of genetic variation to growth and reproduction in the white-tailed deer. In *Biology and management of the Cervidae*, edited by C. M. Wemmer, 168–177. Smithsonian Institution Press, Washington, D.C. *6*

Chesser, R. K., M. H. Smith, P. E. Johns, M. N. Manlove, D. O. Straney, and R. Baccus
1982.   Spatial, temporal, and age-dependent heterozygosity of beta-hemoglobin in white-tailed deer. *Journal of Wildlife Management* 46:983–990. *6*

Cheverud, J. M., M. M. Dow, and W. Leutenegger
1985.   The quantitative assessment of phylogenetic constraints in comparative analyses: Sexual dimorphism in body weight among primates. *Evolution* 39:1335–1351.

Chew, R. M.
1971.   The excretion of ^{65}Zn and ^{54}Mn as indices of energy metabolism of *Peromyscus polionotus*. *Journal of Mammalogy* 52:337–350. *21*

Chiu, K. W., M. S. Leung, and P. F. A. Maderson
1983.   Thyroid and skin shedding in the rat snake (*Ptyas korros*). *Journal of Experimental Zoology* 225:407–410. *19*

Christens, E., and J. R. Bider
1986.   Reproductive ecology of the painted turtle (*Chrysemys picta marginata*) in southwestern Quebec. *Canadian Journal of Zoology* 64:914–920. *15*
1987.   Nesting activity and hatching success of the painted turtle (*Chrysemys picta marginata*) in southwestern Quebec. *Herpetologica* 43:55–65. *15*

Christian, K., C. R. Tracy, and W. P. Porter
1983.   Seasonal shifts in body temperature and use of microhabitats by Galapagos land iguanas (*Conolophus pallidus*). *Ecology* 64:463–468. *22*

Christiansen, J. L., and R. R. Burken
1979.   Growth and maturity of the snapping turtle (*Chelydra serpentina*) in Iowa. *Herpetologica* 35:261–266.

Christiansen, J. L., and E. O. Moll
1973.   Latitudinal reproductive variation within a single subspecies of painted turtle, *Chrysemys picta belli*. *Herpetologica* 29:152–163. *3, 9, 14*

Christie, W. W.
1973.   *Lipid analysis*. Pergamon Press, Oxford. *8*
1982.   *Lipid analysis*. Pergamon Press, Oxford. *8*

Christy, E. J., J. O. Farlow, J. E. Bourque, and J. W. Gibbons
1974.   Enhanced growth and increased body size of turtles living in thermal and post-thermal aquatic systems. In *Thermal ecology*, U.S. Atomic Energy Commission Symposium Series (CONF-730505), edited by J. W. Gibbons and R. R. Sharitz, 277–284. National Technical Information Service, Springfield, Va. *17, 20*

Ckhikvadze, V. M.
1984.   Classification des tortues de la famille des Emydidae et leurs liens phylogenetiques avec d'autres familles. *Studia Geologica Salmanticensia*, Vol. Especial no. 1, 105–113. *5*

Clark, D. B., and J. W. Gibbons
1969.   Dietary shift in the turtle *Pseudemys scripta* (Schoepff) from youth to maturity. *Copeia* 1969:704–706. *1, 2, 10, 12, 17, 20, 23*

Clark, D. R., Jr.
1970.   Ecological study of the worm snake *Carphophis vermis* (Kennicott). University of Kansas Publications of the Museum of Natural History, vol. 19, no. 2, 85–144. *10*

Clark, J.
1937.   The stratigraphy and paleontology of the Chadron Formation in the Big Badlands of South Dakota. *Annals of Carnegie Museum* 25:261–350. *5*

Clark, J. M., and J. Maynard Smith
1955.   The genetics and cytology of *Drosophila subobscura*, XI: Hybrid vigour and longevity. *Journal of Genetics* 53:172–180. *3*

Cloudsley-Thompson, J. L., C. Constantinou, and D. K. Butt
1985.   Carapace coloration and latitudinal distribution in testudinae. *British Herpetological Society Bulletin* 14:10–12. *19*

Clutton-Brock, T. H., P. H. Harvey, and B. Rudder
1977.   Sexual dimorphism, socionomic sex ratio, and body weight in primates. *Nature* 269:797–800.

Clutton-Brock, T. H., F. E. Guinness, and S. D. Albon
1982.   *Red deer: The ecology and behavior of the two sexes*. University of Chicago Press, Chicago. *3*

Cochran, D. M., and C. J. Goin
1970.   *The new field book of reptiles and amphibians*. Putnam, New York. *2*

Cody, M.
1971.   Ecological aspects of reproduction. In Vol 1. of *Avian biology*, edited by D. S. Farner and J. R. King, 461–512. Academic Press, New York. *3*

Cole, C. J.
1984.   Unisexual lizards. *Scientific American* 250:94–100.

Cole, L. C.
1943.   Experiments on toleration of high temperature in lizards with references to adaptative coloration. *Ecology* 24:94–108. *19*
1954.   The population consequences of life history phenomena. *Quarterly Review of Biology* 29:103–137. *3, 15*

Coleman, D. C., and J. T. McGinnis
1970.   Quantification of fungus–small arthropod food chains in the soil. *Oikos* 21:134–137. *21*

Collins, J. P., and H. M. Wilbur
1979.   *Breeding habits and habitats of the amphibians of the Edwin S. George Reserve, Michigan, with notes on the local distribution of fishes.* Occasional Papers of the Museum of Zoology, University of Michigan, no. 868. *2*

Comar, C. L., R. H. Wasserman, and A. R. Twardock
1961.   Secretion of calcium and strontium into milk. *Health Physics* 7:69–80. *21*

Comfort, A.
1956.   *The biology of senescence.* Rinehart and Co., New York. *3*
1979.   *The biology of senescence.* 3d ed. Churchill Livingstone, Edinburgh. *3*

Conant, R.
1951.   *The reptiles of Ohio.* University of Notre Dame Press, Notre Dame, Ind. *19*
1958.   *A field guide to reptiles and amphibians of the United States and Canada east of the 100th meridian.* Houghton Mifflin Co., Boston. *1, 2*
1963.   Semiaquatic snakes of the genus *Thamnophis* from the isolated drainage system of the Río Nazas and adjacent areas in Mexico. *Copeia* 1963:473–499. *7*
1975.   *A field guide to reptiles and amphibians of eastern and central North America.* Houghton Mifflin Co., Boston. *1, 2, 4, 5, 11, 19*

Congdon, J. D.
1977.   Energetics of the montane lizard *Sceloporus jarrovi:* A measurement of reproductive effort. Ph.D. dissertation. Arizona State University. *21*
1989.   Proximate and evolutionary constraints on energy relations of reptiles. *Physiological Zoology.* In press.

Congdon J. D., and J. W. Gibbons
1983.   Relationships of reproductive characteristics to body size in *Pseudemys scripta. Herpetologica* 39:147–151. *3, 6, 8, 9, 11–13*
1985.   Egg components and reproductive characteristics of turtles: Relationships to body size. *Herpetologica* 41:194–205. *3, 6, 8, 9, 11–13*
1987.   Morphological constraint on egg size: A challenge to optimal egg size theory? *Proceedings of the National Academy of Sciences of the United States of America* 84:4145–4147. *3, 8, 9*
1989a.   Biomass productivity of turtles in freshwater wetlands. In *Freshwater wetlands and wildlife,* edited by R. R. Sharitz and J. W. Gibbons. Technical Information Center, Oak Ridge, Tenn. In press. *1*
1989b.   Posthatching yolk reserves in hatchling American alligators. *Herpetologica.* In press. *8*

Congdon, J. D., and D. W. Tinkle
1982a.   Energy expenditure in free-ranging sagebrush lizards (*Sceloporus graciosus*). *Canadian Journal of Zoology* 60:1412–1416. *3, 21*
1982b.   Reproductive energetics of the painted turtle (*Chrysemys picta*). *Herpetologica* 38:228–237. *8, 9, 11, 19*

Congdon, J. D., W. W. King, and K. A. Nagy
1978.   Validation of the HTO-18 method for determination of CO_2 production of lizards (genus *Sceloporus*). *Copeia* 1978:360–362. *21*

Congdon, J. D., R. E. Ballinger, and K. A. Nagy
1979.   Energetics, temperature, and water relations in winter aggregated *Sceloporus jarrovi* (Sauria: Iguanidae). *Ecology* 60:30–35. *21*

Congdon, J. D., A. E. Dunham, and D. W. Tinkle
1982.   Energy budgets and life histories of reptiles. In Vol. 13 of *Biology of the Reptilia,* edited by C. Gans and F. H. Pough, 233–271. Academic Press, New York. *2, 3*

Congdon, J. D., J. W. Gibbons, and J. L. Greene
1983a.   Parental investment in the chicken turtle (*Deirochelys reticularia*). *Ecology* 64:419–425. *2, 3, 8, 9, 11*

Congdon, J. D., D. W. Tinkle, G. L. Breitenbach, and R. C. van Loben Sels
1983b.   Nesting ecology and hatching success in the turtle *Emydoidea blandingii. Herpetologica* 39:417–429. *3, 6, 8, 15, 16, 21*

Congdon, J. D., D. W. Tinkle, and P. C. Rosen
1983c.   Egg components and utilization during development in aquatic turtles. *Copeia* 1983:264–268. *3, 8*

Congdon, J. D., J. L. Greene, and J. W. Gibbons
1986.   Biomass of freshwater turtles: A geographic comparison. *American Midland Naturalist* 115:165–173. *1, 2, 6, 8, 17, 23*

Congdon, J. D., G. L. Breitenbach, R. C. van Loben Sels, and D. W. Tinkle
1987.   Reproduction and nesting ecology of snapping turtles (*Chelydra serpentina*) in southeastern Michigan. *Herpetologica* 43:39–54. *3, 8, 9, 15, 16*

Conger, A. D., and J. H. Clinton
1973.   Nuclear volumes, DNA contents, and radiosensitivity in whole-body irradiated amphibians. *Radiation Research* 54:69–101. *21*

Cooper, W. E., Jr.
1984.   Female secondary sexual coloration and sex recognition in the keeled earless lizard, *Holbrookia propinqua. Animal Behaviour* 32:1142–1150. *19*

Cooper, W. E., and N. Burns
1987.   Social significance of ventrolateral coloration in the fence lizard, *Sceloporus undulatus. Animal Behaviour* 35:526–532. *19*

Cooper, W. S., and R. H. Kaplan
1982.   Adaptive "coin-flipping': A decision-theoretic examination of natural selection for random individual variation. *Journal of Theoretical Biology* 94:135–151. *8*

Cope, E. D.
1875.   *Check-list of North American Batrachia and Reptilia; with a systematic list of the higher groups, and an essay on geographical distribution.* Bulletin of the United States National Museum, vol. 1. *1, 4*

Cosgrove, G. E.
1965.   The radiosensitivity of snakes and box turtles. *Radiation Research* 25:706–712. *21*

1971. Reptilian radiobiology. *Journal of the American Veterinary Medical Association* 159(11):1678–1684. *21*

Cothran, E. G., R. K. Chesser, M. H. Smith, and P. E. Johns
1983. Influences of genetic variability and maternal factors on fetal growth in white-tailed deer. *Evolution* 37:282–292. *6*
1987. Fat levels in female white-tailed deer during the breeding season and pregnancy. *Journal of Mammalogy* 68:111–118. *6*

Coughtrey, P. J., and M. C. Thorne
1983. *Radionuclide distribution and transport in terrestrial and aquatic ecosystems: A critical review of data.* Vol. 1, 93–239. A. A. Balkema, Rotterdam. *21*

Courty, Y., and J. P. Dufaure
1980. Levels of testosterone, dihydrotestosterone, and androstenedione in the plasma and testis of a lizard (*Lacerta vivipara* Jacquin) during the annual cycle. *General and Comparative Endocrinology* 42:325–333. *19*

Cranmore, G., and F. L. Harrison
1975. Loss of Cs-137 and Co-60 from the oyster *Crassostrea gigas*. *Health Physics* 28:319–333. *12*

Crawford, K. M., J. R. Spotila, and E. A. Standora
1983. Operative environmental temperatures and basking behavior of the turtle *Pseudemys scripta*. *Ecology* 64:989–999. *22*

Creger, C. R., L. B. Colvin, and J. R. Couch
1967. Absorption, deposition, and excretion of ^{89}Sr by the chick in relation to route of administration. *Proceedings of the Society for Experimental Biology and Medicine* 124:445–448. *21*

Crenshaw, J. W.
1965. Serum protein variation in an interspecies hybrid swarm of turtles of the genus *Pseudemys*. *Evolution* 19:1–15. *4, 6*

Crews, D.
1979. Endocrine control of reptilian reproductive behavior. In *Endocrine control of sexual behavior,* edited by C. Beyer, 167–222. Raven Press, New York. *19*
1984. Gamete production, sex hormone secretion, and mating behavior uncoupled. *Hormones and Behavior* 18:22–28. *19*

Crews, D., B. Camazine, M. Diamond, R. Mason, R. R. Tokarz, and W. R. Garstka
1984. Hormonal independence of courtship behavior in the male garter snake. *Hormones and Behavior* 18:29–41. *19*

Crofton, H. D.
1971. A quantitative approach to parasitism. *Parasitology* 62:179–193. *23*

Crossley, D. A., Jr.
1963. Use of radioactive tracers in the study of insect-plant relationships. In *Radiation and radioisotopes applied to insects of agricultural importance,* 43–54. International Atomic Energy Agency Publication no. STI/PUB/74, Vienna. *21*

Crouse, D. T., L. B. Crowder, and H. Caswell
1987. A stage-based population model for loggerhead sea turtles and implications for conservation. *Ecology* 68:1412–1423. *15*

Crow, J. F., and M. Kimura
1970. *An introduction to population genetics theory.* Harper and Row, New York. *6*

Cunningham, B., and E. Huene
1938. Further studies on water absorption by reptile eggs. *American Naturalist* 72:380–385. *8*

Cunningham, B., and A. P. Hurwitz
1936. Water absorption of reptilian eggs during incubation. *American Naturalist* 70:590–595.

Cutler, R. G.
1978. Evolutionary biology of senescence. In *The biology of aging,* edited by J. A. Behnke, C. E. Finley, and G. B. Moment, 311–360. Plenum Press, New York. *3*

D

Dana, S. W., and D. W. Tinkle
1965. Effects of x-irradiation on the testes of the lizard *Uta stansburiana stejnegeri*. *International Journal of Radiation Biology and Related Studies in Physics, Chemistry, and Medicine* 9:67–80. *21*

Danforth, S. T.
1925. Porto Rican herpetological notes. *Copeia* 1925:76–79. *19*

Dapson, R. W., and L. Kaplan
1975. Biological half-life and distribution of radiocesium in a contaminated population of green treefrogs *Hyla cinerea*. *Oikos* 26:39–42. *21*

Darwin, C. R.
1859. *On the origin of species by means of natural selection; or, The preservation of favoured races in the struggle for life.* Murray, London. *8*
1871. *The descent of man, and selection in relation to sex.* 2 vols. Appleton, New York.

Davidson, J. M.
1971. Geographic variation in the pond slider, *Pseudemys scripta,* in Alabama. Master's thesis. Auburn University. *5*

Davis, J. D., and C. G. Jackson, Jr.
1970. Copulatory behavior in the red-eared turtle, *Pseudemys scripta elegans* (Wied). *Herpetologica* 26:238–239. *9*
1973. Notes on the courtship of a captive male *Chrysemys scripta taylori*. *Herpetologica* 29:62–64. *4, 7*

Davis, J. J., and R. F. Foster
1958. Bioaccumulation of radioisotopes through aquatic food chains. *Ecology* 39:530–535. *21*

Decuypere, E., E. R. Kuhn, B. Clijmans, E. J. Nouven, and H. Michels
1982. Prenatal peripheral monodeiodination in the chick embryo. *General and Comparative Endocrinology* 47:15–17. *19*

Deevey, E. S.
1947. Life tables for natural populations of animals. *Quarterly Review of Biology* 22:283–314. *15*

Deitz, D. C., and D. R. Jackson
1979. Use of American alligator nests by nesting turtles. *Journal of Herpetology* 13:510–512. *8*

Della Rosa, R. J., M. Goldman, A. C. Anderson, C. W. Mays, and B. J. Stover
1965. Absorption and retention of ingested strontium and calcium in beagles as a function of age. *Nature* 205:197–198. *21*

Deraniyagala, P. E. P.
1939.   *Testudinates and crocodilians.* Vol. 1 of *The tetrapod reptiles of Ceylon.* Columbo Museum, Columbo, Ceylon.

Derickson, W. K.
1976.   Lipid storage and utilization in reptiles. *American Zoologist* 16:711–723. *19*

DeRosa, C. T., and D. H. Taylor
1982.   A comparison of compass orientation mechanisms in three turtles (*Trionyx spinifer, Chrysemys picta,* and *Terrapene carolina. Copeia* 1982:394–399. *1*

Derr, J. N., J. W. Bickham, I. F. Greenbaum, A. G. J. Rhodin, and R. A. Mittermeier
1987.   Biochemical systematic and evolution in the South American turtle genus *Platemys* (Pleurodira: Chelidae). *Copeia* 1987:370–375. *6*

DeSola, C. R., and A. M. Greenhall
1932.   Two species of terrapin in Cuba: The Antillean terrapin, *Pseudemys rugosa,* and the Cuban terrapin, *Pseudemys decussata. Copeia* 1932:129–133. *19*

Dessauer, H. C.
1955.   Seasonal changes in the gross organ composition of the lizard *Anolis carolinensis. Journal of Experimental Zoology* 128:1–12. *19*

Dessauer, H. C., W. Fox, and J. R. Ramirez
1957.   Preliminary attempt to correlate paper-electrophoretic migration of hemoglobins with phylogeny in Amphibia and Reptilia. *Archives of Biochemistry and Biophysics* 71:11–16. *5*

Dice, L. R., and P. J. Clark
1953.   *The statistical concept of home range as applied to the recapture radius of the deer mouse* (Peromyscus). Contributions from the Laboratory of Vertebrate Biology, University of Michigan, no. 62. *18*

Diemer, J. E.
1986.   The ecology and management of the gopher tortoise in the southeastern United States. *Herpetologica* 42:125–133. *15*

Dixon, J. R.
1987.   *Amphibians and reptiles of Texas.* Texas A&M University Press, College Station. *5*

Dixon, W. J.
1983.   *DMDP: Statistical software.* University of California Press, Berkeley. *7*

Dmi'el, R.
1967.   Studies on reproduction, growth, and feeding in the snake *Spalerosophis clifford* (Colubridae). *Copeia* 1967:332–346. *8, 10*

Dobie, J. L.
1971.   Reproduction and growth in the alligator snapping turtle, *Macroclemys temmincki* (Troost). *Copeia* 1971:645–658. *9, 10, 14, 15*

1981.   The taxonomic relationships between *Malaclemys* Gray, 1844, and *Graptemys* Agassiz, 1857 (Testudines: Emydidae). *Tulane Studies in Zoology and Botany* 23:85–102. *5*

Dobson, F. S., and W. T. Jones
1985.   Multiple causes of dispersal. *American Naturalist* 126:855–858. *17*

Dobzhansky, T.
1950.   Evolution in the tropics. *American Scientist* 38:209–221. *3*

Dogiel, V. A.
1962.   *General parasitology.* Oliver and Boyd, Edinburgh. *23*

Domby, A. H., and R. W. McFarlane
1978.   Feeding ecology of little blue herons at a radionuclide-contaminated reservoir. *Wading Birds* 7:361–364. *2*

Douglas, M. E.
1979.   Migration and sexual selection in *Ambystoma jeffersonianum. Canadian Journal of Zoology* 57:2303–2310. *2*

Dozy, A. N., C. A. Reynolds, J. M. Still, and J. H. J. Huismann
1964.   Studies on animal hemoglobins, I: Hemoglobins in turtles. *Journal of Experimental Zoology* 155:343–348. *5*

Drane, C. R.
1981.   The thermal conductivity of the skin of crocodilians. *Comparative Biochemistry and Physiology* 68A:107–110. *22*

Drane, C. R., and G. J. W. Webb
1980.   Functional morphology of the dermal vascular system of the Australian lizard *Tiliqua scincoides. Herpetologica* 36:60–66. *22*

Drummond, H.
1983.   Adaptiveness of island nest-sites of green iguanas and slider turtles. *Copeia* 1983:529–530. *12, 15*

Dryden, L. S.
1985.   Phylogenetic analysis of emydine turtles [abstract]. 65th Annual Meeting of the American Society of Ichthyologists and Herpetologists, University of Tennessee at Knoxville. *5*

Dubinina, M. N.
1949.   Ecological studies on the parasite fauna of *Testudo horsfieldi* Grau in Tadzhikistan. *Parazitologicheskii Sbornik* 11:61–97. *23*

Duellman, W. E.
1961.   *The amphibians and reptiles of Michoacan, Mexico.* University of Kansas Publications of the Museum of Natural History, vol. 15, no. 1. *7*

Duellman, W. E., ed.
1979.   *The South American herpetofauna: Its origin, evolution, and dispersal.* University of Kansas Museum of Natural History Monograph no. 7. *12*

Dumeril, A. M. C., and G. Bibron
1835.   *Erpétologie générale ou histoire naturelle compléte des reptiles.* Vol. 3. Librairie Encyclopédique de Roret, Paris. *7*

Dunham, A. E.
1978.   Food availability as a proximate factor influencing individual growth rates in the iguanid lizard *Sceloporus merriami. Ecology* 59:770–778. *10*

1980.   An experimental study of interspecific competition between the iguanid lizards *Sceloporus merriami* and *Urosaurus ornatus. Ecological Monographs* 50:309–330. *1*

1981.   *Populations in a fluctuating environment: The comparative population ecology of the iguanid lizards* Sceloporus merriami *and* Urosaurus ornatus. Miscellaneous Publications of the Museum of Zoology, University of Michigan, no. 158. *10*

1982.   Demographic and life history variation among populations of the iguanid lizard *Urosaurus ornatus:* Implications for the study of life history phenomena in lizards. *Herpetologica* 38:208–221. *3*

Dunham, A. E., and D. B. Miles
1985. Patterns of covariation in life history traits of squamate reptiles: The effects of size and phylogeny reconsidered. *American Naturalist* 126:231–257. *3, 8*

Dunham, A. E., D. W. Tinkle, and J. W. Gibbons
1978. Body size in island lizards: A cautionary tale. *Ecology* 59:1230–1238.

Dunham, A. E., D. M. Miles, and D. N. Reznick
1988a. Life history patterns in squamate reptiles. In Vol. 16 of *Biology of the Reptilia*, edited by C. Gans and R. Huey, 441–522. A. R. Liss, New York. *3, 8, 10*

Dunham, A. E., P. J. Morin, and H. M. Wilbur
1988b. Methods for the study of reptile populations. In Vol. 16 of *Biology of the Reptilia*, edited by C. Gans and R. Huey, 331–386. A. R. Liss, New York. *10*

Dunson, W. A.
1964. Sodium balance in the softshell turtle, *Trionyx s. spinifer*. *American Zoologist* 4:390. *21*

1966. A new site of sodium uptake in freshwater turtles. *American Zoologist* 6:320. *21*

1967. Sodium fluxes in freshwater turtles. *Journal of Experimental Zoology* 165:171–182. *21*

1969. Concentration of sodium by freshwater turtles. In *Symposium on radioecology*, U.S. Atomic Energy Commission Symposium Series (CONF-670503), edited by D. J. Nelson and F. C. Evans, 191–197. National Technical Information Service, Springfield, Va. *21*

Dunson, W. A., and E. O. Moll
1980. Osmoregulation in sea water of hatchling emydid turtles, *Callagur borneoensis*, from a Malaysian sea beach. *Journal of Herpetology* 14:31–36. *12*

Dunson, W. A., and R. D. Weymouth
1965. Active uptake of sodium by softshell turtles. *Science* 149:67–69. *21*

E

Earhart, C. M., and N. K. Johnson
1970. Size dimorphism and food habits of North American owls. *Condor* 72:251–264.

Eberhardt, L. L.
1969. Similarity, allometry, and food chains. *Journal of Theoretical Biology* 24:43–55. *21*

Eckert, K. L.
1987. Environmental unpredictability and leatherback sea turtle (*Dermochelys coriacea*) nest loss. *Herpetologica* 43:315–323. *15*

Edney, E. B., and R. W. Gill
1968. Evolution of senescence and specific longevity. *Nature* 220:281–282. *3*

Ehrenfeld, D. W.
1979. Behavior associated with nesting. In *Turtles: Perspectives and research*, edited by M. Harless and H. Morlock, 417–434. John Wiley and Sons, New York. *15*

Ehrhart, L. M.
1982. A review of sea turtle reproduction. In *Biology and conservation of sea turtles*, edited by K. A. Bjorndal, 29–38. Smithsonian Institution Press, Washington, D.C. *1, 9*

Eik-Nes, K. B.
1969. Patterns of steroidogenesis in the vertebrate gonads. *General and Comparative Endocrinology* 2:87–100. *19*

Einem, G. E.
1956. Certain aspects of the natural history of the mudturtle *Kinosternon bauri*. *Copeia* 1956:186–188. *8*

Eisenbud, M.
1973. *Environmental radioactivity*. Academic Press, New York. *21*

Eldredge, N.
1985. *Time frames*. Simon and Schuster, New York. *12*

Eldredge, N., and S. J. Gould
1972. Punctuated equilibria: An alternative to phyletic gradualism. In *Models in paleobiology*, edited by T. J. M. Schoepf, 82–115. Freeman, Cooper and Co., San Francisco. *12*

Ellinger, F.
1940. Goldfish as a new biologic test object in experimental radiation therapy. *Radiology* 35:563–574.

Emerson, D. N.
1967. Preliminary study on seasonal liver lipids and glycogen and blood sugar levels in the turtle *Graptemys pseudogeographica* (Gray) from South Dakota. *Herpetologica* 23:68–70. *19*

Emlen, J. M.
1970. Age specificity and ecological theory. *Ecology* 51:588–601. *3*

Emlen, S. T.
1969. Homing ability and orientation in the painted turtle, *Chrysemys picta marginata*. *Behaviour* 33:58–76. *2*

Endler, J. A.
1986. *Natural selection in the wild*. Princeton University Press, Princeton, N.J.

Enlow, D. H.
1969. The bone of reptiles. In Vol. 1 of *Biology of the Reptilia*, edited by C. Gans, 45–80. Academic Press, New York. *10*

Erben, H. K.
1970. Ultrastrukturen and Mineralisation rezenter and fossiler Eischalen bei Vögeln und Reptilien. *Biomineralisation Forschungsberichte* 1:1–66. *8*

Erben, H. K., and H. Newesely
1972. Kristalline Bausteine and Mineralbestand von kalkigen Eischalen. *Biomineralisation Forschungsberichte* 6:32–48. *8*

Ernst, C. H.
1968a. Homing ability in the spotted turtle, *Clemmys guttata* (Schneider). *Herpetologica* 24:77–78. *16*

1968b. A turtle's territory. *International Turtle and Tortoise Society Journal* 2:9,34. *16, 18*

1970. Home range of the spotted turtle, *Clemmys guttata* (Schneider). *Copeia* 1970:391–393. *18*

1971a. Growth of the painted turtle, *Chrysemys picta*, in southeastern Pennsylvania. *Herpetologica* 27:135–141. *8, 10*

1971b. Observations on the egg and hatchling of the American turtle, *Chrysemys picta*. *British Journal of Herpetology* 4:224–227. *3*

1971c. Population dynamics and activity cycles of *Chrysemys picta* in southeastern Pennsylvania. *Journal of Herpetology* 5:151–160. *1, 8, 14, 15, 18*

1971d. Sexual cycles and maturity of the turtle *Chrysemys picta*. *Biological Bulletin* (Woods Hole) 140:191–200. *1, 8, 9*

1972. Temperature-activity relationship in the painted turtle, *Chrysemys picta*. *Copeia* 1972:217–222. *18, 20*

1975. Growth of the spotted turtle, *Clemmys guttata*. *Journal of Herpetology* 9:313–319. *10*

1976. Ecology of the spotted turtle, *Clemmys guttata* (Reptilia, Testudines, Testudinidae), in southeastern Pennsylvania. *Journal of Herpetology* 10:25–33. *14, 15, 18*

1977. Biological notes on the bog turtle, *Clemmys muhlenbergii*. *Herpetologica* 33:241–246. *10*

1978. A revision of the neotropical turtle genus *Callopsis* (Testudines: Emydidae: Batagurinae). *Herpetologica* 34:113–134. *19*

1982. Why are more tropical emydid turtles black? *Biotropica* 14:68. *19*

1983. Geographic variation in the neotropical turtle, *Platemys platycephala*. *Journal of Herpetology* 17:345–355. *19*

1986. Ecology of the turtle, (*Sternotherus odoratus*), in southeastern Pennsylvania. *Journal of Herpetology* 20:341–352. *15*

Ernst, C. H., and R. W. Barbour

1972. *Turtles of the United States*. University of Kentucky Press, Lexington. *1, 2, 4, 7, 9, 12, 16, 18, 19*

1989. *Turtles of the world*. Smithsonian Institution Press. In press.

Ernst, C. H., and E. M. Ernst

1973. Biology of *Chrysemys picta bellii* in southwestern Minnesota. *Journal of the Minnesota Academy of Science* 38:77–80. *19*

1980. Relationships between North American turtles of the *Chrysemys* complex as indicated by their endoparasitic helminths. *Proceedings of the Biological Society of Washington* 93:339–345. *1, 4, 5, 23*

Ernst, C. H., and B. G. Jett

1969. An intergrade population of *Pseudemys scripta elegans* × *Pseudemys scripta troosti* in Kentucky. *Journal of Herpetology* 3:103. *4*

Ernst, C. H., and J. E. Lovich

1986. Morphometry in the chelid turtle, *Platemys platycephala*. *Herpetological Journal* 1:66–70. *10*

Ernst, C. H., R. W. Barbour, and M. F. Hershey

1974. A new coding system for hardshelled turtles. *Transactions of the Kentucky Academy of Science* 35:27–28. *2*

Ernst, E. M., and C. H. Ernst

1977. Synopsis of helminths endoparasitic in native turtles of the United States. *Bulletin of the Maryland Herpetological Society* 13:1–75. *23*

Erskine, D. J., and J. R. Spotila

1977. Heat-energy-budget analysis and heat transfer in the largemouth blackbass (*Micropterus salmoides*). *Physiological Zoology* 50:157–169. *22*

Esch, G. W., and J. W. Gibbons

1967. Seasonal incidence of parasitism in the painted turtle, *Chrysemys picta marginata* Agassiz. *Journal of Parasitology* 53:818–821. *23*

Esch, G. W., J. W. Gibbons and J. E. Bourque

1975. An analysis of the relationship between stress and parasitism. *American Midland Naturalist* 93:339–353. *23*

1979a. The distribution and abundance of enteric helminths in *Chrysemys s. scripta* from various habitats on the Savannah River Plant in South Carolina. *Journal of Parasitology* 65:624–632. *23*

1979b. Species diversity of helminth parasites in *Chrysemys s. scripta* from a variety of habitats in South Carolina. *Journal of Parasitology* 65:633–638. *23*

Eure, H. E.

1976. Seasonal abundance of *Neoechinorhynchus cylindratus* taken from largemouth bass (*Micropterus salmoides*) in a heated reservoir. *Parasitology* 73:355–370. *23*

Eure, H. E., and G. W. Esch

1974. Effects of thermal effluent on the population dynamics of helminth parasites in largemouth bass. In *Thermal ecology*, U.S. Atomic Energy Commission Symposium Series (CONF-730505), edited by J. W. Gibbons and R. R. Sharitz, 207–215. National Technical Information Service, Springfield, Va. *23*

Evans, L. T.

1946. Endocrine effects upon the claws of immature turtles, *Pseudemys elegans*. *Anatomical Record* 94:64. *19*

1951. Effects of male hormone upon the tail of the slider turtle, *Pseudemys scripta troostii*. *Science* 114:277–279. *19*

1952. Endocrine relationships in turtles, II: Claw growth in the slider, *Pseudemys scripta troostii*. *Anatomical Record* 112:251–263. *19*

Ewert, M. A.

1979. The embryo and its egg: Development and natural history. In *Turtles: Perspectives and research*, edited by M. Harless and H. Morlock, 333–413. John Wiley and Sons, New York. *8, 15*

1985. Embryology of turtles. In Vol. 14 of *Biology of the Reptilia*, edited by C. Gans, F. Billett, and P. F. A. Maderson, 75–268. John Wiley and Sons, New York. *8, 13*

Ewert, M. A., and J. M. Legler

1978. Hormonal induction of oviposition in turtles. *Herpetologica* 34:314–318. *2, 13*

Ewing, H. E.

1943. Continued fertility in female box turtle following mating. *Copeia* 1943:112–114. *9*

F

Fabens, A. J.

1965. Properties and fitting of the Von Bertalanffy growth curve. *Growth* 29:265–289. *10*

Fagerström, T.

1977. Body weight, metabolic rate, and trace substance turnover in animals. *Oecologia* (Berlin) 29:99–104. *21*

Fahey, K. M.

1980. A taxonomic study of the cooter turtles, *Pseudemys floridana* (Le Conte) and *Pseudemys concinna* (Le Conte), in the lower Red River, Atchafalaya River, and Mississippi River basins. *Tulane Studies in Zoology and Botany* 22:49–66. *4*

Fairbanks, L. B., and G. E. Burch

1968. Whole body turnover of sodium in adult *Drosophila* (Drosophiladae) and *Megaselia* (Phoridae). *Physiological Zoology* 41:401–411. *21*

Feaver, P. E.

1977. The demography of a Michigan population of *Natrix sipedon* with discussions of ophidian growth and reproduction. Ph.D. dissertation. University of Michigan. *10*

Feder, J. L., M. H. Smith, R. K. Chesser, M. J. Godt, and K. Asbury
1984.   Biochemical genetics of mosquitofish, II: Demographic differentiation of populations in a thermally altered reservoir. *Copeia* 1984:108–119. *6*

Ferguson, G. W., and T. Brockman
1980.   Geographic differences of growth rate of *Sceloporus* lizards (Sauria: Iguanidae). *Copeia* 1980:259–264. *10*

Ferguson, M. W. J.
1982.   The structure and composition of the eggshell and embryonic membranes of *Alligator mississippiensis*. *Transactions of the Zoological Society of London* 36:99–152. *8*
1985.   Reproductive biology and embryology of the cordilians. In Vol. 14 of *Biology of the Reptilia*, edited by C. Gans, F. Billett, and P. F. A. Maderson, 329–491. John Wiley and Sons, New York. *8*

Ferner, J. W.
1979.   *A review of marking techniques for amphibians and reptiles.* Society for the Study of Amphibians and Reptiles, Herpetological Circular no. 9. Miami University, Oxford, Ohio. *21*

Fisher, R. A.
1930.   *The genetical theory of natural selection.* Dover, New York. *3, 8, 14, 15, 24*

Fisk, A., and M. Tribe
1949.   The development of the amnion and chorion of reptiles. *Proceedings of the Zoological Society of London* 119:83–114. *8*

Fitch, H. S.
1960.   Autecology of the copperhead. University of Kansas Publications of the Museum of Natural History, vol. 13, 85–288. *10*
1965.   An ecological study of the garter snake, *Thamnophis sirtalis*. University of Kansas Publications of the Museum of Natural History, vol. 15, 493–564. *10*
1981.   *Sexual size differences in reptiles.* University of Kansas Museum of Natural History Miscellaneous Publication no. 70.
1982.   *Reproductive cycles in tropical reptiles.* Occasional Papers of the Museum of Natural History, University of Kansas, no. 96.
1985.   Variation in clutch and litter size in New World reptiles. University of Kansas Museum of Natural History Miscellaneous Publication no. 76. *13*

Fitch, H. S., and B. Glading
1947.   A field study of a rattlesnake population. *California Fish and Game* 33(2):103–123. *10*

Fitch, H. S., and P. L. von Achen
1977.   Spatial relationships and seasonality in the skinks *Eumeces fasciatus* and *Scincella laterale* in northeastern Kansas. *Herpetologica* 33:303–313. *21*

Florence, T. H., Jr.
1975.   A telemetric study of the activity of the red-eared turtle, *Chrysemys scripta elegans*. Master's thesis. Middle Tennessee State University. *18*

Foley, R. E.
1976.   Energy budgets and a climate space diagram for the turtle *Chrysemys scripta*. Master's thesis. State University of New York College at Buffalo. *22*

Foley, R. E., and J. R. Spotila
1978.   Effect of wind speed, air temperature, body size, and vapor density difference on evaporative water loss from the turtle *Chrysemys scripta*. *Copeia* 1978:627–634. *10, 22*

Fowler, L. E.
1979.   Hatching success and nest predation in the green sea turtle, *Chelonia mydas*, at Tortuguero, Costa Rica. *Ecology* 60:946–955. *15*

Fowler de Neira, L. E., and J. H. Roe
1984.   Emergence success of tortoise nests and the effect of feral burros on nest success on Volcan Alcedo, Galapagos. *Copeia* 1984:702–707. *15*

Fox, A. M.
1961.   Transport of monosaccharides by intestinal segments of the painted turtle, *Chrysemys picta*. *Comparative Biochemistry and Physiology* 3:285–296. *20*

Fox, A. M., and X. J. Musacchia
1959.   Notes on the pH of the digestive tract of *Chrysemys picta*. *Copeia* 1959:337–339. *20*

Frair, W.
1982.   Serological studies of *Emys*, *Emydoidea*, and some other testudinid turtles. *Copeia* 1982:976–978. *5*

Frazer, N. B.
1983a. Demography and life history evolution of the Atlantic loggerhead sea turtle, *Caretta caretta*. Ph.D. dissertation. University of Georgia. *15*
1983b. Survivorship of adult female loggerhead sea turtles, *Caretta caretta*, nesting on Little Cumberland Island, Georgia, USA. *Herpetologica* 39:436–447. *15*
1986.   Survival from egg to adulthood in a declining population of loggerhead turtles, *Caretta caretta*. *Herpetologica* 42:47–55. *24*
1987.   Preliminary estimates of survivorship for wild juvenile loggerhead sea turtles (*Caretta caretta*). *Journal of Herpetology* 21:232–235. *15*

Frazer, N. B., and J. I. Richardson
1986.   The relationship of clutch size and frequency to body size in loggerhead turtles, *Caretta caretta*. *Journal of Herpetology* 20:81–84. *9*

Frazier, J.
1971.   Observations on sea turtles at Aldabra Atoll. *Philosophical Transaction of the Royal Society of London on Biological Sciences* 260:373–410. *14*

Freeman, H. W.
1955a. The amphibians and reptiles of the Savannah River Project area: Caudate Amphibia. In *An ecological study of the land plants and cold-blooded vertebrates of the Savannah River Project area*. University of South Carolina Publications, 3d ser. (Biology), vol. 1, no. 4, 227–238. *2*
1955b. The amphibians and reptiles of the Savannah River Project area: Chelonia. In *An ecological study of the land plants and cold-blooded vertebrates of the Savannah River Project area*. University of South Carolina Publications, 3d ser. (Biology), vol. 1, no. 4, 239–244. *2*
1955c. The amphibians and reptiles of the Savannah River Project area: Crocodilia, Sauria, and Serpentes. In *An ecological study of the land plants and cold-blooded vertebrates of the Savannah River Project area*. University of South

Carolina Publications, 3d ser. (Biology), vol. 1, no. 4, 275–291. *2*

1956. The amphibians and reptiles of the Savannah River Project area: Caudate Amphibia. In *An ecological study of the land plants and cold-blooded vertebrates of the Savannah River Project area*. University of South Carolina Publications, 3d ser. (Biology), vol. 2, no. 1, 26–35. *2*

1960. A unique environmental situation in Steed's Pond, Savannah River Plant area, South Carolina. University of South Carolina Publications, 3d ser. (Biology), vol. 3, no. 1, 99–111. *2*

Freiberg, M. A.
1967a. Diferencias sexuales secundarias y descripcion del alotipo macho de la tortuga *Pseudemys dorbignyi* (D. et B.). *Acta Zoológica Lilloana* 23:389–394. *19*

1967b. *Tortugas de la Argentina*. La Seccion Herpetologia del Museo Argentino de Ciencias Naturales "Bernardino Rivadavia," Buenos Aires. *7*

1969. Una nueva subespecie de *Pseudemys dorbignyi* (Duméril et Bibron) (Reptilia, Chelonia, Emydidae). *Physis* 28:299–314. *19*

Froese, A. D., and G. M. Burghardt
1975. A dense natural population of the common snapping turtle (*Chelydra s. serpentina*). *Herpetologica* 31:204–208. *14*

Frye, F. L.
1973. *Husbandry, medicine, and surgery in captive reptiles*. VM Publishing, Bonner Springs, Kans. *20*

Fukada, H.
1959. Biological studies on the snakes, VI: Growth and maturity of *Natrix tigrina tigrina* (Boie). *Bulletin of the Kyoto Gakugei University*, ser. B (Mathematics and Natural Science), vol. 15, 25–41. *10*

1960. Biological studies on the snakes, VII: Growth and maturity of *Elaphe quadrivirgata* (Boie). *Bulletin of the Kyoto Gakugei University*, ser. B (Mathematics and Natural Science), vol. 16, 6–21. *10*

G

Gadgil, M., and W. H. Bossert
1970. Life historical consequences of natural selection. *American Naturalist* 104:1–24. *3, 15*

Gailbraith, D. A., and R. J. Brooks
1987a. Addition of annual growth lines in adult snapping turtles *Chelydra serpentina*. *Journal of Herpetology* 21:359–363. *10*

1987b. Survivorship of adult females in a northern population of common snapping turtles, *Chelydra serpentina*. *Canadian Journal of Zoology* 65:1581–1586. *3, 15*

Galbreath, E. C.
1948. A new extinct emydid turtle from the Lower Pliocene of Oklahoma. University of Kansas Publications of the Museum of Natural History, vol. 1, 265–280. *5*

Gallagher, K. J., D. A. Morrison, R. Shine, and G. C. Grigg
1983. Validation and use of ²²Na turnover to measure food intake in free-ranging lizards. *Oecologia* (Berlin) 60:76–82. *21*

Gallegos, A. F., and F. W. Whicker
1971. Radiocesium retention by rainbow trout as affected by temperature and weight. In *Radionuclides in ecosystems*,

Proceedings of the Third National Symposium on Radioecology, U.S. Atomic Energy Commission Symposium Series (CONF-710501–P1), edited by D. J. Nelson, 361–371. National Technical Information Service, Springfield, Va. *12*

Gallegos, A. F., F. W. Whicker, and T. E. Hakonson
1970. Accumulation of radiocesium in rainbow trout via a non–food chain pathway. In *Proceedings, Fifth Annual Health Physics Society Midyear Topical Symposium*, 477–498. Pergamon Press, New York. *21*

Ganzhorn, D., and P. Licht
1983. Regulation of seasonal gonadal cycles by temperature in the painted turtle, *Chrysemys picta*. *Copeia* 1983:347–358. *13*

Garrett, A. J.
1986. Results of analysis of turtle from Stephen's Lake. Interoffice memorandum, Savannah River Laboratory, Aiken, S.C. *21*

Garstka, W. R., A. Halpert, and D. Crews
1983. Metabolic changes in male snakes, *Thamnophis melanogaster*, during a breeding period. *Comparative Biochemistry and Physiology* 74A:807–811. *19*

Garton, D. W., R. K. Koehn, and T. M. Scott
1984. Multiple-locus heterozygosity and the physiological energetics of growth in the coot clam, *Mulinia lateralis*, from a natural population. *Genetics* 108:445–455. *6*

Gates, D. M.
1962. *Energy exchange in the biosphere*. Harper and Row, New York. *22*

1980. *Biophysical ecology*. Springer-Verlag, New York. *22*

Gatten, R. E., Jr.
1974a. Effect of nutritional status on the preferred body temperature of the turtles *Pseudemys scripta* and *Terrapene ornata*. *Copeia* 1974:912–917. *9, 10, 22*

1974b. Effects of temperature and activity on aerobic and anaerobic metabolism and heart rate in the turtles *Pseudemys scripta* and *Terrapene ornata*. *Comparative Biochemistry and Physiology* 48A:619–648. *22*

1974c. Percentage contribution of increased heart rate to increased oxygen transport during activity in *Pseudemys scripta*, *Terrapene ornata*, and other reptiles. *Comparative Biochemistry and Physiology* 48A:649–652. *22*

1981. Anaerobic metabolism in freely-diving painted turtles (*Chrysemys picta*). *Journal of Experimental Zoology* 216:377–385. *22*

1985. The uses of anaerobiosis by amphibians and reptiles. *American Zoologist* 25:945–954.

1987. Cardiovascular and other physiological correlates of hibernation in aquatic and terrestrial turtles. *American Zoologist* 27:59–68. *22*

Gaymer, R.
1968. The Indian Ocean giant tortoise *Testudo gigantea* of Aldabra. *Journal of Zoology* (London) 154:341–363. *10, 14*

Gazin, C. L.
1957. Exploration for the remains of giant ground sloths in Panama. *Smithsonian Institution Annual Report* 4279:341–354. *5*

Gemmell, D. J.
1970. Some observations on the nesting of the western

painted turtle, *Chrysemys picta belli*, in northern Minnesota. *Canadian Field Naturalist* 84:308–309. *3*

Georges, A.

1982. Diet of the Australian freshwater turtle *Emydura krefftii* (Chelonia: Chelidae), in an unproductive lentic environment. *Copeia* 1982:331–336. *20*

1985. Reproduction and reduced body size of reptiles in unproductive insular environments. In *Biology of Australasian frogs and reptiles*, edited by G. Grigg, R. Shine, and H. Ehmann, 311–318. Surrey Beatty and Sons, Sydney. *9*

Gerking, S. D.

1957. Evidence of aging in natural populations of fishes. *Gerontologia* 1:287–305. *3*

Gettinger, R. D., G. L. Paukstis, and W. H. N. Gutzke

1984. Influence of hydric environment on oxygen consumption by embryonic turtles *Chelydra serpentina* and *Trionyx spiniferus*. *Physiological Zoology* 57:468–473. *8*

Gibbons, J. W.

1967a. Possible underwater thermoregulation by turtles. *Canadian Journal of Zoology* 45:585. *18, 20, 22*

1967b. Variation in growth rates in three populations of the painted turtle, *Chrysemys picta*. *Herpetologica* 23:296–303. *1, 10, 17*

1968a. Carapacial algae in a population of the painted turtle, *Chrysemys picta*. *American Midland Naturalist* 79:517–519. *10*

1968b. Observations on the ecology and population dynamics of the Blanding's turtle, *Emydoidea blandingii*. *Canadian Journal of Zoology* 46:288–290. *9, 14*

1968c. Population structure and survivorship in the painted turtle, *Chrysemys picta*. *Copeia* 1968:260–268. *1, 2, 16*

1968d. Reproductive potential, activity, and cycles in the painted turtle, *Chrysemys picta*. *Ecology* 49:399–409. *1, 3, 9, 16*

1969. Ecology and population dynamics of the chicken turtle, *Deirochelys reticularia*. *Copeia* 1969:669–676. *2, 3, 8, 9, 15*

1970a. Reproductive characteristics of a Florida population of musk turtles (*Sternothaerus odoratus*). *Herpetologica* 26:268–270. *24*

1970b. Reproductive dynamics of a turtle (*Pseudemys scripta*) population in a reservoir receiving heated effluent from a nuclear reactor. *Canadian Journal of Zoology* 48:881–885. *9–13, 20, 22*

1970c. Sex ratios in turtles. *Researches on Population Ecology* (Kyoto) 12:252–254. *14*

1970d. Terrestrial activity and the population dynamics of aquatic turtles. *American Midland Naturalist* 83:404–414. *1, 2, 6, 9, 20, 22*

1972. Reproduction, growth, and sexual dimorphism in the canebrake rattlesnake (*Crotalus horridus atricaudatus*). *Copeia* 1972:222–226. *10*

1976. Aging phenomena in reptiles. In *Experimental aging research*, edited by M. F. Elias, B. E. Elefteriou, and P. K. Elias, 454–575. Experimental Aging Research, Bar Harbor, Maine. *10*

1978. Reptiles. In *An annotated checklist of the biota of the coastal zone of South Carolina*, edited by R. G. Zingmark, 270–276. Belle W. Baruch Institute for Marine Biology and Coastal Research, University of South Carolina. *2*

1982. Reproductive patterns in freshwater turtles. *Herpetologica* 38:222–227. *3, 6, 9, 11–13, 15*

1983a. Reproductive characteristics and ecology of the mud turtle *Kinosternon subrubrum* (Lacepede). *Herpetologica* 39:254–271. *2, 9–11, 14, 24*

1983b. *Their blood runs cold: Adventures with reptiles and amphibians*. University of Alabama Press, Tuscaloosa.

1986. Movement patterns among turtle populations: Applicability to management of the desert tortoise. *Herpetologica* 42:104–113. *3, 14, 16–18, 22, 23*

1987. Why do turtles live so long? *BioScience* 37:262–269. *1–3, 6, 10, 15, 16, 24*

Gibbons, J. W., and D. H. Bennett

1974. Determination of anuran terrestrial activity patterns by a drift fence method. *Copeia* 1974:236–243. *2*

Gibbons, J. W., and J. W. Coker

1977. Ecological and life history aspects of the cooter, *Chrysemys floridana* (Le Conte). *Herpetologica* 33:29–33. *2, 9*

Gibbons, J. W., and J. D. Congdon

1986. Why did the turtle cross the road? *Science 86*, no. 7: 74–75. *16*

Gibbons, J. W., and J. L. Greene

1978. Selected aspects of the ecology of the chicken turtle, *Deirochelys reticularia* (Latreille) (Reptilia, Testudines, Emydidae). *Journal of Herpetology* 12:237–241. *2, 3, 9, 15, 16*

1979. X-ray photography: A technique to determine reproductive patterns of freshwater turtles. *Herpetologica* 35:86–89. *2, 3, 9, 15, 20*

Gibbons, J. W., and J. E. Lovich

1990. Sexual dimorphism in turtles, with emphasis on the slider turtle. *Herpetological Monographs*. In press. *10*

Gibbons, J. W., and D. H. Nelson

1978. The evolutionary significance of delayed emergence from the nest by hatchling turtles. *Evolution* 32:297–303. *1, 8, 15, 16, 24*

Gibbons, J. W., and K. K. Patterson

1978. *The reptiles and amphibians of the Savannah River Plant*. U.S. Department of Energy, Savannah River National Environmental Research Park, Aiken, S.C. *2*

Gibbons, J. W., and R. D. Semlitsch

1981. Terrestrial drift fences with pitfall traps: An effective technique for quantitative sampling of animal populations. *Brimleyana* 1981(7):1–16. *2, 14, 21*

1982. Survivorship and longevity of a long-lived vertebrate species: How long do turtles live? *Journal of Animal Ecology* 51:523–527. *1–3, 6, 15, 24*

1989. *A guide to the reptiles and amphibians of the SRP*. U.S. Department of Energy, Savannah River National Environmental Research Park, Aiken, S.C. In press. *2*

Gibbons, J. W., and R. R. Sharitz

1974. Thermal alteration of aquatic ecosystems. *American Scientist* 62:660–670. *2*

1981. Thermal ecology: Environmental teachings of a nuclear reactor site. *BioScience* 31:293–298. *2, 18*

Gibbons, J. W., and D. W. Tinkle

1969. Reproductive variation between turtle populations in a single geographic area. *Ecology* 50:340–341. *9, 24*

Gibbons, J. W., J. Harrison, D. H. Nelson, and C. L. Abercrombie III
1976. Status report: The reptiles. In *Proceedings of the First South Carolina Endangered Species Symposium*, edited by D. N. Forsythe and W. B. Ezell, Jr., 79–81. South Carolina Wildlife and Marine Resources Department and the Citadel, Charleston, S.C. [2]

Gibbons, J. W., J. W. Coker, and T. M. Murphy, Jr.
1977. Selected aspects of the life history of the rainbow snake (*Farancia erytrogramma*). *Herpetologica* 33:276–281. [2]

Gibbons, J. W., D. H. Bennett, G. W. Esch, and T. C. Hazen
1978a. Effects of thermal effluent on body condition of largemouth bass. *Nature* 274:470–471. [16, 18]

Gibbons, J. W., J. L. Greene, and J. P. Schubauer
1978b. Variability in clutch size in aquatic chelonians. *British Journal of Herpetology* 6:13–14. [9]

Gibbons, J. W., G. H. Keaton, J. P. Schubauer, J. L. Greene, D. H. Bennett, J. R. McAuliffe, and R. R. Sharitz
1979. Unusual population size structure in freshwater turtles on barrier islands. *Georgia Journal of Science* 37:155–159. [2, 9, 11, 14, 19, 20]

Gibbons, J. W., R. D. Semlitsch, J. L. Greene, and J. P. Schubauer
1981. Variation in age and size at maturity of the slider turtle (*Pseudemys scripta*). *American Naturalist* 117:841–845. [1, 3, 6, 9–11, 13–15, 19]

Gibbons, J. W., J. L. Greene, and K. K. Patterson
1982. Variation in reproductive characteristics of aquatic turtles. *Copeia* 1982:776–784. [3, 8, 9, 11–13, 24]

Gibbons, J. W., J. L. Greene, and J. D. Congdon
1983. Drought-related responses of aquatic turtle populations. *Journal of Herpetology* 17:242–246. [1, 2, 6, 16, 18]

Giersberg, H.
1922. Untersuchungen über Physiologie und Histologie des Eileiters der Reptilen und Vögel; nebst einem Beitrag zur Fasergenese. *Zeitschrift fuer Wissenschaftliche Zoologie* 120:1–97. [8]

Gill, D. E.
1978. The metapopulation ecology of the red-spotted newt, *Notophthalmus viridescens* (Rafinesque). *Ecological Monographs* 48:145–166. [2]

Gilmore, C. W.
1933. A new species of extinct turtle from the Upper Pliocene of Idaho. *Proceedings of the United States National Museum* 82:1–7. [5]

Glidewell, J. R.
1984. Life history energetics of the red-eared turtle, *Pseudemys scripta*, in North Central Texas. Ph.D dissertation. North Texas State University. [20]

Gloyd, H. K.
1947. Some rattlesnake dens of South Dakota. *Chicago Natural History Museum Annual Report* 9:87–97. [2]

Goin, C. J., and C. C. Goff
1941. Notes on the growth rate of the gopher turtle, *Gopherus polyphemus*. *Herpetologica* 2:66–68.

Goldberg, S. R.
1972. Seasonal weight and cytological changes in the fat bodies and liver of the iguanid lizard *Sceloporus jarrovi* Cope. *Copeia* 1972:227–232. [19]

Goldby, F., and H. J. Gamble
1957. The reptilian cerebral hemispheres. *Cambridge Philosophical Society, Biological Reviews* 32:383–420. [20]

Goldman, J. M., and M. E. Hadley
1969. *In-vitro* demonstration of adrenergic receptors controlling melanophore response of the lizard *Anolis carolinensis*. *Journal of Pharmacology and Experimental Therapeutics* 166:1–7. [19]

Goldman, M., and R. J. Della Rosa
1967. Studies on the dynamics of strontium metabolism under conditions of continual ingestion to maturity. In *Strontium metabolism*, edited by J. M. A. Lenihan, J. F. Loutit, and J. H. Martin, 180–194. Academic Press, New York. [21]

Golley, F. B., and J. B. Gentry
1964. A comparison of variety and standing crop of vegetation on a one-year and a twelve-year abandoned field. *Oikos* 15:185–199. [2]

Goode, J., and J. Russell
1968. Incubation of eggs of three species of chelid tortoises, and notes on their embryological development. *Australian Journal of Zoology* 16:749–761. [8]

Goodman, D.
1982. Optimal life histories, optimal notation, and the value of reproductive value. *American Naturalist* 119:803–823. [3]

Gordon, D. M., and R. D. MacCulloch
1980. An investigation of the ecology of the map turtle, *Graptemys geographica* (LeSueur), in the northern part of its range. *Canadian Journal of Zoology* 58:2210–2219. [14]

Gorman, G. C., and J. Renzi, Jr.
1979. Genetic distance and heterozygosity estimates in electrophoretic studies: Effects of sample size. *Copeia* 1979:242–249. [6]

Graham, T. E.
1971. Growth rate of the red-bellied turtle, *Chrysemys rubriventris*, at Plymouth, Massachusetts. *Copeia* 1971:353–356. [10, 20]

Graham, T. E., and T. S. Doyle
1979. Dimorphism, courtship, eggs, and hatchlings of the Blanding's turtle, *Emydoidea blandingii* (Reptilia, Testudines, Emydidae) in Massachusetts. *Journal of Herpetology* 13:125–127. [14]

Graham, T. E., and V. H. Hutchison
1979. Effect of temperature and photoperiod acclimatization on thermal preferences of selected freshwater turtles. *Copeia* 1979:165–169. [22]

Grant, C.
1940. *The herpetology of the Cayman Islands*. Bulletin of the Institute of Jamaica, Science Series, vol. 2. [19]

Grant, C., and C. R. DeSola
1934. Antillean tortoises and terrapins: Distribution, status, and habits of *Testudo* and *Pseudemys*. *Copeia* 1934:73–79. [19]

Gray, J.
1928. The role of water in the evolution of the terrestrial vertebrates. *Journal of Experimental Biology* 6:26–31. [8]

Gray, J. E.
1831. *Synopsis Reptilium; or, Short descriptions of the species of rep-*

tiles, part I: Cataphracta, tortoises, crocodiles, and enaliosaurians. Treuttle, Wurtz and Co., London. *4, 7*

1855.   *Catalogue of shield reptiles in the collection of the British Museum, part I: Testudinata (tortoises).* Taylor and Francis, London. *4, 7*

1873.   *Damonia unicolor, a new species of water-tortoise from China, sent by Mr. Swinhoe. Annals and Magazine of Natural History* (London) 12:77–78. *19*

Green, B., and J. D. Dunsmore
1978.   Turnover of tritiated water and [22]Na in captive rabbits (*Oryctolagus cuniculus*). *Journal of Mammalogy* 59:12–17. *21*

Green, B., D. King, and H. Butler
1986.   Water, sodium, and energy turnover in free-living Perenties, *Varanus giganteus. Australian Wildlife Research* 34:589–595. *21*

Gregory, P. T.
1982.   Reptilian hibernation. In Vol. 13 of *Biology of the Reptilia,* edited by C. Gans and F. H. Pough, 53–154. Academic Press, New York. *22*

Griffiths, I.
1962.   Skeletal lamellae as an index of age in heterothermous tetrapods. *Annals and Magazine of Natural History* (London) 13:449–465. *10*

Grigg, G. C., and J. Alchin
1976.   The role of the cardiovascular system in thermoregulation of *Crocodylus johnstoni. Physiological Zoology* 49:24–36. *22*

Groombridge, B., E. O. Moll, and J. Vijaya
1983.   Rediscovery of a rare Indian turtle. *Oryx* 17:130–134. *19*

Gross, M.
1986.   Gametogenesis and the reproductive function of the kidney in the male pond slider turtle, *Pseudemys scripta.* Master's thesis. University of Alabama in Huntsville. *19*

Gross, M., and W. R. Gartska
1984.   Sperm storage and capacitation in the male slider turtle, *Pseudemys scripta. Journal of the Alabama Academy of Science* 55:141. *9*

Grubb, P.
1971.   The growth, ecology, and population structure of giant tortoises on Aldabra. *Philosophical Transaction of the Royal Society of London on Biological Sciences* 260:327–372. *10, 14*

Gude, W. D.
1968.   *Autoradiographic techniques: Localization of radioisotopes in biological material.* Prentice-Hall, Englewood Cliffs, N.J. *21*

Gunning, G. E., and W. M. Lewis
1957.   An electrical shocker for the collection of amphibians and reptiles in the aquatic environment. *Copeia* 1957:52. *2*

Günther, A.
1885.   *Biologia Centrali-Americana: Reptilia and Batrachia.* Dulau and Co., London. *4, 7*

Gupta, B. B. Pd., C. Halda-Misra, M. Ghosh, and J. P. Thapliyal
1987.   Effect of melatonin on gonads, body weight, and lutenizing hormone (LH) dependent coloration of the

Indian finch, Lal Munia (*Estrilda amandava*). *General and Comparative Endocrinology* 65:451–456. *19*

Gutzke, W. H. N., and G. C. Packard
1985.   Hatching success in relation to egg size in painted turtles (*Chrysemys picta*). *Canadian Journal of Zoology* 63:67–70. *8*

1986.   Sensitive periods for the influence of the hydric environment on eggs and hatchlings of painted turtles (*Chrysemys picta*). *Physiological Zoology* 59:337–343. *8*

Gutzke, W. H. N., G. C. Packard, M. J. Packard, and T. J. Boardman
1987.   Influence of the hydric and thermal environments on eggs and hatchlings of painted turtles (*Chrysemys picta*). *Herpetologica* 43:393–404. *8*

H

Hadley, N. F.
1985.   *The adaptive role of lipids in biological systems.* John Wiley and Sons, New York. *8*

Hakonson, T. E., and F. W. Whicker
1969.   Uptake and elimination of [134]Cs by mule deer. In *Symposium on radioecology,* U.S. Atomic Energy Commission Symposium Series (CONF-670503), edited by D. J. Nelson and F. C. Evans, 616–622. National Technical Information Service, Springfield, Va. *12*

Hakonson, T. E., A. F. Gallegos, and F. W. Whicker
1975.   Cesium kinetics data for estimating food consumption rates in trout. *Health Physics* 29:301–306. *12*

Haldane, J. B. S.
1941.   *New paths in genetics.* Allen and Unwin, London. *3*

Halford, D. K., J. B. Millard, and O. D. Markham
1981.   Radionuclide concentrations in waterfowl using a liquid radioactive waste disposal area and the potential radiation dose to man. *Health Physics* 40:173–181. *21*

Hamilton, J. G.
1947.   Metabolism of the fission products and the heaviest elements. *Radiology* 49:325–343. *21*

Hamilton, R. D.
1944.   Notes on mating and migration in Berlandier's tortoise. *Copeia* 1944:62. *16*

Hamilton, W. D.
1966.   The moulding of senescence by natural selection. *Journal of Theoretical Biology* 12:12–45. *3, 15*

Hamilton, W. H., III
1973.   *Life's color code.* McGraw-Hill, New York. *19*

Hammer, D. A.
1969.   Parameters of a marsh snapping turtle population, La Creek Refuge, South Dakota. *Journal of Wildlife Management* 33:995–1005. *10, 14, 16, 18*

Hammond, K. A., J. R. Spotila, and E. A. Standora
1988.   Basking behavior of the turtle *Pseudemys scripta:* Effects of digestive state, acclimation temperature, sex, and season. *Physiological Zoology* 61:69–77. *20, 22*

Hanson, W. C.
1967.   Radioecological concentration processes characterizing arctic ecosystems. In *Radioecological concentration processes,* edited by B. Aberg and F. P. Hungate, 183–192. Pergamon Press, New York. *21*

Harding, J. H., and T. J. Bloomer
1979.   The wood turtle, *Clemmys insculpta:* A natural history.

Bulletin of the New York Herpetological Society (HERP) 15:9–26. *14*

Harless, M., and H. Morlock, eds.
1979. *Turtles: Perspectives and research.* John Wiley and Sons, New York.

Harris, B. A.
1964. *Life of the rainbow lizard.* Hutcheson and Co., London. *10*

Harrison, J. R.
1978. Amphibians. In *An annotated checklist of the biota of the coastal zone of South Carolina,* edited by R. G. Zingmark, 262–269. Belle W. Baruch Institute for Marine Biology and Coastal Research, University of South Carolina. *2*

Hart, D. R.
1979. Resource partitioning among Louisiana turtles of the genus *Chrysemys.* Ph.D. dissertation. Tulane University. *20*
1983. Dietary and habitat shift with size of red-eared turtles (*Pseudemys scripta*) in a southern Louisiana population. *Herpetologica* 39:285–290. *12, 20, 23*

Hartweg, N.
1939. A new American *Pseudemys.* Occasional Papers of the Museum of Zoology, University of Michigan, no. 397. *4, 7, 19*
1944. Spring emergence of painted turtle hatchlings. *Copeia* 1944:20–22. *8*
1946. Confirmation of overwintering in painted turtle hatchlings. *Copeia* 1946:255. *8*

Harvey, M. J., and R. W. Barbour
1965. Home range of *Microtus ochrogaster* as determined by a modified minimum area method. *Journal of Mammalogy* 46:398–402. *18*

Harwood, P. D.
1932. The helminths of parasites in amphibia and reptiles of Houston, Texas, and vicinity. *Proceedings of the United States National Museum* 81:1–71. *23*

Hasanen, E., S. Kolehmainen, and J. K. Miettinen
1967. Biological half-time of Cs-137 in three species of freshwater fish: Perch, roach, and rainbow trout. In *Radioecological concentration processes,* edited by B. Aberg and F. P. Hungate, 921–924. Pergamon Press, New York. *21*

Hattan, L. R., and D. H. Gist
1975. Seminal receptacles in the eastern box turtle, *Terrapene carolina. Copeia* 1975:505–510. *9*

Hay, O. P.
1908. *The fossil turtles of North America.* Carnegie Institution of Washington Publication no. 75. *5*
1916. Descriptions of some Floridian fossil vertebrates, belonging mostly to the Pleistocene. In *Eighth Annual Report, Florida State Geological Survey,* 39–76. State Geological Survey, Tallahassee, Fla. *5*

Hayne, D. W.
1949. Two methods for estimating population from trapping records. *Journal of Mammalogy* 30:399–411. *18*

Hazen, T. C.
1978. The ecology of *Aeromonas hydrophila* in a South Carolina cooling reservoir. Ph.D. dissertation. Wake Forest University. *18*

Heath, M. E., and S. M. McGinnis
1980. Body temperature and heat transfer in the green sea turtle, *Chelonia mydas. Copeia* 1980:767–773. *22*

Heller, H. C., and D. M. Gates
1971. Altitudinal zonation of chipmunks (*Eutamias*): Energy budgets. *Ecology* 52:424–433. *22*

Hews, E. A., and D. E. Kime
1978. Testicular steroid biosynthesis by the green lizard, *Lacerta viridis. General and Comparative Endocrinology* 35:432–435. *19*

Hildebrand, H. H.
1982. A historical review of the status of sea turtle populations in the western Gulf of Mexico. In *Biology and conservation of sea turtles,* edited by K. A. Bjorndal, 447–453. Smithsonian Institution Press, Washington, D.C. *15*

Hildebrand, S. F.
1929. Review of experiments on artificial culture of diamondback terrapin. *Bulletin of the United States Bureau of Fisheries* 45:25–70. *3, 9*

Hillestad, H. O., and S. H. Bennett, Jr.
1982. *Set-aside areas, National Environmental Research Park.* U.S. Department of Energy, Savannah River National Environmental Research Park, Aiken, S.C. *2*

Hillestad, H. O., J. I. Richardson, C. McVea, Jr., and J. M. Watson, Jr.
1982. Worldwide incidental capture of sea turtles. In *Biology and conservation of sea turtles,* edited by K. A. Bjorndal, 489–495. Smithsonian Institution Press, Washington, D.C. *15*

Hinton, T. G., and F. W. Whicker
1985. The kinetics of radium and strontium in pond sliders *Pseudemys scripta* as a function of two temperature extremes. National Environmental Research Park, Savannah River Ecology Laboratory, Aiken, S.C. *21*

Hirsch, K. F.
1983. Contemporary and fossil chelonian eggshells. *Copeia* 1983:382–397. *8*

Hirshfield, M. F., and D. W. Tinkle
1975. Natural selection and the evolution of reproductive effort. *Proceedings of the National Academy of Sciences* 72: 2227–2231. *3, 8, 15*

Hirth, H. F.
1980. Some aspects of the nesting behavior and reproductive biology of sea turtles. *American Zoologist* 20:507–523. *15*

Hirth, H. F., and A. Carr
1970. The green turtle in the Gulf of Aden and the Seychelles Islands. Verhandelingen der Koninklijke Nederlandse Akademie van Wetenschappen, AFD. *Natuurkunde,* vol. 58. *14, 19*

Hirth, H. F., R. C. Pendleton, A. C. King, and T. R. Downard
1969. Dispersal of snakes from a hibernaculum in northwestern Utah. *Ecology* 50:332–339. *21*

Hogue, D. E., W. G. Pond, C. L. Comar, L. T. Alexander, and E. P. Hardy
1961. Comparative utilization of dietary calcium and strontium-90 by pigs and sheep. *Journal of Animal Science* 20:514–517. *21*

Holbrook, J. E.
1836. Vol. 1 of *North American herpetology.* J. Dobson and Son, Philadelphia. *4, 7, 19*

Holcomb, C. M., C. G. Jackson, Jr., M. M. Jackson, and S. Kleinbergs
1971. Occurrence of radionuclides in the exoskeleton of turtles. In *Radionuclides in ecosystems,* Proceedings of the Third National Symposium on Radioecology, U.S. Atomic Energy Commission Symposium Series (CONF-710501–P1), edited by D. J. Nelson, 385–389. National Technical Information Service, Springfield, Va. *21*

Holgate, P.
1967. Population survival and life history phenomena. *Journal of Theoretical Biology* 14:1–10. *3*

Holleman, D. F., J. R. Luick, and F. W. Whicker
1971. Transfer of radiocesium from lichen to reindeer. *Health Physics* 21:657–666. *21*

Holman, J. A.
1977. Comments on turtles of the genus *Chrysemys* Gray. *Herpetologica* 33:274–276. *4*

Holmes, J. C., and P. W. Price
1980. Parasite communities: The roles of phylogeny and ecology. *Systematic Zoology* 29:203–213. *23*
1986. Communities of parasites. In *Community ecology: Pattern and process,* edited by D. J. Anderson and J. Kikkawa, 187–213. Blackwell Scientific Publications, Oxford. *23*

Holmes, W. N., and J. G. Phillips
1976. The adrenal cortex of birds. In *General, comparative, and clinical endocrinology of the adrenal cortex,* edited by I. Chester-Jones and I. W. Henderson, 293–420. Academic Press, New York. *19*

Holub, R. J., and T. J. Bloomer
1977. The bog turtle, *Clemmys muhlenbergi:* A natural history. *Bulletin of the New York Herpetological Society (HERP)* 13:9–23. *19*

Hopkins, S. R., T. M. Murphy, K. B. Stansell, and P. M. Wilkinson
1978. Biotic and abiotic factors affecting nest mortality in the Atlantic loggerhead turtle. *Proceedings of the Annual Conference, Southeastern Association of Fish and Wildlife Agencies* 32:213–233. *15*

Horn, H. S.
1983. Some theories about dispersal. In *The ecology of animal movement,* edited by I. R. Swingland and P. J. Greenwood, 54–62. Oxford University Press, New York. *17*

Huey, R. B.
1982. Temperature, physiology, and the ecology of reptiles. In Vol. 12 of *Biology of the Reptilia,* edited by C. Gans and F. H. Pough, 25–91. Academic Press, New York. *22*

Hughes, G. M., R. Gaymer, M. Moore, and A. J. Waokes
1971. Respiratory exchange and body size in the Aldabra giant tortoise. *Journal of Experimental Biology* 55:651–665. *21*

Hughes, G. R.
1976. Irregular reproductive cycles in the Tongaland loggerhead sea-turtle, *Caretta caretta* L. (Cryptodira: Chelonidae). *Zoologica Africana* 11:285–291. *15*

Hughes, G. R., A. J. Bass, and M. T. Mentis
1967. Further studies on marine turtles in Tongaland, I. *Lammergeyer* 7:5–54. *10*

Hulse, A. C.
1976. Growth and morphometrics of *Kinosternon sonoriense* (Reptilia, Testudines, Kinosternidae). *Journal of Herpetology* 10:341–348. *14, 19*

Hurlbert, S. H.
1969. The breeding migrations and interhabitat wandering of the vermilion-spotted newt *Notophthalmus viridescens* (Rafinesque). *Ecological Monographs* 39:465–488. *2*
1984. Pseudoreplication and the design of ecological field experiments. *Ecological Monographs* 54:187–211.

Hurly, T. A.
1987. Male-biased sex ratios in a red squirrel population. *Canadian Journal of Zoology* 65:1284–1286. *14*

Husting, E. L.
1965. Survival and breeding structure in a population of *Ambystoma maculatum. Copeia* 1965:352–362. *2*

Hutchison, V. H.
1979. Thermoregulation. In *Turtles: Perspectives and research,* edited by M. Harless and H. Morlock, 207–228. John Wiley and Sons, New York. *22*

Hutchison, V. H., and J. L. Larimer
1960. Reflectivity of the integuments of some lizards from different habitats. *Ecology* 41:199–209. *19*

Hutchison, V. H., A. Vinegar, and R. J. Kosh
1966. Critical thermal maxima in turtles. *Herpetologica* 22:32–41. *18, 22*

Hutton, K. E., and C. J. Goodnight
1957. Variations in the blood chemistry of turtles under active and hibernating conditions. *Physiological Zoology* 30:198–207. *19*

Hutton, K. E., D. R. Boyer, J. C. Williams, and P. M. Campbell
1960. Effects of temperature and body size upon heart rate and oxygen consumption in turtles. *Journal of Cellular and Comparative Physiology* 55:87–94. *22*

I

Imler, R. H.
1945. Bullsnakes and their control on a Nebraska wildlife refuge. *Journal of Wildlife Management* 9:265–273. *2*

Istock, C. A.
1967. The evolution of complex life cycle phenomena: An ecological perspective. *Evolution* 21:592–605. *3*

Ivanovich, M., and R. S. Harmon
1982. *Uranium series disequilibrium: Applications to environmental problems.* Clarendon Press, Oxford. *21*

Iverson, J. B.
1977a. Geographic variation in the musk turtle *Sternotherus minor. Copeia* 1977:502–517. *14*
1977b. Reproduction in freshwater and terrestrial turtles of north Florida. *Herpetologica* 33:205–212. *11*
1979a. Another inexpensive turtle trap. *Herpetological Review* 10:55. *2, 11*
1979b. Reproduction and growth of the mud turtle *Kinosternon subrubrum* (Reptilia, Testudines, Kinosternidae) in Arkansas. *Journal of Herpetology* 13:105–111. *9*
1979c. A taxonomic reappraisal of the yellow mud turtle, *Kinosternon flavescens* (Testudines: Kinosternidae). *Copeia* 1979:212–225. *14*

1980. The reproductive biology of *Gopherus polyphemus* (Chelonia: Testudinidae). *American Midland Naturalist* 103:353–359. *16*

1981. Biosystematics of the *Kinosternon hirtipes* species group (Testudines: Kinosternidae). *Tulane Studies in Zoology and Botany* 23:1–74. *7*

1982. Biomass in turtle populations: A neglected subject. *Oceologia* 55:69–76. *1, 17*

1985. Geographic variation in sexual dimorphism in the mud turtle *Kinosternon hirtipes*. *Copeia* 1985:388–393.

1986. *A checklist with distribution maps of the turtles of the world.* Paust Printing, Richmond, Ind. *1, 7, 19*

J

Jackson, C. G., Jr.
1964. A biometrical study of form and growth in *Pseudemys concinna suwanniensis* Carr (order: Testudinata). Ph.D. dissertation. University of Florida. *12*

1969. Agonistic behavior in *Sternotherus minor minor* Agassiz. *Herpetologica* 25:53–54. *2*

1970. A biometrical study of growth in *Pseudemys concinna suwanniensis*, I. *Copeia* 1970:528–534. *14*

Jackson, C. G., Jr., and J. D. Davis
1972. A quantitative study of the courtship display of the red-eared turtle, *Chrysemys scripta elegans* (Wied). *Herpetologica* 28:58–63. *4, 7, 9*

Jackson, C. G., Jr., C. M. Holcomb, and M. M. Jackson
1972. Strontium-90 in the exoskeletal ossicles of *Dasypus novemcinctus*. *Journal of Mammalogy* 53:921–922. *21*

Jackson, C. G., Jr., C. M. Holcomb, S. Kleinbergs-Krisans, and M. M. Jackson
1974. Variation in strontium-90 exoskeletal burdens of turtles (Reptilia: Testudines) in southeastern United States. *Herpetologica* 30:406–409. *21*

Jackson, D. C.
1968. Metabolic depression and oxygen depletion in the diving turtle. *Journal of Applied Physiology* 24:503–509.

1971. The effect of temperature on ventilation in the turtle *Pseudemys scripta elegans*. *Respiration Physiology* 12:131–140. *22*

Jackson, D. R.
1976. The status of the Pliocene turtles *Pseudemys caelata* Hay and *Chrysemys carri* Rose and Weaver. *Copeia* 1976:655–659. *4*

1977. The fossil freshwater emydid turtles of Florida. Ph.D. dissertation. University of Florida. *5*

1978a. *Chrysemys nelsoni*. Society for the Study of Amphibians and Reptiles, Herpetological Circular, 210.1–210.2. *5*

1978b. Evolution and fossil record of the chicken turtle *Deirochelys*, with a re-evaluation of the genus. *Tulane Studies in Zoology and Botany* 20:35–55. *5*

1988. A re-examination of fossil turtles of the genus *Trachemys* (Testudines: Emydidae). *Herpetologica* 44:317–325. *5*

Jackson, J. F., and S. R. Telford, Jr.
1974. Reproductive ecology of the Florida scrub lizard, *Sceloporus woodi*. *Copeia* 1974:689–694. *10*

Jackson, O. F., and J. E. Cooper
1981. Nutrition diseases. In Vol. 2 of *Diseases of the Reptilia*, edited by J. E. Cooper and O. F. Jackson, 409–428. Academic Press, New York. *20*

Jacobson, K. C.
1987. Infracommunity structure of enteric helminths in the yellow-bellied slider, *Trachemys scripta scripta*. Master's thesis. Wake Forest University. *23*

Jaeger, E. C.
1944. *A source-book of biological names and terms.* C. C. Thomas, Springfield, Ill. *1*

Jenkins, J. D.
1979. Notes on the courtship on the map turtle *Graptemys pseudogeographica* (Gray) (Reptilia, Testudines, Emydidae). *Journal of Herpetology* 13:129–131. *7*

Jennrich, R. J., and F. B. Turner
1969. Measurement of non-circular home range. *Journal of Theoretical Biology* 22:227–237. *18*

Jolicoeur, P., and J. E. Mosimann
1960. Size and shape variation in the painted turtle: A principle component analysis. *Growth* 24:339–354. *10*

Jones, H. G., and W. S. Mackie
1959. The metabolism in sheep of the alkaline earth products of fission: The absorption and excretion of Ca-45 and Sr-90 by blackface wethers. *British Journal of Nutrition* 13:355–362. *21*

Juvik, J. O., A. J. Andrianarivo, and C. P. Blanc
1980–81. The ecology and status of *Geochelone yniphora*: A critically endangered tortoise in northwestern Madagascar. *Biological Conservation* 19:297–316.

K

Kaplan, H. M.
1958. Marking and banding frogs and turtles. *Herpetologica* 14:131–132. *2*

1960. Electrophoretic analysis of protein changes during growth of *Pseudemys* turtles. *Anatomical Record* 138:359. *5*

Kaplan, H. S., and L. E. Moses
1964. Biological complexity and radiosensitivity. *Science* 145:21–25. *21*

Kaplan, R. H.
1980. The implication of ovum size variability for offspring fitness and clutch size in several populations of salamanders (*Ambystoma*). *Evolution* 34:51–64. *8*

Kaplan, R. H., and W. S. Cooper
1984. The evolution of developmental plasticity in the reproductive characteristics: An application of the "adaptive coin-flipping" principle. *American Naturalist* 123:393–410. *8*

Karig, L. M., and A. C. Wilson
1971. Genetic variation in supernatant malate dehydrogenase of birds and reptiles. *Biochemical Genetics* 5:211–221. *6*

Karlstrom, E. L.
1957. The use of ^{60}Co as a tag for recovering amphibians in the field. *Ecology* 38:187–195. *21*

Kaufmann, R.
1975. Studies on the loggerhead sea turtle, *Caretta caretta* (Linné) in Colombia, South America. *Herpetologica* 31:323–326. *9*

Kennedy, C. R., A. O. Bush, and J. M. Aho
1986. Patterns in helminth communities: Why are birds and fish different? *Parasitology* 93:205–215. *23*

Kenyon, W. A.
  1925.   Digestive enzymes in poikilothermic vertebrates: An investigation of enzymes in fishes, with comparative studies on those of amphibians, reptiles, and mammals. *Bulletin of the United States Bureau of Fisheries* 41:179–200. *20*

Kepenis, V., and J. J. McManus
  1974.   Bioenergetics of young painted turtles, *Chrysemys picta*. *Comparative Biochemistry and Physiology* 48A:309–317. *20*

Kephart, D. G., and S. J. Arnold
  1982.   Garter snake diets in a fluctuating environment: A seven-year study. *Ecology* 63:1232–1236. *3*

Kettlewell, H. B. D.
  1965.   Insect survival and selection for pattern. *Science* 148:1290–1296. *19*

Kevern, N. R.
  1966.   Feeding rate of carp estimated by a radioisotopic method. *Transactions of the American Fisheries Society* 95:363–371. *21*

Kiester, A. R., C. W. Schwartz, and E. R. Schwartz
  1982.   Promotion of gene flow by transient individuals in an otherwise sedentary population of box turtles (*Terrapene carolina triunguis*). *Evolution* 36:617–619. *16*

Killebrew, F. C.
  1977.   Mitotic chromosomes of turtles, IV: The Emydidae. *Texas Journal of Science* 29:245–253. *4, 5*

Kimball, F. A., and M. J. Erpino
  1971.   Hormonal control of pigmentary sexual dimorphism in *Sceloporus occidentalis*. *General and Comparative Endocrinology* 16:375–384. *19*

King, D. P. F.
  1985.   Enzyme heterozygosity associated with anatomical character variance and growth in the herring (*Clupea harengus* L.). *Heredity* 54:289–296. *6*

King, F. W.
  1982.   Historical review of the decline of the green turtle and the hawksbill. In *Biology and conservation of sea turtles*, edited by K. A. Bjorndal, 183–188. Smithsonian Institution Press, Washington, D.C. *3*

Kirk, R. E.
  1968.   *Experimental design: Procedures for the behavior sciences*. Brooks-Cole, Belmont, Calif. *18*

Kirkwood, T. B. L.
  1985.   Comparative and evolutionary aspects of longevity. In *Handbook of the biology of aging*, 2d ed., edited by C. E. Finch and E. L. Schneider, 27–44. Van Nostrand Reinhold Co., New York. *3*

Kitchings, T., D. Digregorio, and P. Van Voris
  1976.   A review of the ecological parameters of radionuclide turnover in vertebrate food chains. In *Radioecology and energy resources*, edited by C. E. Cushing, Jr., 304–313. Dowden, Hutchinson and Ross, Stroudsburg, Pa. *21*

Klauber, L. M.
  1937.   A statistical study of the rattlesnakes, IV: The growth of the rattlesnake. *San Diego Society of Natural History* 3:1–56.

Kleiber, M.
  1975.   Metabolic turnover rate: A physiological meaning of the metabolic rate per unit body weight. *Journal of Theoretical Biology* 53:199–204. *21*

Knight, A. W., and J. W. Gibbons
  1968.   Food of the painted turtle, *Chrysemys picta*, in a polluted river. *American Midland Naturalist* 80:558–562.

Knight, J. L., and R. K. Loraine
  1986.   Notes on turtle egg predation by *Lampropeltis getulus* (Linnaeus) (Reptilia: Colubridae) on the Savannah River Plant, South Carolina. *Brimleyana* 1986(12):1–4. *15*

Kolehmainen, S. E.
  1972.   The balances of ^{137}Cs, stable cesium, and potassium of bluegill (*Lepomis macrochirus* RAF.) and other fish in White Oak Lake. *Health Physics* 23:301–315. *21*

Kotb, A. K., and T. D. Luckey
  1972.   Markers in nutrition. *Nutrition Abstracts and Reviews* 42:813–845. *21*

Kraemer, J. E., and S. H. Bennett
  1981.   Utilization of post-hatching yolk in loggerhead sea turtles, *Caretta caretta*. *Copeia* 1981:406–411. *8*

Kramer, M.
  1986.   Field studies on a freshwater Florida turtle, *Pseudemys nelsoni*. In *Behavioral ecology and population biology*, edited by L. C. Drickamer, 29–34. Privat, Toulouse, France. *19*

Kreith, F.
  1973.   *Principles of heat transfer*. 3d ed. Intext Educational Publishers, New York. *22*

Kuchling, G., R. Skolek-Winnisch, and E. Bamberg
  1981.   Histochemical and biochemical investigation of the annual cycle of testis, epididymis, and plasma testosterone of the tortoise, *Testudo hermanni hermanni* Gmelin. *General and Comparative Endocrinology* 44:194–201. *19*

Kushlan, J. A.
  1980.   Everglades alligator nests: Nesting sites for marsh reptiles. *Copeia* 1980:930–932. *8*

L

Lacépède, B. G. E.
  1788–89. Vol. 1 of *Histoire naturalle des quadrupèdes ovipares et des serpens*. Paris. *4*

Lack, D.
  1947.   The significance of clutch size, I. *Ibis* 89:302–352. *8*
  1948.   The significance of clutch size, II. *Ibis* 90:25–45. *8*
  1954a. The evolution of reproductive rates. In *Evolution as a process*, edited by J. Huxley. Allen and Unwin, London. *3*
  1954b. *The natural regulation of animal numbers*. Clarendon Press, Oxford. *8*
  1966.   *Population studies of birds*. Metheun and Co., London. *15*
  1968.   *Ecological adaptations for breeding in birds*. Metheun and Co., London. *8, 15*

Lagler, K. F.
  1943.   Food habits and economic relations of the turtles of Michigan with special reference to fish management. *American Midland Naturalist* 29:257–312. *9*

Lagler, K. F., and V. C. Applegate
  1943.   Relationship between the length and the weight in the snapping turtle *Chelydra serpentina* Linnaeus. *American Naturalist* 77:476–478. *14*

Lahanas, P. N.
  1982.   Aspects of the life history of the southern black-nobbed

sawback, *Graptemys nigrinoda delticola* Folkerts and Mount. Master's thesis. Auburn University. *14*

Lal, P., and J. P. Thapliyal
1982.   Role of thyroid in the response of bill pigmentation to male hormone of the house sparrow, *Passer domesticus. General and Comparative Endocrinology* 48:135–142. *19*

Lamb, T., and J. D. Congdon
1985.   Ash content: Relationships to flexible and rigid eggshell types of turtles. *Journal of Herpetology* 19:527–530. *8*

Lambert, M. R. K.
1982.   Studies on the growth, structure, and abundance of the Mediterranean spur-thighed tortoise, *Testudo graeca*, in field populations. *Journal of Zoology* (London) 196:165–189. *14*

Lande, R.
1980.   Sexual dimorphism, sexual selection, and adaptation in polygenic characters. *Evolution* 34:292–305.
1982.   A quantitative genetic theory of life history evolution. *Ecology* 63:607–615. *3*

Landers, J. L., J. A. Garner, and W. A. McRae
1980.   Reproduction of gopher tortoises (*Gopherus polyphemus*) in southwestern Georgia. *Herpetologica* 36:353–361. *3, 15, 16*

Landers, J. L., W. A. McRae, and J. A. Garner
1982.   Growth and maturity of the gopher tortoise in southwestern Georgia. *Bulletin of the Florida State Museum Biological Sciences* 27:81–110. *19*

Lardie, R. L.
1983.   Aggressive interactions among melanistic males of the red-eared slider, *Pseudemys scripta elegans* (Wied). *Bulletin Oklahoma Herpetological Society* 8:105–117. *17, 19*

Lawson, G. O., and W. R. Garstka
1985.   Castration of turtles, *Pseudemys scripta* [abstract]. *Journal of the Alabama Academy of Science* 56:89. *19*

Lawton, M. F., and C. F. Guindon
1981.   Flock composition, breeding success, and learning in the brown jay. *Condor* 83:27–33. *19*

Lawton, M. F., and R. O. Lawton
1985.   The breeding biology of the brown jay in Monteverde, Costa Rica. *Condor* 87:192–204. *19*
1986.   Heterochrony, deferred breeding, and avian sociality. *Current Ornithology* 3:187–221. *19*

Lazell, J. D., Jr., and P. J. Auger
1981.   Predation on diamondback terrapin (*Malaclemys terrapin*) eggs by dunegrass (*Ammophila breviligulata*). *Copeia* 1981:723–724. *15*

Leggett, W. C., and J. E. Carscadden
1978.   Latitudinal variation in reproductive characteristics of American shad (*Alosa sapidissima*): Evidence for population specific life history strategies in fish. *Journal of the Fisheries Research Board of Canada* 35:1469–1478. *11*

Legler, J. M.
1954.   Nesting habits of the western painted turtle, *Chrysemys picta bellii* (Gray). *Herpetologica* 10:137–144. *3, 8*
1956.   A simple and practical method of artificially incubating reptile eggs. *Herpetologica* 12:290.
1960a.   Natural history of the ornate box turtle, *Terrapene ornata ornata* Agassiz. University of Kansas Publications of

the Museum of Natural History, vol. 11, 527–669. *3, 10, 15*
1960b.   A new subspecies of slider turtle (*Pseudemys scripta*) from Coahuila, Mexico. University of Kansas Publications of the Museum of Natural History, vol. 13, 73–84. *2, 7, 19, 20*
1960c.   Remarks on the natural history of the Big Bend slider, *Pseudemys scripta gaigeae* Hartweg. *Herpetologica* 16:139–140. *1, 20*
1963.   Further evidence for intergradation of two Mexican slider turtles (*Pseudemys scripta*). *Herpetologica* 19:142–143. *7*
1965.   A new species of turtle, genus *Kinosternon*, from Central America. University of Kansas Publications of the Museum of Natural History, vol. 15, 615–625.
1977.   Stomach flushing: A technique for chelonian dietary studies. *Herpetologica* 33:281–284. *2, 20*
1982.   *Turtle measurements.* Videotape. University of Utah, Salt Lake City. *7*

Legler, J. M., and J. Cann
1980.   *A new genus and species of chelid turtle from Queensland, Australia.* Contributions in Science (Los Angeles), vol. 324. *19*

Legler, J. M., and R. G. Webb
1961.   Remarks on a collection of Bolson tortoises, *Gopherus flavomarginatus. Herpetologica* 17:26–37.
1970.   A new slider turtle (*Pseudemys scripta*) from Sonora, Mexico. *Herpetologica* 26:157–168. *4, 7*

Leone, C. A., and F. E. Wilson
1961.   Studies of turtle sera, I: The nature of the fastest moving electrophoretic component in the sera of nine species. *Physiological Zoology* 34:297–305. *5*

Leshner, A. I.
1978.   *An introduction to behavioral endocrinology.* Oxford University Press, New York. *19*

Leslie, P. H.
1945.   On the use of matrices in certain population mathematics. *Biometrika* 33:182–212. *15*
1948.   Some further notes on the use of matrices in population mathematics. *Biometrika* 35:213–245. *15*

Levins, R.
1968.   *Evolution in changing environments.* Princeton University Press, New York. *6*

Lewin, R.
1985.   Why are male hawks so small? *Science* 228:1299–1300.

Lewis, W. M., Jr.
1974a.   An analysis of surface slicks in a reservoir receiving heated effluent. *Archiv für Hydrobiologie* 74:304–315. *18*
1974b.   Evaluation of heat distribution in a South Carolina reservoir receiving heated water. In *Thermal ecology*, U.S. Atomic Energy Commission Symposium Series (CONF-730505), edited by J. W. Gibbons and R. R. Sharitz, 1–27. National Technical Information Service, Springfield, Va. *18*

Lewontin, R. C.
1958.   The adaptations of populations to varying environments. *Cold Spring Harbor Symposia on Quantitative Biology* 22:395–408. *3*
1965.   Selection for colonizing ability. In *The genetics of coloniz-*

ing species, edited by H. G. Baker and G. L. Stebbins, 79–91. Academic Press, New York. *15*

Licht, P.
1974.   Response of *Anolis* lizards to food supplementation in nature. *Copeia* 1974:215–221. *10*

Licht, P., G. L. Breitenbach, and J. D. Congdon
1985.   Seasonal cycles in testicular activity, gonadotropin, and thyroxine in the painted turtle, *Chrysemys picta*, under natural conditions. *General and Comparative Endocrinology* 59:130–139.

Lidicker, W. Z., Jr.
1975.   The role of dispersal in small mammals. In *Small mammals: Their productivity and population dynamics*, edited by F. B. Golley, K. Petrusewicz, and L. Ryszkowski, 103–128. Cambridge University Press, New York. *6*

Lifson, N., and R. McClintock
1966.   Theory of use of the turnover rates of body water for measuring energy and material balance. *Journal of Theoretical Biology* 12:46–74. *21*

Lifson, N., G. B. Gordon, M. G. Visscher, and A. O. Nier
1949.   The fate of utilized molecular oxygen and the source of the oxygen of respiratory carbon dioxide, studied with the aid of heavy oxygen. *Journal of Biological Chemistry* 180:803–811. *21*

Limpus, C. J., T. Reed, and J. D. Miller
1983.   Islands and turtles: The influence of choice of nesting beach on sex ratio. In *Proceedings, Inaugural Great Basin Reef Conference*, edited by J. T. Baker, R. M. Carter, P. W. Sammarco, and K. P. Stork, 397–402. J.C.U. Press, Townsville, Australia. *14*

Liu, C., and S. Hu
1939–40. Notes on growth of *Geoclemys reevesii. Peking Natural History Bulletin* 14:253–266, 1 plate. *19*

Long, D. R.
1985.   Lipid utilization during reproduction in female *Kinosternon flavescens. Herpetologica* 41:58–65. *19*
1986.   Clutch formation in the turtle, *Kinosternon flavescens* (Testudines: Kinosternidae). *Southwestern Naturalist* 31:1–8.

Loomis, F. B.
1904.   Two new river reptiles from the Titanothere Beds. *Journal of Science* 18:427–432. *5*

Lotka, A. J.
1922.   The stability of the normal age distribution. *Proceedings of the National Academy of Sciences of the United States of America* 8:339–345. *15*

Loveridge, A., and E. E. Williams
1957.   Revision of the African tortoises and turtles of the suborder Cryptodira. *Bulletin of the Museum of Comparative Zoology* 115:161– 557. *5*

Lovich, J. E.
1988.   Aggressive basking behavior in eastern painted turtles (*Chrysemys picta picta*). *Herpetologica* 44:197–202. *19*

Lovich, J. E., S. W. Gotte, and C. H. Ernst
1983.   Clutch and egg size in the New Guinea chelid turtle *Emydura subglobosa. Herpetofauna* 14:95. *15*

Lovich, J. E., C. H. Ernst, and S. W. Gotte
1985.   Geographic variation in the Asiatic turtle *Chinemys reevesii* (Gray) and the status of *Geoclemys grangeri* Schmidt. *Journal of Herpetology* 19:238–245. *10, 14, 19*

Lowe, C. H., P. J. Lardner, and E. A. Halpern
1971.   Supercooling in reptiles and other vertebrates. *Comparative Biochemistry and Physiology* 39A:125–135. *8*

Lucey, E. C.
1974.   Heart rate and physiological thermoregulation in a basking turtle, *Pseudemys scripta elegans. Comparative Biochemistry and Physiology* 48A:471–482. *22*

Luckenbill, L. S., M. J. Clare, W. L. Krell, W. C. Cirocco, and P. A. Richards
1987.   Estimating the number of genetic elements that defer senescence in *Drosophila. Evolutionary Ecology* 1:37–46. *3*

Lynn, W. G., and C. Grant
1940.   *The herpetology of Jamaica*. Bulletin of the Institute of Jamaica, Science Series, vol. 1. *19*

Lynn, W. G., and T. von Brand
1945.   Studies on the oxygen consumption and water metabolism of turtle embryos. *Biological Bulletin* (Woods Hole) 88:112–125. *8*

M

MacArthur, R. M., and E. O. Wilson
1967.   *The theory of island biogeography*. Princeton University Press, Princeton, N.J. *3, 15*

MacCulloch, R. D.
1981.   Variation in the shell of *Chrysemys picta belli* from southern Saskatchewan. *Journal of Herpetology* 15:181–185. *19*

MacCulloch, R. D., and D. M. Secoy
1983a. Demography, growth, and food of western painted turtles, *Chrysemys picta belli* (Gray), from southern Saskatchewan. *Canadian Journal of Zoology* 61:1499–1509. *14*
1983b. Movement in a river population of *Chrysemys picta belli* in southern Saskatchewan. *Journal of Herpetology* 17:283–285. *6*

Maderson, P. F. A.
1984.   The squamate epidermis: New light has been shed. In *The structure, development, and evolution of reptiles*, edited by M. W. J. Ferguson, 111–126. Academic Press, Orlando, Fla. *19*

Madison, D. M.
1977.   Chemical communication in reptiles and amphibians. In *Chemical signals in vertebrates*, edited by D. Muller-Schwartze and M. M. Mozell, 135–168. Plenum Press, New York. *19*

Madison, D. M., and C. R. Shoop
1970.   Homing behavior, orientation, and home range of salamanders tagged with tantalum-182. *Science* 168:1484–1487. *21*

Mahmoud, I. Y.
1967.   Courtship behavior and sexual maturity in four species of kinosternid turtles. *Copeia* 1967:314–319. *14*
1968a. Feeding behavior in kinosternid turtles. *Herpetologica* 24:300–305. *18, 20*
1968b. Nesting behavior in the western painted turtle, *Chrysemys picta belli. Herpetologica* 24:158–162.
1969.   Comparative ecology of the kinosternid turtles of Oklahoma. *Southwestern Naturalist* 14:31–66. *14, 16, 18*

Mahmoud, I. Y., and J. Klicka
1979.   Feeding, drinking, and excretion. In *Turtles: Perspectives*

and research, edited by M. Harless and H. Morlock, 229–243. John Wiley and Sons, New York. *20*

Mahmoud, I. Y., and N. Lavenda
1969. Establishment and eradication of food preferences in red-eared turtles. *Copeia* 1969:298–300. *20*

Manchester, D., Sr.
1982. Red-eared sliders in Pennsylvania. *Testudo* 2:27–30. *4*

Manlove, M. N., J. C. Avise, H. O. Hillestad, P. R. Ramsey, M. H. Smith, and D. O. Straney
1975. Starch gel electrophoresis for the study of population genetics in white-tailed deer. *Proceedings of the Annual Conference, Southeastern Association of Game and Fish Commissioners* 29:392–403. *6*

Manolis, S. C., G. J. W. Webb, and K. E. Dempsey
1987. Crocodile egg chemistry. In *Wildlife management: Crocodiles and alligators*, edited by G. J. W. Webb, S. C. Manolis, and P. J. Whitehead, 445–472. Surrey Beatty and Sons, Sydney. *8*

Manton, M. L.
1979. Olfaction and behavior. In *Turtles: Perspectives and research*, edited by M. Harless and H. Morlock, 289–301. John Wiley and Sons, New York. *20*

Manwell, C., and C. V. Schlesinger
1966. Polymorphism of turtle hemoglobin and geographical differences in the frequency of variants of *Chrysemys picta* "slow" hemoglobin—an example of "temperature anti-adaptation?" *Comparative Biochemistry and Physiology* 18:627–637. *5*

Mao, S. H.
1971. *Turtles of Taiwan*. Commercial Press, Taipei, Taiwan. *19*

Marchand, L. J.
1942. A contribution to a knowledge of the natural history of certain freshwater turtles. Master's thesis. University of Florida. *10, 20*
1945. Water goggling: A new method for the study of turtles. *Copeia* 1945:37–40. *2*

Marcus, C. S., and F. W. Lengemann
1962. Absorption of Ca-45 and Sr-85 from solid and liquid food at various levels of the alimentary tract of the rat. *Journal of Nutrition* 77:155–160. *21*

Marey, A. N., V. A. Knizhnikov, and A. N. Karmaeva
1967. The effect of calcium in drinking water on the accumulation of ^{226}Ra and ^{90}Sr in the human body. In *Radioecological concentration processes*, edited by B. Aberg and F. P. Hungate, 333–336. Pergamon Press, New York. *21*

Marquardt, D. W.
1964. *Least squares estimation of nonlinear parameters*. Harvard University Computing Center Library Share Distribution no. 3094, Cambridge, Mass. *10*

Márquez M., R., and T. Doi
1973. Ensayo teórico sobre el análisis de la población de tortuga prieta, *Chelonia mydas carrinegra* Caldwell, en aguas del Golfo de California, México. *Bulletin of Tokai Regional Fisheries Research Laboratory* 73:1–22. *15*

Márquez M., R., C. Peñaflores S., A. Villanueva O., and J. Díaz F.
1982a. A model for diagnosis of populations of olive ridleys and green turtles of west Pacific tropical coasts. In *Biology and conservation of sea turtles*, edited by K. A. Bjorndal, 153–158. Smithsonian Institution Press, Washington, D.C. *15*

Márquez M., R., A. Villanueva O., and M. Sanchez P.
1982b. The population of the Kemp's ridley sea turtle in the Gulf of Mexico—*Lepidochelys kempii*. In *Biology and conservation of sea turtles*, edited by K. A. Bjorndal, 159–164. Smithsonian Institution Press, Washington, D.C. *15*

Martin, R. G.
1977. Density dependent aggressive advantage in melanistic male mosquitofish *Gambusia affinis holbrooki* (Girard). *Florida Scientist* 40:393–400. *19*
1986. Behavioral response of female mosquitofish, *Gambusia affinis holbrooki*, to normal versus melanistic male mosquitofish. *Journal of the Elisha Mitchell Scientific Society* 102:129–136. *19*

Martof, B. S., W. M. Palmer, J. R. Bailey, and J. R. Harrison III
1980. *Amphibians and reptiles of the Carolinas and Virginia*. University of North Carolina Press, Chapel Hill. *2, 19, 23*

Masat, R. J., and H. C. Dessauer
1968. Plasma albumins of reptiles. *Comparative Biochemistry and Physiology* 25:119–128. *5*

Masat, R. J., and X. J. Musacchia
1965. Serum protein concentration changes in the turtle, *Chrysemys picta*. *Comparative Biochemistry and Physiology* 16:215–225. *19*

Mattox, N.
1935. Annual rings in the long bones of turtles and their correlation with size. *Transactions of the American Fisheries Society* 28:255–256. *10*

Mayhew, W.
1965. Hibernation in the horned lizard, *Phrynosoma M'calli*. *Comparative Biochemistry and Physiology* 16:103–119. *22*

Maynard-Smith, J.
1978. Optimization theory in evolution. *Annual Review of Ecology and Systematics* 9:31–56. *3*

McCauley, R. H., Jr.
1945. *Reptiles of Maryland and the District of Columbia*. Hagerstown, Md.

McClellan, R. O., J. R. McKenney, and L. K. Bustad
1962. Changes in calcium ^{90}Sr discrimination with age in young miniature swine. *Life Sciences* 12:669–675. *21*

McCort, W. D.
1987. Effects of thermal effluents from nuclear reactors. In *Environmental consequences of energy production: Problems and prospects*, edited by S. K. Majumdar, F. J. Brenner, and E. W. Miller, 386–401. Pennsylvania Academy of Science, Easton, Pa. *2*

McCort, W. D., L. C. Lee, and G. R. Wein
1988. Mitigating for large-scale wetland loss: A realistic endeavor? In *Proceedings of the National Wetlands Symposium: Mitigation of impacts and losses*, edited by J. A. Kusler, M. L. Quammen, and G. Brooks, 359–367. Association of State Wetlands Managers, Berne, N.Y. *2*

McCoy, C. J.
1968. The development of melanism in an Oklahoma population of *Chrysemys scripta elegans* (Reptilia: Testudinidae). *Proceedings of the Oklahoma Academy of Science* 47:84–87. *19*

McCullough, E. M., and W. P. Porter
1971. Computing clear day solar radiation spectra for the terrestrial ecological environment. *Ecology* 52:1008–1015. *22*

McDonald, H. S.
1976. Methods for the physiological study of reptiles. In Vol. 5 of *Biology of the Reptilia*, edited by C. Gans and W. R Dawson, 19–126. Academic Press, London. *21*

McDowell, S. B.
1964. Partition of the genus *Clemmys* and related problems in the taxonomy of the aquatic Testudinidae. *Proceedings of the Zoological Society of London* 143:239–279. *1, 4, 5, 7*

McFarlane, R. W., R. F. Frietsche, and R. D. Miracle
1978. *Impingement and entrainment of fishes at the Savannah River Plant*. E. I. du Pont de Nemours and Co. Report no. DP-1491. Aiken, S.C. *2*
1979. Community structure and differential impingement of Savannah River fishes. *Proceedings of the Annual Conference, Southeastern Association of Fish and Wildlife Agencies* 33:628–638. *2*

McGinness, J., and P. Proctor
1973. The importance of the fact that melanin is black. *Journal of Theoretical Biology* 39:677–678. *19*

McKeown, S., J. O. Juvik, and D. E. Meier
1982. Observations on the reproductive biology of the land tortoises *Geochelone emys* and *Geochelone yniphora* in the Honolulu Zoo. *Zoo Biology* 1:223–235.

McNab, B. K.
1963. Bioenergetics and the determination of home range size. *American Naturalist* 97:133–140. *18*

McNeill, K. G., and O. A. D. Trojan
1960. The cesium-potassium discrimination ratio. *Health Physics* 4:109–112. *21*

McPherson, R. J., and K. R. Marion
1981a. The reproductive biology of female *Sternotherus odoratus* in an Alabama population. *Journal of Herpetology* 15:389–396. *3, 8, 16*
1981b. Seasonal testicular cycle of the stinkpot turtle (*Sternotherus odoratus*) in central Alabama. *Herpetologica* 37:33–40. *9*

McRae, W. A., J. L. Landers, and G. D. Cleveland
1981. Sexual dimorphism in the gopher tortoise (*Gopherus polyphemus*). *Herpetologica* 37:46–52.

Medawar, P. B.
1952. *An unsolved problem of biology*. H. K. Lewis, London. *3*

Medem, F.
1962. La distribución geográfica y ecología de los Crocodylia y Testudinata in el departmento del Choco. *Revista de la Academia Colombiana de Ciencias Exactas Fisicas y Naturales* 11(44):279–303. *7, 8, 12*
1966. Contribuciones al conocimiento sobre la ecología y distribución geográfica de *Phrynops* (*Batrachemys*) *dahli* (Testudinata, Pleurodira, Chelidae). *Caldasia* 9:467–489. *14*
1975. La reproducción de la "icotea" (*Pseudemys scripta callirostris*) (Testudines, Emydidae). *Caldasia* 11:83–106. *12*

Medica, P. A., R. B. Bury, and F. B. Turner
1975. Growth of the desert tortoise (*Gopherus agassizi*) in Nevada. *Copeia* 1975:639–643. *10*

Meek, S. E.
1904. *The fresh-water fishes of Mexico north of the Isthmus of Tehuantepec*. Zoological Series, Field Columbian Museum, no. 93. *7*

Mendonca, M. T.
1983. Movements and feeding ecology of immature green turtles (*Chelonia mydas*) in a Florida lagoon. *Copeia* 1983:1013–1023. *18*

Merkle, D. A.
1975. A taxonomic analysis of the *Clemmys* complex (Reptilia: Testudines) utilizing starch gel electrophoresis. *Herpetologica* 31:162–166. *6*

Mertens, H.
1985. Population structure and life tables of African buffalo, topi, and Uganda kob in the Virunga National Park, Zaire. *Revue d'Ecologie la Terre et la Vie* 40:33–52.

Mertz, D. B.
1970. Notes on methods used in life-history studies. In *Readings in ecology and ecological genetics*, edited by J. H. Connell, D. B. Mertz, and W. W. Murdoch, 4–17. Harper and Row, New York. *15*
1971. Life history phenomena in increasing and decreasing populations. In *Symposium on statistical ecology*, edited by G. P. Patil, E. G. Pielou, and W. E. Waters, 361–400. Pennsylvania State University Press, University Park. *3, 15*
1975. Senescent decline in flour beetle strains selected for early adult fitness. *Physiological Zoology* 48:1–23. *3*

Michael, E. D.
1972. Growth rates in *Anolis carolinensis*. *Copeia* 1972:575–577. *10*

Millen, J. E., H. V. Murdaugh, Jr., C. B. Bauer, and E. D. Robin
1964. Circulatory adaptation to diving in the freshwater turtle. *Science* 145:591–593.

Miller, J. D.
1985. Embryology of marine turtles. In Vol. 14 of *Biology of the Reptilia*, edited by C. Gans, F. Billett, and P. F. A. Maderson, 269–328. John Wiley and Sons, New York. *8*

Miller, K., G. C. Packard, and M. J. Packard
1987. Hydric conditions during incubation influence locomotor performance of hatchling snapping turtles. *Journal of Experimental Biology* 127:401–412. *8*

Miller, L.
1955. Further observations on the desert tortoise, *Gopherus agassizi* of California. *Copeia* 1955:113–118. *10*

Miller, R.
1976. Models, metaphysics, and long-lived species. *Bulletin of the Ecological Society of America* 57:2–6. *3*

Minckley, W. L.
1969. *Environments of the bolsón of Cuatro Ciénegas, Coahuila, México*. University of Texas at El Paso Science Series, no. 2. Texas Western Press, El Paso. *7*

Minckley, W. L., D. A. Hendrickson, and C. E. Bond
1986. Geography of western North American freshwater fishes: Description and relationships to intracontinental tectonism. In *Zoogeography of North American freshwater fishes*, edited by C. H. Hocutt and E. O. Wiley, 519–613. John Wiley and Sons, New York. *7*

Minnich, J. E., and V. H. Shoemaker
1970. Diet, behavior, and water turnover in the desert iguana, *Dipsosaurus dorsalis*. *American Midland Naturalist* 84:496–509. *21*

Minton, S. A., Jr.
1972. *Amphibians and reptiles in Indiana*. Indiana Academy of Sciences Monograph no. 3. *14, 19*

Minyard, V.
1947. The food habits of the turtle *Pseudemys scripta troosti*. Master's thesis. Tulane University. *12, 20*

Mitchell, J. C.
1982. Population ecology and demography of the freshwater turtles *Chrysemys picta* and *Sternotherus odoratus*. Ph.D. dissertation. University of Tennessee at Knoxville. *11*
1985a. Female reproductive cycle and life history attributes in Virginia population of painted turtles, *Chrysemys picta*. *Journal of Herpetology* 19:218–226. *3, 11*
1985b. Female reproductive cycle and life history attributes in a Virginia population of stinkpot turtles, *Sternotherus odoratus*. *Copeia* 1985:941–949. *11*
1988. Population ecology and life histories of the freshwater turtles *Chrysemys picta* and *Sternotherus odoratus* in an urban lake. *Herpetological Monographs* 2:40–61. *15*

Mitton, J. B., and M. C. Grant
1984. Associations among protein heterozygosity, growth rate, and developmental homeostasis. *Annual Review of Ecology and Systematics* 15:479–500. *6*

Moesteller, F., and J. W. Tukey
1977. *Data analysis and regression*. Addison-Wesley, Reading, Mass. *10*

Mohr, C. O.
1947. Table of equivalent populations of North American small mammals. *American Midland Naturalist* 37:223–249. *18*

Mohr, C. O., and W. A. Stumpf
1966. Comparisons of methods for calculating areas of animal activity. *Journal of Wildlife Management* 30:293–304. *18*

Moll, D.
1976a. Environmental influence on growth rate in the Ouachita map turtle, *Graptemys pseudogeographica ouachitensis*. *Herpetologica* 32:439–443. *9, 10*
1976b. Food and feeding strategies of the Ouachita map turtle (*Graptemys pseudogeographica ouachitensis*). *American Midland Naturalist* 96:478–482. *20*
1977. Ecological investigations of turtles in a polluted ecosystem: The central Illinois River and adjacent flood plain lakes. Ph.D. dissertation. Illinois State University. *9, 12*
1986. Ecological characteristics of a tropical freshwater stream turtle community in northern Belize. Paper presented at the Neotropical Turtle Symposium, Estación de Biología "Los Tuxtlas," Universidad Nacional Autónoma de México, Veracruz, Mexico, March 6, 1986. *12*

Moll, E. O.
1973. Latitudinal and intersubspecific variation in reproduction of the painted turtle, *Chrysemys picta*. *Herpetologica* 29:307–318. *3, 9, 14*
1978. Drumming along the Perak. *Natural History* 87:36–43.

1979. Reproductive cycles and adaptations. In *Turtles: Perspectives and research*, edited by M. Harless and H. Morlock, 305–331. John Wiley and Sons, New York. *3, 8, 9, 12, 15*
1980. Natural history of the river terrapin, *Batagur baska* (Gray), in Malaysia (Testudines: Emydidae). *Malaysian Journal of Science* 6A:23–62. *9, 14, 18, 19*
1986a. Nesting biology of *Callagur borneoensis*, an unusual tropical Asian river turtle. Paper presented at the Neotropical Turtle Symposium, Estación de Biología "Los Tuxtlas," Universidad Nacional Autónoma de México, Veracruz, Mexico, March 6, 1986. *12*
1986b. Survey of the freshwater turtles of India, part I: The genus *Kachuga*. *Journal of Bombay Natural History Society* 83:538–552. *19*

Moll, E. O., and J. M. Legler
1971. The life history of a neotropical slider turtle, *Pseudemys scripta* (Schoepff), in Panama. *Bulletin of the Los Angeles County Museum of Natural History Science* 11:1–102. *1–5, 7–20, 22, 24*

Moll, E. O., E. K. Matson, and E. B. Krehbiel
1981. Sexual and seasonal dichromatism in the Asian river turtle *Callagur borneoensis*. *Herpetologica* 37:181–194. *19*

Moll, E. O., B. Groombridge, and J. Vijaya
1986. Redescription of the cane turtle with notes on its natural history and classification. *Journal of Bombay Natural History Society Supplement* 83:112–126. *19*

Monteith, J. L.
1973. *Principles of environmental physics*. Arnold, London. *22*

Montgomery, R.
1957. Determination of glycogen. *Archives of Biochemistry and Biophysics* 67:378–386. *19*

Moors, P. J.
1980. Sexual dimorphism in the body size of mustelids (Carnivora): The roles of food habits and breeding systems. *Oikos* 34:147–158.

Morafka, D. J.
1982. The status and distribution of the Bolson tortoise (*Gopherus flavomarginatus*). In *North American tortoises: Conservation and ecology*, Wildlife Research Report no. 12, edited by R. B. Bury, 71–94. U.S. Fish and Wildlife Service, Washington, D.C. *16*

Morafka, D. J., and C. J. McCoy, eds.
1988. The ecogeography of the Mexican Bolson tortoise (*Gopherus flavomarginatus*): Derivation of its endangered status and recommendations for its conservation. *Annals of Carnegie Museum* 57. *19*

Morgareidge, K. R., and F. N. White
1969. Cutaneous vascular changes during heating and cooling in the Galapagos marine iguana. *Nature* 223:587–591. *22*

Morreale, S. J., and J. W. Gibbons
1986. *Habitat suitability index models: Slider turtle*. United States Fish and Wildlife Service Biological Report no. 82(10.125). *4, 12, 22*

Morreale, S. J., G. J. Ruiz, J. R. Spotila, and E. A. Standora
1982. Temperature-dependent sex determination: Current practices threaten conservation of sea turtles. *Science* 216:1245–1247. *14*

Morreale, S. J., J. W. Gibbons, and J. D. Congdon
1984.   Significance of activity and movement in the yellow-bellied slider turtle (*Pseudemys scripta*). *Canadian Journal of Zoology* 62:1038–1042. *1, 6, 14, 16, 17, 19, 21–23*

Morris, K. A., G. C. Packard, T. J. Boardman, G. L. Paukstis, and M. J. Packard
1983.   Effect of the hydric environment on growth of embryonic snapping turtles (*Chelydra serpentina*). *Herpetologica* 39:272–285. *8*

Mortimer, J. A.
1981.   The feeding ecology of the west Caribbean green turtle (*Chelonia mydas*) in Nicaragua. *Biotropica* 13:49–58. *14, 16*

Mosimann, J. E.
1956.   *Variation and relative growth in the plastral scutes of the turtle* Kinosternon integrum *Leconte*. Miscellaneous Publications of the Museum of Zoology, University of Michigan, no. 97. *14*
1958.   An analysis of allometry in the chelonian shell. *Revue Canadienne de Biologie* 17:137–228. *10*

Mosimann, J. E., and J. R. Bider
1960.   Variation, sexual dimorphism, and maturity in a Quebec population of the common snapping turtle, *Chelydra serpentina*. *Canadian Journal of Zoology* 38:19–38. *14*

Mount, R. H.
1963.   The natural history of the red-tailed skink, *Eumeces egregius* Baird. *American Midland Naturalist* 70:356–385. *10*
1975.   *The reptiles and amphibians of Alabama*. Auburn University Agricultural Experiment Station, Auburn, Ala. *2, 4, 19*

Mrosovsky, N.
1982.   Sex ratio bias in hatchling sea turtles from artificially incubated eggs. *Biological Conservation* 23:309–314. *8*

Mueller, H. C., and K. Meyer
1985.   The evolution of reversed sexual dimorphism in size: A comparative analysis of the Falconiformes of the western Palearctic. *Ornithological Monographs* 2:65–101.

Mullen, R. K.
1973.   The $D_2{}^{18}O$ method of measuring the energy metabolism of free-living animals. In *Ecological energetics of homeotherms*, edited by J. R. Gessaman, 32–43. Monograph Series, vol. 20. Utah State University Press, Logan. *21*

Müller, L.
1940.   Über *Pseudemys callirostris* (Gray). In *Tier und Umwelt Sudamerika*. Ibero-amerikanische Studien, vol. 13, 107–126. *7*

Müller, P.
1968.   Zur verbreitung der gattung *Hydromedusa* (Testudines, Chelidae) auf den sudostbrasilianischen inseln. *Salamandra* 4:16–26.

Murdoch, W. W.
1966.   Population stability and life history phenomena. *American Naturalist* 100:5–11. *3*

Murphy, G.
1968.   Pattern in life history and environment. *American Naturalist* 102:391–404. *3*

Murphy, M. T.
1983.   Ecological aspects of the reproductive biology of eastern kingbirds: Geographic comparisons. *Ecology* 64:914–928. *11*

Murphy, R. W.
1983.   *Paleobiogeography and genetic differentiation of the Baja California herpetofauna*. Occasional Papers, California Academy of Sciences, vol. 1, no. 137. *7*

Murphy, T. M., Jr., and I. L. Brisbin, Jr.
1974.   Distribution of alligators in response to thermal gradients in a reactor cooling reservoir. In *Thermal ecology*, U.S. Atomic Energy Commission Symposium Series (CONF-730505), edited by J. W. Gibbons and R. R. Sharitz, 313–321. National Technical Information Service, Springfield, Va. *16, 18*

Muth, A.
1980.   Physiological ecology of desert iguana (*Dipsosaurus dorsalis*) eggs: Temperature and water relations. *Ecology* 61:1335–1343. *8*

Myers, G. S.
1966.   Derivation of the freshwater fish fauna of Central America. *Copeia* 1966:766–773. *12*

N

Nagy, K. A.
1973.   Behavior, diet, and reproduction in a desert lizard, *Sauromalus obesus*. *Copeia* 1973:93–102. *10*
1975.   Water and energy budgets of free-living animals: Measurement using isotopically labelled water. In *Environmental physiology of desert organisms*, edited by N. F. Hadley, 227–245. Dowden, Hutchinson and Ross, Stroudsburg, Pa. *21*
1982.   Energy requirements of free-living iguanid lizards. In *Iguanas of the world*, edited by G. M. Burghardt and A. S. Rand, 49–59. Noyes Publications, Park Ridge, N.J. *21*
1987.   Field metabolic rate and food requirement scaling in mammals and birds. *Ecological Monographs* 57:111–128. *21*

Nagy, K. A., and D. Q. Costa
1980.   Water flux in animals: Analysis of potential errors in the tritiated water method. *Journal of Physiology* (London) 238:454–465. *21*

Nagy, K. A., and V. H. Shoemaker
1975.   Energy and nitrogen budgets of the free-living desert lizard *Sauromalus obesus*. *Physiological Zoology* 48:252–262. *21*

Nakahara, M., T. Koyanagi, and M. Saiki
1977.   Temperature effect on the concentration of radionuclides by marine organisms. *Journal of Radiation Research* 18:122–131. *21*

Needham, J.
1931.   Vol. 3 of *Chemical embryology*. Cambridge University Press, London. *8*

Nei, M.
1978.   Estimation of average heterozygosity and genetic distance from a small number of individuals. *Genetics* 89:583–590. *6*

Neill, W. T.
1971.   *Last of the ruling reptiles: Alligators, crocodiles, and their kin*. Columbia University Press, New York. *2*
1974.   *Reptiles and amphibians in the service of man*. Pegasus Press, New York. *19*

Netting, M. G.
1936. Hibernation and migration of the spotted turtle, *Clemmys guttata* (Schneider). *Copeia* 1936:112. *16*

Nevo, E., B. Lavie, and R. Ben-Shlomo
1984. The evolutionary significance of genetic diversity: Ecological demographic and life history correlates. *Lecture Notes in Biomathematics* 53:77–125. *6*

Nichols, J. D., L. Viehman, R. H. Chabreck, and B. Fenderson
1976. *Simulation of a commercially harvested alligator population in Louisiana.* Louisiana State University Agricultural Experiment Station Bulletin no. 691. Baton Rouge, Louisiana. *3*

Norris, D. O.
1980. *Vertebrate endocrinology.* Lea and Febiger, Philadelphia. *19*

Norris, K. S.
1967. Color adaptation in desert reptiles and its thermal relationships. In *Lizard ecology: A symposium,* edited by W. M. Milstead, 162–229. University of Missouri Press, Columbia. *19*

Novak, S. S., and S. J. Morreale
1985. Survivorship and growth of hatchling *Pseudemys scripta* in saline environments [abstract]. Joint Annual Meeting of Society for the Study of Amphibians and Reptiles and the Herpetologists' League, Tampa.

O

Obbard, M. E.
1977. A radio-telemetry and tagging study of the activity in the common snapping turtle, *Chelydra serpentina.* Master's thesis. University of Guelph, Ontario. *18*
1983. Population ecology of the common snapping turtle, *Chelydra serpentina,* in north-central Ontario. Ph.D. dissertation. University of Guelph, Ontario. *3, 8*

Obbard, M. E., and R. J. Brooks
1979. Factors affecting basking in a northern population of the common snapping turtle, *Chelydra serpentina. Canadian Journal of Zoology* 57:435–440. *16, 18, 22*
1980. Nesting migrations of the snapping turtle (*Chelydra serpentina*). *Herpetologica* 36:158–162. *8*
1981a. Fate of overwintering clutches of the common snapping turtle (*Chelydra serpentina*) in Algonquin Park, Ontario. *Canadian Field Naturalist* 95:350–352. *8*
1981b. A radio-telemetry and mark-recapture study of activity in the common snapping turtle, *Chelydra serpentina. Copeia* 1981:630–637. *18, 22*

O'Brien, G. P., H. K. Smith, and J. R. Meyer
1965. An activity study of an isotopically-tagged lizard, *Sceloporus undulatus hyacinthinus* (Sauria: Iguanidae). *Southwestern Naturalist* 10:179–187. *21*

O'Brien, J. P., and W. L. Gojmerac
1956. Radiosensitivity of larval and adult amphibia in relation to temperature during and subsequent to irradiation. *Proceedings of the Society for Experimental Biology and Medicine* 92:13–16. *21*

Obst, F. J.
1985. *Schmuckschildkröten. Die Gattung* Chrysemys. A. Ziemsen Verlag, Wittenberg Lutherstadt. *1, 4, 7*

Odum, E. P.
1961. Excretion rate of radio-isotopes as indices of metabolic rates in nature: Biological half-life of zinc-65 in relation to temperature, food consumption, growth, and reproduction in arthropods. *Biological Bulletin* (Woods Hole) 121:371–372. *21*
1962. Relationships between structure and function in the ecosystem. *Japanese Journal of Ecology* 12:108–118. *21*
1971. *Fundamentals of ecology.* 3d ed. W. B. Saunders, Philadelphia.

Odum, E. P., and F. B. Golley
1963. Radioactive tracers as an aid to the measurement of energy flow at the population level in nature. In *Radioecology,* edited by V. Schultz and A. W. Klement, Jr., 403–410. Reinhold, New York. *21*

Odum, E. P., and E. J. Kuenzler
1963. Experimental isolation of food chains in an old-field ecosystem with the use of phosphorus-32. In *Radioecology,* edited by V. Schultz and A. W. Klement, Jr., 113–120. Reinhold, New York. *2, 21*

O'Hara, J.
1968. The influence of weight and temperature on the metabolic rate of sunfish. *Ecology* 49:159–161. *21*

Oliver, J. A.
1955. *The natural history of North American amphibians and reptiles.* Van Nostrand, New York. *3*

Orr, H.
1967. Excretion of orally administered zinc-65 by the cotton rat in the laboratory and field. *Health Physics* 13:15–20. *21*

Osorio, S. R., and R. B. Bury
1982. Ecology and status of the desert tortoise (*Gopherus agassizii*) on Tiburón Island, Sonora. In *North American tortoises: Ecology and conservation,* Wildlife Research Report no. 12, edited by R. B. Bury, 39–49. U.S. Fish and Wildlife Service, Washington, D.C. *14*

Overton, W. S.
1971. Estimating the numbers of animals in wildlife populations. In *Wildlife management techniques,* 3d ed., edited by R. H. Giles, 403–495. The Wildlife Society, Washington, D.C. *17*

P

Packard, G. C., and M. J. Packard
1980. Evolution of the cleidoic egg among reptilian antecedents of birds. *American Zoologist* 20:351–362. *8*
1984a. Comparative aspects of calcium metabolism in embryonic reptiles and birds. In *Respiration and metabolism of embryonic vertebrates,* edited by R. S. Seymour, 157–179. Junk, Dordrecht. *8*
1984b. Coupling of physiology of embryonic turtles to the hydric environment. In *Respiration and metabolism of embryonic vertebrates,* edited by R. S. Seymour, 99–119. Junk, Dordrecht. *8*

Packard, G. C., C. R. Tracy, and J. J. Roth
1977. The physiological ecology of reptilian eggs and embryos, and the evolution of viviparity within the class Reptilia. *Biological Review* 52:72–105. *8*

Packard, G. C., T. L. Taigen, T. J. Boardman, M. J. Packard, and C. R. Tracy
1979a. Changes in mass of softshell turtle (*Trionyx spiniferus*)

eggs incubated on substrates differing in water potential. *Herpetologica* 35:78–86. *8*

Packard, G. C., T. L. Taigen, M. J. Packard, and R. D.
Shuman
1979b. Water-vapor conductance of testudinian and crocodilian eggs (class Reptilia). *Respiration Physiology* 38:1–
10.

Packard, G. C., T. L. Taigen, M. J. Packard, and T. J.
Boardman
1980. Water relations of pliable-shelled eggs of common
snapping turtles (*Chelydra serpentina*). *Canadian Journal of
Zoology* 58:1404–1411. *8*

Packard, G. C., M. J. Packard, and T. J. Boardman
1981a. Patterns and possible significance of water exchange
by flexible-shelled eggs of painted turtles (*Chrysemys
picta*). *Physiological Zoology* 54:165–178. *8*
1982. An experimental analysis of the water relations of eggs
of Blanding's turtles (*Emydoidea blandingii*). *Zoological
Journal of the Linnean Society* 75:23–34. *8*

Packard, G. C., M. J. Packard, T. J. Boardman, and M. D.
Ashen
1981b. Possible adaptive value of water exchanges in flexible-
shelled eggs of turtles. *Science* 213:471–473. *8*

Packard, G. C., M. J. Packard, T. J. Boardman, K. A. Morris,
and R. D. Shuman
1983. Influence of water exchanges by flexible-shelled eggs of
painted turtles, *Chrysemys picta,* on metabolism and
growth of embryos. *Physiological Zoology* 56:217–230. *8*

Packard, G. C., M. J. Packard, K. Miller, and T. J. Boardman
1987. Influence of moisture, temperature, and substrate on
snapping turtle eggs and embryos. *Ecology* 68:983–
993. *8*

Packard, M. J.
1980. Ultrastructural morphology of the shell and shell
membrane of eggs of common snapping turtles
(*Chelydra serpentina*). *Journal of Morphology* 165:187–
204. *8*

Packard, M. J., and K. F. Hirsch
1986. Scanning electron microscopy of eggshells of contemporary reptiles. *Scanning Electron Microscopy* 4:1581–
1590. *8*

Packard, M. J., and G. C. Packard
1979. Structure of the shell and tertiary membranes of eggs of
softshell turtles (*Trionyx spiniferus*). *Journal of Morphology*
159:131–144. *8*
1986. Effect of water balance on growth and calcium mobilization of embryonic painted turtles (*Chrysemys picta*).
Physiological Zoology 59:398–405. *8*

Packard, M. J., G. C. Packard, and T. J. Boardman
1982. Structure of eggshells and water relations of reptilian
eggs. *Herpetologica* 38:136–155. *8, 12*

Packard, M. J., G. C. Packard, J. D. Miller, M. E. Jones, and
W. H. N. Gutzke
1985. Calcium mobilization, water balance, and growth in
embryos of the agamid lizard *Amphibolurus barbatus.*
Journal of Experimental Zoology 235:349–357. *8*

Packer, W. C.
1960. Bioclimatic influences on the breeding migration of
Taricha rivularis. Ecology 41:509–517. *2*

Parker, G. A., and M. Begon
1986. Optimal egg size and clutch size: Effects on environment and maternal phenotype. *American Naturalist*
128:573–592. *8*

Parker, H. W.
1935. A new melanic lizard from Transjordania, and some
speculations concerning melanism. *Proceedings of the
Zoological Society of London* (April 1935), part 1, 137–
142. *19*

Parker, W. S.
1984. Immigration and dispersal of slider turtles *Pseudemys
scripta* in Mississippi farm ponds. *American Midland Naturalist* 112:280–293. *1, 6, 14, 16, 17, 19*

Parker, W. S., and E. R. Pianka
1975. Comparative ecology of populations of the lizard *Uta
stansburiana. Copeia* 1975:615–632. *10*

Parker, W. S., and M. V. Plummer
1987. Population ecology. In *Snakes: Ecology and evolutionary
biology,* edited by R. A. Seigel, J. T. Collins, and S. S.
Novak, 253–301. Macmillan, New York. *3*

Parmenter, R. R.
1980. Effects of food availability and water temperature on
the feeding ecology of pond sliders (*Chrysemys s. scripta*).
Copeia 1980:503–514. *1–3, 9, 11, 17, 18, 20, 21*
1981. Digestive turnover rates in freshwater turtles: The influence of temperature and body size. *Comparative Biochemistry and Physiology* 70A:235–238. *2, 20, 21*

Parsons, T. S.
1960. The structure of the choanae of the Emydinae (Testudines, Testudinidae). *Bulletin of the Museum of Comparative Zoology* 123:113–127. *5*
1968. Variation in the choanal structure of Recent turtles.
Canadian Journal of Zoology 46:1235–1263. *1, 4*

Patt, H. M., and H. Quastler
1963. Radiation effects on cell renewal and related systems.
Physiological Reviews 43:357–396. *21*

Patt, H. M., and M. N. Swift
1948. Influence of temperature on the response of frogs to
x-radiation. *American Journal of Physiology* 155:388–
393. *21*

Patten, B. M.
1958. *Foundation of embryology.* McGraw-Hill, New York. *8*

Payne, R. B.
1972. Mechanisms and control of molt. In Vol. 2 of *Aviation
biology,* edited by D. S. Farner, J. R. King, and K. C.
Parkes, 103–149. Academic Press, New York. *19*

Peabody, F. E.
1958. A Kansas drouth recorded in growth zones of a bull-
snake. *Copeia* 1958:91–94. *10*
1961. Annual growth zones in living and fossil vertebrates.
Journal of Morphology 108:11–62. *10*

Pearse, A. S., S. Lepkovsky, and L. Hintze
1925. The growth and chemical composition of three species
of turtles fed on rations of pure foods. *Journal of Morphology and Physiology* 41:191–216. *20*

Pendleton, R. C.
1956. Uses of marking animals in ecological studies: La-
belling animals with radioisotopes. *Ecology* 37:686–
689. *21*

Pendleton, R. C., and A. W. Grundmann
1954. Use of ³²P in tracing some insect-plant relationships of the thistle, *Cirsium undulatum*. *Ecology* 35:187–191. *21*

Pendleton, R. C., C. W. Mays, R. D. Lloyd, and B. W. Church
1965. A trophic level effect on ¹³⁷Cs concentration. *Health Physics* 11:1503. *21*

Peters, E. L.
1986. Radiocesium kinetics in the yellow-bellied turtle (*Pseudemys scripta*). Master's thesis. University of Georgia. *21*

Petokas, P. J., and M. M. Alexander
1980. The nesting of *Chelydra serpentina* in northern NY. *Journal of Herpetology* 14:239–244. *8*

Petter-Rousseaux, A.
1953. Recherches sur la croissance et le cycle d'activité testiculaire de *Natrix natrix helvetica* (Lacépède). *Terre Vie* 4:175–223. *10*

Pianka, E. R.
1970. On "r" and "K" selection. *American Naturalist* 104:592–597. *3, 15*

1972. r- and K-selection or b- and d-selection? *American Naturalist* 106:581–588. *3, 15*

1974. *Evolutionary ecology.* Harper and Row, New York. *8*

1986. *Ecology and natural history of desert lizards.* Princeton University Press, Princeton, N.J. *1*

Pianka, E. R., and W. S. Parker
1972. Ecology of the iguanid lizard *Callisaurus draconoides*. *Copeia* 1972:493–508. *10*

1975. Ecology of horned lizards: A review with special reference to *Phrynosoma platyrhinos*. *Copeia* 1975:141–162.

Pieau, C.
1972. Effects de la température sur le development des glands genitales chez les embryons de deux chelonians *Emys orbicularis* (L.) et *Testudo graeca* (L.). *Comptes Rendus Hebdomadaires des Seances de l'Académie des Sciences* (Paris) 274:719–722. *8*

1974. Différenciation du sexe en fonction de la température chez les embryons d'*Emys orbicularis* L. (Chelonien): Effets des hormones sexuelles. *Annales d'Embryologie et de Morphogenese* 7:365–394. *14*

Pieau, M. C.
1982. Modalities of the action of temperature on sexual differentiation in field-developing embryos of the European pond turtle *Emys orbicularis* (Emydidae). *Journal of Experimental Zoology* 220:353–360. *8*

Plummer, M. V.
1977. Activity, habitat, and population structure in the turtle, *Trionyx muticus*. *Copeia* 1977:431–440. *14*

Plummer, M. V., and H. W. Shirer
1975. *Movement patterns in a river population of the softshell turtle* Trionyx muticus. Occasional Papers of the Museum of Natural History, University of Kansas, no. 43. *16, 18*

Poinar, G. O., Jr., and D. C. Cannatella
1987. An Upper Eocene frog from the Dominican Republic and its implication for Caribbean biogeography. *Science* 237:1215–1216. *5*

Pope, C. H.
1935. *Natural history of central Asia.* Vol. 10 of *The reptiles of China.* American Museum of Natural History, New York.

Porter, K. R.
1972. *Herpetology.* W. B. Saunders Co., Philadelphia. *19*

Porter, W. P.
1967. Solar radiation through the living body walls of vertebrates with emphasis on desert reptiles. *Ecological Monographs* 37:273–296. *19*

Porter, W. P., and D. M. Gates
1969. Thermodynamic equilibria of animals with environment. *Ecological Monographs* 39:227–244. *22*

Porter, W. P., and F. C. James
1979. Behavioral implications of mechanistic ecology, II: The African rainbow lizard, *Agama agama*. *Copeia* 1979:594–619. *22*

Porter, W. P., and C. R. Tracy
1983. Biophysical analyses of energetics, time-space utilization, and distributional limits of lizards. In *Lizard ecology: Studies of a model organism*, edited by R. B. Huey, E. R. Pianka, and T. W. Schoener, 55–83. Harvard University Press, Cambridge. *20*

Porter, W. P., J. W. Mitchell, W. A. Beckman, and C. B. Dewitt
1973. Behavioral implications of mechanistic ecology: Thermal and behavioral modeling of desert ectotherms and their microenvironment. *Oecologia* (Berlin) 13:1–54. *22*

Pough, F. H.
1970. A quick method for permanently marking snakes and turtles. *Herpetologica* 26:428–430. *2*

Powell, C. B.
1967. Female sexual cycles of *Chrysemys picta* and *Clemmys insculpta* in Nova Scotia. *Canadian Field Naturalist* 81:134–140. *3, 9*

Prange, H. D., and R. A. Ackerman
1974. Oxygen consumption and mechanisms of gas exchange of green turtle (*Chelonia mydas*) eggs and hatchlings. *Copeia* 1974:758–763. *8*

Pregill, G.
1981a. An appraisal of the vicariance hypothesis of Caribbean biogeography and its application to West Indian terrestrial vertebrates. *Systematic Zoology* 30:147–155. *5*

1981b. *Late Pleistocene herpetofaunas from Puerto Rico.* University of Kansas Museum of Natural History Miscellaneous Publication no. 71. *5*

Preston, R. E.
1966. Turtles of the Gilliland faunule from the Pleistocene of Knox County, Texas. *Papers of the Michigan Academy of Science, Arts, and Letters* 51:221–239. *5*

Prestt, I.
1971. An ecological study of the viper *Vipera berus* in southern Britain. *Journal of Zoology* (London) 164:373–418. *10*

Price, P. W.
1980. *Evolutionary biology of parasites.* Princeton University Press, Princeton, N.J. *23*

1984. Communities of specialists: Vacant niches in ecological and evolutionary time. In *Ecological communities: Conceptual issues and the evidence*, edited by D. R. Strong, Jr., D. Simberloff, L. G. Abele, and A. B. Thistle, 510–523. Princeton University Press, Princeton, N.J. *23*

Price, P. W., and K. M. Clancy
1983.   Patterns in number of helminth parasite species in freshwater fishes. *Journal of Parasitology* 69:449–454. *23*
Price, T. D.
1984.   The evolution of sexual size dimorphism in Darwin's finches. *American Naturalist* 123:500–518.
Pritchard, P. C. H.
1969.   Sea turtles of the Guianas. *Bulletin of the Florida State Museum Biological Sciences* 13:85–140. *10*
1971.   Galapagos sea turtles—preliminary findings. *Journal of Herpetology* 5:1–9. *19*
1979.   *Encyclopedia of turtles.* TFH, Neptune, N.J. *7, 19*
Pritchard, P. C. H., and P. Trebbau
1984.   *The turtles of Venezuela.* Society for the Study of Amphibians and Reptiles, Contributions to Herpetology, vol. 2. Miami University, Oxford, Ohio. *4, 5, 7, 12, 14, 16, 20*
Pritchard, P. C. H., P. R. Bacon, F. H. Berry, A. F. Carr, J. Fletemeyer, R. M. Gallagher, S. R. Hopkins, R. R. Lankford, R. M. Márquez, L. H. Ogren, W. G. Pringle, Jr., H. A. Reichert, and R. Witham
1983.   *Manual of sea turtle research and conservation techniques.* Center for Environmental Education, Washington, D.C. *15*
Prosser, C. L.
1986.   *Adaptational biology: Molecules to organisms.* John Wiley and Sons, New York. *22*
Pulliam, H. R., G. W. Barrett, and E. P. Odum
1969.   Bioelimination of tracer ^{65}Zn in relation to metabolic rates in mice. In *Symposium on radioecology,* U.S. Atomic Energy Commission Symposium Series (CONF-670503), edited by D. J. Nelson and F. C. Evans, 725–730. National Technical Information Service, Springfield, Va. *21*

Q

Quay, W. B.
1972.   Sexual and relative growth differences in brain regions of the turtle *Pseudemys scripta* (Schoepff). *Copeia* 1972:541–546.

R

Radcliffe, C. W., and T. P. Maslin
1975.   A new subspecies of the red rattlesnake, *Crotalus ruber,* from San Lorenzo Sur Island, Baja California Norte, Mexico. *Copeia* 1975:490–493.
Ralls, K.
1976.   Mammals in which females are larger than males. *Quarterly Review of Biology* 51:245–276.
Ralls, K., and P. H. Harvey
1985.   Geographic variation in size and sexual dimorphism in North American weasels. *Biological Journal of the Linnean Society* 25:119–167.
Ralph, C. L.
1969.   The control of color in birds. *American Zoologist* 9:521–530. *19*
Ralph, C. L., B. T. Firth, and J. S. Turner
1979.   The role of the pineal body in ectotherm thermoregulation. *American Zoologist* 19:273–293. *19*
Ramirez, J. R., and H. C. Dessauer
1957.   Isolation and characterization of two hemoglobins found in the turtle *Pseudemys scripta elegans. Proceedings of the Society for Experimental Biology and Medicine* 96:690–694. *5*
Rand, A. S.
1964.   Ecological distribution in anoline lizards of Puerto Rico. *Ecology* 45:745–752. *10*
Randolph, J. C., P. A. Randolph, and C. A. Barlow
1976.   Variations in energy content of some carabid beetles in eastern Canada. *Canadian Journal of Zoology* 54:10–18. *2*
Raney, E. C., and E. A. Lachner
1942.   Summer food of *Chrysemys picta marginata* in Chautauqua Lake, New York. *Copeia* 1942:83–85. *14*
Rathke, H.
1848.   *Uber de Entwicklung der Schildkroten.* Fredrich Vieweg, Brunswick. *8*
Rausch, R.
1947.   Observations on some helminths parasitic in Ohio turtles. *American Midland Naturalist* 38:434–442. *23*
Ream, C., and R. Ream
1966.   The influence of sampling methods on the estimation of population structure in painted turtles. *American Midland Naturalist* 75:325–338. *14*
Ream, C. H.
1967.   Some aspects of the ecology of painted turtles, Lake Mendota, Wisconsin. Ph.D. thesis. University of Wisconsin—Madison.
Regan, J. D.
1961.   Melanism in the poeciliid fish, *Gambusia affinis* (Baird and Girard). *American Midland Naturalist* 65:139–143. *19*
Reichle, D. E., and R. I. Van Hook, Jr.
1970.   Radionuclide dynamics in insect food chains. *Manitoba Entomologist* 4:22–32. *21*
Reichle, D. E., P. B. Dunaway, and D. J. Nelson
1970.   Turnover and concentration of radionuclides in food chains. *Nuclear Safety* 11:43–55.
Rensch, B.
1960.   *Evolution above the species level.* Columbia University Press, New York.
Rhodin, A. G. J., R. A. Mittermeier, and J. R. McMorris
1984.   *Platemys macrocephala,* a new species of chelid turtle from central Bolivia and the Pantanal region of Brazil. *Herpetologica* 40:38–46.
Richardson, C. J., and P. E. Marshall
1986.   Processes controlling movement, storage, and export of phosphorus in a fen peatland. *Ecological Monographs* 56:279–302. *21*
Richardson, J. I., and T. H. Richardson
1982.   An experimental population model for the loggerhead sea turtle (*Caretta caretta*). In *Biology and conservation of sea turtles,* edited by K. A. Bjorndal, 165–176. Smithsonian Institution Press, Washington, D.C. *15*
Richardson, T. H., J. I. Richardson, C. Ruckdeschel, and M. W. Dix
1978.   Remigration patterns of loggerhead sea turtles (*Caretta caretta*) nesting on Little Cumberland and Cumberland Islands, Georgia. In *Proceedings of the Florida Interregional Conference on Sea Turtles,* edited by G. E. Henderson, 39–44. Florida Department of Natural Resources, St. Petersburg. *15*

Richmond, C. R.
1958.   *Retention and excretion of radionuclides of the alkali metals by five mammalian species.* U.S. Atomic Energy Commission Report no. LA-2207. Los Alamos Scientific Laboratory, N.Mex. *21*

Ricklefs, R. E.
1979.   *Ecology.* Chiron Press, New York. *15*

Ricklefs, R. E., and J. Burger
1977.   Composition of eggs of the diamondback terrapin. *American Midland Naturalist* 97:232–235. *8*

Ricklefs, R. E., and J. Cullen
1973.   Embryonic growth of the green iguana *Iguana iguana.* *Copeia* 1973:296–305.

Riddle, O.
1909.   The rate of digestion in cold-blooded vertebrates: The influence of season and temperature. *American Journal of Physiology* 24:447–458. *20*

Riggs, M. R., A. D. Lemly, and G. W. Esch
1987.   The growth, biomass, and fecundity of *Bothriocephalus acheilognathi* in a North Carolina cooling reservoir. *Journal of Parasitology* 73:893–900.

Rising, J. D.
1987.   Geographic variation of sexual dimorphism in size of savannah sparrows (*Passerculus sandwichensis*): A test of hypothesis. *Evolution* 41:514–524.

Risley, P. L.
1933.   Observations on the natural history of the common musk turtle, *Sternotherus odoratus* (Latreille). *Papers of the Michigan Academy of Science, Arts, and Letters* 17:685–711. *8, 14*

Robertson, R.
1971.   *Lepidoptera genetics.* Pergamon Press, Oxford. *8*

Robin, E. D., J. W. Vester, H. V. Murdaugh, Jr., and J. E. Millen
1964.   Prolonged anaerobiosis in a vertebrate: Anaerobic metabolism in the freshwater turtle. *Journal of Cellular and Comparative Physiology* 63:287–297.

Rogers, A. W.
1973.   *Techniques of autoradiography.* Elservier, New York. *21*

Rogers, K. L.
1976.   Herpetofauna of the Beck Ranch local fauna (Upper Pliocene: Blancan) of Texas. *Publications of the Museum, Michigan State University,* Paleontological Series 1, 163–200. *5*

Rohwer, S.
1975.   The social significance of avian winter plumage variability. *Evolution* 29:593–610. *19*

Rohwer, S., and P. W. Ewald
1981.   The cost of dominance and advantage of subordination in a badge signaling system. *Evolution* 35:441–454. *19*

Romanoff, A. L.
1967.   *Biochemistry of the avian embryo.* Wiley-Interscience, New York. *8*

Romanoff, A. L., and A. J. Romanoff
1949.   *The avian egg.* John Wiley and Sons, New York.

Romer, A. S.
1956.   *Osteology of the reptiles.* University of Chicago Press, Chicago. *4*

Root, R. B.
1973.   Organization of plant-arthropod association in simple and diverse habitats: The fauna of collards (*Brassica oleracea*). *Ecological Monographs* 43:95–124. *23*

Rosado, R. D.
1967.   La "Jicotea." *International Turtle and Tortoise Society Journal* 1(3):16–19, 42. *12*

Rose, F. L.
1969.   Desiccation rates and temperature relationships of *Terrapene ornata* following scute removal. *Southwestern Naturalist* 14:67–72. *10*

Rose, F. L., and J. L. Dobie
1983.   *Chrysemys-Pseudemys-Trachemys:* A taxonomic dilemma [abstract]. *26th Annual Meeting of the Society for the Study of Amphibians and Reptiles,* 86. *5*

Rose, F. L., and F. W. Judd
1982.   The biology and status of Berlandier's tortoise (*Gopherus berlandieri*). In *North American tortoises: Conservation and ecology,* Wildlife Research Report no. 12, edited by R. B. Bury, 57–70. U.S. Fish and Wildlife Service, Washington, D.C. *14, 16*

Rose, F. L., and W. G. Weaver
1966.   Two new species of *Chrysemys* (= *Pseudemys*) from the Florida Pliocene. *Tulane Studies in Geology* 5:41–48. *4, 5*

Rose, M. R., and B. Charlesworth
1980.   A test of evolutionary theories of senescence. *Nature* 287:141–142. *3*
1981.   Genetics of life-history in *Drosophila melanogaster,* II: Exploratory selection experiments. *Genetics* 97:187–196. *3*

Rose, M. R., and E. W. Hutchinson
1987.   Evolution of aging. In *Review of biological research in aging,* edited by M. Rothstein, 23–32. Alan R. Liss, New York. *3*

Ross, J. P.
1982.   Historical decline of loggerhead, ridley, and leatherback sea turtles. In *Biology and conservation of sea turtles,* edited by K. A. Bjorndal, 189–195. Smithsonian Institution Press, Washington, D.C. *3*
1984.   Adult sex ratio in the green sea turtle. *Copeia* 1984:774–776. *14*

Ruby, D. E.
1976.   The behavioral ecology of the viviparous lizard, *Sceloporus jarrovi.* Ph.D. dissertation. University of Michigan. *10*

Ruckdeschel, C., and G. R. Zug
1982.   Mortality of sea turtles *Caretta caretta* in coastal waters of Georgia. *Biological Conservation* 22:5–9.

Ruibal, R., R. Philibosian, and J. L. Adkins
1972.   Reproductive cycle and growth in the lizard *Anolis acutus.* *Copeia* 1972:509–518.

Rundo, J.
1967.   Kinetics of Sr-85 deposition in the skeleton during chronic exposure. In *Strontium metabolism,* edited by J. M. A. Lenihan, J. F. Loutit, and J. H. Martin, 131–148. Academic Press, New York. *21*

Rundquist, E. M.
1985.   Life history: *Pseudemys scripta elegans* (red-eared slider). *Herpetological Review* 16:113. *17*

Russell, L. S.
1934.   Fossil turtles from Saskatchewan and Alberta. *Transactions of the Royal Society of Canada,* ser. 3, vol. 28, 101–111. *4*

Ryan, M. J.
1985.   *The Tungara frog*. University of Chicago Press, Chicago.

[S]

Sacher, G. A., and E. Staffeldt
1971.   Species differences in sensitivity of myomorph and sciuromorph rodents to life shortening by chronic gamma irradiation. In *Radionuclides in ecosystems*, Proceedings of the Third National Symposium on Radioecology, U.S. Atomic Energy Commission Symposium Series (CONF-710501–P2), edited by D. J. Nelson, 1042–1047. National Technical Information Service, Springfield, Va. *21*

Sachsse, W.
1975.   *Chinemys reevesii* var. *unicolor* and *Clemmys bealei* var. *quadriocellata*—Ausprägungen von sexualdimorphismus der beiden "Nominatiformen." *Salamandra* 11:20–26. *19*

Sampedro, A., V. Berovides, and A. Perera
1985.   Variaciones etareas de *Pseudemys decussata* en la Ciénega de Zapata. *Poeyana* 287:1–7. *19*

Sanders, H. L.
1968.   Marine benthic diversity: A comparative study. *American Naturalist* 102:243–282. *23*

Sanderson, R. A.
1974.   Sexual dimorphism in the Barbour's map turtle, *Malaclemys barbouri* (Carr and Marchand). Master's thesis, University of South Florida. *2, 14*

Sandor, T.
1969.   A comparative survey of steroids and steroidogenic pathways throughout the vertebrates. *General and Comparative Endocrinology* 2:284–298. *19*

SAS Institute
1982.   *SAS user's guide: Statistics*. Edited by A. A. Ray. SAS Institute, Cary, N.C. *21*

Savage, J. M.
1966.   The origins and history of the Central American herpetofauna. *Copeia* 1966:719–766. *12*

Schad, G. A.
1963.   Niche diversification in a parasitic species flock. *Nature* 198:404–406. *23*

Schaffer, W. M.
1974a. Optimal reproductive effort in fluctuating environments. *American Naturalist* 108:783–790. *3*
1974b. Selection for optimal life histories: The effects of age structure. *Ecology* 55:291–303. *3*

Schaffer, W. M., and P. F. Elson
1975.   The adaptive significance of variations in life history among local populations of Atlantic salmon in North America. *Ecology* 56:577–590. *3*

Schaffer, W. M., and M. D. Gadgil
1975.   Selection for optimal life histories in plants. In *The ecology and evolution of communities*, edited by A. Cody and J. Diamond, 142–157. Harvard University Press, Cambridge. *3, 8*

Schaffer, W. M., and M. L. Rosenzweig
1977.   Selection for optimal life histories, II: Multiple equilibria and the evolution of alternative reproductive strategies. *Ecology* 58:60–72. *15*

Schalles, J. F.
1979.   Comparative limnology and ecosystem analysis of Carolina bay ponds on the Upper Coastal Plain of South Carolina. Ph.D. dissertation. Emory University. *2*

Schalles, J. F., R. R. Sharitz, J. W. Gibbons, G. J. Leversee, and J. N. Knox
1989.   Carolina bays of the Savannah River Plant, Aiken, South Carolina. U.S. Department of Energy, Savannah River Plant National Environmental Research Park, Aiken, S.C. *2*

Scheffe, H.
1959.   *The analysis of variance*. John Wiley and Sons, New York. *18*

Schell, S. C.
1980.   *Trematodes of North America north of Mexico*. University of Idaho Press, Moscow, Idaho. *23*

Schmidt, K. P.
1953.   *A checklist of North American amphibians and reptiles*. 6th ed. American Society of Ichthyologists and Herpetologists. University of Chicago Press, Chicago. *7*

Schmidt, K. P., and D. D. Davis
1941.   *Field book of snakes*. J. P. Putnam's Sons, New York. *2*

Schmidt, W. J.
1943.   Über den Aufbau der Kalkschale bei den Schildkroeteneiern. *Zeitschrift fuer Morphologie der Tiere* 40: 1–16. *8*

Schoener, T. W., and A. Schoener
1978.   Estimating and interpreting body-size growth in some *Anolis* lizards. *Copeia* 1978:390–405. *10*

Schoepff, J. D.
1792–1801. *Historia testudinum iconibus illustrata*. Ionnis Iacobi Palmii, Erlangae. *4, 7*

Schreckhise, R. G.
1974.   Strontium kinetics in mule deer. Ph.D. dissertation. Colorado State University. *21*

Schreckhise, R. G., and F. W. Whicker
1976.   A model for predicting Sr-90 levels in mule deer. In *Radioecology and energy resources*, edited by C. E. Cushing, Jr., 148–156. Dowden, Hutchinson and Ross, Stroudsburg, Pa. *21*

Schubauer, J. P.
1981a. The ecology and behavior of an aquatic turtle, *Pseudemys scripta*, inhabiting a thermally altered reservoir, Par Pond, South Carolina. Master's thesis. State University of New York College at Buffalo. *18*
1981b. A reliable radio-telemetry tracking system suitable for studies of chelonians. *Journal of Herpetology* 15:117–120. *18, 20*

Schubauer, J. P., and R. R. Parmenter
1981.   Winter feeding by aquatic turtles in a southeastern reservoir. *Journal of Herpetology* 15:444–447. *10, 16, 18, 20, 22*

Schueler, F. W.
1983.   Reticulate melanism in Canadian western painted turtles. *Blue Jay* 41:83–91. *19*

Schuett, G. W., and R. E. Gatten, Jr.
1980.   Thermal preference in snapping turtles (*Chelydra serpentina*). *Copeia* 1980:149–152. *22*

Schultz, V., and F. W. Whicker
1982.   *Radioecological techniques*. Plenum Press, New York. *21*

Schwartz, C. W., and E. R. Schwartz
1974. *The three-toed box turtle in central Missouri: Its population, home range, and movements.* Missouri Department of Conservation, Terrestrial Series, no. 5. *14*

Schwartz, J. H., and W. Flamenbaum
1976. Heavy metal–induced alterations in ion transport by turtle urinary bladder. *American Journal of Physiology* 230:1582–1589. *21*

Schwarzkopf, L., and R. J. Brooks
1985. Application of operative environmental temperatures to analysis of basking behavior in *Chrysemys picta. Herpetologica* 41:206–212. *20, 22*
1986. Annual variations in reproductive characteristics of painted turtles (*Chrysemys picta*). *Canadian Journal of Zoology* 64:1148–1151. *11, 15*
1987. Nest-site selection and offspring sex ratio in painted turtles, *Chrysemys picta. Copeia* 1987:53–61. *8*

Scott, D. E., F. W. Whicker, and J. W. Gibbons
1986. Effect of season on the retention of ^{137}Cs and ^{90}Sr by the yellow-bellied slider turtle (*Pseudemys scripta*). *Canadian Journal of Zoology* 64:2850–2853. *16, 21*

Scott, J. R., C. R. Tracy, and D. Pettus
1982. A biophysical analysis of daily and seasonal utilization of climate space by a montane snake. *Ecology* 63:482–493. *22*

Scott, T. R.
1979. The chemical senses. In *Turtles: Perspectives and research,* edited by M. Harless and H. Morlock, 267–287. John Wiley and Sons, New York. *20*

Scribner, K. T., and M. H. Smith
n.d. Genetic variability and antler development. In *Horns, pronghorns, and antlers: Evolution, morphology, and social significance of cranial appendages in ruminants,* edited by G. A. Bubenik and A. B. Bubenik. Vol. 2 of *Morphology, physiology, and management.* Kluwer Academic Publishers, Dordrecht, Netherlands. In press. *6*

Scribner, K. T., M. H. Smith, and J. W. Gibbons
1984a. Genetic differentiation among local populations of the yellow-bellied slider turtle (*Pseudemys scripta*). *Herpetologica* 40:382–387. *15*

Scribner, K. T., M. H. Smith, and P. E. Johns
1984b. Age, condition, and genetic effects on incidence of spike bucks. *Proceedings of the Annual Conference, Southeastern Association of Fish and Wildlife Agencies* 38:23–32. *6*

Scribner, K. T., M. C. Wooten, M. H. Smith, and P. E. Johns
1985. Demographic and genetic characteristics of white-tailed deer populations subjected to still or dog hunting. In *Game harvest management: Proceedings of a symposium on game harvest strategies,* edited by S. L. Beasom and S. F. Roberson, 197–212. Caesar Kleberg Wildlife Research Institute, Kingsville, Tex. *6*

Scribner, K. T., J. E. Evans, S. J. Morreale, M. H. Smith, and J. W. Gibbons
1986. Genetic divergence among populations of the yellow-bellied slider turtle (*Pseudemys scripta*) separated by aquatic and terrestrial habitats. *Copeia* 1986:691–700. *6, 15–17*

Searle, A. G.
1968. *Comparative genetics of coat colour in mammals.* Logos Press, London. *19*

Segal, S. J.
1957. Response of weaver finch to chorionic gonadotropin and hypophyseal luteinizing hormone. *Science* 126:1242–1243. *19*

Seidel, M. E.
1988. Revision of the West Indian emydid turtles (Testudines). *American Museum Novitates* 2918:1–41. *5, 19*

Seidel, M. E., and M. D. Adkins
1987. Biochemical comparisons among West Indian *Trachemys* (Emydidae: Testudines). *Copeia* 1987:485–489. *5, 6*

Seidel, M. E., and S. J. Inchaustegui Miranda
1984. Status of the trachemyd turtles (Testudines: Emydidae) on Hispaniola. *Journal of Herpetology* 18:468–479. *1, 4, 5, 19*

Seidel, M. E., and R. V. Lucchino
1981. Allozymic and morphological variation among the musk turtles *Sternotherus carinatus, S. depressus,* and *S. minor* (Kinosternidae). *Copeia* 1981:119–128. *6*

Seidel, M. E., and H. M. Smith
1986. *Chrysemys, Pseudemys, Trachemys* (Testudines: Emydidae): Did Agassiz have it right? *Herpetologica* 42:242–248. *1, 4, 5, 7, 23*

Seidel, M. E., S. L. Reynolds, and R. V. Lucchino
1981. Phylogenetic relationships among musk turtles (genus *Sternotherus*) and genic variation in *Sternotherus odoratus. Herpetologica* 37:161–165. *6*

Seigel, R. A.
1980a. Nesting habits of diamondback terrapins (*Malaclemys terrapin*) on the Atlantic Coast of Florida. *Transactions of the Kansas Academy of Science* 83:239–246. *8*
1980b. Predation by raccoons on diamondback terrapins, *Malaclemys terrapin tequesta. Journal of Herpetology* 14:87–89. *14, 15*

Seigel, R. A., and N. B. Ford
1987. Reproductive ecology. In *Snakes: Ecology and evolutionary biology,* edited by R. A. Seigel, J. T. Collins, and S. S. Novak, 210–252. Macmillan, New York. *3*

Seigel, R. A., J. T. Collins, and S. S. Novak, eds.
1987. *Snakes: Ecology and evolutionary biology.* Macmillan, New York.

Selander, R. K.
1966. Sexual dimorphism and differential niche utilization in birds. *Condor* 68:113–151.

Selander, R. K., and D. R. Giller
1963. Species limits in the woodpecker genus *Centurus* (Aves). *Bulletin of the American Museum of Natural History* 124:261–271.

Semlitsch, R. D.
1980. Growth and metamorphosis of larval dwarf salamanders (*Eurycea quadridigitata*). *Herpetologica* 36:138–140. *2*
1981a. Effects of implanted tantalum-182 wire tags on the mole salamander, *Ambystoma talpoideum. Copeia* 1981:735–737. *21*
1981b. Terrestrial activity and summer home range of the

mole salamander (*Ambystoma talpoideum*). *Canadian Journal of Zoology* 59:315–322. *2, 21*

1983.   Terrestrial movements of an eastern tiger salamander, *Ambystoma tigrinum*. *Herpetological Review* 14:112–113. *21*

Semlitsch, R. D., and J. W. Gibbons

1978.   Reproductive allocation in the brown water snake, *Natrix taxispilota*. *Copeia* 1978:721–723. *8*

Semlitsch, R. D., and M. A. McMillan

1980.   Breeding migrations, population size structure, and reproduction of the dwarf salamander, *Eurycea quadridigitata*, in South Carolina. *Brimleyana* 1980(3):97–105. *2*

Semlitsch, R. D., and G. B. Moran

1984.   Ecology of the redbelly snake (*Storeria occipitomaculata*) using mesic habitats in South Carolina. *American Midland Naturalist* 111:33–40. *2*

Semlitsch, R. D., and J. H. K. Pechmann

1985.   Diel pattern of migratory activity for several species of pond-breeding salamanders. *Copeia* 1985:86–91. *2*

Semlitsch, R. D., K. L. Brown, and J. P. Caldwell

1981.   Habitat utilization, seasonal activity, and population size structure of the southeastern crowned snake *Tantilla coronata*. *Herpetologica* 37:40–46. *2*

Sergeev, A.

1937.   Some materials to the problem of the reptilian post-embryonic growth. *Zoological Journal* (Moscow) 16:723–735. *10*

Service, P. M., E. W. Hutchinson, and M. R. Rose

1988.   Multiple genetic mechanisms for the evolution of senescence in *Drosophila melanogaster*. *Evolution* 42:708–716. *3*

Sexton, O. J.

1958.   The relationship between habitat preferences of hatchling *Chelydra serpentina* and the physical structure of the vegetation. *Ecology* 39:751–754. *18*

1959a.   A method of estimating the age of painted turtles for use in demographic studies. *Ecology* 40:716–718. *3, 8, 10*

1959b.   Spatial and temporal movements of a population of the painted turtle, *Chrysemys picta marginata* (Agassiz). *Ecological Monographs* 29:113–140. *1, 3, 14, 16, 18, 20, 22*

1965.   The annual cycle of growth and shedding in the midland painted turtle, *Chrysemys picta marginata*. *Copeia* 1965:314–318. *8*

Sexton, O. J., G. M. Veith, and D. M. Phillips

1979.   Ultrastructure of the eggshell of two species of anoline lizards. *Journal of Experimental Zoology* 207:227–236. *8*

Seymour, R. S.

1982.   Physiological adaptations to aquatic life. In Vol. 13 of *Biology of the Reptilia*, edited by C. Gans and F. H. Pough, 1–51. Academic Press, New York.

Shapiro, H. S.

1968.   Deoxyribonucleic acid content per cell of various organisms. In *CRC handbook of biochemistry*, edited by H. A. Sorber, H52–H61. Chemical Rubber Co., Cleveland. *21*

Sharitz, R. R., and J. W. Gibbons

1982.   *The ecology of southeastern shrub bogs (pocosins) and Carolina bays: A community profile*. U.S. Fish and Wildlife Service,

Division of Biological Services Report no. FWS/OBS-82/04. Washington, D.C. *2*

Sharitz, R. R., K. W. Dyer, N. C. Martin, C. E. Mitchell, and R. L. Schneider

1986.   *Wetlands*. Vol. 1 of *Comprehensive cooling water report*. Savannah River Ecology Laboratory, Aiken, S.C. *2*

Sharp, P. J., and H. Klandorff

1985.   Environmental and physiological factors controlling thyroid function in galliformes. In *The endocrine system and the environment*, edited by B. K. Follett, S. Ishii, and A. Chandola, 175–188. Springer-Verlag, New York. *19*

Shaw, G.

1802.   *General zoology; or, Systematic natural history*. Vol. 3, part 1. G. Kearsley, London. *19*

Shealy, R. M.

1976.   The natural history of the Alabama map turtle, *Graptemys pulchra* Baur, in Alabama. *Bulletin of the Florida State Museum Biological Sciences* 21:47–111. *3, 14*

Sheeler, P., and A. A. Barber

1965.   Reticulocytosis and iron incorporation in the rabbit and turtle: A comparative study. *Comparative Biochemistry and Physiology* 16:63–76. *5*

Shellabarger, C. J., A. Gorbman, F. C. Schatzlein, and D. McGill

1956.   Some quantitative and qualitative aspects of I-131 metabolism in turtles. *Endocrinology* 59:331–339. *21*

Shields, W. M.

1982.   *Philopatry, inbreeding, and the evolution of sex*. State University of New York Press, Albany. *6*

Shine, R.

1978.   Sexual size and male combat in snakes. *Oecologia* (Berlin) 33:269–277. *10*

1979.   Sexual selection and sexual dimorphism in amphibia. *Copeia* 1979:297–306.

Shively, S. H., and J. F. Jackson

1985.   Factors limiting the upstream distribution of the Sabine map turtle. *American Midland Naturalist* 114:292–303. *14*

Shoop, C. R.

1965.   Orientation of *Ambystoma maculatum*: Movements to and from breeding ponds. *Science* 149:558–559. *2*

1968.   Migratory orientation of *Ambystoma maculatum*: Movements near breeding ponds and displacements of migrating individuals. *Biological Bulletin* (Woods Hole) 135:230–238. *2*

1974.   Yearly variation in larval survival of *Ambystoma maculatum*. *Ecology* 55:440–444. *2, 21*

Shoop, C. R., and T. L. Doty

1972.   Migratory orientation by marbled salamanders (*Ambystoma opacum*) near a breeding area. *Behavioral Biology* 7:131–136. *21*

Sidis, I., and A. Gasith

1985.   Food habits of the Caspian terrapin (*Mauremys caspica rivulata*) in unpolluted and polluted habitats in Israel. *Journal of Herpetology* 19:108–115. *20*

Silas, E. G., M. Rajagopalan, S. S. Dan, and A. Bastian Fernando

1984.   Observations on mass nesting and immediate postmass nesting influxes of the olive ridley, *Lep-*

idochelys olivacea, at Gahirmatha, Orissa—1984 season. In *Sea turtle research and conservation*, Bulletin of the Central Marine Fisheries Research Institute, no. 35, 76–82. Cochin, India.

Silva, A. M. R., G. S. Moraes, and G. F. Wassermann
1984. Seasonal variations of testicular morphology and plasma levels of testosterone in the turtle *Chrysemys dorbigni*. *Comparative Biochemistry and Physiology* 78A:153–157. *19*

Simanek, D. E.
1978. Genetic variability and population structure of *Poecilia latipinna*. *Nature* 276:612–614. *6*

Simpson, G. G.
1950. History of the fauna of Latin America. *American Scientist* 38:361–389. *12*

Sites, J. W., Jr., I. F. Greenbaum, and J. W. Bickham
1981. Biochemical systematics of neotropical turtles of the genus *Rhinoclemmys* (Emydidae: Batagurinae). *Herpetologica* 37:256–264. *6*

Sites, J. W., Jr., J. W. Bickham, B. A. Pytel, I. F. Greenbaum, and B. A. Bates
1984. Biochemical characters and the reconstruction of turtle phylogenies: Relationships among Batagurinae genera. *Systematic Zoology* 33:137–158. *5*

Skoczylas, R.
1978. Physiology of the digestive tract. In Vol. 8 of *Biology of the Reptilia*, edited by C. Gans, 589–717. Academic Press, New York. *20*

Skorepa, A. C.
1966. The deliberate consumption of stones by the ornate box turtle, *Terrapene o. ornata* Agassiz. *Journal of the Ohio Herpetological Society* 5:108.

Slatkin, M.
1981. Estimating levels of gene flow in natural populations. *Genetics* 99:323–335. *6*

Slobodkin, L. B.
1967. Toward a predictive theory of evolution. In *Population biology and evolution*, edited by R. C. Lewontin, 187–205. Syracuse University Press, Syracuse, N.Y. *23*

Smith, C. C., and S. D. Fretwell
1974. The optimal balance between size and number of offspring. *American Naturalist* 108:499–506. *8, 11*

Smith, D. C.
1977. Interspecific competition and the demography of two lizards. Ph.D. thesis. University of Michigan. *10*

Smith, E. M., S. L. Robertson, and D. G. Davies
1978. Cutaneous blood flow during heating and cooling in the American alligator. *American Journal of Physiology* 235:R160–R167.

Smith, H. M.
1946. *Handbook of lizards: Lizards of the United States and of Canada*. Comstock, Ithaca, N.Y. *2*

Smith, H. M., and E. D. Brodie, Jr.
1982. *A guide to field identification: Reptiles of North America*. Golden Press, New York. *2*

Smith, H. M., and R. B. Smith
1979. *Guide to the Mexican turtles*. Vol. 6 of *Synopsis of the herpetofauna of Mexico*. John Johnson, North Bennington, Vt. *7, 12, 19, 20*

Smith, H. M., D. C. Kritsky, and R. L. Holland
1969. Reticulate melanism in the painted turtle. *Journal of Herpetology* 3:173–176. *19*

Smith, M. H., and R. K. Chesser
1981. Rationale for conserving genetic variation of fish gene pools. *Ecological Bulletins* (Stockholm) 34:13–20. *6*

Smith, M. H., C. T. Garten, Jr., and P. R. Ramsey
1975. Genic heterozygosity and population dynamics in small mammals. In *Genetics and evolution*, Vol. 4 of *Isozymes*, edited by C. L. Markert, 85–102. Academic Press, New York. *6*

Smith, M. H., H. O. Hillestad, M. N. Manlove, D. O. Straney, and J. M. Dean
1977. Management implications of genetic variability in loggerhead and green sea turtles. In *XIII International Congress Game Biologists, Atlanta, Georgia*, edited by J. J. Peterle, 302–312. Wildlife Management Institute and the Wildlife Society, Washington, D.C. *6*

Smith, M. H., M. N. Manlove, and J. Joule
1978. Spatial and temporal dynamics of the genetic organization of small mammal populations. In *Populations of small mammals under natural conditions*, Special Publication Series, Pymatuning Laboratory of Ecology, University of Pittsburgh, vol. 5, edited by D. P. Snyder, 99–113. *6, 22*

Smith, M. H., R. K. Chesser, E. G. Cothran, and P. E. Johns
1982. Genetic variability and antler growth in a natural population of white-tailed deer. In *Antler development in Cervidae*, edited by R. D. Brown, 365–387. Caesar Kleberg Wildlife Research Institute, Kingsville, Tex. *6*

Smith, N. L., and R. R. Miller
1986. The evolution of the Rio Grande basin as inferred from its fish fauna. In *Zoogeography of North American freshwater fishes*, edited by C. H. Hocutt and E. O. Wiley, 457–485. John Wiley and Sons, New York. *7*

Smith, P. W.
1951. A new frog and a new turtle from the western Illinois sand prairies. *Bulletin of the Chicago Academy of Sciences* 9:189–199.

1961. *The amphibians and reptiles of Illinois*. Illinois Natural History Survey Bulletin no. 28. *4, 19*

Snow, J. E.
1980. Second clutch laying by painted turtles. *Copeia* 1980:534–536. *3*

1982. Predation on painted turtle nests: Nest survival as a function of age. *Canadian Journal of Zoology* 60:3290–3292. *8*

Sokal, R. R.
1970. Senescence and genetic load: Evidence from *Tribolium*. *Science* 97:1733–1734. *3*

Sokal, R. R., and N. L. Oden
1978. Spatial autocorrelation in biology, I: Methodology. *Biological Journal of the Linnean Society* 10:199–228. *6*

Sokal, R. R., and F. J. Rohlf
1969. *Biometry: The principles and practice of statistics in biological research*. W. H. Freeman and Co., San Francisco. *6, 18*

Sokol, O. M.
1971. Lithophagy and geophagy in reptiles. *Journal of Herpetology* 5:69–70. *20*

Solomon, S. E., and T. Baird
1976.   Studies on the eggshell (oviductal and oviposited) of *Chelonia mydas* L. *Journal of Experimental Marine Biology and Ecology* 22:145–160. *8*

Solomon, S. E., and J. Reid
1983.   The effect of the mammillary layer on eggshell formation in reptiles. *Animal Technology* 34(1):1–10. *8*

Sorensen, T.
1948.   A method of establishing groups of equal amplitude in plant sociology based on similarity of species content and its application to the analyses of the vegetation on Danish commons. *Kongeligie Danske Videnskabernes Selskab Biologiske Skrifter* 5:1–34. *23*

Soule, M.
1966.   Trends in the insular radiation of a lizard. *American Naturalist* 100:47–64.

Sparrow, A. H.
1962.   *The role of the cell nucleus in determining radiosensitivity.* U.S. Atomic Energy Commission Report no. BNL 766(T-287). Brookhaven National Laboratory, New York. *21*

Sparrow, A. H., A. G. Underbrink, and R. C. Sparrow
1967.   Chromosomes and cellular radiosensitivity: The relationship of D_0 to chromosome volume and complexity in seventy-nine different organisms. *Radiation Research* 32:915–945. *21*

Sparrow, A. H., A. F. Rogers, and S. S. Schwemmer
1968.   Radiosensitivity studies with woody plants: Acute gamma irradiation survival data for 28 species and predictions for 190 species. *Radiation Botany* 8:149–186. *21*

Sparrow, A. H., C. H. Nauman, G. M. Donnelly, D. L. Willis, and D. G. Baker
1970.   Radiosensitivities of selected amphibians in relation to their nuclear and chromosome volumes. *Radiation Research* 42:353–371. *21*

Sparrow, R. C., and A. H. Sparrow
1965.   Relative radiosensitivities of woody and herbaceous spermatophytes. *Science* 147:1449–1451. *21*

Spencer, H., M. Li, J. Samachson, and D. Laszlo
1960.   Metabolism of strontium-85 and calcium-45 in man. *Proceedings of the Society for Experimental Biology and Medicine* 117:59–63. *21*

Spinage, C. A.
1972.   African ungulate life tables. *Ecology* 53:645–652.

Spotila, J. R., and E. A. Standora
1985a. Energy budgets of ectothermic vertebrates. *American Zoologist* 25:973–986. *22*

1985b. Environmental constraints on the thermal energetics of sea turtles. *Copeia* 1985:694–702. *22*

Spotila, J. R., O. H. Soule, and D. M. Gates
1972.   The biophysical ecology of the alligator: Heat energy budgets and climate spaces. *Ecology* 53:1094–1102. *22*

Spotila, J. R., P. W. Lommen, G. S. Bakken, and D. M. Gates
1973.   A mathematical model for body temperatures of large reptiles: Implications for dinosaur ecology. *American Naturalist* 107:391–404. *22*

Spotila, J. R., R. E. Foley, J. P. Schubauer, R. D. Semlitsch, K. M. Crawford, E. A. Standora, and J. W. Gibbons
1984.   Opportunistic behavioral thermoregulation of turtles, *Pseudemys scripta*, in response to microclimatology of a nuclear reactor cooling reservoir. *Herpetologica* 40:299–308. *18, 20, 22*

Spray, D. C., and M. L. May
1972.   Heating and cooling rates in four species of turtles. *Comparative Biochemistry and Physiology* 41A:507–522. *20, 22*

SPSS, Inc.
1986.   *SPSS^x user's guide.* 2d ed. McGraw-Hill, New York. *11*

Stamps, J. A.
1983.   Sexual selection, sexual dimorphism, and territoriality. In *Lizard ecology: Studies of a model organism,* edited by R. B. Huey, E. R. Pianka, and T. W. Schoener, 169–204. Harvard University Press, Cambridge.

Standora, E. A.
1982.   A telemetric study of the thermoregulatory behavior and climate space of free-ranging yellow-bellied turtles, *Pseudemys scripta.* Ph.D. thesis. University of Georgia. *20, 22*

Stara, J. F., N. S. Nelson, R. J. Della Rosa, and L. K. Bustad
1971.   Comparative metabolism of radionuclides in mammals: A review. *Health Physics* 20:113–137. *21*

Staton, M. A., I. L. Brisbin, Jr., and R. A. Geiger
1974.   Some aspects of radiocesium retention in naturally contaminated captive snakes. *Herpetologica* 30:204–211. *21*

Stearner, S. P.
1950.   The effects of x-irradiation on *Rana pipiens* (leopard frog), with special reference to survival and to response of the peripheral blood. *Journal of Experimental Zoology* 115:251–262. *21*

Stearns, S. C.
1976.   Life-history tactics: A review of the ideas. *Quarterly Review of Biology* 51:3–47. *3, 15*

1977.   The evolution of life-history traits: A critique of the theory and a review of the ideas. *Annual Review of Ecology and Systematics* 8:145–171. *3, 15*

1980.   A new view of life-history evolution. *Oikos* 35:266–281. *15*

1984.   The effects of size and phylogeny on patterns of covariation in the life history traits of lizards and snakes. *American Naturalist* 123:56–72. *15*

Stearns, S. C., and R. C. Crandal
1981.   Quantitative predictions of delayed maturity. *Evolution* 35:455–463. *3*

Stearns, S. C., and J. C. Koella
1986.   The evolution of phenotypic plasticity in life-history traits: Predictions of reaction norms for age and size at maturity. *Evolution* 40:893–913. *3*

Stewart, J. R.
1979.   The balance between number and size of young in the live bearing lizard *Gerrhonotus coeruleus. Herpetologica* 35:342–350. *3, 8*

Stewart, J. R., and R. E. Castillo
1984.   Nutritional provision of the yolk of two species of viviparous reptiles. *Physiological Zoology* 57:377–383. *8*

Stickel, L. F.
1950.   Populations and home range relationships of the box turtle, *Terrapene c. carolina* (Linnaeus). *Ecological Monographs* 20:351–378. *3, 14*

1978.   Changes in a box turtle population during three decades. *Copeia* 1978:221–225. *3, 15*

Stock, A. D.
1972.   Karyological relationships in turtles (Reptilia: Chelonia). *Canadian Journal of Genetics and Cytology* 14:859–868. *4*

Storer, R. W.
1966.   Sexual dimorphism and food habits in three North American accipiters. *Auk* 83:423–436.

Storm, R. M., and R. A. Pimentel
1954.   A method for studying amphibian breeding populations. *Herpetologica* 10:161–166. *2*

Storr, J. F., A. L. Costa, and D. A. Prawel
1982.   Effects of temperature on calcium deposition in the hard-shell clam, *Mercenaria mercenaria*. *Journal of Thermal Biology* 7:57–61. *21*

Stubbs, D., and I. R. Swingland
1985.   The ecology of a Mediterranean tortoise (*Testudo hermanni*): A declining population. *Canadian Journal of Zoology* 63:169–180. *14*

Stubbs, D., I. R. Swingland, and A. Hailey
1985.   The ecology of the Mediterranean tortoise *Testudo hermanni* in northern Greece (The effects of a catastrophe on population structure and density). *Biological Conservation* 31:125–152. *14*

Studier, E. H., A. L. Studier, A. J. Essy, and R. W. Dapson
1977.   Thermal sensitivity and activation energy of intrinsic intestinal motility in small vertebrates. *Journal of Thermal Biology* 2:101–105. *20*

Suzuki, H. K.
1963.   Studies on the osseous system of the slider turtle. *Annals of the New York Academy of Sciences* 109:351–410. *10*

Svardson, G.
1949.   Natural selection and egg number in fish. *Institute of Freshwater Research Drottingholm Report* 29:115–122. *3, 8*

Swingland, I. R.
1983.   Intraspecific differences in movement. In *The ecology of animal movement*, edited by I. R. Swingland and P. J. Greenwood, 102–115. Oxford University Press, New York. *17*

Swingland, I. R., and C. M. Lessells
1979.   The natural regulation of giant tortoise populations on Aldabra Atoll: Movement polymorphism, reproductive success, and mortality. *Journal of Animal Ecology* 48:639–654. *3, 15, 16*

T

Talbert, O. R., Jr., S. E. Stancyck, J. M. Dean, and J. M. Will
1980.   Nesting activity of the loggerhead turtle (*Caretta caretta*) in South Carolina, I: A rookery in transition. *Copeia* 1980:709–718. *15*

Tamarin, R. H., M. Sheridan, and C. K. Levy
1983.   Determining matrilineal kinship in natural populations of rodents using radionuclides. *Canadian Journal of Zoology* 61:271–274. *21*

Tamayo, J. L., and R. C. West
1964.   The hydrography of Middle America. In Vol. 1 of *Handbook of Middle American Indians*, edited by R. Wauchope and R. C. West, 84–121. University of Texas Press, Austin. *7*

Tanaka, S., and F. Sato
1983.   Brief observation of the mating behavior of the box turtle *Cuora flavomarginata flavomarginata* in nature. *Biological Magazine, Okinawa* 21:75–76.

Tanner, J. T.
1978.   *Guide to the study of animal populations.* University of Tennessee Press, Knoxville. *15*

Taylor, E. H.
1933.   Observations on the courtship of turtles. *University of Kansas Science Bulletin* 21:269–271. *7*

1970.   The turtles and crocodiles of Thailand and adjacent waters. *University of Kansas Science Bulletin* 49:87–179. *19*

Taylor, H. M., R. S. Gourley, C. E. Lawrence, and R. S. Kaplan
1974.   Natural selection of life history attributes: An analytical approach. *Theoretical Population Biology* 5:104–122. *3*

Telford, S. R., Jr.
1970.   Seasonal fluctuations in liver and fat body weights of the Japanese lacertid *Takydromus tachydromides* Schlegel. *Copeia* 1970:681–689. *19*

Temeles, E. J.
1985.   Sexual size dimorphism of bird-eating hawks: The effect of prey vulnerability. *American Naturalist* 125:485–499.

Terrell, C. W., and W. R. Garstka
1984.   Melanism and reproduction in the male slider turtle, *Pseudemys scripta* [abstract]. *Journal of the Alabama Academy of Science* 55:144. *19*

Tester, J. R., F. McKinney, and D. B. Siniff
1968.   Mortality of three species of ducks—*Anas discors*, *A. crecca*, and *A. clypeata*—exposed to ionizing radiation. *Radiation Research* 33:364. *21*

Thapliyal, J. P., and B. B. Pd. Gupta
1984.   Thyroid and annual gonad development, body weight, plumage pigmentation, and bill color cycles of Lal Munia, *Estrilda amandava*. *General and Comparative Endocrinology* 55:20–28. *19*

Thapliyal, J. P., and P. D. Tewary
1961.   Plumage in Lal Munia (*Amandava amandava*). *Science* 134:738–739. *19*

Thompson, M. B.
1985.   Functional significance of the opaque white patch in eggs of *Emydura macquarrii*. In *Biology of Australasian frogs and reptiles*, edited by G. Grigg, R. Shine, and H. Ehmann, 387–395. Surrey Beatty and Sons, Sydney. *8*

1987.   Water exchange in reptilian eggs. *Physiological Zoology* 60:1–8. *8*

Thornhill, G. M.
1982.   Comparative reproduction of the turtle, *Chrysemys scripta elegans*, in heated and natural lakes. *Journal of Herpetology* 16:347–353. *1, 10, 12, 13, 15, 18, 20*

Tietz, N. W.
1982.   *Fundamentals of clinical chemistry.* W. B. Saunders, Philadelphia. *19*

Timken, R. L.
1968.   *Graptemys pseudogeographica* in the upper Missouri River of the northcentral United States. *Journal of Herpetology* 1:76–82. *14*

Tinkle, D. W.
1961.   Geographic variation in reproduction, size, sex ratio,

and maturity of *Sternotherus odoratus* (Testudinata: Chelydridae). *Ecology* 42:68–76. *9, 10, 14, 24*

1962. Reproductive potential and cycles in female *Crotalis atrox* from northwestern Texas. *Copeia* 1962:306–313. *10*

1967. *The life and demography of the side-blotched lizard,* Uta stansburiana. Miscellaneous Publications of the Museum of Zoology, University of Michigan, no. 132. *3, 10*

1969. The concept of reproductive effort and its relation to the evolution of life histories of lizards. *American Naturalist* 103:501–516. *3, 15*

1979. Long-term field studies. *BioScience* 9:717. *3*

Tinkle, D. W., and R. E. Ballinger
1972. *Sceloporus undulatus:* A study of the intraspecific comparative demography of a lizard. *Ecology* 53:570–584. *10, 11*

Tinkle, D. W., and R. K. Selander
1973. Age-dependent allozymic variation in a natural population of lizards. *Biochemical Genetics* 8:231–237. *6*

Tinkle, D. W., H. M. Wilbur, and S. G. Tilley
1970. Evolutionary strategies in lizard reproduction. *Evolution* 24:55–74. *3, 10*

Tinkle, D. W., J. D. Congdon, and P. C. Rosen
1981. Nesting frequency and success: Implications for the demography of painted turtles. *Ecology* 62:1426–1432. *1, 3, 9, 15*

Towns, A. L.
1987. [137]Cs and ^{90}Sr in turtles: A whole-body measurement technique and tissue distribution. Master's thesis. Colorado State University. *21*

Tracy, C. R.
1976. A model of the dynamic exchanges of water and energy between a terrestrial amphibian and its environment. *Ecological Monographs* 46:293–326. *22*

1982. Biophysical modeling in reptilian physiology and ecology. In Vol. 12 of *Biology of the Reptilia*, edited by C. Gans and F. H. Pough, 275–320. Academic Press, New York. *22*

Tracy, C. R., G. C. Packard, and M. J. Packard
1978. Water relations of chelonian eggs. *Physiological Zoology* 51:378–387. *8*

Trinkaus, J. P.
1948. Factors concerned in the response of melanoblasts to estrogen in the brown leghorn fowl. *Journal of Experimental Zoology* 109:135–169. *19*

Trivers, R. L.
1972. Parental investment and sexual selection. In *Sexual selection and the descent of man*, edited by B. Campbell, 136–179. Aldine, Chicago. *8, 10, 14*

1976. Sexual selection and resource-accruing abilities in *Anolis garmani. Evolution* 30:253–269. *10*

1985. *Social evolution.* Cummings, Menlo Park, Calif. *8*

Troyer, K.
1983. Posthatchling yolk energy in a lizard: Utilization pattern and interclutch variation. *Oecologia* (Berlin) 58:340–344. *8*

Tucker, J. K., R. S. Funk, and G. L. Paukstis
1978. The adaptive significance of egg morphology in two turtles (*Chrysemys picta* and *Terrapene carolina*). *Bulletin of the Maryland Herpetological Society* 14:10–24. *3, 8, 11*

Turner, F. B.
1975. Effects of continuous irradiation on animal populations. *Advances in Radiation Biology* 5:83. *21*

Turner, F. B., and K. H. Berry
1986. *Population ecology of the desert tortoise at Goffs, California, in 1985.* Report prepared for the Southern California Edison Company UCLA #12–1544. Laboratory of Biomedical and Environmental Sciences, University of California, Los Angeles. *3*

Turner, F. B., J. R. Lannom, H. J. Kania, and B. W. Kowalewsky
1967. Acute gamma irradiation experiments with the lizard *Uta stansburiana. Radiation Research* 31:27–35. *21*

Turner, F. B., P. A. Medica, and C. L. Lyons
1984. Reproduction and survival of the desert tortoise (*Scaptochelys agassizii*) in Ivanpah Valley, California. *Copeia* 1984:811–820. *15*

Turner, F. B., P. A. Medica, and R. B. Bury
1987. Age-size relationships of desert tortoises (*Gopherus agassizi*) in southern Nevada. *Copeia* 1987:974–979. *3*

Uden, P., P. E. Colucci, and P. J. Van Soest
1980. Investigation of chromium, cerium, and cobalt as markers in digesta: Rate of passage studies. *Journal of the Science of Food and Agriculture* 31:625–632. *21*

Ultsch, G. R., and D. C. Jackson
1982a. Long-term submergence at 3° C of the turtle, *Chrysemys picta bellii*, in normoxic and severely hypoxic water, I: Survival, gas exchange, and acid-base status. *Journal of Experimental Biology* 96:11–28. *22*

1982b. Long-term submergence at 3° C of the turtle, *Chrysemys picta bellii*, in normoxic and severely hypoxic water, III: Effects of changes in ambient PO_2 and subsequent air breathing. *Journal of Experimental Biology* 97:87–99. *22*

Ultsch, G. R., C. V. Herbert, and D. C. Jackson
1984. The comparative physiology of diving in North American freshwater turtles, I: Submergence tolerance, gas exchange, and acid-base balance. *Physiological Zoology* 57:620–631. *22*

Van Denburgh, J.
1895. A review of the herpetology of lower California, part I: Reptiles. *Proceedings of the California Academy of Sciences* 2(5):77–162. *4, 7*

Van Devender, R. W.
1978. Growth ecology of a tropical lizard, *Basiliscus basiliscus. Ecology* 59:1031–1038. *10*

Van Pelt, A. F.
1966. Activity and density of old-field ants of the Savannah River Plant, South Carolina. *Journal of the Elisha Mitchell Scientific Society* 82:35–43. *2*

vanTienhoven, A.
1983. *Reproductive physiology of vertebrates.* 2d ed. Comstock, Ithaca, N.Y. *19*

Vigerstad, T. J., and D. L. Kiser
1977. Par Pond circulation patterns and plankton sampling. In *Savannah River Laboratory, Environmental Transport Division annual report*, 93–96. Savannah River Laboratory, Aiken, S.C. *18*

Viosca, P., Jr.
1933. The *Pseudemys troostii-elegans* complex, a case of sexual dimorphism. *Copeia* 1933:208–210. *14, 19*

Vitt, L. J., and W. E. Cooper
1985. The evolution of sexual dimorphism in the skink *Eumeces laticeps:* An example of sexual selection. *Canadian Journal of Zoology* 63:995–1002.

Vitt, L. J., and H. J. Price
1982. Ecological and evolutionary determinants of relative clutch mass in lizards. *Herpetologica* 38:237–255. *12*

Vogt, R. C.
1978. Systematics and ecology of the false map turtle complex, *Graptemys pseudogeographica*. Ph.D. dissertation. University of Wisconsin—Madison. *2, 19*

1980a. Natural history of the map turtles *Graptemys pseudogeographica* and *G. ouachitensis* in Wisconsin. *Tulane Studies in Zoology and Botany* 22:17–48. *13, 14*

1980b. New methods for collecting aquatic turtles. *Copeia* 1980:368–371.

1981. Turtle egg (*Graptemys:* Emydidae) infestation by fly larvae. *Copeia* 1981:457–459. *15*

n.d. The female reproductive cycle in neotropical freshwater turtles. Unpublished manuscript. *13*

Vogt, R. C., and J. J. Bull
1982. Temperature controlled sex-determination in turtles: Ecological and behavioral aspects. *Herpetologica* 38:156–164. *14*

1984. Ecology of hatchling sex ratio in map turtles. *Ecology* 65:582–587. *14*

Vogt, R. C., and C. J. McCoy
1980. Status of the emydine turtle genera *Chrysemys* and *Pseudemys*. *Annals of Carnegie Museum* 49:93–102. *1, 4–6*

Volsoe, H.
1944. Structure and seasonal variation of the male reproductive organs of *Vipera berus* (L.). *Spolia Zoologica Musei Hauniensis* (Copenhagen) 5:1–172. *19*

W

Waagen, G. N.
1972. Musk glands in Recent turtles. Master's dissertation. University of Utah. *7*

Wade, S. E., and C. E. Gifford
1965. A preliminary study of the turtle population of a northern Indiana lake. *Proceedings of the Indiana Academy of Science* 74:371–374.

Wagner, J. G.
1979. *Fundamentals of clinical pharmacokinetics*. Drug Intelligence Publications, Hamilton, Ill. *21*

Wahlund, S.
1928. Zusammensetzung von populationen und Korrelation sercheinungen vom standpunkt der vererbungslehre aus betrachtet. *Hereditas* 11:65–106. *6*

Ward, F. P., C. J. Hohmann, J. F. Ulrich, and S. E. Hill
1976. Seasonal microhabitat selections of spotted turtles (*Clemmys guttata*) in Maryland elucidated by radio-isotope tracking. *Herpetologica* 32:60–64. *21*

Ward, J. P.
1980. Comparative cranial morphology of the freshwater turtle subfamily Emydinae: An analysis of the feeding mechanisms and the systematics. Ph.D. dissertation. North Carolina State University at Raleigh. *5*

1984. *Relationships of chrysemyd turtles of North America (Testudines: Emydidae)*. Special Publications, the Museum, Texas Tech University, no. 21. *1, 4, 5, 7, 19*

Wathen, P., J. W. Mitchell, and W. P. Porter
1971. Theoretical and experimental studies of energy exchange from jackrabbit ears and cylindrically shaped appendages. *Biophysical Journal* 11:1030–1047. *22*

Watrous, L. E., and Q. D. Wheeler
1981. The out-group comparison method of character analysis. *Systematic Zoology* 30:1–11. *5*

Wattiaux, J. M.
1968. Cumulative parental age effects in *Drosophila subobscura*. *Evolution* 22:406–421. *3*

Weathers, W. W., and F. N. White
1971. Physiological thermoregulation in turtles. *American Journal of Physiology* 221:704–710. *22*

Weaver, W. G., and J. S. Robertson
1967. A re-evaluation of fossil turtles of the *Chrysemys scripta* group. *Tulane Studies in Geology* 5:53–66. *4, 5*

Weaver, W. G., and F. L. Rose
1967. Systematics, fossil history, and evolution of the genus *Chrysemys*. *Tulane Studies in Zoology* 14:63–73. *1, 4, 5, 7, 19, 23*

Webb, G. J. W., and C. R. Johnson
1972. Head-body temperature differences in turtles. *Comparative Biochemistry and Physiology* 43A:593–611. *22*

Webb, G. J. W., and G. J. Witten
1973. Critical thermal maxima of turtles: Validity of body temperature. *Comparative Biochemistry and Physiology* 45A:829–832. *22*

Webb, G. J. W., S. C. Manolis, K. E. Dempsey, and P. J. Whitehead
1987. Crocodilian eggs: A functional overview. In *Wildlife management: Crocodiles and alligators*, edited by G. J. W. Webb, S. C. Manolis, and P. J. Whitehead, 417–422. Surrey Beatty and Sons, Sydney. *8*

Webb, R. G.
1961. Observations on the life histories of turtles (genus *Pseudemys* and *Graptemys*) in Lake Texoma, Oklahoma. *American Midland Naturalist* 65:193–214. *12, 14, 18–20*

1962. North American Recent soft-shelled turtles (family Trionychidae). University of Kansas Publications of the Museum of Natural History, vol. 13, 429–611. *19*

Webb, R. G., and J. M. Legler
1960. A new softshell turtle (genus *Trionyx*) from Coahuila, Mexico. *University of Kansas Science Bulletin* 40:21–30. *19*

Weichert, C. K.
1970. *Anatomy of the chordates*. McGraw-Hill, New York. *23*

Weinheimer, C. J., D. R. Pendergast, J. R. Spotila, D. R. Wilson, and E. A. Standora
1982. Peripheral circulation in *Alligator mississippiensis:* Effects of diving, fear, movement, investigator ac-

tivities, and temperature. *Journal of Comparative Physiology* 148:57–63. *22*

Weins, J. A.
1977. On competition and variable environments. *American Scientist* 56:590–597. *3*

Whicker, F. W.
1983. Radionuclide transport processes in terrestrial ecosystems. *Radiation Research* 94:135–150. *21*
1984. Transport of radionuclides through aquatic food chains. In *The fate of toxics in surface and ground waters*, Proceedings of the Second National Water Conference, edited by J. Wilson, 145–156. Philadelphia Academy of Natural Sciences, Philadelphia. *21*

Whicker, F. W., and L. Fraley, Jr.
1974. Effects of ionizing radiation on terrestrial plant communities. *Advances in Radiation Biology* 4:317. *21*

Whicker, F. W., and T. B. Kirchner
1987. PATHWAY: A dynamic food-chain model to predict radionuclide ingestion after fallout deposition. *Health Physics* 52:717–737. *21*

Whicker, F. W., and V. Schultz
1982. *Radioecology: Nuclear energy and the environment.* Vols. 1 and 2. CRC Press, Boca Raton, Fla. *21*

Whicker, F. W., G. C. Farris, and A. H. Dahl
1967. Concentration patterns of Sr-90, Cs-137, and I-131 in a wild deer population and environment. In *Radioecological concentration processes*, edited by B. Aberg and F. P. Hungate, 621–634. Pergamon Press, New York. *21*

Whicker, F. W., W. C. Nelson, and A. F. Gallegos
1972. Fallout Cs-137 and Sr-90 in trout from mountain lakes in Colorado. *Health Physics* 23:519–527. *21*

Whicker, F. W., J. J. Alberts, J. W. Bowling, and J. E. Pinder III
1984. Unpublished data. Savannah River Ecology Laboratory, Aiken, S.C. *21*

White, F. N., and G. Ross
1966. Circulatory changes during experimental diving in the turtle. *American Journal of Physiology* 211:15–18. *22*

Whitfield, D. P.
1987. Plumage variability, status signalling, and individual recognition in avian flocks. *Tree* 2:13–18. *19*

Whittaker, R. H., and D. Goodman
1979. Classifying species according to their demographic strategy, I: Population fluctuations and environmental heterogeneity. *American Naturalist* 113:185–200. *3*

Whittow, G. C.
1973. Evolution of thermoregulation. In *Special aspects of thermoregulation*, Vol. 3 of *Comparative physiology of thermoregulation*, edited by G. C. Whittow, 201–258. Academic Press, New York. *22*

Wickham, M. M.
1922. Notes on the migration of *Macrochelys lacertina*. *Proceedings of the Oklahoma Academy of Science* 2:20–22. *18*

Wickler, W.
1968. *Mimicry in plants and animals.* McGraw-Hill, New York. *19*

Wied, M. zu.
1839. *Reise in des innare Nord-America in den Jahren 1832 bis 1834.* J. Hoelscher, Coblenz. *4, 7, 19*

Wilbur, H. M.
1975a. The evolutionary and mathematical demography of the turtle *Chrysemys picta*. *Ecology* 56:64–77. *1, 3, 15*
1975b. A growth model for the painted turtle *Chrysemys picta*. *Copeia* 1975:337–343. *3, 10, 11*

Wilbur, H. M., and P. J. Morin
1988. Life history evolution in turtles. In Vol. 16 of *Biology of the Reptilia*, edited by C. Gans and R. Huey, 387–439. A. R. Liss, New York. *3, 8, 15*

Wilbur, H. M., D. W. Tinkle, and J. P. Collins
1974. Environmental certainty, trophic level, and resource availability in life history evolution. *American Naturalist* 108:805–817. *3*

Wiley, E. O.
1981. *Phylogenetics: The theory and practice of phylogenetic systematics.* John Wiley and Sons, New York. *5*

Wiley, R. H.
1974. Evolution of social organization and life-history patterns among grouse. *Quarterly Review of Biology* 49:201–227. *3*

Wilhoft, D. C.
1986. Eggs and hatchling components of the snapping turtle *Chelydra serpentina*. *Comparative Biochemistry and Physiology* 84A:483–486. *8*

Wilhoft, D. C., M. G. del Baglivo, and M. D. del Baglivo
1979. Observations on mammalian predation of snapping turtle nests (Reptilia, Testudines, Chelydridae). *Journal of Herpetology* 13:435–438. *15*

Williams, C. K., and M. G. Ridpath
1982. Rates of herbage ingestion and turnover of water and sodium in feral swamp buffalo, *Bubalus bubalus*, in relation to primary production in a cyperaceous swamp in monsoonal northern Australia. *Australian Wildlife Research* 9:397–408. *21*

Williams, E.
1956. *Pseudemys scripta callirostris* from Venezuela with a general survey of the *scripta* series. *Bulletin of the Museum of Comparative Zoology* 115:145–160. *5, 7*

Williams, E. C., and W. S. Parker
1987. A long-term study of a box turtle (*Terrapene carolina*) population at Allee Memorial Woods, Indiana, with emphasis on survivorship. *Herpetologica* 43:328–335. *3, 15*

Williams, G. C.
1957. Pleiotropy, natural selection, and the evolution of senescence. *Evolution* 11:398–411. *3*
1966a. *Adaptation and natural selection.* Princeton University Press, Princeton, N.J. *3, 8*
1966b. Natural selection, the cost of reproduction, and a refinement of Lack's principle. *American Naturalist* 100:687–690. *3*

Williams, J. D., and K. Dodd, Jr.
1978. Importance of wetlands to endangered and threatened species. In *Wetland functions and values: The state of our understanding*, edited by P. E. Greeson, J. R. Clark, and J. E. Clark, 567–575. American Water Resources Association, Minneapolis.

Williams, K.
1978. *Systematics and natural history of the American milk snake,*

Lampropeltis triangulum. Milwaukee Public Museum, Publications in Biology and Geology, no. 2.

Williamson, L. U., J. R. Spotila, and E. A. Standora
1989. Growth, selected temperature, and CTM of young snapping turtles, *Chelydra serpentina*. *Journal of Thermal Biology*. 14:33–39. *22*

Willis, D. L., and W. L. Lappenbush
1975. The radiosensitivity of the rough-skinned newt (*Taricha granulosa*). In *Radioecology and energy resources*, edited by C. E. Cushing, Jr., 363–375. Dowden, Hutchinson and Ross, Stroudsburg, Pa. *21*

Willis, D. L., and M. M. McCourry
1968. Radiosensitivity of the western fence lizard (*Sceloporus occidentalis*) and the desert crested lizard (*Dipsosaurus dorsalis*). In *Radiation Research Society, 16th Annual Meeting, Abstracts*, 96. Academic Press, New York. *21*

Wilson, E. O.
1975. *Sociobiology*. Belknap Press of Harvard University Press, Cambridge. *14*

Winokur, R. M., and J. M. Legler
1975. Chelonian mental glands. *Journal of Morphology* 147(3):275–292. *7*

Witschi, E.
1961. Sex and secondary sex characters. In Vol. 2 of *Biology and comparative physiology of birds*, edited by A. J. Marshall, 115–168. Academic Press, New York. *19*

Witschi, E., and R. P. Woods
1936. The bill of the sparrow as an indicator for the male sex hormone, II: Structural basis. *Journal of Experimental Zoology* 73:445–459. *19*

Witzell, W. N.
1982. Observations on the green sea turtle (*Chelonia mydas*) in western Samoa. *Copeia* 1982:183–185.

Wolff, J. O., and D. F. Holleman
1978. Use of radioisotope labels to establish genetic relationships in free-ranging small mammals. *Journal of Mammalogy* 59:859–860. *21*

Wood, F. E., and J. R. Wood
1977. Quantitative requirements of the hatchling green sea turtle, *Chelonia mydas*, for valine, leucine, isoleucine, and phenylalanine. *Journal of Nutrition* 107:1502–1506. *20*

Wood, J. R.
1974. Amino acids essential for the growth of young sea turtles (*Chelonia mydas*). *Proceedings, World Mariculture Society* 5:233–248. *20*

Wood, J. R., and F. E. Wood
1977. Quantitative requirements of the hatchling green sea turtle for lysine, tryptophan, and methionine. *Journal of Nutrition* 107:171–175. *20*

Wood, R. A., K. A. Nagy, N. S. MacDonald, S. T. Wakakuwa, R. J. Beckman, and H. Kaaz
1975. Determination of oxygen-18 in water contained in biological samples by charged particles activation. *Analytical Chemistry* 47:646–650. *21*

Woodbury, A. M.
1951. Symposium: A snake den in Tooele County, Utah. *Herpetologica* 7:1–52. *2, 10*

1953. Methods of field study in reptiles. *Herpetologica* 9:87–92. *2*

1956. Uses of marking animals in ecological studies: Marking amphibians and reptiles. *Ecology* 37:670–674. *2*

Woodbury, A. M., and R. Hardy
1948. Studies of the desert tortoise, *Gopherus agassizii*. *Ecological Monographs* 18:145–200. *3, 10, 14, 16*

Woody, J. B.
1986. On the dollar value of the Oaxacan ridley fishery. *Marine Turtle Newsletter* 36:6–7. *15*

Woolley, P.
1957. Colour change in a chelonian. *Nature* 179:1255–1256. *19*

Woolverton, E.
1961. Winter survival of hatchling painted turtles in northern Minnesota. *Copeia* 1961:109. *8*

1963. Winter survival of hatchling painted turtles in northern Minnesota. *Copeia* 1963:569–570. *8*

Wright, A. H.
1918. Notes on *Clemmys*. *Proceedings of the Biological Society of Washington* 31:51–58.

Wright, A. H., and A. A. Wright
1949. *Handbook of frogs and toads of the United States and Canada*. Comstock, Ithaca, N.Y. *2*

1957. *Handbook of snakes of the United States and Canada*. 2 vols. Comstock, Ithaca, N.Y. *12*

Wright, R. E., H. W. Florey, and A. G. Sanders
1957. Observations on the gastric mucosa of Reptilia. *Quarterly Journal of Experimental Physiology* 42:1–14. *20*

Wright, S.
1931. Evolution in Mendelian populations. *Genetics* 16:97–159. *6*

1943. Isolation by distance. *Genetics* 28:114–138. *6*

1969. *The theory of gene frequencies*. Vol. 2 of *Evolution and the genetics of populations*. University of Chicago Press, Chicago. *6*

1970. Random drift and the shifting balance theory of evolution. In *Mathematical topics in population genetics*, edited by K. Kojima, 1–31. Springer-Verlag, New York. *6*

Wurth, M. A., and X. J. Musacchia
1964. Renewal of intestinal epithelium in the freshwater turtle, *Chrysemys picta*. *Anatomical Record* 148:427–439. *21*

Wygoda, M. L.
1981. Notes on terrestrial activity of the crayfish *Procambarus alleni* (Faxon) in west-central Florida. *Florida Scientist* 44:56–59. *2*

Y

Yamaguti, S.
1963. *Nematoda*. Vol. 3 of *Systema helminthum*. Interscience Publishers, New York. *23*

Yntema, C. L.
1960. Effects of various temperatures on the embryonic development of *Chelydra serpentina*. *Anatomical Record* 136:305–306. *8*

1970. Observations on females and eggs of the common snapping turtle, *Chelydra serpentina*. *American Midland Naturalist* 84:69–76.

Young, J. D.
 1950.   The structure and some physical properties of the tes-
         tudinian eggshell. *Proceedings of the Zoological Society of
         London* 120:445–469. *8*

Z

Zar, G. H.
 1974.   *Biostatistical analysis.* Prentice-Hall, Englewood Cliffs,
         N.J. *11*
Zug, G. R.
 1966.   *The penial morphology and the relationships of cryptodiran tur-
         tles.* Occasional Papers of the Museum of Zoology,
         University of Michigan, no. 647. *1, 4, 5, 23*
 1969.   Fossil chelonians, *Chrysemys* and *Clemmys*, from the Up-

per Pliocene of Idaho. *Great Basin Naturalist Memoirs*
19:82–87. *5*
 1971.   *Buoyancy, locomotion, morphology of the pelvic girdle and
         hindlimb, and systematics of cryptodiran turtles.* Mis-
         cellaneous Publications of the Museum of Zoology,
         University of Michigan, no. 142. *5*
Zug, G. R., A. H. Wynn, and C. Ruckdeschel
 1986.   *Age determination of loggerhead sea turtles,* Caretta caretta,
         by incremental growth marks in the skeleton. Smithsonian
         Contribution to Zoology no. 427. *10, 24*
Zweig, G., and J. W. Crenshaw
 1957.   Differentiation of species by paper electrophoresis of
         serum proteins of *Pseudemys* turtles. *Science* 126:1065–
         1067. *5*

Turtle Species Index

Contributors

This volume benefited greatly from the contributions of certain investigators who have conducted original research on the biology of slider turtles. Their addresses (as of October 1988) are included for anyone wishing to communicate directly with a particular individual.

HAROLD W. AVERY
Department of Biology
University of California, Los Angeles
Los Angeles, CA 90024–1606

JUSTIN D. CONGDON
Savannah River Ecology Laboratory
Drawer E
Aiken, SC 29802

ARTHUR E. DUNHAM
Department of Biology
University of Pennsylvania
Philadelphia, PA 19104

CARL H. ERNST
Department of Biology
George Mason University
4400 University Drive
Fairfax, VA 22030

GERALD W. ESCH
Department of Biology
Wake Forest University
Winston-Salem, NC 27109

ROBERT E. FOLEY
New York Department of
    Environmental Conservation
Hale Creek Field Station
Gloversville, NY 12078

NAT B. FRAZER
Department of Biology
Mercer University
Macon, GA 31207

WILLIAM R. GARSTKA
Department of Biological Sciences
University of Alabama
Huntsville, AL 35899

J. WHITFIELD GIBBONS
Savannah River Ecology Laboratory
Drawer E
Aiken, SC 29802

TIMOTHY M. GOATER
Department of Biology
Wake Forest University
Winston-Salem, NC 27109

JUDITH L. GREENE
Savannah River Ecology Laboratory
Drawer E
Aiken, SC 29802

THOMAS G. HINTON
Savannah River Ecology Laboratory
Drawer E
Aiken, SC 29802

DALE R. JACKSON
Florida Natural Areas Inventory
The Nature Conservancy
254 E. Sixth Avenue
Tallahassee, FL 32303

KYM C. JACOBSON
Department of Biology
Wake Forest University
Winston-Salem, NC 27109

JOHN M. LEGLER
Department of Biology
University of Utah
Salt Lake City, UT 84112

JEFFREY E. LOVICH
Savannah River Ecology Laboratory
Drawer E
Aiken, SC 29802

DAVID J. MARCOGLIESE
Department of Biology
Wake Forest University
Winston-Salem, NC 27109

CLARENCE J. McCOY
Carnegie Museum of Natural History
4400 Forbes Avenue
Pittsburgh, PA 15213

JOSEPH C. MITCHELL
Department of Biology
University of Richmond
Richmond, VA 23173

DON MOLL
Department of Biology
Southwest Missouri State University
Springfield, MO 65804

EDWARD O. MOLL
Zoology Department
Eastern Illinois University
Charleston, IL 61920

CHRISTOPHER A. PAGUE
Department of Biological Sciences
Old Dominion University
Norfolk, VA 23508

Current address:
Virginia Natural Heritage Program
203 Governor Street, Suite 402
Richmond, VA 23219

WILLIAM S. PARKER
Division of Science and Mathematics
Mississippi University for Women
Columbus, MS 39701

ROBERT R. PARMENTER
Department of Biology
Utah State University
Logan, UT 84322

Current address:
Department of Biology
University of New Mexico
Albuquerque, NM 87131

JOSEPH P. SCHUBAUER
Institute of Ecology and
    Department of Zoology
University of Georgia
Athens, GA 30602

Current address:
Marine Sciences Research Center
State University of New York
    at Stony Brook
Stony Brook, NY 11794

DAVID E. SCOTT
Savannah River Ecology Laboratory
Drawer E
Aiken, SC 29802

KIM T. SCRIBNER
Savannah River Ecology Laboratory
Drawer E
Aiken, SC 29802

MICHAEL E. SEIDEL
Department of Biological Sciences
Marshall University
Huntington, WV 25701

MICHAEL H. SMITH
Savannah River Ecology Laboratory
Drawer E
Aiken, SC 29802

JAMES R. SPOTILA
Department of Biology
State University College
1300 Elmwood Avenue
Buffalo, NY 14222
and
Savannah River Ecology Laboratory
Drawer E
Aiken, SC 29802

Current address:
Department of Bioscience and
    Biotechnology
Drexel University
Philadelphia, PA 19104

EDWARD A. STANDORA
Department of Biology
State University College
1300 Elmwood Avenue
Buffalo, NY 14222

RICHARD C. VOGT
Estación de Biología Tropical "Los
    Tuxtlas"
Instituto de Biología
Universidad Nacional Autónomo de
    México
Apartado Postal 94
San Andres Tuxtla, Veracruz, México